"Öcalan's works make many intellectuals uncomfortable, because they represent a form of thought that is not only inextricable from action but also directly grapples with the knowledge that it is."
—David Graeber author of *Debt: The First 5,000 Years*

"Öcalan's writings, written in captivity, are in the tradition of the ideology of the PKK, a left national liberation movement that seeks to change its own society. However, Öcalan, apparently also one of those whose political thinking have been sharpened by the forced abstinence from daily politics, has succeeded in further developing his political thought in captivity."
—Thomas Schmidinger, author of *The Battle for the Mountain of the Kurds: Self-Determination and Ethnic Cleansing in the Afrin Region of Rojava*

"Öcalan's plea to build a strong and complex self-organized civil society without taking direct action against the state is similar to Zapatismo in Chiapas.... Finally, this calls to mind Karl Marx's realization: 'An idea becomes material violence when it seizes the masses.' And Abdullah Öcalan's message has seized the masses in Kurdistan."
—Nikolaus Brauns, historian and journalist, author of *Partisanen einer neuen Welt: Eine Geschichte der Linken und Arbeiterbewegung der Türkei*

"Öcalan is the Gramsci of our time."
—Tamir Bar-On, author of *The World through Soccer* and *Beyond Soccer*

Beyond State, Power, and Violence

KAIROS

In ancient Greek philosophy, *kairos* signifies the right time or the "moment of transition." We believe that we live in such a transitional period. The most important task of social science in time of transformation is to transform itself into a force of liberation. Kairos, an editorial imprint of the Anthropology and Social Change department housed in the California Institute of Integral Studies, publishes groundbreaking works in critical social sciences, including anthropology, sociology, geography, theory of education, political ecology, political theory, and history.

Series editor: Andrej Grubačić

Recent and featured Kairos books:

Building Free Life: Dialogues with Öcalan edited by International Initiative

The Art of Freedom: A Brief History of the Kurdish Liberation Struggle by Havin Guneser

The Sociology of Freedom: Manifesto of the Democratic Civilization, Volume III by Abdullah Öcalan

The Battle for the Mountain of the Kurds: Self-Determination and Ethnic Cleansing in the Afrin Region of Rojava by Thomas Schmidinger

Taming the Rascal Multitude: Essays, Interviews, and Lectures 1997–2014 by Noam Chomsky

A New World in Our Hearts: Noam Chomsky in Conversation with Michael Albert

Between Thought and Expression Lies a Lifetime: Why Ideas Matter by Noam Chomsky and James Kelman

Mutual Aid: An Illuminated Factor of Evolution by Peter Kropotkin, illustrated by N.O. Bonzo

Asylum for Sale: Profit and Protest in the Migration Industry edited by Siobhán McGuirk and Adrienne Pine

Autonomy Is in Our Hearts: Zapatista Autonomous Government through the Lens of the Tsotsil Language by Dylan Eldredge Fitzwater

For more information visit www.pmpress.org/blog/kairos/

Beyond State, Power, and Violence

Abdullah Öcalan

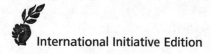

International Initiative Edition

KAIROS

Beyond State, Power, and Violence
©2023 PM Press

ISBN: 978-1-62963-715-0 (paperback)
ISBN: 978-1-62963-763-1 (hardcover)
ISBN: 978-1-62963-780-8 (ebook)
Library of Congress Control Number: 2019933027

Cover Image: Zümrüd-ü Anka by Ahmet Güneştekin

Cover by John Yates/www.stealworks.com
Interior design by briandesign

10 9 8 7 6 5 4 3 2 1

PM Press
PO Box 23912
Oakland, CA 94623
www.pmpress.org
Printed in the USA.

Published with International Initiative Edition
International Initiative
"Freedom for Abdullah Öcalan—Peace in Kurdistan"
P.O. Box 100 511
D-50445 Cologne
Germany
www.freeocalan.org

Original title: Bir Halkı Savunmak
First published in 2004 by Mezopotamien Verlag, Neuss
Translation by Michael Schiffman and Havin Guneser
Edited by Havin Guneser

Contents

FOREWORD *by Andrej Grubačić*   xiii

PREFACE **In Defense of a People**   xix

ONE **Social Reality and the Individual**   1
Introduction   1
Natural Society   4

TWO **Hierarchical Statist Society: The Birth of Slave Society**   12
On Method   12
The Advent of Hierarchy   15
Patriarchy   21
Gerontocracy   23

THREE **The Statist Society: The Formation of Slave Society**   32

FOUR **Feudal Statist Society**   50
The Mature Slave Society   50
The Capitalist State and Capitalist Society: The Crisis of
Civilization   64

FIVE **The Democratic and Ecological Society**   88
The Historical Essence of Communal and Democratic
Values   88
Prophets and Barbarians   118
Monasteries, Witches, and Alchemists   128
From the Renaissance to Marxism   133

SIX   **A Blueprint for a Democratic and Ecological Society** 164

Democracy as a System for a Way Out of Crisis   176

Women's Liberation   192

The Return to Social Ecology   201

SEVEN   **Chaos in the Middle East Civilization and Ways Out**   211

Introduction   211

Understanding the Middle East Correctly: What Is the
Problem and How Did It Develop?   216

    The Mentality of the Middle East   216

    The State in the Middle East   222

    The Family in the Middle East   233

    Further Particularities of Society in the Middle East   242

       Ethnicity and Nation   243

       Homeland   244

       Class   245

       Property   248

       Economy   249

       Dynasty   250

       Tariqat   252

       Civil Society   253

Violence and Dictatorship in the Civilization in the
Middle East   253

EIGHT   **The Current Situation in the Middle East and
Probable Developments**   260

The Middle East Today   263

    State Power   268

    Theocracy as the Foundation of Every State   269

    The Situation of Women   272

    The Economy   274

Scenarios   277

The Future of the Region   286

Democratic Politics   294

The Freedom of Women   302

Economy   304

Ecology   305

NINE   **The Kurdish Phenomenon and the Kurdish**
Question in the Chaos of the Middle East 312
Introduction 312
Some Distinctive Lines in the Kurdish Society 314
     A Short Sketch of the History and Concepts of
     "Kurds" and "Kurdistan" 314
     The Struggle Over Kurdistan, War, and Terror 324
     The Policy of Forced Assimilation Targeting the
     Culture of Kurdistan 342
     Ethnicity, Class, and Nation in Kurdistan 346
     Official Ideology and Power in Kurdistan 357
     Self-Awareness and Resistance in Kurdistan 374

TEN   **The PKK Movement: Critique, Self-Critique, and**
Its Reconstruction 383
Section A—Historical Sketch of the PKK 383
     First Phase: Emergence 383
     Second Phase 391
     Some Thoughts on the PKK 394
Section B—Critique and Self-Critique in the Name of
the PKK 405
     The Concept of the Party 408
     Power and Violence 410
     Democracy 413
     Self-critique of the PKK 415
     National Liberation 419
Section C—The Questions in the Restructuring of the
PKK 422
     Kurdish-Turkish Relations 428
     First Contacts 429
     The Strategic Alliance 432
     Capitalism in Turkey 435
     The Era of the Republic 437
     1920–1940 440
     1940–1970 443
     1970 to Today 444

Section D—Reform and Social Transformation in
Turkey   445
    Nationalists   451
    The Liberal Bourgeoisie   453
    Democrats   455

ELEVEN   **Contribution to the Debate about the Refoundation
of the PKK**   461
Introduction   461
Tasks in Reconstructing the PKK and the Time of Koma
Gel   463
Theory   465
Practice   466
Program   467
    Political Objectives   469
    Social Objectives   474
    Women   476
    Ecology and Economics   478
    Internationalist Aspect   479
    Individual Rights   480
Organizing   482
    Cadres   482
    The People's Congress   493
The People's Defense Forces   507
Options for Democratic Action and a Democratic
Solution   515
The Second Path   516

TWELVE   **The Role of the ECtHR and the EU in the Lawsuit
against Abdullah Öcalan**   519
Critique of the ECtHR   526

THIRTEEN   **An Identity That Must Be Accurately Defined**   541

AFTERWORD   575

APPENDIX   **Letter**   584

ANNEX A   **Modern History of Turkey**   605

ANNEX B   **Chronology of the Recent History of Kurdistan**   607

ANNEX C   **Chronology of the PKK**   609

NOTES   612

INDEX   638

ABOUT THE CONTRIBUTORS   652

PUBLICATIONS BY ABDULLAH ÖCALAN IN ENGLISH   654

FOREWORD

Andrej Grubačić

There is no doubt that *Beyond State, Power, and Violence* is an unusual book. This is a book of omnivorous contradictions, in which almost everything overlaps: myth and fact, past and present, dream and reality; it displays Abdullah Öcalan's preternatural powers of observation, his astonishing grasp of history and anthropology, as well as his love of the colors and smells of the mountains. It feels like a work of art in the wrong genre: when I first read it, I was immediately reminded of Maupassant, who compared a novel to an "opera in prose." The book, written in prison, was published in 2004, and is, in part, an original interpretation of world history, a revolutionary manifesto, an intellectual autobiography, a program for a unified social science, a courageous analysis of the PKK (Kurdish Workers' Party), a learned treatise on Kurdish and Middle Eastern history, a critique of political economy, all the while being an incredibly lively and readable text, despite, or because of, all the learning and research that went into it (Öcalan's analysis deftly integrates Foucault's biopower and power/knowledge, Wallerstein's world-system, Bookchin's organic society, and a number of other concepts and thinkers). André Breton once offered the image of a man cut in two by a window as the model of the surrealist picture. This is close to what Öcalan presents: neither window nor mirror but an artful combination of the two, in which exterior mingles with the interior, the two sides reflecting each other, while reminding us that *women* and *life* are the same word in some languages. I won't test the reader's patience with yet another summary of Öcalan's fascinating life and politics; the book includes a very competent biography and chronology of his revolutionary journey. Instead, as a fellow world historian, I will say a few things about his historical method and the ("wrong") genre of this book (which, incidentally, changed the entire course of the Kurdish revolutionary politics, but more on that later).

Breton's mirror and window describe well the historical method Öcalan uses. The parts are not cut in two but, rather, creatively juxtaposed: if the window corresponds to dialectical critique, the mirror reflects insightful self-critique. As we learn in chapter seven, critical self-interrogation of the concepts of power, state (party), and violence (war), while carefully balancing analytical and emotional intelligence, led Öcalan to embrace democratic, ecological, and women-centered revolutionary politics. His critique and self-critique are braided through and shape his historical method. Öcalan understands it takes more than seeing to make things visible. He knows that certain processes, shooting like arrows across the whole field of study, evade the historians' attempt to fix them in words. With dazzling virtuosity, he debunks the idea of finding absolute truth in conventional historical assessments. Is it possible, Öcalan seems to ask, to separate the idea of scientific truth from that of a true society? While dialectical knowledge seeks to raise the stone under which the monster of modern capitalism lies brooding, positivist historical research into facts opposes such a desire. Within positivism, curiosity is punished, utopia is expelled, fantasy prohibited, and knowledge resigns itself to being a mere repetitive reconstruction. It becomes impoverished, like life under factory discipline. The felicity of knowledge, as Adorno put it, is not to be. In this scientistic syndrome of thought the goal of knowledge is confused with the means of knowledge. For positivists, the system is something "positive." For dialecticians like Öcalan, the system is the core of what must be criticized. For a good positivist, always eager to quantify, art, mythology, and imagination all serve as a rubbish bin for everything that is excluded from this restricted experience. Social sciences are political concepts, as Öcalan convincingly suggests, constructed in the service of the state and capital; one of the principal concerns of liberal social science was precisely to establish a modern society organized around the triad of power, state, and violence.[1]

In *History and Class Consciousness* Lukács defined the social type of the historian as the dialectical extreme of reification. We could politely disagree and say that a professional historian, lost in fragmentary analysis of discrete shreds of the past, is even less attuned to the resounding echo of history. Like the great world historian William McNeill, Öcalan argues not for history but for a *mythhistory*, a project by which historians provide a sense of the past, a broad but intelligible and meaningful interpretation as a basis for a rebellion against the present.

Clearly, this rebellion is filled with signs and traces of antagonistic temporalities whose contents and forms are expressions of a much older history. From this point of view, nonhierarchical forms are not archaic forms or stages but antagonistic temporalities and contemporary alternatives. However, Öcalan investigates the past not to restore some form of new age obscurantism but, to the contrary, to reconstruct the truth left out of the official sources. Like Sheldon Wollin, Öcalan asks us what time it is, but his answer is that democratic time was, since the beginning of hierarchical society, out of sync with the normative rhythms and temporalities. The task of his mythhistory is to look for those possibilities and examples of different social relations obscured by the temporalities of capital and the state. Residual faith would have it that the truth resides in original documents, while moving closer and closer to those documents, in fact, means moving closer and closer to incoherence. What we need is an intelligible world, and there is no sense in pretending that all we need is more detail.

Of course, this does not imply a total reproduction of experience. Let us remember McNeill's adjunction:

> Pattern recognition of the sort historians engage in is the chef d'oeuvre of human intelligence. It is achieved by paying selective attention to the total input of stimuli that perpetually swarm in upon our consciousness. Only by leaving things out, i.e., relegating them to the status of background noise deserving only to be disregarded, can what matters most in a given situation become recognizable. Suitable action follows. Here is the great secret of human power over nature and over ourselves as well.... Only some facts matter for any given pattern. Otherwise useless clutter will obscure what we are after: perceptible relations among important facts.[2]

On that basis, relegating the background noise of conventional interpretation and positivist accumulation of swarming facts, Abdullah Öcalan had established perceptible relations among the facts that allows us to comprehend how the tradition can be revitalized to change the present.

Öcalan's method is a practical mode of intervention into history. He presents an entirely different consideration of time and space to open a new terrain of possibilities. His take on history is like that of an archeologist who investigates an archeological site not as a space of the past but as centuries and millennia that exist contemporaneously before our eyes. Unlike Enkidu, he refuses to escape to the city and the state, and he is not seduced by the liberal ordering of official time. He searches for the antagonistic temporalities revealed by his historical method, moving through the "useless clutter" of official facts.

Just like the positivist historian confuses the means and ends, so does the modern revolutionary. Öcalan's signature contribution is to recognize that both revolutionary socialists and liberal reformers belong to the same temporal logic of capitalism. Soviet socialism was realized by this logic through gulags, and today the same logic still excuses imperial interventions. Both the Leninist conception of brick-and-mortar socialism and the productivist visions of traditionalist Marxism are complicit in the progressivist myth that is emblematic of the liberal conception of history.[3] A new political temporality beyond state, power, and violence is necessary and is already present in the layers of antagonistic past; it needs to be recovered, rather than invented. The democratic and socioecological communal society is neither the break nor the accelerator; it is an alternative to the entire course of hierarchical society.

This is a revolutionary politics that rejects facile restitutionism (because a return to the "archaic" past would still involve a linear model of time). Rather, it cautions us that a mistake made by modern revolutionaries and scholars was to assert that unilinear temporality (with the modern nation-state at the other end of the developmentalist arrow) banishes antagonistic temporalities and political forms (Bookchin's "legacy of freedom"). Organized on these different temporal registers, the book shows that a historical method can have connections with one's own lived experience. It is striking how original a move this is. The result is a qualitatively different regime of historical times: not to restore the premodern past but to make a detour via the past toward a future in which we could recover the art of democratic and communal living. At the center of all this is the figure of a woman, the first slave and the first colony of patriarchal-statist society. Öcalan accords special salience to the restored dignity of women, as the premise and conditio sine qua non of egalitarian politics.

Capitalism and the US hegemonic model is in crisis, and the contemporary "chaos interval" of capitalist civilization is a key moment in time and space in which we—all of us, not only, or not exclusively, the industrial proletariat—might be able to rectify history for the future. In this restorative historicity, history is narrated into the future and capitalist modernity becomes the backward past, violent and morally unjustifiable. As we walk into the present, we have the future behind us, and the past in front of us. Time has looped on itself to reveal a solidarity of women and men across the centuries.[4] It is tradition that is subversive, not the act of abolishing it.

What comes into full view is the poverty of liberal utopia. The essence of this parochial concept is the idea of the sovereign nation-state anchored to a bounded territory, as well as to a certain utopian temporal and spatial order, a belief in the inevitability and moral quality of progress, the nation-state, and capitalism. Öcalan turns this idea upside down. His appropriation of history challenges the Eurocentric divisions of time and space, inferiority and superiority, civilization and barbarism, the entire geography of modernization, including the essential dichotomy between nature and society. Against the fantastical finality of liberal politics, he speaks of democratic intervals, existing time-spaces of mutual aid and democracy, as practices retrieved from both the past and the present but entirely integral to democratic modernity.

Öcalan reminds us that history is forever unresolved, a field of unfinished possibilities. We reach back to refuse some possibilities, and we reach back to select others. He urges us to refuse the liberal vision of civilization and progress, but he is not kind to Lenin's vision of state-centered internationalism and national liberation project either. If politics is a process of liberation of the natural and moral society from the state, national liberation should be thought of then as a rupture with the modern concept of the nation. It is the right time (Wallerstein's "kairos") to wake the people from their utopian dream of nation-states and focus our collective energy on the project of democratic world confederalism.

To conclude: the result of Abdullah Öcalan painstaking research, of his elaboration of an original historical method in the "wrong genre," is a mythhistorical manifesto for a new politics and social science. This book was much debated in Kurdish revolutionary circles. Its publication has eventuated a far-reaching self-critique within the Kurdish freedom movement (the reader would do well to pay careful attention to the parts of the book devoted to the history of PKK and Kurdish identity). The result of this process has been reevaluation and reconstruction, a birth of a new organizational paradigm that has informed (and made possible) the social revolution in Rojava. I use this word, *birth*, intentionally. Öcalan had suggested elsewhere that he had not one but three births. One was biological, another political (the birth of PKK), and the last was shaped by his rejection of the state. This book is his first and most comprehensive expression of this belief. It's historical and theoretical value is immeasurable. Considering its impact, both in and beyond Rojava, it does not seem like a terrible exaggeration to suggest that it is the most influential revolutionary manifesto of the twenty-first century.

In Defense of a People

Escaping from social reality is more difficult than one might think. This is especially true for the kinship-based society that one is from. The competition entered into with one's mother in terms of socializing at around seven years of age, continues, as the people say, until the age of seventy. The fact that the mother is the main socializing force is a scientifically proven fact. My first crime—as to my own self—was to view this mother's right as doubtful and to make decisions about my own socialization early on and on my own. That I dared to live alone within human society, according to the latest scientific findings, a unique creation of at least twenty billion years, without a mother and a master, is worthy of examination. Had I taken my mother's grave warnings and her attempts at choking me seriously, the road to the tragedies I have faced might have gone unpaved. My mother was the last remnant of the millennium-old goddess culture that was going extinct and was at an impasse. As a child, I did not hesitate to feel free, neither fearing this symbol nor feeling the need for its love. However, I never forgot that the only condition for my existence was my mother's honor and dignity, and that these should be protected. I intended to protect her dignity, but in a way that I thought was right. After I learned this lesson, my mother no longer existed for me. As that remnant of the goddess faded from my attention, I never felt the need to question what she felt for me. Although a cruel separation, this was the reality. I don't know whether to call them prophecies or curses, but I began to remember all that she said during worsening tragic moments. She offered such truths as would have gone undetected by even the best of sages. One major truth she had ascertained was: "You trust your friends a lot, but you will be very lonely." Whereas my truth was that I would establish sociality together with my friends.

This is the beginning of my life story. Even if my mother had wanted to, there was no society that she could have passed on to me. Her society had long since disbanded. What she wanted to do was to offer me something to hold on to in life. She wanted to give me the opportunity that she was unable to acquire. My father's story was a little different but still largely similar. I have always considered the reality of my family as the most unassertive legacy of a disbanded, enervated, ancestral culture that grounded itself in the remnants of the clan cult. I was never inclined toward village society or the official state society that began with primary school, nor did I understand much of either. With seemingly outstanding success, I had climbed to the final year of Turkey's oldest and most well-known faculty of political science. The result was that my ability to learn had been delivered a fatal blow. The school of revolution that I chose later was a ruthless mill wheel that grinded life down even further. Had I pursued my early passion for the mountains, I might have avoided the tragedy. My concern for saving and developing my friends never allowed for this. As I threw myself at the eastern and western gates of Europe—the last representative of our civilization—I would find myself adrift in the icy cold environment of capital and profit calculations. At this point, I lacked the cogency necessary to advance. Perhaps there was no breeze that I could allow myself to drift upon—by this point, it no longer interested me in any case, even had there been one. During this time, some of my comrades immolated themselves. Many bold and courageous young women and men were ready to give all they had. None of this can be denied. They carried out a far-reaching resistance and showed incredible commitment. None of this achieved anything but the exacerbation of my loneliness.

When the masters of all continents conspired in unison to take me by force and brought me to the İmralı Island, a legend came to mind: the Greek god Zeus, who chained the demi-god Prometheus to the Caucasian mountains and each day fed his liver to giant eagles. I am talking about the Prometheus who stole fire and freedom from the gods for humanity! It was as if the legend was coming true in my case.

A question may come to mind as to the kind of relationship that might exist between this short life story and my court (European Court of Human Rights; ECtHR) defense. This is the relationship that I would like to shine some light upon. In doing so, I have the additional important goal of proving that the sorcery of the relationship between capital and profit is far greater than any sorcerer and more cruel than the most cruel god-king. No other century has been as cruel and bloody as the twentieth century. I was a child of this century, and I had to untangle it.

However, it is difficult to subject this reality to a cogent evaluation under the blackout conditions created by the incredible ideological influence of Western civilization. It is not that easy to escape the wizard's web. At the endgame, the phenomenon we call *the Turk* will also lose, and perhaps the residue of humanity that is unfit to live will be left behind.

Therefore, if the court is truly the sort of judicial power it claims to be, it might make sense to take it seriously and to advance a meaningful defense. The Middle East has been under the supervisory machinery of European civilization for the last two centuries. Complete chaos and daily tragedies are what is experienced today. Those who judge have always been the masters. Their judgments have always been one-sided. In their hands, the scales of justice, it would seem, is law that measures and distributes rights. What is distributed is punishment in exchange for the seized values and profits.

European civilization has established the EU, the European Convention of Human Rights, and the European Court of Human Rights as its judicial power against the brutal twentieth-century wars and injustices that were of its own creation. If the Court does not wish to exist in name only, it has to correctly determine what is being prosecuted in my case. Let me point out right away that an ex gratia clemency within the narrow limits of individual rights cannot be seen to offset the aggravated isolation that has already carried on for seven years. Such an approach would indeed constitute real punishment for both myself and the people I represent. In my defenses, I will question this punishment. It is clear that I have developed an approach that is far from official law and from the logic of a traditional defense. I have to develop it in such a manner. Bringing at least some clarity to the tragedy of peoples experienced under the influence of Europe and contributing to a solution, even if only to a certain extent, would constitute a certain remuneration for all that has happened. In particular, avoiding new open-ended tragedies will depend on the strength of the defense and the response it receives. That is why I saw the need to focus on social history, the Middle East, and the Kurdish phenomenon. It is thus of great importance to bring a new interpretation, based on self-critique and the lessons drawn from recent history, to the PKK as a movement—a new actor that needs to be taken seriously—and to the Kurdish solution that, if successful, would set off a chain reaction in the Middle East.

The foundation of this tragedy—resembling the Arab-Israeli tragedy but in contemporary attire—was laid by the 1916 Sykes-Picot Agreement, which was the Middle East Project of its era. At the outset, it did not seem to aim for the grave developments seen in the present day. The other established political formations were intended as instruments for a solution. But, in fact, the end result was a "modern" polish over the despotic statist society tradition of the Middle East. This polish is coming off abundantly and continuously. What emerged from beneath this polish was the power of the tribal-ethnic tradition of the last five thousand years or more, and a state tradition that offers no solution but is the residue of the hollow despotisms. As the polish has lost its luster, it has become clear that the left and the right, nationalist Islamists, so-called intellectuals, and political currents offer nothing different from this sociopolitical reality. The capitalist society system is experiencing one of the most significant offensives of globalization. In a nutshell, the Middle East's share in the general crisis of the capitalist society system is "chaos." Periods of chaos have their own unique characteristics. They represent the critical "interval" where the laws that rendered meaning to the old structures are dissolved and new ones begin to flourish. What will emerge from this creative "interval" will be determined by the efforts of the forces of life to create new meaning and structures. These efforts constitute what is called ideological, political, and moral struggle.

The Kurds are entering this period of chaos with the negative burden of a ruthless tradition—being in a constant state of crisis, with a culture of massacre breathing down its neck. If they are not guided by a highly sensitive approach in terms of meaning and corresponding structures, they might easily become an element of a conflict that transcends the Arab-Israeli tragedy in intensity. Their social characteristics have been crippled and frayed by the despotic state, leaving them open to the use by all kinds of external factors. In any event, traditionally they perceive this type of rule as their destiny, as an unchanging paradigm. However, as the US—the hegemonic power that leads the new globalization offensive, with its new Middle East Project—has made the Kurds an essential element of its agenda, the process is becoming even more sensitive. The

US is carrying out policies through crude experimentation. This, in turn, is causing tragedies in society in the Middle East, with every step they take, as well as leading to the—intentional or unintentional—imposition of an agenda with an unclear objective. The EU will do nothing but follow this process more slowly and more rationally based on its profit margins. The despotic state understanding does not traditionally see the Kurds as a reality and approach them in friendship. "If they raise their heads, crush them" is the only policy, and it is learned by rote. In conjunction with this, a totally treacherous and collaborationist Kurdish tradition—familial-ism—is always maintained to be used when necessary. It is in character that they do not hesitate to engage in all sorts of unprincipled coopera-tion, not only with the local despotic state structures but also with the new imperial masters.

The remaining Kurdish phenomenon has been torn to pieces and narrowed down to the largest possible extent and, beyond being ignorant, is made up of familial objects that have been the subject of massacre—both in terms of the mind and of the form. Kurds are not even aware of "how to be themselves." In the chaos of the Middle East, this Kurdish object can be instrumentalized to any end. It is an extremely convenient material, which could be used in a brutal way, but even more so could serve to structure a Middle East worth living in.

If the Kurds successfully answer the question of "how to be themselves" in a democratic way, no doubt they will be a leading force in successfully exiting the chaos. They will not only reverse their own ill fate but also that of all of the people in the region. In this way, they will be able to put an end to the bloody balance sheet of the five-thousand-year-old ruthless tradition of civilization. By ending the lineage of the masters of civilization whom they initially gave rise to and always served blindly to feed, the Kurds will make the most important contribution to the age of free lineage of the peoples. Otherwise, as the offensives of the imperial masters drag on, become more pervasive, and fail, they will be unable to avoid playing roles as a "die and kill" force that do not fall short of those of Israel-Palestine throughout the region. What is already happening is nothing more than the sparks for even bigger conflicts. If we look at the ploys of the Israel-Palestine states, we do not need an oracle to predict the future of "Kurdish state" ploys. The difference in principle between legitimate armed defense and violence that aims to create a state as the tool for a solution must be clearly understood.

Therefore, a realistic "solution based on democratic and peaceful method" that is not state-oriented but that will not accept this blind chaos as an ongoing way of living is vital. One must think deeply about both their profound meaning and their creative structures and implement them with passion; this must be the most sacred of all of our efforts. In my defense, I will try to alleviate both the great pain brought about by having the PKK's responsibility and to expand on this option for a solution with some depth, having engaged in genuine self-critique and learned from it.

I think I did the right thing by making using of the İmralı trial period as a search and call for democratic peace, even if under very unfavorable conditions. This phase was valuable because of the possibility for a qualitative transformation. It was a time when the need to abandon the aspiration for a hierarchical and statist society became, in principal, more intense, both consciously and practically. I believe that I have learned the instructive lesson of difficult times. I resisted so that I would neither fall into crude opposition nor into letting myself go in a dastardly way. My defense made a significant contribution to the transformation of Turkey, the political formation called the AKP benefitting most consciously from it. What can be considered a significant loss is that, despite all my efforts, I could not get the allegedly democratic left-wing forces to benefit from it in a similar way. Democracy was being discussed by the right, but not by the left. Therefore, it followed that the right would be on the winning side.

The main objective of my defenses to the European Court of Human Rights (ECtHR) was to draw a correlation between the civilization in Europe and that in the Middle East and to offer a democratic option, particularly to the Kurds, but also regarding developments in general.[1] The withdrawal of the PKK to South Kurdistan was the result of this. Later developments and the US occupation of Iraq have proven this to be the right decision. The discussions around the world in relation to the Middle East is taken up extensively in this book, and the importance of this discussion is becoming clearer every day. I harbor neither a meaningless primitive hostility toward nor the usual submissive approach to Western civilization. I have tried to display an original and creative attitude that is open to a synthesis.

My defense at the court in Athens was an attempt to deftly demonstrate how a more concrete issue can be treated and what the oligarchies are doing to the people.[2] I tried to show, once again, the necessity and importance of evaluating historical problems from the perspective of peoples.

My most recent defense, which you are now reading,[3] will complement the previous ones. Here I take into account the negotiation process
that Turkey-Asia Minor has entered toward the legal and political integration process with the EU.[4] The Kurdish question will play a leading role
in the successful development of the process. Political, democratic, and
human rights criteria can also be seen as the criteria for the solution of
the Kurdish question. However, instead of being wholeheartedly adopted,
Turkey's decision, both in terms of the state and the government, has been
perceived as an obligation. This approach shows Turkey's traditional fear
of the West. However, the hope is that Turkey will come to understand
that a wholehearted and libertarian approach to the question will bring
great benefits not losses to Turkey. It is time to end the game of playing the
Kurdish card with the West, which began with Mosul and Kirkuk when the
Republic in Turkey was founded. Playing such a game has only brought
about undermining the revolutions of the republic and oligarchic degeneration, and, at present, have not resulted in anything but a change in its
characteristic. Treating the synthesis of the democratic republic and a free
Kurdish citizenry as important and achieving a solution will prove the way
to attain true unity and democratization. Western civilization's option of
democratic rights and human rights will not allow for another approach.

Given the criteria of positive law, it does not seem likely that my
rights will be seriously addressed. Besides, the political and economic
background underlying my legal case and the power of the reality of the
plot is way beyond the power of the rule of law. Moreover, law itself is
nothing but politics tied to long-term rules and institutions. This is also
the case for the European Court of Human Rights. All the same, exercising
the right of defense is a moral, political, and juridical duty. I believe that
my defense struggle that has been going on for the last six years is far
superior to my previous ideological-practical defenses, both in terms of
substance and configuration. Those who feel they can make life and death
decisions about others must also be able to judge themselves. Those who
want to defend others must first know how to defend themselves. And, of
course, those who hope to liberate others must first know how to liberate
themselves. In this way, our children's right to be born free, which has
never been the case, will become a reality.

ONE

Social Reality and the Individual

Introduction

My trial has now been dragging on for quite some time. It would be difficult to find another important political trial that has lasted this long.[1] It is still unclear how much longer it will go on for. While, on the one hand, I am imprisoned as the sole inmate under very severe isolation conditions, on the other hand, I press on with my legal defense.

When the ECtHR allowed my "individual complaint" to be heard, it was careful to exclude all political and social aspects of the case. Obviously, this was done to hide an important aspect of the overall reality. It is obvious that this approach has major shortcomings and brings with it the possibility of an unfair trial. A fundamental issue that needs to be clarified is the attempt to detach the individual from the society by "putting the individual in possession of rights," and then asserting that the judicial process is to be conducted on that basis. This procedure constitutes the essence of European culture. Large sections of my first submission were devoted to the attempt to analyze this culture.[2]

Sociality is the condition for the existence of the human species. The separation of humans from the previously existing family of primates and the transition to becoming human proceeded in parallel with the development of sociality. This is a basic fact of social science.

It is impossible to theorize the individual and "society" separately, regardless of the level of abstraction involved. There is no solitary individual. There may be a lonely individual whose society has fallen apart, but at least that individual lives with the memories of the fallen society. With

1

these memories, a new socialization is only a matter of time. The survival and development of the human species is closely related to the level of sociality it has developed. Isolating and condemning an individual to solitude is the most brutal way to weaken and enslave that individual. Even groups of slaves, serfs, and workers in the city constitute a society. From time to time, they remind themselves of their own existence by rebelling. On the other hand, solitude is highly instructive. The process of seclusion of all the famous sages and prophets in history reflects this fact.

Individualism is a highly contradictory concept. Its flip side is when it is totally and insanely turned loose and directed against the society. Society's life according to rules that are not based on coercion is called morality. Individualism strains this morality. More precisely, the development of individualism in European civilization is associated with a weakening of morality. While in Eastern civilization society is the main focus of attention, in Western civilization the individual is the focus of attention. This definition of the individual can end in two different ways: while the individual who rules and exploits can rise to the rank of emperor, the exploited and condemned individuals live in the deepest slavery. It is not by coincidence that the brutal face of the twentieth century emerges from this generalized, deepened slavery of the capitalist system that spreads across all levels of society. This sort of order, with its ubiquitous masters, has lost its fundamental moral values and is, in the final analysis, capable of anything because of its ambition for profit and acquisition.

The loneliness, imprisonment, and isolation that I live with is linked to this general structure of the system. If a society—a people—is prevented from being "itself," this means: you are the prisoner of the weakest of all types of loneliness—that of the individual who has been broken off from the society, ever since birth. To the extent that you cease to be yourself, you integrate into another society. But then you are, again, no longer yourself. The choice between great solitude or surrendering to another reality is a dire dilemma that I have referred to as the "Kurdish trap"—a choice tantamount to that between the devil and the deep blue sea.

Today, concepts like difference and sharing with *the Other* are increasingly part of the debate.[3] It is correct to say that social wealth and the creation of diversity will develop by sharing with the other—so long as it is voluntary. The system, however, has its eyes set on a completely different policy, one of planned uniformity and homogenization. This is ethnic cleansing, genocide, assimilation, and ceasing to be yourself. It is this type of policy that is intensely experienced in the Kurdish reality. The sources of this policy are nineteenth- and twentieth-century biopower,[4] racism, and fascism; all totalitarian understandings of power. While aiming to create a strong nation and race, the result is aggression and war, with roots undoubtedly stretching back to the origins of hierarchical society. It was, however, in the twentieth century that it became a systematic and widespread state policy. Two major world wars and a large number of regional and local wars finally forced Western civilization into a sine qua non unity, primarily based on the principles called the European Union (EU) norms. In this sense, it is effectively Europe's self-critique before the rest of humanity.

An individual that run amok and a state power that develops in contradiction to moral values are capable of any misdeed, all the more so when the accumulation of capital's greed for profit is the driving force. Even laying aside the plot behind my being handed over, my trial under the existing conditions calls for the most severe penalty, because I have transformed a society that had dropped all legitimate claims into a society that makes demands, which is a radical action against a system that indulges in the greed for power and profit.

Even raising the question about one's own society, culture, mother tongue, and freedom is treated as insurrection, separatism, and treason against the fatherland. It is a "crime," the corollary of which didn't even exist in either the Ottoman civilization or in the Turkish tribal system. This crime is an invention of biopower, racism, fascism, and all of the totalitarian regimes of European civilization, and in the twentieth century it was exported to the Turkish state system. The whole world has suffered under it.

If I am guilty of any crime, it is that I too was to some degree infected by the culture of power and war. I also got involved in this game because state power was understood as necessary for freedom and, to this end, war was also viewed as a necessity, like a religious order for believers. Almost no one who acted in the name of the oppressed was able to escape this malady. From that perspective, I am guilty not only from the vantage point of the ruling system but also from that of the freedom struggle for which I have sacrificed everything.

To the end, I will commit myself to this self-critique, not only in theory but also in the noble practice of my solitude. But how will the system pay for its crime of preventing a society and a people to be itself by force and subterfuge? If this trial is to be fair, the arguments of both sides must be heard in a balanced way and a decision made accordingly. A jurisdiction that has lost its ties with science can never be fair. Clearly, social science will be the main weapon that I will resort to. That I walk on the right path to the extent that I am enlightened by such social science is a requirement if I am to be a dignified human being.

We also must not neglect the destruction of nature brought about by a system that subjugates society in such an extreme way. Ecological and feminist thinking and practice can contribute to a reestablishment of our relationship to a natural social life that has been lost. In my view, defining "democracy" correctly—the political option of peoples—and revealing the potential democracy has to solve problems is one of the most pressing issues. While the new wave of globalization presents a sugarcoated free market of commodities that it fetishizes as the only solution—knowing that what it actually offers us is the oldest thief and the usurper—we should further elucidate our ecological and democratic option and raise it as our symbol of a new life. Thus, not only shall we render the ideals of freedom and equality in history more current and livable, we will show that not a single step taken to this end is in vain. Just as something that exists in nature never disappears, no social value that has existed ever completely disappears.

That in my defenses I am once again drawing closer to social reality is related to the philosophical depth I've reached. Philosophy as a social science must again play the role it did in the period of its birth. A return to philosophy, as opposed to today's science enmeshed in power, is the departure point of a free society.

Countless contemporary and historical examples have shown that a democracy that does not rest on philosophy can quickly degenerate or even be misused by demagogues as the foulest tool for ruling the people. One way to prevent this from happening is to carry out a political struggle that integrates the tradition that considers ethics and science as an inseparable whole. If we shoulder that responsibility, we will be able to create a way of life and a world based on freedom and equality out of the system's crisis.

Natural Society

The relationship between society and nature is an area that social science is increasingly focusing on. Even though it is obvious that the environment has an influence on society, this fact has only recently become a topic of scientific research and philosophy. This interest was triggered by the recognition of the catastrophic extent to which the social system affects the environment. When we search for the source of this problem, we encounter the dominant social system, which is dangerously at odds with nature. It is becoming increasingly scientifically clear that alienation from the natural environment is the source of thousands of years of conflict within society; the more conflicts and wars within society have arisen, the more society's contradiction with nature has increased.[5] Today's watchword is the subordination and enslavement of nature and the ruthless appropriation and exploitation of its resources.

It is claimed that nature is cruel, which is certainly not the case. The fact is that humans, who have developed an enormous amount of intra-species cruelty also treat nature cruelly, as the current environmental problems indicate. No other species has exterminated as many species of plants and animals as humans have. Should this process of extermination continue unabated, humans might well meet the same fate as the dinosaurs. If the speed of population growth is not reduced and human's current destructive frenzy and misuse of technology is not stopped, we will soon reach a point where the continuation of human life is no longer possible.

This reality together with an increase in war, even within society itself, very dangerous forms of politics, increasing poverty and unemployment, the loss of the moral foundations of society, and a robot-like, alienated existence represent existential threats to humanity. Without a sufficiently clear analysis of the causes of these social developments, we will be unable to describe civilization, with its class struggles and its wars, in a theoretically accurate way or find solutions. The fact that sociology offers fewer answers to today's problems than does religion only shows that the social sciences and, therefore, the entire structure of science must be subjected to scrutiny.

Science has allegedly made massive advances, so why is there such madness? As is well known, the twentieth century was many times bloodier than all of human history that preceded it. This suggests serious errors and flaws in the structure of scientific thought. One may, with some justification, object that these errors are perhaps not a result of the scientific findings themselves but, rather, flaws in the way that governments implement them. However, this alone would not relieve science and scientists and their institutions of their responsibility.

In my view, today's scientists and their institutions are more backward and irresponsible in their dependence on the rulers both in terms of morality and faith than the priests in ancient Egypt and Mesopotamia's first kingdoms. The religions and prophets within the Abrahamic tradition rebelled against the kingly lineages of the Nimrods and pharaohs and played a huge role in the development of humanity in terms of morality and faith.[6] This is the positive aspect of the priestly tradition. On the other hand, scientists under the command of power routinely provided those in power with instruments of destruction, even facilitating the detonation of the atomic bomb against humanity. Thus, there is a serious problem in the relationship between science and power. We may see science as a social achievement and an important value, but we cannot explain why science has led to so many catastrophes. Since we cannot simply ignore these catastrophes as if they never happened, we cannot accept or even forgive these scientists and their institutions.

Until we find an explanation for this primary contradiction, sociology and the other sciences must be subjected to scrutiny. Unless we can determine where the system has made a fundamental error, leading humanity astray and threatening its future, the development of a theory and practice of liberation, freedom, and equality will not allow us to achieve our lofty goals. However much we may try, in the end, we will only carry water to the mills of the dominant social system once again. If we do not clarify this contradiction, we will also be unable to clearly pinpoint the other defects in the system.

In this book, I would like to uncover just how this contradiction lies at the root of European civilization. The Western social system has been better than any other at disguising itself at its most crucial points. It is the system that has used propaganda to achieve a pronounced distortion of ethics and morality. We can easily show that we don't live in the age of greatest freedom but, rather, in the age of the most sophisticated enslavement. As a result, I feel obliged to define the various social forms in my own terms.

By the term "natural society,"[7] I mean an order of human communities that began with the dissociation of the human species from the primates and existed for a long time until the emergence of hierarchical society. In anthropology, these communities of twenty to thirty people are usually called "clans." Based on the stone tools they used, they are also called Paleolithic and Neolithic humanity. These people primarily subsisted as hunters and gatherers on the basis of what they found in nature. In a certain sense, they got by with the products provided by nature. Their eating habits were similar to those of related animal species. For that reason, we can't speak of a social problem. The clan was continuously on the lookout, hunting and gathering whatever it found. With the use of tools and the discovery of fire, the yield increased, and, concomitantly, the species developed faster and the distance from other primates increased. The natural rules of evolution determined this development.

The mentality and communication system of natural society are still largely unexplored. Even the intriguing question of the stage of intellectual development at which we can speak of "humans" is an issue that remains important. In this context, the question of whether the mentality or the structure and tools are primary criteria is important. Historically, this distinction underlies the separation between idealist and materialist philosophy.

The latest scientific findings, for example, the quantum physics of subatomic particles and waves, have opened up entirely new fields for this discussion. The possibility of being two different things at the same time, the so-called particle-wave duality, has been proven. Heisenberg's uncertainty principle refers to the existence of an ambiguity that for structural reasons humans can never completely eliminate. Even phenomena like intuitive orders with free will have been postulated. The notion of coarse and inanimate matter is increasingly abandoned. On the contrary, we are confronted with a universe very much alive and free. The real mystery, however, is humans, especially their thoughts. I am not suggesting a slide into idealism and subjectivism, but it is now assumed that the origin of all of the diversity in the universe is to be found at the boundaries of its tiniest parts, in the quantum realm.

All the processes that takes place in and beyond the realm of atomic particles, in the wave-particle universe, constitute all kinds of beings, especially the "liveliness" feature. This is what we mean when we say the intuitiveness of the quantum. Indeed, such a diversity of nature only seems possible by a great inherent intelligence and preference for freedom. How could so many plants, flowers, living beings, and, in the end, humans derive from coarse, inanimate matter? Even though it is asserted that all living metabolism is based on molecules, it does not seem possible to satisfactorily explain the diversity of nature without explaining what takes place *in* the system of molecules, atoms, and subatomic particles and at the level of particles and waves.

We can carry out an analogous analysis of the cosmos. What happens at the outer limit of the universe—provided it is actually finite—is similar to what happens in the realm of the quanta. What we are confronted with here is the concept of a "living universe." Cosmology is faced with the question of whether the universe itself can perhaps be described as a living being with mind and matter.

The human, who is right in between the cosmos and the quantum, can be called a "microcosm." The result: if you want to understand both universes—the quantum and the cosmos—unravel the human being! The subject of all perception is the human being. The knowledge of all areas from the quantum to the cosmos is the product of humans. This also brings the perception process of the human being into focus. In a certain way, this process mirrors the evolutionary history of the approximately twenty-billion-year history of the universe. We can regard humans as some sort of a microcosm. In them, we can trace the evolutionary history of matter from subatomic particles and waves right up to highly complicated DNA molecules. In addition, in humans we can also observe the history of all developmental processes beginning with the first stages of plants and animals. In the development of a human being, known as ontogeny, embryos go through all developmental stages of biology from simple to more complicated living beings (phylogeny). The rest is complemented by society and evolution. It is with social evolution that science has attained its present level. In this sense, we can consider humans as a "summary of the universe."

Were it not for the fact that all materials of which humans are composed possess qualities such as vitality, intuition, and freedom, then human vitality, intuition, and freedom would not have developed as an overall expression of these qualities. From something that does not exist, nothing new arises. This statement is in contrast to the concept of "inanimate matter." There is no doubt that consciousness only develops within a human type of organization and society. But it should also be clear that consciousness could not develop if the matter of which this form of organization and society is composed and with which it interacts did not have qualities such as knowledge, intuition, sense, and originality. If a thing is not already present in the essence, how could it be created?

This analysis suggests that humans did not acquire knowledge either through a simple reflection of external nature or through a form of Cartesian idealism. It makes more sense to assume that the origin of humans followed a pattern similar to what we find in the cosmos and in the quantum universe. Of course, these laws operate in keeping with human specificity. The universes express themselves in the human being. Therefore, a better understanding of humans leads to a better understanding of the universe. The well-known philosophical principle "know thyself" also reflects this fact. Self-knowledge is the foundation of all knowledge. All knowledge acquired without knowing oneself will, in the end, be nothing more than an aberration.

Therefore, in human society, all institutions and behaviors that lack self-reflection inevitably assume an errant and distorted character. This explains the anomalous, contradictory, bloody, and repressive character of all social systems that are based on knowledge without self-knowledge. Therefore, we can assume as a fundamental, universal, and, therefore, also social rule that a natural process of development acceptable for human society arises from knowledge of the self.

On the basis of this assumption, what can we say about the nature of human self-knowledge in natural society? We can at least say that in natural society each human being was duty bound to safeguard the survival of other clan members along with their own. None of the clan members could imagine having a more privileged life than other clan members, nor could they imagine life outside the clan. They might hunt, there might even be cannibalism, but all of this is for the survival of the clan. The rule of life in the clan is "all or nothing," i.e., "everyone or no one." Anthropology emphasizes this feature of clans and speaks of a kind of group personality. In that context, nobody can imagine an autonomous individual personality or personal decisions. The particular significance of the clan lies in the fact that it is the first and fundamental form of human existence.

This was a form of society that was free of privilege, class, and hierarchy and that knew no exploitation. It existed for millions of years.[8] We can conclude that for a long time the development of the human species as a society was not based on relations of domination but on the principle of solidarity. Nature took its place in collective memory as a "mother" that raises humans in its fold. Humans lived harmoniously with each other and with nature.

The symbol of clan consciousness was the totem. The totem probably represented the first abstract conceptual system. This system, often called totem religion, formed the first concept of "sacredness" and "taboos." The clan declared itself sacred in the symbolic value of the totem. In that way, it arrived at the first concept of morality. The knowledge that there was no chance of survival without the clan community gave this social form of existence the aura of sacredness, which had to be symbolized and revered as the highest value.

This is the source of the power of religious belief. Here we have the primordial form of religion in the broadest sense. Religion was the first form of social consciousness and was inseparably linked to moral concepts. It was only much later that religion gradually turned from a collective consciousness into a rigid belief.

After the stage of the totem, the further development of social consciousness took place in the form of religion. Thus, religion is the first fundamental memory of society, its deep-rooted tradition, and the source of its moral beliefs. Any consciousness that the clan community developed through its practice always connected it to the totem and, through the totem, to its own abilities. The growing success of the human community brings with it constant veneration, taking the symbolic form of the totem. The blessing of the totem is the power of the "sacred," but the sacred itself is nothing other than the power of society.

The sanctity of this power comes openly to the fore in magic. The attempt to influence the environment through magical rituals was originally an attempt to strengthen society. Magic is, in this sense, also the mother of science. In clan society, women were regarded as wise, because they alone possessed the knowledge of the origin of life and birth and constantly observed nature. For this reason, in many societies magic was performed by women.

The clan was a unit with the women at its center. Men did not yet possess power over women. The male role in procreation was either unknown or considered to be of secondary importance. The children only knew who their mothers were. However, the central role of women is not just a matter of biology. Almost all sculptures that have survived from this period show the traits of women. In natural society, their life practice meant women were the ones with the broadest knowledge. The fact that they gave birth and raised children led them to perfect their gathering and sustaining skills. Scholars also attribute a leading role in the development of language to women. All these facts led to women's social influence.

The bellicose and power-hungry character traits of men are often ascribed to their role as hunters. Men's physical traits forced them to look for game that was farther away and to protect the clan from danger. This secondary social role explains why men remained more or less pale and lacking in profile. Private relationships had not yet developed within the clan. What was procured by gathering and hunting belonged to everyone. The children were the children of the whole clan. Neither men nor women had yet become exclusive. Because of these particular features, this form of society is also called primitive communism.

The emergence of the clan's way of life meant the birth of society, its first memory, and the basis for the development of its primal consciousness and concepts of "faith." What remains is the insight that a healthy society must be based on its natural environment and the power of women, and that human existence was realized by a strong solidarity that knew neither exploitation nor oppression. In that sense, humanity is the intersection of these fundamental values.

It would be absurd to believe that the social experience of millions of years has vanished into thin air. In nature, nothing is ever destroyed, and this is all the more true for society, which *is* a form of nature. It is an important insight of the dialectical view of history that a later stage of development supersedes the previous one in the precise sense that it also includes it. The idea that development takes place when opposites cancel each other out through mutual annihilation in the course of development is erroneous.[9] On the contrary, the law of dialectics states that thesis and antithesis continue their existence in syntheses in a richer formation. In the same way, clan values also undergo further developments through new syntheses.

The concepts of "freedom" and "equality" remain fundamental today because of life in clan society, which I call natural society. Even before freedom and equality were consciously formulated, they were, in their natural form, already hidden in the clan way of life. Wherever freedom and equality are lost, these concepts—which secretly live on in social memory and are, in fact, the basic principles of every developed society—will quickly come to the fore again. As society develops in the direction of hierarchy and state institutions, these institutions will be pursued relentlessly by freedom and equality. At heart, it is clan society itself that is struggling here.

TWO

Hierarchical Statist Society:
The Birth of Slave Society

On Method

There are different ways to categorize the history of human societies using different criteria. If, for example, we focus on the fundamental mode of thinking, then mythological, metaphysical, and positivist scientific ages is an important classification. Marxism, on the other hand, concentrates on class and divides the ages into primitive communism, slavery, feudalism, capitalism, and socialism and its aftermath. Another suggestion has been the division of ages into fundamental cultural civilizations.

I would like to suggest another division. Here I refer to dialectics with its triad of thesis, antithesis, and synthesis, which was worked out by Hegel and became his main philosophical method. According to dialectics, all entities in the universe possess a dualist quality. It is this contradictory structure that enables movement. Of course, this movement is not a mechanical movement but, rather, a creative inner movement that brings about change and diversity. For example, we can describe the beginning of the universe as a contradiction between being and nonbeing. The contradiction between being and nonbeing gave rise to something new, movement itself. Being could not unfold without nonbeing, nor could it set itself in motion. The essence of becoming was the resistance of being against nonbeing. While being attempted to terminate nonbeing, and nonbeing attempted to terminate being, a third current, a kind of synthesis, the becoming universe, finally appeared.[1] It is similar with the dualism of particle and wave. Particles and waves are both impossible on their own; every particle also has wave character, just as every wave also has particle character. Through the synthesis of these two contradictory properties, they can form movement and, therefore, also becoming. Another example is the contradiction between sameness and diversity. The concept of "sameness" only makes sense in contrast to diversity. Where there is no diversity, sameness is a sort of nonbeing, of nonexistence.

A more vivid contradiction is the one between animate and inanimate. The emergence of life represents an extraordinary leap in the development of the universe, which science, all its efforts notwithstanding, has not yet been able to fully explain. The fact that scientists are now able to sequence and chart genes and clone living beings does not mean that they have actually understood the phenomenon of life. The molecular structure of life alone cannot explain the phenomenon. A suitable external environment (atmosphere and hydrosphere) and corresponding molecular structures are prerequisites for the emergence of life, but these are only the structural building blocks of life, its material order. The decisive aspect is the relationship of this material order to immaterial facts, such as liveliness and sense.

The most significant vulgar materialist error was to equate subjectivity—or liveliness and sense—with the material configuration. Even in quantum physics, this sameness is collapsing, and people feel compelled to resort to an intuition-like explanation.

The human intelligence (brain) among living beings is even more interesting. One definition of humans is "nature rendered self-conscious."[2] Here, we face the decisive question: Why does nature need self-reflection? Where does the real origin of the capacity of matter to think lie? In posing these questions, our intention is not to once again problematize the search for god. Rather, we have to analyze the phenomena of the universe, existence, and nature in conceptual terms that go far beyond such extremely simplistic explanatory attempts. My paradigm is based on the assumption that the universe is enormously rich, productive, and diverse, with unbounded developmental possibilities.

Peoples' conception of the universe in previous ages, for example, the mythological, the metaphysical, or the positivist-science paradigms, led to totally different notions and attitudes. Whereas in mythology each phenomenon was correlated with a god, in metaphysics the Aristotelian concept of "God as the first mover," the "unmoved mover," was predominant. Positivist science, in turn, looked for vulgar materialist explanations for all phenomena and developed a philosophy of strict causality and linear development.

Of course, it would be interesting to know the approach in the animal world. I wonder with what feelings the reptiles, the birds, and the mammals perceive their surroundings. And the perception of stones and sand particles? They too have an attitude. The universe and the nature as a whole is an attitude—one that is in unlimited motion, at that.

The existence of humanity is also a phenomenon related to all things that developed before or after its emergence. For us, the most important question is: How can we construct the thesis, antithesis, and synthesis of this phenomenon? If we define the human and their society as a being with the most developed capacity to sense, determining the fundamental contradiction in this phenomenon, as well as the final synthesis, will allow us to achieve the highest stage of scientific conceptualization. Since the human being is at the center of our interest, we also want to know how the fundamental dialectics of this being proceed and what potential synthesis this being is moving toward or transforming into.

First and foremost, the social sciences have to analyze these fundamental notions. The most interesting state of being of the general universal becoming—the human attitude—cannot reach a correct social science without doing this and will drown in a sea of innumerable individual phenomena. This is one of the reasons for the lack of direction in today's social science. The concepts, assumptions, and theories of social phenomena that people developed early on, since the mythological age, were not only insufficient for explaining the facts but were also grossly distorted. This was especially so as social phenomena became more complex and complicated with the onset of monotheistic religions and metaphysical philosophy and finally ended in the cul-de-sac with positive science. These explanatory patterns for social phenomena are largely responsible for a bloody and exploitative system like capitalism gaining power over humanity. If humans are unable to correctly analyze sociality—the form of their own being—they may well go the way of the dinosaur.

In the wake of two world wars, many social scientists attempted a renewal, but these efforts did not go beyond determining some limited facts. Even most aspiring schools of thought, including Marxism, made limited contributions to a solution. Marxism attached the world of the oppressed and exploited, in whose name it specifically spoke, to a new dogma and understanding of politics that functioned as a substitute for the ruling social system, and, this, as a result, is precisely why Marxism failed to reach its ideals.

That a whole number of other schools in the area of social science were no more successful than many philosophical or religious groups of the ancient world or the medieval age is clear in light of their contribution to what's happening in the world of today. Social science and its institutions have played an important role in the genocidal dimensions of wars, unbridled greed for profit, and the ever-increasing destruction of the ecology. They serve those who hold political power and the forces of war in an unprecedented manner and must thus be assigned a major share of responsibility. Their inability to stop those who hold political power and their wars or to circumvent the unlimited greed for profit shows the bankruptcy of social science and its institutions and proves its betrayal of humanity. Therefore, a new and sufficient understanding and restructuring of social science suitable for and adapted to addressing the current fundamental problems of humanity remains especially important. This is a precondition for effective political action and organization.

These connections are the background for the kind of understanding of social science that we hope to develop here. The fundamental concepts and hypotheses I will be presenting should be seen as efforts in that direction. To the extent that efforts like this intensify and institutionalize themselves, the possibility of finding solutions to important problems will increase, and that is the approach that will be taken in this attempt to form a very general conceptualization.

The previous section represented my attempt to define the sense in which it is possible to speak of a "natural society." After this excursion into the world of social science concepts and my own epistemological paradigm, we can now turn to the origins of hierarchical society.

The Advent of Hierarchy
The clan-type social organization spread over time and space, gradually gaining diversity and increasing in numbers. Over time, this community grew and perfected its identity around the mother-woman. In the Neolithic Age, the mother-woman took the lead in developing the domestic order. In this system, the women took care of food, clothing, and other daily-use items. Through observations made, the woman acquired knowledge and attained the position of a "wise woman." She was also a powerful mother-woman to the extent that she succeeded in tightly integrating many of children and men close to her into this system. The widespread religious system of the goddesses, the feminine elements in the language, and the

numerous female figures in artistic portrayals are all clear evidence of the mother-woman's rising power. As such, we can speak of the development of an unbridled feminine cult.

There was probably a certain amount of dissatisfaction among men at that time. There was jealousy and anger toward the children who gathered around the mother-woman and toward the men who got more of the woman's attention and supported her. In fact, a significant number of the men were, of course, distant from this system. It is likely that those the mother-woman did not find useful and the elderly men were largely left outside the system.

This contradiction was initially insubstantial, but over time it gradually developed. Developments in hunting not only increased men's capacity to fight but also their knowledge. The old men who were excluded tended to develop a patriarchal ideology. The shamanist religion shows this tendency in a particularly striking way. Shamans were something like the prototype of the male priest. They worked systematically to develop a countermovement and a house order meant to undermine women.

In contrast to the mother-woman's advanced domestic order, the men had lived in relatively simple huts in semi-wilderness, and, with shamanism, they were now able to form an opposing house order. The alliance of the shamans with older and more experienced men is an important development. By virtue of their ideological power over some of the young men who joined them over time, they grew increasingly powerful within the community. This made the sources of men's power more important. Both hunting and the defense of the clan against external threats had a military character and were based on killing and wounding. This is the beginning of war culture. In life-or-death situations, there is always an automatic fixation on authority and hierarchy, with the most capable person taking on the position with the highest authority. This was the beginning of another culture that would predominate over the mother-woman cult.

The emergence of authority and hierarchy even before the development of class society represents one of the most important turning points in history. This authority and hierarchy were qualitatively distinct from the mother-woman culture, which was generally characterized by peaceful activities that did not necessitate war of any kind, including gathering and, later on, the cultivation of crops. Hunting, however, an activity that was based on the culture of war and harsh authority, was predominantly the purview of men. The result was that patriarchal authority took root.

Hierarchy and authority were fundamental components of patriarchal culture. The concept of "hierarchy" is the first example of the leadership approach of the authority that amalgamated with the sacred authority of the shaman. This institution of authority, which increasingly placed itself above society, would, with the eventual development of classes, transform itself into state authority. Hierarchical authority, however, was primarily tied to particular persons and not yet institutionalized. Therefore, it could not rule over society in the same measure as state institutions later would. Compliance was still half voluntary, and loyalty was determined by the interests of society. All the same, this process, once it began, was wide-open to the emergence of the state. Nonetheless, primordial communal society did resist this process for a very long time.

Those who accumulated produce enjoyed respect and loyalty only if they shared their surplus with the community. Personal accumulation was considered a major offense. Only those who redistributed what they had accumulated were considered to be good people. The concept of "generosity," still so common among tribal societies, has its roots in this ongoing powerful tradition. Even feasts emerged as a kind of ritual for the distribution of the surplus. From the beginning, the community saw accumulation as the most significant threat it faced and turned resistance against it into the foundation of morality and religion. Traces of this tradition can be found in all religious and moral teachings.[3] Society approved hierarchy only when its usefulness and generosity redounded to its benefit. This sort of hierarchy played a positive and useful role.

This quality of the mother-woman based hierarchy is also the historical basis of the concept of "mother," which is still regarded with much respect and as authority in all societies. Being a mother meant giving birth and nurturing even under the harshest conditions. Not surprisingly, the culture, hierarchy, and authority formed on this basis gained great loyalty. The real explanation of the continuing power of the concept of "mother" is that it forms the foundation of social existence, not some abstract biological capacity to give birth. In this sense, we must understand "mother" and "mother-goddess" as the most important social phenomena and concepts. This culture was completely closed to the phenomenon of the state and embodied all the features that would prevent it from arising.

Against this background, we can locate natural society, which represented the initial thesis, at the beginning of human existence. Before that point, life had been animalistic. Thereafter, however, life was characterized by a development of hierarchical and statist forms of society that stood in contradiction to natural society and dislodged it. The antithetical character of this development is tied to the constant suppression and regression of the natural society.

Natural society, the thesis, existed wherever humans lived and was an effective social system until the end of the Neolithic Age (c. 4000 BCE in the Middle East). It continues to exist to this very day in all social pores, even though it has been suppressed. This continuity is clearly visible in fundamental social concepts. "Family," "tribe," "mother," "fraternity," "freedom," "equality," "friendship," "generosity," "solidarity," "feasts," "bravery," "sacredness," and many other phenomena and concepts are relics of that social system. The oppositional hierarchical and statist society has continued to cause regression and to suppress this system. This is the reason why it represents the antithesis to the older system. The nested and simultaneous existence of two social systems is in accord with the fundamental laws of dialectics.

On the basis of this interpretation of dialectics, the characters of thesis and antithesis don't develop such that one annihilates the other but in the manner that leads to regression and suppression. As in nature overall, when social systems take the form of thesis and antithesis, these subsume one another within themselves. Nonetheless, the struggle between them undoubtedly leads to important upheavals. The thesis never remains in its old state, but the antithesis is also unable to totally devour the preceding thesis. It can only develop by nourishing itself upon it.

It would be useful at this point to say a few more words about dialectics. During the period of dogmatic Marxism, society understood the dialectic as the annihilation of the thesis by the antithesis, but such an interpretation was a fundamental theoretical error. In all sciences, most of all in biology, we see that symbiosis is of great importance to the development and transformation of phenomena. Annihilation or similar developments occur only in exceptional cases. Rather, the symbiosis of thesis and antithesis is in the foreground. The simplest expression of that symbiosis is the relationship between mother and child. The child develops in dialectical contradiction to the mother. But this contradiction can't be interpreted in such a way that the child annihilates the mother. Rather, there is a symbiosis, which is carried on through the succession of generations. An extreme example of this dialectic is the duality of the snake and the mouse.[4] But even there, balance is retained between the extremely fast propagation

18

of mice and the very slow propagation of snakes. Every day it becomes clearer that beings in nature are not meaningless, and that they all have a certain ecological meaning. Thus, even though "extremes" and "absolute limits" can be valid concepts within very limited parameters, it has by now become scientific common sense that mutual dependence is the fundamental law of nature.

One change I want to make when evaluating social systems relates to inevitableness and randomness. The idea of a linear and continuous progress and strict causality in the Western system of thought, which is rooted in the assumption of divine laws, has lost its validity because of the developments in quantum and cosmos physics mentioned above. In the dialectics of development, the "chaos interval" manifests itself in each phenomenon, and all qualitative changes require such an interval. This shows that continuity and continuous linear progress are intellectual abstractions and a metaphysical approach. It is not always possible for this chaotic interval to lead to linear progress. The interaction of numerous factors at that particular interval can lead to multiple and multifaceted developments.

In human societies, these intervals are called "times of crisis." The social conditions that emerge from a crisis depend on the struggle of the forces involved. Many different systems can develop, with both progressive and regressive developments possible. Besides, concepts like "progress" and "regression" are relative. A permanent march forward actually doesn't fit the universal theory. If this principle of universal progress were valid, metaphysical idealism would be correct, but the assumption of absolute truths is inconsistent with the principle of universal formation. Nature doesn't develop in absolute qualities. Absoluteness means unalterability and sameness. The way our own species developed proves that no such thing exists.

Thus, we can deduce from the characteristics of the laws of physics, chemistry, and biology that the laws of nature are based on these chaotic intervals, and that, as we move toward the development of human beings, these laws take even more flexible forms. In human society in particular, the laws have a more flexible quality. This means that many new laws can emerge during these short intervals. From that perspective, a high level of freedom leads to an enormous diversity of human society. Flexibility creates freedom, and freedom creates diversity. In this sense, humans are a natural wonder who very frequently create their own laws in abundance.

This allows human society to constitute the laws of its own system with the same richness of frequency and abundance.

Thus, there is no law dictating an inevitable development of the hierarchical and statist society from natural society. Perhaps it is possible to speak of a tendency in that direction, but it would be completely wrong to assume that this tendency is compulsory, uninterrupted, and will go to the full possible extent. In the following chapters, I will occasionally talk about how the Marxist assumption that class society is imperative for development has been one of the biggest errors committed in the name of the oppressed and exploited. It meant that from the outset socialism was left to class domination.

In my view, this error was the main reason that Marxism, in the course of its 150-year history, became capitalism's stand-in. Regarding the state, class, and violence as necessary phases of social development and progress belittles or even ignores the fantastic resistance of natural society that continues to this day. It automatically relinquishes history to the ruling forces. People who see the existence of classes as fate become unwitting ideologues of the ruling classes. In this sense, Marxism has played a very dangerous role and has done so in the name of the oppressed and exploited.

Hierarchy and class rule developed, but this was not an inevitable development. It was a development contrived by the forces that established hierarchy and statehood based on hierarchy and enforced it with tyranny and fraud. The core forces of natural society tirelessly resisted this process but were continuously pushed back and forced into the narrowest of areas and spaces. There were certain areas from which they were totally excluded. The politics and propaganda of the ruling system succeeded in convincing almost everyone that any society will consist of class and state hierarchies. The game called *fate* is the metaphysical epithet for this praxis. Practically all religious, confessional, philosophical, and scientific schools have played this game. This is the result of enormous physical and mental oppression and the policies and propaganda of priestly ideology and the god-king state, with roots that reach back thousands of years. Some have called this game *mythology*, others, *philosophy*, and still others, *science*. Finally, we have reached the current situation in which ideology and science are all but totally amalgamated with the state. The part Marxism has played in all of this cannot be stressed enough. I will try to show how this game was played and who the players were.

Patriarchy

The first victim of hierarchical society was the domestic order of the mother-woman. Women were perhaps the very first social group to be oppressed in this system. As a result of the established and firmly rooted values of male dominated society, this oppression, which essentially started even before the beginning of written history, has hitherto been all but ignored the social sciences. Drawing women step-by-step into hierarchical society, with the loss of all of their prominent social attributes, was the first momentous counterrevolution in society. To this very day, if we examine the situation of women within the family, we will be horrified when we see the far-reaching dimensions of this repression and deception. For example, the so-called "honor killings" and "love killings" that are the monopoly of men are a small indicator of what is going on. It would be totally wrong to ascribe this process to biological differences between the sexes. The role or the laws of biology cannot determine the course of social relations. At most, the reciprocal relationships of female and male traits can be evaluated, as is the case for all species. The mother-woman cult was primarily subjugated for social reasons. The reasons for oppression and the accompanying ideology are, thus, essentially social in nature. Here, explanations based on the sex drive or other psychological phenomena are nothing more than perfidious diversionary maneuvers.

The "strongman" who developed his mettle in hunting and organized a group around him became aware of his power and made sure that it was accepted. Then he gradually took control of the mother-woman's domestic order. This process took until the founding of the first Sumerian city-states in the fourth millennium BCE. On the basis of surviving cuneiform tablets, we can reconstruct the process surprisingly well. The Epic of Inanna, the goddess of Uruk, the first city-state, is particularly instructive. It describes an era when the woman cult and the patriarchal cult were in equilibrium but depicts a sharp dispute: Inanna, the goddess of Uruk, goes to see Enki, the god of the city of Eridu, at his palace. Once there, she demands the return of the 104 *me*, the fundamental discoveries and inventions of civilization, which she regards as her rightful property. By various means, she succeeds in bringing them back to Uruk. This legend is a key narrative that helps us to understand this period. In the epic, Inanna forcefully stresses the fact that the *me*, as the achievements of civilization, belong to the mother-goddess, and that the male god Enki had played no role in these achievements but had robbed them from her using violence and subterfuge. Inanna's efforts are an attempt to reestablish the culture of the mother-goddess.

It is generally assumed that this and similar epics stem from around 3000 BCE, i.e., the point at which patriarchy and the influence of mother-woman were still in balance in the Middle East. Immediately thereafter, however, this mother-woman cult and culture went into a gradual decline and were subjected to extreme cruelty. As a result, women found themselves in temple prostitution in the ziggurat. The Sumerian priests created a harem for themselves and a bordello for the ordinary people. Nippur, then the center of the civilization and a kind of Sumerian New York City, saw the emergence of the world's first brothel, the so-called *musakkatdim.*[5]

In the Babylonian creation myth Enuma Elish from the second millennium BCE,[6] the goddess Tiamat is presented as a horrible witch and represents the woman who must literally be torn to pieces. This gruesome myth reflects a subjugation of women that actually took place. The monotheistic religions and the bourgeois social system continued this tradition of degrading women, and even intensified it by completing the picture with dolled up and caged woman with a sweet voice. The inferior status that had been—and is—assigned to women in these historical and social systems was always accompanied by such intense and far-reaching ideological propaganda that, for the most part, women themselves saw their situation as a matter of fate and regarded it as a necessity to fulfill its requirements. Greek philosophy regarded women as a source of weakness. In monotheistic religions, their secondary status is seen as a divine commandment. Women were described in a multiplicity of humiliating ways that designated them as "passive, indeterminate materiality,"[7] a "field to be tilled by men," and so on.[8]

Without a precise look at the changed status of women that began with hierarchical society, we can explain neither the structure of the class society on which the state is based nor the state itself, making the most fundamental misconceptions unavoidable. Women were ripped out of natural society and subjected to the most extensive slavery, not simply as a gender but as human beings. All other forms of slavery and serfdom developed as a consequence of the enslavement of women. That is why it is impossible to analyze the other forms of serfdom and slavery without first analyzing the enslavement of women. Nor will we be able to overcome other forms of slavery if we do not overcome the enslavement of women.

The wise women of natural society practiced the cult of the mother-goddess for thousands of years. The mother-goddess had always been seen as the highest value. How was it that this long-lasting and far-reaching social culture came to be suppressed, with women turned into today's dolled up and caged nightingale? Men may adore this nightingale, but she is a prisoner. Without overcoming this longest-lasting and deepest captivity, no social system can talk about equality and freedom. So far, nobody has written a history of women that satisfactorily addresses these issues. None of the social sciences assign women their due place.

Whether or not freedom and equality prevail in a society depends on whether or not women enjoy freedom and equal rights. Even those men who allegedly respect women often only do so to the extent that women are the tool of their passions. Even today, women are rarely accepted by men simply as a human being and a friend beyond sexual interest. Friendship exists between men, but, for men, having women as friends all but immediately results in sexual scandal. One of the main steps toward freedom will be finding or creating men who are able to overcome this pattern. I will have more to say about this later.

Gerontocracy

We must also talk about the pressure and the dependency that experienced elders in hierarchical society bring to bear on the young. This is called *gerontocracy*. While the elders, on the one hand, become stronger by virtue of their experience, on the other hand, with old age, their physical strength decreases, making them increasingly weak. This induces them to put the young in their service. By bringing the youth under their intellectual influence, they make them dependent in all they do. This is also an important pillar of patriarchy. The old make the physically stronger youth do what they, the old, would like to see done. Establishing the dependency of the youth has continued, becoming more profound every day. The dominance of experience and ideology cannot be easily broken. The urge of the young for freedom is rooted in this historical phenomenon.

From the time of the sages long past to today's scientists and their institutions, the youth have been deprived of decisive and vital strategic knowledge. The information that the young get tends to lull them to sleep, to euthanize them, and to make their dependence permanent. If knowledge is imparted at all, the recipients are deprived of the means to put it into practice. One constant tactic of the rulers consists of permanent delay. The strategies, tactics, and systems of oppression and ideological and political propaganda established against women are also employed against the youth. The urge for freedom on the part of the youth is not only due to their physical age but also to this specific social pressure. Notions such as "greenhorns" or "hooligans" are the basic propaganda terms used to humiliate the youth. The efforts to prevent the energy of the young from being directed against the system work in parallel to this. This and the shoring up of the social order are the real purpose of the early fixation on the sex drive, drugs, and the inculcation of rigid dogmas that the adolescents are subjected to.

Youth who strive for freedom are hard to stop. Youth are the social group that, more than any other, are a potential nuisance for the system. Because the powerful have always known this, the young, in the name of "education," were spared nothing, from human sacrifices of young people to even more incomprehensible practices. Next to the subjugation of women, the subjugation of the youth played the decisive role in the emergence of hierarchical society. All subsequent statist societal systems have treated young people in a very similar manner. It is no coincidence that the systems that exert reliable control over their youth regard themselves as the strongest. A brainwashed youth can be induced to do any kind of work and to go into the most difficult professions, including warcraft. The youth continue to be kept dependent and under control, a fact that actually and paradoxically results from both the weakness and the strength of the old. This relationship still plays an important role in supporting the existing ruling systems without losing any of its speed and intensity. To emphasize it once more: just as with femininity, youth is not a physical but a social category. One important future task of social science should be to liberate these two phenomena from the distortions that supersede and mask them.

In this connection, it is also necessary to mention children. Anyone who turns women and the youth into captives will automatically, if indirectly, also integrate the children into the desired system. It is important to expose the distorted aspects of the approach the hierarchical and statist society takes to children. Because of the enslavement of the mother, children are deprived of a decent education, and this gives rise to a distorted and mendacious subsequent social development. In the final analysis, the educational system to which children are subjected is also based on repression and lies. Various methods are used right from the cradle to make children dependent on the system. Children are permitted to long for the freedom of natural society but never allowed to live this dream. One of the most noble tasks is to make sure that the children live in accordance with their dreams.

I want to emphasize once more that we must not regard the increasing dominance of patriarchal relations as a necessary outcome. It was not an innocent development that all but followed from natural law. It is especially important to show that patriarchy was a fundamentally important stage on the path to the emergence of classes and the state. It was in line with the essence of natural society that the relations established around the mother-woman were not founded on power and authority but were organic and based on solidarity. They were not an aberration or deviation and were totally closed for state authority. Because of the organic emergence of these relations, they do not rest on or resort to lies and violence. This latter point also explains why shamanism is a primarily male-dominated religion. If we take a close look at shamanism, we will immediately discover that it is a profession in which illusions and demonstrations of power play a huge role. It was here that the forms of power and mythology were carefully prepared for the crafty authority that later on came to dominate and strangle the innocence of natural society. The shaman was on the road to becoming a priest, a cleric. He strove to turn the relations with the ancestral elders into an alliance. Then, to complete and perfect their rule, the two needed the help of the mighty hunter and the men surrounding him. The group that was most confident in its strength and hunting skills had the tendency to gradually transform itself into the first military core unit. Then, step by step, this triad accumulated values and abilities. The system of mother-woman was gradually dismantled through malice and guile. Gradually, control was gained over the domestic order. Women had been an influential force whose word was also respected by men, but they were gradually subjected to the rule and control of the new authority.

It was no coincidence that the first strong authority established was over women. Women had been the voice and power of organic society. Without removing them from the scene, the system of patriarchy could not have triumphed, and it would also have been impossible to make a further transition to the institutions of the state. Thus, overcoming the power of women was strategic. The information we have from Sumerian sources clearly shows that this process led to intense conflicts. The female figures of Lilith and Eve, who were integrated into monotheistic religions, represent this process in a particularly succinct manner. Lilith represents the unrelenting woman,[9] whereas Eve represents the woman who capitulated. The claim that she was created from a man's rib only demonstrates the extent of the dependency into which she had been forced. On the other hand, the characterizations of Lilith as a rebellious, spiteful witch, a friend of Satan, and similar maledictions document what must have been a huge conflict. This reveals a lot about the culture of the following millennia, its convictions, and its articles of faith. Without analyzing how the women were socially overwhelmed, it is impossible to understand the fundamental particularities of the later male-dominated society culture, let alone the social construction of masculinity. And without understanding the social construction of masculinity, it is impossible to understand the institution of the state, making it impossible to correctly define the culture of war and power associated with the state. I am dealing with this topic in such detail to create real clarity about the horrible "divine personalities," as well as all sorts of boundaries, exploitation, and massacres, that developed because of the later emergence of classes. The paradigm shift that led people to regard political power and the state, these two curses of humanity, as sacred represents the dirtiest mental counterrevolution in the history of humanity. Nonetheless, it did take place. To describe this counterrevolution as the inevitable consequence of progress is a dangerous error that Marxism also fell prey to. If we are unable to critically review and correct this interpretation from the perspective just sketched, no revolution will be able to avoid rapidly becoming a counterrevolution.

The world of natural society of, first, the women, and, with it, that of the youth and children, was destroyed and replaced by a hierarchy built on force and lies (mythology). This became the dominant form of the new society, but, simultaneously, there was another, second, deep-rooted counterrevolution: the process of alienation from nature, the process that began its destruction. It is incorrect to presume that society cannot survive or develop without a hunter or warrior approach. Animal species that do not feed on flesh are thousands of times more common than carnivores. Only a small number of species are carnivorous. When we take an in-depth look at nature, we see that, above all, animal life needs rich plant life for its continued existence. The development of animal life is the result of the development of plant life; this is a dialectical relationship. The first animal did not have another animal to eat. It fed on plants. Thus, eating meat should be viewed as an anomaly. If all animals ate one another, the animal species would not have formed at all. This would have been contrary to the developmental rule of evolution. There are always departures from a fundamental tendency, but if these departures from the norm replace the norm, then that species will die off. The most obvious example would be homosexuality, if it were the general rule the human species would, as a result, die off spontaneously.

The material and, even more so, immaterial and intellectual consequences of a culture of killing are grave. A community that develops a culture of killing animals and its own conspecifics "beyond necessary defense" will also begin to develop all the essential tools and institutions necessary for a war machine. As the state was increasingly shaped into the fundamental institution of power, more refined arrows, spears, and axes were developed for war and were increasingly seen as the most important tools of all. The development of a patriarchal society from the natural mother-oriented society was the most dangerous anomaly in history and laid the foundation for all of the later horrendous forms of killing and exploitation. But this was not fate, a natural development, or a necessity for progress but, rather, a complete anomaly. It resembles the snake and the mouse dialectic. Calling theories on state the "snake and mouse" theory is an evaluation that is closer to the truth. Most men are called lions, and this is something they long to be. But I ask, "Who will you eat?"

I don't get much news about what is going on out there, but I just learned that the last film in *The Lord of the Rings* series, *The Return of the King* recently won an Oscar. The essence of the film, apparently, was the destruction of the ring that represents power. A virtual reality expected from the US. Perhaps it is a precautionary measure and brainwashing exercise to allow for even subtler implementations of power globally, as the mask obscuring power falls away. This is an era for forming new paradigms. They must have prepared for this to some degree. They are smart, and they know very well that if the true face of classical power is revealed, they will find themselves powerless. The dominant powers that rule the world consider doing what is necessary to maintain their divinity and further flawlessly develop it to be their most basic duty.

In the end, the culture of hunting and war led to a military form of organization, which developed to the degree that natural ethnic society fell apart. While the organization around the mother-woman builds the preliminary relationships in connection with ancestry, family, kin, and relatives, the military organization is dominated by the strongman who is detached from all of this. It is clear that ultimately no natural form of society could continue to exist once confronted with this form of power. Social violence has now begun to intrude into society—what people call civilized relations—and decisive power is always in the hands of those who control the means of violence.

This, in turn, paved the way for private property. It is quite clear that violence is the basis of property. The sense of self is excessively strengthened by seizure through violence and shedding of blood. Violence as a means could not be developed and used until dominance became part of human relationships. Dominance and rule have an immediate relationship with ownership—the ownership that is inherent in being ruled is a dialectical relationship. Ownership is central to all property regimes, and with it a new era had begun. The community, women, the youth, and children, as well as the fertile hunting grounds and gathering sites, were now regarded as property. The strongman increasingly came to the forefront in all his glory. From there, it was only a small step to the god-kings.

At the same time, the shaman-priest was at work to construct the mythology of this new process. His task was to anchor this new formation in the minds of the ruled, extolling it as a magnificent development. The struggle for legitimacy requires efforts at least as refined as those required for naked violence. To achieve his goal, the shaman-priest had to implant in the minds of the people a belief so strong that it could become an absolute law. Research into the history of religion tells us that this is when the concept of the "ruling god" arose.

The belief in the "totem" so omnipresent in natural society had nothing to do with ruling. As a symbol of the clan, the totem was taboo, sacred, sacrosanct. As a symbolic expression, it functioned as the precise reflection of the life of the clan, a life not closely bound to the clan and its rules was unthinkable. For that reason, the totem was regarded as the highest and loftiest expression of the clan's existence, as untouchable and sacred. It was respected and enjoyed the highest veneration. In the process, some object of significance, an animal or a plant, is chosen as a totem. Anything in nature that gave life to the clan could be chosen as a symbol to be believed in. Thus, the religion of natural society is integrated with nature. It was not a source of fear but a fountain of strength that provided the people with character and fortitude.

The god that was venerated in the new society overcame and masked the totem. To locate this god, people looked for a place on the peak of the mountains, at the bottom of the sea, in the sky. They stressed his ruling power. How very much he resembled the newly emerging class of masters! One of the names of the God in the Old Testament, and therefore also in the Gospels and the Koran, is *adonai*, meaning *lord*, or *Rab* in the Koran. The new class emerged by idolizing itself. Two of the best-known additional names, *Elohim* and *El*,[10] mean *majesty* and heralded the rule of a patriarch or sheikh over the nomadic desert tribes. In all holy scriptures, the birth of patriarchy and the birth of a new God are interwoven in a notable way. These connections are also present in Homer's Iliad, the Indian Ramayana,[11] and the Finnish Kalevala. The new society would have hardly been able to survive without establishing its legitimacy through a "struggle for the hearts and minds." No social unit will tolerate being ruled for long without being convinced of its legitimacy. The effect of violence is generally short-lived—in the long run, it is belief that counts.

Investigating this state of affairs by looking at the example of the old Sumerians is particularly important, because they provide the first written record. The creation of the gods by the Sumerians was a grandiose affair. The essence of all epics is the overthrow of the mother-goddess and the imposition of the rule of the father-god. The struggles between Inanna and Enki, as well as, in later Babylonian versions, between Marduk and Tiamat, take up a lot of space in these epics. A sociological examination of these epics—whose content subsequently found its way into all epics and holy scriptures—provides an enormous amount of information. It is not for nothing that people say: "History begins at Sumer."[12] The analysis of religions, literary epics, the law, democracy, and the state using the cuneiform tablets of the Sumerians would perhaps provide one of the most fundamental approaches that could lead to some progress in social science.

The patriarchal counterrevolution sketched above is possibly the biggest distortion and aberration in history. Its roots in the mentality of both individuals and society run so deep that we are still far from even partially overcoming them. The Sumerian priests still rule us. The state institutions they invented and the gods they conjured up to legitimize these bodies still direct us without giving us a chance to recover; they dominate our perspectives and paradigms in very fundamental ways. It is as if Albert Einstein had tailored his famous statement, "It is harder to crack a prejudice than an atom," to describe these very relations.

Isn't it this discourse that continues in the country of the ziggurats, in the sacred priest palaces of the Sumerians, between the Euphrates and the Tigris, in Iraq—the cradle of civilization and the birth of the state—and the ruthless wars and exploitation that have been raging uninterruptedly beyond any measure of humanity since their invention?

Patriarchal society and its transition into a state do not serve the well-being of humanity but, rather, represent its greatest plague. Since first arising, this new vessel has spread destruction like a snowball rolling downhill and has come close to making our planet—the sacred of all—uninhabitable. Thomas Hobbes famously chose the picture of the Leviathan—an Old Testament monster that rises from the sea—for the state,[13] a truly fitting metaphor for this dangerous "creature."

The geographical and historical bases of this culture, which I have tried to describe schematically, show themselves in their clearest form on the slopes of the mountain ranges of the Taurus-Zagros system in Upper Mesopotamia. In this region, researchers found many traces and artifacts of the mother-woman-oriented natural society that began to develop there at the end of the last Ice Age, around 20,000 BCE.[14] In the statuettes that were found, the design of the habitations, the weaving tools, and the hand mills, we always find the traces of women.

Beginning in the fourth millennium BCE, we can observe an intensified spread of patriarchal authority. Archeologically detectable traces of annihilation and destruction demonstrate that military formations increasingly gained influence in the new society, and that there were intense feuds between the tribes. The fact that the tribes themselves still exist today may be seen as a sign of the extent of the resistance they put up at the time.

When patriarchy spread through the region, this was accompanied by the emergence of the classes and the state. Around 3000 BCE, history witnessed the birth of a city-state. The most splendid example for this was the city of Uruk. In fact, the oldest surviving literary work in the world, the epic of Gilgamesh, can be seen as the founding epic of the city of Uruk. One can even say that the largest transformation in history actually took place under the conditions of this city-state culture. The story of Inanna and Enki recounts the conflict between the mother-woman society and the patriarchal society in marvelously poetic language. The Gilgamesh epic is the original example of a work about the kind of "heroic age" that we find in every society. Here, we see the first conflict between city dwellers and "barbarians." Women were still by no means defeated, but the "strongman," accompanied by his military entourage, gradually habituated society to his rule and dominance. His ideological fictions, his religious institutions, and his initial dynasties and palaces heralded the advent of "civilization."

THREE

The Statist Society: The Formation of Slave Society

Hierarchical society represented the intermediate link between natural society and statist society based on class. A typical feature of this era was that both authority and military fealty were bound to a particular person. The subsequent institutionalization of authority implies a qualitative change. The state basically was an authority that gained continuity by its institutionalization.

Even though the state is possibly the most dangerous instrument in history, it remains one of the least understood. The culture it contains and the diversity of the interests that it carries out play a decisive role. Everything said and written about the state contributes to making it more mysterious and obfuscating its true meaning. Just as it is erroneous to regard the state as no more than a tool of coercion, the idea that it is a sacrosanct authority also obscures what is going on.

The analysis of the state is a fundamental problem that social science has yet to successfully grapple with. But without a comprehensive analysis of the state, no genuine solution to any social phenomenon or problem can be found. I think I am able to show that even a revolutionary like Lenin committed his greatest mistake when it came to analyzing the state.

What we have presented so far in our analysis of the state is far from adequately defining this phenomenon and must be supplemented. In doing so, we must always keep in mind the Sumerian model, since it is the original and has been transmitted to us by its written documents. When we try to define the "state" institution and its notion, we must be careful to free ourselves from some faulty ideas. For example, the view that states are established and then destroyed and replaced by others needs to be abandoned. We should also beware of overly focusing on the different forms of the state and the distance between the communities where the state is located, which could cause us to erroneously speak of a large number of states. These issues all have serious drawbacks.

It might be helpful to conceive of the state as a "society within society" or as a second society within the first society or, put another way, the lower society's upper society. A second useful basic assumption is that the state, as a concept and as an institution, fragments lower society and has continuity over it. A complementary assumption is that the state is not just some arbitrary form of authority but is fundamentally a military-political authority.

Because of the respective perspectives and interests involved, the definitions of the state used by the various clerics, philosophers, or scientists are by no means objective. Moreover, for the most part, they attach importance only to one particular aspect. If the state is an obstacle to their interests, they are even prone to ignoring objective facts, embracing a fierce subjectivism and cursing the state. The approach of revolutionaries, on the other hand, seems to be susceptible to a moral pragmatism according to which the state is particularly evil when the task is to smash it, while it is a very good thing when the task is to establish one.

If one is not the founder of a state or inclined to philosophize about it, the state is a social instrument that has always turned people's heads with the irresistible seduction of power and of possessing it and, in the process, has promoted them either to the rank of divinity or delivered them to annihilation.

The state is generally defined as a "republic," a "democracy," a "monarchy," an "oligarchy," or a "dictatorship," making it even more difficult to understand its core and essence.

Observing how the Sumerian priests established a state-like institution gives us perhaps the most realistic information for understanding the state. At the outset, they established the temple, called the Ziggurat. They raised it toward the sky and dedicated the top floor to God and the bottom floor to their servants. The intermediate floors were then opened to the representatives of the middle classes. The surrounding houses and land were mere extensions of the temple. Their productive technology was stored in a section of the temple, and they kept very precise records of their quite substantial production. It was clear that this institution was a new society that obviously subsumed elements of the previous hierarchical and natural societies. They integrated from these societies whatever was useful for building the new one; anything that was useless or presented an obstacle was discarded.

The concept of "social engineering," although new, is, nonetheless, a good description of what the Sumerian priests did. They functioned like "holy engineers of society" and created an apparatus that was initially greeted by the people with enthusiasm and festivity. A big mill wheel had been established; it was driven by the waters of the Euphrates and the Tigris to create a historically unmatched surplus.[1] Could there have been a greater feast for humanity than this? If this arrangement is not the greatest divinity, what is?

Undoubtedly, the essential nourishment for all of this came from the achievements of Neolithic natural society, the magnificent establishment in the foothills of the Zagros-Taurus Mountains. The means of production and the species of plants and animals in the area had been turned into a culture by the mother-woman society over thousands of years. The dexterity of the priests lay in their reorganization of all of this to create an upper society and to achieve a new mode of production by introducing artificial irrigation in the fertile lower Euphrates and the Tigris basin. This lies at the core of the invention of the state, an enormously important historical event. Subsequent processes were to add new floors to this state edifice and to erect the edifice anew in other places.

The congenial location for this upper society was the city. The mentality of the city and the state hasn't by any means been exhaustively analyzed. This location, often described as "civilized society," brought revolutionary changes both to the humanity's mentality and the material structure of production—or perhaps one should say it forms the basis of a great counterrevolutionary change in comparison to natural society. It improved rationality, writing, and many forms of the arts and crafts, but at what price? Whether this was an urban *revolution* or an urban *counterrevolution* is still of great importance, something that we must comprehensively reflect upon. In that context, we must not forget that many historical movements, especially the monotheistic religions, were also directed against these structures. The vice-like grip of urban society on humanity resembles hell much more than paradise, or, to put it more precisely, as illustrated by examples to this day, has brought paradise to a very few, while condemning the overwhelming majority to a life in hell.

The substance of the society of the city-state is such that it invites domination, property, and oppression in every respect. It was not easy to habituate people who came from a natural society to this system. Among the absolutely necessary preconditions for this system were domination of the minds of the city dwellers by frightening gods and the use of women as instruments of seduction—the initial prostitution. Entrenching servitude was only possible with these two deep-seated institutions, religion and prostitution, and by constant and daily supervision. Both institutions have profound opiate-like characteristics.

This structure of mentality and production formed around the first original exemplar of city-state society has since been perfected in all areas. It was created in Sumer and never disappeared. It is that structure of mentality that has reached the present like so many links in a chain. The Egyptian, Hittite, and Greek city-states represented slight variations on the original. That the roots of this trio stretch back to Sumer as the first link in the chain is further corroborated by an increasing number of historical documents.

The next links in the chain, China, India, and Rome, achieved universal significance. Because this is not a historical treatise, we will not deal further with these epochs here.[2] Rather, we are trying to establish the unity and continuity of the state—unity in the sense of existence and continuity in the temporal sense are important factors in the life of the state. To describe each occurrence as a distinct and separate founding of a state would not provide a useful basis for analysis. Repeatedly analyzing the same essence does not enhance its meaning; it only repeats it.

When we examine the Sumerian example closely, we discover right from the outset that two functions have been interwoven in state society. On the one hand, the state serves as an instrument of authority and repression and, on the other, as a public productive system that feeds the whole city. From that point on, this double quality would preoccupy the people as the fundamental contradiction of the state. One cannot do with it or without it. As an instrument of repression and power, the state is all but unbearable, but, as an instrument of public safety and production, it has become indispensable.

Here, the main problem is whether or not public safety and production—the common good of society—require repression and authority from the start. Is it not possible for the society to have common safety and production for all without the state? If it is possible, this would make the state as an instrument of force superfluous. This is the crucial point of this problem. In a way, the state has turned into a huge conglomerate of interests, a configuration where a certain amount of a drug is mixed into a good meal. The very subtlety of the clerical state system is demonstrated by the way that it enables the emergence of an exploitative and parasitic group by obfuscating this distinction.

Even an anarchist theorist like Mikhail Bakunin, who considered the state absolutely "evil," had to concede that it is a *necessary* evil. Marxism has likewise considered the state as necessary at a certain stage of social development. In what follows, I will show in detail that the state as an instrument of force and repression is neither a necessary instrument of progress nor a necessary evil. It is an instrument that has been an unnecessary and superfluous plague right from the start and has gradually transformed itself into the equivalent of a gang of thugs. Seen from that perspective, it would be best to regard it as a social metastasis from the very first day, something that should have been denounced, isolated, and removed immediately. We ought to treat it as an instrument of collective security and production for society and define it as a social instrument that would no longer be called a state in the classic sense. It is more realistic and appropriate to call such a social entity "democracy." This is something I will go into in more detail in the next sections.

The prototype of democracy can be seen in the beneficial hierarchy that exists in natural society. Both the mother-women and the experienced old men are essential and useful fundamental elements that ensure collective safety and the management of the community, a community not based on accumulation and property, and are, thus, accorded great uncoerced respect.

As soon as this is taken advantage of, and authority and selfish interests take the place of voluntary loyalty and considerations of utility, the superfluous instrument of violence establishes itself over society. It is part of the essence of all exploitative and repressive systems that the instrument of force masks itself as an instrument of collective security and collective production. This was the most malign of all inventions and would bring with it all later forms of slavery, terrorizing mythologies and religions, systematic annihilation and plunder, massacres and genocides.

Marxism's explanation for the emergence of this process is that a more advanced society is born from the womb of the previous backward society, with violence as its midwife. But this belief, which we all once shared, fundamentally deforms our understanding of the state, as well as of revolution, democracy, and the practices of organization. I don't think any movement for freedom and equality in history has succeeded in overcoming this approach within this scope through the articulation of such a self-critique. Because of these deformed views, all religious orders and philosophical schools and all states and political movements supposedly working for the benefit of the oppressed in effect achieved the opposite of what they originally set out to achieve.

As the comparison with the Leviathan suggests, the tradition of the state as an instrument of domination is indeed that of a monster with an insatiable thirst for blood and exploitation. It sustains itself on blood down to its very last cell. Many examples have shown how this monster destroys and sacrifices the most valuable individuals, including its own apparent masters, without batting an eye, and how it crushes all of society's moral traditions to dust without the slightest hesitation. If an Ottoman sultan murders his seventeen brothers in a single night "for the well-being of state," even he, as the "master" of this instrument, knows that he is merely following its rules.[3] In Roman history, the history of Iran, and in all histories of the state as a tool of arbitrary force, we likewise find innumerable examples of the ideological cover-up of all forms of cruelty.

Here, it is particularly important to investigate the mentality and social institutions formed by the phenomenon of the state. The alienation of mentality from nature, unimaginable class formations, and a whole series of special organizations and military institutions are all inventions of this coercive instrument. The sultan, the emperor, the shah, the raja, and the imperator turned into almost godlike beings, even though they merely represented a culture characterized by total contempt for work and the praise of plunder and robbery—a world of parasites with an understanding of a "god" who orders what they want done, and which includes both bogus paradises and bogus netherworlds. For thousands of years, rivers of blood have been flowing for the glory of these foul highnesses.

Filling this instrument of domination and force with revolutionary content is like giving a fox in charge of a henhouse a revolutionary role. On the other hand, stressing only the repressive side of the state, while simultaneously denying its effect on the social forms, leads to anarchism. The state is a Janus-faced phenomenon that, thus far, has always had the last word.

The real challenge is to make the distinction between the necessary and unnecessary aspects of state power. We should regard this phenomenon neither as a necessary evil nor as a sacred being. It is just such one-sided approaches that have led to the biggest errors of the human intellect.

When we say that the state has essentially remained the same over time, we are, of course, not saying that it did not change form. On the contrary, the sameness of the essence has *required* changes in form. This dialectical principle applies to every phenomenon.

We can learn more about the state by observing it in the era of slavery, the state-based form of society that existed for longer than any other where the state became deep-seated. We can see slaveholding states in their purest form in the Sumerian and Egyptian societies. The Sumerian and Egyptian slave state forms entrenched fundamental changes in the way the mental, social, and economic institutionalization developed in society. The mindset of natural societies is based on an understanding of animate nature. People believed that each phenomenon of nature has a soul. These souls or spirits are understood as the carriers of life.

In totemistic belief, there was no concept of a "transcendent god" who is different from humans and who rules from the outside. People strove to be in consonance with the spirits of nature. To deviate from this practice was tantamount to death. This fundamental view of nature necessarily leads to the need for extraordinary harmony. We see a life lived according to the most basic principle of ecology. Contradictions between social life and the forces of nature were something people tried their utmost to avoid. Life in consonance with the environment—the forces of nature—was, thus, the basic principle kept in mind while a belief system and morality were being developed. This life principle was so deeply rooted in the minds of all human beings that it occupied a privileged place in their religious and moral traditions.

Actually, this is tantamount to the transfer of the principle of the general flow of natural life to human society. Nothing and nobody can exist without concern for the environment. Under new internal and external conditions, transient deviations from the main flow will always reunify with it, because otherwise they would remain outside of the system and cease to exist. The particular significance of the ecological principle in human society is due to this fundamental subjectivity of nature.[4]

The emergence of statist slave society resulted in a clear departure from this vital and essential principle. The problems of ecology and the environment are closely related to the emergence of the society in this manner, to the beginning of civilization; class society stands in contradiction to nature. The main reason for this is the new society's paradigm based on a slave mentality that was formed through a profound counterrevolution. In natural society, all members of the community participated in all aspects of life in an organic way. Each person counted as a genuine, true member of society. Beliefs and feelings were shared by all, and the concepts of "lying" and "cheating" had not yet developed. They seemed to speak in the same child-like language as nature. To rule over nature and to misuse it was considered the greatest sin and was taboo in their morality and religions—their newly developed laws of society.

In the new statist slave society, these fundamental religious and moral views were turned into their opposite. From that point on, gaining social legitimacy not only required resorting to violence but also to lies. It is impossible to run the system of slavery exclusively by force. The system cannot be maintained without binding the society to deep-seated beliefs. This was the historical phase when the fundamental ideological inventions of the Sumerian and Egyptian priests made their first appearance, inventions that have pervaded all of history until today. The most fundamental basis for legitimacy and "acceptance" of the system is the mythological framework of thought that the priests grouped around a number of concepts they had invented. The most important feature of this mythology was that it put the new world of the gods above natural events. En, Enlil, and Ra, as the initial gods, were perfectly suited to the task of elevating the new class of the masters—*Rab*—and mystifying them.[5] The gods and the rule of the slaveholder class were intertwined when they emerged. Just as the new masters now led a hitherto unknown palace life from a throne, without working but through commanding alone, the gods, as their fictional symbols, were also enthroned above all forces of nature. Rule over society was thus projected as rule over nature. It was the beginning of the rule of the religion of the commanding gods superseding animism, the religion of natural spirituality. The shift to explaining natural events by gods instead of by spirits led to radical changes in mentality.

There are lucid reasons for not calling this a revolution but, rather, a counterrevolution. It was the beginning of the most dangerous and negative period in history. As I briefly mentioned in the discussion of quantum physics, today the conception of nature as something that is actually alive is once again widely discussed in scientific circles, albeit in a manner quite different from the way it was understood in natural society. Indeed, the assumption that every natural object has subjectivity, a "law in which it acts and a level of meaning," has something revolutionary to it. The subjectivity that governs materialized matter is the energy it holds. Energy is a reality that is not matter; in a sense, it is the spirit of matter.

In the end, albeit differently, this understanding bases itself on an ecological life that is in consonance with the natural flow in a way similar to the understanding of initial society. The rupture from this basic principle constitutes the reason that environmental problems have become the greatest danger that faces humanity today. The mentality and mode of production of class society are what lies at the foundation of this rupture.

A second important related turning point that sparked a huge and perilous leap was the rupture between emotional intelligence and analytical intelligence. All living beings have emotional intelligence. In a certain sense, it represents subjectivity, the state of mind that is specific to natural processes. On the other hand, the evolutionary development of humans was accompanied by a tendency toward analytical intelligence.

Analytical intelligence enables faster decisions and, therefore, faster changes, but, along with this, the rate of aberration also increases. Emotional intelligence is simple, but it deploys the "certainty of instincts." Instincts develop through the transformation of conditioned reflexes into unconditioned reflexes. Even though they represent the simplest form of learning, they have proven to be very stable. Since they are the product of hundreds of thousands of years of experience, they are not easily fallible. They have close relations to life and, thus, immediately react to internal or external conditions that are threatening life or are otherwise relevant to it. These aspects quickly prevent them from playing the role of analytical intelligence. Nevertheless, emotional intelligence remains the prevalent force at work for life. It doesn't interpret things—it enables survival. Increased interpretation always leads to a greater rate of aberration.

Analytical intelligence, on the other hand, mostly through interpretation, tries to tailor new courses and new forms of behavior to emotional intelligence. The fact that human species live in a social manner is related to the level of development of analytical intelligence. It is analytical intelligence that provides rapid social development, but because, alone, it lacks the emotional dimension, it becomes dangerous when given free reign. Analytical intelligence becomes particularly frightening once human beings get used to the culture of power and war. Among the most telling expressions of this form of intelligence are the recent wars of annihilation. Analytical intelligence is literally cold mechanical precision without empathy and sympathy or feelings of compassion, fear, or love, making this destructive feature extremely dangerous. On the other hand, if it works in harmony with emotional intelligence, it can play a decisive role in the formation of healthy and competent individuals and communities.

Within the society of the slave state, a grand rupture developed between these two forms of intelligence. Perhaps one could speak of a class intelligence, a mind that breaks away from the emotional intelligence that dominated natural society, an intelligence that instead exclusively specializes in the art of repression and exploitation. This is a development that would lead to extremely harmful results. The material basis for the formation of the class we are talking about is the abundant surplus product of the slave production mode,[6] which developed based on the surplus product of Neolithic society. Only by administering production did this class acquire the ability to seize a large part of the production for itself. At this point, the only thing missing was a new mentality that justified this mode of production. The mythologies woven around the new ruling gods were the result of the search for this mentality. What we have before us is a phase of radical reorientation toward analytical intelligence, an intelligence mainly preoccupied with designing laws for the subordination of the servants and presenting this process as a commandment that came from the immortal gods. The immense historical importance of the Sumerian and Egyptian priests was a result of this issue having played such a large role in the history of humanity. Their particular form of intelligence, which broke with natural life and with natural society, has succeeded in creating an enormous mythological and fictional system. To make the servants believe all of this, they created a system of schools, temples, and statues designed to impress and mesmerize them. By replacing the harmless animistic religions of natural society with religions dominated by ruling gods, they increasingly extended the realm of submission. By contorting and exploiting the feelings of fear, they carefully explained why one had to be afraid of these new gods and what the reward would be if one followed their commandments. For the first time, they invented utopias that featured *both* heaven and hell. They developed an ideological system designed to guarantee a perfect consonance with the new class of masters. The fact that their way of thinking was mythological suited the spirit of the time. The religion of animism was actually libertarian and egalitarian. This new religion, primarily characterized by mythology, was a class religion, a religion of inequality and slavery. It demanded absolute subordination to its gods—i.e., to the "masters."

This counterrevolution in mentality was actually one of the greatest triumphs of analytical intelligence in human history; it was the development of the class mind. From that point on, history, literature, the arts, law, and politics were reproduced with this class mentality. We can see the clearest, most unadulterated expression of this process in Sumerian and Egyptian mythology. At this point, the ideology of the ruling exploiter class was on its way to creating an upper society—a statist society. Each step in this direction was carried out in the name of the whole society and was, accordingly, attributed to it. Little by little, the ideology of the mother-goddess that had been transmitted from natural society was exploited, emptied of its content, and assimilated. In this way, everyone was pushed into the service of the system of male gods. In the same way, women were pushed into the service of men. This was the beginning of both public and private prostitution.[7] The free and equal members of natural society were transformed into the new class of servants. A Sumerian myth describes how humans were created from the excrement of the gods. The claim that the first woman was created from a man's rib also first figured in Sumerian mythology. Sumerian mythology was indeed a truly remarkable success that greatly influenced all later mythologies. It is, thus, the primordial source of the monotheistic religions, as well as of literature and law. A similar influence can be attributed to the Gilgamesh epic, which has found an echo in legends all across the world.

As an extended analysis of the structure of the Sumerian mentality is not the topic of the present remarks, it is sufficient to state that what was at the beginning of history and, therefore, of civilization, was not just coercion but also analytical intelligence. Sumerian mythology was undoubtedly the main source of the process. And the origin of later metaphysical thought should be sought in this intelligence. A handful of masters at the top did not stop at simply living in their heavenly palaces but simultaneously laid the foundation for the world of legends and utopias that has tantalized and consoled humanity ever since. Indeed, this "big society lie" took root in the minds of all of humanity and institutionalized itself in a most powerful manner through all sorts of mythologies, legends, temples, and schools.

This counterrevolution in Sumerian society was actually the most radical change in mentality of all time and radically changed the paradigm, that is, the fundamental view of nature and the universe, first in society in the Middle East, then in that of all humanity. Natural society and its concept of an "animate nature and universe" are both colorful and productive. Its members don't see nature as vengeful and evil but regard her as a mother. *Amargi*, the Sumerian word for *freedom*, simultaneously means *return to the mother*. This word alone illustrates an important aspect of the counterrevolutionary mindset. From the perspective of the new mythology, however, both nature and the universe are full of dominating and punitive gods. These gods—in reality, oppressive and exploitative despots—are elevated outside of nature and increasingly hide themselves. It is as if they had dried up nature itself. Thereafter, the perception of inanimate nature and inanimate matter were developed. Just like servants created from the excrement of the gods, all living beings were increasingly humiliated in the same way. This paradigm, which increasingly became more deep-seated, paralyzing the mentality of the society in today's Middle East, must be seen as a key reason for the region's failure to pull itself together. European society only succeeded in demolishing this paradigm with the Copernican Revolution and the Christian Reformation. Giordano Bruno, a genius of the Renaissance, was burned alive at the stake, because he vehemently advocated the perception of animate nature.[8] But the paradigm never really managed to penetrate formations like Chinese and Japanese societies, which is why these societies adapt to positive developments much more quickly. One reason for this is their perception of an animate universe. There was a similar factor at play in the development of Greek and Roman civilization, namely, the fact that the philosophical way of thinking overcame Sumerian-Egyptian mythologies and replaced them with metaphysical and dialectical constructions.

While "the state" as a concept and its core features emerged in the priests' temples, it was the domain and responsibility of the hierarchical society's council of elders and the military chief's entourage to institutionalize it and to elevate it to a ruling power. The power of the state is determined by the intense and long-term relationships and contradictions between these three groups. First, we witness the rule of priest-kings, who then gradually retreat into the background and are replaced by a council of elders—a primitive form of democracy. Later, we see the development of the rule of a military chief whose power was the ultimate determinant. This process is reflected in the poetic-mythological language of the Gilgamesh epic. Gilgamesh himself represents the military chief, the "hero." Compared to him, the once powerful priests and priestesses appear quite pale. Enkidu represents the first known example of the military recruitment of other ethnic groups, who are called "barbarians." This was the point at which organization beyond family ties first emerged.

The intoxicating effect of power led to the subjugation of the powerless and the self-representation of the owners of the surplus product as god-kings. An era began in which the human ego conceived of itself as "the greatest of all." Nature and society were now reinterpreted as the creations of a god-king. This interpretation occupies a privileged place in all mythologies. The apprehension that God is the "master of all things" has its roots in Sumerian and Egyptian mythology. They are the source from which it made its way into the Holy Scripture. In this way, the power of the state was to be eternalized.

If the state hadn't undergone further development, in particular, if it had not armed itself with mythology, it would have never been more than a gang of thieves. The impressive productivity of state power at that time led to a situation in which it was presented as the reflection of an extraordinary divine institution and could, thereby, dominate people's minds. In this sense it could be understood as the most refined organization of extortion. At this point, we encounter the power of ideology. It persuaded people to regard this great extortive organization as the sacred institution of a divine commandment. Whenever the power of the state is praised beyond measure, we have to assume that some great robbery accompanied by a mystification of interests is taking place. The god-kings knew this very well when they presented and institutionalized themselves. Magnificent palaces, a military entourage composed of the strongest men, an effective secret service, an impressive harem, a renowned dynasty, a lineage showing which god a particular god-king descended of, and groveling ministers and subordinates who rendered homage—these were all indispensable elements in this institutionalization. The pyramid tombs were actually more like a permanent earthly palace. Garments, scepters, and seals were standard accessories that were always with them. Now, the role of other members of society was to constantly worship this supreme divine establishment and show gratitude. The attributes of God recounted in the Holy Scripture are mostly reiterations or partially altered versions of those of the Sumerian and Egyptian god-kings.

When they died—or, rather, when they made the transition to the afterlife—their whole entourage was buried alive with them, because the existence of an entourage separated from the body of the king was unthinkable. Another reason for their burial was the fact that the king needed their services in the afterlife. The descendants left in the world had the task of continuing their existence. This also played a part in the emergence of the concept of "immortality." This striking example clearly shows how analytical intelligence transformed society by detaching from reality.

The construction of a single pyramid required the work of hundreds of thousands of slaves, who were often worked to death. The form of state power erected at that time has been a permanent and destructive catastrophe for humanity. From then on, concepts like "atrocity," "judgment day," and "savior" became part of humanity's vocabulary. Under these circumstances, the concept of "prophetic personalities" as freedom fighters takes shape. The prophets would emerge as the ones who could provide salvation from this great disaster. Again, the source is Sumerian society.

One social group that lost out, along with all of natural society, was women. Sumerian mythology reads like the lamentation of women who lost. The Inanna cult carries the traces of the previous women-centric society and reflects the major struggles waged against the rising male-dominated society. While the majority of the gods of the first cities were of female origin, they were increasingly replaced by gods of male identity. And, again, the temples were the key institutions when the fall of women was prepared. The temples devoted to the mother-goddess Inanna, led by female priestesses, that had been widespread in the beginning, were now taken over one by one and gradually transformed into brothels.

The domestic order of natural society around the mother-woman was a completely different institution. While women were no one's property, the mother-woman herself was the leader of her children and the man she desired. At this time, the institution of marriage in the classic sense had not yet developed. The patriarchal family under the rule of the male became widespread as male-dominated society took shape on the basis of the state institution. This is how the institution of the family first took shape, lasting until the present day, even if in a modified form. Within the patriarchal family, the position of women grew weaker and weaker until, like the children, they became the property of men. For women this kind of family is nothing but a cage.

Leading social scientists agree that there is no other form of slavery that is as deeply entrenched and permanent as the patriarchal family under male rule. To be able to analyze the degree of enslavement in a particular society, you must analyze the degree of enslavement of women in its many forms. It is not just about the practical and mental dependency that materializes in women. Her emotions, her physical movements, her voice, and her way of dressing herself all reflect the way in which she is enslaved. Rings were affixed to her nose, her ears, her wrists, and her ankles. They were symbols of the chains of slavery. In medieval times, she was even forced to wear a chastity belt. A very one-sided code of honor and moral understanding developed. Women were ideologically nullified. They were stripped of all the valuables they possessed and were themselves transformed into merchandise. They were reduced to the value of their bride price.

Women's slavery, which has its roots deeply embedded in Sumerian society, is a topic that remains seriously understudied. The bondage that began with hierarchical society continued through the temple of the priests and ended with them being forced into men's huts and assigned the lowest status. Since then, in effect, it is this status that has been continuously fostered. As far as women are concerned, the basic focus of education, morality, and literature is on how they are to serve their men with all their feelings and actions, all the while "minimizing their mental power."

Male slaves gain a certain status by using their physical strength and by providing a lot more surplus product. Their slavery is primarily economic. Women, however, are enslaved, body, mind, and soul. If released from his bondage, a male slave can possibly become a free person. If women are set free, they are then often re-enslaved in an even worse way. This phenomenon shows how intensely this slavery has been internalized. On close inspection, it is easy to see how everything about women has been mercilessly designed according to the wishes of men. The way they walk and talk, their gaze and bodily posture, everything seems to say: "I've been forced to submit and surrender." The primary reason that the enslavement of women is not analyzed is the insatiability of men, the satisfaction that they get from this dictatorship. The prototype of the god-king in society is the man as the master of the woman at home; he is not just a husband but, in effect, the "god-husband." This quality, without losing anything essential, is one that has continued its effect into the present.

Economically, slave state society functioned like a huge factory, although it was different from the modern factory with regard to technical equipment and property relations. The masters drove the slaves like a herd of cattle. The surviving buildings and edifices from that ancient time are testimony to the unbelievable amount of slave labor exerted in the fields, in the quarries, and on the construction sites. Driving slaves required more force and violence than driving animals. The slave was a work animal, a matter of property and a mere means of production. Slaves were outside the scope of the law, without emotions, as if they were merchandise. The form of analytical intelligence in men can best be seen in the reality of slaves.

Another institution that made a solid start in slave state society was the institution of property. In its essence, the system was based on a process whereby upper society turned lower society and all they had into property. The god-kings and their representatives owned everything. Ownership was the natural consequence of domination. If the human ego was given the opportunity to put on airs, there was no longer any limit. The lack of factors that could have a constraining effect during the system's founding period led to the cult of the god-king. Beginning with and from the state, a property order unknown to natural society infiltrated all institutions, including the family, and created a sense of property as central among all members of society. Property was regarded as the foundation of the state and declared sacred. From then on, there was a drive to turn the whole world into property. To this day, property boundaries—as state borders, dynastic landholdings and homeland borders—are in various forms engraved into the consciousness of humans as almost God-given.

Actually, property as the source of unearned income is indeed theft. Of all the institutions, it is the one that disrupts the collective solidarity of society the most. But it is indispensable as the fundamental institution for nurturing upper society.

We defined natural society as the spontaneous state of ecological society. One of the most fundamental social contradictions to date is the fact that ecological society is continuously pushed back by the expansion and deepening of state society. The more the internal contradictions of a society develop, the greater its contradiction with its external environment becomes. Domination of humans is accompanied by the domination of nature. Of course, a system that has no mercy on human beings will not hesitate to do all kinds of damage to nature. In any case, dominance and conquest have firm places within ruling-class morality. Ruling over nature is regarded as a right and honorable behavior as is ruling over humans. Natural society's animist approach to nature and the sacredness attributed to it are ignored. It is conquered as if it were enemy territory. As long as these concepts dominate the mentality of statist society, the way is paved for ongoing environmental disasters, which have already taken on colossal dimensions.

All this may suffice as a definition of statist society in its foundational phase. It might be asked why I speak of "slave state society" rather than simply "slave society." I think the former notion is more concrete and serves the purpose if the state is seen as upper society.

Slavery is unthinkable without the state. State power is the fundamental condition for its existence. The state is not an abstract institution. It is the joint organization of those who have taken control of the instruments of repression and exploitation. We should view public safety and all its other public works as necessary services to mask its real purpose and gain greater legitimacy in the eyes of society. Another important reason to call it a statist society is the fact that the feudal and the capitalist forms of society had also come into existence in rudimentary forms and continue their development based on this very same state. The common and indispensable institution for those groups that exploit and repress is the state. With regard to repression and exploitation, no other institution has ever been more effective and successful.

While Sumer and Egypt were the original forms of the slave state society, the Hittite, Chinese, and Indian examples are like a second ring that replicate these forms. Institutions that are the same at the core reemerge in different forms. The more original examples of Iran and the Greek and Roman civilizations have attained an important transformation in the realm of mentality, with philosophical thought making significant progress in the area of a morality of freedom. As a result, the institution of slavery was somewhat relaxed. As such, we can talk about the archaic and primitive founding phase of the system from 3000 to 2000 BCE, the time of its maturation from 2000 to 1000 BCE, and its classical period from 1000 to 300 BCE.

Of course, humanity also continued to develop during the phase of slavery, the foundational social system of class-based civilization. The system of slavery did not, however, determine everything. For example, the urban revolution should not be regarded as the result of slavery. Cities were possible with neither a state nor slavery. There are numerous examples of cities that did not become states. It would also be a terrible mistake to regard slavery as the necessary precondition for writing, mathematics, other sciences or skilled crafts, architecture, or the various arts that developed alongside the city.

The idea that slavery is a lever of progress in this sense is a fundamental error that many schools of thought—including Marxism—have subscribed to. This, in fact, only proves that science and the arts were not able to detach themselves from the state. Instead, the state took control of them whenever it could, thereby preventing their free development and putting them to use for its own interests. History shows us that science and the arts did not develop as a *consequence* of slavery. Actually, they were seriously hampered by its very existence. The most important inventions and discoveries made between 6000 and 4000 BCE, when there was no slavery, were unparalleled until the period from 1600 to 1900 CE. In the five thousand years in between, comparatively little happened. It is well known that from 1600 to 1900 CE, it was primarily individual researchers who contributed to scientific advances. The state, for its part, always monopolized the results.

Even though the emergence of analytical thought has much to do with the development of the cities, the slave state society proceeded to distort this way of thinking to advance its own class interests. It was not slavery that brought about the development of analytical thought. The slave system came upon humanity like a nightmare by misusing this mode of thought to create a gigantic world of lies. The fact that people have located the development of science and the arts, the common culture of humanity, in slavery and other classed society forms can only be explained by the existence of a power-knowledge complex,[9] i.e., by the power of the state over the arts and sciences. If evaluations of the above sort made in the name of ideologies and movements for freedom and equality are not the result of conscious efforts, they must be the subconscious consequence of a loyalty to this power complex. Even when talking about Marxism-Leninism, this assessment remains accurate.

In the following chapters, I will try to show in detail that even Marxism-Leninism was unable to free itself completely from the dominating power-knowledge complex, and that this was one of the main reasons for the collapse of real socialism.

Between 250 BCE and 500 CE, the slave society form of the state fell into a general crisis and came to an end with the rule of feudal society as the upper form. Decisive factors were external attacks by "barbarians"— having the characteristics of natural society—and internal social erosion, along with the struggle with emerging Christianity. What dissolved, however, was not the state but only its slaveholding form. As events showed, the state would fortify itself and transform into the feudal state.

FOUR

Feudal Statist Society

The Mature Slave Society

It is of great importance that we see the state as a mindset and an institutional flow throughout history. Definitions of the state based on the assumption that states rise and fall, are quickly founded and destroyed, and are then newly built by another class or group, or that states are based on religious or national concepts, don't bring us any closer to understanding this phenomenon but, rather, obfuscate it and tear it out of its context. It would be more correct and enlightening to regard the state as society's most fundamental conceptual system and most uninterrupted institutional reality. The state can be compared to "a snowball" that grows continuously, sometimes freezing and at other times burning those around it. Since its inception, the state has both proliferated and diversified, but, in essence, it has never changed. Most importantly, the state has existed without interruption. It hasn't ceased to exist for even one second. If there had been even a single interruption in its existence, this would certainly have led to its destruction, in a way comparable to the separation of the soul from the body. The body is unable to continue its existence once the soul leaves it, and the soul can no longer be returned to the body. In the same way, we can regard the state as an animate creature. Given its diversity and scope, the state can be compared to a genus. Just like animal and plant genera, it may consist of many different species of varying magnitude, but its basic properties will remain the same. This explanatory model is not undermined by the fact that some species can be described as better and some as worse *exemplars* of the genus.

When Lenin advocated the replacement of the "bourgeois state" by the "proletarian state," he thought he was engaging in honest and accurate reasoning, but there simply cannot be a "proletarian" version of the state as a social form. Many since Spartacus have attempted this, but they have all failed. Even the Soviet experiment could not avoid collapse, despite the fact that it was carried out in roughly a third of the world. The main reason being that the state form exists essentially to serve the lifestyle of the oppressive and exploitative groups and classes. That is why it was created. It cannot provide the form for equality and freedom for those groups and classes who are subjected to oppression and exploitation. Not only is its essence not suitable, its form also contradicts freedom and equality.

Our snowball that began with the Sumerians has grown steadily. There is significant data confirming that other regions of the world, including China and South America, were also nourished by this model. Of course, they "enriched" it with regional material, but the primary inspirational source of the ideas and institutions remained the Sumerian priest state. Science generally assumes that this model served both directly and indirectly as "divine" inspiration. The scientific investigation of the details of this process is a task for historians. We, on the other hand, need to correctly decipher and explain the soul and substance of it. The primitive slaveholding model of the state that began in Sumer and Egypt continued through time and across space with the Hittites, the Medes, the Aztecs, and other smaller states, in Iran, India, China, Greece, and Rome, reaching its mature stage in the feudal form like a growing and proliferating example of a genus. The state has continued to this day to infiltrate the most hidden nooks and crannies of natural society, creating many new realms and turning subjugation and exploitation into a magnificent art.

What is meant by the so-called "art of politics and war" is actually the art of systematically killing and suppressing people, as well as exploiting them in all kinds of ways. The fundamental artistic forms used to prepare the basis of legitimacy for this "art" were mythology and legends, partially the content of the Holy Scripture, sculpture, painting, music, and other forms of culture and art. These arts were certainly not *created* by the slaveholding class, but it developed a particular ability to use them for its own purposes: the art of fundamentally transforming the human mindset. And they did this by using these basic material and immaterial instruments of life that humanity had created with enormous effort over the course of millennia. The system of slavery didn't make any positive or creative contribution but only served to distort and deform. I want to draw attention to this, as it has often been falsely interpreted, even being presented in the name of freedom and equality.

Let me briefly summarize what the institution of the state already included when it arrived at the feudal state stage. When the Sumerian and Egyptian god-kings died, they had thousands of their female and male servants buried alive so that they could serve them in the afterlife. For the erection of each sepulchral monument they sacrificed hundreds of thousands by working them to death. While a corner of paradise was made for a group of rulers, the rest were treated worse than a herd of cattle. Their fundamental policy was to obliterate all the social structures, such as clans or tribes, that opposed slavery. Erecting towers and ramparts consisting of human skulls was considered a glorious deed. The art of premeditated killing—something totally unnatural—entered human society for the first time. Women were successfully locked in a cage. The natural dreams of children were impeded. People who wanted to live freely were left only the deserts, mountains, and forests. The slaves were transformed into economic means of production not only with their labor power but with all their bodies. Analytical intelligence was used to create a grand mythology based on lies.

As if naked violence and material exploitation of the masters were not enough, the masters also made the immaterial oppression and exploitation of the priests' world of the gods the central element of belief and worship of the human mindset. Morality and the arts were now primarily used to praise and flatter them. In contrast to the understanding of a living universe, they filled the natural environment and human society with soulless and punitive gods who lived either beneath the earth or in heaven. While the masters never experienced even one day of scarcity, all other groups constantly suffered from illness and hunger. Even during their games and ceremonies people were killed for entertainment.

This overview could easily be extended. Slave states are known to us from historical records, and their remnants are still visible and present in our conscious. No state, big or small, without exception, has refrained from operating within this framework and adding to it whatever it considered necessary for the art of politics and the art of war.

Even a mere list of the deeds of the Roman and the Byzantine emperors would make it difficult for any normal human being to reconcile the resulting canvas of horror with conscience and reason, though the truth would be a little more elucidated. The designation of the slave state as "Leviathan," inspired by the Holy Scripture, is only too fitting.

It is not necessary to investigate the disintegration of this social form of the state more closely here. We know, however, that it was severely weakened by resistance and attacks from the outside, by tribes, called "barbarians," that still embodied features of natural society. Because of the resistance and the attacks of various tribes and peoples—among them the Teutons, Huns, and Scythians in the north and the Arabs and Berbers in the south—the centers of the slaveholding civilization, i.e., China, India, and Iran in the East and the two Roman Empires in the West, could no longer sustain their existence in the previous form. To call these groups "barbarians," however, simply reflects the language of the slaveholders.

It is actually more correct to describe them as the fundamental revolutionary forces that created developments that are closer to freedom and equality. For our purposes, it is important to treat tribal leaders who tried to emulate the slaveholding masters separately from the mass of the people. Internally, the system of slaveholding society was undermined and could not be sustained due to gnostic religious currents, key among them Christianity, Manicheism, and Islam, which were primarily based among the poor masses and those who were striving for freedom. One cannot really say that these movements based themselves on conscious concepts of "freedom" and "equality," but it is clear that, in essence, they wanted to free themselves from slavery. "Redemption" and "redeemer" are the most popular concepts. Jesus was called the "Messiah," i.e., the "redeemer." Mani was an apostle of peace and an opulence of colors. The meaning of the word *Islam* is *submission to peace*. The most important demands leading to the disintegration of the system were peace and redemption.

Because of the mentality of the time, these demands were inevitably formulated in religious terms and, therefore, could only lead to liberation and peace in a fairly limited way.

It is clear that gnostic religions, denominations, and philosophical schools that grew in the shadow of the empires would be affected by these systems, in terms of mentality, as well as politically and militarily. They would not reestablish a system of classical slavery, which, by this point, they knew well and had fiercely condemned. But it was not yet clear what to replace the old system with. Besides, many people who had artfully mastered the system of slavery were quite at ease with politically adopting the new religions and turning them into their legitimate base. As a matter of fact, Constantine the Great, the Roman emperor who came into office in 306 CE, did so on the basis of adopting Christianity. He moved the empire's capital to today's Istanbul and, with his Edict of Tolerance in 313 and the Council of Nicaea in 325, paved the way for Christianity to become the official religion. The religion that had fought against slavery for three hundred years now struck a deal with the slave system, much like Mani, who was protected by Shapur I, the second great king of the Sasanian dynasty. The more radical Mohammad, however, based his system primarily on Jewish and Christian theology and the legacy of the Byzantine and Persian Empires.

They all consciously took up the struggle against the classical system of slavery and succeeded in overcoming it. Nevertheless, they fell back into the general templates of the priest state invented in Sumer. They made them a little bit more flexible and transformed them into instruments that were at least bearable for humans. It did not even cross their mind to renew natural society under new conditions. In fact, they condemned this system, not the system of slavery, as "idolatry." All of this should be sufficient to show that the new state phenomenon that will be encountered was no more than a refurbished version of the previous one. As for the barbarian communities that were closer to natural society, they had no choice but to accept a new state form that was more bearable, because their chiefs had long been involved in the system of slavery.

These radical changes in human history took place during the fifth and sixth centuries CE. There had been a similar process during the sixth and fifth centuries BCE, when Buddha, Confucius, Zarathustra, and Socrates morally and philosophically opposed the classical mentality of slavery. The result was the development of more advanced forms of state in the social systems in Greece, Rome, Iran, India, and China.

In historical developments of this sort, Marxism attributes the decisive role to the means and relations of production. For Marxism, the struggle between mentalities plays a secondary role. Marxism also attributes too little significance to the struggle of ethnic and religious groups. This amounts to little more than a dogmatic interpretation of the dialectical method and is far from an integral understanding of history. Ignoring society's massive mobilization, which can include mentality and politics, and interpreting reality exclusively in economic terms will inevitably lead to a flagrantly limited understanding.

If we don't understand the mobilization of large communities and instead stress the role of technology and the structure of production as the force of change, we will fall prey to the ideology of the state without recognizing it. An interpretation of history that lacks an analysis of the great movements of religious and ethnic groups—clans, tribes, and peoples—will lead to serious errors and shortcomings, both methodologically and in terms of content.[1] This oversight is the main reason that interpretations of history made by the Marxist method have been sterile and have led to erroneous results. While attempting to overcome the idealism based on the traditional exaltation of the upper society, they fell into the opposite trap of vulgar materialism, with an analysis of a very narrow class and economic structure.

Another historical and social problem relates to what we mean by overcoming the past. The law of development, substantiated by change in nature and evolution in biology, shows that previously existing phenomena continue to exist within later ones. So, for example, the fusion of two hydrogen atoms leads to helium. The hydrogen continues to exist in the helium. If the helium atom is split, the hydrogen reemerges. But the fusion into helium has led to a qualitative change; helium is an element that is different than hydrogen. We find something similar in biology with regard to the emergence of species. The previous species is, in a sense, contained in the emerging one. The change in societies is similar. The upper society carries the lower society within itself. The lower society does not, however, contain the upper society, because there is no new phenomenon. Thus, feudal society emerges as a consequence of the internal and external attacks on the slave system by adopting new elements, but it continues to carry with it many of the values of slave society. These values do not continue on in their old form; as a result of a synthesis with the new values, they take new forms.

The old is not superseded by being eliminated; it continues to exist in a different form. Thus, the Roman system of slavery was able to rejuvenate itself through the "fresh blood" of the barbarians and Christians. It is only in this way that one can apply dialectics to historical processes and come to correct conclusions that are not suffocated in dogma.

The transformation of the mentality against natural society continued to deepen in the feudal society system. Great developments have been achieved through analytical intelligence. Both religious and philosophical ways of thinking form the dominant mentality of the new society. Both ways of thinking once again became dominant within the transforming elements of the old society. Just as the Sumerian society synthesized the values of Neolithic society within its new system, feudal society synthe-sized the immaterial values of the oppressed classes within the internal structures of the old system and that of the resisting ethnicity in the periph-ery. In this process praxis is decisive. Praxis, in a sense, is the constituting entity of time, like a force. Time is praxis that is constituted.

The mentality renews its mythological qualities with religious and philosophical concepts. The rising imperial power represented the form of an evolution toward the greatest god, which represents the universal power, rather than many weak and powerless gods. In a mutually rein-forcing process, what goes on in material life finds its counterpart in the mentality. The transition from polytheism to monotheism was closely related to this process. The thousands of years of state practice has now eroded the concept of the "god-king." The East-West synthesis that began with Alexander the Great was also very important stage in this sense. Alexander, who was raised with the Aristotelian mentality, clearly under-stood what lay behind the idea of a god-king. He even lets the scribes in his entourage know how artificial he found the concept of "god-king." Even so, to guarantee his authority he continued to benefit from it and declared himself a god and forced a resistant Athens to accept this. It is only with the epoch of the Roman emperors that the era of the god-kings cult would finally come to an end. When the emperor died, people would say that he had risen up to the gods, showing that the distinction slowly grew between god-kings and human kings.

The concept of "God as a Trinity" that was introduced by Jesus led to great historical contortions. The mentality revolution that began with Jesus is a great development that constituted a long transition period between the era of god-king and the era of human kings. While, up to that time, the kings had presented themselves as gods, Jesus, who was influ-enced by that culture but whose concern was the kingdom of Jerusalem, described himself not as God but as the *Son* of God.

Actually, the concept "Son of God" in the Holy Scripture has profound sociological significance. Being the "Son of God" instead of being God is something new, while the "Holy Spirit," in fact, signifies being from the lineage of God.

Jesus tried to reform that mentality he was born into, and in doing so he changed both the Roman and Jewish religious cults. The kingdom of Judea and the Roman prefect collaborated to crucify Jesus because of the revolutionary character of the new message. At the time, there were a growing number of poor and unemployed people. They and the lower clerics and officials took an interest in Jesus, which is to say, the Jesus phenomenon didn't come out of the blue. It was connected to the Essene community, which played a significant role at the time. John the Baptist, who was seen as a prophet, named Jesus his rightful successor, and even before Jesus was crucified, John was decapitated. In brief, the system of slavery was in a severe crisis. The mentality revolution in the form of Christianity was the result of an evolution spanning several centuries. In a way, Christianity was very much like the Marxist, social democratic, or socialist movements of recent times. Its expansion followed well-trodden paths within the Roman Empire and in its shadow, so to speak. One can properly regard the Christian movement as the first and most comprehensive party of the poor in history. It was a movement that was based not on ethnicity but on humanism.

This was another way in which Christianity followed Roman cosmopolitism. In their resistance against the Roman emperors, the Christians' most important thesis was the claim that the emperor couldn't possibly be a god. "There is only God the Father, and Jesus is His Son." This sentence was to bring about the collapse of the foundations of the Roman imperial mentality. However, what appeared to be a religious conflict was, in reality, primarily a political conflict. Through the work of the apostles and, later, the work and sacrifice of numerous men and women venerated as martyrs and saints, Rome's immaterial mentality was conquered. With Constantine the Great the political conquest was complete. Christianity became the official religion of Byzantium, the newly created state. Throughout its existence, this state was to be the battlefield of enormous confessional disputes that remain unresolved to this very day, disputes based on the conflicting interests of different classes and ethnic structures.

Theological research has yielded vast knowledge about the development of religions. Christianity emerged as a Jewish sect, whereas Judaism can be traced back to Abraham, an important representative of the prophetic tradition of resistance against the Sumerian and Egyptian god-kings and their rule. Moses led the exodus, an important departure, and this series continued, with important figures in the chain like David and Isaiah and on to Jesus, as was discussed earlier. Islam would be the last of its sects.

Even though the mentality component of the movements led by these prophets was the predominant feature, they also had a strong political society component. They were searching for a system that was less harsh and more bearable than the archaic slavery of the god-kings. They were all strongly influenced by Sumerian and Egyptian mythologies. Even so, they considered many of the fictions of the mythologies and the conception of god as obsolete due, among other things, to the influence of the times. They regarded a continuation of the archaic form of slavery as intolerable. Another of their goals was to give the formation of the merchant and the craftspeople more breathing room and to provide an autonomous space for the development of their class. They found the necessary ideological material in those very mythologies of yore. Since they came from the lower strata of the city populations, they also found resonance in the natural society in rural areas.

They resemble today's petite bourgeoisie. Because of their structure, they were unable to develop a radically independent ideology. The ideology of such movements, it is safe to say, was and will always be eclectic. The mentality that they constructed is a sort of ideology of the middle class—an ideology that picks from both the upper and underclasses. They created their own system of mentality by adding upper-class concept of "class rule" to the concepts of "freedom" and "equality" drawn from the lower classes and the ethnic groups, turning it into a tradition and successfully trans-forming it into a different culture.

The Islamic version of this tradition gave more room to analytical intelligence. It completely broke with the claims of the god-kings. Islam didn't see Jesus as the Son of God but as a prophet, a *messenger* of God. The distinction between God and humans is strongly and unequivocally empha-sized. The most important claim for the Koran as Islam's holy scripture is its universal conception of God. Its delineation of God is very abstract. In a sense, he is perceived as the energy of the universe. But the outweigh-ing aspect of this concept is its relation to the social. The unity of a state concept, which became more centralized and increasingly abstract, and the new abstract conception of "God" were closely related. With "Allah," the development of "El" reaches the summit of perfection:[2] this is Sumerian theology arriving at its final stage. With the existence of Allah, whose every word is absolute law, the adventurous journey of the gods, who began as mythological beings, comes to an end. Seen from that angle, it is under-standable that Mohammad approached the concept of the last prophet as he did. Sumerian mythology had already been undermined to the extent that it was of no use to the new religions. It was now time for the development of the metaphysics of those times. The broader social practice had come to know nature better and has begun to scientifically define natural processes.

As a result, the mentality of the feudal system reached a point where a separation of worldly affairs and religious affairs could be postulated. It was more appropriate for the human mind to accept descriptions such as "representative of God on earth" or "shadow of God."[3] It had become difficult to inculcate people with the belief that a human was a god.

All of the more developed religions came to the conclusion that God could not be a human being, and that a human being could not become a god. From this point onward, nature was no longer explained with divine concepts but with rational concepts. Life in this world and life in the netherworld were thoroughly and carefully separated. All the same, the idea of a God who controls all human actions and who rewards good works and punishes bad deeds remained strongly in place. Actually, a reflection of the increasingly centralist and abstract state institution was intensely intertwined with the concept of "God."

When Hegel, in his *Outlines of the Philosophy of Right*, written in the nineteenth century, said it "is God's way in the world that the state should exist. The basis of the state is the power of reason actualizing itself as will" and, thus, described the state as virtually the embodiment of God on earth, he openly pronounced this fact.[4] There was a close connection between the concept of the "state," which to a large extent parted company with individual kings and became more abstract and attained a strong central structure, and a concept of "god" that moved from polytheism toward a single, powerful God with a stronger central position. Actually, in that sense, both Christianity and Islam developed the theory of a centralist state. Indeed, during Mohammad's lifetime, we saw the development of both the Islamic state and the papal god state putting this theory into practice.

Feudal mentality's renewal of concepts, as well as its dogmas on many different issues, was often intertwined with the old mythologies and Greek and Zoroastrian philosophies and morality, constituting an eclectic blend of all three. From their depictions of heaven and hell to their understanding of the universe, from good and bad deeds to angels and djinns, from forms of worship to juridical rules, the fundamental sources were Sumerian mythology, Greek philosophy, and Zoroaster's morality of freedom.

This mentality played a dominant ideological role from approximately the fourth to the fifteenth centuries, retaining its dominance in the main areas of civilization. First, it spread to Europe and, from there, to all other continents. Its decline started in the early fifteenth century, when a new revolution of the mindset began with the Renaissance. Even today, one cannot say that the mentality of the medieval age has been completely overcome. In the Middle East, in particular, it carries on in many areas and in numerous disguises.

The political and military institutions of feudal state society were also the product of a process of maturation. The state was exuberant with self-confidence. It was the most sacred embodiment of God on earth. Its soldiers were the soldiers of Allah. The mask of holiness is fitted thoroughly. Politics was the first force, the clergy, the second, the military, the third, and the fourth was the bureaucracy. The basic institutions of the state were, by this point, well-established. Even though dynasties came and went, the state as an institution didn't lose any of its value. What counted was not this or that dynasty but the institution itself. The same was true for individuals. The world was conceived of as the God-given property of the rulers. Servants were not only expected to agree with this but even be grateful for it. Wars were embroidered with the label *holy*. They were led in the name of the divine order. Even though humanity as a whole was addressed in terms of freedom and equality, loot and tribute were the main institutions of exploitation. In this respect, classical slavery was simply maintained. Their armies were organized in a more systematic and permanent manner. The transition from a military entourage to an orderly standing army as an institution had long since occurred. During the medieval period, armies were formed on the Persian, Greek, and Roman models and were qualitatively and quantitatively superior to their predecessors. The institution of knighthood was pompously in full flower, and the knight and the sword were military symbols of that time.

The bureaucracy was also institutionalized. Ministers and officials gained a fixed status, a distinction was made between the military and *ilmiye* classes.[5] Taxation was fixed on sound principles, and communication-intelligence became widespread as an institution.

War came to be seen as a form of production. Conquests were important sources of profit. The conquest of new lands meant new surplus products. The most powerful state was the state that was best at waging war and conquering new areas. Neither greed for blood nor exploitation knew any limit. But the war in the name of Allah could only be concluded with the conquest of the whole world. This, however, was tantamount to universal and endless holy war. Eventually, the statist system couldn't expand any further, which meant it was also incapable of any further maturation. It had reached its final stage of growth. That, in turn, meant that the institution of the state had reached its mature phase in the course of history. The subsequent phase could only be a stage of crisis.

In social life, being a servant was regarded as a natural, Allah-given state of affairs. Servitude is the state of life from birth, not something that occurs later in life. People were born and died as servants. A way of life other than servitude was inconceivable. There was Allah, and there were His servants, and, in between, there were angels and prophets, as emissaries who relayed His orders. Translated into sociological terms, this meant that Allah represented the institutionalized abstract authority of the state. Here, the angels were the army of public officials, while the prophets and the archangels were the ministers and top level of the bureaucracy. Society was ruled by a gigantic "system of symbols." There was a close relationship between visible rule and symbolic rule. Without analyzing the relationship between symbolic and concrete rule, we cannot really reach a sound understanding of society. If we want to understand the rule of society in its naked form, we must lift the veil of the pantheon, the system of the gods, that obscures it. Then we will see how the true ugly and cruel face of oppressors and exploiters has been veiled for thousands of years in the name of sanctity.

Social servitude is not just a class phenomenon. Apart from the despot—and even he was a prisoner of the system—everybody, all social classes and strata, was shackled by it. The system of subjugation was more effectively hidden than the slave-holding system. Mollifying it also meant that the system reached deeper. The basic paradigm of society was a system of servitude without beginning or end. From time immemorial and for all eternity—this too was more of a concept of the era of the mature state—this system has existed and will exist unchanged. Scrutiny and change only takes place in the afterworld. Not only was actual physical resistance against the system considered the greatest sin, so was spiritual or intellectual opposition.

For those who know absolute obedience best, servitude was the embodiment of virtue and perfection. The creators, who in natural society and in the age of the heroes of positive hierarchy best served the community, were condemned in the age of servitude as extremely dangerous to God, i.e., the masters. They were said to be sinful and fiendish, that is, devilish and satanic, personalities who needed to be punished. Actually, the concept of "devilry," of the "pact with the devil," was used against all of the groups that rejected slavery. With roots from the Middle East, this concept was applied to groups that resisted being integrated into the system. For that very reason, those among the Kurds who had not adopted any of the mono-theistic religions and had remained true to their traditions of natural life were called "devil worshipers." It is quite meaningful that this group of Kurds sanctify the devil as divine.[6]

The mature period of the servitude system regarded the world as a place of temptation and sin. Life was to be avoided. The maxim was: the more you want to live, the more you are bound to sin. The best way to live consisted of preparation for death in every way. This view regarded nature as dead matter that should not be approached at all, which made any creativity impossible from the outset. For servants, the conception of an animate nature was unthinkable. Actually, we can see the traces of terrible oppression and exploitation at the very beginning of this system of thought. This approach to nature is the main spiritual reason that even today the society in the Middle East cannot come to its senses. On the other hand, for the world of the masters there was a lively world on earth that was in no way inferior to heaven. They and the gods—who have the same name (*Rab* means *lord*)—lived comfortably and satisfactorily like something out of the *Arabian Nights*. These tales are the mythological representation of the mature state system in the Middle Ages.

As for the situation of women held in a cage, the only change was the development in the way they sounded and the ornaments they wore. Their slavery was deepened and veiled to an incredible degree. In the Middle Ages, women experienced the second major cultural rupture of sexist soci-ety. The first major cultural rupture occurred at the time of the emergence of slave state, within the culture of the goddess Inanna (later, Ishtar).[7] This can also be seen later: as the system reaches maturity, a cultural rupture against women occurs with Miriam, the older sister of the prophet Moses,[8] and the Virgin Mary, the mother of the Prophet Jesus, as well as Aisha, the wife of the Prophet Mohammad.[9] However, it was not just that, in the end nothing remained of their divinity—rather, by this point, women were regarded as the closest thing to the devil. Even the slightest objection would see a woman declared the devil. She might at any time sell her soul to the devil or seduce men, in which case, she would be burned alive as a witch. In this culture of massacre, girls might be buried alive and women debased into sexual objects or stoned to death by a mob. For millennia, women's most profound state of slavery within the society grew ever more complex, reaching unbearable dimensions. It is impossible to understand the level of enslavement in this system without analyzing the situation of women. The rings affixed to them, the bride price, and all the ornamentation were symbols of this culture of slavery. They are rendered thoughtless, as if their tongues have been severed. Dried-out mothers were like fields that the men could use as they wished. They had long since lost their status as agent-subjects and been turned into objects. No longer were there any traces of the goddesses of natural society. Nothing remained of the wise leader, the woman that all of the children, the youth, and the men revolved around.

The situation of the children and the youth was similar to that of the women. The general system of servitude deprived children of the soul of childhood before they were seven years old. Because of the extraordinary educational methods of the system, the years of adolescence result in total satellite personalities. All modes of behavior had already been conditioned. Freedom had become unthinkable, even as a word.

In general, we can evaluate this as a period when society was intellectually and emotionally obliterated. The only things that were heard were the roaring voice of the upper society with the sounds of "Allah, horseshoe, and sword." All sagas and legends were some kind of a drama based on killing and conquering. This may sound slightly exaggerated, but it reflects the essence of the state of mind at that time fairly accurately. The archaic version of slavery was replaced by the more solid system of classical slavery. The state and the society it represented entered their highest stage, their mature period. All of the system's fundamental concepts and institutions have now been established. Mosques, churches, and synagogues declared the sanctity of the system with their daily prayer calls and ringing bells. Even though the capitalist state that was to follow appeared to grow stronger, it would, in essence, represent the last stage of a social form that was entering a general crisis. As is well known, splendid pinnacles are generally succeeded by crisis-ridden phases of dissolution. This general law of nature is even more valid for social processes.

We did not use medieval concepts like "serfdom," "the village," and "the city" much, which is another possible form of conceptualization. We did not repeat the class analysis—its method and results—because it is already known. This method, however, might also clarify some facts. The serf, peasant, merchant, town-dweller, artisan, and those working in the arts and sciences can be conceived of as different segments of the society. It may be necessary to deal extensively with the land as a means of production and, thus, the property relations it was ruled by, as well as law that is developing. The land was the most important means of production. Conflicts and wars always revolved around the conquest of land, and the middle class grew stronger and developed the potential to play a greater role in social developments—all of which is worthy of more careful consideration. But since my goal here is an overall definition of the state, it seems more appropriate to provide an outline and only address in greater detail those aspects that are directly related to this goal.

It was mainly internal factors that led to the dissolution of the slave state system of the Middle Ages. Neither new attacks by ethnic groups from the outside nor attacks by new religions from the inside were necessary for its dissolution. The accumulated internal problems were sufficient. The uppermost strata of the ethnic group that have been incorporated within the borders of the state, the middle stratum of the rising bourgeoisie, and those who rebelled in the name of religious confessions and other peoples were the key forces that led the uprising against the monarchy, which was considered as the absolute state. The intersection of the demand of the ethnicity movement for a national state and the demand of the urban middle class, particularly the trade bourgeoisie, for national borders led to one of the greatest historical turning points: the rise of the national state and capitalist society. This process, which began around the fifteenth century and continues to this day, represents the final stage of the state as society's superstructure. Because of the level of progress in both mentality and material technology, it became possible for the society to recognize the state form of organization—at least in its archaic and classical forms—as unnecessary, as an institutional process that is a hindrance.

The Capitalist State and Capitalist Society: The Crisis of Civilization
Lenin was right when he noted that in times of general crisis the issue of the state and revolution is a vital one. People expected him to provide an accurate definition of the state and society. The oppressed and exploited of the twentieth century believed in him as if he were a prophet. He was honest in his thinking and his actions, and he was very capable.

He did, indeed, come close to an accurate definition. Nevertheless, the state knew how to continue eluding definition, like a spellbound object, and frustrate Lenin's intentions. It is as if the state, for all the prophets, sages, philosophers, and scientists up to this day, has presented something like a "quantum dilemma." This dilemma says that if one knows the location of a particle, one will be unable to measure its time (or, rather, its momentum), and that if one knows its momentum, one cannot measure its location. After its discoverer, this principle is called the "Heisenberg uncertainty principle." This could be a principle for the most advanced sensibility—*knowing*. I believe, indeed know, that the moment of *knowing* is when we take form. Since knowing and formation occur at the same moment, I could not find a remedy for half-knowing despite all my efforts. This is, however, a dilemma that occurs at the macro and micro boundaries of the universe. It makes itself felt in the most magnificent formations of the universe.

I do not believe that the state is such a phenomenon. Just as Engels ingeniously sensed, the day will come when the state is thrown onto the scrapheap of history like a dysfunctional tool that ends up in a museum.[10] But the misfortune is that it is difficult to understand, because no one knows exactly who its real owner is or where and how it was formed, and because it assumes a completely different reality when it is owned. Thus, it appears similar to a "quantum dilemma."

We live in capitalism. Even the motor of capitalism, the US, is now declaring a worldwide battle to downsize the state.[11] In fact, the destruction of the ring in the *Lord of the Rings* that we mentioned above intends a critique of the extreme power that has become a major obstacle. At the same time, the US does not hesitate to wrap itself around the whole world as a state. This means that the problem of the state continues in all its intensity at the highest level of upper society. The situation of the other states that should be like provincial governors could probably not be better analyzed. It seems as if there is no government that doesn't think of reforming the state in some manner. But, oddly enough, none of these reforms has any effect beyond exacerbating the crisis. The goal of the latest Middle East adventure is supposed to be a "Great Middle East Reform Project." It is on the agenda of the whole world, but whether the ground covered will take us forward or backward, whether it will lead to some kind of solution or further deepen the deadlock, remains unclear. In my view, all these assessments and uncertainties stem from the same problem: we do not dare to define the state.

The situation of social scientists, whose task it would normally be to develop that definition, is no better than that of the Sumerian priests who tried to determine the fate of humans from the movements of the stars. Even though the horrible record of war and violence in the twentieth century outstrips several times all previous wars and acts of violence combined, some people don't hesitate to produce whole filing cabinets of lies about so-called individual or organized terrorism, despite the fact that these are actually a by-product of the system. It seems as if all they do is to ensure that the state is not understood for what *it is*—organized violence. Even those who try their best to arrive at a definition of the state continue to grope in the dark. These social scientists seem to be unaware that they are shattering the totality of the factual reality in the name of "methodology," and, thus, they are rendering it unrecognizable.

Interestingly, not having a correct definition of the state seems to be a problem even for the state itself. The state—which sometimes disguises itself and on other occasions makes itself attractive but also often intimidates and punishes, thereby making itself unrecognizable—has become the basis of the social crisis. It is highly likely that this aspect of the crisis can be found everywhere around the world. The things happening daily in Lower Mesopotamia alone seem like the revenge for a cursed past. As if a snake were biting its own very long tail. Or, to use the language of the Holy Scripture, it seems like the Leviathan wages a struggle for its own annihilation at its place of birth by devouring its own tail.

Just like any other social system based on exploitation and oppression, capitalism could not arise without the state. The dogmatism of the archaic system of slavery was of a mythological nature, whereas the feudal system's dogma was religious in nature. In the first, god is embodied in the king and his dynasty and, in the latter, god is represented—rendering itself invisible—in the abstract existence of the state. The respective mentality of each epoch necessitated this.

In the mentality of the Islamic world, science and philosophy would succumb to religious dogmatism at the end of the twelfth century CE. From then on, the door to the *ijtihad* was truly closed,[12] and the templates of the dogmas besieged the mentality of society in the Middle East like a web of ignorance. Europe, on the other hand, would begin to lay the foundations of a historical revolution in mentality by drawing upon the legacy of the East and Ancient Greece from the twelfth century on.[13]

All the oppressive methods of Christianity notwithstanding, it could not, on the other hand, refrain from stoking the curiosity for knowledge. Since the memory of natural society and its remnants was still alive, overcoming Christian dogmas, which were very much open to interpretation, would prove to be as difficult as overcoming the Islamic community's dogmas.

Just as the fresh memories of the natural society did not succumb to the Roman Empire, they would also not succumb to Christian dogmatism. Rather, this memory countered the Christian concept of "nature as dead matter" with an animated, hopeful view of nature. There are many theories as to why capitalism was successful in Western Europe. In my view, the most important reason was that dogmatism hadn't so thoroughly taken root there, not having had the opportunity as it had in the Middle East. The Inquisition primarily targeted three groups: heretics (deviants from the denomination), alchemists (the vanguard of science), and witches (the remaining wise women). The very existence of these three groups was the antidote to dogmatism. It was from the ashes of hundreds of thousands of people burned at the stake that the mentality of the Renaissance emerged.

The birth of the capitalist social system from this process—one of the greatest revolutions in mentality—had nothing to do with fate; there was no certainty about the development of capitalism. So how did capitalism take advantage of this revolution and become the dominant system?

To answer this, we must take a closer look at the ways of thinking and belief that established a connection of linearity and certainty between revolutions in mentality and social systems in history. This way of thinking is nothing more than the reflection of the Levh-i Mahfûz understanding in the Holy Scripture to scientific thought.[14] The dogmatic belief expressed by the people in the phrase "what is written will happen" shows how widespread this way of thinking actually is.

In all previous analysis, I have tried to carefully emphasize the connection between this understanding and the hierarchical statist will and its understanding of ruling. The goal of this approach is to instill in society a system of *commands* as divine law. This can be understood as a draft concept of "law and legislation." This several thousand–year tradition led to the emergence of a linear development model that began with the *golden age* and ended with *the last judgment* and *heaven and hell*. Fatalism is a requirement of this understanding. There were heated discussions in the Islamic world between the representatives of the Levh-i Mahfûz and those of the *Mu'tazilites*.[15] The origin of this understanding, which renders meaningless the necessity for freedom of discussion and a preference for multichoice free will, is much older. It goes further back, namely, to the time of mythology, when people believed that supernatural gods created and ruled everything, and continues as philosophical idealism. The form it takes in European civilization, beginning with the Renaissance and continuing into the present, is the understanding that progress is the norm. Both the strong Enlightenment belief in "progress" and the Marxist belief in the "inevitable development toward communism" have their roots in this dogmatic way of thinking.

Proven phenomena in the physics of subatomic particles, i.e., quantum physics, have broken the power of this way of thinking. The realization that neither natural nor social development follow a straight, uninterrupted line, but that development occurs within a chaos interval in the subatomic world that is open to multiple preferences, including the option of freedom, is one of the greatest intellectual revolutions of all time. Actually, we can achieve this way of thinking intuitively and speculatively, without the need for subatomic physics, because, without developmental power that leaves room for freedom of preference in all the events and phenomena in the world, it would be impossible to explain the infinite diversity of the universe and of nature as it has emerged. Diversity requires freedom, whereas the linear approach enforces uniformity and, thus, lack of choice. We are resorting to this scientific and philosophical way of thinking to facilitate a more creative approach in our effort to understand the process that accelerated from the fifteenth century onward and resulted in the victory of capitalism.

In short, the victory of capitalism was not fate; things could have turned out differently. We need to evaluate the causes for the success of capitalism more accurately. Marxism—which influenced all of us—declared capitalism and the preceding forms of society based on class divisions as "inevitable historic progress." By doing this, Marxism, inadvertently and contrary to its own convictions and hopes, made an enormous contribution to the capitalism that it has so rigorously fought. The essence of what I want to articulate to the court in this defense is my conviction that there is *no* principle of inevitability in systems of society, even though the most fundamental modes of thinking, including Marxism, assert that there is. Regardless of whether they concern forms of upper society or the state, all claims about "inevitable development" bear the traces of the official propaganda of the last several thousand years. Under a scientific cloak, the old belief in fate lives on with a new name: "mandatory laws of social development."

But the dynamics of social transformation work in a different way. They can't be explained simply in terms of base and superstructure. All transformations are subject to highly complicated factors. The dogmatic interpretation of dialectical materialism that influenced a great many contemporary intellectuals did *not* correspond to reality, as evidenced by the dissolution of real socialism. All those who had pinned their hopes on this interpretation were gravely disappointed.

We would come closer to a solution if we were to relate the historical social systems to the ideological, political, and moral forms of struggle typical for the time in question rather than viewing it as the result of mandatory laws. Laws, in humans—as individuals and in a social matrix—are both very flexible and capable of rapid transformation. The strict laws that we find in physical, chemical, and biological phenomena are valid only in the realms of physics, chemistry, and biology. For other realms, human intelligence and society are the decisive factors.

Consequently, not anchoring humans and society in fatalistic under-standings is of great importance in terms of the opportunity and likelihood of becoming free. Both prejudices in advance and fatalistic final judgments impede the dynamics of free creation. As for the social science, we must not lose sight of the fact that most of what social scientists say is the rhetoric that has been filtered down from the dominant social systems that stretch back thousands of years, has donned different masks in different eras, and fulfills its current stakeholder task in the guise of scientism.

In this context it would be helpful to look at the connection between the Renaissance—the revolution in mentality—that has gained great speed and depth since the fifteenth century, on the one hand, and capitalism, on the other hand. Two aspects of Western European society play a particular role in the emergence of Renaissance mentality. The weakness of state culture and fresh memories of natural society created favorable conditions for creative and free thought. Even the rigid dogmas of Christianity were unable to prevent these conditions. The knowledge and culture of the Middle East entering Europe as a consequence of the Crusades and the combined effect of the Greco-Roman culture coalesced with these conditions, making it possible to overcome Christian dogmatism. The emergence of Christian sectarianism in the thirteenth century played a role both as the cause and the result of these developments. The Dominican and Franciscan orders were noteworthy developments. During this period, similar brotherhoods, the Mu'tazilites and the Ishraqiyun,[16] were being suppressed in Islam.

The contributions made by the new observations of the world provided by the geographical discoveries of this period were also quite important. These two developments, that is, the weakness of state culture and the memory of natural society, on the one hand, and the synthesis of the positive legacy of Christianity and Islam, with Judaism effective as the stem culture, with the Greco-Roman culture, as well as the geographic discoveries, on the other hand, gave rise to the Renaissance mentality. One can regard the Renaissance as the third greatest expression of the power of understanding in the history of humanity. The first one was the Neolithic mentality, which reached its zenith around 4000 BCE in the inner arc of the Taurus-Zagros mountain system. We know that all of the technical devices required by humanity for the transition to civilization were created during that period. The wheel, weaving, devices for working the soil, including the plough, large villages, the languages and ethnic structures that were becoming distinct, heroic epics—all of these created the wonders arising from the woman-mother's great productive power. Goddess religion actually represents an exaltation of a great mentality and the blessing of women's productivity, as is corroborated by all findings from that time. The root word *star* in Arian, the language and culture of the time, that sparked the emergence of an era, which still today means *star* in English, meant *goddess* at the time. In Kurdish, the language in the region, even today the exclamation *ya star*, which corresponds to the present-day *ya Allah—by the strength of Allah*—still expresses great astonishment, grandeur, and the strength of faith.

This is such an ancient creation that, even if in varied forms, it is still found in all languages of Aryan origin. You might say that the heaven on earth was first created in that mountain arc. Humanity experienced hundreds of "firsts" in production and social life. The musical instruments and rhythms of that time continue to envelop our souls with their most shivery and deeply staggering impact even today. Research shows that this culture spread to the lower courses of the Euphrates and the Tigris, the Nile and the Punjab valleys, and laid the base for the Sumerian, Egyptian, and Indian cultures that arose. It was, as such, the first link in the chain of civilization.

The second great mentality period occurred between 600 and 300 BCE on both shores of the Aegean. This is a stage at which the mentality of philosophy and science made a big leap forward against slaver mythology. This period is, therefore, also referred to as the "centuries of wisdom." Western Anatolia can be thought of in the way we now think of Western Europe. It is the echo of the civilizational wave from the East lapping the

Aegean coast. Here, the role that Christianity would later play in Europe was played by the ensemble of the Hittite, Median, Egyptian, and Cretan civilizations. Here too, among the factors that enabled the emergence of a new mentality were the absence of a deeply rooted state tradition, the strong presence of a culture of natural society, a fecund and beautiful natural world, and the existence of magnificent seas and islands. As excavations in Troy make clear that the extensive trade between East and West was also undoubtedly an important factor.

First and foremost, these two grand renaissances provided the foundation for the Western European Renaissance. Unless we understand the renaissance in the foothills of the Taurus-Zagros, we will not understand the renaissance at the shores of the Aegean, and without understanding the latter, we will, likewise, be unable to understand the European Renaissance. To go further: if we fail to consider the spread of the Neolithic Aryan revolution, culture, and languages that formed inside the same arc that encompassed China, Europe, North Africa, and the Caucasus from the fifth to the fourth millennium BCE, we will be unable to understand either the Neolithic communities that arose there or the subsequent formation of civilizations. To understand this history, in which the consecutive parts are interwoven like links in a chain, is of central importance if we are to comprehend the great mentality revolutions, religions, and social structures.

I emphasize these points, because for each European, and even for their grandchildren, the Greco-Roman era and the Renaissance come to mind when they think of the "civilization" and Christianity. But, actually, the developments in these areas were only a stop on the civilization eras' sacred river that had been flowing for thousands of years, constantly hitting rock bottom, growing wider, paving its way forward, and exalting its upper ranks.

The most important features of Renaissance mentality include regaining the human soul that had been destroyed by the medieval period, a return to the world and to nature, which had been continuously vilified, a rupture with dogma, and a new confidence in human reason.

Since the time of the Sumerian priests, knowledge had been monopolized by the state and turned into one of the crucial instruments for strengthening the state's power. Not only the surplus product and the most advanced means of production but also the most useful knowledge and those who held that knowledge were immediately transferred to the state institution. The new science was not allowed to create areas of free activity, because allowing space for free science would have meant a new society. It is in the nature of the slave state to regard such structures as a threat and to act against them, either to bring them under control or to eradicate them.

It is no accident that the Church's Inquisition began at this point: when individuals began to attain their souls, they became free. Those whose free thinking led them to question religious dogmatism were condemned as heretics. The women who were tried as witches were those who carried with them a non-Christian identity. For their part, alchemists were looking for knowledge beyond what existed. These three currents were able to open a breach in dogmatism. When the art movements began to display the beauty of life, it spelled the surpassing of the mentality that saw matter and nature as dead. Painting, music, architecture, and literature began to reshape the content and form of the individual's soul. An individual with a new spirit and a new way of thinking was a person who was lively and who could not be constrained by the existing mold. We will see later how, with this individual, the attempt was made not only to conquer a new land but nature itself.

This was also a time that served as a stimulant in conceiving new utopias. The old clothes no longer fit. Since the material conditions were not yet ripe for more far-reaching developments, the utopias had to remain within the framework of the existing system.[17] People did not want to go back to the oppressive old world, but they also did not know exactly how to open the door of the new world. This pursuit would compel the search for a new philosophy and science. The greater the rupture with the old world, the more they enter the new one.

Nicholas of Cusa moved from religion to philosophy, while Copernicus pushed the door ajar, making way for the scientific revolution. Descartes laid the foundational step for the philosophical revolution, when he addressed the dilemma of matter and the mind, leaving God, at least provisionally, out of the picture. Galileo Galilei introduced the experimental method into science, thereby making one of the most important contributions to the daisy chain process of revolution. With Newton, the universe gained the power to be in motion according to its own laws, independently of God. The philosophical, scientific, and artistic revolution took root during the period stretching from the fifteenth to the seventeenth centuries. Even though the wheels of the Inquisition continued to grind on, Protestantism would deliver a further blow to the rigid dogmatism of the Church, making religion a private matter. The rupture with the Church was essentially a rupture with state power: on the one hand, the Catholic Church was the state, and, on the other hand, it provided the armor that surrounded and protected the feudal state. A state without the Church was unthinkable; the Church basically fought in the name of the state.

The revolution in mentality liberated the individual, which also meant the dissolution of servitude to the state. What superficially looked like a confessional controversy, in reality amounted to the destruction of the legitimacy of the state.

Developments in the eighteenth century increased the foundational base of the Renaissance among the masses. The revolution in mentality was no longer a new idea, a new hope, and the spirit of just a handful of people but had become the concern of a broad range of people. Like a new religion, including Christianity or Islam, it reached its own masses.

The existence of such a free mass of people in every Western European country posed a great threat to the Catholic Church (clergy) state and the states of the various kingdoms. It was no longer possible to use the Inquisition to deal with these masses. War was necessary. The Hundred Years' War (1337–1453), the Wars of the Roses (1455–1485), and the Thirty Years' War (1618–1648) demonstrated this reality very clearly. Finally, the Catholic Church and the monarchies were defeated by the awakening European nations. With the English Revolution of 1640, the American Revolution of 1776, and the French Revolution in 1789, the triumphant era of the national denominations and their states began.

If we want to resolve crises periods in a way that favors democratic tendencies, it is important that we rethink the current concept of "revolution." Categorizing the European revolutions simply as "bourgeois revolutions" reflects the narrow class approach of Marxism; it is a gift to the bourgeoisie, all in the name of proletarianism. Undoubtedly, a dogmatic interpretation of dialectic materialism played a huge role in this development. If we regard this as the modern version of a belief in the Levh-i Mahfûz, a belief in fate, with history unfolding in a linear, predetermined manner, we may come closer to the concrete reality. We cannot analyze the extraordinarily rich content of the reality without overcoming this dogmatism, which I also experienced as a strong influence.

In none of the capitalist schoolbooks is there anything on the underlying ideas, theories, and programs of the English, American, or French

Revolutions. Those who played their role in these revolutions never claimed to represent the bourgeoisie. The masses involved in these revolutions were mostly poor and wanted freedom and equality. It would be a huge exaggeration to even claim that the bourgeoisie played a decisive role in the movements behind the Renaissance, the Reformation, and the Enlightenment. By and large, the rise of bourgeoisie as a class focused on the accumulation of capital through profit; this was its "total effort." Undoubtedly, this class was aware of the link between the path to profits and the path to state power. Thus, it actively tried to influence and take hold of power but lacked revolutionary theory or practice, even in the narrowest sense. The objective conditions underlying the revolutions mentioned above were the product of a long evolution of history. The subjective members, the thinkers or political activists, did not advance a specific bourgeois revolutionary program; they didn't even have parties. They were nothing more than a current, a tendency that was primarily sponsored by some of the rich, who were mostly defenders of feudalism interested in science and the arts. The prominent demands were generally humanistic and centered on the desire for a free and equal world.

All of the written utopias presented a social structure that was the opposite of capitalism. Given that, how is it that these thinkers and militants were regarded as bourgeois and their revolutions as bourgeois revolutions? Over the course of time, we know that the bourgeoisie, as is the case with every force that aspired to dominate, achieved this by either partially or completely attaining power. Hierarchical and statist forces have come to and lost power thousands of times based on the requirements of the art called "politics," but the instrument suitable for exploitation and oppression continued to exist uninterruptedly. The most recent similar force to rise will not, it must be kept in mind, behave otherwise. All revolutions are the work of the people. Every now and then the old hierarchical statist forces also participate. They behave very intelligently and with great resourcefulness, particularly once the victory of a revolution is on the horizon. They are masters at exploiting the demands of the oppressed for their own purposes. We find similar efforts in all revolutions, successful or not.

For example, when Jesus planned his actions, he did not have the foundation of the Byzantine Empire in mind. Essentially, he opposed the cult of the emperor. In the end, however, the movement he gave rise to could not escape becoming an instrument of this form of state, which was the scene to the most scheming of emperors. Even Mohammad couldn't escape becoming an instrument in the hands of the aristocracy in Mecca, which he had toppled with his ideas and action, in the founding of its empire, the "Umayyad Caliphate," while murdering his relatives (*ehl-i beyt*; people of the house). No one can claim that Mohammad planned to build a feudal empire. There are hundreds of similar examples in history. "Then," one might object and say, "there is no revolution in which people have been successful." I will address this issue thoroughly in the next chapter, showing that a different analytical approach is required.

At this point, it is sufficient to note that the efforts were not in vain, although it is true that the problem of power has not yet been resolved. The main purpose of this defense is to cut through this deadlock, and one of the most important lessons to be learned is that the social armor most difficult to pierce is the ideology of domination.

The demands for "freedom, equality, and fraternity" that were common to the European revolutions were at their core no different than the demands that have been raised against domination and exploitation since the emergence of hierarchy. Just as state power developed as links in a chain, the people's oppositional movements also had their own history of development. These two dialectical phenomena are in a constant interaction rife with relationships and contradictions. It is very difficult to grasp fundamental social transformations, especially revolutionary processes, with abstract generalizations without considering this dilemma of social dialectics in their historical development, especially in terms of both their generalities and their respective particularities.

The nation and capitalist society are fundamental forms of European civilization, but they don't necessitate each other. The formation of the nation and the configuration of capitalist society follow different logics. Even though they emerged at roughly the same time, this does not mean that they share the same logic. The fact that the bourgeoisie presents itself as the leading force in the nation is closely linked to its ideological, political, and economic goals. These links are "nationalism" in terms of ideology and "liberalism" in the case of politics and economics. Both are ideal weapons for influencing both the state and the people, but they are fictitious phenomena, nothing more than propaganda tools, and they are the primary tools used by the bourgeoisie to gain and retain power.

During the Renaissance, the Reformation, and the Enlightenment— the developments that transformed old Europe into the Europe we know—these propaganda tools played a very limited role. It was only in the nineteenth and twentieth centuries that they wreaked havoc. The concepts of "proletariat" and "communism" employed by the oppressed and exploited were used in a similar way. But given the nature of these groups, they were less successful at mastering the art of power.

Revolutions as important breaking points and moments of restructuring in the transformation of societies cannot be realistically understood using the nineteenth- and twentieth-century "right-" or "left-"wing logic structures. It is, nonetheless, important to correctly define these movements, which made enormous sacrifices in the name of humanity. The importance of the need for redefinition becomes particularly clear when we consider the gigantic sacrifices millions of people made for the Soviet revolution, the way in which the Soviet Union dissolved, and the consequences of this. After two hundred years of blood, violence, and pain in the name of modernity, the horrors of World War II marked a particularly important turning point, after which at least a limited discussion of power, violence, and the ideological instruments that disguise them began.

Bourgeois reality, which is the basic class form of capitalism, needs to be understood in this context. Describing it as a new oppressive and exploitative class tells us nothing in particular but only enumerates the properties that are common to all ruling classes. The specific feature of the bourgeoisie is that it uses both individualism and analytical intelligence with maximum efficiency against sociality and, thus, has been able to dissolve the moral fabric that envelops society to a degree that no ruling power before it achieved. At the beginning of its dissolution, natural society was also strongly against the accumulation of value that was detrimental to society. Those who distributed the greatest amount of accumulated values were held in the highest esteem. People were aware of the dangers inherent in accumulation.

Unfettered accumulation was only possible with the presence of a special ruling power and the subsequent transition to a hierarchical society and the state. Accumulation initiated the process that both fostered the establishment of this power and made way for that accumulation to subsequently be used by this power. This is how the logic of the chain reaction came into existence. Those who accumulated the most were generally the ruling power. On close inspection, in fact, accumulation was nothing but a kind of theft from society, because value itself is not possible without society. The understanding found in natural society in this regard is, thus, correct, leading it to establish its most fundamental moral principle. Since the decisive agent of all values is society, there must be neither individual accumulation nor accumulation by any particular group without the consent of society—i.e., unless society has some self-interest in that accumulation.

Looting and the subsequent division of the spoils, an aspect of all wars, was the degeneracy of this understanding in class society. Those in power have adopted the principle of deprivation from the accumulation of value in order to weaken one another. They are infallible when identifying the fundamental source of power. The craftsmen and the merchants—prototypes of the bourgeois way of becoming a class—have existed from the outset in any civilization but have been seen as dangerous and, therefore, have been kept under control. This control was constant, and they could not escape frequently being plundered. The slave and feudal state powers based on land ownership always viewed the development of a third category besides themselves and the slaves—or serfs—with great suspicion and, therefore, always tried to keep them under control. Within the history of civilization, apart from the class of servants, they found all other formations contrary to nature. Until the emergence of the civilization shaped by the bourgeoisie, there was an established morality and worldview in this system. War and power followed fundamental laws. The equilibrium that had emerged was stable enough to prevail for thousands of years. Although violence and law were employed to rule society, both had only a very limited reach. Primarily, society was held together by its moral fabric. Even though the ruling power constantly eroded morality, this feature was maintained. The fact that the ruling power only represented a numerically small minority when compared to society overall also contributed to this state of affairs.

The emergence of the bourgeoisie as a class destroyed this far-reaching equilibrium. Both as a ruling and exploitative power, this class had such weight that it became unbearable for society. In order to rule and exploit, it had to exploit the whole of society. Marxism came to the correct conclusion that, as a result, it would be the last ruling and exploiting class. To ascend as a class, it had to continuously atomize society. To achieve that, the first thing it had to do was to tear down morality, society's fundamental system of safeguard. Without tearing down the morality that was still based on a longing for the freedom and equality of natural society, capitalist society could not have developed.

Even though Marx and Engels's remarkable formulation in the *Communist Manifesto*, according to which "the bourgeoisie, wherever it has got the upper hand, has put an end to all feudal, patriarchal, idyllic relations" is true, this was not a revolutionary act; it was destructive and antisocial. To render society defenseless is not a revolutionary act but, rather, at most, a move that is anti-humanity.[18] In the hands of the bourgeoisie, ruling and exploitative power is a cancerous tumor that has seeped into society's core. It is not necessary to be a scientist to detect the connection between the widespread cancer, AIDS, or any other similar illnesses afflicting people and this social cancer. At a time when capitalist society was still at its very beginning, Hobbes defined the need for power, namely, the state, as a necessity "to prevent man from becoming a wolf to man."[19] But the shoe was on the other foot. Capitalism established its rule *to* turn the human being into a wolf to all others. In the modern era, humans have become wolves, not just to other humans but to all of nature. Which section of society or element of nature could this class, which strives to maximize its profit and accumulation, exempt from exploitation once in power?

Marxism has analyzed concepts such as "value," "profit," "labor," "distribution," "imperialism," and "war" well, but understanding their function in capitalism within this framework is more instructive. The descriptions in the Holy Scripture of the "false Messiah,"[20] who will arrive briefly before the apocalypse, are rather fitting for this class. No dominant social system has attacked and destroyed the foundations of society and the natural environment as extremely as capitalism. This class that transforms the nation into a site of racist nationalism and fascism, the domination of nature into an ecological catastrophe, and profit into enormous unemployment is now at a stage where it is beginning to devour itself. It is increasingly losing its specific properties and beginning to fall apart. It is this class, not the proletariat, that is enacting a counterrevolution against itself. A new social era cannot sustain this class reality and can only be established on the basis of its dissolution.

Here, I present but a few theses. Addressing some fundamental processes, including the incorporation of the previous systems into capitalism, how capitalism became a state, the way in which the sciences and the arts got caught up in power, capitalism's development into imperialism, its uneven development, and its wars could fill a book and is not possible here. What is important for us is the logic underlying these processes.

The concept of "class" can also be extended to other dimensions. Its function in dissolving real socialism, its ability to transform national liberation movements and their states into its reserve power, and its capacity to use the social democrats are all important examples. Our currently dominant class reality is able to turn everything toward making profit by advertising even the most unnecessary of things in the realms of science and technology or in society. Sports and cultural events are used like opium. The rebelliousness of the proletariat and the intellectuals is eliminated, and they are made to beg for work from this new dominant class. It drains all that is sacred of its essence and leaves the Renaissance's sparkling and vivid image of the world to robotic gazes.

One innovation that capitalism brings to the power structure is the depth of its institutional character. Instead of connecting power to a particular person, capitalism switched to a system that binds people, parties, and even social systems to power, and, with this, the invisible, abstract character of power was developed. Ideology, politics, and economics now serve multilayered functions. With nationalism, derived from the concept of "nation," entire nations are made to believe that power actually belongs to them. In essence, a nation can never hold power. Always and everywhere, only a minority within an ethnic group, a dynasty, or a nation truly holds power.

A system was created in which individuals hold power with those at the bottom being oppressed. An extremely poor husband in a family at the lower end of the social hierarchy can still see himself in the role of the "little emperor" in relation to his wife, and the wife, in a chain-like manner, plays this role in relation to her children. As for the children, what else can they do but play their roles in the same system once they are adults? The fact that the chain of achieving power is established in this manner is a feature of this system.

Like individuals, political parties are overly oriented toward power. Their main function is to bring the state to society and society to the state. Society itself becomes a state possession. Like an invisible god, the state lurks everywhere in society.

The mindset of power created by ideology is perhaps the greatest falsifier. The role of the "art of politics" is to convince individual groups in society that the state is theirs, and that it is necessary that they serve it, which essentially represents political demagoguery at its most developed. Politics is not just an instrument for taking power, as one might think. It is also an instrument to defend, expand, and perpetuate power. This is the role of politics, particularly against democracy. There is probably no other phenomenon that negates democracy as much as the art of politics, and this has been the case since the classical Athenian age.

The economy, more than ever before, has coalesced with power. The economy is run as a "political economy." We are living in a time when there is almost no individual or group that cannot be brought into line using the economy as a weapon. The saying that there is no value or power that money cannot buy is the most popular slogan of this era.

The definition of the essence of holding power and ruling can be further developed in relation to nation-state. The nation-state is the contemporary form of what in earlier times was called the priest state, the dynastic state, or the religious state. None of these are anything more than signatures left on the essence of power. In the capitalist developmental phase, borders that delimit a common language and traditions are the geographic parameters for ideal accumulation. This is primarily to create a lucrative and profitable area for accumulation that is not about a sacred fatherland. For those in power, this area—cordoned off to external competitors—is ideal for securing their capital accumulation and consolidating their power. The birth of nationalism was a consequence of this material development. A new ideological veil was required as the religion of "worldliness" declined with laicism. The ideology of nationalism, with its connection to the phenomenon of the nation, developed rapidly.

Essentially, nationalism can be thought of as a more developed form of the ethnic "tribal" feelings of the past, that is, as a faith system replacing the prevailing ethnic sentiments and religion. When its proponents began to internally oppress and exploit ethnic, confessional, religious, and other ideological groups and to proceed similarly against social systems on the outside, nationalism assumed the concept of a "master race." Where there was once a "true belief superior to all other beliefs," now there was the "belief in the master nation or race." Nationalism began to infiltrate the society that had once been enlightened by the scientific mentality, submerging it in darkness once again, as religion had previously done.

Just like the previous concept of "holy war," in the nineteenth and twentieth centuries, nationalist mentality offered the most useful legitimating instrument for mobilizing society for war and violence of all sorts. While the seventeenth and eighteenth centuries saw the birth of nations, the nineteenth and the twentieth centuries was the period when nationalism spread like fire. The destructiveness of the age of nationalism, with state power reaching its apex during World War II, simultaneously marked the beginning of the general and final crisis of capitalism. It became clear that nationalism and humanity cannot coexist. The system going into crisis early on did not simply mean that it lost power. It raised the risk that it would be even less likely to adhere to the established rules and would grow even more aggressive.

The revolts of 1968 represented the most comprehensive critique of the system. Capitalism—whether in the form of real socialism or fascism—reached an understanding of an all-encompassing authority, and, thus, proved unsustainable. Unsustainability means crisis, and this is exactly what humanity is living through right now. This period, which could simply be called chaos, is different from the Renaissance. While the Renaissance represented an exit from the crisis of feudal society, in the 1970s, capitalism entered a period of chaos. The innovations and diversity that will result from this chaos will depend on both the nature and strength of the struggles waged. One very remarkable thing is the fundamental shift in the world-view—the paradigm—that has accompanied this period. The unraveling of all moral values at the core of society, the massive growth of a nationalism that has infiltrated every mentality, and the consequences of ecological destruction, which have spread and created a robotic sameness, a gray, zest-less, hopeless, faithless, and aimless worldview. The dominant psychology and social atmosphere of the crisis is characterized by stress, anger, hatred, violence, extreme compulsiveness, individual loneliness, social worthless-ness, and a relationship logic totally locked into self-interest, infidelity, disinterest in humanism, extreme selfishness, and the increasing loss of any sacred meaning to life. Radically new quests only appear under such circumstances. The perpetual nature of the crisis makes this necessary.

For the first time in history, the imperialist system and the oppression of nations and classes by capitalist rule became so comprehensive that it engulfed the world. By the end of the nineteenth century, there was no longer anywhere on the map that was not occupied. With this, domina-tion, assimilation, and even genocide on national, class, ethnic, religious, and sexual grounds became more widespread than it had ever previously been. It was the beginning of a time when humans were nothing more than wolves to other humans. Viewed in terms of imperial practice, the United States of America represents an ultimate stage. We are in the final imperial era.

From a theoretical point of view, imperial rule took the following course: state power surpassed the limits of a city, a country, or a nation; it was concentrated in one person, continually expanded, and then came to a standstill, regressed, and collapsed. Its establishment in the social system led to a chain reaction, with every new power forced to establish its empire on the remnants of the previous one.

As far as we know, this historical continuity began around 2350 BCE with the Akkadian dynasty in Sumer and continues today with the Bush dynasty in the United States.[21] It is interesting that the last empire is now involved in a conflict in a part of the world where the first empire once emerged. We can think of the principle of plants drying out at their roots.

In an empire, there can be no completely independent states, nations, or societies—or, rather, complete independence can be idealized, but it is very rare that it can put it into practice. The prevailing reality is dependence on the dominant empire. This dependence can play out on various levels, but that does not change the fact that it is always present.

Within the empire, which has exerted influence on the social structures for around 4,350 years, many ruling groups, small or large, from the closest ally to the most unimportant satellite state, have been directly or indirectly dependent on the hegemonic state and are in a state of dependency within their own existing borders. This is also true in the era of the allegedly independent national states—which are all actually controlled by an internal minority.

To influence society, nationalism promises complete independence from the hegemonic power; this is its political assertion and the core of its game. To be a hegemon is to have the most influential mentality, power, social and economic structure, and science and technology, as well as the greatest military strength. Because the US meets these criteria, it is today's primary hegemonic power, which means it is also one of the most problematic aspects of the entire systemic crisis, the way the crisis is managed, and the way it will conclude.

It is very instructive to analyze the social characteristics of the system, particularly with regard to women. However, it is important to clarify from the outset that there are serious drawbacks to examining any social phenomenon by making distinctions like political, social, economic, cultural, etc. Societies that are constantly being constituted within a historical whole have all of their base and superstructure systems work as a whole, like parts in a clock. The disease of excessive fragmentation stems from Western science's loss of fact-based integrity. As we make use of this approach, which makes grasping the truth scientifically difficult, it is of utmost importance not to ignore the totality. Women should be regarded as an epitome of the whole system and analyzed accordingly. Just as capitalist society is the continuation and apex of all previous exploitative societies, women experience the apex of the enslaving effects of all these systems. Without understanding how women have been shaped by the oppressive and exploitative grip of the oldest and most concentrated hierarchical and statist society, we cannot correctly define society. The correct understanding of ethnic, national, and class slavery is only possible if the enslavement of women is correctly understood. A limited amount of research on the topic, always very studiously ignored by social science, was conducted in the final quarter of the twentieth century when it was no longer possible to ignore it. Both the feminist movement and the horrific destruction of the environment by rulers and their wars has drawn our attention to the sexist character of the history and domination. This alone shows us the sexist nature of science as a whole, including the social sciences, which, in theory, ought to be the most neutral. Science is sexist.

We will defer the positive interpretation of women to the next section. Let us first ask what kind of change capitalism has brought to traditional enslavement. First, we must assert that it would be contrary to the essence of capitalism to bring freedom. The claim that capitalism has broken women's chains by abolishing the old traditions is a massively misleading distortion.

To be sustainable, an oppressive system's relationship to freedom is a matter of coarser or subtler methods. The women praised in love poems and the women who are subjected to the harshest and ugliest slavery are one and the same. Women are like canaries in cages—houses under the domination of men. She may be cute, but she is a captive. Just like a bird will immediately fly away given the opportunity, there is no turning back on the part of a woman once she begins to become conscious of her situation. If she knows that she can go somewhere that offers her freedom, there is no house or palace, no wealth, no power, and no individual that she cannot escape from. Women have the potential to break away from it all. No other creature has ever been condemned to a captivity as complete as that of women. By captivity, I mean suppressing and destroying the objective and subjective conditions for free development. The failure of all previous social analyses, the frustration of all their plans and programs, and the emergence of inhumane developments are all related to women's level of slavery. Therefore, without ensuring a solution to women's enslavement and guaranteeing women's freedom and equality, no social phenomenon can be competently resolved, nor can equality or freedom be achieved.

If we regard women's physical appearance, which has been commodified as the result of being integrated into the system by capitalism, we may come closer to reality. We know that during classical slavery, it was primarily women who were bought and sold in the slave markets. In feudal slavery, this continued extensively in the form of concubinage. What is sold here is the woman as a whole. The bride price and political rentier are forms of this process that have found their way into the family. Capitalism, however, like a butcher, has divided the body into pieces, and each piece has been given its own price tag.

From head to toe, from chest to waist, from stomach to sexual organ, from shoulders, knees, back, thighs, eyes, lips, and cheeks to neck, no part of a woman is left unevaluated. Unfortunately, no one asks whether she has a soul or not, and, if so, no one thinks of what it is worth. In terms of her brainpower, she is the eternally "insufficiently intelligent."

Women are the commodity that gives pleasure to both the private and the public houses.[22] They are the baby-making machines. Nothing is more difficult than giving birth to children, but it does not count as work. Even for as demanding a job as raising children, there is no remuneration. In all of the important economic, social, political, and military institutions, women are at most symbolically represented, but they are indispensable material for advertising. They are the only creatures whose sex is so frequently turned into a commodity and offered on the market. They are the target of most cursing and abuse. They are widely instrumentalized in the lie called love. There is always someone interfering in whatever they do. They are an identity for which there is a unique language and particular way of speaking—the womanly way. They are humans with whom one cannot be friends in a human way. The woman is the human being whom even the most decent man wants to pounce on. Women have become the objects over which every man regards himself as an emperor.

One could continue enriching the definition. The interesting thing is that the male dominant society continues to hold the belief that life with such an identity, inscribed with so many negative properties, is easily lived. This is because women are regarded as thoroughly domesticated slaves. Nonetheless, it is difficult and humiliating for any man with a scrap of honor to live with someone who has been organized to such negative ends. Plato has been criticized for excluding women from his concepts of "state" and "society," but this was a consequence of this humiliation. There are many philosophers who can be interpreted similarly. Nietzsche, for example, also wrote that living with someone with these characteristics definitely corrupts a person. Why, then, is there such a strong lust for women in all societies? Because these societies are debased, and because the men in them are also debased. This is because slavery is contagious. Such a useful slave would surely be the most sought-after partner for people accustomed to slavery. Birds of a feather flock together. For this reason, the ruin of women is simultaneously the ruin of society, and the debasement of men.

In short, as long as social phenomena concerning women are not sufficiently elucidated, as long as there is no unity of the free mother-woman of natural society with the free and conscious womanhood of class-based civilization, there can be no equal and balanced life partners. In any case, such unity cannot be achieved if its equivalent masculinity is also not restructured in a similar manner.

In the social realm, we can observe how capitalism creates and rules over many different phenomena, particularly in the areas of men, family, work, civil service, education, health, and the law. A thumbnail definition of the family would be: the basic institution of hierarchical and statist society. This hearth is the stem cell and the smallest molecule of this system. The "little imperator" in the family is a reflection of the imperator at the top. It is the worksite that most reflects the slavery of society.

Slavery in the family is the main guarantor of slavery in society. The system reproduces itself daily, even hourly, in the bosom of the family. The family also carries the greatest burden. It is hierarchical and statist society's obedient donkey; mount it, and it will carry you. Because of the close connection between the two, the general disintegration of the capitalist system has most strikingly projected itself on to the family.

It is superfluous to talk about capitalism's economy. Capital itself is the core of the economy. It is the most abusive, brutally competitive system and is willing to risk anything for profit. There is no social phenomenon that hasn't been turned into a commodity. However, turning society into a commodity means society is to be disposed of. Such a society represents a system whose life span has expired, and, therefore, it needs to be ended.

The system tries incessantly to extend its life, using science and the arts. But the goal here is not to foster science, technology, or the arts; it is all about the system's survival using the extraordinarily advanced power of science and the arts. This calls to mind the situation of a sick person approaching the end of their life, with science and technology mobilized to cure that person. Science and the arts mostly play an indispensable and decisive role in the construction of new and habitable systems when faced with these processes of the system and the pursuant chaos.

The historical significance of capitalism rests on the fact that it is the last of the dominant systems. The system, whose pores descend from early hierarchical society, was able to take advantage of the freer environment opened up by the Renaissance to become the dominant system and express its full potential. At this point, however, it seems unlikely that it can continue to develop in any significant way in either essence or form. There is nothing in society or nature that it hasn't abused. What has been done, however, is entirely quantitative and nothing more. Society endures such extreme manipulation because of the unprecedented use of violence—including the use of the atomic bomb. No other system has ever been so intertwined with violence and war. Both society and the individual are tossed around like a bull rider at the rodeo; there is no forward movement, only up and down. If the present social conditions are not overcome, the individual's search for the new, for hope, for finding their orientation, and for becoming a creative talent will stagnate and wither. The system's state citizenship is in dissolution, both in terms of meaning and of structure.

There are no "new" territories or societies in this world of ours that could overcome US-led capitalism in terms of its scheme. Europe is in the process of self-critically assessing the huge devastation of the system, and this will be the case for some time to come. Latin America has neither the historical nor the social conditions to become like the US. The fate of the countries on that continent depends on what happens to the US. The situation in Africa is similar, with Africa even further behind. On the west coast of the Pacific, China and Japan can, at best, help the US maintain the system. They have neither the assertiveness necessary to develop a new and creative form of capitalism nor the conditions necessary to do so. They may, however, be existent capitalism's best practitioners. Russia— the former Soviet Union—has strategically accepted its defeat and has adopted progress based on receiving US aid as its new policy.

What remains is the troubled region of the Middle East. It is no coincidence that the Middle East, given its geographic location and culture, is a source of difficulty for the system. The stem cells of society lie in the Middle East, the roots of those who once founded civilization and of those who would maintain it. Their gods are from the Middle East. Sooner or later, the son returns to his father's house to settle old scores. With the Greater Middle East Initiative, this role befitting the US mission has now entered the phase of implementation. Relations and contradictions, which will become more intense, will determine what emerges from the chaos. Even today, one could say that the situation in the Middle East reflects the system moving from its late phase toward its unraveling. Therefore, what is happening is very important and must be correctly analyzed. These are areas where the breaking points of contradictions and the chaos is at its most concentrated. Such areas mostly play the role of a womb and the cradle of the new. Will the ruins of the Sumerian priest temples now be the grave of the civilization they gave birth to?

FIVE

The Democratic and Ecological Society

The Historical Essence of Communal and Democratic Values
One of the most fundamental shortcomings of social science is that it does not demonstrate the other side, the "counterpart," that throughout history has been and must be in dialectical contradiction with hierarchical and state-based societies. They act as if history is free of contradictions and consists of nothing but the linear development of the dominant social system. In reality, the historical development of hierarchical and statist society has occurred in contradiction with the values of natural society—playing the role of an antithesis, given that all phenomena emerge in contradiction with their opposite pole. The hierarchical and statist society nourishes and feeds itself on its antithesis and is, thereby, able to grow and differentiate itself.

We must not underestimate the power of natural society. This society plays the role of the main stem cell. Just as all cells of the various tissues of the body emanate from the stem cell, it is from the natural society that all institutions—which we can compare to tissues—emerge. Just as organs and systems of organs form from tissues, the primordial institutions of natural society lead to the emergence of "primitive hierarchical institutions," as well as the other more complex organs and social systems. It is possible to suppress, beat back, and restrict natural society, but it can never be destroyed, for this would be the end of society as such. The fact that social science has not comprehended these relationships is one of its greatest shortcomings. What nourished the hierarchy and the state was the natural societies whose formation is the result of a developmental process lasting millions of years. How else could the dialectical contradiction have arisen?

If you carry out social analyses exclusively with narrow class or economic means, you exclude one of the most essential elements of reality from the outset. This great mistake, delusion, and error was made and was exacerbated by the fact that even Marxism, with its great aspirations, perceived natural society, which it called "primitive communism," as extinct, as having ceased to exist thousands of years ago.

In reality, natural society has never ceased to exist. Even though hierarchical and statist societies have fed upon it, natural society has never been completely consumed and has always managed to sustain its existence. Whether as a point of reference for ethnic groups, slaves, and serfs as a foundation for overcoming proletarianization and the rise of the new society, as nomadic communities in deserts and forests, or as the free peasant and the mother-based family—despite all of the destruction, it has always been present as a living morality of society. Contrary to a widely held view, it is not narrow class struggle alone that is society's driving force for progress but the strong resistance of communal social values. Of course, the importance of class struggles cannot be denied, but, at the same time, they represent just one of several historical dynamics. The leading role is played by the itinerant nomads in the mountains, deserts, and forests. In terms of their form, they are the ethnic movements, including tribe, *aşiret*, and people. It has been the strength of ethnicity to survive all of the merciless attacks and all of the natural hardships for millennia: it created language and a culture of resistance, as well as simple and noble humane values and a corresponding morality.

Among the most discussed issues is what kind of systems can emerge from the crisis of capitalism. There was also a crisis in the aftermath of World War I. The Bolshevik Revolution was closely linked to Lenin's analysis in that regard. World War II demonstrated that the crisis was still not over, and that it had a character of permanency. After that, however, capitalism regained its strength. The second great scientific-technological revolution allowed it to make quite a leap forward. These short-term outbursts couldn't prevent the crisis-driven cracks in the system from branching out. After the 1970s, and with the dissolution of the Soviet Union, not only has the crisis not been alleviated, it has, in fact, become worse. In the end, the Soviet experience objectively proved to be an effective palliative for the system.

Recently, there have been an increasing number of analyses of the crisis by both opponents of the system and proponents of neoliberalism.

Is neoliberalism really a caricature of the past? Or is it, in the guise of "globalization," really something new, as its protagonists claim? While these discussions are in full swing, it has become increasingly urgent for the people of the world to find an alternative system, especially following the crisis of real socialism. Where are the tensions within the system that includes the United States, the European Union, and Japan, the North-South conflict, and the increasing overall social polarization taking us? The environmental, feminist, and cultural movements stepped in as new actors. Human rights and civil society became increasingly important for solving problems. The left has constantly striven to renew itself. What kind of a world did the "club of the rich"—the World Economic Forum in Davos— on the one hand, and the "club of the poor"—the World Social Forums in Porto Alegre—on the other hand, visualize? These shallow discussions never got beyond the necessities of the day. Having a program and planned action was limited, and systematic and theoretical farsightedness was a rare phenomenon on both sides. In short, the proponents of freedom and equality had neither the knowledge nor the necessary structures to successfully transform the crisis into a departure point for something new.

In modern history, liberalism has repeatedly succeeded in pulling the waves of many revolutions into its own waters, as it did during the revolutions led by laborers and peoples in 1848, 1871, and 1917, co-opting these revolutions and influencing their course in its own interests. To prevent neoliberalism from doing the same, so as not to drown in its so-called new waters, it is necessary to avoid repeating the same mistakes. What's required is the power of correct knowledge, the restructuring of society, and uncovering successful forms. Particularly in the Middle East, where the contradictions are intensifying daily, and crises and conflicts are frantically experienced, a "people's option" must become meaningful and light must be shed on its structure. In the face of the new US offensive, also called the 9/11 crisis, which displays the most profound conspiratorial quality, the people of the world must have their *own* range of options ready, if they are not to fall into a radical error once again, and if they are not to become the putty for repairing the rotting structures of the system. History awaited a modest answer, one that was serious and did not mislead—solidly closing its door on well-worn repetitions that proved futile and didn't hold out any further hope.

In this book, I am taking up the challenge to find answers to these questions, which have preoccupied me for a long time. Both the grave situation of the Kurdish people, who expect a comprehensive and feasible solution, and whose expectations we absolutely have to be worthy of, and the problems faced by the PKK, which took upon itself the responsibility to lead the people, required me to find the power of meaning and the structural instruments necessary for a successful solution. In facing this responsibility, I am fully aware of the need to act in the name of a transnational option for all peoples, while struggling in the name of our own people. A humanism and a view of nature and the universe that go far beyond my earlier narrow understanding of "patriotism and internationalism" provide the basis for all of my efforts. With this in mind, I am presenting my thoughts on a democratic and ecological society for discussion and evaluation.

First, the primary question is what our theoretical framework should be. What are the consequences of having no theory? What are the results of inadequate and false theories? What would the features of a competent theoretical framework that fits the purpose be?

Even though "information society" is a buzz term these days, it is essentially an accurate definition of our era. It indicates that without the necessary knowledge it will be difficult to address and manage even ordinary phenomena, let alone the comprehensive meaning and structuring problems of social transformation. Anyone who tries to solve these problems simply by trial and error will for the most part be bitterly disappointed. Moreover, even successes will always harbor the risk of a coming defeat if they are simply fortuitous. However, a movement or a life that becomes nothing more than a routine is a gradual loss of the meaning of real life. Real life consists not only of movement but of movement with momentum.

As a result, it is very likely that in crisis-ridden societies, efforts to achieve fundamental transformation will be futile or even harmful if they are not elucidated and guided by capable theoretical perspectives fit for the purpose. Therefore, times of historical crisis are often accompanied by intense intellectual efforts. It is for this reason that we observe the development of new schools of thought and communities of faith before and after the emergence of civilizations and the formation of new systems.

Since Marxism-Leninism played such a dominant role for the resistance movements of the twentieth century, we have to take a closer look at it. This worldview has also affected us, and we should have understood earlier—not after seventy years—that we could not proceed without uncovering its fundamental flaw.

The essence of my theoretical approach to my understanding of the system that I call democratic and ecological society is fundamentally to form it outside of any state power—that is, to search for a solution not only outside of the capitalist system's concept of "power," but outside of all classic hierarchical forms of state power in all state-based societies. This approach is not utopian; it is so closely tied to social reality that I see it to be the most important accomplishment of my struggle. My personal and social origins have surely played a role in attaining this theoretical capacity, but the most important factor was to *understand* the overall systemic structure of the historical society. Beneath this ability to *understand* lies the particularities of our struggle and the ability to successfully be a responsible person. The place of decades of seclusion and prison, of treachery and suffering, in the formation of great religions and schools of thought is indisputable. The values of natural society, as well as the struggle of ethnic groups and the poor for survival, have their indispensable place in this mentality.

Clearly, conceiving of history as a chronicle of important events in the orbit of political power cannot constitute our historical basis. It seems more meaningful to try to understand the system in its totality and to draw the appropriate lessons.

The history upon which we must base ourselves is that of those who live at the opposite pole of hierarchical and class-based social development. The official political narratives of history either do not mention them or regard them as anarchist groups or useless mobs or herds only worthy of exploitation in the service of their interests. Such an understanding of history is not just idealistic and abstract; it is cruel. Our history only becomes meaningful when it is written from the perspective of all kinds of thought and action that stood against hierarchy and political power going back to the time of natural society—the resistance of those who suffered discrimination because they belonged to a certain ethnic group, class, or sex.

Moreover, as we define the historical basis of our theoretical approach, another important aspect is that it must incorporate the power of actual knowledge in the society as much as possible. If these two cannot be integrated, our capacity to *understand* and our structures will remain deficient for addressing the future. If a theory does not include the entire system's capacity to know within its own horizon of knowing, it will be inadequate and will inevitably be absorbed within the horizons of opposing theories. This is a fundamental fact of our ideological struggle.

Thus, sketching this theoretical framework for the democratic and ecological society system is our first step. The degree to which this system will conform to the ideals of freedom and equality depends on the substance we give to this framework and on our success in developing a suitable practice. We can safely assume that such a system would be neither the old hierarchical and classic statist system nor the slave system of the defeated, oppressed, and exploited society. It will be a moral system in which there is a sustained dialectical relationship with nature. It will not be founded on internal domination, and the common good will be determined by direct democracy.

The communal quality in the formation of the societal entity is its essence, not just its form, which clearly shows that in the long run a society can only exist communally. Losing communality is tantamount to ceasing to be a society. Any development against communal values means the loss of some of society's values. That is why it's realistic to regard communal life as the fundamental way of life. The human species cannot continue to exist without communal way of life. I stress this here to expose the following misconceptions. According to the discourse of civilization, hierarchy and power are valuable because they are what keep society alive and venerated. Everyone lower in the hierarchy and without power is regarded as part of a herd that must be led. This understanding is the first major systematic lie, a lie that is the most ancient and that firmly occupies the human mind. As society is made to believe this idea, it legitimates a process that is contrary to its own interests. This is such a powerful idea, however, that even today almost everyone is deceived by it. Even though the communal order is society's essential mode of existence, the values that sustain it and are revered are incorrectly ascribed to hierarchical and ruling power. This is a paramount contradiction that must be resolved. This discourse, which distorts social history, is the basic norm of the entire superstructure, especially in historiography, literature, and politics. In the end, society's true mode of existence is thus turned into a voiceless object lacking in discourse.

Unless we stop calling the primordial society "primitive," the postulates of social science will inevitably be built on false premises. Here, we must again return to the analogy of the stem cell. It may well be that compared to the more differentiated cells, the stem cell is "primitive." However, it is not primitive in the sense that it is backward and should be eroded but primordial in the sense of being primary and foundational. Without this perspective on the values of communal society, the analysis of all other institutions must be considered baseless and seriously devoid of meaning.

If we want to be consistent in our social struggle, we must first of all respect the way society exists and look at it realistically. But even the most radical contemporary socialists shy away from communality, not just in their analyses but also in their practice. It is a deception to say that a person is private but their thought is communal. It is the outcome of capitalism's moral impoverishment of society. Until almost the end of the twentieth century, phenomena such as ethnicity, tribe, aşiret, and people seem to have been underappreciated and to have remained unexamined by social science. However, if ethnic societies (in the sense of non-state societies) are not recognized as just as important as political power, it will be impossible to understand and find appropriate solutions to social problems. The form of the communal essence can be seen more clearly in ethnicity and ethnic groups. What remains of society when we remove ethnicity? Until quite recently, all contemporary schools of thought, including Marxism, regarded ethnicity as an archaic form without function. Even more so, its communal essence was presented as something makeshift, as a reactionary feature! The more social influence individualism gained, the more it dominated social values and, thus, the more important and respected it became. It is not without reason that I see social scientists in a more negative light than I see Sumerian priests. The priests, as particularly conscious members of their society, lived for and with the society—which also constituted the basis for their thought and beliefs. The most important criterion here is not whether or not their knowledge was right or wrong; the essential criterion was their commitment to the communality of society. For "social scientists," however, regardless of the correctness or incorrectness of their knowledge, social communality is never something they base themselves on. They approach things technically—and this is where the disaster begins. To the extent that they fail to acknowledge the sanctity of society's communality and devote themselves to it, all scientists in general, but social scientists in particular, cannot avoid being called the "great class of the immoral." Had people continued to adhere to the communality of society, we would not have war and power or oppression and exploitation on the scale we have them today. What communality would explain the nuclear bomb?

Communal society entered its most critical phase when it reached the threshold where it underwent hierarchical structuring. The accumulated social experience led to richness of meaning with objects and gestures and, thereafter, to language and finally to the symbol. With the totemistic religion, this phase acquired a sacred expression. The particular importance of religion stems from its development as society's original self-identity. The identification of society with a totem signified a state of primordial consciousness. The sacredness of consciousness in this form arises from social life itself. The rupture from primatial life brings with it the first important difference in meaning. The novelty of the difference is staggering. In all its important steps, social practice led to exciting developments, which, in turn, increased consciousness. In the course of this process, consciousness came to be articulated with words, with words becoming names and names becoming symbols. This development of consciousness was vital to productivity. A life without consciousness became increasingly difficult, and the poor quality of such a life was immediately apparent. The improvement in the quality of life and increased qualitative development went hand in hand with differentiation in consciousness. This was when religion acquired its full importance and sacredness. However, it contained a contradiction from the very beginning. On the one hand, life without religion became difficult, because religion was an expression of the consciousness of the first socialization, an expression of identity. On the other hand, it is conservative in relation to the future, as it carries with it a set of rules in relation to what is sacred and taboo—not to be touched, to be left alone, a forbidden area. It was not open to new elements of consciousness, thereby preventing further development. Therefore, from the outset multiple religions were necessary. Multiple religions and multiple gods were the expression of increasing differences and distinctions in consciousness. This was positive. In the beginning religion imputed a soul to everything; that the world was explained in animist terms was the result of a social paradigm and a naturalist view of the world. That too was positive. The increasing transition to a veneration of the "great spirit" and from there to divinity symbolized a society developing specific qualities, in short, developing an identity. In the beginning, God was the community itself.

In this connection, the story of the prophet Abraham's concept of "God" is interesting. Famously, with his uprising against Nimrod and the pantheon of the Babylonian-Assyrian god-kings—the divine group—whose statues he smashed as "graven images," Abraham started one of the most impressive revolutions in mentality in history.[1] The tribe whose leader he was could not do without a god for even a day. This god, however, could not be the totem of the primordial era, because there had just been a revolutionary rebellion against the veneration of idols, but creating a new conception was difficult and required a new richness of meaning. Essentially, a radical reorientation of religion was necessary. It would, of course, be affected by the religious and divine system of the time. At the same time, however, there was an enormous desire and necessity for innovation and, with it, the freedom it entailed.

In the prophetic tradition, the process of seclusion is meant for reaching intensity of meaning. The new thoughts awakening in the mind and their concepts and structures are seen as inspiration, illumination, and revelation. Revelation represents the voice of God in a rather abstract way. Compared to the previous system of idols, the abstract concept of "God" represents a leap to a more advanced system of meaning. Having gone through this process, Abraham laid the foundations of his own religion. It was probably at a point when he was beset by numerous problems that Abraham retreated into solitude, where he responded to the traditional voice: "Who are you!?" The voice responded, "I, yah-weh"—meaning *He is*, the one who speaks. What is more interesting is that the Kurdish word *va hev* also means *He is*. Studies on the origin of the Hebrew language show that it was influenced by Aryan languages—the basis of Kurdish. The origin of this development can be even better elucidated if we consider that the Abrahamic cult is from the prophetic tradition that is particularly developed in Urfa—you could even call Urfa its birthplace. At the same time, it was a region with a strong mixture of Semitic and Aryan cultures. This Semitic-Aryan interlace in Hebrew was also reflected in the newly developing religious culture. *Yahweh* later became *Jehovah*, and they are connected with the word *Jew*. The words *Israel* and *Allah* are the result of the reflection of this development in the Semitic culture.

Let me continue a little bit more with this well-known example, so that we can better understand the development in communal society. The root of the concept of "Allah," which has occupied the hearts and the minds of people for centuries is *El*. El is a divine figure. The word probably emerged around 2000 BCE from the Canaanite branch of the Semitic languages. As nomads in areas that are part desert and part plains, the Canaanite tribes were closer to an abstract understanding of God. Life in nomadic communities was only to a limited degree determined by a local river, mountain, or agricultural land. Nature was uniform. The earth and the sky were infinite expanses. In this situation, the tribe seemed to be the only entity.

Within these tribes, there developed a hierarchy, namely, sheikhdom. The sheikhs were the wise old men of the tribe, before the prophetic institution emerged, in a way like the shaman within the Semitic culture—a precursor to the time of prophets. As their authority increased, they were accorded more and more respect and sacredness. They were literally the brain of the tribe. The more the respect and sacredness attained were conceptually framed, the more they became religious. During the transition from tribal totemism to abstract god, the concept of "sublimity" developed, a concept that is translated as *el*. In today's Arabic, *'ala* has a similar meaning. When the Hebrews settled down in Canaan in the region that today is called Israel and Palestine, they were, of course, influenced by the local culture they found there. They adopted the concept of "Elohim," which is also derived from the stem *el*, but which, in terms of its significance, corresponds to the older *Jehovah*. Over the course of time, *Elohim* developed into the concept of "Allah."

In connection with the development and strengthening of society, as well as attaining contradictory features, the concept of "Allah" also changed. From the simple concept of "el," i.e., "sublimity," it was charged with complex meanings during the time of Mohammad. It is ascribed ninety-nine attributes. It would be difficult to find a sociological model that fully projected the collective, most important, and sacred properties of society more impressively.

Let me also add that it would be wrong to vulgarly assess my evaluation—Allah as the figure of the memory of social development—to be the denial of God. On the contrary, the development of this concept, particularly among the Hebrew tribe, then made the leap from social laws to physical, chemical, and biological laws, finally arriving at today's science and attaining the power of meaning. With its development, both the depth and sublimity of the cosmos and the quantum have been arrived at. The decryption of the genes and the living cell, as well as how they can be constructed, is now within our reach. Therefore, the correct analysis of the concept of "Allah" is a measure of true divinity. That we set this bar so high is a clear indication for how religion should be understood. Real sacredness requires a correct sociological analysis of our times. Otherwise, it would be an even more dangerous denial of Allah than the idolatry of the past to have the masses call out dryly to Allah by rote, devoid of any meaning. In our social reality, it is this that must be cursed and overcome— rote "abstract idol worship."

The sociology of religion is still far from reflecting social reality. Skillfully establishing the connection between epistemology, the science of knowledge, and sociality is a necessity that must be addressed. The current state of sociology forces us to resolve even the simplest of issues.

It should be emphatically stressed that the nature of communal society has to be the starting point for an analysis, or it will be impossible to understand the subsequent developments. Just as the hydrogen atom with one proton and one electron must be understood before it is possible to explain the other elements, the communal community within the root structure of society must be grasped before the diversity of social phenomena can be understood—an incomplete narrative will bring about a flawed social science. If mythology and theology are dismissed as mere flights of fancy, a patchwork like sociology does nothing but create confusion. This would mean power had unfettered maneuvering room, for if we don't understand communality, we cannot understand power. Communality is the soil from which hierarchy and state power emerged. The Greek word *hierarchy* means *rule of the sacred*. It reflects the increasing authority of the wise old men. At the time of its birth, it had a positive function. Guiding the youth and motivating and leading the clan or the commune was an advanced stage of development, and the benefit to the wise men was to easily overcome the troubles of old age. The more talented among the young rallied around them understood that they would be more successful if they benefited from the experiences of the old. The shaman, as the first example of a religious interpreter, would also become a close ally. As the shaman increasingly became the spokesperson in the field of religion, his transformation into a priest occurred, while the young men who rallied around a masterful chief among the hunters became the prototype of a military entourage. The alliance of the priest, chief, and wise man was the expression of the rising hierarchy. The state as an institution did not yet exist. Loyalties were bound to particular persons, but the power around the domestic system-mother was gradually dissipating.

The mother, the creative force of communal society, fought a major struggle against this new tripartite alliance. Historical relics provide clear evidence that this was an intensive phase. The era of the domestic system-mother reached its peak from 10000 to 4000 BCE but was overcome by the alliance of the shaman, chief, and wise man—representing the birth of patriarchy.

The conflict between Inanna and Enki in Sumerian mythology and that between Marduk and Tiamat in Babylonian mythology are symbolic of the prehistoric era of transition. This is clear even from a simple interpretation of the mythology. Inanna is the strong mother symbol emanating from prehistory. She insistently demands the return of the 104 *me*, i.e., the means, concepts, and laws of civilization. She claims that the god Enki (the first patriarchal abstraction) stole the values she had created. The most exciting passage of the legend recounts how she moves from the town of Uruk to Eridu, i.e., from her town to Enki's town, and manages, with great difficulty, to seize the *me* from him. This legend reflects a major social struggle that actually took place at the time.

On the other hand, the conflict between Marduk and Tiamat in the later Babylonian epic reflects more deeply the struggle over authority.[2] It makes manifest the mercilessness of the transition from matriarchy to patriarchy in mythological language. The second and third versions of these epics can be seen with Isis and Osiris in Egypt and Zeus and Hera in Greece, and we find similar conflicts in the epics of the Hittites and the Urartians.

As with mythology, we can learn a lot from religions, particularly monotheist religions. The contribution of Moses to the Abrahamic tradition was the absolute subduing of women. At the time of Abraham, women were not yet so deeply humiliated. In the relationship between Abraham and Sarah there was close to equal power. But in the conflict between Moses and Miriam—acting as his sister—Miriam was doomed to a painful defeat, losing the last remnant of her power. By the time of David and Solomon, women had been reduced to a one-dimensional objects of desire. It appears that they no longer had any authority. They were the objects of pleasure for the rising kingdoms and instruments for the perpetuation of the lineage. Personalities like Esther and Delilah emerged, but even they didn't play a role beyond being instruments of exploitation.

Within the Jesus and Mary dilemma, we don't hear a single word from Mary, as if her tongue had been cut out. Christianity represented a giant step toward the situation that women find themselves in today. But if we look at Mohammad and Aisha, we see a tragedy. Aisha, who is still a child, bitterly complains about the rising feudal Islamic authority. Historians often report that she complained: "O Lord, it would have been better if you had created me as a stone rather than given birth to me as a woman." Even though, in the midst of all the power intrigues, she remains Mohammad's most beloved wife, she curses herself with the frustration of knowing she is unable to achieve anything.

In the stateless societies still existing today it is possible to observe how hierarchy is primarily strengthened by the patriarchal society's conflict with matriarchal power. With this defeat of women, there were major ruptures in their social situation. Once the decision maker, she was reduced to a commodity to be bought and sold. The woman, who had previously organized the men, and who had long resisted the loss of her authority, remained a female figure, an identity who had lost her will and was forced to conform to male preference. That this transition was far from smooth can be seen in the rites in which the aspirants to the throne married the mother-goddess and were sacrificed in a sacral ceremony at each year's anniversary of their sacred wedding. These ceremonies, which we come across in many societies, symbolized the woman long resisting the loss of her authority. They conducted these sacrificial rites to symbolically prevent men from gaining authority and dominating women. The conflict between Marduk and Tiamat shows that in Sumerian society this process ended around 2000 BCE, with a defeat for women. Over the course of civilization, we encounter similar examples in all societies with roots in the Middle East.

Even though hierarchical society played a positive role in the beginning, it was bound to either disintegrate or become a state. It was the transitional stage between communal society and the state. But its strength emanated from the process of attaining its societal character. This form of authority was deeply embedded and remained valid for a long time, reaching its zenith among ethnic groups in particular.[3]

It is hierarchical patriarchal society that enforces the subjugation of women, youth, and other members of the ethnic group. The most important thing here is *how* this authority is procured. Authority is not exercised through laws but on the basis of morality, with morality being the society's power of rules that must be conformed to. This power is not exercised by force but is voluntarily respected because of its vital role in maintaining social existence. The difference from religion is that morality stems from worldly need rather than sacredness. Undoubtedly, religion is also worldly, but the beguiling aspect of its concepts and its ancient origin wraps it in greater sacredness. It is more abstract and ritualized. Morality, however, is more everyday and worldly and is based on necessary practical rules. Even though the two are closely interwoven, morality constantly makes arrangements for the management of the worldly work, while religion is responsible for finding an answer to the questions of belief and the after-life. Religion is the theory of the primordial society, while morality is its practice.

Until the stage of statehood, these two institutions were sufficient to rule society. It can also be seen as the period when society was ruled by customs, traditions, and beliefs. The communal characteristic of society still had more influence than the individual. Loyalty to the community meant conforming to its religious and moral framework. Noncompliance meant chaos and crisis in society, which was tantamount to destruction and disintegration. Therefore, at the time, religion and morality enjoyed the power to persuade or to sanction. If anybody did not conform to reli-gion and morality, this was seen as causing great damage to society. It was hard for society to tolerate this, and it had to respond with the most severe punishment. It either expelled those concerned or forced them to undergo a strict process of education. The important thing was to prevent any damage to the communal aspect of society. The fact that religions still regard the failure to conform to certain rules and rites as the greatest sin demonstrates the power of community. It emphasizes the divine quality of the communal relationship.

Nowadays, religion is firmly presented as a personal matter. This is wrong. Religion is never personal; it is the first conceptual, moral, and administrative form of social phenomena. The concept of "hierarchism," i.e., the rule of the sacred, expresses this fact very succinctly.

Communal society is in permanent conflict with hierarchy. The two societies follow different paths with regard to religious and moral values. In one society, the material and immaterial values that have been created flow back to the society, whereas, in the other, they are increas-ingly monopolized. While in the religious phenomenon that reflects the values of the patriarchal society there is a tendency toward an abstract and monotheist concept of "God," the matriarchal authority of natural society resists with a multi-goddess concept. In the domestic mother order, the essential rule was that people worked and produced, and everyone was given what was necessary to keep them alive. While patriarchal moral-ity legitimizes accumulation and paves the way for private property, the morality of communal society regarded this as offensive and as a source of evil, instead encouraging the distribution of everything among all. This is the origin of the concept of "generosity." The goal was to protect collective property against private property, lest harmony in society deteriorate and tensions increase. Potential solutions to this contradiction were seen either in a return to the old values or a strengthening of both internal and external power. This is how the social basis of violence and war based on oppression and exploitation was formed.

The hierarchical groups that grew around material and immaterial values constantly and jealously made a systematic effort to sanctify authority and the legitimacy of private property to prevent their disintegration. The dispersed and smaller communities had few resources with which to oppose this development. The oppressed clans and tribes could ensure their freedom only through constant migration. The purpose of the nomads' historical march toward the depths of deserts, forests, and mountains was not just for hunting and gathering but also for the preservation of their communal values.

This constant march, which carries within itself a love of freedom, is one of the most important driving forces of history. The necessity for self-preservation forced the clans and smaller tribes (*kabile*) to become an aşiret.[4] This is not just about increasing physical numbers; it is a form of resistance to hierarchy. At first, the existence of authority within the aşiret had a positive quality and, thus, was morally praised in legends and songs. The head of the aşiret was the symbol of the existence and freedom of the aşiret, i.e., its mentality, dignity, and security.

The contradictory process described above continued until the stage when the state became the institutionalized authority based on permanent coercion. The birth of the state marked the second great phase in the history of society. It brought radical changes to the structure of production, social life, power, and society's mentality. The erratic tribal and aşiret conflicts continually eroded accumulation and property. The remedy found to counter this was the institutionalization of authority on the basis of might. The priest was born from the shaman, the king from the sage, and the commander from the chieftain. In all three cases, the person was transient but the institution was permanent. The sedentary rural phase was over, and the age of the city began. In village society, the communal system initially prevailed—it was the basis of life in Neolithic society. The village was the sacred location of the agricultural revolution that lasted from 10000 to 3000 BCE. It was also the place where communal society and hierarchical society coexisted side by side. At this point, there were still no agas or beys.[5] The village was the splendid expression of the domestic system of the mother, because all values regarding it arose from her mind. The animals she domesticated and the plants she cultivated provided an unparalleled and miraculous life. Thousands of discoveries and inventions of that time were the work of the mother-woman. It was the time of the anonymous "women's inventions." The crafty and increasingly strong hierarchical groups longed to possess these inventions and the wealth of products they generated, so they usurped them and gave birth to the state to perpetuate their position. From that period's peasantry living in the foothills of the Taurus-Zagros Mountains, where thousands of mounds can be found even today, descending to the plains irrigated by the Euphrates, the Tigris, the Nile, and the Punjab rivers, they built cities that would lead to the state (polis) order.

In the establishment of village and city, the second important factor for the division in society was added: a sedentary nomadic lifestyle. The hierarchical division is vertical, while sedentary nomadism had a horizontal character. All later historical social systems were shaped by the contradictions caused by this dividing line.

The revolution in mentality that began with the village and intensified with the city was first reflected in the culture of religious belief. The order of the gods tried to distinguish itself completely and persistently from the order of nature and human beings. To achieve this, the gods were invested with various properties: they were almost immortal, they lived in heaven but sometimes retreated beneath the earth, and they did not allow humans among them and punished them at a whim. In the case of the Sumerian mythological gods, these attributes became increasingly diverse. An extensive pantheon or "team of gods" developed: gods that protected cities, gods of rivers, mountains, and the sea, and gods of heaven and the netherworld. This order of conceptualization represents the power of an ascending class in society intertwined with the forces of nature. This partly mythological, partly religious formation of mentality, which is based on sanctifying and perpetuating the existence of the ruling classes who divide the earth among themselves, was crucial for legitimacy in the new order. While communal society's fundamental forms of belief and morality collapsed, the new ones were able to provide a stronger and more permanent mentality. This distinction showed itself most poignantly in the transition from a goddess-dominated religious order to a god-dominated religious order. This was the true significance of the conflicts between Inanna and Enki and between Tiamat and Marduk.

No mythology could possibly attain the storytelling power of Sumerian mythology; it describes the emergence of class division and state formation poignantly, creatively, and poetically. What we have in front of us is a fantastic narrative. We encounter the "firsts" of all religious, literary, political, economic, and social concepts and institutions in Sumerian society. As such, we can say that this originality is one of the most important historical developments that would significantly shape the structure of the basic concepts and institutions of society. As a result, the solutions found by Sumerian society have universal ramifications.

Researchers believe that the emergence of the city and the state happened as a consequence of the agricultural village revolution in the foothills of the Taurus-Zagros Mountains. The concepts and tools of this most comprehensive and long-lasting revolution in the history of humanity were carried to Lower Mesopotamia by a hierarchically structured group mainly consisting of priests. It is highly likely that they also brought all of the necessary techniques of soil cultivation, house building, weaving, and transportation, as well as some of the animal species, samples of seeds, and fruit trees, otherwise it would not have been possible to attain all of this in an area that, without irrigation, was nothing but a desert. Available research has clearly shown the road map of this culture carried over with the incoming communities. These migrations took place around 6000–5000 BCE, and after 4000 BCE village units with up to five thousand inhabitants are documented. Uruk, the famous city whose tutelary is the goddess Inanna, emerged as a state around 3200 BCE. It was only appropriate that Uruk was immortalized in the Epic of Gilgamesh, the first great written testimony of the urban revolution, as the gift of the mother-goddess. Just like many other Sumerian words, the word *Gilgamesh* might be of Aryan origin. In modern Kurdish, *gil-gir* means *big*, while *gamesh* means *buffalo*. In local culture, strong men are still described as "strong as a buffalo." *Gilgamesh* could thus simply mean *big buffalo*, i.e., the strongest man of all. His description in the epic seems to confirm this interpretation. It is always interesting to study what happens to historical values on the road map of cultures.

The Gilgamesh epic recounts the story of the birth of the kingdom and, therefore, of the state. Since it was the first epic ever, it is the main source and model and was later frequently imitated. Major works from Homer's *Iliad* to Vergil's *Aeneid*, from the *Arthurian Romance* to Dante's *Divine Comedy*, have carried on this tradition. Nobody knows how many once famous but unwritten epics the first great agricultural revolution might have inspired. We find traces of them in the Sumerian, Hittite, and Ionian written narratives. And we can still feel them in the musical patterns and instruments that have been retained until today. The majority of them reflect aşiret culture. The similarity between the values still existing among the aşiret of today and their traces in Sumerian writings is truly striking.

This brief historical excursion provides a clearer understanding of the new social system that arose at this point. We can trace the rise of statist society throughout its history. We see that both institutions, the city and the state, develop in an interwoven way around the great cult of the temple. The Sumerian example lets us give a more accurate definition of religion than Marxism, which says that religion is a superstructural institution that later, as the base, reflects the economic order. The temple itself was both the productive area for the concept of "god" *and* the center of economic production (the upper floor of the ziggurat is divine; the ground floor is human and reserved for production). The upper floor of the ziggurat belonged to the pantheon of gods, the ground floor was full of tools of production and the stocks. The floors in between overflowed with workers. We must not look at these temples as we do today's churches and mosques. When they emerged, they mainly served as centers of the new mentality and material production, as is clearly corroborated by available data. We should not forget that it was the priest, as a human, who founded the temple. This very fact shows that mentality was decisive in the revolution in the productive infrastructure, just as much as it was in the case of the city and the state. The temple was an institution where mentality was of the utmost importance. In Hellenic language, theory can be understood as "gazing at the divine"—meaning the fundamental paradigm. Strikingly, in this connection, what must be noted is that the Sumerian temples—the ziggurats—as both theoretical-political and the technological-economic centers, were the stem cells, or prototypes, of the city that would later develop.

The ziggurats were the seed from which both the city and the state emerged. There, in the head of the priest, the interests of the hierarchical society are synthesized and a theoretical model for their more comprehensive development is created and put into practice with the means available. The city is born from the temple, the civilization from a city, the state from the civilization, the empire from the state, and a whole new world is born from an empire. Could one imagine a greater miracle? It is no coincidence that this region is called the "land of miracles."

We know that the first Sumerian kings were of priestly origin. As the state institutionalized and developed its bureaucracy, the potential of the priest-king had to be curtailed. Politics—i.e., the administrative problems of the growing city—became increasingly important. A development from the sacred character of the state to a more secular and worldly character occurred. While the priests were primarily concerned with the theoretical work, the political element dealt with the practical issues. Although everything is tightly intertwined, this situation would gradually bring the politician to the forefront. The growing city also meant the growing role of the politician. A step after this, particularly if the external security of the city becomes an important issue, was for the role of the military commander to come to the fore. The kingdom, thus, nourished itself from these three sources—and all three were said to emanate from the divine. Since then, what we have seen is the proliferation of this model with a limited amount of diversification. The temple was the stem cell of the state, and what later developed resembled new cells, tissues, organs, and organ systems—just as we see with human beings.

To sum up, this entire formation constitutes the state as the superstructure. In mythology, the state as an institution is likened to a golden throne. On it sat the kings, like the immortal gods, who, intent on never leaving this life, separated their lineages and *class* from that of all other human beings. Since they ruled as part of a dynasty, they proclaimed their lineages immortal. In this way, kings acquired seats of honor in history as immortal gods. What is even more striking is that this social split gives us all the clues necessary for understanding the later periods. Monotheistic religions, literature, the arts, and politics enter the stage of history as milestones of this original emergence. If we take a closer look at the source of state power, we will better understand why it must be so incessant, intense, and merciless.

In this new historical social system, the contrast with communal society shaped itself as the upper society. It magnified the depth of the difference between them. The crucial question regarding our topic is: Was this development inevitable?

Many theories of society represent the emergence of class society as the basic condition for progress. We will, however, get closer to the truth if we analyze the dynamics of the development. The surplus product due to the irrigation systems developed around the temple facilitated the integration of more people into production. The conditions in which thousands of people could work more efficiently were present. The extensive irrigation canals, the vastness of arable land, bronze and, later, iron tools, and vessels that could navigate canals and rivers allowed for large-scale production and trade. The combination of all these factors meant the city as settlement. At first, the rule of the priests came pretty close to primitive communism, indicating that the city does not necessitate the state. Essentially, the state, dominated by the political and military elements, would be formed when the problems of administering an expanding city and defending it against the tribes from the mountains and the deserts became increasingly important preoccupations. However, could the administration and security of a city not be ensured without a state? The example of the self-defense of many cities, particularly Athens, shows that a democratic administration can do so successfully, and that the state is far from necessary. This model is encountered at the initial stage of the Sumerian society. A council of prominent representatives from the tribes makes up the administration, with defense groups formed drawing upon the city's youth when necessary. A commander was chosen on the basis of what his duties would require. In Athenian society, this development occurred in a very concrete and systematic way.

Therefore, making the birth of the state a basic necessity of history is incompatible with the facts. Instead, it is more accurate to define the state as a tool for rule and repression that arose to facilitate the confiscation of the surplus product made possible by increased production. To do so, it uses the regulation of public life and public security as cover—camouflage and a promotional tool for the creation of the state. Because public administration—the common good of society—and public security can easily be taken care of by a democratic assembly of the city, exploitation of this opportunity, in fact, its confiscation—which is not necessary—must be understood to be a counterrevolution. It is realistic to define this power, which imposes itself on the pretext of ensuring the city's common good and security, both of which could be assured with democracy, as a reactionary and tyrannical power that has existed since the beginning of history. Even today, there are more politicians and security forces than necessary, and they do little more than develop despotic qualities. This power must be seen more as an additional burden than as a benefit. Essentially, this is no different from the situation of yore, when this whole drama began.

However, it was not the power of democratic governance that grew throughout history but the rule of despotic power. In this process, each step in the development of the state as an accumulation of despotic power was not only unnecessary, it was the essence of the most reactionary, conservative, and distorting development. In a narrow sense, it is important to view power and war as the fundamental passion, mind, and will of this tradition that has very effectively hidden itself within the state. It is, therefore, necessary to separate the "art" of politics and war from general administration and public security. Anyone who has scientific and practical intuition cannot help but see this distinction. The consequence of not making this distinction when analyzing the state is extremely negative. Differentiating between democratic governance and despotic and arbitrary rule serving personal interests in both theoretical and practical dimensions is fundamental and must be the basis of our historical approach.

In hierarchical and statist society systems, the most important political phenomenon is the conflict between the democratic element and the war and power clique. There is a constant struggle between the democratic elements based on communality—society's mode of existence—and war and power cliques that disguise themselves as hierarchy and the state. In this sense, it is not the narrow class struggle that is the motor of history. The actual motor is the struggle between the mode of existence of the demos (the people), which *includes* class struggle, and the warrior ruling power clique, which thrives on attacking this mode of existence. Societies essentially exist on the basis of one of these two forces. Which mentality dominates, who comes to possess authority, what the social system and the economic means look like—all of this depends on the outcome of the struggle between these two powers. Depending on the level of struggle, one of three, often intertwined, outcomes have occurred throughout history.

The first is the total victory of the warrior ruling power clique. It is a system of total enslavement imposed by the conquerors who present their glorious military victories as the greatest of historical events. Everyone and everything must be at their disposal; their word is the law. There is no room for either objection or opposition. To even think of deviating from the ruler's preordained plan is not permitted. You have to think, work, and die in exactly the way you are ordered to! What is sought is the zenith of dominant order with no alternatives—empires, fascism, and all kinds of totalitarian practices fall into this category, and monarchies generally strive to achieve such a system. This is one of the most common systems in history.

The second possible outcome is the exact opposite, society's system of free life—clans, tribes, and aşiret groups with similar language and culture—against the oligarchy of warrior ruling power veiled as the hierarchy and the state. This is the way of life of undefeated and resisting peoples. All manner of ethnic, religious, and philosophical groups not affiliated with the oligarchy that are resisting attacks in the deserts, mountains, and forests essentially represent this social way of life. The most important force of the resistance struggle for social freedom and equality was the way of life of the ethnic groups, based on emotional intelligence and a lot of physical labor, and that of the religious and philosophical groups, based on analytical intelligence. The libertarian flow of history is the result of this way of life based on resistance. Important concepts, including creative thought, honor, justice, humanism, morality, beauty, and love, are very closely related to this lifestyle.

The third possibility is "peace and stability." In this situation, there is a balance between the two forces at various levels. Constant war, conflicts, and tensions pose a threat to the survival of society. Both sides might well conclude that it is not in their interest to be in constant danger or always at war and may reach a compromise on a "pact for peace and stability" through various forms of consensus. Even though the outcome might not entirely correspond to the goals of either side, conditions make compromise and an alliance inevitable. The situation is thusly managed until a new war arises. In essence, the order characterized as "peace and stability" is actually a state of partial war, where the power of war and the ruling power and the undefeated power and resistance of the people are both present. It's more accurate to call the state of equilibrium in the war-peace dilemma a partial war.

A fourth eventuality, in which there is no war and peace problem, would arise if the conditions that led to the emergence of both sides were to disappear. A permanent peace is possible only in societies that have either never experienced these conditions or where the primordial communal natural society order and the war-and-peace order have been transcended. In such societies, there is no place for the concepts of "war" and "peace." In a system where there is neither war nor peace, these concepts cannot even be imagined.

During the historical periods when hierarchical and statist systems of society prevail, all three situations coexist in an unbalanced way, with none able to function alone as a historical system. In that situation, there wouldn't even *be* history, as such. We have to understand that "absolute rule" and "absolute freedom and equality" should be considered as two extremes that are, in fact, idealized conceptual abstractions. In the case of social equilibrium, as with natural equilibrium, neither of the two extremes can ever fully prevail. Actually, we can talk about the "absolute" only as a concept with very limited spatial and temporal dimensions. Otherwise the universal order cannot survive. Just imagine that there were no symmetry and no equilibrium. The preponderance of one tendency would certainly have already led to an end of the universe. But we haven't yet seen this kind of finiteness, so we can conclude that the absolute exists only in our imagination not in the world of actual phenomena. The language and logic of the universal system, including that of society, is one of almost balanced dialectical dualisms that grow richer or poorer in constant flux.

The validity and complexity of the social system prevailing in a wide variety of communities is the state of partial war and peace known as "peace and stability." The people are in a constant ideological and practical battle with the forces of war and power to swing the situation in their favor and to improve their social, economic, legal, and artistic conditions, as well as their mentality. War is the most critical and most violent state of this process. The essential force behind war is the force of this warrior ruling power, and its raison d'être is to seize the people's accumulation in the easiest possible manner. People and oppressed classes are forced to respond with a war of resistance to defend their existence against this insistent plunder and to survive. Wars are never the people's choice; they are imperative, however, to defend their existence, their dignity, and their system of free life.

It is interesting and instructive to look at democracy in historical systems from this perspective. To this day, the dominant historical conceptions basically correspond to the paradigm of the warrior ruling power group. The expeditions of massacre for booty and plunder could easily be labeled as "holy wars," thus, developing an apprehension of a "God that commands war." Narratives presented wars as extraordinarily splendid events. Even today, the dominant view is that war is a winner take all situation, that what is taken through war has been earned. The understanding of rights and legal frameworks based on war is the dominant mode of existence of states.

All of this established the common notion that the more one wages war, the more rights one has. "Those who want their rights will have to fight for them." This mindset is the essence of the "philosophy of war."

Nonetheless, it is praised by most religions, philosophies, and art forms. This goes as far as the action of a handful of usurpers being described as the most "sacred" action. Heroism and sacredness have been turned into the title of this act of usurpation. Honored in this way, war became the dominant way of thinking and gained a reputation as the instrument for solving all social problems. A morality that portrayed war as the only acceptable solution, even if there were other possible ways, bound the society. The result was that violence became the most sacred tool for solving problems. As long as this understanding of history continues, it will be difficult to analyze social phenomena in a realistic way to find solutions to problems other than through war. The fact that even representatives of the most peaceful ideologies have resorted to war shows the strength of this mindset. That even the major religions and the contemporary class and national liberation movements, which have all striven for permanent peace, have nonetheless fought in the style of the warrior ruling power cliques is further testimony to this fact.

The most effective way to impose constraints on the warrior ruling power mindset is for the people to adopt a democratic stance. This stance is not "an eye for an eye, a tooth for a tooth" situation. Even though a democratic position includes a system of defense that encompasses violence, essentially it is about gaining a culture of free self-formation by struggling against the dominant mentality. We are talking here of an approach that goes far beyond wars of resistance and defense; it focuses on and implements an understanding of a life that is not state-centered. To expect the state to handle everything is to be a fish caught on the warrior ruling power clique's fishing line. You may be offered bait, but only so that you can be hunted. The first step toward democracy is enlightening people about the nature of the state. Additional steps include extensive democratic organization and civil action. In this context, defensive democratic wars will be on the agenda only if they are necessary. To wage war without having first taken every other possible steps results in being the instrument of wars of pillage, which, historically, has very often been the case.

Tracing the developmental process of democratic existence in history is one of the main goals of my analysis. A correct struggle for democratization is possible only on the basis of a correct understanding of history.

Through the interweaving of hierarchy, class, city, and the state, we emphasized that the social being, which we tried to define up to the Sumerians, has acquired a contradictory character. This is a society that was different in every imaginable way, from its economy to its mentality. A clique that has wrapped itself in the instrument of "state" emerged and developed a system using permanent violence and war. The accumulated domestic and external seizure of wealth became the fundamental element of its art of politics. In addition, with the creation of a mindset and literature—mythology—that sanctifies war, an effort was made to convince all of the related segments of society that this is a system of gods that have existed since time immemorial. Objections and resistance to this system, which existed in its pure form from 4000 to 2000 BCE, gradually emerged. At first, the city councils, formed from the ranks of reputable tribal representatives, took an insistently democratic stance. Faced with the clique of priests, kings, and military chieftains, the councils did not forego a democratic approach without resistance,[6] and, for a long time, there was a mixed system of part state and part democracy. Eventually, more and more people broke off or were separated from their tribe for internal and external reasons. A symbolic description of this is offered in the Gilgamesh epic. Gilgamesh's closest friend, Enkidu, is seduced by a woman and lured into the city. This is also the first example of the use of a woman as an agent. Many of the tribal members who gravitated to the city were employed in the more conducive and wealthy city life and within the administration as public servants, soldiers, or working slaves. This development upset the state-democracy balance, which were actually based on the tribal system, to the detriment of the city councils. With the development of this process, one after another, they were liquidated. We can observe a similar development in many new state formations.

The internal struggle resulted in the defeat of the democratic forces, but there was always a certain balance of power held by the tribes in the state that could never be completely liquidated, preserving its existence to different degrees. Meanwhile, the statist society system was also put under serious pressure from the outside. Nomad movements were mobilizing against those who had settled. Such movements, which the Hellenic-Roman literature generally called the "barbarians," must be analyzed in a dialectical totality. The city, as the sedentary society, constantly expanded its wealth because of the slave labor within the city and uneven trade and repression externally. The city also gave rise to contradictions similar to those found in today's relationship between imperialism and the states held in conditions of artificial underdevelopment. It was not the nomads who attacked "barbarically"; it was the city. Unfortunately, since the city was dominant in our conceptual order, it succeeded in presenting itself as "civilized" and all the "Others" as "savages" who were shouting the curious noise ("bar bar"), thereby legitimizing itself. We can compare the great movement of the nomads against the city to the democratic national liberation movements of our time. The form of nomadic societies, in fact, reflected the different stages of ethnicity. The movements they created can essentially be considered as forms of democratic resistance, stance, and existence. Moreover, there is the whole issue of who attacked whom that needs to be carefully researched. The city-states, and later the empires, possessed better tools of coercion and exploitation and sought to constantly grow and expand, objectively positioning them as aggressors. On the other hand, we can characterize the position of the ethnic groups in the opposite way, as being on the defensive and resisting. In another sense, it can be regarded as the process of the first freedom movement targeting incipient slavery.

It is likely that Sumerian society was confronted by tribes of Aryan origin from the mountains in the north and east (where those that founded the society themselves also probably originally came from) and by tribes of Semitic origins called the Amorites, the forebears of the Arabs, from the deserts in the south and the west. This was when the cities began to be ringed with ramparts and fortresses. The relentless waves of attack and counterattack went on for centuries. From this first and greatest historical dialectical contradiction emerged the power of ethnicity strengthened by advanced civilizations. We can observe that this important contradiction took shape in the agricultural revolution alongside the emerging agrarian society when the first language and ethnic groups were formed in Middle East culture around 10000 BCE. This important contradiction began in modern-day Iraq, where it continues to exist in a concrete form. After ethnicity became deeply rooted, around 4000 BCE, its expression made itself felt in specific cultures and languages. We can imagine that before the urban revolution, the ethnic groups were in conflict with each other, fighting over fertile land, as well as ore and stone deposits. While, in the Zagros-Taurus Mountains, the Aryan cultural group came to the fore, in Arabia, which at that time was more fertile than today, it was the Semitic cultural group that stood out. In places where these two cultural groups met between mountains and deserts, mixed systems emerged. Examples of cultures that carried elements of both groups include the Sumerians, the Hebrews, and the Hyksos.[7] The Arabs and the Kurds, on the other hand, continue to exist as the deep-rooted groups of the Semitic and Aryan cultures to this day. Many of the cultural groups that emerged later were absorbed by these two main groups. It is possible that the powers that play a role in the relationship and the conflict between Arabs and Kurds today are trying to create a bicultural state in Iraq, replicating the approach taken in the establishment of the original Sumerian state.

The Sumerians knew well both the Semitic groups coming from the south and west and the Aryans coming from the north and the east. Both groups frequently turn up in their literature and mythology. This tells us something about both cultures, at least indirectly. However, it was the stronger Sumerian city culture that expanded within these two cultural groups, a process that essentially continued until the conquest of Babylon by Alexander the Great in 331 BCE.

In a certain sense, history is shaped by the dialectical relationship between the sedentary population and the nomads of these two cultural groups. The outcome spread everywhere in waves, from the Atlantic to the Pacific, from the Sahara to Siberia. To the degree that urban civilization expanded outward and imposed itself, the nomadic societies from the outside would be integrated into it. Therefore, a historical understanding that excludes nomadism and solely considers the city dwellers is seriously flawed. Alongside and connected with the development of the state in sedentary civilization, a democratic stance developed accordingly.

The correct understanding of the relationship between the state and democracy is of decisive importance. I call "democracy" the self-governance of a people who have not become the state and resist statehood. This kind of self-governance has a relationship with the state, but it is not absorbed by this relationship and doesn't deny itself. The boundaries of the state, on the one hand, and of democracy, on the other hand, are among the most sensitive of political problems. Defining the intermediate point where the state does not deny democracy and democracy does not deny the state is the essence of "peace and stability." The complete denial of either one or the other will mean war. The various modern conceptions that regard democracy either as an extension of the state or as something coextensive with the state are either erroneous or are designed to obfuscate.

In that case, we may ask: Where *can* democracy be found in history? Primarily it can be found in the resistance and stance of ethnic groups against the state and civilization to protect their communal characteristics and retain their freedom. The reason for the perennial failure of the sociologists to figure this out is that they are totally permeated by urban culture. Scientists are, in fact, to an extent few people would suspect, the modern priests of the bourgeoisie. They are as loyal to the values of urban culture as believers are to the Holy Scripture.

We could describe the ethnic mode of existence, if it is not defeated, as semi-democracy. To this we must add the attribute "primordial." Ethnicity is primordial democracy. Commitment to communal values internally and resistance to the dominant state imposing itself from the outside force the popular groups to engage in democratic, free, and equal relationships. If their relationships lacked this quality, their resistance would be meaningless. The definition of democratization in the Middle East has always been hampered by treating ethnicity as a barrier to democracy. But democracy based on the individual in Western civilization cannot be the sole determinant of the definition of democracy. Basing democracy exclusively on the individual is as erroneous as basing it on the state. Pluralist democracy requires society to consist of *both* communities and free individuals. An approach based on the homogenization of individuals and communities is unnecessary and provides no assurance for democracies. The fundamental feature and specialty of democracies is that they always lead to a novel synthesis while preserving differences.

Regarding ethnic communities as a specialty of democracy can only be possible through the true implementation of democracy. When the leadership of a state, using its own criteria, describes its hunt for votes as "democratic competition," the system that will emerge is demagogy. We have to regard ethnic diversity as an opportunity for democracy. It can contribute even more to democracy than a free individual.

It is the task of democratic politicians who are active day in and day out to integrate the stance of the people who have internalized a millennia-old culture of resistance with contemporary democratic standards. What would be wrong would be to see the democratic potential of society in the Middle East as an obstacle.

The preponderance of the warrior ruling power within the state structures first manifests itself in the form of the god-kings and imperators. To the extent that their power increases, the significance of the demos, the people, decreases. Sargon, who was of Amoritic origin, was regarded in Sumerian society as the first imperator in history. He stated with great appetite that he had expanded his rule into the interior of the mountainous areas. What was created was something of a symbol of dependence in the silence of the graveyard. This process, which started around 2350 BCE, paved the way for all subsequent empires. Each one of them expanded the boundaries of the previous one. If Gilgamesh was the initial symbol of the kingdom, Sargon was the father of imperators. Therefore, it is appropriate to consider every stance against this growing process to the detriment of communal order as democratic accumulation. The fact that ethnic groups succeeded in living in the depths of deserts, mountains, and forests, despite all difficulties, defying hunger, disease, and attacks, is in itself a great democratic accumulation for humanity. Had these forms of resistance not existed, who would have maintained the pluralism and the wealth of these cultures? Had it not been for those many thousands of years of resistance, how could we have created the popular arts? Thousands of means of production, a multitude of social institutions, dignity, passion for freedom, human solidarity—how could any of it have been achieved?

As Sargon's Akkadian Empire passes over into the Babylonian and Assyrian dynasties, we see a further increase in imperial power. Each imperator ramps up the bar for subjugation, as if the goal was to break all previous records. There are proud narratives of fortresses and ramparts allegedly built of human skulls. Shouldn't the lengthy resistance of the ethnic groups in the mountains, deserts, and forests against these unlimited expeditions of annihilation be part of the history of democracy? If they are not part of the history of democracy, then what are they? Should we simply not mention them at all and just ignore them? Would history actually make sense if we did that? Would it then be anything other than the history of robbery and tyranny? Even an attempt to understand how the resistance of some small aşiret found its way into the legends would put us in a much better position to understand the democratic values of the nomads and the ethnic groups. If we were to look at the human beings who belong to an ethnic group and compare them to the allegedly free individual deprived of substance by capitalism, we would find that the former, if evaluated properly, would constitute a more far-reaching democratic power. The real democratic potential is in Eastern societies.

We must clearly understand that the democratic potential of Western society, which has totally absorbed the culture of warrior ruling power, is actually quite limited. The existing form of democracy is a veil for the state, tied to thousands of conditions and strongly influenced by the bourgeoisie. Because of the theories and lifestyles that were invented to devalue our own societies, we have forgotten how to see the enormous democratic potential of our people belonging to different communities.

The Hurrians, that is, predecessors of the Kurds of Aryan origin, were called *kurti* by the Sumerians. *Kur* means *mountain*, while *-ti* is an inflectional ending that expresses belonging. Which is to say, the *kurti* are *mountaineers*, a people of the mountains. They have been resisting since the birth of the Sumerian state. *Guti*, *Kassites*, and *Nairi* are different names for the same people. The resistance of the Urartian and Median semi-states against the Assyrian Empires is one of the noblest struggles in history. Their victory, after a resistance of more than three hundred years against one of the most brutal empires in history, left traces in the form of a festival celebrated by all the people in the region, including the Assyrians themselves.[8] If this resistance is not to be recorded as part of the culture of democracy, how then should it be recorded? The Medea in the legend of Theseus of Athens is actually a reverberation of this resistance.[9] It is no coincidence that even Athens, so highly praised for its democracy, talks of hapless Medea. During the democratic period, the Athenians saw their proximity to the Medes as an important guarantee for their survival—a glimpse of this can be seen in the Medes being one of the most discussed topics in *The Histories of Herodotus*.

The Medes, who carried the great tradition of the resistance of the people of the Middle East right to Athens, made the most important contribution to the history of democracy, a contribution that has yet to be acknowledged. It was not by chance that Alexander the Great tried to establish a kinship with the people of Media. He knew the place of these people in Hellenic history and regarded them as a model. As imperator, Alexander swept over the civilization of the East like a steamroller, but he was also appreciative of the influence they exerted *on him*. The East-West cultural synthesis he created would later make a major contribution to Christianity, and Christianity, in turn, would make major contributions to Western civilization. So, in fact, the instruments of the empire did not just serve the warrior ruling power. The peoples' cultures of resistance also surreptitiously flowed through these channels and, in this way, wrote the history of peoples' democracy.

The Roman Empire was perhaps the most powerful and empowering representative of the warrior ruling power culture in history, and it produced the most ferocious of emperors. This empire systematized the most horrible forms of killing humans—they were crucified or fed to the lions. But is it not also true that the democratic culture of the East sparked a great movement of humanity, a movement of the poor against this power? Did not Jesus, as a link in the prophetic tradition, spark a historical turning point? Would there even be a Western culture, a Western democracy, had it not been for the Christian movement based on the cult of Jesus of Nazareth? Therefore, we also have to look at the prophetic tradition from a democratic perspective.

Prophets and Barbarians

While nomadic society attacked the warrior ruling power from the outside (in what was actually an act of self-defense), on the inside, the social force that we will call the prophetic and priestly tradition served as a channel for the poor seeking to resist. This is a movement with a class aspect. Researchers deduce that the prophetic tradition that has its roots in the culture of the Middle East first emerged, like so many other things, in Sumerian society. In Sumerian culture, we find hints of the first prophet Adam and the paradise from which he was expelled. We can assume that Adam and Eve refused to fully adapt to the system of slavery—the lifestyle of the upper society of the state—and this presumably is the reason for their expulsion from paradise. This might also be a semi-mythological narrative dealing with individual freedom. Since Adam and Eve's contradictions with the system are so obvious, it might be said that with their expulsion they became the progenitors of a strain of resistance. They represented something along the lines of an estate of free peasants and craftspeople.

It would perhaps prove enlightening to see the middle-class townspeople, who are not slaves, as the class basis of this tradition. That the second great prophet, Noah, was a craftsman is evident, as he built the ark. That he was able to build and equip a ship that could withstand the great flood is testimony to the high level of craftsmanship at the time. The class character became even clearer when the god Enki told him, in secret and without the knowledge of the other gods, "A great flood is coming; equip your ship in such a manner that you can begin a new life."[10] That craftsmen as important as shipbuilders were among those that had a special relationship with members of the ruling strata is only to be expected. The story of the flood narrates the migration that, as with Adam, was probably the result of some sort of uprising against the harassment of the rulers. Noah's ark reportedly hit land at the mountain Cûdî.[11] In Kurdish, the word *Cûdî* means *he saw land.* This calls to mind a migration to the north from Lower Mesopotamia, something that happened frequently for various reasons.

Around 2000 BCE, Sumerian city systems were built in abundance at the headwaters of the Euphrates and the Tigris. One of the most important centers was Urfa. The name calls to mind the important Sumerian cities of Ur and Uruk. The syllable *Ur* means *settlement on a hill.* Urfa and its surroundings (Harran) are something like the center of the prophetic tradition.[12] It seems as if those who were dissatisfied with the state of affairs in the cities of Lower Mesopotamia, who rebelled, and who were seeking freedom and justice were turning to Urfa. There were many such cultural centers throughout history, with Babylon, Alexandria, and Antioch emerging later to play a similar role, while under capitalism it was Paris, London, and, today, New York. It is highly likely that beginning around 2000 BCE, Urfa was such a center of enlightenment. The oldest known temple in Göbekli Tepe, which is dated to 9000 BCE, is not very far from Urfa. Even the traditions that dominate the region to this day would fit into such a course of history. Around 300 BCE, Urfa played a central role for Hellenic culture and the Sabians,[13] and around 1000 CE it was a center of Christianity. Urfa was the cradle of numerous prophets, including Job and Idris, who are revered there to this very day.[14] Quite rightfully, it is also called "the city of the prophets."

The story of the emergence of Abraham,[15] which researchers believe took place around 1700 BCE, makes all of this even clearer. The fact that he smashed the idols in the pantheon of Nimrod, a god-king in the Assyrian-Babylonian style, showed that he dared to instigate a revolution in mentality. That he faced the grave punishment of being thrown into the fire projects his rebellious position as a historical tradition.[16] As a result, he had to head toward Canaan during his second great migration, i.e., to the land of today's Israel and Lebanon. During the hard days in Canaan, he made an important contribution to the prophetic tradition. He had both the courage and the understanding necessary to lay the basis for an abstract, monotheistic concept of "God."

Even before Abraham, we had Job as a historic figure in the culture of resistance. In a historically significant way, he openly raised an objection against Nimrod, to the effect: "You are hurting the people." Such behavior toward a god-king was unprecedented and required enormous courage. He was sentenced to rot in a dungeon. His body was infested with maggots. Even so, he carried on. This made him a symbol of patience and led to him being seen as a prophet.

Once we understand how important the monotheistic religions are to our current civilization, we should also be able to see the importance of correctly interpreting the Abrahamic tradition. Another one of Abraham's skills was his ability to effectively combine the Aryan and the Semitic cultures. That Abraham lived in both cultures gives us an opportunity to understand this combination as a new synthesis that, like the East-West synthesis, led to creativity. A third important characteristic of Abraham's cult was that he represented the first *human* authority, as the messenger of God against the Sumerian (Nimrod) and the Egyptian (the pharaoh) systems of the god-kings. During a time when slavery was at its height and a pursuit of freedom was beginning, the Abrahamic option was a way out and represented an important alternative. The fact that he offered a response to the radical searching of humanity laid the base for the most important social movement in history. Even though the ethnic groups waged a strong resistance against both of the slave systems externally, this internal resistance, with its social character, was equally important and offered an alternative.

The uprising against the cult of the god-kings, the pronouncement that it was impossible for human beings to be gods, was a great social revolution. It was a blow against the most important ideological pillar of the slave system. The unmasking of the god-kings as mere human beings led to major cracks in the Sumerian and Egyptian mythological structure. This, in turn, gave rise to the social current that came to be called monotheistic religion, which affirmed the unity of God. It is no accident that there is insistence that the chain starts with Adam.[17] It demonstrates the roots and the tradition's chain-like continuity. The great prophets represent this tradition's historical milestones, much like the prophets of Marxism or liberalism.

The prophet Moses was yet another groundbreaking figure of this tradition. Moses, who lived around 1300 BCE, and whose lineage could be traced back to Abraham, first appeared leading a similar rebellion in Egypt. He knew Egyptian culture well, and the fact that he dared to instigate the rebellion within the Hebrew tribe, which was slavishly loyal to the pharaoh, indicates that he was a leader with social and libertarian foundations. He has kinship with the Hebrew tribal traditions. The Hebrew tribe's religion was different from that of the Egyptians. Even though Moses was reportedly influenced by the semi-monotheism of the pharaoh Akhenaten, who pronounced Aton to be the greatest of all gods, he continued to draw primarily on the Abrahamic religious tradition. The

Holy Scripture describes the famous march through the Sinai Desert, the impression made on him by a volcano,[18] his rejection of idolatry, and his proclamation of the Ten Commandments. Basing himself in the Hebrew tribe, Moses waged a great battle for the new religion. This ideological struggle prevented the disintegration of the tribe and finally led it to the promised "Holy Land." This ideological firmness represents one of the major developments in Hebrew history. This development and others in Hebrew religious culture offer powerful examples of how a minority can influence a majority.

But prophetic movements cannot be attributed to the Hebrews alone. This tradition gained a universal place through Jesus, who was closer to the Arameans, and Mohammad, who was an Arab.

The prophetic movement that developed as a social tradition from within and in opposition to warrior ruling power stands closer to the democratic stance, not just in the general history of humanity, but also particularly in the historical society system of the Middle East. If we add to this the aspect of poverty, we can say that it represents something like the first "social democratic" movement in history. And, with regard to the strata and classes that form its social base, we can indeed draw a parallel to today's social democratic movement; it was the middle class, craftspeople, traders, free peasants, and the tribes. In fact, we can go even further. Just as the social democrats gave the system a somewhat milder character but were unable to escape being its substitute, sooner or later, prophetic social democracy also proved unable to escape integrating into the established class society systems or itself building a similar system.

The system they gave rise to in opposition to the rigid slavery of antiquity was the feudalism of the Middle Ages. The prophetic tradition certainly didn't consciously strive for a feudal system. The goal was peace and justice for all of humanity, but the huge transformative power of the dominant system rendered the god-state of the prophets not overly distinguishable from the original system.

Stripped of any sociological interpretation, theological discourse is incapable of explaining the social reality of the institution of prophecy that so pervasively influenced the history of humanity, even though it has a large collection of works at its disposal. The language of the period no doubt expresses the mentality of those times, but in the absence of an interpretation for what it would mean today it cannot go beyond a boring, stultifying, rote narration. Correctly defining this institution as one that, compared to ancient slavery of the Sumer and Egypt, was founded on social and individual freedom and justice is of great importance. It reflected the important social struggles of the peoples in light of the appearance of religion, which suited the mindset of the time. The institution of prophecy was the first major institution of social leadership. The acquisition of prophetic qualities meant being able to synthesize the concepts and thoughts, i.e., the patterns of mentality that dominated the general worldview at the time, and to elevate them to a higher level. Prophets played a socially liberating role to the extent that they broke with the official mythology and the religion of slavery. This was undoubtedly, as always, accompanied by both radical ruptures and compromises with the dominant system.

What is expected from a sociological history of religion is that it be able to analyze the prophets, or at least the most important ones, within their respective cultural environments, which includes the mentality, the ruling power, and the social and economic aspects of their time, thereby enabling an integrated and holistic interpretation of history written in a more realistic way that not only deals with sultanate and heroic legends of "booty plunder" but also features social, popular, and ethnic dimensions. This would also help make sense of the current discussion about laicism. We must clearly understand who actually benefits from the hundreds of thousands of employees and the related budgets.[19]

In the Roman Empire, the process just described continued in a similar way. Right from the beginning (50 BCE to the beginning of common era), internal religious currents with a social content and external ethnic nomadic movements enveloped themselves around the hitherto most concentrated and greatest warrior ruling power in history. In its phase of gestation and early development, Christianity was a political party movement of the poor (tribes, families, and similar kinship groups) that was at least as universal as Rome in just about every respect. It was the first universal social party of the poor. Just as Rome mobilized its own clique as the greatest warrior power of its time, Christianity mobilized the movement of the poor in line with this. During the capitalist period, a similar class concentration would occur. This is the continuation of the dialectical contradiction between the state's most repressive and exploitative structure, on the one hand, and the most stringent structures of the toiling masses, on the other hand.

The history of these two currents of resistance and the violent repression in Rome is long. The kind of historiography that consists of stories about the Roman emperors ought to be seen as nothing but a distortion disseminated by official historians. Just as the warrior ruling power, accumulating like a snowball, is the outline of repressive and exploitative history, the nomadic ethnic groups and the social and religious currents represent the outline of communality. The history of peoples as social and ethnic reality still remains largely unwritten. The dominant class character of historiography has probably made the biggest contribution to the distortion of social phenomena and to ignoring the main constituents. Preventing a true historiography combined with extensive distortions is the most effective way to capture the human mind. Societies robbed of their historical consciousness are subjugated to conditions that are even worse than annihilation, that is, losing their purpose and identity.

Societies that have been habituated to such conditions can easily be induced to accept any burden. In this respect, the tradition of monotheistic religions is also significant, because these religions are like the memory of social reality. The chronicle of the prophets is effectively an alternative to the chronicle of the sultanate. Through the institution of the episcopacy, Christianity created a tradition equivalent to that of the Roman emperors, so to speak. A similar development also took place among the leadership of the ethnic groups. The fact that both currents emulated the emperor led both of them to compromises with the system, sometimes in the form of total integration and sometimes as transformation into more sustainable higher-level social structures.

It might make sense to give a crude historical overview of ethnicity, starting with the birth and institutionalization of agricultural culture between 15000 and 10000 BCE.

Much archeological and etymological data show that ethnicity first took shape during this period in the inner arc of the Taurus-Zagros mountain system. The agricultural revolution was the existential condition for the rise of ethnic movements. There was no other way to shake free of clan society. Clan society, on the other hand, could never go beyond being a large family group, a limit set by the productive technology. The linguistic level was also limited at this point; the great language families had yet to emerge. Researchers assume that the history of the language families that we know today begins at around 20000 BCE, yet again, in the same geographic region for similar reasons. The establishment of language led to developments in production, which raised sociality to a higher level. Many scientists, including Gordon Childe, Colin Renfrew, and Vyacheslav Ivanov, assume that the primeval Aryan language group formed in the aforementioned arc.[20] The Aryan language group is the work of the primordial communal groups that carried out the agricultural revolution. The oldest words of agricultural origin are found among all people who share this language structure. Another commonly accepted view is that this initial period of ethnic formation spread to all continents by cultural rather than physical expansion. Another assumption is that the expansion to the American continent occurred through the migration of what were to become the first Americans across the Bering Strait sometime around 11000 BCE.

Until the development of Sumerian civilization around 3500 BCE, this culture of ethnicity primarily developed along the foothills of the mountains on the shores of the Euphrates and the Tigris. Relics of the oldest settlements and many elements that carry on in popular culture today testify to this. The period from 6000 BCE to 400 BCE was of particular importance in terms of arriving at a sustained ethnicity with distinct identities. Almost all of the inventions and knowledge that led to the beginning of both history and civilization were developed during this chalcolithic period, known also as the Copper Age. By this point, the basic institutions of the arts, religion, and hierarchy had developed. The Hurrians, as the oldest group of Aryans, lived at the center of this emerging culture, and many scientists feel they should be regarded as the earliest ancestors of today's Kurds. Their name is derived from *ur*, or *hilly location*, i.e., they were the inhabitants of places at a certain altitude. Evidence of their existence reaches back to about 6000 BCE. At the time of their founding, they were both relatives and neighbors of the Sumerians. The Sumerians and the Assyrians called a number of groups that shared a similar culture the Gutians, Kassites, Lori, Nairi, Urartians, and Medes.

Around 9000 BCE, the wave of Aryan agricultural culture reached Anatolia. Around 6000 BCE, it reached the Caucasus, North Africa, and Iran. Then, between 5000 and 4000 BCE, it reached China, southern Siberia, and the interior of Europe. Data show that agricultural culture spread across the world. To a lesser extent, this also happened physically through Aryan migrants who traveled as far as India, England, Greece, Italy, the Iberian Peninsula, and northern Europe in the period from 3000 to 2000 BCE. It is assumed that around 2000 BCE, reacting to certain developments, they turned, in a countermovement, in the direction of the areas that had become rich as a consequence of the Sumerian civilization. In this way, they became part of the civilizational processes in India, Iran, Anatolia, and Egypt.

This was a very agitated period in history. The seductiveness of Sumerian civilization can be compared to that of the United States today. Its appeal radiated out to all of the immigrants and rural societies in the vicinity, pulling them to itself. In the history of the ethnic groups, the time of the great migrant movements, around 2000 BCE, is the phase of the most far-reaching expansion. As a consequence of this expansion, the foundations of the Chinese, Indian, Hellenic, Anatolian, and Iranian civilizations were laid. In a certain sense, after Mesopotamia, this was urbanization's—the state's—second leap forward following the Sumerian trail. Even so, at that time, the cities of the civilization were no more than islands in a sea of migrants. Actually, those taking action were the nomads. The third major immigrant leap forward began around 1000 BCE, from Europe, the Caucasus, and Central Asia to the areas of civilization in the south, replacing the initial phase in the system of civilization, dynasties, and principalities. The major ethnic groups known for this leap forward are the Dorians in Greece, the Phrygians in Anatolia, the Medes where the Zagros and Taurus converge, and the Etruscans in Italy. These groups played an important role in the development of civilization within the Roman state in the first millennium BCE. The Greek, Phrygian, Urartian, Med, and Etruscan civilizations were the most important civilizations established by some of the major ethnic groups in this leap forward.

Organizationally, the movement based on a culture of ethnicity did not go beyond the hierarchical stage. If it was not dispersed by internal or external forces, it was confronted with the problem of founding a state. Becoming a state on the Sumerian model was only possible for those groups that successfully mastered these stages. They imitated the models of civilization they had the closest contact with. The hierarchical structure did not offer the potential for anything else. It is in this situation that classes emerged. Part of the lower stratum remained in the rural areas partially safeguarding its lifestyle. Others turned to the city, becoming slaves or soldiers or integrating into one or another stratum of the sedentary population. In this way, they completed class society.

For class society, ethnic groups always mean fresh blood. They fulfilled a function in ancient civilizations that was comparable to that of the peasantry under capitalism. If we want to draw a general parallel with the present, the national resistance against the expansion of capitalism and the subsequent foundation of a national state have ethnic resistance and the founding of states in the form of principalities based on their ethnic grassroots as their counterpart in ancient civilizations.

The source of religious prophetic movements that we defined as a kind of class struggle of antiquity can be found in these civilizations' phases of maturation. They were of urban origin and were shaped by the middle class. They were courageous enough to claim that the system of slavery was contrary to reason. They were the first critics and the first actors in a social uprising. They were also influenced by the old traditions of shamanism and sheikhdom that had no influence in the institutions of kingdoms. The abstract character of their concepts of "religion" and "God" and their opposition to idolatry should be seen as a differentiation of mentality. Their most fundamental claim was that human kings could not be gods. The idea of the godly kingdom, on the one hand, and the refusal of rational human beings to believe in it, on the other hand, actually reflected the contradiction and the struggle between the ruling class and the townspeople. Grasping the difference between the laws of urban society and natural animism set the stage for unraveling the belief in the god-king. The differentiation of mentality developed faster in an urban environment. The city offered more room for new quests, concepts, and ways of thinking. The commodity system based on buying and selling stimulated the mind even more. Together, this further strengthened the leadership role of analytical intelligence. At a certain point, the increasing knowledge and the abstract conceptualization began to erode the official ideology—the mythology in which people believed. The search for new ideologies cleared the way for the period of the prophets' idealism.

This process probably began around 3000 BCE, and, until the time of Abraham, was generally limited to the Sumerian metropoles. Whenever the prophets could no longer find shelter, they moved to peripheral regions that offered them a certain amount of freedom. The period from Adam to Enoch and Job might well be called the era of pre-Urfa prophecy. I hypothesize that Urfa played a central role in the second and the first millennia BCE. This is probably when the prophetic tradition became well-established and developed a strong institutional foundation. Several prophets, including Abraham, were "exported" from this area. This hypothesis is supported by numerous legends.

My second hypothesis is that between the first millennium BCE and the fall of Rome, Jerusalem came to the fore as the second center for prophecy.

The Holy Scripture contains an extensive list of prophets from this time. The rich and powerful narratives imbued in the prophetic passages, which began with Saul, David, and Solomon, can be regarded as the moral rules that organize social life and the longing for a kingdom. The social component was strongly emphasized. Preventing people from worshiping idols and binding them to (God) is in essence a religious narrative of the effort to protect the Hebrew tribe from disintegration and its formation as a kingdom. Just as Sumerian mythology is the fairy tale version of the history of the god-kings, the Holy Scripture is the religious story of the history of turning a tribe into a kingdom. The reigning mentality and literature of those times necessitated the biblical language. What is important is to grasp the essential content beneath the shell of the outer form. In the end, Jesus's actual goal was to become the king of Jerusalem, which he calls the "daughter of Zion." For his attempt, he paid with his life.

The third and last period of prophecy was from 1 CE to 632 CE, i.e., from the birth of Jesus to the death of Mohammad. For the Hebrews, thereafter, the time of the Sephardic scribes began,[21] while Christianity expanded enormously among other peoples, first through the actions of the apostles and then of the priests and bishops.

The prophetic literature that was translated primarily into Greek and Latin, that is, the Gospels, radically transformed the mentality of Western civilization. In the struggle with the demigod Hellenic and Roman emperors, this tradition finally deprived the latter of their putative sacredness.

Constantine the Great's adoption of Christianity in 312 CE, making it the official religion, was the final step in a historical process. This is the success of the idea that started with the first prophets, who said that a human being cannot be God, although it lost much of its essence along the way. The branch of this tradition led by Mohammad that emerged as Islam declares its mission as a messenger and "shadow of God" right from the outset. It also rejected the Christian trinity of Father, Son, and Holy Spirit and proclaimed as its most important revelation that human beings could only be the servants of God. But even the understanding of the servant of God still shows the influence of the culture of god-kings. The god-king was replaced by "Allah," but, even so, this was a poignant example of how far the struggle over mentality in this area had already evolved. All of this demonstrates that the struggle of humans against the god-kings had already been going on for many thousands of years, which shows us very clearly that the struggle for liberation from severe slavery was far from easy.

While the era of the god-kings ended with the fall of the Roman Empire, with Mohammad this chapter of history ends completely. The basic idea of prophecy was that humans should not declare themselves gods. Like a single-issue party program, when the goal is fulfilled there is no point in continuing to exist. What remains are traces, stories, and shadows.

Monasteries, Witches, and Alchemists

The main product of the monotheistic religions of the Middle East was the feudal state of the Middle Ages. Serfdom is a milder, or, rather, more refined, form of classical slavery. It is a step up on the ladder of slavery. Classical slavery also continued within feudalism. The sultan—the warrior ruling power—was seen as the "shadow of God," and we should regard feudalism as the continuation of the god-king cult. In terms of their democratic stance and communal qualities, both movements, Christianity and Islam, were nonetheless contributions to freedom and justice that should not be underestimated.

The millennia-old tradition of resistance against ancient and classical slavery led to important achievements in mentality, as well as in the political, social, and economic realms. Even if these achievements are often barely mentioned in written history, their existence cannot be doubted. Culture itself is largely based on these two channels of resistance, both of which have provided the primary substance of all of the arts. The monuments, in the form of temple structures, are preserved to this day in all their splendor. If there are still fragments of a social morality, then this is also due to these traditions. Immortal epics, saints, and the lore of the walis reflect the great human stance. It is these traditions that make the wisdom of people who spent years in a hermitage so valuable. The same is true for those who rotted away in dungeons, were nailed to crosses, or ascetically fasted, eating only bread, olives, and dates. These traditions felt the pain suffered by the people and valued wisdom highly. These are also the traditions that valued communal life, the monastic order, and knowledge, as well as the development of arts and crafts, giving them the rank of a school rather than propagating individualism. Once more, it was these noble channels of tradition that helped the people to think about peace, defend human dignity, and base themselves on solidarity, as well as to emphasize fraternity and remain open to universality, even in situations where the warrior ruling power clique gave them no other alternative but to kill or die. While these movements couldn't establish class society, they also largely failed to prevent their own integration into the dominant social systems. Sometimes they became just as hierarchical and statist as their former masters, but respect for the truth requires us to emphasize that these movements are responsible for the humane values that remain alive today. Today's democratic stance, freedom, equality, the search for natural environment, human rights, and cultural identities would be unthinkable today without the contributions of these two great traditions. The public realm, which is at least as indispensable a basis for democracy as contemporary individualism, must be regarded as the most important legacy of these two great movements, and doing so will allow us to better understand and analyze the positive effects of this tradition.

The framework of the democratic stance and communalism that we have just outlined can help us better understand the Roman imperial society. Just like all of its predecessors, after a few centuries, the Roman Empire would also collapse as a result of the internal social-communal movement and the waves of defensive attacks on the part of ethnic communities from the north, which were still close to being natural societies. The decay and the collapse of a part of Rome at the end of the fourth century represented—if only indirectly—the combined victory of the relationship between ethnicity and the religious communality. It is one of the great victories of peoples and the communal order, even if their relationship was a complicated one. The statist mentality and its cult were certainly not destroyed. Although it fragmented like a snowball hitting a surface, this did not stop it from reestablishing its existence in many areas rather than melting away. Once again, we see that the warrior ruling power would not endure prolonged fragmentation. New links were added to the chain and it would continue to grow, multiplying these links. In a new form, it would continue as Byzantium in the East and Charlemagne's Frankish Empire and the Holy Roman Empire in the pristine lands of Europe.

Rome was primarily defeated by Germanic tribes with Aryan cultural roots. The Huns from Central Asia also hemmed the empire in for decades. It is unthinkable that the powerful Roman military machine would have been rendered inoperative without the power of the ethnic groups. Democratic communalists should never talk about the "sad fall of the Roman civilization brought about by the onslaught of the barbarians"; this would not be the language of truth. When we think of the whole chain of imperators, the frightening character of the warrior ruling power becomes even clearer. Regardless of objections, we see the fact that the barbarians—essentially, popular liberation forces—smashed this kind of power as a great step toward freedom.

The decline of Rome serves once more to show what actually determines history. It is the struggle between those who turn war and violence into the basis of the political, social, economic, and moral framework and those who resist this process and insist on democratic stance and a free, egalitarian communal life. If we do not ignore that this constant state of war underlies what is called the order of "freedom and stability," we can better understand this social reality.

The history just sketched is the background for the unfolding of the Middle Ages in Europe from the fifth to the fifteenth centuries, without which Europe would not have been able to create a civilization; it wouldn't even have learned of the number zero. Brooding over things for a long time during the feudal period, and then its effort to attain and use the new knowledge with a zest for action and actively, and to strive toward a new mentality—all of this would have been unthinkable without this historical background. Later, Europe duly turned toward science and history, drawing strength from both. With the use of these two powers, effective historical and scientific methodologies, an entirely new and important level in civilization would be created.

The positive contribution of Christianity to the Middle Ages is quite limited. In fact, the Inquisition was a conscious effort to prevent the birth of something new. It tried to dry out the positive channels of the past by setting them on fire: heretics and believers in different confessions, witches, the remnants of free women, and alchemists, who were the pioneers of science. Faced with the still fresh memory of the more natural life of the ethnic groups and the force of Protestantism, the Inquisition was finally defeated, and the mentality and will of the new civilization grew clearer and stronger. Protestantism broke the ossified conservatism of the predominant form of religion and paved the way for nationhood based on the culture of ethnicity.

There is no evidence to support the claim that a plan to develop the later capitalist system lay behind this great historical development. Rather, there is more evidence of an effort to develop a democratic civilization.

The feudal system of the Middle Ages took up the dogmatism of the ancient slavery, although with changes and imposing limits. A sultan replacing the god-kings as the "shadow of God" signaled a shift in dogma, but the essence was preserved. The warrior power structure grew even stronger, by expanding into large areas of Europe and Asia. Instead of the weary Roman and Persian Empires, fresh blood flowed into the construction of the Arab-Islamic, the Germanic-Catholic, and the Slavic-Orthodox systems, a process that continued with the Turkish-Islamic and the Mongol-Islamic systems later on. The decisive factor in these new forms of empire was their ability to absorb the "fresh blood" of new cultural elements. Although during their ascendance to power they all tried to emulate the Romans and Persians, Christianity and Islam represented a much more powerful mentality and faith framework. This framework was rich enough to provide the warrior ruling power the fuel needed to preserve the system over a long period of time. On the other hand, the Arab, Germanic, Turkish, and Mongolian hierarchical forces, accustomed to the strongest and longest nomadic and migrant life, were able to recruit however many soldiers they wished from their own tribes. The more comfortable and wealthy city life had such great appeal that it even expanded into the areas predominantly inhabited by these new tribes.

The reality is that the lower strata of the ethnic groups and the poor within the Christian monasteries of Christianity and the Islamic tariqa sought salvation and a different world and life. They joined these movements because they detested the repression and exploitation of the state and hierarchy. In a nutshell, they had expectations in a universal humanist democracy based on a synthesis of the religious orders, the monasteries, and the old natural communal life.

In both religions, there were many people like Mawlana, who represented the universal mind and heart of the time.[22] Mawlana welcomed everyone, with an approach that can be summarized as: "Come, whichever people you belonged to among the seventy-two peoples. Come, regardless of the sins you have committed in the past." This embodied a universal democratism. In this way, Mawlana became the voice of the democracy and universalism of the Middle Ages.

This interpretation of these widespread monastic and Sufi currents of that period is stimulating. Whereas the upper strata of the ethnic and religious groups became the feudal state forces, the poor lower strata lived as the forces of the communal order spread over vast areas, living in the monasteries or the Islamic counterpart, the religious orders and *dergah*.[23] This was a profoundly significant class division. In a certain sense, what we find here is the split between the warrior ruling power specific to the Middle Ages, with its dependent collaborators, and the democratic, communal people—and the struggle between these two groups. The contradictions between Batiniyyas and Sunnis in the Islamic world and between Catholics and Heretics in Christianity reflects this.[24] We can observe similar divisions within ethnic groups. The contradictions between Seljuks, Ottomans, and Turkmens, or between the Arab caliphs and the Kharijites,[25] represent contradictions and struggles between different classes within an ethnic group. Some of the movements of the poor managed to politicize themselves at an advanced level. The Qarmatians, Assassins, Fatimids, and Alevites are expressions of the reaction of the poor to class differentiations;[26] they are examples of the primitive democracy of the Middle Ages. However, the understanding of rule and power that dominated the social system did not allow for more progressive democratic organizations in these movements.

In any case, as a result of external repression and internal degeneration, they were quickly liquidated and lost their influence. Formations that can be called the "monastic culture," and which had lasting effects in Europe and Central Asia, proved more viable. Monasteries played an important role in science and the development of productive techniques, becoming the driving force of science and social life. The birth of universities and madrassas in the Middle Ages was also closely related to the monasteries and dergah. Following a major struggle, the warrior ruling power groups managed to become the dominant force in the system. The decisive factors were the mentality and the traditional power of the state as an institution. Its organizational and administrative style was so refined that primitive and semi-democratic formations never had a chance. But even more important than the question of dominance was that this aspect of history is intertwined with major struggles.

Gaining acceptance for the new form of state as the "shadow of Allah, the supreme sultanate," required a massive propaganda campaign. This new form which was interwoven with intrigues, tyranny, and plunder required much disguising. During medieval feudalism, the warrior ruling power inherited from the Romans and the Persians, which I compared above to a snowball and a fireball, dressed itself in the religious garb of both Islam and Christianity and made itself permanent. Contrary to its own claims, it surpassed the Roman and the Persian Empires in its tyranny and plunder by a long shot. On the other hand, even though they were betrayed by their hierarchies, the neglected, subdued, and impoverished ethnic groups, the monasteries, and the heretical and denominational movements and religious orders represented and characterized the democratic society with a communal spirit and the reality of the people to a far greater extent than would be assumed. If we want to understand our conditions today, we must take the blinkers off when looking at the Middle Ages, including the earlier periods, and move beyond the ossified heart that the rulers have worked to instill in us for thousands of years. We must try to understand and sense theses eras as they are described above, for their spirit and consciousness of freedom.

Those who fail to correctly experience history with both their soul and consciousness can never claim to represent freedom and equality and can never be true democrats.

From the Renaissance to Marxism

The European civilization of the Middle Ages, which had succeeded in taking what is necessary from the positive legacy of Eastern societies—the monastic movement played a decisive role in this—from the thirteenth and fourteenth centuries on, prepared the Renaissance with steps accelerated by the creativity of its youthfulness.

It is important to understand why feudalism in its classic form didn't last long. Class society had evinced this potential to a great extent by having existed in the form of ancient slavery for a very long time—4000 BCE to 500 CE. It had displayed whatever it could conceive of. If the contribution of feudal class structure to this process was relatively minor, that was because of its own limited potential. Feudalism was in no position to make much of a contribution to the social system. Moreover, the objective of both the ethnic and the religious movements required a radical overcoming of this system. Their main goal was not the imperial emulation of hierarchies. In a certain sense, they had attained the new warrior ruling power by exploiting both the social revolution of religion and the tribal revolution of the ethnic groups. Long before the French Revolution, the flag of the resistance of the poor masses carried the message of "equality, fraternity, and peace." All this happened during the millennia of divine reign. Their utopias were to be eternal with "Armageddon and paradise." But the hierarchy, masterful in the art of plundering with intrigue and tyranny, proceeded to enforce its own will through deception and suppression.

That this era didn't last long in Western Europe was the result of the genuine power to enlighten of the Christian monasteries, which were less influenced by monarchs than were Islamic monastic communities, and the still fresh spirit of natural society among the ethnic groups, particularly among the Teutons. As has always been the case historically, these two forces maintained freedom of conscience and free will. With great curiosity and enthusiasm, these two forces carried the flag of science and freedom onto the fertile soil of Western Europe. Neither the medieval princes and kings—poor copies of the Roman emperors—nor the official Church's Inquisition, which de facto became their very soul, could block their way. If we want to learn the truth about today's Western civilization, we should treat this period of creation with respect and sensitivity, since at the time there were free-spirited people capable of great thought. The values created at the time were at least as significant as those of the Neolithic village agricultural revolution and the urban civilization revolution. It is the continuation of the spirit of creative consciousness and freedom that is slowly withering away in the East. The consciousness and freedom that was nurtured by the European people was the spirit of wisdom and of natural society that we had carried with us for thousands of years and whose pioneers we had once been. This is not something that is alien to us; on the contrary, it is a reality that is our very own.

The Renaissance, or rebirth, that is said to begin in the fifteenth century was actually the last child of a millennium-old lineage whose primordial mother and father hail from the East. The belief that it originates from some Adams and Eves of Europe is a grave error. It might, in fact, be a child of the East born in exile. One thing is certain: the Renaissance was the accelerated continuation of the thirteenth and fourteenth centuries. It didn't develop in the palaces of the kings and bishops, those copies of Rome, nor did the political-military force or the economic force of the feudal traders play a decisive role. That honor fell to the rural monasteries and the emerging urban universities, which were independent places of study, surviving on their own labor, that raised the level of freedom and consciousness, supported and nourished by the ordinary people who had placed their hopes in them. I must stress that the road to the Renaissance does not pass through the palaces of the kings and the Church but through the communal schools of ordinary people. Neither the class of feudal lords nor the absent bourgeoisie "showed the way."

To temporally and spatially locate the Renaissance in the flow of civilization's river, it is helpful to begin at the source, the Sumerians.[27] From its places of origin around Ur and Uruk, it expanded, from 3500 to 2500 BCE, in northward waves along the Euphrates and Tigris to Nippur, Babylon, and

Nineveh. We distinguish the era of Nippur from 2500 to 2000 BCE, the era of Babylon from 2000 to 1300 BCE (old and middle period), the era of Assur from 1300 to 600 BCE and, the last Babylonian period from 600 to 300 BCE. Outside of Mesopotamia, from 1700 to 1200 BCE, there was a Hittite civilization in Anatolia, which was directly influenced by the Sumerians, and then from 900 to 550 BCE, there was the Medes, and from 550 to 300 BCE, the Persian civilization. I regard this whole era as the first link in the chain of civilization.

The classical Greek and Roman civilizations, as its second link, should be considered in connection with the second great intellectual revolution, the transition from the mythological to the philosophical way of thinking that developed after the fall of Troy, the last great outpost of the East in the West. Until then, the Hellas and Etruscans settling in today's Greece and Italy had not reached any specific autonomous development. They had not really transcended the role of migrations of traditional expansion. From 1000 BCE on, the first elements of the Greek and Roman civilizations emerged, and by 500 BCE, with the development of philosophical thought, they were able to make the transition to a civilization with originality. This originality was the result of their long nourishment from the legacy of the Sumerian and Egyptian civilizations, their synthesis with the migration from the north, and the influence of the geographical particularities. The developments on the Greek and the Italian peninsulas represented the continuation of Hittite civilization's development in Anatolia. Once we consider the rich contributions of Egypt and the Phoenicians in the Eastern Mediterranean, the underpinnings of this original development are better understood. The further expansion of this second link from 1000 BCE to 500 CE came to a halt on the European Atlantic Coast.

The third great link in the chain of civilization was accompanied by other temporal and geographical conditions. When the river of civilization surged against the shores of Western Europe, it entered another very fertile period. Around 1500 CE, the third great revolution of the civilization began. If we connect the Renaissance to the chain of world civilization, a flow in this direction makes sense.

The most accurate definition of the Renaissance is as a revolution in mentality that was deep-seated in a number of respects, the first being the rebirth of the individual, who, in the name of divinity, had quite literally been obliterated by religious thought. Christian theology reached the summit of scholasticism around 1250 CE, after integrating Aristotle's philosophy. We can also characterize this as the most advanced form of metaphysics. Humans, as such, were close to completely forgotten, having been exorcised from life to such a degree that they even ceased to be good enough to play the role of God's puppets. An extreme form of sociality based on religion had been arrived at. However, human nature cannot endure this state of affairs for long, because this form is incompatible with the practical and concrete life. The efforts of heretics, dissident confessions, and witches (women from the non-Christianized natural society) represented the resistance of the autonomous spirit against Christian dogmatism. Even the alchemists' scientific experiments attempting to turn natural elements into gold can be seen in this light. The goal of the Inquisition was to suppress anything that might give rise to a free individual. Perhaps the most pertinent example of a break from Christian dogmatism and the leap into the idea of free nature was Giordano Bruno. As a passionate lover of nature, Bruno didn't distinguish between God and nature. It was as if he was intoxicated by his understanding of a living nature, of a living universe. He admired the independent functioning of nature. This enthusiastic Renaissance pioneer was finally burned alive in Rome in 1600, a sacrifice just as worthy of note as those of Spartacus and St. Paul.

Another important consequence of this perspective that broke with dogmatism in approaching nature was the development of scientific methodology. The human mind, which had been broken away from natural reality by metaphysical and speculative methodology, had managed to turn to nature again, but with a new methodology. By imposing observation, experimentation, and measurement on nature, the "prophets" of the empirical method, Roger Bacon, Francis Bacon, and Galileo Galilei, pushed the door wide open for the development of science. The gradual development of a scientific mindset was closely connected to its methodology. A philosophical approach meant approaching nature with hope, while methodology meant turning this hope into reality. While philosophical predictions and hypotheses illuminated scientific fields and their facts, observation, experimentation, and measurement supplied scientific evidence. It is impossible to benefit from nature through philosophical hypotheses without experimentation and measurement. Without the application of experimentation and measurement to a phenomenon, no results can be anticipated. Although steps taken in this direction in the Islamic world yielded some results, they only made a limited contribution to scientific knowledge, because a systematic methodological basis was lacking. The solution of the problem of basic methodology led to a scientific revolution that encouraged the rapid growth of scientific knowledge, one of the foundations of Western civilization. The search for scientific methodologies during the Renaissance also contributed to the emergence of new philosophical schools. The proximity and close connection of philosophy and science have not only led to the development of a more productive science but also to the emergence of advanced philosophical structures that are linked to science.

We can regard this way of thinking and feeling, which completely broke with God, as the foundation of the Renaissance and perhaps the greatest paradigm shift in history. The revolution in mentality that has taken place should not be underestimated. This is the kind of revolution that was the most difficult to carry out. The most important achievement of Western civilization was to have liberated itself from religious dogmatism and to have given meaning to life on the basis of the individual's capacity to feel and think. A nature that is totally alive, vibrant, and colorful excites us with all that it encompasses and, being full of possibility, engenders great hope. The fact that humans, after thousands of years, and with a significant accumulation of consciousness, once again returned to nature is the source of all subsequent developments.

The second great shift was reform in religion. A reaction to Christian dogmatism, which was in sharp contradiction to the understanding of natural society, was inevitable. The Germanic people's traditions of natural society and the fact that they became acquainted with religion only fairly late were the necessary preconditions for the reform to come from this culture. Protestantism was actually a Germanic interpretation of Christianity. It represented a revision and reformation that softened and undermined dogmatism and cleared the way for science. We can speak of a counterreaction to the reign of religion. It represented a blow against the strong conservatism of religion that was overly politicized, obstructed practical developments, and had left no room for freedom and the specific characteristics of various people. It was the theological reflection of the revolution in mentality. The breakdown of dogmatic patterns of thought inaugurated a phase of rapid development in philosophical thought. Just as overcoming mythological thought in West Anatolia in the seventh century BCE launched the classical age of philosophy, overcoming religious dogmatism led to a more advanced philosophy. One might say that philosophy, which represents the most advanced development of the revolution in mentality, found its prophets in Baruch Spinoza and René Descartes.

The third development accompanying the Renaissance was a way of life that placed the human being at its center. The idea that a human being was the absolute property of God was a different form of slave mentality. As the mythological thought form that found its way from the cult of the god-kings into the monotheistic religions, it came close to eradicating the individual from social life. It was the residue of a situation in which the slave was entirely the tool of his master. The loss of individuals within the identity of the master and of God to such a degree meant that they didn't have lives of their own. God didn't belong to the individual; the individual belonged to God. This situation translated into the extreme dependency of humanity on the religious hierarchy, which transformed itself into the state. Every religion contains a hidden form of slavery that favors the ruling class. The Renaissance resuscitated respect for human beings, and this also neatly fits in with the definition of society as the way of existence that makes individual lives more meaningful. Wherever the social being annihilates the individual aspect, slavery begins to take hold. What happened in Soviet socialism and in the Sumerian priest's state socialism was essentially the same. Once the individual is merged into the mass, the result must be called slavery, regardless of the purpose this condition supposedly serves. The totemic religions and polytheisms of clan society and antiquity, which were, in a certain way, a projection of society onto certain concepts, supplied the individual with power. Because it erased the individual, the predominant religious understanding that marked the Middle Ages represented a serious deviation from genuine sociality.

By pulling the human being into the center of life, humanism, individuality, and reform were able to mount serious opposition to the deviation in the way of societal existence. In that regard, the Renaissance was one of the most fundamental stages of mentality in history. It was a very important step for human creativity and naturalness and established a foundation upon which an ecological society could develop. When, later on, the mentality of capitalism became dominant, this did not only mean the destruction of all previous achievements by a transition from individuality to individualism, it also paved the way for the greatest ecological deviation in history. The reason for the ecological catastrophe should not be sought in the mentality of the Renaissance but in its capitalist *distortion* that emptied it of its essence and, in exactly the opposite manner, separated it from the state of social being. While the deviation from the reality of societal existence that mythology and religious dogma introduced consisted of their drive to turn society into God's society, capitalism commits exactly the opposite deviation, eradicating sociality in favor of individualism. We will come back to this topic when we talk about the ecological deviation, one of the main problems of our time.

Over just three centuries of accumulation (1400 to 1700 CE), the Renaissance essentially shaped Western civilization's way of thinking. By connecting the human mind, which had been detached from nature and society, with a more profound philosophical and scientific path, it paved the way required for a new civilization.

In connection with this development, there is a particular methodological problem that needs to be addressed. The biggest mistake of the extremely materialist interpretation of the Marxist concept of "history" in particular is its linear presentation of the development of the social systems. The notion that the development of capitalism and its establishment as a system was inevitable may have served capitalism more than any capitalist ideologue ever could—and, even worse, it did so in the name of anti-capitalism. It may seem like a contradiction, but, looking back, we understand better that no capitalist ideologue has served this system as well as the vulgar materialists of Marxist origins.

Along with evaluating the Renaissance as one of the most important revolutions in mentality in history, we must pose the important question as to which social system it was connected to. Classic historical conceptions regard the Renaissance as the mentality trailblazer of the system of capitalist society. The Marxist concept of "history" treats the emergence of this system almost like a divine commandment. Both of these views are the consequence of a life that is dependent on capitalism.

Capital accumulation has existed throughout history to a greater or lesser extent. Beginning with the Sumerians, we see the accumulation of capital and wealth frequently, particularly with the development of trade. Some groups built economic empires and became rich, among them the Jewish elite have a historical reputation in this regard. But, despite this, these groups were unable to become the dominant system. Both the upper state society and the lower communal societies viewed accumulation with suspicion and as something dangerous. They were always well aware that accumulation could easily become the midwife of malice. The most important factor was the fear that it could tear apart the morality of society. Even the warrior ruling power, regardless of how much it reigned over society, could not risk tearing apart the morality of society. For the existence of hierarchy, it is essential that the social phenomenon is preserved, because this is the basis of its institutionalization. When hierarchy destroys a society, it also destroys its morals. Separating a society from its basic moral traditions meant exposing it, bare, defenseless, and vulnerable, to any danger. The fact that capitalist capital could transform itself into a system was closely related to the dissolution of morality and, thus, the dissolution of society. This happened entirely independent of any subjective goal. Without the dissolution of sociality a system cannot be formed from capital, and once capital was on the path to becoming a system, it became extremely destructive.

In the *Communist Manifesto*, Marx and Engels poignantly described this process. But they were also a little bewildered. Even when they conceded a revolutionary role to capitalism, they insistently reiterated its destructiveness and ruthlessness and the necessity to overcome it as soon as possible. Capitalism isn't a social system like any other; it is a cancerous system of society. We must perceive and examine civilization, both class society in general and capitalist civilization in particular, as a social malady. Cancer is not a congenital disease. It is a disease that emerges once the body is worn out and its immune system has begun to break down. Society functions in a similar way. In civilizational systems, a worn-out society is afflicted by the intrusion of the cancer into all of its tissues—its institutions—as capital infiltrates. Society is exposed to a more or less lethal effect, depending on the type of capitalism. Here, the analysis of the twentieth-century wars can illuminate this reality in a number of respects. But extreme competition, maximum profit, unemployment, hunger, poverty, racism, nationalism, fascism, totalitarianism, the art of demagogy, ecological destruction, excessive finance, individuals who are wealthier than whole states, nuclear bombs, biological and chemical weapons, and extreme individualism must all be regarded as types of cancer related to the capitalist system.

I provide this brief description of capitalism in order to correctly understand its connection with the Renaissance. Definitionally, the Renaissance is to all intents and purposes passionately and undogmatically based on an understanding and love of nature, society, and the individual. It is a return to the sacredness of nature and the individual. This individual is not a capitalist individual but an individual equipped with knowledge of nature, the arts, and philosophy, who avoids war and seeks a free and equal society. The Renaissance utopias were not capitalist but communalist. There is no research that convincingly proves that the emerging social system was capitalism. Life in the monasteries was communal. The dominant spirit of the newly developing cities tended toward democracy. The scientists, philosophers, authors, and artists were all hardworking people who were barely scraping by. Few people accumulated capital, and these, particularly the moneylenders, were hated by the rest of society. Until the Industrial Revolution, the feudal aristocracy and the popular classes born as a nascent nation formed a social system that did not yet have a definite character.

Even this brief assessment shows that one cannot really speak of a capitalist social system until the nineteenth century. It would, therefore, be a grave error to regard the Renaissance as a preliminary stage and a process for forming the mentality that automatically led to capitalism. In reality, it was an interval of chaos that was open-ended to any development. It was an intermediate phase during which the feudal system crumbled and disintegrated, but a new society was not born; only its earliest birth pangs were palpable. During this intermediate phase the reemergence of the feudal system in a stronger form or the birth of an individualistic capitalist system were both possibilities—but, at the same time, developments toward the emergence of a democratic, egalitarian, and free society with an already present solid infrastructure were not impossible. Theoretically, any of a number of systems might have emerged in their entirety, depending on what resulted from the consciousness and political abilities of the diverse groups struggling for particular systems.

In fact, the adherents of a capitalist society and those who sought an egalitarian and libertarian society were locked in a direct battle until the end of the French Revolution. The English Revolution of 1640 had a predominantly democratic character. In it could be found a number of strong personal and collective views about equality and freedom. It was not a bourgeois revolution but a revolution of the ordinary people. The city communes in Spain in the sixteenth century were also democratic in nature. A freedom-loving and democratic quality clearly characterized the American Revolution of 1776, and there were many tendencies in the French Revolution of 1789, including communists. In brief, when considering how the social chaos of the Renaissance might have ended, a free, egalitarian, and democratic society was no less possible an outcome than capitalist individualism.

It was only with the Industrial Revolution that capitalism gained the upper hand in the social war. In the nineteenth century, it increased its dominance everywhere, and, in the late nineteenth and early twentieth centuries, the system largely completed its expansion across the world for the first time. The struggle for a more egalitarian, free, and democratic society missed the chance to become the dominant social system with the defeat of the revolutions of 1848 and 1871.

To complete the definition of this process, we must also discuss the phenomena of the nation and the national state in connection with the newly emerging social system. It is important to understand that shaping of societies as national phenomena is not a direct product of capitalism. In this regard, the idea that capitalism creates the nation is a grave error shared by Marxism. The process of the formation of clans, tribes, aşirets, nationality, and nation within societies has its own specific dialectics and is not the product of class society. A nation is possible without capitalism. Language, culture, history, and political strength play a more decisive role in the formation of a nation. Free, egalitarian, and democratic social structures lead to healthier nations.

In Western Europe, nations took shape by the twelfth century. But the question of what system within the nations would prevail was only settled at the end of the eighteenth century, with the victory of the bourgeoisie. With the victory of capitalism *within* the nation, capitalism also replaced religion with nationalism as the dominant ideology. Both developing the market internally and external expansion are closely linked to strong nationalism. These particular aspects of strong nationalism lead to the nation-state. The nation-state developed by piercing the religious ideological veil with secularism. Actually, the concept of a "state for the whole nation" is completely erroneous. Talking about the nationality and national unity of a *society* reflects a certain reality, but the nationality of a *state* is more of an ideological attitude rather than a social reality,[28] because the state cannot belong to society as a whole. The state is always in the service and at the disposal of a minority within the nation. Just as was the case previously with religion, the state transformed the phenomenon of the nation into an ideological phenomenon, thereby creating a foundation to legitimize itself. All nationalisms of the nineteenth and twentieth centuries can be traced back to this claim to social legitimacy.

Nationalism plays a huge role in covering up internal class contradictions and fostering aggression abroad. We have to understand nationalism as an ideological weapon of the capitalist state if we want to gain a better grasp on its period of expansion.

At the same time, nationalism bolsters the centralism of the state. Contrary to democratic federal structures, state nationalism tends toward centralized unitary structures. From there, a transition is made to a fascist and totalitarian understanding of the state. The social disease turning into hysteria and the capitalist system tending toward a fascist and totalitarian form of the state develop neck and neck. The result is the suicide of capitalism. In that sense, World War I and World War II can be understood as suicidal acts on the part of the system, resulting from the excessive use of nationalism. It is a process whereby capitalism, which itself represents a crisis of civilization, slides down into the most general and deep crisis, and from there into chaos.

Examining the system of capitalist society from a more comprehensive and holistic theoretical perspective exposes how much it is the sum of the most exploitative elements that have infiltrated human society. Exploitation can be understood as a form of opportunism meant to turn everything into immediate profit. It is the high art of opportunism. Material values are the primary goal. However, to the extent that it benefits material interests, immaterial values, such as ideas, beliefs, and the arts, can also be drawn upon. It is fundamental to the philosophy of capitalism to expect to profit from all social phenomena. All values encountered, whether natural communal or hierarchical state values, are indiscriminately exploited. This is why we have compared capitalism to a hungry wolf or a cancerous tumor—we could even think of it as a woodworm in a tree. As long as the wolf doesn't attack the whole herd, as long as the cancer doesn't spread to the whole body, as long as the woodworm doesn't gnaw away at the stem and cause the tree to fall, it remains under control and its hosts can carry on. But as soon as capitalism becomes the dominant system and, with this, drifts into extreme forms, which is its nature, it reaches its most dangerous phase—fascism and totalitarianism. In this situation, society is in a permanent state of war beyond the recognized global wars like World War I and World War II. Even more perfidiously, wars take place within all institutions and relationships of society. At this point, the logic underlying the statement "man is a wolf to man" begins to operate with full force. The war extends to spouses, to children, and to the entire natural environment.

The atomic bomb is the symbolic expression of this reality. A surreptitious, step by step but continuous atomization takes place throughout society.

If we look at the national state and the process of globalization, the situation becomes even clearer. Once the national phenomenon becomes uncompromising and completely conquers the state, the individual, whose existence was nurtured heretofore, begins to be quite literally transformed into an "ant."

Humanity, humanism, and the individual that developed in the context of the Renaissance are now subjected to the inverse process. They come under attack. This alone should be sufficient to demonstrate the contra-diction between the values of the Renaissance and those of capitalism. As the capitalist grows, the individual shrinks. Humanism becomes an empty concept or, in light of the ferocious global wars of conquest by the large corporations under the name of globalization, a concept that is a source of embarrassment. Not only the national state but all institutions must be dismantled or colonized in the era of globalization. Adopting an extreme version of the principle that "no value can be above the nation-state" provided the nation-state with a veneer of holiness that no previous state had ever possessed. Everything for the national state! In fact, this whole deceptive camouflage and craftiness around the national state only serves the capitalist. The state, particularly the national state, is a magical shortcut for raking in exorbitant profits, leading to the conver-sion of nationalism, as the ideology of the nation-state, into a system of belief and faith unequaled by any mythological, philosophical, or reli-gious perception or belief. It literally blinds all eyes and seals all hearts. When juxtaposed with the overblown symbols of the nation, other values no longer seem meaningful. Holiness is latent only in these overblown elements of national values. On the other hand, there is an attempt to bind the individuals as citizens to the "brotherhood of the state," using a style of the proselytizing similar to that of a medieval sect.

Citizenship is another concept that needs to be properly analyzed. In a way, it has taken the place of the relationships of slavery and serfdom, the shape the bond to the state took in antiquity and the Middle Ages. In this sense, it denotes a transformation to a relationship of slavery to the bourgeoisie—i.e., to the state. State citizenship shapes the modern form of the slave that the system requires. The individuals it creates are individu-als made useful to the bourgeoisie. They are assigned a number of duties, first among them, the draft and the obligation to pay taxes. They give birth to the might needed by the state and the ruling class. Childbirth is turned into a cost-efficient affair for the bourgeoisie. Regardless of all the talk about economic, social, political, and cultural rights, it is to all intents and purposes only the ruling class that can actually access these rights.

Even more dire are the consequences of the grip of capitalism on science and the arts, which have, for the most part, been turned into tools of state power. Capitalism, and with it the know-how of ruling power, reaches unprecedented dimensions with the power of scientific revolution. The monopolization of science and the arts results in terrible domination and exploitative power, giving capitalism the opportunity to shape the individual as it wants for its own benefit. Capitalism doesn't limit itself to transforming the mentality and fundamental paradigms to suit its principles but also shapes an individual with blinkers and a heart of stone. With such eyes and hearts, humans are turned into a parochial, self-seeking, egotistical, indifferent, cruel, callous, abstract, robot-like beings. Instead of the extremely lively and sacred world and human-centered viewpoint of the Renaissance, the world and society are now engulfed by a gray, lifeless, loss of sacredness, an uninspired, uninteresting, tense, and weary atmosphere. The laborers, the wage-earning elements of society, have the status of hens laying eggs. Food (their salary), which has become the sole purpose in life, is used to force them to lay these eggs. The *homo economicus* constructs all that they have so that they will be sated. Even worse is the potential of the system to create the highest level of unemployment in history. To keep a steady reservoir of cheap labor, it increases the reserve army of the unemployed.

The relationship between the bourgeoisie and the worker changed in a way that made the heretofore rebellious workers meek as lambs and more dependent on their masters than the serfs of the Middle Ages had ever been. The labor force ceases to be a class in whose name the revolution is made; in the face of huge unemployment and the even greater danger of lower wages, it lost its identity, acquiring in its place one that pretty much resembles that of slaves loyal to their master. In this case, the workers were no longer a value in themselves but became an appendage of the bosses or the institution providing them their sense of self.

The situation of the women, the children, and the elderly, who already lived in the most perilous circumstances, became even more brutal. The woman, who moans while being crushed under the weight of the insatiable appetite, insensitivity, and brute force of the dominant man since the establishment of hierarchy, is subjected to yet another set of fetters in the capitalist system. The being that men fabricate the most lies about is the woman. The final words of Freud, who carried out the most comprehensive study of sexuality, before his death are said to have been: "What is the woman?" All of this cannot be regarded as normal. This is a situation created by the terrible ideology of male domination of women. The dominant male, who actually doesn't want to get to know the woman at all, resorts to "fake love" purple prose—one of his most important weapons to obfuscate her situation. For the dominant male, love amounts to the concealment of lies, implicit disrespect, the blindness of his consciousness, and his brute instinct gaining increasing space and becoming established. That the woman is put into a position where she must swallow this is related to the depth of her despair under repression. She is cut off from the material and immaterial conditions of life to such a degree that she has only the misery of accepting man's most despicable insults and attacks as the latter's natural right.

I have always been astonished by how the woman brings herself to live with this developed "status." But I must openly confess that I have sensed this: when a butcher leads an animal to the slaughtering block, the animal realizes that it is about to be killed and begins to tremble from head to foot. The posture of the woman before a man always reminds me of this tremor. Unless she trembles before him, the man is not at ease, because this is the main requirement for him to be sovereign. The butcher slaughters only once, but the male slaughters repeatedly throughout his lifetime. This is the truth that must be exposed. Hiding this with love songs is a despicable act. The most worthless objects and concepts of civilization are the ones about love. What a man has never been able to do, what he does not even want to do, is to have the power to approach a woman with everyday naturalness. I would regard any man who did so as a real hero. This problem doesn't stem from a simple weakness or a biological difference between the sexes but from the fact that the hierarchical statist society has placed the woman right at the bottom, as the first object of stratification. This is the deepest problem of the society because of the features of the status embedded in the society. That sociology has finally taken an interest in the topic, even if only to a limited degree and only very recently, is certainly the result of the current crisis of capitalism.

Once things are finally laid bare, we can expect the phenomenon of woman to manifest itself in all its aspects. The elements of oppression and exploitation capitalism adds to the phenomenon of womanhood require a more comprehensive understanding. The woman is allegedly the most valuable commodity, so to speak. No previous system has ever subjected the woman to such a degree of commodification. There was no big difference between slavery in general and the enslavement of women or concubinage—which was part of general slavery, in any case—in antiquity and in the Middle Ages from the point of view of the system. There was no women-specific slavery or commodification. There were also male harems. There were eunuchs and *iç oğlanları*.[29] Of all systems, it is actually capitalism that makes the biggest distinction between the sexes. A woman literally does not have a single feature that has not been commodified. This is done using supposed artistic embellishments, including literature and novels. But the main function of this art is to make women take on the lion's share of the unbearable burden of the system. While a fee is charged for all other work, the most difficult work, that is, pregnancy, child-rearing, and all kinds of housework, are free of charge. Nor is there a fee for being a man's sex slave. In many private homes, the woman is not even accorded a value that is as much as the wage in a brothel.

What is called the virtue or honor of marriage is essentially putting up with the tribulation of the "little emperor." Just as the great emperor regards it a reason for war if something happens to his state property, which he considers to his honor, the little emperor regards it as a matter of great virtue, and therefore a reason for fighting, if something is done to the woman as the property he considers to be his honor. An even stranger phenomenon is the fact that the woman is completely drained of her soul, but physically she is transformed into an extreme femininity, an embellishment, a "caged bird" with a beautiful voice. The voice and makeup scheme, based on the overwhelming denial of her own identity, is far removed from the natural woman and destroys her personality. Above all, this extreme femininity is a special deprivation of her personality that the woman suffers. It's a man's invention, and he imposes it. Even so, he does not hesitate to blame the woman, as if this is her natural posture. Though the system itself is responsible for her being used as advertisement and exhibition material, it is a condition that is ascribed to woman as her natural essence. With capitalism, woman's dignity has reached an absolute low. At the same time, the values of communal society have hit rock bottom alongside the identity of the woman. The logic of the system is both dependent upon it and highly skilled at ensuring it.

Abstracted from all her sacredness by pornography, under capitalism, she is reduced to the status of the early primates. The eradication of woman from society over the course of the history of civilization depends not only on the development of hierarchy and classes but also on the glorification of the dominant male society by men. Even where women have not completely lost their social influence, they have diverged very far from their place within societies based on communal values.

Actually, the woman's nature is closer to the values of communal society, because her intelligence is more sensitive to the characteristics of nature and, thus, closer to reality, with emotional intelligence at the forefront. Because analytical intelligence is more speculative, its ties to life are limited. The fact that analytical intelligence is developed in man is related to the deceitful and repressive character of his social position.

The system also hangs like a shadow over the world of children. The dream world in which children live is diametrically opposed to the world of icy calculation. Children and capitalism do not fit together. The elderly are like aged children. For capitalist production, the venerated sacred sage has now become a burden, an unnecessary object. While children can still be used once they grow up, the elderly no longer have any value, because they are going to die. In society's relationship with the elderly, we can see how it completely drifts away from sublimity and sacredness. The way the elderly are shuffled into retirement homes shows the ugly face of the system in all its aspects, including its cruelty and meaninglessness. The problem of old age raises enough damning questions to prove how unnecessary this system is for society in its various dimensions.

While the people in the capitalist metropole are fully satiated, the people in the periphery live with hunger and every form of deprivation. The dialectical relationship between obese people and those who are basically reduced to skeletons makes the extreme-profit feature of the system even clearer. It seems hardly possible for the contradictions within society to become more extreme. Excessive repetition of social contradictions and the disintegration of some institutions are effectively the definitive proof of the permanence of the crisis and that we have entered a state of chaos. Just as in every natural process, here too there is a moment when the chain can be broken, and that moment is now. Old laws are becoming invalid. Structures have become meaningless, because they are dysfunctional. The time has come to create new laws of meaning and the structures they require.

148

The problem of social ecology begins with civilization. In a way, natural society is an ecological society. The power that curtails society from within also curtails any meaningful bond with nature. Without the curtailment from within, no extraordinary ecological problems would have arisen. The aberration is the loss of meaningfulness in civilized society, a meaningfulness that is normally inherent in all natural processes. The new situation is similar that of a baby that has been weaned. The enchantment of emotional intelligence is gradually wiped away.

Analytical intelligence, which frequently moves away from the voice of conscience and nature, increasingly develops its contradiction to the environment in its artificial world. Life's bond with nature becomes hazy and is replaced by abstract thoughts and gods. Creative nature gives way to the creator God. Nature, which should be understood as a tender mother, is now stereotyped as "cruel." Finally, it becomes an act of heroism to fight against nature, which is conceived of as mute and cruel. Exterminating animals and plants in all sorts of uncontrolled ways and pollution of the land, water, and air are normalized, as if this were the most basic right of human society. The natural environment is blunted as a dead, hopeless, and transient habitat. Once a boundless source of hope, nature is now seen as no more than a dried-up, uncomprehending, and crude agglomeration of matter.

Even though this understanding of nature was demolished by the Renaissance, in the capitalist system the exploitation and abuse of society is supplemented by the exploitation and abuse of nature. Capitalism wants to complete the conquest of all of humanity with the conquest of nature. It sees it as both a right and an accomplishment to exploit nature at its whim. The result of the Industrial Revolution and its aftermath is that the natural environment, the indispensable source of society's life, blew a fuse.

As it turns out, it is not nature that is unreasonable but the system. But this realization arrived too late. The environment is sending out a nonstop "SOS" signal. It is literally crying out that it is unable to bear the current social system. In this respect too, the crisis of the system seems to have entered an interval of chaos. But unless the meaning and structure of ecological society is understood in the discussion about ecology, there will be no way out of this chaos.

When we discuss the social system, we need to guard against overgeneralization. For example, when defining capitalism, it would be wrong to come to the conclusion that it is present in every nook and cranny of society, or, even worse, to literally identify capitalism with society. No dominant system can ever constitute the entire society. This would contradict the fact that there must always be dialectical opposition. A one-sided development that does not generate its own opposite is an idealistic and a factually invalid concept. Contrary to what one might think, there is always a substantial social realm outside of the dominant system. Here we find the remnants of old systems, the poles in opposition to the ruling system, and future alternatives intertwined together. Society functions in a very lively way and by frequently developing its laws perpetuates its own change. Schematizing systems is useful to gain a better understanding of them, but *replacing* reality with these schemata creates the risk of succumbing to dogmatic approaches. Therefore, one must not identify the schemata with the highly complex structure of reality itself.

Capitalism is also often described in schematized ways. In some respects, these remain far from capturing reality as a whole, while possibly exaggerating certain aspects. That is why we put so much effort into developing a definition. When we look at the developmental process of the system, we must not exaggerate either the negative or the positive sides if we want to arrive at an objective evaluation. A fatalistic development model is incorrect, but it is also impossible to prophesize a future where the fulfillment of predictions is inevitable. The lifespan of social laws is short. Development of meaning and associated structures is also frequently possible. Nevertheless, scientific knowledge offers the advantage of understanding systems within the context of their own dynamics, without having to resort to fatalism or prophesy, and of acquiring meaning based on the concrete. Philosophy and mythology, however, can also contribute to the richness of meaning. Quite obviously, we can't define a phenomenon like society, which in itself includes the whole of natural evolution, using laws that resemble simple physical laws. Since we, as observers, are also part of any phenomenon, some uncertainties will therefore be unavoidable. This has been proven by quantum physics.

But it was not only the values that led to capitalism that were inherited from the Renaissance. Finding the necessary power of meaning for collective social structures was one of the other possibilities resulting from the extraordinarily rich material it made available. The first utopists, Tommaso Campanella, Thomas More, and Francis Bacon, and later Charles Fourier, Robert Owen, and Pierre-Joseph Proudhon, conceptualized a large number of communal social systems and occasionally even tried

to concretely organize them.[30] During the Enlightenment, many philosophers once again pondered upon the question of the qualities of the new
emerging society. The most important revolutions always included a
component that was open to the left and had an unfinished aspect. The
capitalist system in its established form is not based on the conception
of any important thinker. The social utopias these serious thinkers were
striving for always had a collective character and assigned a crucial role to
morality. Nevertheless, there were objective reasons for the success of capitalism, for example, the power of the cult of the state, the great influence of
the former aristocracy, and the fact that the new bourgeois class was better
developed than its counterpart. It is understandable that the new socialists,
who carried with them the clear traces of the old dominant society, were
easy to take advantage of, because any power struggle carried out without
the power of thought and a structural program geared to overcoming the
system of state power cannot end in anything other than power changing
hands, with the new force saying, "Me instead of you."

The accumulation of capital and property is the essence of this system.
The most important factors making it the ruling system are the pursuit
of booty, which has a historical basis; enormous wealth provided by the
geographical conquests, the transition from manufacture to the Industrial
Revolution brought about by scientific discoveries, the climb from political revolutions to power, and the move from mercantilist statism to the
power center of the nation-state. When, in the nineteenth century, capital
thwarted the expectations of the utopists and used the Industrial Revolution
to become a system, the necessity for a more radical and more solidly
grounded theoretical approach and political struggle became clear. This
is when Karl Marx and Friedrich Engels entered the scene like prophets.

The nineteenth century, when capitalism ensured its victory within
the system of civilization, can also be characterized by the systematic development of the current of thought opposed to capitalism and the transition
of that current into political action. The Renaissance, the Enlightenment,
and the Industrial Revolution formed the basis of both currents. The
religious perspective lost its predominance, and the secular worldview
gained weight. In reality, the scientific revolution and currents of modern
art served as a real source of inspiration for developing yardsticks and
perspectives required to facilitate this development.

Among the intellectual currents directed against the system, Marxism
increasingly stepped into the foreground. Marx and Engels called the

oppositional currents predating their own system of thought "utopian socialism"; they explained that the decisive aspect of the utopian character of these currents was that they were developed before capitalism had become the predominant mode of production. Their own thought system was distinct from the others, because it was based on a strict economic determinism.

They based their intellectual system on Hegel's dialectic, claiming to have stood it on its feet. As further foundational sources of inspiration, they referred to English political economy and French utopian socialism. Of course, it was the philosophical inspiration that became Germany's contribution. It is clear that they succeeded in creating a synthesis that was very powerful in their time. While there was the fresh victory of a systematized society, the ability to form such a systematic opposition really testifies to an effort with great foresight and a great sense of responsibility. The first product of their effort was the *Communist Manifesto*.[31] It was well-nigh a party program and was soon adopted as the programmatic basis of the Communist League. Karl Marx and Frederick Engels called themselves "scientific socialists" to separate themselves from other socialists.

Clearly, for their time, they developed the most realistic approach to defining capitalism. *Capital*,[32] Karl Marx's masterpiece, can rightly be regarded as a sophisticated elaboration on the nature of capitalism. On the other hand, Frederick Engels's *The Origin of Family, Private Property and the State* was an effort to complete their system of thought by extending the historical analysis of society as far as possible.[33]

The results of Marxist socialism from around 1850 to the present have sufficiently revealed both its accuracy and the inadequacies and errors in its systemic analysis. For a better understanding of its analyses of the social system it is helpful to compare it with its historical counterparts. The first manifesto that we know of from written sources is the Ten Commandments, in which Moses formulated the break with the system of slavery in ancient Egypt. He was inspired by the pharaoh Akhenaten's monotheist "sun god" religion and influenced by the Jewish belief of his ancestors in Yahweh. With the Ten Commandments, he tried to create order in his society, the Hebrew tribe. As is well known, this manifesto, which is believed to have been proclaimed around 1300 BCE, has continued to have a great influence until today. The Old Testament, the first part of the Holy Scripture, is a collection of works that emerged from the Ten Commandments. The Old Testament consists of many different parts, including prophet's manifestos in all critical periods, and was handed down whole from generation to generation until Jesus.

We can regard the Gospel as the second great manifesto. This tradition, based on Christ, was a declaration that was published and developed in opposition to the slaveholding Roman Empire, essentially in the name of all the poor and unemployed people oppressed by it. This was perhaps a first manifesto in the name of the oppressed classes. The consequences of this, in the name of Christianity, are no less effective today than they historically were. Apart from the prophetic tradition, Christianity also possesses a tradition of holy men and women. As with the *awliyā*, the Islamic saints, we can still learn a lot from these saints today.

The third great historical manifesto is the Koran. This work, in which Mohammad combines his observations about the Arab tribal and aşiret society of his time with his interpretation of the Torah (the first five books of the Old Testament) and the Gospel is a kind of declaration of the "conditions" of medieval feudal society. While Europe had been conditioned by the Gospel, there was an effort to use the Koran to condition the Middle East. These examples can realistically be described as manifestos and social solutions, albeit with a religious mindset.

The most important question that can be asked about Marx's *Capital* is: Has it torn down capitalism, or has it strengthened it even further? The same question also ought to be posed about other similar manifestos defining particular systems. To better clarify the issue requires an understanding of the process of thesis, antithesis, and synthesis that is the basis of dialectical thought. As mentioned at the beginning, the system of the universe has a dualist quality in that "one" is split into two.

Today, the unity ("one") in the energy and matter relationship is no longer in doubt. Here, the formula $E = mc^2$ shows us the way. Energy appears as the factor that moves and changes matter. It could also be defined as the essence of matter that is freer. The photon, a particle that moves at the speed of light, is essentially energy that broke away from matter. All matter turning into photons becomes light. This happens, for example, in radioactive processes. Despite this identity, the duality of matter and energy is also a fact. The fact that they are essentially the same does not prevent them from becoming a duality. The actual secret is why or how a "one" is pushed into simultaneously being two things. What is this tendency to dualism, and how does it arise? It is very likely that intra-atomic processes shape all diversity and movement. The latest research shows that the unimaginably small, fast, and short-term formation and transformation of particles determines the atom formation process and the process by which atoms form molecules and molecules form compounds, that is to say, the emergence of different elements and their compounds can be understood. Various magnetic domains probably also play a role.

It is inevitable that this process in nature is adapted to society. Although laws of society are very different, it can be conjectured that they are based on the same system. At least in rough outline, we know that transformations to the social system are also derived from the "one," the clan. We also know that hierarchical society emanated from the clan and from there gave rise to the various forms of statist society right down to capitalism.

If we don't interpret the concept of "opposition"—or "dichotomy"—in dialectics as the destruction of one by the other but, rather, as one being impacted by the other and transformed into a different formation at a higher level, we enhance our ability to understand phenomena. What is even more important here is the fact that this is not a straight and linear transformation. The transformation of opposites does not happen according to the schema $a \times b = ab$. This formula of classic logic may be valid in a very limited moment, but in the world of phenomena the transformation can have a more of a zigzag or spiral, fimbriated feature, as well as at times being faster and at other times being slower, and, instead of having no beginning or end, it can have features of instant eternity. We can safely assume that transformation includes features from linear to spherical that vary with chaos intervals.

When opposition to capitalism appears, it would be nothing more than an abstract hypothesis to think it will destroy capitalism and reach the envisaged society, that is, socialism, in a linear way. Reality is very different from that, and, as such, its formation takes place in a different way. The dominant system can absorb its opposite, colonize it, turn it into something identical or into a partner, or it can evolve in a long-term transformation with not much loss of power. It can also suddenly break apart and turn into the material for a new system.

The most basic thing one can say about the development of the Marxist line is that its theory and practice were unable to prevent it from dissolving in capitalism. This took place in three forms: social democracy, real socialism, and national liberation. One cannot, however, claim that these three developments or phenomena had no effect on capitalism. There have been important changes, including changes going in a relatively liberal direction, but the system succeeded in extending its own existence as a result of these forms. It would not be satisfactory to explain this away with "counterrevolutions," as the issue is much deeper and related to the fundamental qualities in the adopted understanding of socialism.

The root of the error lies in the distinction between capitalists and workers. In essence, this distinction is no different than the distinction between masters and slaves on a Roman latifundium. The analogy also applies to the relationship between the aga and serfs. Let's look at another example: when we compare the way a "patriarchal" man organizes and his support system within the family and compare that to the condition of the tied-down woman, the winner of the conflict is obvious from the outset. Apart from rare exceptions, the man—as the winner of a particular fight, will emerge stronger than the battered woman at the end of the fight. After which, she becomes even more his. The contradiction remains, but to the degree she transforms, she takes another step in disintegrating within the male-dominant system. We can extend this example to the whole social system. In class society's civilization, and even in the hierarchical society that preceded it, under conditions where the woman was under the domination of men and bound in thousands of ways, it would be illusionary to adopt a theory and a practical form and expect the liberation of the woman. This would be no different than saying: "Be ready to be beaten even more and put yourself into even tighter bondage." From the moment the woman agrees to housewifization, she is inevitably on the road to defeat. The lamb can whine as much as it wants, but will that save it from the hand of the butcher? The chances of the lamb surviving depend solely on the butcher's mercy and his interests. Maybe he will let the lamb live if he needs milk or wool, but he also might slaughter it.

As opposed to what was once assumed, the worker who opposes the capitalist is not in an antagonistic contradiction. If we look at today's capitalism, a worker with a good job and a decent salary is part of the cream of society. Those actually suffering under the system are the gigantic army of the unemployed, colonized peoples, ethnic and religious groups, and the overwhelming majority of women. The character of the system is determined by hundreds of centers of contradiction, including the situation of children and youth, the elderly, and ecology and the environment. Finally, it is also determined by the internal contradictions and those between various levels of the profit networks within the capitalist society, as well as those between the city and rural areas, between big cities and small towns, between knowledge and power, between morality and the system, between the military and the political, and a whole host of other things. With a deeper understanding of society, it is easy to recognize that a revolutionary theory of change will not have much of a chance if it is not based on *these* phenomena but instead on the privileged workers who are easily instrumentalized by the system.

But the Marxist approach has more fundamental shortcomings. It has not analyzed civilization as a whole. Engels's attempts remained very limited. He considered the fundamental contradiction between class society and natural collective society a long gone and backward relic of the past. However, our comprehensive historical definition has shown that there is a continuous and encompassing conflict between communal and democratic positions and hierarchical and statist positions. Communal democratic values are not backward nor have they been annihilated. They continue to play a dynamic role in the emergence of all systems, including capitalism. In the emergence, the development, and the crisis of dissolution of the capitalist system, of all the contradictions those associated with communal democratic values are primary.

The system is quite successful in retaining and instrumentalizing many groups, including peasants and workers. Sometimes, it even manages to turn them into strong allies. By fanning the flames of the scourge of individualism, it succeeds in continuing to mask its rule, thereby perpetuating it. But it cannot prevent society from being a society, and society is essentially communal and democratic. Because capitalism is well aware of this, it reinforces individualism to the detriment of society. It stirs up the instincts. In many ways, it turns human society back into a society of primates, "turning the society into an ape-like existence." Only if society resists this process and finally succeeds in completely destroying it will there be a chance for something completely new to develop. Social transformation projects have the chance of success if they take into account this fundamental aspect of the contradictions from the outset. In connection with this, no contradiction can technically be resolved without a basis in the moral fabric that capitalism has systematically destroyed.

Without social morality, it is not possible to rule or to change a society using juridical, political, artistic, and economic means alone. By "morality," I mean society's spontaneous way of existence. Here I am not talking about the narrow traditional morality; I define morality as society's conscience and heart in implementing itself. A society that has lost its conscience is doomed. It is not by accident that capitalism is the system that has most thoroughly and profoundly destroyed morality. Being a system whose end is near, it is understandable that capitalism is destroying social conscience. The systematic destruction of morality is the concrete expression of the fact that the system's potential for exploitation and oppression is exhausted. For all of these reasons, the struggle against capitalism absolutely requires an ethical—i.e., consciously moral—effort. A struggle without this is a struggle lost from the outset.

In Marxist analysis, the life of the person unfolds completely within the capitalist value system. Urban life is prevalent. The individual is bound to the capitalist system in a thousand different ways through city's way of life—a summary of domination. Even Marx himself was bound to the system in a thousand ways. While a great many Christians and Muslims broke with the system and retreated to hermitages, to the monasteries and the dergah, this only had a limited effect. Most Marxist fighters are not even aware of this sort of moral formation. They assume that it is possible to live with one or another version of capitalism and nonetheless succeed in a theoretical and practical struggle.

Even more serious is the fact that Marxist theory regarding the political revolution and its aftermath has a hierarchical and statist character. War, the dictatorship of the proletariat, and statism are close to being sanctified concepts. But state and power, war and the army, are all products of the civilization of class society and are absolutely indispensable tools for the life of the ruling and exploiting class. To put these tools into the hands of the proletariat means to decide, right from the beginning, to emulate them. And, indeed, they were used quite competently by real socialism to attain victory. But, seventy years later, it became clear that it had created the most rapacious form of capitalism, in comparison to which Western European capitalism looked like Sunday school. It was the most totalitarian and antidemocratic form of capitalism. It was the understanding of state that lies behind this phenomenon.

The state, which Engels once wrote must "slowly wither away," actually reached its highest stage with real socialism, but to look for ulterior motives or counterrevolution behind this makes little sense. The reality is that the tools used do not lead to socialism but to capitalism—and this would remain true even if "the state were fully conquered." Socialism requires socialist means, including full democracy at all levels, an environmental movement, a women's movement, human rights, and self-defense mechanisms for society.

A further factor in the failure of real socialism was that in many social phenomena, such as parties, unions, peace movements, national liberation fronts, and politics, the official regime could not be overcome. Since these tools are not viewed from a general strategic and philosophical perspective that is democratic and ecological, using them as a means of struggle ultimately makes it impossible to avoid integration into the system.

Another critique of Marxism concerns the conjuncture. During the time of Marx, capitalism had reached maturity. As a result, Marx and Engels drew the conclusion that capitalism was inevitable. They saw capitalism playing the role of a bulldozer that paves the way for socialism. If we further generalize, they saw the civilization of class society as inevitable progress and believed that these were necessary preliminary stages of the system they idealized. We have already demonstrated that this should be treated as a fundamental error. As tools of domination for classes and rulers, all the various means of existence, forms, and institutions of the state, except for the compulsory security and public administration that is "indispensable for society," are not only unnecessary but reactionary and an obstacle. Many institutions, such as state capitalism, excessive domination on the inside and outside, and the welfare state that bloats the bureaucracy, are obstacle to genuine social democracy and a healthy environment. From a moral point of view, for example, war and the army are institutions that must be rejected—except in the case of necessary democratic defense.

When Marx says that they adopted the theory of class struggle from the French historians, he actually takes the nature of the tool he uses as given, which amounts to accepting the ruling class's way of fighting in an institutional manner. The same is true of the notion of the "dictatorship of the proletariat." He has no qualms in adopting historical dictatorial practices as they are.

Under Lenin and Stalin, dictatorship evolved into a permanent state. Democracy was negated without ever being implemented. But Lenin was closer to the truth when he noted that democracy is indispensable to socialism. In later processes, the method and policies of the dominant ruling class became even more centralized. A complete overlap of the state and the party developed. The party turned into a completely antidemocratic institution, both internally and externally. The policies of war and peace within the system could no longer go beyond powering the mills of capitalism. Fundamental flaws and errors like these, and there are many more, would lead to the inevitable conclusion that no radical change that went beyond reproducing and strengthening capitalism could be permitted, even after seventy years.

Nonetheless, Marxism is undoubtedly a major historical development in the struggle for freedom and equality. It made a rich contribution to social struggle. It introduced the significance of the economy and class into sociology. It forced the bourgeoisie to resort to milder forms in matters of national liberation, human rights, and the welfare state. However, its narrow tactical approach to democracy, its inability to see ecology and women's freedom differently than they were seen under capitalism, and the inability to overcome bourgeois structures as the basic paradigm of life greatly facilitated its integration into the system. Moreover, social democracy and national liberation, which were both inspired by Marxism and succeeded under the influence of real socialism, always represented weaker versions of socialism and never really parted ways with capitalism. Sections within them even perceived capitalist development favorably. They didn't fight for a different life but for a larger slice of the pie for their social base within the *existing* order. The problem of developmentalism and distribution is completely related to the laws of the system. As such, looking at real socialism, social democracy, the national liberation movements, liberalism, and conservatism as nothing more than denominations of capitalism provides us a more realistic perspective. Just as the denominations of Islam, Christianity, and Judaism differ from what was at their origins, these denominations that have emerged from capitalism also differ to an equal degree from their stem cell, capitalism. Put differently, the distinction is as great as that between different species of the same family. Religion also continues to exist in a limited way, and currents like anarchism do not offer much under capitalism other than marginality.

After World War II, the atmosphere of the "anti-fascist" victory didn't last very long. The revolutionary perspectives of 1968 and the youth movements led to important paradigm shifts. A hatred against the system as a whole emerged. It had become clear that real socialism, social democracy, and national liberation would not be able meet the expectations of those seeking change. The world these currents promised was no better than the existing one. In the 1970s, many intellectual currents that had been based on Marxism since the 1848 Revolutions grew weaker, and other currents came to the fore, particularly the New Left, ecology, and the women's movement. There was a deep loss of trust in real socialism in its various versions that equaled the distrust of capitalism, and the second great scientific revolution since the 1950s, as well as the new developments in the social sciences and in the cultural realm, brought far-reaching surge in feminism, ecology, and ethnology.

Contrary to general opinion, the unraveling of real socialism in 1989 was not to the advantage but to the disadvantage of capitalism. It meant that one of the most fundamental links in the chain of the system had broken. The system that had rallied its masses with the Cold War and kept the rest of the world's masses distracted with real socialism and national liberation states had collapsed. As a result, for the first time, the worldwide approval for statist society declined and a deep-seated belief that it wasn't a tool for achieving a solution began to arise. The national state and nationalism have significantly lost their ability to distract people. The social welfare state in the highly developed capitalist states was short-lived and became ineffective in most countries. The system has entered a new phase in all respects. When we look at the history of capitalism, we see that it emerged from the chaos interval of the Renaissance as one of the best organized social systems. It skillfully benefited from political revolutions. With the Industrial Revolution, capitalism reached the peak of its maturity, making it the first system to complete its worldwide expansion.

At the end of the nineteenth and beginning of the twentieth century the system faced profound crises, with contradictions that could only be resolved by world wars. Actually, the whole twentieth century is characterized by a general crisis of capitalism. The periods before, in between, and after the two world wars showed that the system could only be sustained by war. When real socialism and its variants intensified the polarization, the war changed in quality and transitioned from a hot war to the Cold War. The unraveling of real socialism in 1989 deprived the system of this opportunity, and it literally fell into a kind of void, having no one to attack. It had to produce a new enemy, which it soon found in Islam with Middle Eastern roots.

In the terminology of this new era, we encounter notions such as "globalization" or "US Empire" with increasing frequency. Globalization indicates the expansion of systems, thus there is nothing new about it. From the time of the primitive clans to our day, all systems have been "globalist." Every successful system has a greater or lesser chance of expanding.

The notion of an "empire" is also very old. The conditions for the rise of an empire emerged when the city-states multiplied and the state became the state of all cities. Because the number of the cities grew continuously, the expansion of the empire was inevitable, and specific areas and styles of empires developed. The tradition of empires began with Sargon and the conquest of the Sumerian cities by the Akkadians and has continued to develop since then. At the time, the slaveholding Roman Empire was the largest and most powerful empire the world had ever seen. Later, the feudal Byzantine and the Ottoman Empires arose to replace it and continued the tradition. Similar empires also emerged in China and India. This tradition then continued during the emergence of capitalism with the Portuguese, followed by the Spaniards, and then the British Empire, upon which the sun never set, and on to the end of World War II. After the war, the dichotomy of the US and Soviet Russian Empires dissipated to the seeming advantage of the United States in 1989. Now there was nothing left standing in the way of the Rome of capitalism.

Empires have a character: their structure is not particularly unitary and centralized; they are generally divided into several provinces. Because they have absorbed many state traditions from earlier times, they also often display a tendency toward a loose federation. The more powers the empires bring under their control outwardly, the greater the number of provinces and dependent states under their control. When the expansion reaches global dimensions, this tradition repeats itself to an even greater degree.

In the era of US imperialism, we find a similar dual obstacle at home and abroad. It must be stressed that the United States did not build an empire from scratch but continued a tradition that has existed for millennia. It is forced to sustain it, as the world system of the states cannot exist without an empire. The existence of states that are completely independent of each other is pure conjecture. In reality it does not exist. What does exist is an interdependency among all states. This interdependency, which reaches from the strongest to the weakest states within the system, turns some states into empires. The one regarded as the most powerful of all by the system becomes the greatest empire, and its word carries the greatest weight. It is this tradition that the US has taken over from its most recent predecessors, the British and the Russian Soviet Empires. It has to spread its dominance at various levels both in depth and breadth across a wide geography containing hundreds of languages, cultures, political entities, and economic arrangements. The system's inherent necessities, i.e., profit and maximum accumulation of capital, require the permanent perpetuation of this process. The continuous flow of profit depends on the expansion of the system. The fact that this collides with the interests of many other powers leads to tension in their relationships. Since the issue is always around being the strongest, this tension cannot lead to the emergence of a second pole, as this would contradict the logic of the system.

Since the 1990s, globalization and the US Empire have been seeking a balance within this framework. The "systemic chaos" that capitalism is undergoing shows that the crisis cannot be overcome as it was in the past. As a result, the globalization of our time will be ridden with crises. Although the factors that intensify the crisis are inherited from the past, they tend to increase in severity. All countermeasures notwithstanding, the falling rate of profit, the increasing cost due to environmental pollution and taxes, expenses rising from the welfare state practices, and the increasing democratic opposition diminish the capital accumulation rate of the system. The distinction between the internal and the external is further reduced. Globalization forces everyone to behave almost as if they were a single state. In this phase, new arrangements between the system and its allies are inevitable. The nation-state, which at the emergence and during the maturity of capitalism had shown limited independence, is now an obstacle. Neither the tendency toward becoming the greatest power nor the economic character of globalization can endure the old nationalism and the nation-state.

The republican tradition going back to the French revolutionary tradition is in particularly dire straits. It is the new example of conservative resistance. This is the source of the contradiction between the United States and European Union. European republicanism and its democracy are grudging in relation to their previous independence. This once again reminds Europe of its colonial past. Europe has not forgotten that capitalism is its Kaaba. For these reasons, the tension between the US and the EU is serious. Although the Pacific—China and Japan, in reality—are assumed to be the locus of a new flowering of capitalism and have the potential to become a third focal point of the system, this region can only maintain a partial independence. Those in this group are masters at imitating systems individually or in combination. Countries like Russia and Brazil also have to be content with equally limited independence. The power logic of the system necessitates this. Countries like Turkey that find themselves betwixt and between will also find themselves in greater difficulty.

States that refuse to align themselves with all of this are regarded as rebellious or rogue states and are brought into line by the system's military, economic, and cultural power. Far from being completely absorbed by the system, the Middle East presents a totally rebellious stance together with its strong civilizational tradition, Islam, and grave economic problems. Cold War "communism" has been replaced by the "green authoritarianism" of the Middle East.[34] The profound reactionary and authoritarian structures hidden under the Islamic veil must now be shattered. The Jewish—the Hebrew tribe—lobby with its influence now wants to realize its millennium-old dream in Israel. The logic of the system can no longer tolerate the Middle East in its current form. The new phase, which had a complicated beginning, including the conspiratorial attack on the Twin Towers of the World Trade Center on September 11, 2001, faces dynamics that will redefine not only the Middle East but also the fate of the system. The encounter between the oldest and the newest in the cradle of civilization's birthplace promises to be full of surprises that will determine the future form of civilization.

SIX

A Blueprint for a Democratic and Ecological Society

The world social system entered the chaos interval required for change as a result of the dissolution of real socialism in 1989 for structural reasons. But there is also qualitative difference between the previous crises of capitalism and the current one—namely, the "chaos interval." Generally speaking, radical changes within societies do not materialize through just any sort of crisis, but at the end of a process of crises that have a *chaotic* property. When faced with normal periods of crises, the system will generally succeed in restoring itself, that is, in restructuring itself on its existent basis and carrying on. For example, following the first and second generalized depressions—periods of crises—the capitalist system managed to restore and further strengthen itself following a war. An important objective reason for capitalism's ability to absorb even real socialism is linked to the nature of the crisis. Although an important factor was that Marxist-Leninist approaches could not completely detach themselves from the dominant values of class society, the systemic crisis reached by real socialism was of a character that it could have been overcome with its own efforts. If the objective reason for the dissolution was not of this nature, there would never have been such an abject surrender. Real socialism even hoped for its salvation through an intervention on the part of the dominant system. At the time, the leading capitalist countries did, in fact, act to prevent worse decay.

This reality alone points to the striking effect real socialism had both in overcoming the systemic crisis and in its decline into chaos. If capitalism hadn't split into different denominations in the aftermath of the

1848 revolutions, it might have entered into chaos even earlier. In particular, capitalism was able to continue beyond the twentieth century under the rubric of three denominations: real socialism, social democracy, and national liberation. Together they helped delay the systemic chaos by at least a hundred years. Had the capitalist system continued unchanged, it would have entered the chaos interval—the crisis of qualitative transformation—by the beginning of the twentieth century.

The capitalist system brought upon humanity the misery of terrible wars, including the use of nuclear weapons, creating the monsters of colonialism, nationalism, fascism, and totalitarianism in the process, while allowing real socialism, social democracy, and national liberation movements to play a role in developing "solutions" to these problems, which should be understood as historical, political, and military maneuvers to extend the life of the system.

The chaos interval denotes the hodgepodge necessary for changes, such as new forms, new types, and new structures in the world of phenomena. The contradictory aspects within a phenomenon are, at this point, no longer able to maintain either their interrelationship or the existent structuring. The form becomes unable to preserve the essence; it becomes insufficient, narrow, and destructive.

In that situation, we will see a process of disintegration, with the hodgepodge we call "chaos" emerging. The essence has liberated itself from its old form but has not yet reached a new one. The fragmented old form can do no more than provide material that can be used to construct a new form. Within this interval, it seems that a universal principle is actually at work. Embraced by chaos, the structural particles of the universe undergo a rapid reordering into a new form. If this reordering is suitable for containing the particles, it becomes a permanent structure, and a new system emerges around this new permanent structure.

Let me try to elucidate this with an example from the realm of material facts. The H_2O molecule represents a form called "water." It emerges when two hydrogen atoms connect with one oxygen atom. The action-reaction relationship between the subatomic particle ordering of both elements and the water molecule continuously ensures a state of liquidity that is highly fluid. Fragmentation, however, is the beginning of chaos. When all the H and O atoms are released, and if, for example, elements like carbon or sulfur intervene, after a short reaction time a variety of new compounds emerge. This means new structuring. In the place of water, other liquids, acids, bases, or even toxic gasses, such as carbon monoxide, can emerge.

This universal rule for the development of structures also holds for societies. For a new structure to emerge, the old structure must first crumble. But this crumbling and hodgepodge alone cannot *replace* a structure. We have a situation similar to a dough that needs to be kneaded and shaped. Let's give an example from society. Around the end of the fifteenth century, the feudal system and its mentality began to unravel. At the time, various new classes, the "barbarians," and pre-Christian feudal formations had forced their way into the system. With the disintegration of feudalism, a number of democratic forms and a number of capitalist bureaucratic forms emerged.

Many signs indicate that together with the capitalist system its opponents too began to fall into decay in the nineties. One of the first signs is the fact that globalization of capital is particularly concentrated in the financial sector. The financial system is where money makes money from money, not unlike a casino. Such a structure can only be an element of decay. Financial capital upsets the established structures. National institutions, whether states or ideologies, economies or the arts, can no longer sustain themselves by their own efforts. The globalization of power and the US Empire displays how much the old structures and the former balance of power are obsolete and meaningless around the world, and that they are no longer considered valid. This has led to crises, coups, and bloody ethnic and religious conflicts in many regions and within many nation-states. This reality is also system-related and shows the signs of chaos.

The system is unable to relieve its internal tensions; there is constant tension and imbalance, particularly between the US and the EU, and in the relations between those two and Japan and China. The gulf between extremely poor and extremely rich countries, called the "North-South conflict," also continues to deepen. On all sides, crisis and chaos have become a constant feature.

The rupture of peoples from the state institution is becoming increasingly deep. Once people began to understand that the phenomenon of the state—accepted for millennia as a god-king, the "shadow of God," or God himself (the bourgeois state in Hegel)—essentially masks the power that is the source of exploitation, repression, and violence, the state comes to be increasingly isolated. In the fairy tale "The Emperor's New Clothes," the child cries out: "But the emperor is naked!" Just as this child sees that the emperor is naked, people slowly begin to see the state in all its nakedness. This is an important starting point for chaos.

Equally important is the extremely high level of unemployment. Unemployment with a structural character will continue to increase as long as this system exists. The system is the source of the exponential growth of unemployment. In no other social system has there been such a high number of jobless people. Unemployment is one of the leading phenomena that most clearly demonstrate the chaotic quality of the crisis. A high level of unemployment means a corresponding degree of chaos. Apart from the many other negative aspects of joblessness, unemployment is essentially a state of not being social; in a way, it is the bankruptcy of society.

At the same time, because of the impressive production technologies, there is an excess of goods that can't be absorbed. The problem is not scarcity but the reverse—surplus. There are enormous populations that not only live in a state of deprivation but in a state of hunger, while the surplus of goods is piled up in large quantities, even in overabundance. There can be no clearer sign of a state of chaos. Additionally, we are seeing the cancerous growth of the cities. This growth is one of the best examples of a social development that, from a sociological point of view, has nothing to do with the city as such.[1] It is a process whereby the cities simultaneously turn into villages and proliferate beyond what is intended, thereby ceasing to even be cities. The chaos is even more intense in the cities, where society has been completely transformed into a commodity. There is no value left that cannot be bought or sold. Sacredness, history, culture, nature—everything is being turned into a commodity. This reality is the development of social cancer and leads to chaos.

The pollution and the environmental destruction resulting from all the other qualities of this chaos demonstrate that this chaos feature has also inundated the environment. The greenhouse effect, the ozone hole, the pollution of the water and the air, as well as the far-reaching extinction of species, are each a symbol of this. The actual disaster is the fact that the relationship between the society and nature, which is an ecological phenomenon, is becoming divided by a deep gulf. If this gulf isn't closed immediately, today's society will go the way of the dinosaurs of yore.

The population explosion must also be seen as a consequence of the general structural contradictions within the system. Capitalism's population policy is based on the premise "the more worthless a person, the more

they multiply." The population problem will intensify as long as capitalism exists. The population explosion is one of the most important factors
intensifying the chaos.

The social structures at the opposite pole of the system are also in a
state of hodgepodge and crumbling. The family in particular is experiencing one of the most intense processes of disintegration in history. Half of
all marriages fail, and immoral and uncontrolled sexual relationships are
growing exponentially. The "sacred marriage" of days gone by is considered
dead. Children and the elderly, victims of the decay of parental relationships
and the family, find themselves in a situation that is particularly senseless
and destructive from a social point of view. To the degree that the age-old
exploitation and oppression of women comes to light, the women's question
also descends into a total crisis. As the woman gets to know herself, in her
rage against her degradation, she becomes a decisive factor in the dynamics
of the chaos. The analysis of the woman leads to the analysis of the society,
and the analysis of the society leads to the analysis of the system.

The scarcity of social morality becomes an indication of the general
immorality. The depletion of morality leads to uncurbed individualism
and the destruction of social values. From a capitalist perspective, acting
morally is tantamount to stupidity. A society that has lost its moral foundation—i.e., its conscience—can only be in a state of chaos. It cannot be seen
otherwise. The state tries to prevent social problems with welfare policies
but fails because of the general structure of capitalism and the related scarcity of resources, so the problems continue to grow exponentially. The only
meaningful activity of the state—serving the "common good"—completely
loses its essence. Society's "common safety" is now also under a similar
threat. The fact that capitalism turns everybody into "a wolf preying on
everyone else" leads to a common problem of safety. When this point
is reached, the safety of society is no longer solely threatened from the
outside or by criminals or legally defined crimes, but, among other things,
the hunger and the unemployment produced by the system give rise to a
basis for fundamental safety issues. Because of mounting costs, on the one
hand, and a growing population, on the other hand, education and health
care are not sufficient to resolve the situation. Chaos-like illnesses, such
as cancer, AIDS, and stress, are spreading. Society is faced with a situation
in which it is increasingly severed from the indispensable necessities of
life, such as the environment, housing, health, education, work, and safety,
and is becoming aware that it is unable to find far-reaching solutions and

is, thus, caught in the grip of chaos. The current situation is one where the inability to find a solution is actually dizzying. The defense mechanisms, such as the arts, science, and technology, that need to intercede in these processes taking place in the historical society systems cannot play their roles because the extreme monopoly held by official power.

As communal solidarity dissolves, the traditional defense grows weaker, giving way to individual and gang-related violence. Against the terror of the rulers, the terror of the tribe and the clan is revived. As the warrior ruling power within the state becomes evident, society's right to legitimate defense arises. If the most general principles of equality dictated by the rule of law are not applied and human rights and the democratic right to free speech are pushed aside, popular defense forces will inevitably emerge. This, in turn, will lead to a spiral of violence and counterviolence that doesn't, however, contribute to a solution to the crisis but only exacerbates it.

When state nationalism is excessively escalated, the reaction will be the development of ethnic nationalism, and this is another channel of violence.

While institutional activities such as sports and the arts are meant to ameliorate and reduce material contradictions and to contribute to mutual understanding, they are actually turned into tools of numbing and contribute to the emergence of a fabricated situation. Religion, denominations, and cults play a similar role, helping to prevent society from becoming aware of reality. Alongside transcendental worlds, conservative religious communities are created and turned into obstacles on the road to a real solution. The triad of sports, the arts, and religion is thus robbed of its actual historical and social essence and is used to desensitize people by imposing blinkers and hearts of stone, creating fabricated and illusionary paradigms that impose a no-solution situation on society as its fate. This kind of resistance to chaos has a result opposite to that desired, making chaos more profound.

It is mostly during these periods that science and technology play an enlightening, guiding, and facilitating role in transforming society. However, the onerous monopoly of power prevents them from reaching far enough to find a social solution. Science has been limited to the role of analyzing partial aspects without a view to the whole and to using a sledge-hammer to kill a fly. The enormous means necessary to solve the problems are funneled into senseless armaments and wars and into creating entirely profit-oriented products that are not suitable to the basic needs of society. Therefore, they serve the development of chaos.

It would be possible to further develop our definition of the chaos that the system causes by incorporating the whole society. But what we have already said is sufficient for our purpose. If we don't bring clarity to the situation of chaos and, instead, continue to think and act as if we are living in normal circumstances, we will not be able to avoid certain fundamental errors and, thus, rather than finding a solution, will live through the no-solution situation over and over again. In times like these, intellectual efforts are much more important than is generally the case. Because both the former scientific structures, such as universities and religion, increasingly contribute to misunderstandings rather than to clarity about what is happening, enlightening intellectual efforts become all the more valuable. Science and religion beholden to power become extremely effective in distorting the analysis of the conditions and presenting false paradigms. As such, in times like these, we should pay more attention to the counterrevolutionary role of science, religion, the arts, and sports. There is a constantly growing need for an unwavering science and scientific structures that do not mislead but offer society real projects and true paradigms, structures that I would call "schools and academies of social science." The struggle must be won primarily in the intellectual realm, that is, in the realm of mentality. We are living in a period when a revolution in mentality is of decisive importance.

This struggle over mentality should go hand in hand with moral values. If achievements in mentality are not accompanied by moral and ethical advances, the result will remain questionable and at best fleeting. Keeping in mind the system's enormous immoralizing reality, it is necessary that adequate ethical and moral behavior that can meet society's needs is expressed in the personalities of the individuals and institutions. An encounter with chaos in the absence of ethics and morality might result in the individual and society being devoured. A new social ethic must be added to morality, one that does not ignore social tradition but harmonizes with it. As the dominant system has used the period of chaos to turn the political institutions and their tools into means of demagoguery, it is necessary to pay particular attention to the political ways and means necessary to restructure society. For political institutions, such as parties, elections, parliaments, and communal governments, to play their role in the realization of the democratic ecological society, they have to develop problem-solving instruments, both in terms of form and of content. There has to be an adequate and optimal connection between a political organization and its practice and the democratically, communally, and ecologically oriented society. In the face of this period of chaos, there is a need to concretely embody these general approaches. For society and the system, the way out of the chaos might be in sequential fimbrias—small interventions can have significant results. The time it takes to exit the chaos may be longer or shorter, "perhaps no less than several decades but also no more than fifty years."[2]

Within this framework, we will now assess the solutions the various parties are likely to offer. How we exit this chaos will be determined by the struggle between the sequential approach of the dominant system forces led by the US and that of the people. The crisis alone will neither lead to the collapse of systems nor to the construction of new ones. Moreover, the notions of "collapse" and "dissolution" are relative. Analyses, once common in socialist parlance, such as "dying capitalism," "imperialism is a paper tiger," or "capitalism can't survive the current crisis," have nothing but propaganda value. The belief-based approaches, such as that of the inevitability of "progress," also have only limited validity. Of course, regression is also entirely possible. It remains an open question just how "progressive" capitalism as a whole is. The forces of the dominant system are more knowledgeable than the popular forces and equipped with an army, power, and experience. They also have immense wealth at their disposal. As such, they may well be able to form a new system and subdue the oppositional system or, if that does not work, buy their way out or resort to one or more of a broad range of possible compromises.

We must also make clear that a critique of capitalism isn't a blanket rejection nor is every individual capitalist merely a cog in the machine. The capitalist system has access to a variety of approaches to finding a way out. First, it could reestablish itself. It succeeded in doing this after both world wars. Many countries were able to reestablish themselves after their own wars. Second, the system could try to exit the crisis by renewing its previously tested denominations. The frequently tested alternation of conservatives and social democrats could be refurbished. The system has both a broad spectrum of possible alternations of this sort, as well as experience in the development of new models. Third, it could go the "middle way" and enter into far-reaching compromises with opposition forces, should it become clear that another course would entail lasting damage.

BEYOND STATE, POWER, AND VIOLENCE

Fourth, it could institute substantive changes to prevent a complete defeat. Throughout history, dominant systems have made many similar changes during times of severe crisis, and capitalism has also frequently done so over the course of its own history. The past perception that the system is inflexible and that once it goes into a crisis it is difficult for it to survive is no longer terribly realistic. This might seem like a left-wing assessment, but, in essence, it is right-wing, because it fosters a futile hope and expectation that the system will collapse of its own accord, and that people can just wait for it to drop into their laps—without doing anything. But even the ripest fruit cannot be eaten unless it is plucked. An even worse situation arises when people begin to doubt their own thoughts and beliefs because the system doesn't simply dissolve as expected. This is the result of a faulty definition of the system and incorrect assumptions about changes to and transformations of systems.

The effort made by the US to manage the system in crisis is perfectly clear. It is conscious of its responsibility to ward off severe damage. Therefore, the conjecture that it is planning to expand the empire is insufficient. Undoubtedly, the system is already showing most of the portents that once pointed to the impending doom of Rome. Just as Rome did, the US is engaging in numerous efforts at reconstruction and renovation. Obviously, the concentration of the system's imperial power in a single pole requires an additional effort. After the dissolution of the Soviet Union in 1990, the expansion was close to inevitable, not because the US had grown stronger, but because the system simply doesn't tolerate a vacuum. It must be stressed that the empire is not a US invention; it is as old as the system itself and has found its latest expression in capitalism and, through that, in the US. It was the British that delivered the empire to the US. It is not that the US became an empire but, rather, that the empire became the US. Perhaps the US was the power that made the transition into an empire in the world the most easily. Although with some reluctance, but also out of necessity! Nevertheless, the expansion of the empire will not contribute to a way out of the crisis but to its sinking further into the crisis.

The areas into which it can expand are regions that are already in deep chaos. The additional crises Iraq and Afghanistan brought with them are hard to miss. In essence, the US of the 2000s, as the power that comes closest to being an empire, cannot avoid providing the new formations required, but this does not fit in with the reality of "power struggle." Even with the limited military, economic, and scientific means available, the US cannot afford to withdraw. Its most important task is to manage the system from within the crisis. This includes managing relations with the EU and with other countries, including Japan, China, and Russia, and preventing the tensions from exploding into open conflict. The US does not enter into a conflict with the various system powers in a way that resembles the two world wars, nor does it any longer wage indirect wars against any of these powers, as it did during the Vietnam War. On the contrary, it tries to convince such countries to join it in shouldering the aggregate burden of the system. It tries to resolve the crises that arise as a result of finance and trade disagreements through cooperation. To do so, it uses the services of global and regional organizations like the International Monetary Fund (IMF), the World Bank, and the World Trade Organization (WTO). The US will work to deter Latin America and Africa from exacerbating the crises and further straining the system. It will also take care to not allow radical ruptures in the weakest links of the chain. It will try to establish control over the forces opposing the system that have emerged or may emerge in countries like Cuba, Venezuela, Haiti, and Liberia but, if the necessary conditions arise it will destroy them.

Within the Islamic countries in the wider Middle East, which, for the US, is the most geopolitically critical region, a new project is being prepared, as the imperialist system's second Marshall Plan. This initiative, called the Greater Middle East Initiative, seems necessary if the system is to come out of the crisis without suffering a heavy blow. Both the basic energy resources and the sociocultural and religious phenomena have created a situation in the region that means the US cannot adopt a laissez-faire attitude about any incapacity to integrate the region into the system. Powers in imperial positions cannot remain silent in the face of such realities. For the last two hundred years, there has been an effort to govern the region through capitalist colonialism or semi-colonialism. The respective forces relied on despotic state structures that didn't leave the people any breathing room, but, even so, they were not integrated into capitalism in any meaningful way. The strategic Arab-Israeli conflict has become deeper. Radical Islam turned against the US, its creator. The nation-state model established inside borders that were drawn with a ruler created a deadlocked reactionary status quo. Nationalism, religionism, and statism were like a coat of armor unprecedented in the world that suffocated the societies in the Middle East. Therefore, a new project idea is required. However, the important questions are: How and with what forces will this come alive? What political and economic system will it be based on? And how will the people of the region respond?

As well as being the main problem, geopolitically this is also the main contradiction facing the US-led NATO and UN system. The target, which was once fascism or communism, is now "radical Islam," or "Islamic fascism." The system's forces and its vassals are uncomfortable with the wave of globalization engulfing the world under US leadership. The European republics and democracies in particular are reacting more vigorously every day. They are trying to prevent the EU—as the nation-state and the über-nation—from being squashed. Under the shield of the EU, an attempt is being made to create a human rights and democratic bourgeois alternative. One key policy being pursued is balancing the US. Similar efforts are also being made by Russia, China, Japan, and Brazil. In general, the nation-state is the institution that faces the most difficulty in the face of the US's imperial proclivities. The efforts of small and medium-size states—which actually should have become provincial states long ago—are to some degree swimming against the tide. It is reasonable to think that eventually they will openly admit their dependency, give up their national pride, and adapt to the rules of this new globalization. They have no other choice. The internal and external conditions necessary to resist the system based on some sort of second Soviet experience and to, thereby, retain at least a modest amount of independence seem to be lacking. At this point, the old revolutionary illusions no longer offer a progressive option vis-à-vis the system but, instead, represent conservatism. Progressive national liberation or conservative bureaucratism no longer seem to be suitable instruments. The system is no longer in a position to continue believing in its potential effectiveness, nor are the US or the people in the lowest social positions. The time of the national despotism and oligarchies, which was based on a balance of power between the US and the Soviet Union, is over.

While the system has the capacity to further develop science and technology, the social conditions pose a serious obstacle. Since supply exceeds demand, science and technology become dysfunctional when it comes to producing genuine innovation, although they could easily play a very important role in solving the problems of the great majority of the population. To make the possibility a reality a democratic and ecological society would be necessary.

It is to be expected that the ascent of the US-led system will come to an end and the US will go into decline in the next twenty-five to fifty years.

The evidence of decline outweighs the signs of survival and maintenance. If the system wants to survive, it can only achieve this only by downsizing, not by expanding. Therefore, the system's military presence, which grew massively during the struggle against the national liberation movements and the Soviet Union, will continue to shrink. There will be a transition to a period with smaller armies that use high-tech.

While terrorism, drug cartels, and the nuclear, biological, and chemical weapons of rogue states are described as the targets, the real targets are the developments in the Middle East, because this is the region where the system runs the highest risk of imploding. Contrary to what is believed, it's more likely that the developments will move the region closer to democratic and communal systems, making it possible to overcome imperialism and despotism, rather than toward a pronounced radical Islamic character. If the Middle East is not controlled by despotic, nationalist, religious, and statist regimes, it could guide us out of the chaos by developing new structures that could provide models for solutions. The social dynamism that began with Afghanistan and Iraq will continue, at first in Israel and Palestine, and then, even more profoundly, in Kurdistan, will have to point to new ways forward, or they will contribute to deepening of the chaos. This is the geopolitical basis upon which the system's military forces (above all, NATO), the coalition in Iraq, and the UN as a whole will look for a solution.

The contradictions in the region must be addressed economically and democratically rather than militarily. If fewer military interventions and more economic and democratic support were to bring the Middle East out of the chaos it is in, this would essentially determine the model for the whole world for the next fifty years or more. The essence of this model is *smaller armies and states and an extensive economic and democratic system.* It seems unlikely that the system will come out of the crisis, unless the states decide to reduce their huge sources of expenditure—financial crises and budget deficits.

In an effort to overcome the nineteenth-century nation-state, the development of local public administration, an economy based on multinational corporations, and the information society seems to be something like a joint program for the US-led system. Broader regional, EU-style, or despotic unions could also develop in the region.

It is safe to assume that world wars are not to be expected, and that global and regional unions will be of growing importance. The nineteenth-century state, corporations, nation, and ideologies may be replaced by semi-states, semi-democratic political institutions, transnational economic unions, regional cultural groups, and social and philosophical mentality and behavior that put morality first.

Until the end of the nineteenth century, the capitalist system ran the world unilaterally and almost exclusively as it wished, but the twentieth century saw major wars. One of the most important results of these wars was the insight that the world could no longer be ruled against the people's will. Even though the people have not succeeded in building their own systems, they are now in a position to impose their democratic will upon politics and against state power. It is highly likely that the next twenty-five to fifty years will bring us closer to popular democratic systems. Another possibility is the revitalization of their cultures, the most precious treasures that have been almost lost in the process, and their transformation into an inventive life. Severing the people from their cultural reality had consequences that were even worse than physical massacres and economic plunder.

To sum up: there is a strong possibility of a period when the unilateral will of capitalism reaches an end and the people overcome both chauvinism and war-laden nationalism, impose democratization and peace, and connect with their cultural and local reality. It is also essential in the context of this option that this is not carried out alone but in tandem with the state-centered but downscaled structures of the dominant system in a principled way. Our civilization can be transformed from a structure dominated by class, gender, and ethnic groups and cultures into a "global democratic civilization," as a historical stage that recognizes the communal and democratic values of the people, is receptive to woman's freedom, overcomes ethnic-national oppression, and is based on cultural solidarity. This would represent a new historical stage.

Democracy as a System for a Way Out of Crisis

The way out of crisis for the people, conceptualized as all non-state social forces that exist in the world social system, could be sequential. It cannot be assumed that there will be a single way out. Instead, various paths to a solution are possible and can be expected, depending on the level of activity of the forces involved in the project and its implementation.

We must still say a bit more about what we mean by *the people of the world*. There are many categories or sections of society that remain outside of the state or are excluded because it serves the state's interests. The scope of groups implicated vary across time and from state to state. We must understand that the concept of "people" is dynamic, which is to say, it is subject to rapid change. We can call those sections clustering around the state and profiting from it materially and immaterially, both economically and in terms of knowledge, upper society or the oligarchy—or, as more commonly referred to by the general public, the "great and wealthy" sector.[3] On the other hand, we can call all groups that are on the opposite side of the dialectical contradiction—the oppressed classes and the oppressed ethnic, cultural, religious, and gender groups—the "people." As the content of the variables shift, the number of the groups comprising the people will increase or decrease. The nature of the oppression and exploitation may also vary. Class, national, ethnic, cultural, racial, religious, intellectual, and sexist oppression can manifest themselves in various shapes and forms, from harassment to massacre. Correspondingly, there are many forms of exploitation that can be identified as material or immaterial and that act through assimilation or denial, through plunder or theft, legally or illegally, using force or deception. Over the course of history, these categories have shifted from system to system, and more complicated social groups have evolved.

The global crisis that began with the 1968 youth movement accelerated with the 1989 dissolution of Soviet real socialism and was further intensified by the September 11, 2001, attacks on the Twin Towers has clearly strongly affected the people. With the invasion of Iraq on March 20, 2003, the upheaval in the world acquired a dimension that can rightly be called historic. The crisis now continuously ramps up in regular short intervals and shifts both in location and character.

The lava that the contradictions within the system spew onto the people becomes increasingly painful. Unemployment, hunger, worsening health, a deteriorating environment, and declining education occupy the agenda of various social sectors. We tried above to ascertain the potential of the system's dominant forces finding a solution, and we showed that, as opposed to the nineteenth century, they have essentially lost the capacity to solve any problems on their own. The solutions imposed don't even come close to producing meaningful results that we can live with but, instead, only intensify the chaos. In other words, we concluded that the source of the crisis cannot also be the source of the solution, but that if these forces change they can play a role as a party to a compromise based on acceptable principles.

The people, on the other hand, develop their solutions according to their experience handed down over the course of history. Whether one calls it historicity, tradition, or culture, each group of people has a history. These communities, which have taken shape over time, beginning with clan society, have developed their form using their existential reflexes in the face of the geocultures—spatial conditioning—and political structures they have come up against throughout history. As noted in the previous section, their position has a communal and democratic character. We cannot ignore the communal and democratic position they have taken by instead looking at the individual that the capitalist system has hollowed out and transformed into a primate. Even at the most primitive stage, the individual could not live for even a single day outside of the communality of society. A panoply of brainwashing operations based on denying the social element served to diminish the significance of this reality, but this remains to be the fundamental social reality.

Individuality cannot survive for long without ties to the existing society. Without elucidating the reality of the people in all its dimensions, none of the calculations designed to find a way out of the present chaos will work. I want to once more emphasize: if the capitalist system in the twentieth century, and "particularly its state structure," had not rested on the three derivative denominations—social democracy, real socialism, and national liberation—to prop itself up, it might not have survived long enough to enter its current crisis. The most important property of all three denominations is that they came to power by giving hope to the people. For more than 150 years, i.e., since the 1848 revolutions, they have rhetorically claimed, "First we will conquer the state, and then everyone will get their due," as if the state had access to inexhaustible sources of life—one spontaneously tends to think of the state as a paradise with endless layers. The state is turned into a program of hope. Parties are founded, and wars are waged. When one side wins, the values that are transferred from society to the state—becoming the state's assets—are distributed among its supporters. When it comes to the large masses of society, there is nothing left. The same old story. And if your side doesn't win, that only means that the war continues.

Even in their contemporary form these denominations continue to feel compelled to have each step they take blessed in the name of the people. The people were active throughout the twentieth century. But since the dominant system paradigm could not be overcome, in the end, all the great heroic deeds, the sacrifices, and the joy and the sorrow benefited the system. When, above, we looked into the depths of history, we saw that similar situations have arisen in the past.

Insofar as history is an attempt to learn from the past, we must, in the present crisis-ridden and chaotic situation, produce a solution for the people that is lasting, deep-seated, and principled. No task is more meaningful than this and no effort more sacred. In my view, the crucial failure that led to defeat was not taking the communal and democratic position of the people as the starting point. No matter how profound the analysis of society is, the strategies and tactics developed, the organizations created, and the actions taken, even the victories won will, yet again, be integrated into the system in the worst possible way.

Lenin, the ingenious twentieth-century revolutionary, was absolutely right in noting that democracy is indispensable to socialism. But even he was quickly infected by the malady of power and came to believe that it was possible to take a short cut to socialism—without the experience of democracy. He probably did not think that the power that he rested on would, some seventy years later, lead to a rapacious form of capitalism.

Because of this malady of power, the tremendous Soviet accumulations—the sacrifices and the martyrdom of millions of people, and the loss of thousands of their greatest intellectuals—has in the end only powered the mills of the system that the revolutionaries ostensibly wanted to overcome.

The lesson we can draw from the great October Revolution, this major twentieth-century experience, is that in the struggle against capitalism lasting and principled solutions can be achieved only by transforming the democratic position of the people into comprehensive democratic systems. As long as democratization and democracy are not freed from the malady of statehood, the road to a democratic system will remain closed.

We must once again look at history to acquire a better understanding of the nature of our solution. Let's begin with antiquity. In the end, the slaveholding Roman Empire was defeated by people from the outside who had a communal order, did not recognize the state, and were called "barbarians," while internally, the communal order of monasteries had been gnawing away at the empire. It was these forces that led to the dissolution of the cruel machinery of slavery, forces that were totally communal and democratic. But their chiefs embraced the remnants of power and deceived them. Instead of the democratic Europe that could have been developed, they created a Europe consisting of despotic feudal states and statelets. Similar movements appeared wherever slavery was overcome. With the onset of Renaissance, medieval feudalism was left behind, with cities as islands of democracy rising everywhere. An urban democracy developed, and a democratic Europe became a historical possibility.

The great French Revolution of 1789 and, before it, the English Revolution of 1640 and the American Revolution of 1776 and, similarly, the communards beginning in the sixteenth century in Spain and various other European countries, were the strong voices of democracy. But the warrior ruling power—the always crafty and rampant instrument of violence throughout history—has always worked for oppressive systems, old or new. It succeeded in winning some people over to its side, while crushing others. The genuine democratic forces were engulfed in its historical maelstrom.

The warrior ruling power proliferated like a tumor, feeding on the wars of the nineteenth and twentieth centuries, and hit the world with a plague of maximally inhumane regimes, namely, racist fascism and totalitarianism, and finally transformed itself into the chaos of today, the worst chaos history has ever seen.

Democratic traditions are also universal, and they too are like the links of a chain. They connect us to the earliest historical times and spatially to the remotest regions. We are not alone. History and regions belong to democracy, which, more than any other system, should be ours. Our primary task is to prevent any loss in the process of knowing, to choose the right political tool, and to return to social morality. All these things are related to "knowing." The political tool is what we need to be particularly careful about; in short, it must be understood as non-state democracy. In other words, we shouldn't fall into the same error or heedlessness of embracing statist, even dictatorial, democracy, as even a brilliant man like Lenin did. But this doesn't mean an anarchist absence of authority and order. It represents the meaningful, wholeheartedly approved, and enlightened authority of the popular order, a democracy of the people that doesn't allow itself to be suffocated in bureaucracy, in which the civil servant administration is elected annually and can be recalled at will.

Here, we cannot but recall the famous Athenian democracy. On the one hand, the kingdom of Sparta and Athenian democracy struggled for predominance on the Greek peninsula, while, on the other hand, along with the Roman Empire of their time, they hoped to prevent the Medes and the

Persians from invading. The tiny city of Athens defeated these two famous enemies during the fifth century BCE, with its own weapon, democracy.

It succeeded without resorting to an orderly standing army and a state, equipped only with voluntary militias and commanders voted into office for a year at a time. However, its democracy wasn't a people's democracy but was a democracy limited to the slaveholding class. All the same, Athens left its imprint on the fifth century BCE, turning it into the "century of Athens." Relying on their democracies, the people have defeated every kind of oppressive system, as well as their worst enemies. They have also created their most prosperous periods with these democracies. Without the emerging democracy of the United States, the British Empire, on which the sun never set, would never have been brought into line. Without the people's democracy of the English, the rampant Norman kings and their lineage would never have been overthrown, nor would the system of English democracy that remains exemplary today have been created. Without the marvelous demos of France, the French wouldn't have been able to carry out their great revolutions or create their world-renowned and exemplary republican regime.

Democracy is the most creative of regimes. The more democratic a political regime, the greater its economic prosperity and the more comprehensive its social peace. We know that once democracies lose their inner core and become tools for hunting down people in the hands of the demagogues, first the regime, and then its prosperity, will begin to collapse. This will be followed by conservatism, fascism, war, and destruction. Had social scientists only been a little bit more honest, we would have been able to see that history and society are predominantly characterized and nurtured by a democratic stance. If democracy is curtailed, history comes to a standstill, or we find ourselves considering an aspect of history that is truly cursed.

Here, another important point must be raised. A class-based pseudo-democracy is neither meaningful nor desirable. According to the prevailing social science conceptions, first becoming a "slave," then a "serf," and, finally, a "worker," or "proletariat," are the inevitable consequences of inexorable forward flow of history. This conception also claims that without having undergone all of these phases, any transition to socialism, freedom, and equality is impossible.

Saying "long live the slaves, serfs, or workers," as this conception would appear to demand, leads to a class revolution, a class democracy, which will then be followed by a class dictatorship. Such a theoretical formulation, as is now perfectly clear, serves slavery from top to bottom. In a people's democracy, there is simply no place for slaves, serfs, or workers! In the same vein, there is also no place for slavery, serfdom, or proletarian labor.

A genuine people's democracy doesn't accept but rejects the existence of slaves, serfs, and workers like those found in the systems of slavery, serfdom, and capitalism. Sanctifying the oppressed classes and groups is an old disease. Democracies do not suffer from this disease. Just as the name suggests, wherever there is democracy, there is no oppression or unjust exploitation. Being herded like sheep is unacceptable. In democracies, people are not ruled by others. There is self-governance. They are not the subjects of any sovereign; they *are* the sovereign. Domineering systems may enslave people and institutionalize serfdom and proletarian labor, but wherever there is a true development of democracy, slavery, serfdom, and proletarian labor cease to exist. People will still work, but they will do so as the masters of their own labor and as members of their own working commune. Communalism and democracy are bound together as the fingernail is to the finger. This is how we define the democracy we strive for and the history it is based on. Class democracies, on the other hand, require a ruling power, and the ruling power needs a state, and every state means the negation of democracy. Class democracies are essentially state power, not democracy. The experiences of the Soviet Union, China, and Cuba clearly prove this. *The larger the state, the less democracy; or, the more democracy, the smaller the state* should be learned by heart as a golden rule.

The connection between democracy and freedom and equality is obvious. They are in no way alternatives to one another. The greater the level of democracy, the more various freedoms will develop, and, as they do, equality emerges. Democracy is a true oasis, where freedom and equality can flower. Freedom and equality that aren't based on democracy can only be class-oriented.

Under such circumstances, freedom and democracy can only exist for a class, a group, or a few privileged groups. What remains for all the others is to be ruled and enslaved. Since self-governance is essential in people's democracy, the equality and freedom it manifests must also be for all. Therefore, the most comprehensive freedom and equality can be found in people's democracies, democracies without a state or a ruling power.

Democracies are neither the negation of the state nor its fig leaf. Trying to achieve democracy by destroying the state is an illusion. It may prove more effective to implement a principled unity of the state—one which needs to wither away gradually—and democracy.

We do not live in an era of boundless democracy. In today's world, where the power of the state is absolutely overbearing, a viable democracy requires a principled compromise with state power. Having learned this lesson well—albeit late in the game and insufficiently—European civilization is trying to operate its own intertwined form of democracy and the state. After terrible wars, Europe can perhaps see the profound power of democracies for achieving solutions and the bellicose character of ruling power. Focusing on ruling power may perhaps procure a minority much advantage and power, but it also paves the way for major catastrophes for the land, the nation, and the people. Before the emergence of nation-states, democracy was not held in particularly high esteem by Europeans, but the experience of fascism clearly showed that even the nation-state cannot be preserved unless democracy is accorded primacy. The idea of first securing the nation-state and then proceeding to democracy is the cause of all the catastrophes of fascism and totalitarianism. As soon as Europe, in the form of the EU, gave priority to human rights and democracy, it paved the way for lasting prosperity and peace. This is the model of the EU, the actual magical power that attracts the world to Europe! Europe can atone for its past sins to the extent that it spreads this magical power to the world, making this positive essence the common value of all people, as has happened with every civilization.

But let's not forget that there is an experienced bourgeois class at the foundation of European civilization that always maintains its influence and pursues domination and has crafty, ice-cold calculations of profit. As contemporary aristocrats, they will not easily renounce the luxury of living on the back of democracies.

However, the democracies will succeed in removing them from their thrones and bringing about the step-by-step withering away of their state without recourse to the guillotines. This is not something that Europe can do alone, but as democracy develops throughout the world, Europe will become "global" in a positive sense, and, as it is democratized, the world will become "European." This might very well be the historical course that will allow us to overcome the present chaos. Without renewed democratization around the world, it seems unlikely that the US, with its corporations and wars, or Europe, with its law and democracy, can come out of the chaos, as they have on previous occasions.

The social content of "democracy" as a concept must be approached carefully. No distinctions, whether they be of class, sex, ethnicity, religion, intellect, occupation, or otherwise can exist within this concept. Moreover, there can be individual or group participation. Individual citizenship cannot be taken as a basis for being democratic, nor can the grassroots participation of groups be prevented. Neither individual nor group power constitute an advantage. Ideas of power are as undesirable between groups as they are between individuals. The basic principle must be that the common good—the common interest of society in all areas— and individual initiative should not hinder each other. This establishes the optimal—most efficient—combination of individuality and common interests. The communal feature nurtured by individuality gives rise to an individual who is balanced, can take initiative, and is creative, drawing strength from the society's communal values. On the other hand, if the emphasis focuses solely on the communal feature, democracy is in danger of sliding into totalitarianism.

However, if everything is considered legitimate in the name of individualism, this leads to anarchy, on the one hand, and to an extreme prioritizing of the individual over society, on the other. Ultimately, both tendencies lead to dictatorship, arbitrary rule, and the decay of society. Democracy is in urgent need of people who are devoted heart and mind to the interests of society and the well-being of the individual. Democracy cannot be implemented by institutions and principles alone. More than just political parties is needed. They need to be complemented by democrats who keep society alive and dynamic, constantly educate the people about democracy, and continuously encourage their vigilance. Democracy as a dynamic phenomenon is like a plant that needs a steady supply of water (education). If it is not nurtured by its devoted children, it will dry out, degenerate, and might even become a tool of antidemocratic machinations.

Democracy is indisputably the most effective instrument for solving social problems and, most importantly, for establishing peace. Except in cases of legitimate and inevitable self-defense, it draws its strength not from war but from the ability to persuade. By comparing what will be lost in a war with what will be gained through persuasion, one can always develop solutions that suit the genuine interests of the people. Courageous and sober discussion will illuminate problems, and problems identified in this way can be resolved by the widest participation of all parties concerned and through deep-seated reconciliation. No other system is as successful as democracy when it comes to clarifying facts and discussing issues. Democracy is the true oasis where science and the arts can freely develop. Athenian democracy, for example, proved to be the ideal environment for philosophy.

Without Athenian democracy, Socrates, Plato, and Aristotle would have been unthinkable. If the city democracies of the Renaissance had not existed, revolutions in science and the arts would not have occurred.

Democracy also provides the best way for people to revitalize their rich cultural traditions. Culture is not just a people's past but a form of self-existence that enlaces it. A people isolated from its culture is not simply separated from its cultural form, but the soul that led to this form is also destroyed. As such, democracy is the most appropriate political system if a people are to live freely and equally on the basis of their own culture.

If people live their cultures freely in democracies, there is a greater chance that they will resolve the national, ethnic, and religious problems, which generally stem from national oppression. In countries or areas where there is real democracy, there is no need for any form of oppression nor is there any opportunity to use oppression as a tool for achieving particular interests. Instead of the nationalism of the oppressors and of the oppressed, the basis is taken to be democratic integrity.

The contribution of democracy to the economy must not be underestimated. Once society is organized democratically, economic values can neither be relinquished to monopoly leadership nor to plunder or individual inefficiency. Democracy permits neither extreme greed for profit nor institutional or individual laziness and irresponsibility. Here too an optimal balance is achieved, including eventually establishing the best possible balance between public and private economies. A significant body of research demonstrates the relationship between democracy and economic efficiency and development. Democracies offer the best conditions for both efficient production and just distribution, as well as for appropriate investments and necessary research. Developing production that meets the actual needs of the people is the main factor in achieving a balance of supply and demand. This is the only way that a genuine social market can actually emerge. Deadly competition is replaced by fair contest. Democracy reduces to a minimum the main causes of crises, including the imbalance of supply and demand, price manipulation, inflation, and similar financial games, thus proving its power for finding solutions and ways out of economic problems. The problem of system-immanent unemployment is fundamentally solved in this manner.

In light of the democratic social struggle, we must take a separate look at the youth. When the youth enter the process of socialization, they are faced with dangerous traps. While the youth vacillate under the conditioning of traditional patriarchal society, on the one hand, and the official ideology of the system, on the other hand, they are dynamic and structurally open to novelty. As a result of the influence of the old society, they are entirely inexperienced with regard to what is happening around them and still far from understanding what awaits them. They can't even breathe in the face of the 1001 seductive tricks of capitalist society. All these realities necessitate a social education of the youth that is especially designed for them, appropriate to their essence, and which helps them to avoid falling into the traps. The education of the youth is a task requiring great effort and patience. On the other hand, the youth possess an agility that is legendary for its dynamism. As soon as they have a good grasp of purpose and method, there is nothing that they cannot successfully accomplish. If they orient themselves around a life with purpose and a method, mobilize on that basis, and can muster the necessary patience and perseverance, they can make the most important contribution to a historical cause.

An offensive by a democratic youth movement led by cadres who have acquired these properties guarantees success in the overall struggle for a democratic society. A social movement that lacks the dynamism of the youth will only have a limited chance of success. The experience of elderly people and the dynamism of the young are phenomena that make themselves felt at all stages of history. Those who have succeeded in establishing a strong bond between these two elements have had a high success rate in their struggle. The exalted aspirations of today's youth will only become meaningful once they are directed toward finding a way out of the social system's crisis. Youth without aspirations can only avoid decay and entirely losing life by a return to genuine aspirations.

Understanding the chaotic situation—the fatal crisis of the capitalist system—is the condition for the youth offensive. In addition, internalizing the values of democracy, woman's freedom, and an ecological society will give them the opportunity of historical success, while restructuring themselves will give them a real role in structuring the society that is longed for. Everything will be determined by the correct and skillful participation of the youth in the historical social offensive.

Just as important as self-definition are the forms of organization and action that democracies adopt. While self-definition illuminates the purpose, forms of organization and action necessitate a correct definition of the indispensable means. It is difficult to move forward in democracies unless the correct concord between purpose and means and a suitable balance in their correlation is achieved. Democracies based solely on purpose or on means resemble a one-legged person. How far and how well can someone walk with only one leg?

The basic forms of democratic organization include, among other things, a congress at both the highest level and at the level of the grassroots local communes, cooperatives, civil society organizations, human rights organizations, and municipal organizations. A large number of broad issue-oriented organizations are necessary. Democracies require a society that is maximally organized. Such organizations are indispensable for articulating social demands. A society that does not succeed in organizing itself will be unable to democratize itself. It is essential that all areas, including the political, social, economic, and cultural realms, create their own specific organizations. Parties, as the fundamental political organizations, are indispensable for democracy. In the social realm, civil society organizations are the leading forms of organization. In the judicial realm, human rights organizations, bar associations, and foundations are of particular importance. The main organizational form within the economic realm could be commercial, financial, or industrial in nature and include cooperatives, working groups, and other structures like public transport.

Health care and education are the public institutions that need to be most urgently addressed. The organization of sports and the arts is also indispensable for the overall education of the people. Villages require village presidents and councils of elders, less as instruments of the state than as tools of democracy. Every village needs a community cultural center. Communes—independent from similar forms—must be turned into meaningful grassroots organizations in the towns, and city councils are also indispensable. Regional intercity municipal associations are important. All of these institutions and organizations should be represented at the highest decision-making body, the General People's Congress. People's congresses provide an indispensable organizational model for solving the fundamental problems of all people. Without a people's congress, it makes no sense to talk about people's democracy.

People's congresses must not be seen either as alternatives *to* the state or as institutions *of* the state. As there is no people's state, they cannot aim to replace the existing state. As has been repeatedly stressed above, the state is as old as the hills and is the upper society's most fundamental organizational form. It did not come into existence in a democratic way. It is traditional and run by appointment. The upper society may well apply democracy within its own sphere, which could be called the democracy of the upper classes. This serves the state as a fig leaf. Most democracies that follow the model of the Western republics are based on the state. In these republics, the state comes before democracy, and democracy without a state is unthinkable. But in a people's democracy the goal is neither ruling power nor conquering the state. A democracy that aims to become a state digs its own grave.

When the modern European states, the US, and the Soviet Union were founded, there were brief periods of democracy in each case. But since they all immediately made the transition to a state, the incipient democracies were rendered obsolete without ever being systematized. This has generally been the case throughout history. The upper society has always been afraid of democracy.

Today's crisis cannot be overcome by going against the will of the people, which raises the necessity of the people's participation. The participation of the people is tantamount to its self-democratization. This cannot be done without a congress system. Though the capitalist state may not have been forced to share social authority with people's congresses in the nineteenth and twentieth centuries, today, the crisis-ridden states cannot move toward a solution if they antagonize the people and do not concede them any initiative. The severity of the crisis makes the comprehensive, permanent, and institutionalized participation of the people necessary. Therefore, the people's participation, which found limited meaning in the nineteenth and twentieth centuries, can be much more meaningful today only through people's congresses. Congresses of this sort are neither a party nor a semi-state entity. They are functional institutions of the people that arise from historical conditions. The people have bid farewell to the capitalist denominations, i.e., real socialism, social democracy, and national liberation, and have said an even more decisive goodbye to the state, inaugurating an era of congresses. The state is neither completely rejected nor accepted as it previously was. Therefore, it is possible for them to take part in the solution of social crises together, as long as a framework that includes certain principles is followed. The gradual downsizing of states, along with the introduction of new state models, necessitate the congress model even more.

Congress models can be of critical importance as safeguarding tools in countries with major national problems. Moreover, congresses are also necessary for religious communities and groups at lower levels. Their capacity to unite the participants from all parties, worldviews, and belief systems makes them indispensable for the realization of democracy. As a result, the most realistic approach is to see the solution of congresses not as an alternative to the state but as a model for a solution in the face of severe problems that the state cannot solve alone, which have similarities rather than contradictions.

A plurality of organizations and internal democracy are at least as indispensable as the overall democratic criteria. The democratic formation and functioning of organizations in all areas are essential. There can be no people's democracy if these organizations are not democratic. Therefore, organizational democracies under the immediate control of the people that are electorally renewed at least once year are the best guarantee of overall democracy.

If we do not understand democracy's mode of action, it is difficult to validate its operation. A democracy without action is like a human being without a voice. Actions are the voice of democracy. Each act by the people and every activity of any organization constitutes an action. In the absence of an entire spectrum of actions, simple and complex—from demonstrations, assemblies, rallies, elections, protests, and strikes through legal resistance to rebellion at the right time and in the right place—democracy cannot be realized. Particularly in cases where the fundamental demands of the people are ignored and various democratic norms, goals, and institutions are destroyed, action is imperative to achieve a solution. People and organizations that fail to act cannot democratize themselves. An organization or a people that shows no capacity for action should be regarded as dead. Of course, only organized action is useful, because other action leads nowhere and will be unsuccessful. The more organized the people are, the more action they will engage in. Action goes beyond protest and resistance. Most civil society action is constructive. Overall, a positive understanding of action is essential.

When should popular uprisings and wars be on the agenda? The only way to respond to the conditions and manner of these fundamental forms of action, which have frequently been exploited and used against the people, is by successfully surpassing the most important turning points in people's history. Uprisings and struggles only make sense if all other forms of action have failed to yield results, and there is no other solution to the remaining problems. In particular, when the forces of the warrior ruling power allow no other option for a solution but violence, rather than live under the influence of humiliating slavery, the people must show the strength to revolt and struggle to protect their vital interests. If the laws are not applied to all equally, if the role democracy can play in a solution is ignored, if all peaceful action are invalidated, then deliberating on the need for an uprising or a popular war may well become inevitable. The following criteria can provide clarity: if the state fails to demonstrate any honest interest in and does not allow for a democratic solution in any meaningful and responsive way, and the people are left without any other form of pressure, more or less bloody uprisings or protracted people's wars will come into play, as has been the case at one point or another for most of the peoples around the world.

Not every struggle and uprising pursues separation; on the contrary, they generally seek greater democratic unity. The era of uprisings and national liberation struggles whose goal was the founding of separate states is over. In the final analysis, uprisings and national liberation struggles striving for a state do no more than add little appendages to the capitalist system, which doesn't solve any of the people's problems and may make things even worse. Having twenty-two states has probably not reduced the problems faced by the Arabs but has likely multiplied them. Therefore, the goal of the new era of popular uprisings and struggles is not to gain a state but to achieve a fully operative democracy, both in form and in essence. This is the main role such uprisings and struggles should play. Separation only makes sense when it cannot be avoided. The people's option always favors democratic unity. However much the extreme nationalists on both sides may champion separation and violence, under these conditions, the people's option must be the least violent and most democratic unity. On the other hand, as dangerous as it is to resort to an uprising and war before the time and circumstances are ripe, it is just as humiliating and deadly not to embark on this course if there is no other choice.

A further important question for democracy is how to act in a situation of legitimate self-defense. Legitimate self-defense makes sense only under the conditions of occupation. When an occupying, colonial, or otherwise repressive regime is set up over a people, this constitutes an occupation. Occupation always involves a foreign power but is sometimes carried out in substantial part by local collaborators. When this occurs, the task of self-defense arises, with the goal of ending the occupation and establishing democracy. However, since a foreign factor is at play, it is more correct to call the defense legitimate and national-democratic. In this situation, the conditions for rebellion and war have again emerged. However, the struggle cannot be based on a classic war of national liberation. Even if there is a national dimension, given the particularities of our time, it is more appropriate to speak of a defensive war in favor of broad democratic unity. Uprisings and wars of this sort might develop solely in the cities, only in rural areas, or simultaneously in both. In many countries in Africa, Asia, and the Americas numerous different forms have already been tried. To solve the current problems, it would be more appropriate to focus primarily on democracy not on taking state power. Even if it is of a national nature, against the occupiers and the collaborators who act jointly at the top, it is most appropriate that the people struggle cooperatively in pursuit of democratic unity. In situations like this, other forms of peaceful action must be applied to the fullest. Legitimate self-defense should be carried out and organized primarily to support, develop, and protect the democratization of the people.

While targeting the repressive warrior cliques, it would be an error to overlook the existence of interlocutors prepared to embrace a democratic solution. Being in confrontation with the entire state and the concerned nation is never the right strategy. From a tactical point of view, it is also not right to target any individual and every institution of the occupying nation. What is essential is to determine fairly narrow goals and achieve effective results, to thereby increase the people's options for a democratic solution and protect the people's existence. In this way, a legitimate self-defense movement and its organization should continue and intensify until the powers responsible for the occupation and for blocking a solution are convinced that they cannot continue with the unjust war they are waging and are pulled toward a democratic solution. This may be the main means of getting out of the current crisis.

Even in "normal" times, when there is no emergency to address, the question of peoples' self-defense cannot be neglected. During a crisis, apart from general security considerations, the question of intrinsic security is also important. In many respects, the state's classic security criteria can no longer meet the security needs of the people. If state power were to fall into the hands of oligarchic and dictatorial forces, legal security, which is limited in any case, might well be suspended. The state would be literally parceled, so a multiplicity of mafia-like gangs that are in close cahoots with the state would emerge and practice total terror against the people. Criminality would explode. Those seeking their rights would begin to use surrogate forces instead of legal means, and the law, so to speak, would become a commodity. State security forces themselves would become a security issue. Self-defense would become an inevitable necessity in the face of the arising security problems experienced at present in many crisis-ridden countries. This is why self-defense forces should be set up.

The people's defense forces should not be seen as anti-state or as an alternative to the state but as forces that satisfy the need for security in places where the state does not provide security, does so insufficiently, or is itself the reason security is needed. People's defense units are not classic guerrilla or national liberation armies. People's liberation guerrillas and national liberation armies predominantly seek to attain power and to seize the state. They want to resolve the question of ruling power. For their part, people's defense units should never have the power or the state as their specific goal, except in cases of objective necessities. Their main task is to try and protect the people and to provide space for democratic endeavors when their legal and constitutional rights are violated and when the law fails to perform its duty. Furthermore, they must lead the people's resistance against such attacks and protect the people's cultural and environmental existence.

People's defense can be organized in suitable units both in the city and in rural areas and might also be called the people's protection militia. These units can take on tasks that the local security forces are unable to fulfill. In a crisis, social structures are in a process of continuous dissolution and increasing turmoil, which makes self-defense a vital issue for the very existence of the people and their self-governance. While seeking a way out of the crisis through a democratic solution, the people's defense forces could provide a way out of the increasing environment of insecurity that inevitably accompanies this phase.

Women's Liberation
While constituting the essence of democratization, the main phenomenon that needs to be treated separately is the system of relations and contradictions formed around women. The counterpoise of the communal and democratic stances is something the social sciences have only recently and insufficiently begun to look at, and this is even more the case in the

approach to the phenomenon of women. The presupposition accepted by all scientific, moral, and political approaches is an understanding that what is happening to women is the result of their very nature. Even sadder is the fact that the women themselves have become accustomed to the acceptance of this paradigm as natural. The naturalness and sacredness of the status imposed on the people for thousands of years has been imposed on women even more intensely and has been carved into their mentality and behavior. To the extent that the people are feminized, the women have also turned into a people. This is what Hitler meant when he said, "Peoples are like women."[4]

When the phenomenon of "women" is approached more deeply it is clear that they are treated as more than a biological sex and, instead, as something like a lineage, a class, or a nation—the most oppressed lineage, class, or nation. We should all be aware that no lineage, class, or nation has ever been subjected to slavery as systematic as the enslavement of women.

The history of the enslavement of women has not yet been written. The history of her freedom also awaits being written. The depth of woman's enslavement and the intentional masking of this fact is closely linked to the rise of hierarchical and statist power within a society. As women are habituated to slavery, hierarchies (from the Greek word ἱεραρχία or *hierarkhia*, *rule by the high priest*) are established and the path to the enslavement of the other sections of society is paved. The enslavement of men follows the enslavement of women. But the slavery of a sex is different in some ways from the slavery of classes and nations. It is legitimized through refined and intense repression combined with lies that play on emotions. A woman's biological difference is used to justify her enslavement. All the work she does is taken for granted and treated as unworthy "woman's work." Her presence in the public sphere is presented as prohibited by religion and considered morally shameful; gradually, she is banished from all important social activities. As the dominant power of the political, social, and economic activities is taken over by men, the "weakness" of women becomes even more institutionalized. Thus, the idea of a "weaker sex" is shared as a common belief.

Once all material and immaterial power resources are accumulated in the man's hands, the woman is turned into a being who is dependent on the male hand, at times pleading, at other times accepting her fate by trampling on her own dignity, and often losing all interest in life and becoming immersed in a deep silence. In a way, she can be described as the living dead.

A few analogies allow us to capture the phenomenon even more poignantly. The first analogy is to the bird in a cage. Sometimes she is made as fancy as a beautiful bird, a canary for example, or like a nightingale with its beautiful voice. Everyone likens her to the bird of their choosing—mostly to sparrows. Another analogy is to a cat placed at the bottom of a deep well and made to constantly meow. Feeding her scraps from his meal can be the owner's perfect tool for taming her. These analogies may seem a little vulgar, but it is clear that to capture the depth of slavery requires multifaceted efforts, both scientific and literary.

An extremely sexist society has been created. However, the real vulgarness lies in the fact that raping a woman is seen as a heroic deed on the part of a man, and while the man takes pleasure and pride in it, the woman faces all kinds of atrocities as a result, from being stoned to death through confinement in a brothel to the complete and permanent exclusion from society. Again, it may yet be a little vulgar to say so, but while men are proud of their sexual organs, women's sexual organs have been turned into a source of shame for them. Even the simplest physical differences were used to the disadvantage of women without hesitation. Just *being* a woman has been turned into a source of shame. Even in love, allegedly a very sacred feeling, what women experience is nothing but something recklessly imposed by men. Consistent with this, female children have always been disdained.

The question we must pose is: Why this deep slavery? The answer undoubtedly has to do with the phenomenon of ruling power. The very nature of power itself necessitates slavery. If the system of power is in the hands of men, not only a part of human species but an entire sex must be completely shaped according to this power. Just as the power holders regard the borders of the state as effectively the borders of their household and feel entitled to do anything within these borders,[5] in the micromodel of this system, the family, men as the power holders feel just as entitled to do whatever they want—including killing if they deem it necessary. The woman in the house is such an ancient and profound form of property that the man, driven by an unlimited sense of ownership, says, "This woman is mine." This woman cannot claim the slightest right over the man to whom she is attached by the bond of marriage, while the man's discretionary power over the woman and children is unlimited. The most fundamental source of property should also be sought in the family, in the disposition of women as slaves. The source of property is the enslaved woman.

The slavery and property relations that permeate women expand to the entire social milieu in waves. In this manner, all thoughts and feelings that are anchored in property ownership and slavery suffuse the mentality and behavior of the individual and of society. This is how society is prepared for every sort of hierarchical and statist framework.

This serves to easily and legitimately enable the continuation of all sorts of class structures—called civilization. Thus, it is by no means only women who lose. Apart from a handful of hierarchical and statist forces, it is the whole of society.

For women, the particularities of a special period of crisis are not that important, because they live in a permanent state of crisis. Being a woman is to have a crisis-ridden identity. The only gleam of hope in the chaos of today's capitalist system is the fact that the phenomenon of the woman has been illuminated, to a limited degree at least. In the last quarter of a century, feminism has made the reality of womanhood clearly visible, even though this is still far from sufficient. Since under circumstances of chaos, the likelihood of change increases to the degree that a phenomenon is illuminated, the steps taken in favor of freedom can lead to a qualitative leap. Women's freedom can emerge from the current crisis with great victories.

Women's freedom must find its scope in accordance with its definition as a phenomenon. Generalized social freedom and equality may not automatically mean freedom and equality for women. Specific organizing and efforts are essential. Even though a general movement for democracy can open up opportunities for women, this alone will not automatically bring democracy. First and foremost, women themselves should present their own democratic goal, organization, and effort.

First of all, there is a need for a definition of freedom to counter the slavery that has been incorporated in women. This is particularly because the power of the capitalist system to create a bombastic vision and to substitute virtual reality for reality is so highly developed that even the kind of activities that degrade women the most, like pornography, are identified with freedom.

Even though there are many important elements in the feminist struggle, the struggle still falls far short of transcending the horizons of Western-centered democracies. At its foundations lies not only its inability to transcend the way of life formed by capitalism but also that it has failed to provide a full grasp of it. Their situation calls to mind Lenin's concept of "socialist revolution." Despite all of the far-reaching efforts and the many victorious wars of position, Leninism ultimately could not avoid making an extremely valuable contribution to capitalism from the left. Feminism could suffer a similar fate. The lack of a strong organizational base, an insufficiently developed philosophy, and difficulties with regard to the question of female militancy undermine its claims. As a result, it may not even be able to become the "real socialism" of the women's front. Nonetheless, feminism must be seen as a crucial step that has drawn attention to the problem.

Just like everything else, being a woman has its own nature. Biology supports the increasing evidence that beyond their sociality, in terms of their biological sex, women are the more central element. In short, the physical structure of the female encompasses that of the male, but the physical structure of the male does not encompass the female. Contrary to the Holy Scripture, it is understood that it is not women who are derived from men but men from women. Women's chromosome set is more comprehensive than men's. Even their monthly bleeding, which is generally regarded as a disadvantage, should be seen as a delicate bond that connects women with nature. Bleeding from the uterus should be seen as an unfinished, continuing natural flow of life. The principal vein of life has not ended; rather, its continuation should be understood as an indication of its will. The so-called women's sicknesses are actually phenemona of life. This stems from the fact that women represent the center of life.[6] The complicated processes of life take place in the uterus, in the bellies of women. The child a woman gives birth to and its umbilical cord are effectively the final links in the chain of life. In light of this reality, the man appears as an adjunct, as an appendage of the woman. This is further confirmed by the extreme and senseless jealousy that men feel. While the woman is by nature more self-confident, the man cannot stay still. A man is like trouble that revolves around the woman. All of this indicates that woman's physical structure is not laden with weakness but is more central. Therefore, women must first and foremost reject the definition of "flawed and sick" imposed upon them by the dominant male culture and make the men feel that the opposite is true. This is what we mean when we say a woman should have confidence in her physical structure.

The natural consequence of this physical structure is that women have stronger emotional intelligence—emotional intelligence is intelligence that does not break away from life. It is intelligence that strongly carries within itself empathy and sympathy. Even when analytical intelligence develops in women, because of their more pronounced emotional intelligence, women are more capable of being more balanced and connected to life and are better at avoiding destructiveness. Men do not understand life as well as women. Woman is life itself (in Kurdish, the words for *woman* (*jin*) and *life* (*jîn*) are almost the same), and she has the ability to see all aspects of life in a clear and simple way, far removed from hypocrisy. This ability is strong, as we can all confirm from personal experience.

Men bear responsibility for the ruthless creation of attributes like "scheming," "rotten," and even "whore" to describe women's reality. No woman, of her own initiative, has the need or desire for scheming or whoring. This would simply not correspond to her physical nature and biological existence. The true creators of scheming and whoring are men. We know that it was the male ruling power that opened the first known brothel—called *musakkatin*—in the Sumerian capital of Nippur, sometime around 2500 BCE.[7] Nevertheless, men shamelessly and constantly nurture the impression that prostitution was created by women.

By attributing their own creation and the consequent guilt to women, men establish a false sense of "honor" that results in the unimaginable perdition and beatings, as well as the massacres, that women constantly face. The conclusion we can draw from this little additional excursion is that, above all else, women must be skillful in countering the ideological attacks of men. Against the dominant male ideology, women must arm themselves with "the ideology of women's freedom" by overcoming capitalism, including the form of feminism it generates, and wage their struggle.[8] Against the ruling dominant male mentality, it is necessary, first and foremost, that women understand well how to win in the ideological realm and fully ensure their victory by strengthening their mentality, which is libertarian and close to nature. We must not forget that traditional feminine submission has social not biological roots. It is based on internalized slavery. Therefore, the initial step in the ideological realm must be to defeat the thoughts and feelings of submission.

The woman who struggles for her freedom should be aware that once she begins to tackle the political realm, she will come face to face with the most difficult part of the struggle. Without an understanding of how to achieve victory in the political realm, no gain could be made permanent. To win in the political realm does not mean a women's movement to become a state. On the contrary, combating statist and hierarchical structures means establishing political formations that are not state-oriented, are democratic, and seek woman's freedom and an ecological society. Hierarchy and statism are entirely incompatible with women's nature. Therefore, the women's freedom movement must play a leading role in the creation of political structures that are anti-hierarchical and outside of the state. Any hope of destroying slavery in the political realm is only possible if women know how to win in this realm. The struggle in this realm necessitates women's comprehensive democratic organization and struggle. The areas in which a democratic struggle must be organized and developed include civil society, human rights, and local governments. Just as with socialism, the path to women's freedom and equality is through the most comprehensive and successful democratic struggle. Without achieving democracy, the women's movement will be unable to achieve freedom and equality.

In the social realm, the most important problem for freedom is the reality of marriage and the family. Both pose a situation like that of bottomless pits. Even though they may appear to women as salvation, given the current mentality of the society, at best this amounts to moving from one cage to another. Moreover, it means the forced abandonment of a youthfulness full of life to a butcher's mentality. The family must be regarded as the reflection of the upper society—the society of the ruling power—within the people and as an institution that is an agent of the upper society. The man is the representative of society's ruling power within the family, its most concentrated embodiment. When a woman is married, she actually becomes a slave. It is difficult to imagine another institution that enslaves the way marriage does. The most comprehensive slavery is quite literally established with this institution, and this slavery continues as it takes root in the family. I am not talking about a partnership in general, or about a common life. This is an issue that attains substance depending on how freedom and equality are understood. I am talking about marriage and family in its established and classic sense. For women, this means becoming nothing but property, withdrawing from the political, mental, social, and economic realms, and facing extreme difficulty in any effort to return to their senses. Marriages and relationships arising from individual and sexual needs or from a traditional understanding of the family can generate the most dangerous deviations on the road to free life, if they are not subjected to radical questioning, and if principles of a common life that is free, democratic, and aims to achieve equality between women and men is not ensured. The need is not to form such unions but to fully ensure women's freedom by analyzing the realms of mentality, democracy, and politics and accordingly bring about the will for a common life.

The concept of "love," which has been hashed out and rehashed ad nauseam in today's world, is going through its worst period ever—it is at its most vile and is devoid of content. Never before in history has there been so much conceptual confusion about love. From relationships that only last a fleeting moment to openly murderous behavior, from prosaic relationships to extremely dangerous ones, everything is called "love." Nothing demonstrates more clearly the capitalist system's understanding of life than this relationship.

The "love" of our times is an obvious confession of what the mentality imposed on humans and society by the dominant system has become, even in the most sacred area. Reviving love is one of the most difficult of revolutionary tasks. It requires a great deal of labor, intellectual clarity, and love of humanity. Love requires being at the threshold of the wisdom of the times—one of its most important conditions. Second, it forces us to make a great show of resistance to the system's madness. Third, it requires adopting a moral attitude where we cannot even look into each other's eyes in the absence of liberation and freedom. Fourth, it requires us to limit our sexual drive on the basis of the three imperatives just mentioned. We must be clear that if the sexual drive is not constrained by wisdom, the morality of freedom, and the reality of politico-military struggle, each step taken will negate love. The fact is that for those who do not have the option of freely settling down—not even as much as a bird—to talk about love, relationships, and marriage actually is an act of submission to the slavery of the social order and shows no real appreciation for the ennobling value of the freedom struggle.[9]

If we are to talk about the reality of love in our age, this love will only be possible if we attain personalities that surpass those of Laila and Majnun and the many Sufi masters, and if we act with the meticulousness of scientists,[10] thereby paving the way to social freedom from the current chaos and, in this way, proving our courage, our selflessness, and our ability to succeed.

The problems of the economic and social equality of women can best be addressed by ironing out the issue of political power and a successful process of democratization. Clearly, without democratic politics and actual advances in the realm of freedom, a merely dry legal equality would not have much meaning.

The shift in attitude about women should best be seen as a cultural revolution. Given the problems and the relationship structure involved in the phenomenon, no meaningful and freedom-oriented solution can be achieved within the present culture, regardless of how good the intentions and how great the effort. The development of the most radically freedom-oriented identity possible is dependent upon the approach taken to woman, or, rather, grasping and overcoming the system at play in the overall relationship between women and men. It is high time to understand that we cannot advance even a millimeter if we confuse the early marrying off of young women with tradition and pornography with modernity. There is a need to comprehend both the depth of freedom and the depth of slavery at play in this area and turn that understanding into will power. Those who fail to advance in terms of women's freedom, and therefore freeing themselves must understand that they cannot be a problem-solver and bring about transformation in any area of social or political freedom. Any effort for freedom that does not surpass the dilemma of the dominant man-the enslaved woman cannot attain a truly free identity—the most fundamental criterion for freedom. A relationship between women and men based on freedom cannot be realized if the relations of property and power over women are not destroyed.

It is totally reasonable to see our century as the social period in which the will of free women shall rise. Some thought should go into conceptualizing and establishing lasting institutions that women may well require for at least a century. Women's Freedom Parties may also be needed. The fundamental purpose and primary task of these parties would be to determine the basic ideological and political principles of freedom and execute and supervise their implementation into practice.

Rather than building women's refuges particularly in the cities, organized freedom spaces should be created for the female masses. Perhaps Cultural Parks of the Free Women could be one of the appropriate forms this could take. Cultural Parks of the Free Women are particularly essential in situations where families cannot educate female children as well as because of the well-known structures of the system's schools. These cultural parks could become spaces that include education, as well as production and service units, for eligible women and female children and those who need it, thus, playing the role of contemporary women's temples.

It is said that one cannot live without a woman. But it is not possible to live with the current woman. The most devastating relationship is probably the one between a woman and a man who are submerged up to their necks in slavery. In that case, to exit the fatal chaos of the capitalist system, the great power that is expected from true love can only be created around the free women—and achieving this must be understood as the most noble and sacred deed of the true heroes who have devoted their hearts and minds to love.

The Return to Social Ecology

It is most realistic to look for the origins of the ecological crisis, which is continuing to deepen alongside the crisis of the social system, at the beginning of civilization. We have to understand that the alienation from other humans that develops within society due to domination brings with it alienation from nature, and the two become intertwined. Society itself is, in its essence, an ecological phenomenon. By ecology, we mean the physical and biological nature on which the formation of society is based. The relationship between the physical and the biological formation of planet earth is further illuminated with each passing day. This is one of the areas where science has been most successful. One can scientifically show that life began in water and spread from there to land, where it developed into an almost unimaginable diversity of plant and animal species. The physical and biological environment that the human species can survive in is understood to be connected to these developments. One of the assumptions in establishing that connection is that the human species is the last link in the evolutionary chain of living beings in general and of the animal world in particular. The foremost conclusion to be drawn is that the human species cannot live in an arbitrary way but can only sustain itself if it adheres to the requirements of this evolutionary chain. Should humans destroy the evolutionary links upon which they rest, they will lose their biological integrity and, as a result, the species will inevitably risk being unable to sustain itself. Science now shows us that the integral essence of evolution in nature is based on the mutual dependence of the species to a far greater degree than we previously assumed. As this mutual dependence is undermined, great ruptures will occur in the evolutionary links, which, in turn, will result in a situation in which the survival of many species is seriously threatened.

The problem created by civilization facing this scientific reality is that if no measures are taken the gates of hell have already been half-opened. The most fundamental reason civilization gave rise to the problem is the tyranny and ignorance it rests upon, or, more precisely, "the necessity to be a liar." When they first arose, hierarchy and the state could not make their existence permanent by relying solely on force and oppression. Hypocrisy and lies were indispensable to obfuscate the truth behind events. Power requires domination, the domination of the mentality. On the other hand, to secure power, the mentality developed had to validate falsehoods. The brute side of power will always guarantee that this type of mentality lives and dominates, acting as the subtle expression of power. Shaping mentality in this way also provides the basis for alienation from nature. As it denies the communal bond that creates society and replaces it with the hierarchical state forces that initially developed as an anomaly, the mentality will become open to forgetting and trivializing the bond between nature and life. All subsequent progress based on a civilization that rests on this foundation will mirror both an increased detachment from nature and environmental destruction. The civilization forces will cease to even perceive natural necessities. After all, the underclass that feeds them provides them with everything that is already prepared.

Utopias of divinity and paradise in the Holy Scripture were fabricated based on the mythologies of the Sumerians who were the first civilization forces. They were carved into human mentality—which was then at its childhood—as fundamental patterns. God and paradise only existed as abstractions from nature, or, rather, they were the fake world designs of the rising forces of the ruling power to replace real nature. In essence, they were saying: "We, who have become gods, live in paradise." The second version was: "The sultans, the 'shadows of God,' live as if they are in paradise." The third version boasts: "The exploiter lives in a paradise-like way." These perceptions, which were presented in the form of divine sublime realities—the patterns of mentality that dominate society—forgot all about "mother nature." They even went one step further and pushed relations with nature into a state of encompassing alienation, based particularly on their assumptions about a "cruel" or "blind" nature, a nature that had to be "subdued." Using the accumulations of the ruling power—which are the products of tyranny and lies—to make life as anti-nature as possible is the root cause of ecological problems. Denying the role of nature in life and replacing it with fake religious figures and creators allowed for nature to be called a "blind force." The effectiveness of this mentality, even to this day, is the main reason why a scientific mentality has not developed. A scientific mentality can only develop on the basis of a correct and objective definition of the forces of nature. A belief system that delegates everything to God or jinns will never make sense of a wonderful arrangement like nature. Such a system will sidestep science by insisting that the whole of physical and biological nature was created by an abstract concept, "God."

We saw explicitly that this abstract God is a mental creation of the first rising stratum of exploiters to ensure their legitimacy. The danger is that it will not just serve to bind serfs and slaves to their exploiters, but that the serfs and slaves will themselves be detached from reality. This cuts the human mind's correct bond with nature and leads to alienation from itself and nature. The mother nature of days gone by is now replaced by "cruel nature"—by real villains. When we observe the stages of development of this mentality throughout history, it is impossible not to be horrified. The games of humans vs. predatory animals in the arenas of the Roman Empire were a product of this mentality.

Any interest of the human being in the whole of plant and animal worlds is increasingly hampered and obfuscated. All this is connected to the cruel practices of the ruling power. In fact, playing humans and animals off against one another in this way effectively symbolizes this alienation from nature. During medieval feudalism the earth became an inn that should be abandoned as soon as possible. In fact, it was an immoral place that bound people to itself and seduced them to sin. What was nature when compared to the glory of God? Thus, to leave nature—the world—as soon as possible became the goal for believers. But for the upper layer, however, a paradisaical life would continue, with a 1,001 revelries. We refer to this falsification (distortion) when we talk about the great mental deviance. This millennium-old mental deviance is the basis of the backwardness of societies in the Middle East.

At its heart, the Renaissance was a renewal of the mentality bond that had been broken with nature. The Renaissance developed its revolution in mentality on the basis of the vitality, creativity, and sacredness of nature. It was based on the assumption that everything that is can be found in nature. In the arts, the beauty of nature was much better depicted than had previously been the case, and its scientific approach expanded the limits of nature. With the human being as the basis, the task of science and the arts was to recognize and display the full reality of that human being. The modern age is the result of this shift in mentality. Contrary to the common view, capitalist society was not the natural result of this process but has actually functioned as a distortion and played a regressive role. The methods developed to exploit human beings were now combined with the exploitation of nature. Domination of humans coalesced with the domination of nature, launching the most intense attack of all time against nature. Capitalism grasped the exploitation of nature as its revolutionary role, without wasting a moment considering the sacredness, vitality, or equilibrium of nature. Capitalism totally discarded the perception of nature's sacredness, which had been present in all previous mentalities, even if in a distorted form. This system arrogated to itself the right to do what it likes with the nature, without fear or anxiety.

As a result, the social crisis merged with the environmental crisis. Just as the system's essence carried the social crisis to the chaos interval, now the environmental disasters are leading to SOS signals warning of dangers to life itself. Cities proliferating like a cancer, polluted air, a perforated ozone layer, rapidly accelerating extinction of plant and animal species, destruction of the forests, pollution and contamination of the waters, mounting piles of garbage, and unnatural population growth have driven the environment into chaos and rebellion. No calculation has been made as to how many cities, people, factories, and vehicles or how much synthetic material and polluted air and water our planet can tolerate; instead there is a reckless pursuit of maximum profit. But this negative development is not a matter of fate. It is the result of an imbalanced use of science and technology by those in power. It would be wrong to hold science and technology responsible for this process. In and of themselves, they cannot be blamed for any of this. They reflect and comply with the nature of the system's forces. Just as they can be used to annihilate nature, they could also serve to heal and improve it. The problem is totally social.

Furthermore, there is a major contradiction between the level of science and technology and the living standard of the overwhelming majority of people. This situation is the result of the interests of a minority who hold complete discretionary power over science and technology. In a democratic and freedom-oriented social system, science and technology would play an ecologically positive role.

Ecology is itself a science. It investigates society's relationship with the environment. Even though it is new, it will play a leading role, increasingly intertwined with all other sciences, in overcoming the society-nature conflict. The limited development of environmental consciousness will make a revolutionary leap with such an understanding of ecology.

The bond between primitive communal society and nature was like the bond between a mother and her child. The society perceived nature to be alive. The golden rule of religions at that time was not to do anything against nature to avoid being punished by it. The religion of primordial communal society was a nature-based religion. In the formation of society there was no natural anomaly and contradiction. Philosophy defines human being as "nature rendered self-conscious."[11] Thus, humans are actually the most developed *part* of nature.

This clearly exposes the unnaturalness and anomaly of the social system that puts the most developed part of nature in contradiction with nature as a whole. That this social system has turned human beings, who were once united with nature in festive exuberance—festivities are in fact a reflection of joyful and productive unity with nature—into such a plague upon nature clearly demonstrates how troublesome this social system is.

Being wholly part of the natural environment does not only have economic or social content. Trying to understand nature is also an indispensable philosophical passion. Actually, it is a mutual passion. While nature proved its great curiosity and creative power by taking form as the human, by understanding nature humans become aware of themselves—it is thought-provoking that the Sumerians understood *freedom* (*amargi*) to mean *return to the mother*, i.e., to nature. There is a relationship of one that is in love and one that is loved between nature and humans—this is a great love adventure. To disrupt or separate them is probably, in religious terms, the biggest sin, because a more valuable power of meaning cannot be created. As it is relevant to our topic, we once more see the remarkable importance of our interpretation of woman's bleeding both as a sign of the separation from nature and as our origin within it. The woman's naturalness is due to her proximity to nature, and it is also in this reality that her mysterious attractiveness finds meaning.

The rationality or morality of a social system that does not integrate us into nature cannot be defended. This is why the system that most put humans in contradiction with the natural environment has been transcended rationally and morally. As is already clear from this short description, the relationship between the chaos experienced by the capitalist social system and the environmental disaster is dialectical. Fundamental contradictions with nature can only be overcome by breaking with the system. This issue cannot be resolved by environmental movements alone, due to the nature of the contradiction. On the other hand, an ecological society requires a moral transformation. The anti-morality of capitalism can only be overcome by an ecological approach. The relationship between morality and conscience demands an empathetic and sympathetic spirituality. This, however, is only meaningful if equipped with a sound ecological approach. Ecology means friendship with nature and belief in natural religion. In this respect, ecology stands for an awakened consciousness and a renewed integration into natural organic society.

The practical problems of an ecological way of life are already on the agenda. One of the tasks facing us is to deepen the already existing organizations that are working to stop natural environmental disasters in all respects and make them an integral part of democratic society, as well as to build solidarity with the feminist and freedom-oriented women's movement. Intensifying and organizing environmental consciousness is one of the most important activities of democratization. Just as we once organized intense class and national consciousness, we must now initiate impassioned campaigns to create a democratic and environmental consciousness. Whether it is animal rights, the protection of the forests, or reforestation, each is an indispensable part of any social plan of action, because the social sensitivity of those who have no biological sensitivity is necessarily deformed. The path to a real and meaningful sensitivity is to see the link between the two.

The period ahead must and shall witness great struggles waged for denuded nature to regain its great forests and its flora and fauna. It is necessary to give reforestation a chance. The slogan "the greatest patriotism is expressed in reforestation and the planting of trees" will likely become one of the most precious slogans. It will come to be better understood that those who do not love and protect animals will not be able to love and protect humans. Humans will become more precious as they grasp that animals and plants are entrusted to them.

A social consciousness devoid of ecological consciousness will inevitably be corrupted and fall apart, as was the case with real socialism. Ecological consciousness is a fundamental ideological consciousness. It's a bridge between philosophy and morality. The policy that will rescue us from the contemporary crisis must be ecological if it is to lead to a favorable social system. As with women's freedom, the patriarchal statist understanding of power plays a fundamental role in the long-standing neglect of unresolved ecological problems and an error-ridden life. As ecology and feminism continue to develop, all of the disparate balances within the patriarchal statist system will be further disrupted. A truly unified struggle for democracy and socialism will only be possible when women's freedom and the environment's liberation are targeted. Only the struggle for this sort of new and integrated social system can provide one of the most meaningful forms for coming out of the present chaos.

Capitalist globalization plunged into its third major crisis and a period of chaos with the dissolution of the real socialist system for internal reasons in 1989. Under US leadership, the system is trying to maintain power as an "empire of chaos." The US empire of chaos now resembles the Roman Empire as it disintegrated—albeit with all the distinctions that characterize the capitalist system that we should all be aware of. The EU countries, which have reservations about US hegemony, are trying to put up some resistance with half-hearted criticisms of the US around issues of democracy and human rights, hoping to be able to retain their traditional republics, democracies, and national states. But the nation-state poses an obstacle to capitalist globalization, which will, in turn, prevent the EU from developing into anything more than a weak transnational political union. It seems unlikely that a third global focal point, led by China and Japan, which are getting stronger in the Pacific, will arise in the near future. Russia and Brazil, among others, would join such countries, mostly, it would seem, to protect their nation-states. Many other countries, nations, and groups of states around the world are now having serious problems sustaining their nation-states, which were initially formed in the context of the balance of power between the US and the USSR in the aftermath of 1945. Within the framework of the US empire of chaos, they face being restructured and shrinking, contracting, or partially or completely fragmenting. Many regions, but especially the Middle East, the Balkans, and the Caucasus, are experiencing this process in the extreme.

The empire of chaos, which we could also, in a certain sense, call World War III, is not managed using military and political methods alone but more intensely and decisively by global corporations and the media. Global economic and media corporations do not shrink from physically and mentally starving societies in order to easily manipulate and use them as they see fit.

They hope that by using their scientific and technological superiority they can salvage capitalist society system from chaos and exit the crisis even stronger or, if this is not possible, at least minimize the damage as far as possible, restructuring if necessary. In this chaos, the old-fashioned ways and means are no longer suited to managing, protecting, and sustaining the system with nothing but small changes. Therefore, it would be more realistic to evaluate the new US tactical and strategic approaches and implementations in the light of the chaos process.

Peoples' mostly communal and democratic stance throughout history must be strengthened through theoretical and tactical renewal to the point where it can overcome the chaos. The left of former days, which gave rise to real socialism and the New Left, ecological, and feminist movements of more recent times, as well as the Porto Alegre meetings, are far from being able to grasp and overcome the chaos. There is an urgent need for an intense discussion on the general theoretical perspectives and specific local tactics necessary for a global *democratic and ecological society with women's freedom* and for different solutions—without ignoring the aforementioned movements. In doing so, the first prerequisite will be to say farewell to old theories and tactics that focus on ruling power and on finding a solution by either "destroying or seizing the state." As real socialism has shown us, if we do not abandon a state-oriented mentality and liberationist-developmentalist methods, there is no escape from serving the capitalist system in the worst way. In addition, the people's demands for true freedom and equality cannot be met by mobilizing the masses to revolt and make war with slogans and programs centered around a state, socialism, liberation of the homeland, a nation, or a religion, programs that have been primarily based on abstract and ideological concepts and generalizations of the past like country, nation, class, and religion—this can only end in ultimately dissolving into the capitalist system and further strengthening it.

In the new stage of global capitalism, it is all about revealing the consciousness and will of the people and all the groups that constitute the people based on their self-identity and culture and researching, organizing, and putting into action local and transnational solutions. It is equally indispensable to develop a democratic society organization in the form of an extensive social network as the fundamental organ of local authority, from the democratic municipal movement to village and neighborhood communes, from cooperatives to broad civil society organizations, from human rights to children's rights and animal rights, from woman's freedom to ecological organizations, and vanguard youth organizations. It is also vital to establish political parties that focus on democratic politics as the ideological, theoretical, and administrative coordinators of this type of democratic society. Without the development of democratic parties and alliances, the creation of a democratic society is futile. A people's congress as the highest expression of democratic society and political groups is an inevitable fundamental task for each group of people. These people's congresses are not an alternative to the state but also refuse to submit to it and, provided their principles are preserved, are open to compromises. They are the most important democratic organs for overcoming the present chaos. The role of these people's congresses is to secure the political, self-defense, legal, social, moral, economic, scientific, and artistic needs of democratic society and to meet these responsibilities by leading the appropriate institutions and ensuring the necessary rules, regulations, and control mechanisms.

The basic slogans of the people should be "free nation and homeland" and "socialism through the most comprehensive implementation of democracy"—an understanding of equality that is based on the "equality of unequals" and that goes beyond mere equality before the law,[12] embracing religious freedom and constructing democratic congresses that are not a state.

Taking into account the gigantic economic, military, and scientific potential of global capitalism, all kinds of democratic legal action can be considered as methods of resistance, and when the laws are not applied in the same way to everyone and there is a regime of tyranny, organized uprisings and guerrilla wars based on self-defense can also be considered.

Because capitalist society is based on the negation of morality, to truly build a democratic, and ecological society with woman's freedom, it is an indispensable principle and attitude to act on the basis of an ethical theory and a moral practice.

In overcoming the chaos, science and the arts are the foundations of the mentality that we should base ourselves on the most. Formal education, which is imposed from primary school all the way to university, is based on the creation of state- and hierarchy-driven beings who are alienated from their individuality, their society, and the environment. The traps and deceptions of such an education and training must be overcome. In their place, we must develop a new understanding and paradigm of science and the arts that must be understood, above all, as serving a revolution in mentality and must be internalized and put into practice. This paradigm must present the people and society with their historical realities, freeing the moment in order to carry it into the future. On this basis, a new type of social science academies and schools should become widespread according to needs.

Striving for a "global democratic civilization of the people" as an alternative to capitalism's global empire of chaos not only shows respect for the past resistance traditions but can lead us to the future world, a world that will be more democratic, free, and equal than any before it.

SEVEN

Chaos in the Middle East
Civilization and Ways Out

Introduction

It's true that World War III is taking place in the Middle East in a unique way. However, certain particularities distinguish this war from classic military-political aspects. Although defining it as a clash of civilizations is correct,[1] its content is often incorrectly interpreted. Frequently, not enough attention is paid to its historical and social dimensions—what side particular forces are on and their methods and goals are not clear. Even though there is plenty of talk about various plans and projects, the war in question appears to lack a plan and to almost be running on its own steam. We are, so to speak, faced with a war that aims to create chaos.

The states and societies in the Middle East are literally a pile of problems. Various problems that have been accumulated and suppressed since antiquity suffocate society. The regimes themselves, dictated by the capitalist system, in the hope they would lead to a solution, have become the source of problems. They can neither develop solutions themselves nor allow any domestic or foreign forces to do so. It is, thus, an error to reduce the issue to the crisis of Islam alone. We are dealing with mentalities that predate the emergence of the monotheist religions and that have their roots in the Neolithic Age. There are a number of social structures and systems that can't be defined by the concept of "nation." Not only every aşiret but also almost every family is as complex as the state problem. The abyss separating women and men is just as wide and deep as the rift between society and the state, indicating the depth of their alienation from one another.

This chaos is like the Babylonian confusion of languages in the legend of Tower of Babel. It's as if the legend were playing out anew in the same place, with more than seventy nations forces active.[2] And the chaos gets worse every day. The Arab-Jewish war, a relic of the time of the pharaohs, continues unabated. The same is true of the military operations that have been carried out against the Kurds (previously known as the "Kurti") since the time of the Sumerian kings. Therefore, we must seek a clearer answer to this question: How did all these problems become what they currently are in the Middle East?

Society in the Middle East is the stem cell of all societies. It draws strength from this quality. Stem cell theories are also valid for societies. The capitalist system of the American continental culture has shown an ability to expand into all cultures; from the Pacific and Australia to India, China, and Japan and from Africa to Russia and South Siberia. In a certain sense, it has won the war of cultures and civilizations. However, the system hasn't succeeded in conquering the Middle East, despite numerous attempts since the nineteenth century. This region is riddled with problems that perhaps even surpass those of the world wars, with elements that go beyond asymmetric warfare. The main reason for these difficulties is clearly the social fabric.

The monarchy and feudalism smashed by the French Revolution and the Czar's autocracy and feudalism that disintegrated in the face of the Russian Revolution were very similar; both waged a struggle against a superstructure that lacked structural depth. Even so, analyzing and dissolving *these* structures posed great difficulty. Furthermore, these revolutions played out at a superstructural level and ultimately could not escape being integrated into the capitalist system. The attempt to impose these models on societies in the Middle East and their superstructures aggravated rather than resolving problems. Therefore, there remains a need to understand well the nature of this clash of civilizations. More precisely, what is it that makes the Middle East civilization so obstinate, preventing potential solutions? Why have results been obtained through interventions against other known civilizations around the world, while similar efforts have not been successful in the Middle East?

The answer to this question lies in the reality of the Middle East being the main civilization. It is like the relationship of a mother to her children. A mother doesn't resemble her children; the children resemble their mother. Correspondingly, daughter civilizations cannot reshape the main civilization in their own image. Rather, *they* will resemble *the main civilization* in at least some respects. I want to once again use the metaphor of the stem cell. A stem cell contains the genetic potential for all types of cells, but not all the genes of the stem cell can be found in the differentiated cells. Undoubtedly, one must not push the parallels between social and biological phenomena too far, but this comparison can, nevertheless, be helpful in understanding various trends. It is clear that the civilization of the capitalist system needs to approach the Middle East civilization with greater depth and a better understanding of its particularities.

In attempting to analyze the Middle East civilization, it is particularly important to look at its structure of mentality. The birth of the three monotheist structures of mentality in this region, where they subsequently became firmly rooted, is a basic fact that must be addressed. As a result, there are a number of fundamental issues that the sociology of religion must resolve in this region, and this effort must include literature and the other arts if it is to be concrete.

Drawing a map of the region's mentality without identifying the values of Neolithic society, which are still influential in the region, would be gravely incomplete. On the other hand, denomination, tribe, and family structures as subunits of religions and people who have integrated into the ruling power remain a reality. The mentality patterns that capitalism has introduced are distorted by the reality of the Middle East and, thus, have only limited significance in the area. Looking at the origins of mentality patterns within the mythological world at the beginning of written history, or maybe even earlier, at the time of polytheism, and especially in the context of their relationship to Sumerian mythology, will contribute to a better understanding of the intertwined mentality patterns. In the contemporary Middle East, there is tremendous chaos, entwinement, deterioration, and indistinctness when it comes to what is said and done, concept and fact, fantasy and reality, religion and life, science and ideology, philosophy and religion, morality and law. Along with all of the contamination they have caused, almost all the layers of mentality ever known to humanity remain in the region, stacked up as piles of problems. Both old and the new language structures reflect a mentality that abounds with conservatism. There is a profound ignorance and narrow-mindedness about concepts that have arisen in recent centuries, such as "country," "homeland," "nation," and "a state with set borders." Elements of a modern mentality and medieval, even archaic, elements coexist in a dubious marriage. Therefore, without an assault on the mentality structures of the Middle East, the political, social, legal, and economic attacks on the physical structures that we are witnessing at present will not result in anything other than terror, massacres, and torture in all their official and unofficial dimensions of savagery, which is also, for the most part, essentially a mindset.

The power structures in the Middle East also differ significantly from those in other parts of the world. The phenomena of war and power are no less complex than are their mentality patterns. Although these are some of the oldest institutions in the region, there is a tremendous disconnection and a paradox that has arisen between war and power and social and economic life. These mutual relationships are open to all kinds of demagoguery and oppression, whether subtle or crude. Rationality has little significance in this context. As a phenomenon far from being understood and analyzed in sociology, and "social science," the ruling power and war seem to be effectively hidden within their religious, ethnic, economic, political, and class contexts. It is, however, not really possible to get a realistic picture of the Middle East without properly analyzing all aspects of power and war, from the abstract concept of "God" to the very concrete blow with a club.

Its social structuring institutions, particularly the family, are just as complex as power itself. Men and the women in the Middle East are so complex that they require a specific analysis. An analysis of the family, women, and the dominant male using generic sociological parameters will prove largely insufficient. Political, ideological, and moral reality is mirrored in men and women in their strictest and darkest aspects. The contradictions within the family institution are by no means less than those within the state institution. The family, however, has a meaning that goes beyond its role as a social institution; it is, so to speak, the "black hole" of all societies. If we take a closer look at women, we might well gain insight into the entire drama of humanity.

An analysis of both historical sociality and geosociality requires a firmly dialectical approach. Without analyzing each period of historical time and the different spatial contexts, it is not possible to understand either our present day or the overall civilization systems. In fact, the history that has not been written is even more important than written history, just as the story of the places never mentioned is more important than that of the places everybody talks about.

It is quite clear it wouldn't make much sense to look at the economic backwardness using the dry principles of economic theories without considering all these various social contexts. It is a general malady in social science to analyze the whole by dividing it into parts—like a cadaver. This has probably led to extremely erroneous results in studies of the Middle East civilization. Economics, is at the forefront of such studies. Economic analyses that fail to take into account the intertwined relationship of war and power and mentality and sociality will only lead to greater ignorance. It goes without saying that examining the Middle East with the analytical templates of Western civilization involves important theoretical and practical errors. The present chaos is partly a product of just such approaches.

No one any longer denies the chaos in the Middle East. It is one of the most emphasized issues of the day. Tragically, though, no one has attempted to carry out a meaningful analysis—neither those who claim to be the actual masters of the region nor those who seek to be the new masters. They are all frightened. A realistic analysis of the region would not only open a Pandora's Box but would also lead, in a way, to the landing of Noah's Ark on the new mountain of Cûdî.[3] A new generation of life, both in human and ecological terms, will only germinate at that point. Current life has an all-embracing pattern of lies and violence. The five-thousand-year-old social pores are clogged with the sediment of thousands of years of despotic and exploitative undertakings and the innumerable forms of prostitution—a formal institution stretching back to the Sumerian priest state. While these social pores cannot be pronounced entirely dead, they are, however, breathing lethargically far from vitality.

Alexander the Great collaborated with the Kurdish aristocracy, who had a distinct structure within the Persian Empire, thereby managing to strengthen the movement known as Hellenism. Will the contemporary Alexanders of our day, the US emperors, with their latest projects on the Middle East, be able to bring about developments reminiscent of Hellenism? Will they, the US administrators of their province Iraq, succeed in setting events in motion as Hellenism did in collaboration with the Kurdish aristocracy?

Even more important is whether, as at the dawn of history, Kurds can once again repeat their role by becoming the cradle of a new civilization. That is, will the Kurds be able to play a similar role in the transition to the age of democratic civilization in the Middle East?

The role the Kurdish tribes played in history was mostly the result of their interaction with the civilizations around them—whether externally influencing them or reacting against them. In their own area, civilizational development was limited. Instead they resisted invasions and occupations from the outside based on ethnicity—in the form of aşiret and tribe—to secure their existence, as well as engaging in the cooperation necessary to do so. The Kurds maintain the same qualities today.

On the other hand, it will not be easy to resist, safeguard existence, and develop cooperation based on old motifs in the face of global capitalism's new offensive. Although the traditional aristocratic collaborationist families may want to carry on with their established policy, the democratic people who have transcended ethnicity—as the "people of *serkeftin*"—can no longer be content with the old motifs nor can the people be controlled by one or another power.

It would be most fitting for social libertarians to regard the Kurdish people's inability to establish a classic state as an opportunity rather than a defeat. Are there any social freedom values and social libertarians that were able to be both state-oriented and please their people? Many peoples in Latin America, Africa, and Asia now have their own state. Has this helped them solve their problems? Is it not the case that their problems have, in fact, gotten worse?

The important thing is to unify and institutionalize a communal and democratic identity—which is also historically the basic attitude of the people—integrating contemporary science and technological possibilities. Today, democracy is as essential as bread, air, and water for the people of the Middle East. No option other than democracy will make people happy—everything else has already been tried at some point in history. The Kurds, who have a particular role among these people, will do themselves, their neighbors, and all of humanity a huge favor if they succeed in mobilizing their geography, historical time, and social characteristics, which have become highly strategic factors, to the advantage of democratic civilization in the Middle East.

Understanding the Middle East Correctly: What Is the Problem and How Did It Develop?

The Mentality of the Middle East

It's important to first address conceptual solutions before turning to institutional solutions. If we don't succeed in correctly defining the concepts operative within societies both historically and in their everyday lives, the clarity of our hypotheses will be extremely limited. If, for example, we don't carry out a sociological analysis of the concept of "Allah," how will we be able to properly define any historical period or society?

There is a reason why the European discussion of theology (theodicy) in terms of mentality largely unfolded as they were coming out of the feudalism of the Middle Ages. The intense discussions about *theos*, i.e., God, finally led to philosophy, and then to the natural science. The Europeans believed deeply in God; He was sacred to them. They decided to explore the meaning of this God whom they revered and thoroughly believed in. They had the courage to discuss ideas that risked shattering dogmas and introducing novelties. Theology formed the basis of the intellectual debate that led them out of the Middle Ages. Contemporary scientific and philosophical ideas at the time were closely linked to theology. What was important, however, was that conclusions were drawn on the basis of the ensuing discussion, which provided the basis for reason-based science and philosophy. Islamic theologians, however, failed to draw conclusions from these discussions, instead bringing thought to a standstill by sanctifying dogma. In the early twelfth century, the important Islamic scholar Imam Ghazali condemned philosophy, sharply limiting the possibility of *ijtihad* in the process,[4] causing it to disappear in the darkness of the Middle Ages. Even today, nobody dares to hold such a debate—or, perhaps more correctly, nobody is able to.

Furthermore, intellectual depth in societies in the Middle East dates back to the mythological age. The works of the Sumerian priests and writers, who were masterful mythmakers, were used by all three monotheistic religions as the basis for their improved versions. We know Abraham as the founder of monotheistic religion. However, he grew up in the kingdom of the Babylonian dynasty—under a certain Nimrod. Abraham's father is said to have been a watchman in the pantheon housing the statues of deities in the city of Urfa, where the memory of Abraham is still alive today. As result of his experience there, he underwent a transformation of mentality. If this is the case, how can we understand Abraham's religion if we know nothing about the pantheon of Nimrod?

The discourses of the most important theology professors on this subject do not go beyond fairy-tale-like narratives: Abraham broke the idols with an ax. This made Nimrod angry, and he asked who had broken the idol. Abraham responded that it was broken by the greatest idol of all. Nimrod queries as to how a lifeless idol could break something, and so goes the discussion. Without a sociological analysis of the Sumerian mythology that provides the basis for the pantheon of Nimrod, we cannot define Abraham's religious revolutionism. Without defining him, we will be unable to fully understand the religious revolutions of Moses, Jesus, and Mohammad. In spite of the numerous universities, theological faculties, *imam hatip* schools,[5] religious orders, and deity institutes in the Middle East, a sociological appraisal of theology is nowhere to be found, for if it existed the magic would evaporate. Its true nature would be revealed. It would become obvious that at the root of the idea of monotheism lies two facts: the expression of the unity of the forces of nature and the ascension of the hierarchical chief and the king within society. In other words, the dominant concept of "society" and, with it, the supreme expression of the dominant concept of "nature" was increasingly elaborated until the process finally arrived at Allah with his ninety-nine attributes. However, none of this is ever discussed, and although, at present, God has been blatantly politicized, even militarized by the likes of Hezbollah (Party of God), the deception of seeking his existence in heaven continues.

The institution of prophecy is also treated dogmatically by theology. It is turned into an abstract narrative, as if it has no connection to social development. But actually, the traditions of shamans and sheikhs, on the one hand, and of the vizier institution, as the chief executive under the authority of the emerging kingdom, on the other hand, are effective in its formation. Prophecy developed as a solution to the problems that occurred between the development of the state and the hierarchy. As such, this development is political in nature. It has both a widespread grassroots basis and an operational basis. Therefore, it plays a role in developments both in terms of wisdom and of political leadership. The important thing, however, is to determine where it fits into social reality, even if it is considered holy. If this were done, the historical personalities of some of the prophets might make more sense, and history too might be better illuminated. A dogmatic narration, however, leaves both aspects in the dark. In terms of holiness, many similar theological concepts also serve to obfuscate. This is particularly clear with the concepts of "heaven" and "hell." Their roots stretch back to Sumerian mythology, and their connection to the rise of class society is clear. The situation that the working classes found themselves in actually resembles hell—*Jahannam* literally means *the valley of Hinnom*, a place of filth and putrefaction[6]—while those who seized the surplus product for themselves lived in a virtual paradise.[7] We could adduce many more examples, but our goal is not to point out their ubiquity but to draw attention to the need to illuminate them through social science analysis.

The distinction between mythology and religion within the thought of the Middle East is still not discussed. Moreover, there is also no interpretation of mythology; it is simply dismissed as legend, even though for millennia this way of thinking engrossed the memories of the societies we still live in. This was the basic form of thought for thousands of years. As a poetic narrative of the symbolic expression of society's material life, mythology influenced all of the religions and literary forms that followed, all of which adopt concepts from mythology. To dismiss mythology as a bunch of made-up stories is to be deprived of the richest cultural resource. Without a meaningful appreciation of mythology as the mode of thinking of humanity's childhood era there can be no sound analysis of religion, literature, or the arts. Rather than denying mythology, we should revive it.

The question of when and in what form mythology served as a source for religion deserves a separate discussion. As I have mentioned, mythology is religionized when it becomes an absolute rule of belief. In this sense, becoming religionized is about accepting mythology as an irrefutable truth. Becoming religionized has a twofold value. First, it leads to the concept of "indisputable thought" in our reason, and this is how the idea of *lawfulness* develops. Divine law and the law of nature are increasingly integrated. Second, the thought of dialectic movement in nature and in society was circumvented before it was even born, which paved the way for idealist thinking. Thought broke away from facts to the utmost degree and underwent an uncontrolled development of its own. With that, the endless adventure of idealist thought began, driving social mentality away from the world of facts yet again. The development of religious thought gradually led to rigid dogmas in fundamental areas, such as law, politics, economy, morality, and the arts, becoming the law in the process. In fact, this made it extremely easy for the rising statist class to rule over society. To elevate each religious rule to the rank of a law was tantamount to solving the problems of legality and legitimacy with one stroke. The main reason for the exaltation of religion in antiquity and the Middle Ages was that it made ruling a whole lot easier.

Religion is a meticulously wrought ruling ideology. The ruling class has always been fully aware of the abstract character of religion, but the lower strata of society were made to believe that it was real. Much of the investment in religion—one only needs to think of all the temples and houses of worship—is closely linked to the state's ruling power, as are religious rituals. To disguise this, a ban on discussion was introduced, because any discussion would very soon have focused on two important issues: the rise of the kingdom and natural law. Both are very important issues. It would have made clear how the god-king and the sultan—the "shadow of god"—were glorified, and this would have rid society of a terrifying and punishing understanding of God. Furthermore, addressing nature would have left the door ajar to science. The principles that govern the world of scientific phenomena—from quantum physics to the physics of the cosmos—would have been uncovered. The superiority of Europe is the result of very intense theological analyses carried out as it emerged from the Middle Ages. Of course, this intellectual development cannot be attributed to the discussion of theology (theodicy) alone, but without it the door would not have been pushed open for forward-looking thought. Possibly the Renaissance would not have arisen so easily without the debates of the Dominican and Franciscan orders in twelfth, thirteenth, and fourteenth centuries.

In the Middle East, the ilmiye class closed itself off to discussions precisely during the Middle Ages.[8] They imposed a rigid dogmatism on society, casting debate itself as apostasy. This tendency, which had long been nurtured by the tradition of power, finally caused the Middle East civilization to lose its edge to the West for the first time. The fifteenth century is the century of the great separation. The different approaches taken to theology lie at the base of this increasingly profound split between the East and the West. In fact, from the ninth to the twelfth century, there had been a remarkable development in philosophical thought in the Islamic world, which the West had only adopted by translating key works.[9] There is no doubt that at that point the superiority in terms of thought was to be found in the Middle East. The Mu'tazilite theological school based itself on rationalism and declared war on dogmatism. Ibn Rushd (Averroes) was the greatest philosopher of the twelfth century. The leading Sufi philosophers, including Mansur al-Hallaj and Suhrawardī, defended their thinking at the cost of their lives. The mounting repression toward the end of the twelfth century shaped the character of the Middle East in a way that has lasted to this very day.

The role of religious dogmatism in weakening literature cannot be overestimated. Had literature remained connected to mythological sources it might have developed much further, but prohibitions against this caused it to shrivel. Prohibitions and accusations of "sin" robbed humanity of one of its richest resources. While Europe produced its first classics at this point,[10] in the East, literature was reduced to flattering the sultans and embellishing their biographies. The saddest aspect of all is that today Westerners are producing literature about the religious and mythological reality in the Middle East. The nature of literary writing is a serious question in and of itself.

The revolution in mentality and the resulting developments Europe experienced during the Renaissance, the Reformation, and the Enlightenment can still not be put on the agenda in the Middle East society. The eclectic transmissions of intellectual development do not come to mean to be the Renaissance, the Reformation, and the Enlightenment. One can, on the contrary, even speak of backsliding. Radical Islam does not stand for renewal but, rather, for the revival of conservatism. The concept of "political Islam" is entirely in line with the traditional misuse of religion by the ruling power. It is unlikely that the Middle East will be able embrace the path to intellectual development while skipping the spiritual and intellectual processes that the West went through. A transformation in mentality cannot be achieved by holding fast to religion, or even by pure scientism or with positivist philosophical approaches. For example, the denominational approach at the basis of the current backwardness of Russia and China, that is, real socialism, which is not based on the thought processes of the West, had a decisive impact.

A revolution in mentality is essential in order to overcome and restructure society's institutions, which have reached a dead end. But a revolution in mentality is not simply a matter of absorbing Western thought and conveying it wholesale. Even the limited attempts to do this are eclectic to the point of playing no role that goes beyond patching things up. Rote learning of Western thought won't make anyone creative; not only will it make them unproductive, it will also prevent any possible revolution in thought. There are numerous intellectuals who are rote learners of this type, but there are no genuine social scientists to be found. University pietism abounds and is roaming about—that we can call contemporary mullahs. Their sophistry even falls short of the sophistry of antiquity. Intellectuals, philosophers, and scientists who really put their heart into it are harder to find than the proverbial needle in a haystack. Moreover, there is no belief that there is any need to do so. In fact, Western ideology has been transferred in very deficient ways. Whether nationalism, liberalism, or socialism, these contemporary ideological forms have played a reactionary role in the mentality of the Middle East's intellectuals. It is pretty obvious from current practices that reality in the Middle East cannot be explained using these ideological templates, which only lead to even greater pollution.

If the revolution in mentality is to use Western forms, they must be adapted to reality in the Middle East. Without overcoming the background of meaning that all the fundamental historical and social structures are based upon through a full-fledged intellectual bombardment, a power of meaning upon which new structures can be based is not possible. Structures devoid of meaning have no social value or role. If you have not figured out your own social reality and clarified national, ethnic, and religious phenomena in thought, it will prove difficult to analyze the social and economic institutions based on politics alone. In Western thought, developments regarding issues like religion, nationalism, and racism required a great effort. The paradigm of a new life prevailed only as a result of the constructiveness of such challenging efforts.

The politicians and intellectuals of the Middle East act as if in their concrete case there is no need for the major struggle required for these efforts, and that they can succeed by mere rote learning and technical conveyance. The outcome is the inability to even dare to make one's own revolution in mentality, accompanied by intellectual dependency, helplessness, and a lack of solutions in the face of global capitalism. The chaos in the Middle East cannot be overcome in the people's favor without the region experiencing *its own* Renaissance, Reformation, and Enlightenment; it cannot rid itself of thousands of years of despotism with a two-hundred-year-old Western polish.

The State in the Middle East

The institutionalization of hierarchy and the state is a social phenomenon that is extremely difficult to analyze. It is possible to penetrate the culture of the Middle East by understanding the language of its political culture. With the rise of hierarchy and the state, the web established among class division, religiousness, dynasty, family, and aşiret relations literally placed the social system outside of time and space. The mythological and religious discourse, along with class and ethnic discourses, only serves to further muddle the true nature of things.

This region, which was the center for the Neolithic phase of primordial communal society, still experiences the culture of that time as its deepest social memory. Even in material terms, Neolithic structures are still widespread. The nature of the villages had scarcely changed until recently. Slaveholding and feudal social systems are also deeply rooted cultural values in the region. Layering Western culture onto this cultural sum would amount to applying a thin layer of varnish, nothing more. Therefore, it is highly misleading to just look at the varnish and develop a social analysis on that basis.

There is hardly any social pore that patriarchy, a synonym for hierarchy, has not permeated. It is quite possible that patriarchal traditions ruled society thousands of years before the rise of the state institution. It is also possible that patriarchy's power is not as all-encompassing and stifling anywhere in the world as it is in the Middle East. The influence of patriarchy on moral concepts, the personalities of men and women, the ethnic culture, and the understanding of family and honor is blatantly obvious. The cities, where one would expect a culture opposed would develop, bear the deep traces of the rural areas and, therefore, patriarchy. Hence, they are like islands in a sea of provinciality.

The state rose atop the patriarchal culture that had existed for millennia. Powerful patriarchal groups played a more essential role in its formation than classes did. The most prominent figure within these groups was the wise old man. As the elder with the most experience, the wise man was perhaps the earliest authority of all. It is likely that following the agricultural revolution, in which the wise mother played a major role, the wise and experienced elder who gradually developed took a further step forward in his social status, becoming the shaman, the sheikh, or the prophet. When classes subsequently formed in society and patriarchal institutions evolved into the state, the wise man, along with his allies, culminated in a dynasty and, based on that, a monarchy.

It is likely that the youth who were capable of carrying out an attack were turned into a military entourage, and the shaman became the priest, making a leap to a higher stage of authority in the process. While the priest worked to develop the ideological basis for this new authority, the military entourage slowly morphed into an army. This is the most realistic assumption about how the state emerged in this region. There is no evidence that the legions of slaves existed before this point. Slavery only developed after the state institution grew stronger. In the examples of Sumer and Egypt, we see the substantial influence of the priests and tribes very early on. Enslavement was far from easy, engendering a furious struggle. The habituation of society to slavery was the most important process in the culture of the Middle East and needs to be tracked and analyzed.

The great significance of mythology, the ideology of the Sumerian and Egyptian priests, was its role in the creation of the state. Just as the capitalism's struggle using ideologies such as nationalism and liberalism created capitalist state form, the power of the mythological discourse created the slavery form of antiquity. Had the mythological discourse not had a legitimizing influence on society, the great dynasties of the god-kings would probably never have emerged or, at least, would never have taken root so strongly or lasted so long.

Nimrod and the pharaoh are expressions that represent the institution of the god-kings in the culture of the Middle East. The god-king was a creation of the Middle East. He was more than a person; he was an institution, a culture. Compared to the god-king, all the other members of society were like ants carrying provisions. The difference between the god-king and the "rest of society" was pushed to the limit and manipulated in a way that effectively created two different species: the immortal god-kings and ordinary mortals. The mythological craftiness or skill was to take great care to ensure that those who were slowly transforming themselves into the state were not seen as mere human beings. I believe that the continuity of the state as an institution that secured the life of the rulers was decisive in the emergence of the attribute of "immortality." The connection between the concept of "immortality" in the idea of God and "continuity" in the state institution seems perfectly clear. Before the emergence of the state, the gods also died. The portrayal of the Neolithic gods included designated days each year that marked their births and deaths. Celebrations and mourning ceremonies were a form of worship based on widespread myths and rituals. Once the state institution became permanent—people were temporary, the state permanent—the gods were made immortal. Here, the way in which the lineages and dynasties of the god-kings gained privilege is also important. The fact that they were no longer considered human beings and were now regarded as immortal conferred upon them a certain supernatural greatness and distinction. When the class making up a state was deified and turned into an immortal lineage in this way, it fell upon all the other human beings—everyone else in society—to act as their servants.

This servitude is significantly different from the type of dependence seen later in Greek and Roman slavery, in a way that is similar to the difference between devotion to the master and devotion to God. In divine devotion there is a unity of strong belief and worship. In the priestly tradition, loyalty to the state was framed as loyalty to the god-king with such great genius that the slaves and the army of those rendered servants were turned into ants and reduced to the point that their sole purpose was to carry heavy loads. In Sumerian mythology, humans were presented as having been created from the excrement of the gods, although later there was a slight improvement and they were shown to have been created from earth or mud. Even today, the derogatory way in which humans were created by the gods continues to reverberate and be refined. The woman was too forgotten to be created from God. The honor bestowed on her was being created from the rib of a man.

The particular significance of these narratives is that they reflect the great ideological system of the time when the state class initially emerged. The division among human beings ran so deep that for generations the overwhelming majority of society not only approved of the divinity of the state class but even worshiped this class and perceived working hard as God's command. The prevalent ideology was really deeply rooted. In this way, an institutional trait based on tyranny and lies was transformed into metaphysics, an abstract fetish—a thing to idolize—which is most supreme, worshiped and for which every effort is made.

The basic features of this emerging civilization rippled out from the Middle East to the rest of the world. In the process, it specifically suppressed the very rich and valuable Neolithic elements of the region's culture, while spreading a mythological creation that would provide the basis for the most reactionary thoughts and beliefs through the same channels to a large swathe of the developed societies, especially to the societies in the region. This process had such a powerful and far-reaching influence that it continues to be felt in the way Hegel, the last important representative of idealist philosophy, went as far as to describe the state as the embodiment of God. Current discourses that continue to treat the state as eternal, elevated, and sacred also have their origin in this ancient system of servitude.

An important shift accompanied the transition from state ideology with its roots in mythology to the state based on the ideology of monotheistic religions. The main contradiction—highly symbolic—between

Christianity and the Roman Empire was Christianity's conviction that the emperor couldn't be a god and that Jesus, as the Messiah, should be accepted as the Son of God. This discourse is, of course, essentially true of all monotheistic religions. The prophetic tradition emerged from the rejection of the god-kings and the acceptance of the prophets as the messengers of God. As such, this tradition represented a radical break with the ideology of the god-king. When we compare the divine worldview that dominated social mentality in the world of antiquity with that of the Middle Ages, we can see that a revolution in social mentality took place. In concrete terms, it was a flight from the cults of Nimrod and the pharaoh, i.e., a flight from their state. In other words, it was an exodus, or a hijra.

We see this tendency in the practice of many prophets, from Abraham through Moses to Jesus and then Mohammad. These movements, whose political aspect was as clear as their social aspect, should be seen as serious revolutions in their respective periods. Their main ideological message was: "Humans can't be gods; they can, at best, be messengers of God." In concrete terms, they helped to weaken the god-kings and to impose a compromise on at least part of society. In short, they wanted to limit the unlimited despotism of those who regarded themselves as god-kings.

A despot who insisted he was a god-king would not compromise, let alone take any note of the voices of his subjects. The story of the prophet Job is interesting and instructive in this regard. Here, if we dig deeply into the story of Job in the Holy Scripture, the essence of what it intends to express is: Job had lost everything he once possessed and lay in a cave, or a prison; his body was eaten up by maggots, and, he was in great pain and moaning. For the god-king, i.e., the Nimrod in Urfa, it was unthinkable that his subjects express pain. A subject was obliged to serve the god-king in silence and show no pain. Simply showing pain was an offense. The prophet Job's major achievement was inducing the god-king—i.e., the state—to recognize his pain. For the first time, a god-king understood that one of his subjects was suffering pain. This new "understanding" amounted to a revolution. The figure of Job symbolized the suffering and the poverty of the people.

When the graves of Sumerian and Egyptian god-kings were opened, archeologists found the remains of as many as a couple of hundred human beings, most of them women. Quite obviously, when the king died, his entourage was buried alive with him. In the understanding of the time, a king's entourage did not have any life independent of him. Just as his arms and legs were part of him and died with him, his entourage was regarded as inseparable from his body and also had to die with him. In absolutist and totalitarian regimes, the subjects are also considered to be parts of the body of the monarch or the sovereign—like the flesh and nails or, more precisely, like bodily hair. They are denied any independent life. Though it might take milder forms, this is the "golden rule" that all states expect their subjects to embrace. The understanding of god-kingdom-servant has remained pretty much the same to this very day. Only in Western civilization has it undergone a limited amount of change.

Job's revolution was the expression of a time when the people engaged in a relatively weak revolt by expressing their suffering. This is the basis of Job's holiness, and the significance should not be underestimated. Job's revolution may have been the first time in history that people tentatively objected to the state. Even though we don't know whether or not the state backed down, the cult of the prophets grew exponentially, and around 1000 BCE, David and Solomon established their first known state. The founding of a state by David is very interesting. Ironically, when he founded the state, he was in the position of today's Palestinians. He established his own principality by fighting against the local principalities. In a process that has certain parallels with our time, God and the king were clearly separated. The two were now separate entities. Even though the king is called the "shadow of God," God is actually an abstract figure of the newly rising kingdom: its conceptual expression.

The notion of "zillulah," "shadow of Allah,"[11] which is found in monotheist religions, is notable because it marks a change in the form of state power. Even so, we must be very careful, because the essence of power remained unchanged. A kingdom that was elevated to heavenly heights could still issue dangerous orders from above. An invisible figure that remained totally hidden from the sight of his subjects could make them do whatever he wanted in more insidious and crafty ways. By declaring himself answerable only to God, the "shadow of God," the sultan, could behave even more irresponsibly. Particularly remarkable was the growing relationship between the ascension of God and the abstract institutionalization of the state. As the state developed into an increasingly abstract institutional entity—independent of any individual—the concept of "God" as its ideological reflection also became increasingly abstract.

With Mohammad, this understanding of God in the tradition of Abraham and Moses turned into the theoretical core proposition that superseded almost everything else in the Koran. Mohammad's greatest contribution to the idea of God was to equip God with ninety-nine attributes, creating a new level of sophistication: God is the only one, the indivisible one, the invisible one, the all-seeing one, the one with infinite reach, the one who is both merciful and punitive, the one who tolerates absolutely no other god, and so on. Here, we encounter a higher level of abstraction regarding the state institution. The degree of institutionalization corresponds to the degree of abstract divinity. Before Jesus and Mohammad, prophets tended to simply represent opposition to slave society, creating their own limited political systems that more or less resembled tribal governments or short-lived mini-states. The last two prophets, however, laid the groundwork for the emergence of the feudal state. Better put, their great struggles were placed at the foundation of the feudal state institution as part of a broader compromise, one that did not quite suit their purpose. The monotheist religions corresponded to the expansion of the middle-class reality. While the religions that were centered on god-kings suited the emergence of patriarchal and the slave states, polytheism and personal deities had coincided with the circumstances of the Neolithic Age and the living conditions of the lower classes.

We will understand the relationship between theology and society and politics better if we keep in mind that "divinity" was the collective, abstract expression of a developing social identity and its will. Although in the Middle Ages the state in the Middle East also included the middle class, no real change in its despotic character was observed. The sultan—a new title for the king—was the personal representative of power and was answerable to no one but God. The ilmiye class, the religious scholars, who interpreted God's commandments were nothing more than a group of service personnel. They represented nothing but the will of the sultan. The state's upper society had succeeded in gaining overwhelming sovereignty over society in terms of morality and mindset. Even though the state's control of the city was tighter than elsewhere, there was still room for it to become more widespread in rural areas. The medieval state was at its strongest under both Islam and Christianity. By the sixth and seventh centuries, the Sasanian and Byzantine Empires, the degenerate and last forms of slavery during antiquity, began to make the transition to feudalism. The Islamic state is perhaps one of the leading states to have emerged and made the transition to feudalism in its most radical and harsh form. This could be considered as a new stage in the culture of the Middle East. The Arab-Islamic state was strongest under the Umayyads, the Abbasids, and the Seljuk Turks but was later substantially weakened by the attacks of the Mongols from the East and the crusaders from the West. The collapse of the Ayyubid dynasty around 1250 CE ushered in a period of stagnation. It seems most reasonable to regard the Ottoman Empire as a half-Islamic and half-Byzantine state. The feudal characteristics of both states were integrated into the Ottoman Empire. Both of these states had implemented the strictest form of despotism, and both had tried very hard to prevent the decline of feudal society. The Ottoman Empire, a fresh, still vigorous power, entered into a series of broad compromises that prolonged its rule as the last Middle East state to the greatest degree possible.

The feudal states with similar processes, as in China, India, and Europe, for example, are equally alien to democracy. The common maxim of the people was: "The greatest bliss in this world is found living at a great remove from the state." Despite all the conciliatory efforts of religion, the state and society remained alien to each other. Although with great difficulty, ethnic groups and heretical—against formality—denominations were able to continue to exist in the mountains and deserts and in monasteries and dergah. These communities were the last shelters of the communal and democratic stance. Rebelling against the state was integral to these societies, and resistance became a way of life.

While attempting to define the state in the civilization in the Middle East, our actual goal is to shed light on today. Even though the state's existence in Western civilization is rooted in the Middle East, it eventually went its own way. This separation, which began with states in Athens and Sparta, was carried, via Hellenism, to Rome. Even though the claim of being a god-king continued during Rome's imperial era, albeit in a substantially muted form, the separation was completed with Constantine's acceptance of Christianity. The idea of a Kingdom of God that will last a thousand years is the continuation of an old apocalyptic myth from the Middle East.[12] Compared to its form in the Middle East, the state in Rome was worldlier. There was no augmenting of the state's sacredness. When the Roman Empire collapsed under the crushing blows of the tribal migration, the state lost its remaining reverence even more. The Germanic tribes, which were less acquainted with the state, played an important role in revealing the worldly face of the state. Though they later tried to reanimate the state they inherited from the Roman Empire as the "Holy Roman Empire of the German nation," the city-states and kingdoms became completely devoid of their divine armor. Once a clearer understanding of the nature of the state emerged, peoples and nations turned to political structures with democratic and national traits. The English, American, and French Revolutions extended the secular character of the state even further. Imposing constraints through constitutions buried the despotic state in the depths of history.

In the Middle East, however, there have been no such developments in the state tradition; on the contrary, the state has become increasingly conservative and reactionary. The Ottoman and the Iranian states were exclusively occupied with the attempt to prolong their existence a little longer by carrying out a defensive struggle against the West. While the state in the Middle East was falling apart, the colonialism of the Western state was far from firmly established. As a result, the nineteenth and the twentieth centuries represented a period of crisis for the Middle East. The political formations during these centuries, which can be characterized as semi-colonial and neocolonial, had some aspects not found elsewhere in the world.

Our short historical reflection reveals these differences. The relationship between state and society is particularly resistant to change, which means there are no quick escape routes from the crisis. There are neither the conditions for a rapid absorption of capitalist state forms nor for a rapid disintegration of the region's own traditions. The social traditions lack the necessary creative dynamic to respond to either of those things, or, to be more precise, the power of tradition cannot easily recover since it has been in a consistent nose-dive within its social base since the Neolithic Age. Moreover, the collaborationist upper-class attempts fail to resonate in society and are insufficient for effectively analyzing society. Neither the American way nor the Pacific way represented by, say, Japan are viable options for making the leap to Western-style development.

The Islamic molds are not the only obstacles, but the values of civilization as a whole remain resilient. There is a prevalent hodgepodge constituted of the values of Neolithic society and the values of Sumerian and Egyptian slavery, combined with Islamic values and the rich values of ethnic groups. Civilization in the Middle East does not easily accept a foreign scion to enable transformation and can be compared to an aged tree that cannot endure being grafted. To make way for the new, one must either uproot the tree completely or have access to a suitable scion. But neither of these options are available. The first attempt at grafting was undertaken around 1900 by the Young Turks, and later by Turkey under

Kemalism. Just as real socialism did not work, over the course of more than eighty years, the Western scion also failed to take root, even though it was heavily fertilized with nationalism. In Iran and Afghanistan, the monarchies were swept away when they tried to put on a modernist face. For its part, Arab nationalism is in mortal agony. The situation in Iraq proves how difficult it is to even bury it. Much the same is true of Israel's Zionist nationalism, turning the Israel-Palestine question into complete savagery. Radical Islam and a renewed turn toward Islam are nothing but suicidal, a fluttering triggered by hopelessness in the face of the far-reaching global offensive of capitalism. Radical Islam has no new potential to offer and can provide no solution.

A brief historical summary of the main concepts shows that the phenomenon of the state underlies all the problems in the Middle East. Western civilization has carried out major struggles to unlock the mystery of the state, an institution that originated in the Middle East. Among other things, the Renaissance lifted the ideological veil with which the state had covered itself, and with the revolution in mentality shattered the mythological and religious armor. It allowed for reality to be seen more baldly. The Reformation shattered the immunity and integrity of the same state's god-state ideology, as well as the state's bureaucracy, which was defended by the church. It brought an end to the rule of fear over society, which allowed everyone to freely define their beliefs. In the Middle East quite the opposite occurred; opposing currents, the Mu'tazilites among others, were eliminated. In the West, the collapse of religious reign accelerated freedom of thought and belief. The Enlightenment amplified this development and carried it to the masses. In objective terms, the Renaissance, the Reformation, and the Enlightenment shattered the state's armor of immunity and paved the way for society's democratic power. The English, American, and French Revolutions smashed the classic state, which led to the state's ideological and bureaucratic renewal. The state was constrained by constitutions and human rights and advanced the initiative of social forces, leading to significant civilizational developments during the nineteenth and twentieth centuries.

In the Middle East, the exact opposite took place during these centuries. The forces that organized themselves as the usurping warrior ruling power clique abused the state's need to provide for the general security and common good of "society" right from the beginning and made itself completely dominant using gruesome means. The state became completely despotic and developed into a parasite sucking the blood of society. The period after the fifteenth century is the tragic story of this process. While the West saw an evolution from the Magna Carta to modern constitutions, the Middle East and the East overall developed the most varied forms of despotism. The popular saying "there are many intrigues among the Ottomans" has its origins in that time, and the saying "the greatest bliss in this world is found living at a great remove from the state" reflects this fact. Society in the Middle East is like a tightly bound quarry in the hands of the state. Those who show even the slightest sign of emancipation are immediately cut down to size. Nor is there any constraining of the state with legal and constitutional means; on the contrary, the state has, in fact, become increasingly reactionary and protects its own order ever more vigorously.

In the twentieth century, when the state in the Middle East cringed and became increasingly conservative, both internally against society and externally against the West, it covered itself with the twentieth century nationalist cloak, which only worsened the problems. With state support and by way of nationalism and limited reforms, a small minority modernized, but the bigotry and the backwardness within society in general created a mentality that was unhealthy, simplistic, absurd, and, one might say, from another time and place. While traditionalism lost all its sacredness, modernity only formed a layer of unwitting objective agents around the state. The state in the Middle East was never completely dissolved but, rather, responded in the expected way, given its character of being an agent institution. The West had no desire to destroy it, because it considered the situation sufficient for its short-term interests. For two hundred years, the West sustained the Ottoman and Iranian monarchies, which would have collapsed if left on their own, by finding new ways to maintain the balance of forces. The "comprador capitalism" developed by the capitalist system worldwide,[13] which had become dominant in the West, provided an ideal economic base for this unwitting agency. The many problems of society were not even acknowledged, let alone addressed. Thus, it was like a contemporary version of the god-king state. The technical and military support received from the West functioned as a lifejacket for the state in the Middle East, allowing it to easily sustain itself against its own society. As long as it had its masters behind it, it was not difficult for the warrior ruling power clique to prolong its life. And the more this state was polished by the capitalist system's auxiliary tools or denominations—real socialism, social democracy, and national liberation movements—the more secure it could consider itself.

This so-called reform process lost one base after another in the face of the general crisis and chaos of capitalist imperialist globalization, which accelerated with the dissolution of real socialism in the 1990s. The empire of chaos under the leadership of the US cannot go on with these structures. That would be contrary to the logic of the system. For the system, profit and security are the decisive factors, and in this new situation the state in the Middle East puts both factors at risk. This state is now synonymous with wasteful expenses and insecurity. Its detachment from the masses elevated this wastefulness and insecurity to unbearable dimensions. With this polished patchwork of despotism, it is very difficult to respond to the demands of people who are grappling with the problems of global capitalism from above and the problems from below that have been accumulating since the Neolithic Age.

The Family in the Middle East

The problem of social mentality and behavior shaped around the family and the woman has become at least as aggravated as the state problem. Like heaven and hell, the state above and the family below form a dialectical whole. While the state realizes its micromodel in the family, the growing family demands envisage its macromodel as the state. Each family finds its ideal solution in becoming a state. The reflection of the state despot in the family is the "head of the family," the man, as the "little despot." Just as the great despot called the "state" tries to bring order to the world in an effective, authoritative, and arbitrary manner, the junior chief, the little despot, also exercises the same absolute order over a few women and children.

If we failed to analyze the family as the micromodel of the state in the civilization in the Middle East, our social analysis would be flawed. In today's society in the Middle East, if the women's question has become at least as grave as the question of the state, this is because, as in the case of the state, there is a long and complex history of women's slavery. Without indicating where this Bermuda Triangle is on the map, the woman-family-man relationship will suck down all of the ships carrying a social solution that may pass by. The Bermuda Triangle in the social ocean is the family—the microstate in the Middle East. As hierarchy and the state rise, they cannot help but reflect their projections in the family institution, because hierarchy and a state that does not echo in the family will not survive for very long. In the civilization on the Middle East, this dialectical dilemma is meticulously weaved and cannot be neglected.

It is necessary to formulate a brief history of women's slavery, since there will be great flaws in understanding the family and men, and, thus, from another point of view, the state and society, without treating women as the oldest captive sex, lineage, and class and subjecting them at least to a limited sociological analysis. As I have tried to present a definition of the woman in the previous chapter, I won't repeat it here. However, we should never neglect to say that when women take part in sociality considering them as a biologically deficient and defective sex is entirely ideological and is "a devise of the dominant male mentality." On the contrary, we should never ignore that it is a scientifically proven fact that women are more capable biological and social beings.

The center of the domestic mother culture is the Middle East. Current knowledge suggests that this culture began to develop around 15000 BCE. The flora and fauna of the inner foothills of the Taurus and Zagros mountain range region offered the basic material conditions necessary for domestication. The fact that the climate and the soil structure were suitable for growing wheat and related plants, as well as for breeding small livestock, such as sheep and goats, was key.

Women bearing and raising children can best be realized in sedentary conditions. When this need is combined with a favorable climate and the presence of suitable plants and animals, the basic conditions for domestication arise. Foraging ability and the many plants and fruits met food needs, while the domestication of mountain sheep and goats for wool, milk, and meat further satisfied people's needs.

Trial and error showed that growing plants and trees in fields multiplies the yield. Keeping animals instead of immediately slaughtering them yielded milk products and wool that came in handy in periods of emergency. Thus, the mother-woman had substantial experience both in agriculture and livestock breeding that allowed her to develop the domestic order with the children she raised. Coming out of the caves, growing food, and raising livestock at a fixed location, as well as setting up house, may appear to be a small step, but for humanity it was as big an event as the moon landing.

From constructing huts, it was only a small step to founding villages. In many regions in present day Kurdistan, numerous unique testimonials to this culture, whose history reaches back to the twelfth millennium BCE, can still be found. Examples include Çayönü near Ergani/Diyarbakır, Çemê

Xalan near Batman, Nevalı Çori and Göbekli Tepe, near Urfa, the caves in the region Hakkâri, and archeological sites in the Bradost region. These are the oldest examples of sedentary culture that have been found anywhere in the world. The primary evidence of the intensity of domestic mother culture is that practically all figures and statuettes found are female. Another example is the role of the feminine prefixes in the languages of the region. That, until this day, the domestic mother culture remains an area of mastery for women confirms this fact.

Sumerian sources demonstrate that this culture was influential when the Sumerians founded their first cities and remained strong thereafter. The mythological motif around Inanna, the goddess of Uruk, is highly instructive. Her resistance, especially against men's ascendance to domination, surpasses even the best of feminist movements of our time. In the struggle against the god Enki—the figure representing the rising patriarchy among the Sumerians—she vehemently defended women's civilization. In poetic language, she expounded the view that the 104 *me*, the achievements and concepts of the civilization of that time, belonged to her, and that Enki had deceitfully stolen them and had to return them. This mythological narrative, which can be traced back to 3000 BCE, shows in a spectacular way the extent of women's role in Sumerian civilization. Furthermore, the origin of Inanna is connected to Ninhursag, the ancient mother-goddess. *Nin* means *goddess*, *kur*, *mountain*, and *sag*, *region*. Ninhursag is, thus, the goddess of the mountain region. Given that for the Sumerians in Lower Mesopotamia, *mountain* is synonymous with the mountain ranges and foothills of the Zagros, we can say that goddess culture descended from the mountainous area.

At the time of the Sumerians, who represented the global center of civilization from 4000 to 2000 BCE, the woman-mother culture was still influential. It had equal weight with that of the man. This is reflected in all of the mythological documents of the time. Goddess temples were widespread. A culture of shaming has not yet been developed around the woman. Sexuality in particular was described as a divine act, and, far from women being shamed, the literary expression finds no parallel even in the best erotic stories. Every act and all behavior connected with sexuality finds meaning as something that makes life valuable and beautiful. Female sexuality was presented as something beautiful and worthy of extraordinary respect. There was, at that point, none of the shaming of women that would be seen later, after the great counterrevolution in the way of life that was to come. The female body was constantly praised. Even the sacred wedding ceremony, although distorted—being turned into the man's act of disfigurement—can be traced back to that period. The epics of Memê Alan, of Mem and Zîn, and of Derweşê Evdî, which are still recited in Kurdistan today, reflect the strong position of women in many ways.[14] It is, therefore, realistic to assume that their origins stretch back to the fifth millennium BCE.

In the Inanna mythological motif, both the shepherd and the farmer are represented as her companions. The shepherd Dumuzi—the origin of all male ascension—and the farmer Enkimdu compete in their respect for and loyalty to Inanna.[15] There is nothing they would not do to become the first among her companions. Inanna is still in the leading position. The male—as the farmer and the shepherd—is far from dominant.

In another famous Sumerian epic, the Babylonian creation epic Enuma Elish, we see that the tide has turned. The struggle between the god Marduk, who represents the male who has grown extraordinarily powerful, and Tiamat, the considerably weakened mother, is extremely instructive. In the epic, we find a horrible defamation and shaming culture being instilled against the woman-mother and against the goddess-mother. All the mythological molds are mobilized to represent the woman as without virtue, useless, harmful, and horrible. Patriarchal society had become so powerful that it could render its rule eternal in the epics. Everything about the man was glorified and presented as heroic; while everything about the woman was denigrated, shamed, and declared worthless. This culture, a major change to the detriment of women's social status, became widespread since around 2000 BCE.

This sexual rupture would arguably lead to the greatest change in social life in history. This first change in the culture of the Middle East in relation to women could be called *the first great sexual rupture* counterrevolution. We call it a *counter*revolution, because it did not make any positive contribution to the development of society. On the contrary, it led to an impoverishment of life, by introducing the rigid domination of patriarchal society and excluding women. This gave rise to a monophonic male society, rather than a society that once talked with two voices. This rupture in the civilization in the Middle East was perhaps the first step on the road to its decline. The consequences of this rupture have grown even gloomier with each passing period. The transition was made to a one-dimensional and extremely masculine social culture. While the emotional intelligence of the woman that once worked wonders and was extremely humane and animated was being lost, the cursed—although they would argue the opposite—analytical intelligence of a cruel culture that has surrendered to dogmatism, detached itself from nature, regarded war as the highest virtue, enjoyed spilling streams of human blood, and arrogated to itself the right to treat women and enslaved men arbitrarily emerged. Of course, advocates of this kind of intelligence present it very differently. This sort of intelligence, or thinking, has a structure that is the opposite of the egalitarian woman's intelligence, which is focused on animate nature and humane production.

With the rise of the dominant male structure within society, a serious standstill in creativity was experienced. While there were thousands of inventions and discoveries made from the seventh to the fifth millennium BCE—the period of the mother-woman—after the third millennium, we encounter only a few inventions worth mentioning. In addition, a structure has emerged in which the warrior ruling power culture is widespread and the conqueror—i.e., the profession of the kings—is held in the highest esteem, with conquest becoming the main goal of states. Essentially, the exclusion of women went hand in hand with a growing appreciation of authorities based on conquest, the warrior, and the male. With the state institution attaining its meaning entirely as the invention of men, wars for plunder and booty became something like a mode of production. Women's social effectiveness based on production was replaced by men's social effectiveness based on war and pillaging. Women's captivity and the culture of warrior society are very closely connected. War doesn't produce. War extorts and plunders. Even though the role of force can under some specific conditions be decisive to social development—clearing the way for freedom or resisting occupation, invasion, and colonialism—it is for the most part destructive and negative. Furthermore, wars foster a culture of violence that is internalized by society. The sword of war between states, like the man's hand in the family, is a symbol of domination. Both lower and the upper society face the threat of this sword and are in the grasp of this hand. The culture of oppression is constantly praised. The greatest social figures are proud of the blood of the innocents that they have spilled, seeing it as an expression of virtue. The kings of Babylon and Assur in particular considered it a great honor and glory to erect mountains of human skulls or to build castle ramparts with them. The still widespread culture of social violence and state terror has its roots in this culture.

The culture of the *second great sexual rupture* against women developed during the time of the monotheistic religions, with the culture of the rupture that occurred during the mythological era simply becoming the law, this time as God's command. Practices targeting women since then have been linked to God's sacred command. The relationship between Abraham, Sarah, and Hagar shows how the new religion affirmed male supremacy. Patriarchy was well-established, the institution of concubinage had been formed, and polygamy was approved. The difficult relationship between Moses and his sister Miriam shows that women had also lost their share of inheritance. Moses's society is a true male society; women are not granted a single responsibility. This is the source of the dispute with Miriam. The saying "a woman should not interfere in men's business while her hands are in dough" probably stems from that period.

Sometime around 1000 BCE, in the Hebrew kingdom of David and Solomon, the transition was made to an extensive harem culture. Women were given away as gifts, and a new era in which the woman has no say whatsoever began. She is completely silenced. Women as property were no different than any other property. In the new religious state, this situation was also reflected in the family. It is impossible to talk about any role for women under this double cultural domination, i.e., the domination of the religious state culture and of the patriarchal culture. The best woman was the one who complied most with her man and with patriarchy. Religion was also used to cast aspersion on women. As Eve, she is, first and foremost, the original sinful woman, having seduced Adam and caused his expulsion from paradise. Lilith, who refused to bow down to the God of Adam—the symbol of patriarchy—became Satan's companion—the human figure who refused to fall to his knees before Adam and who refused to become a servant. Mythological aspersions became templates for religious aspersions. The Sumerian story of a woman created from the rib of a man made its way into the Holy Scripture, and there isn't a single woman among the thousands of prophets. Women's sexuality is regarded as a great sin, and constant aspersion and denigration are turned into a moral principle. The woman, who had a magnificent place in Sumerian and Egyptian societies, was now a sinful, seductive, and shameful object.

Let's move on to the time of Jesus. Even though the Mary that we encounter here is perceived to be the Mother of God the Son, she has no divinity of her own. The goddess title of the mother-goddess is replaced by a very quiet and weeping mother, and her decline continues. Becoming pregnant by the breath of God—the man who dominates the woman—is an enormously contradictory concept.

The Trinity of the Father, the Son, and the Holy Spirit represents a synthesis of polytheism and monotheism. At the time, the Gnostics, who acknowledged God, and the pagans, who worshiped idols, were widespread and in a close relationship with Christianity. There was an intense conflict between them and the strict Hebrew monotheism. As a compromise among these three tendencies, a religion with a triple God emerged. This considerably reduces the number of gods. In Mohammad's time, there was also a trio of gods, or, rather, goddesses.[16] It is interesting that even though she should logically also be a goddess, Mary merely appears as an instrument of the Holy Spirit. This phenomenon demonstrates that divinity had by this point become masculinized. In Sumer and Egypt, gods and goddesses had existed in almost equal numbers. Even in the Babylonian period, the voice of the mother-goddess remained strong.

With Jesus and Mary, the role that befalls the woman is to be the weeping and composed woman and mother. She will never again talk about divinity. In her home, she will take particularly good care of her male children, who have become more valuable as "god-sons." She has no social role other than being a good housewife. The public space is completely closed to women. The female saints in Christianity were based on the practice of female virgins, women who went into seclusion to rid themselves of their great sins. It could be that this had a positive side, albeit a very limited one. Sainthood for women at the very least meant liberation from sexual conceptions and reproach. There were strong material and immaterial reasons to prefer this to living the hell at home. There is no doubt that this is a historically significant tradition. This, in a way, can even be characterized as the original destitute women's party. Albeit faintly, it represents the revival of the temple culture of the goddess in the form of the convent culture of the woman. This form of sainthood has an important place in the history of European civilization.

Monogamy was also substantially inspired by the way of life of these holy women. Even though these women lived in very difficult conditions and regarded their own sexuality as a source of danger, as was the case with their virginity, we can still say that this practice contributed to the improvement of the status of women. The downside, however, was that women, in reaction against Catholic marriage—against never being able to divorce—were turned into sexual commodities. This, of course, was due to rising capitalism.

Even though the new status that the woman gained with Mohammad and Islam was to some degree positive when compared to the patriarchal nature of desert tribal culture, it was essentially based on Hebrew culture. The status of women, which was already profoundly shaped by David and Solomon, was the one adopted by Mohammad. In addition, marrying several women for political purposes and living with a great number of concubines was considered normal. While the number of wives was limited to four, this had essentially also been the case in pre-Islamic culture. That the understanding "the woman is your arable land, you can cultivate it as you wish" treats woman as a property is a given. Mohammad's concept of "love" was also quite interesting. The fact that, at fifty years old, he falls in love with the nine-year-old Aisha shows the nature of his interest. On the other hand, his frequent eulogies for his first wife Khadija testify to the significance that he assigned to women. In general, it could be said that he showed some awareness of the situation of women. However, his decision to leave untouched the harem and concubinage as institutions would play out extremely negatively when the state layer later entered the picture.

When Aisha intervened in the power struggle between the caliphs after the death of Mohammad, she was defeated. She learned the hard way about a woman's actual value and cried out: "My God, I'd rather you brought me into this world as a stone and not as a woman!" The fact that there is no place for women within the ruling power had already been made abundantly clear in the dispute between Moses and Miriam. And in the medieval feudal Middle East there was no positive development in the status of women—and these historical molds still prevail.

The symbolic love affair between Layla and Majnun does not end well. There is no place for love in a feudal society. Women went through their most characterless period within the family that remained when faced with the challenges of the state and patriarchy. They were absolute prisoners to the desires of those in power and played a purely instrumental role in strengthening their power. In general, they were entirely isolated from society. While, in the remaining nomadic communities, the traces of the primordial communal order were still imbued with respect for women, the most profound female slavery is experienced by women in the city.

It became increasingly difficult to define a woman's place within an order based on domination and property. Today, women—as the evidence of an implementation of thousands of years—is in a state of total wreckage. Even the seductive effect of the capitalist system is far from being fully reflected. Women remain the principal element at the heart of the backwardness within society in the Middle East. Men in the Middle East, who have been defeated on every front, take out the consequences of their defeat on women, and the more men are humiliated in the outside world, the more they take it out on women, whether intentionally or spontaneously. Men, full of anger because they are unable to defend their society and can't find a way out of the trap they're in, turn their rage into fits of violence against women and children in the family. The phenomenon of "honor killing" is, in fact, the act of a man who allows his honor to be trampled everywhere in the social sphere to dispel his anger by targeting the woman. He thinks that with a symbolic but extremely empty and crude display he has restored his honor—in a way he is engaging in a sort of psychotherapy. A lost history and a lost social cause underlie the problem. One of the fundamental problems is to explain to this "man" that he will never shed the stain on his honor until he confronts its historical social cause and does his part. It is absolutely necessary to teach him that true honor is not found in a woman's virginity but by procuring historical and social virginity, and making sure that it is implemented as such.[17]

I hope that these brief historical observations have contributed to clarifying the fact that the problems of today's family in the Middle East are as important as the problems with the state. These problems are intensified by pressure from both sides. The reverberations of the historical legacy of patriarchal and statist society and the modern molds emanating from Western civilization have not led to a synthesis but have created a Gordian knot. The blockage within the state is paralleled by an even greater impasse within the family. Relationships with several wives and the many children that result from this make the family economically unsustainable. Adolescents can't find work, further rendering the family dysfunctional. The family tuned to the economy and the state finds itself at an impasse where it can no longer function with either as it once did. The current family in the Middle East resembles neither the Western family nor the Eastern family. The result is the erosion of the family. Compared to the more rapidly dissolving social bonds, the family manages to maintain its strength, because it is the only social refuge. The family should not be underestimated, and our criticism of the family is not necessarily premised on a radical rejection of the family, but, nonetheless, it establishes the need to give the family new meaning and the equally urgent need to restructure it.

It is important to raise the men's question, which is far graver than the women's question. Analyzing the concepts of "domination" and "power" in men is no less important than an analysis of the slavery of women—but perhaps more difficult. It's not women but men who are unwilling to transform themselves. Letting go of the figure of the sovereign male triggers a sense of fear and loss similar to that experienced by a ruler who has lost control of his state. We have to show men that this, the rottenest form of domination, also deprives *them* of freedom and turns them into outright conservatives.

The correct approach is not to first solve the state problem and only thereafter that of the family. The two phenomena are dialectically intertwined and must be addressed and resolved simultaneously. The consequences of real socialism's erroneous deferral of the solution of social problems to some point after the problem of the state had been solved are obvious. No serious social problem can be resolved by giving a single problem exclusive priority. We have to look at problems in their totality and give meaning to each problem in relation to the others, and we must approach their resolution in the same integrated way. Thus, just as pursuing a solution in the absence of analyzing the state without first analyzing the mentality, addressing the family without also addressing the state or the man without analyzing the woman would be inadequate, the inverse is also true.

Further Particularities of Society in the Middle East

The problematic of the Middle East includes some other fundamental elements that must be understood. Phenomena such as ethnicity, nation, homeland, violence, class, property, economy, and so on are by no means clearly defined on a conceptual level and still can't be pinned down in a manner that is free of chauvinist ideological armor. At this point, it is still not possible to scientifically determine the true value of these phenomena in the culture of the Middle East. They are either filtered through religious ideology or some form of chauvinist nationalism, in both cases arriving at conclusions that lead to a no-solution situation.

Questions as to what ethnicity, nation, homeland, violence, property, and economics actually mean within this social reality, what they are good for, and how they interrelate are never asked, and, therefore, the reality falls victim to ideological points of view. With an even much worse perspective, politics deteriorate even further, giving rise to greater aggression and selfishness. A rational, just, and democratic approach is never even considered. The rulers live in dread of a substantial scientific elucidation of society's problems free from ideology and politics, which they fear would spoil all of their tricks. Keeping the truth hidden is the key role of education and politics in the Middle East, because, if this is not achieved, the art of ruling power can no longer be exercised. The magic can only be broken by transparency.

Ethnicity and Nation

We have already given a lot of weight to ethnicity—the clan, the tribe, and the aşiret and kavim communities. Even if indirectly, we attempted to trace its emergence, development, and transformation. Though to a lesser extent than before, ethnicity is still a significant reality in the Middle East. Its influence is stronger in the rural areas. In the city, brotherhoods (*tariqat*) and similar religious communities have taken its place.[18] Because full citizenship and democracy are not a reality, most people belong to an ethnic or religious community. As well as the family, the states oversee the other entities of the ethnicity. Successful politics must factor in the strength of the tribes. They have not yet been fully assimilated into classes or nations and, as a result, contribute to social turmoil. They are also important because they carry with them the lineage culture as an element of historical resistance. Their unqualified rejection would be neither realistic nor useful. We must, however, distinguish between two things. Ethnic bonds must be correctly analyzed, because they can make a positive contribution. This is distinct from the micronationalism and political mindcuffs based on ethnicity, which have extremely negative consequences.

In society in Middle East, "the nation" and "nationalism" are concepts that tend to create more problems than they solve. The need for a national market during mercantilism—or merchant capitalism—that is, during the emergence of capitalism, was fulfilled by first creating the nation from the established language boundaries and, later, deriving nationalism from it. The concept of "the nation" corresponds to the concept of "the umma,"[19] a community that is devoted to a religion, but in this case devoted to a language. Essentially, "the nation" is a political concept rather than a sociological one, as it was introduced for political purposes. It satisfies the demand for a state with more substantive borders. The nation is important to the state not so much for its ethnic base but for its political basis. Even when striving for a "pure" nation, political interests are decisive. The determinant factor behind this policy is, of course the question of the market. The market and politics are the womb of the nation. From a sociological point of view, they are not as significant as ethnicity. Ethnicity is one of the strongest sociological phenomena. Ethnicity, e.g., being a kavim, is in some ways much like a nation, with the difference being that the former has not yet developed a market value or any political value. In the Middle East, nationalism, as opposed to the nation, plays the primary role. Nationalism is replacing increasingly weak religious bonds. It is a kind of secular—worldly—religion and, as such, the most significant tool for legitimizing the state. Running a state without resorting to either religion or nationalism would be difficult. Besides, religion provides the state's genes, with nationalism being its modern form.

Today, the nation and nationalism are of no value for finding the solution to any social problem. On the contrary, they make a solution more difficult, because problems are hidden underneath the veil of nation and nationalism. We need to define and evaluate these phenomena and concepts, which are not even a hundred years old in the region, within their own reality. Political and ideological approaches that are solely based on the nation and nationalism can lead to many errors. The role chauvinist forms of nationalism have played in the wars of the nineteenth and twentieth centuries is obvious. This is also true of all forms of nationalism in general and in the Middle East, particularly Arab and the Israeli nationalism, where we see how the application of nationalism to politics has led to dead ends and caused substantial bloodshed and suffering. There is absolutely no role for nationalism in political and ideological activities, and the phenomenon of the nation should only be introduced to the extent that it can contribute to the solution of social problems. Otherwise, it will only serve to deepen the chaos due to the already strong ideological conditioning in the Middle East, as is also the case in Europe.

Homeland

Even though the concept of "homeland," "motherland," or "fatherland" (*vatan*) has ancient roots that refer to the location of a settlement, it now gains a new meaning as the geographical territory that a nation-state claims. The nation-state is based on political rather than ethnic borders. Unlike in Europe, in the Middle East the borders of the nation are not determined by the linguistic boundaries but by the borders of the area the state encompasses. "Homeland," therefore, becomes a political phenomenon. Thus, in current language and contemporary meaning every state is at the same time a homeland. A correct definition of "homeland" is not possible using an ideological and political approach. In addition, linguistic boundaries alone are not sufficient to constitute a homeland either. In my view, considering "homeland" a cultural concept is a little closer to the truth. We can, therefore, define "homeland" as a geographical area that transcends political nationalism, where people who are older than this homeland settled over the long course of history. Just as there can be a homeland for any one people, there can also be a shared homeland for peoples who are intertwined.

If we look at the Middle East as a whole, it becomes obvious that it would be extremely difficult to divide it and create borders using the European model. Its existence as a whole, with specific particularities, is well established. Economic and social bonds have determined what each country is called. Enforced political divisions are never as strong as the values that have developed over the course of history. The political borders drawn after World War I distorted the concept of "homeland," or, rather, they have led to the emergence of a genuine "homeland problem." The integral political reality in the Middle East makes today's political map unrealistic. The political dynamic necessitates the integrity of different geographic regions. The current situation compels international conflicts and provokes nationalism. Israel-Palestine and Iraqi Kurdistan are two examples. The imperial tradition in the Middle East was closer to federalism. From the first empire to last empire, the Ottoman Empire, the administrative, political, and economic structures in the region were always federal in nature. A federation based on large autonomous regions is comparable to the federation in today's United States of America. The real problem in the Middle East with regard to the issue of homeland lies in the contradiction between the traditional federal framework, to which the current structures refuse to return, and unrealistic fragmentation of the region among numerous unnecessary nation-states. If this is not overcome, we will be unable to arrive at a reasonable understanding of either "homeland" *(vatan)* or "citizenship" *(vatandaşlık)*.

Class

In social systems, the phenomenon of class has less of a sociological meaning than is usually assumed. The bonds with the most profound influence on society are ideological, political, ethnic, and religious in nature. Dynamism based on class consciousness is limited. Class division will necessarily emerge in hierarchical and statist societies. And, conversely, hierarchy and the state cannot develop without the phenomenon of class. On the other hand, no hierarchy and no state structure can be destroyed by the class it is based on, because class division and statehood mutually necessitate each other. There may be fierce struggles between the two, but a compromise is inevitable at the end of the day. The class that controls the state and the class enslaved by it are in dialectical contradiction. The state is the status, or mode of stance, at the heart of this dialectical contradiction. The state would cease to exist without the other. Without classes, there is no state. Insisting on class also means insisting on the state. Thus, praise for an oppressed class eventually turns into praise for the state with which the class in some manner have embraced. The term "workers' state" is, therefore, a problematic concept from the outset. Supporting a workers' state is the equivalent of saying, "I will create my own bourgeoisie"; the Soviet example provides striking evidence of this. The most correct form of class struggle is the refusal to experience class division ideologically or practically. This means living as free individuals, ethnic groups, or religious communities. All that would then be left of the state would be a coordinating institution determined by the common will of society called "general security and common good."

In the Middle East, we see the emergence of pure class division in its most original form at the beginning of the Sumerian and Egyptian civilizations. In mythology, it finds its expression as divinity and the creation of the human being from excrement. This is a fundamental division and takes on different forms in the various monotheistic religions. Moses initiated a particular form of class division by giving the authority of priesthood to the tribe of Levi, which was the tribe among the Hebrew tribes closest to him. Jesus's movement, however, began as a movement of the have-nots against the priest class. Later on, Christianity too experienced a class division based on the remnants of the Roman Empire. When the highest Church dignitaries founded a religious state, they were able, under the religious cover, to develop a particular kind of class division at the bottom. In Islam, class division was experienced differently. In that case, a distinction between the family of the prophet (*ahli bayt*) and the umma,[20] the community of the faithful, soon arose. From the residues of the Byzantine and Sasanian Empires, the caliph formed a state that was based on the umma but that did not possess any particular ideological depth. The umma represents the part of the Islamic state that is unreservedly faithful and accustomed to being unquestioningly obedient. In this way, the veil of the umma masks and reconciles the real class division.

In all of this, we encounter the social democratic character of the monotheist religions: class compromise. Jesus was actually a radical class revolutionary. In Christianity, especially during the period when it became the state, Arianism in particular represents the great class resistance of the poor.[21] The same tendency was seen when the Sunni denomination in Islam became the state; the Alevi denomination represented the poor and the oppressed. In the Middle East, classes don't appear as immediately visible structures; instead, they confront us clothed in ethnic, religious, and denominational covers.

Therefore, class division must be looked for and found under many layers of ideological, ethnic, and denominational cover. The same is true of their struggles. There is always a class essence to any ethnic, religious, denominational, or religious community and any ideological struggle. This is a fact we should never lose sight of when analyzing social phenomena. When the classes struggle to control the state in today's Middle East, as is currently the case in Iraq, for example, the struggle is expressed in the relationships and contradictions between the Arab Shiite/Alevi and Sunni denominations, as well as with the Kurdish ethnic group and other minority religious communities. Class division is experienced in the depths of the ideological, religious, and ethnic structure of the state and the people as its subjects. This is why parties based on a particular class, like those in the West, are not that meaningful. Therefore, it is more fruitful when analyzing the situation in the Middle East and developing a practice to take into consideration class division, while realistically understanding the concrete unique forms of this in the region and refraining from simplifications like "the working class" or "the peasant class." Otherwise, the phenomenon of class division will become a tool for deepening the impasse, as is the case today.

One of the reasons for the defeat of the classic communist, social democratic, and national liberation parties was their modern approach to class division. Their vulgar approaches played a decisive role in the failure of the communist, social democratic, and radical nationalist parties in Iran, Iraq, Turkey, Egypt, and Syria and in the fact that, despite enormous efforts, they were defeated in their struggle for power by currents that made masterful use of religious cover, for example, Shiites in Iran, the Muslim Brotherhood, Hamas, and Hezbollah.

Property

The phenomenon of property became more evident at the class division stage of social development, but it was actually formed in the depths of feelings of social belonging and feelings of identity. It might be useful to distinguish between two types of property. In essence, we can define collective property as the will to make decisions about everything that is jointly needed for the livelihood of an organic community (usufruct).[22] Every individual in the community had the same right or "will to use" a thing. In fact, because of this aspect of its nature, it cannot exactly be called property. Collectivism is, in fact, the negation of private property. In contrast, private property is the increased disposition of and "will to use" by individuals or groups of individuals in opposition to common and collective property. The civilization in the Middle East represents the society that has known property the longest, because class division has ancient roots in the region. The state was formed by establishing property that has both collective and private nature intertwined around it. The assumption that owners of private property emerged first and then seized the state is incorrect; the origin of the order of collective and private property and statehood are intertwined. The more the upper layer came to constitute the state, the more property it owned. Becoming the state meant declaring the territory within its borders its property. The state is the largest property partnership. It is a private property unit. The lower and middle segments are permitted a limited amount of private property, but it is frequently confiscated, which serves to limit the development of private property. Private property, other than that of the state, is not secure.

This also explains why private property has not developed in the same way as in the West. The way a state comes into existence is also decisive in how property is constituted. In the West, the state was curbed right from the beginning by aristocratic and, later, bourgeois circles that possessed a lot of private property. This enabled for the strong formation of the private property institution. Western civilization has proven that private property gives rise to more creativity than does state property.

Collective property has lived on in the deepest parts of society, mostly within families, clans, denominations, and religious communities. These forms of collective property must definitely not be confused with the state's collective private property. The most reactionary, parasitic, and uncreative type of property is the property of the state. The extreme preponderance of state property is one of the most important factors contributing to the economic backwardness of the Middle East. Both the state and the state property order grow like cancerous tumors and deprive society of breathing space. In most cases, property and the state are coterminous. Thus *mülk* (estate, state territory), *malik* (king, one of the attributes of Allah), and *maliket* (property) are all derived from the same word stem. This allows us to make a categorical generalization; in the final analysis, if, in the god-king state, God is the owner of all things, the god-king is the owner of all things, and, thus, since the god-king is the state institution, the state is the owner of all things. Unless this relationship between the state and property is fully grasped and resolved, social development will remain difficult. It is the state and property as the totality of the dispositions that the state has seized that completely hinder the relationship between a healthy individual and society.

Economy

The concept of "economy" has a universal meaning. We can define *economy* as *the systematic form of the exchange of material similar to the metabolism of any living being.* The essence of economic activity is the extraction of animating material from dead matter and its renewed transformation into dead matter through consumption. It is quite obvious that society cannot forego this activity in coming into existence and surviving.

On the other hand, the other related fact is that there can be no economy without vitality—most often understood as "mentality" or "soul." Therefore, any analysis that looks only at one of these aspects will arrive at a faulty conclusion. It would be best to analyze mentality and the economy as intertwined—the intermediate social groups are the state and the family, or, more generally, they are the political and social phenomena. Analyzing either the economy or the mentality in isolation, will lead to the mistake of overemphasizing the most insignificant details, while being unable to see the whole. It is obvious that productive thought processes also lead to a productive economy. It is evident from the historical example in the inner foothills of the Zagros, Taurus, and Amanos Mountains, in what is known as the Fertile Crescent, where between 6000 and 4000 BCE the Neolithic revolution took place, that one of the most productive periods of human mentality also took place. Economic prosperity on the Aegean coast gave rise to the Cretan, Greek, and Roman civilizations, which were accompanied by intellectual, philosophical, and scientific revolutions. The mentality of the Renaissance was one of the important sources for the emergence of the bountiful European economy. The outcome was mutually beneficial to the economy and society's mentality.

The economic epochs that resulted from the development in mentality in civilization in the Middle East are evident. On the other hand, the most fundamental factors in the reduction of economic productivity are a delinking from the world of phenomena within the mentality, an increasing chasm between physics and metaphysics, aimless speculation, and an immersion in dream worlds. The more metaphysics of the Middle East—mythological, religious, and philosophical—was delinked from the realm of phenomena and became immersed in abstract concepts, the greater the economic decline. The focus on theology, especially the tendency to be hostile to philosophy, cannot lead to a correct definition of the natural world, and not developing philosophical and scientific thought certainly leads to a more profound economic impasse, an inability to develop, and an incapacity to move beyond millennia-old Neolithic methods.

Without far-reaching intellectual developments similar to the Renaissance, the Reformation, and the Enlightenment, there can be no permanent, institutionalized economic progress in the Middle East. The failure of development programs promoted either by states or individuals is the result of the reality that underlies the enormous misery and unemployment of the masses. This region, which is very resource-rich, cannot hope to master the economic revolution without experiencing a radical revolution in mentality, and it is, therefore, unable to solve its enormous problems, including unemployment and poverty. If, in the search for a solution in the Middle East, we do not place mentality and democracy revolution at the heart of any economic solution, we will not yield any results. Any developments that do occur will be nothing more than a Band-Aid solution. The best method would be to base any effort to achieve a permanent solution on the dialectical relationship between the economy, on the one hand, and democracy and mentality, on the other hand.

Dynasty
The dynasties and the tariqat are also important to these conceptual clarifications. To complete our reflection on the civilization in the Middle East, we need to illuminate their role.

The dynasty is a conspicuous phenomenon with ethnic and mythological religious elements that has its origin within the family and the state. Dynasties have always played an important role in the rise and fall of families and states. States rarely develop without a dynasty—a rule that still largely holds today. This is the result of the strength of the patriarchal family structure. Patriarchy is actually the "genetic source" of the state. That is why the strongest patriarchal family generally controls the dynastic state. The dynasty thus becomes the state. The dynasty as an institution has existed for thousands of years, leaving deep marks on both the state and society. It is, to all intents and purposes, a combination of the ruling class, the ruling ethnic group, and the dominant religion.

Another advantage the dynasty has is that family line has allowed it influence over long periods of time. It has also proven suitable for spatial expansion through interdynastic marriages. These qualities explain why states have primarily been founded within dynasties. The fact that the dynastic institution constitutes a strong focal point not only for social development but also for the development of the state means that its role cannot be overlooked. In a sense, civilization in the Middle East has been sustained by dynasties—with state dynasties having had the greatest historical effect. While non-state dynasties have predominated in the West, in the East, dynasties linked to states have been more successful. A dynasty can, at the same time, be seen as a school, in that it provides a social model. Important developments are carried over to society once they have occurred within the dynasty school, or model. Ethnic groups, and even nations, are often known by the power and name of the dynasties that have been fostered in their midst, and it is not uncommon for them to play a dominant role. To speak of the Umayyads, the Abbasids, the Ayyubids, the Seljuks, the Ottomans, and the Barmakids is to simultaneously speak of the Arab, Kurdish, Turkish, and Persian nations.[23]

The continued existence of dynasties in the mindset and material environment should neither be denied nor exaggerated. The most realistic approach is to treat them as a social phenomenon and to integrate them into the normal democratic social terrain. They shouldn't be idolized in the process but should be recognized as a social reality and approached in an analytical manner. Anything else might lead to serious political and social problems and intensify the crisis. The importance of dynasties may be better understood if we point to the terrible tragedies caused by Saddam's dynastic craze.

Tariqat

The tariqat are similar to the dynasties but operate in the religious and denominational realm. They base their existence on the application of the general principles of religion at specific times and in particular places. The weakness of the general organization of religion is compensated for by the tariqa organization. Religion becomes a concrete organizational power through tariqat and denominations. Thus, it is only natural that denominations and tariqat exist wherever religion is present. Orders, that is, tariqat, provide a way for a more intense and organized religious experience. As such, the head of the tariqa and the personalities of the key organizers play a huge role. Wherever there is a void, we see the emergence of a tariqa. The masses, who are dissatisfied with the state, particularly rush to tariqa-like organizations. When the family becomes too constricted and the state is out of reach, with no other strong organizations in between, there is a high likelihood that a person will turn to a tariqa. The *mezhep* (denomination) can be regarded as a broader and more traditional form of the tariqa.[24] Many tariqat must remain semi-secret to protect themselves from the state and to enable their members to leave the narrow boundaries of families. While some of them are state-driven, others are vehemently anti-state.

The Middle East is almost like a society of the tariqat. The tariqat have played an important role, especially when ethnicity could not completely satisfy all needs, particularly in the cities, where the family became too constricted, and also during historical periods when the state considered itself the one and only. The *batenî*, the "hidden" tariqat of the Middle Ages, were actually class parties of the poor. From 1000 to 1250, one of the best-known tariqa, the batenî Assassin order of Hassan-i Sabbah, caused great distress to many Seljuk sultans and viziers, who represented the ruling dynasty and denomination. The Khawarij, the Fatimids, and the Alevi represent a similar tradition. In a way, the tariqat and similar religious communities are like the nongovernmental organizations in society in the Middle East.

The phenomenon of tariqat must be objectively evaluated, as they developed to meet a social need. Since they are quasisocial and quasipolitical organizations, their role is important to both the ruling power and the opposition. At times and in places where scientific progress is limited and the understanding of democracy has not developed, such organizations are inevitable. They can, however, be overcome by developing social science and democratic struggle. Nowadays, the tariqat have largely degenerated and have become an instrument, much like a corporation, of multiple interest-based relationships. The correct way of dealing with them is to lead the people toward science and democracy. For that, however, we must be at least as convinced of the legitimacy of science as the tariqat are of their beliefs. Democracy requires a zealous, ongoing, and determined effort. It is important not to deny the existence of the religious community groups whose origins date back many centuries and, thus, to approach them in a democratic manner and with the knowledge that there is a place for them within democracy, which is also an effective way to disentangle conservatism.

Civil Society

A similar approach can be taken to some of the civil society and political party organizations, which can be likened to modern tariqat in a broader sense. It is important, particularly nowadays, to examine the phenomenon of civil society from a broader perspective, especially when family, clan, and faith bonds are intertwined with ideological ties. Combining the elements of classic and contemporary civil society may produce better results. Nongovernmental organizations that are not rooted in the past or in tradition may well experience difficulty and risk drying up quickly. No ideological, political, social, or artistic movement's success can be permanent if it is unable to establish a relationship with tradition—if they fail to do so they cannot avoid being temporary, much like a fashion trend. The formation of a wide-ranging civil society and democratic mobilizations that reconnects with tradition, especially by learning from the failures of the left that belittled tradition, could provide a way out of the crisis and, therefore, a route to success.

Violence and Dictatorship in the Civilization in the Middle East

Even though we have already discussed these issues in connection with the state, the analysis of ruling power regarding the form of the state and the question of violence requires a deeper analysis. The state's general essence is the same everywhere. It represents a tradition based on the appropriation of surplus product and surplus value. However, it takes different forms depending on time and place. As a result, many different forms of the state have arisen during different periods and under different conditions. However, in the context of the East-West quandary, two key tendencies become obvious. In the West, we frequently encounter republican and democratic forms, whereas, in the East, the main state form is despotism.

In Europe, we see republics both in the slave systems of classic antiquity and in several of the city-states in the Middle Ages, and they have become even more ubiquitous in modernity. The main difference between the republic and despotism is found in the field of law. Although the slave-owning ruling classes played a role in both state forms during antiquity, with republicanism rules that are the result of intense social struggles prevail. There is a dynamic social structure. Everybody understands their relationship with the state and knows their rights—and, when necessary, they fiercely defend them.

While the republic represents a dynamic society, the opposite is true of despotism, where a single person arbitrarily imposes his will upon society as law, something that is fairly similar to a monarchy. The only difference is that a monarchy is based on a determined dynasty, and there are traditions and rules in place for determining who will be the monarch, and the rules for governance are also based on tradition. Every now and then, the extraordinary occurs in situations of chaos. Then either a new dynasty ascends to power or the old one changes the rules and continues to rule. Self-evidently, in the case of a despot, rules are arbitrarily established and changed at will. The monarchies in the Middle East are closer to despotism in character. The decrees of the Ottoman Empire, called *fermân*, were essentially nothing but despotic commandments. Even though they were treated as law, they actually had nothing in common with the kind of law that is the result of social struggle.

Dictatorship is yet another state form. It is the precondition or prototype for emperors. It is one-person or a small-group rule by people who have been endowed with extraordinary authority by the political elite. Dictators differ from despots insofar as the supervisory power surrounding them has some weight. There is always a group that the dictator is accountable to. While an empire is a long-term, durable regime, dictatorship is temporary and is only resorted to in exceptional situations. Though the state formation in the Middle East is very close to despotism, it is also quite close to monarchy and empire. Thus, in the Middle East, despotism, monarchy, and empire merge in the head of state, which indicates how much influence these heads of state—who equate themselves with the state—have. It is possible that the most pronounced example of the effective application of willpower is found in a head of the state in the

Middle East, which reflects the essence of the state. The powerful traditions of patriarchy, sheikhdom, nobility, and the "gents" (*effendi*) merge in the institution of the head of state and are regenerated as supreme power. That is why it is difficult to find republican and democratic state forms in the Middle East—even as an exception. In all of this, the state seems to act on the basis of its unadulterated essence. Moreover, by having a single form, it hopes to prove its power. In addition, it regards an unchanging image of the state and the permanent nature of its form to reflect political skill and a virtue.

Another obstacle to the development of republicanism in the Middle East is that an understanding of the god-king and the god-state has been seared into the memory of society for centuries. It is against tradition for the human servants to intervene in the affairs of the god-state. The greatest sin is to interfere in God's—the state's—affairs. This motif frequently appears in the Holy Scripture: "Don't meddle with the affairs of God. Don't demand accountability from God. Though shalt have no gods apart from me." This is, expressed in religious terms, the same as: "Don't meddle with the affairs of the head of state. Don't demand accountability from your ruler. You cannot partake in his authority." According to one theory, the Holy Scripture was written to establish a kingdom based on the Hebrew tribe, and there is some truth to this. Some even say that Moses came from an Egyptian principality. This would explain why he outlines his notion of "kingdom" in the Torah.

In addition, Jesus was captured and arrested for allegedly wanting to seize the kingdom in Jerusalem, which he called "the daughter of Zion." In the Koran, this is formulated even more openly. The surahs and verses Mohammad focused most intensely on were along the lines of: "Though shalt not have any gods besides Him. Don't meddle with the affairs of God. God demands accountability from everyone and is accountable to no one." In doing so he consciously or unconsciously paved the way for sultans, padishahs, and emirs—the forms the head of state took in the Middle Ages. In this sense, the Koran is a state charter. In an extraordinarily farsighted manner, it determined and pronounced upon a form of rule as if it would last for several centuries. An analysis of the Koran on the basis of political theory might provide highly instructive results. But, of course, the position of the umma between loyalty to Allah and loyalty to the state is much clearer and more instructive. The religious declarations of the Middle Ages in Islam and Christianity, as well as in the Far East, for example, in China and

India, appear as harbingers of the new state. What is pronounced in the name of God is nothing but the birth and development of the medieval state.

Separating the state from its despotic character in today's Middle East would be very difficult but is absolutely necessary. Even though there may be a few states that call themselves republics, one can hardly say that they have overcome their despotic qualities. Republicanism requires a consensus among the classes. In the entire history of the Middle East, no country has ever been a constitutional state or republic based on a social consensus. Regardless of their progressive or reactionary positions, regimes based on the will of one person are incompatible with the idea of a republic. In a republic, it is not the will of one person that is decisive but the harmony or the compromise among the differing expressions of will of many people of equal strength. Among the reasons why this is not the case in our region is the weakness of the social classes, which fail to articulate their political will, the traditional subservient spirit toward the state, and the fact that there are no republican traditions to build upon. Regardless of what these states are called, and although there may be a difference in the degree of despotism, it is nevertheless important to emphasize and understand that none of these states have overcome their despotic character, especially when waging a struggle for democratic politics and republicanism.

It is even more important that we analyze the culture of violence in civilization in the Middle East. One could say that there is almost no single pore in the society in Middle East that violence has not penetrated and no institution that is not essentially determined by it. In general, the opinion that violence plays a decisive role in political, social, and even economic structures is accepted, but nowhere is this role more evident than in the base and superstructure of society in the Middle East, where it is difficult to find any institution that is not characterized and shaped by violence. Power and violence are like monozygotic twins.

When defining violence, it is meaningless to resort to theses based on biology or theories based on "nature." The social origin of violence is clear. Equally obvious is its relationship to the emergence of class division and states on the basis of surplus product and surplus value. That much seems to be generally accepted in social science.

One remarkable thing about violence is how little is actually said about it. Even though it has played a decisive role in all societies that have known power, it is generally treated as if it were an insignificant or exceptional phenomenon. It is hardly even mentioned that wars, which are certainly the most intense expression of violence, are a form of savagery that is otherwise nonexistent in the animal kingdom. Instead, people spend their time dredging up new pretexts that purportedly explain why war is necessary. The only legitimate reason for war is necessary self-defense, preserving and liberating one's existence. Waging wars to seize, to plunder socially accumulated value, or for domination and permanent state power only serves those who would rule over and dominate society and shape it in the service of their own interests. Even though all of this is straightforward and entirely evident, apologists for war try to obscure these simple and easily observed facts with abstruse subterfuge and false claims. There is probably no other phenomenon that has been more often misrepresented or hidden than the real sources of power and violence. Mythology, religion, philosophy, and, finally, so-called social science actually distort and obscure the most important fact that violence is inhumane in the extreme and is essentially the most brutal act of oppressive and exploitative social parasites.

This characterization is generally valid but is even more pertinent for understanding social reality in the Middle East. Sayings things like "beating comes from paradise" and "violence is sweeter than honey" fairly accurately describes the origins of violence—because "paradise" is the marvelous island of the rulers. Violence is the decisive reason that society has been so entirely crippled and suffocated. Statuses based on violence have been created in all hierarchical and statist society systems, and the corresponding institutions have been protected with armor. No institution that is not part of the spiral of violence has any chance of survival.

It is quite obvious that no free or nonmilitarized society can develop under these conditions. Even new ideas are only accepted once they pass through the filter of violence. There is no room for creative thinking in such an atmosphere; instead, all world affairs are carried out using hackneyed catchwords. Leaders, especially heads of state and of the family, know very well that their power depends on their authority and violence. When Genesis says, "Fill the earth and subdue it,"[25] violence is implied. The violence that has seeped into all of society's pores leaves very little room for the power of meaning. Therefore, social institutions only exist pro forma. Society is formed by institutions that are far from creative and will only move when incited to do so from the outside, because there is no space left for meaning. Thus, clearly, we cannot expect such a society to develop freely.

The tradition of nourishing society with violence is even more oppressive in the family, its smallest subunit, leaving no room to breathe. For women in particular, it is an invisible state of war. There is hardly a single cell within a woman's body that does not shiver from violence. This is also the case for children. Violence is the basic method of education. It's to be expected that a child who was raised violently will resort to violence as an adult. Some take pride in rule by violence and even enjoy it. The feeling of empowerment based on the use of ruling power and violence should be regarded as the most dangerous social disease, but, instead, it is treated as the most sublime and pleasant of feelings. Something that should be cursed is presented to us as the most exalted virtue.

Without exception, none of the current social institutions in society in the Middle East would be imaginable without violence. It is used as a fundamental problem-solving tool everywhere, from state violence and violence within the family, from the violence of revolutionary organizations to fascist, nationalist, and religious violence. Dialogue is dismissed as mere prattle. The power of the word is not deemed to make much sense, even though it is exactly what the superiority of Western civilization is based upon, and its likelihood for success is high, because it first relies on the word, thoroughly explores all options for meaningful dialogue, and, if nothing else works, then resorts to violence. Compared to the East, the West has analyzed its relationship with violence, gained insight thereby, and drawn conclusions. The European Union is relatively cautious and self-critical about violence, and even the United States is quite analytical when it comes to the use of force. It doesn't use force blindly but understands that its successes are due to the strength of its analyses, and that its failures are the result of faulty analyses. Both the EU and the US have learned the necessary lessons.

Freeing society in the Middle East from violence is a far-reaching challenge and has much to do with education. To be successful, trust in the power of meaning is central. It must be understood that violence should only be resorted to if it is inevitable and can be effective. This is a difficult task that requires a sound evaluation not just of the violence emanating from war, revolution, and counterrevolution but of the extent of the violence used in all areas. In opposing it, great mastery is required to prepare and implement appropriate and effective counterviolence. In resurrecting a society that has been scorched by a millennia-old tradition of violence, we can't rely on violence, except in rare conditions where it is necessary as a midwife. We must instead make room for meaning, dialogue, and organizational power. This should be considered and then implemented as the analytical method necessary if we are to leave the chaos behind.

EIGHT

The Current Situation in the Middle East and Probable Developments

The proper definition of the relationship between social tradition and the current situation is still a major challenge for the social sciences. But how well can we understand the current phenomena, events, and processes without establishing their connection with tradition? How much influence does tradition have on the present? To what extent and how does the society experience tradition and present reality coterminously? Until we answer these questions, it will be difficult to come to a realistic and correct assessment of the current situation and the probable developments. Absent the necessary answers, any attempt at implementation will be inadequate and rife with errors. That is why our methodology is to constantly try to link history and the present. I am of the opinion that tradition is always embedded in the present, albeit for the most part encoded. The present moment and conditions change the parameters of tradition less than is generally assumed. But to be able to trace this in the world of facts, it is necessary to break a few of the codes. The reason I am engaging in extensive historical interpretations is to decipher the current implicit codes.

An example will make this clearer. Anyone—or at least those who are ideologically and politically interested in the twentieth century—who has heard of Lenin knows that his revolutionary integrity is beyond doubt. Nevertheless, I do not think that Lenin, in his theoretical and practical engagement with the question of power, succeeded in cracking its codes. And because he couldn't decipher them, he laid the basis for the defeat of his own goals with the kind of system he built, which shows how important it is to correctly crack these codes. There are innumerable sages who analyzed and defined power in ways that are much more accurate than the analyses of today's revolutionaries. They may not have smashed power, but they also did not become tainted by collaborating with it. Can we dismiss them as unimportant? The socialism that Lenin built using the old Russian power blocs from the czarist era survived a mere seventy years. Having provided a historical service to the system it opposed, it simply disintegrated without offering as much resistance as Saddam Hussein, who was just a run-of-the-mill rival power. Soviet socialism did not even warn the worldwide movement it was in agreement with and with which it shared the same goals of its coming collapse, in what was almost a betrayal of sorts. I do not see the point of engaging in endless criticism of the Leninist system. I think our clear observation needs to be that it failed to decipher the heavily encrypted code of power.

Without decoding the many layers of the traditional codes found in all revolutionary phenomena, events, and processes that we are working on currently, particularly those that are defined as periods of qualitative leaps, it would be very misguided to think that we could achieve developments that are genuine, desirable, and in accordance with our goals. My only concern is that without such historical social definitions, including mine, that may be inadequate and rife with errors, we cannot correctly and fully describe the present. The disastrous and horrifying life in the Middle East in the past, and even more today, clearly shows us the importance of deciphering these codes. Even if the latest technology is used, the consensus is that these problems cannot be solved with widespread violence. Nor can this situation, which is worse than brutal, be changed solely by economic, financial, political, and educational efforts. Nonetheless, it is obviously necessary that we strive to resolve the situation. This is why developing key concepts that aid in our effort to unravel tradition is important—and in this regard we are open to criticism. I deeply believe this is necessary for any present-day effort to be meaningful and yield success.

If we start from this point and mentally visualize the Middle East and all its capitals, the denunciation of Babylon in the Old Testament springs to mind, as does the aversion Sumerian poets felt for the Akkadian Empire,[1] along with the Christians' contempt for Rome, of course. Are Baghdad, Jerusalem, Mecca, Ankara, Istanbul, Kabul, Tehran, Cairo, and Islamabad not modern versions of Babylon? How is it possible for people to live in such a violated, desperate, and despicable way, despite the great culture behind them? How were people forced into this situation? Such an understanding and methodology cannot be found in any book—not in any art of war or the art of becoming a ruler?[2] Even cannibalism means something where it occurs. But the same meaning is not to be found in the despotic monsters of the Middle East subjecting people to physical annihilation and the annihilation of meaning. It is difficult to find anywhere else where killing is as despicable, treacherous, and immoderate—the perpetrators call it "masterful"—as in the Middle East.

I still have to address a methodological problem. The contemporary priests of the West, the literary figures, philosophers, scientists, and artists of various sorts, investigate a phenomenon, event, or process by dismembering it and discretely analyzing its parts. They believe that research and study are possible only if its object is dissected and reduced to a cadaver. This always reminds me of the Sumerian priests' method of reading the fate of humans in the movement of the stars in the sky. One is science, the other, mythology, but the outcome is the same.

I am convinced that the conduct of our "contemporary priests" is much more despicable. Why, despite all their detailed knowledge, are they unable to understand the twentieth-century campaigns of physical annihilation and the annihilation of meaning, which exceed anything we have seen in previous centuries many times over? Why are they unable to offer effective solutions? No phenomenon, event, or process that is not looked at in its entirety can be correctly defined. Analyzing things by boundlessly dismembering them, substantially overlooks or misses the truth and is not instructive but prevents a sound learning process.

Humanity's formation needs to continue in a way that does not change its essence. The Western capitalist system results in excessive fragmentation and modification that makes this impossible. This is why it makes sense to call this system the society of crisis. Arts, philosophy, and science determine a person's mentality. Mentality or spirituality cannot be dismembered. Such dismemberment kills. In the West, this is the dominant manner of killing, and it is spreading to the rest of the world. The most important aspect of human wisdom is its representation of this wholeness. Prophecy is a form of wisdom that has attained more sacredness. The difficulties and problems that wise people and prophets have faced were the result of their ability to take a holistic approach. On the other hand, any social institution or representation that doesn't internalize science, philosophy, and the arts impairs the actuality of formation. In the final analysis, every perversion stems from a lack of holistic understanding. To look at phenomena, events, and processes with a singular mindset—more precisely with a dismembered mentality—is the most dangerous form of ignorance, because it destroys reality; this is the disease of this epoch and system. The perspective generally regarded as particularly scientific should actually be considered the most deceitful form of ignorance. A scientism—which is actually unrestrained analytic intelligence—that lacks spirituality and has lost touch with emotional intelligence is open to all kinds of dangers. It's a kind of cancer: discourse cancer.

The problem is not about knowing too much but about living on the basis of that knowledge. The essence of social existence is to carry forward this knowing—science, philosophy, the arts—in all of its dimensions and in its wholeness as society's mentality. This is the reality that our age has destroyed. This is also the reason for the destructive character of science. Nuclear annihilation, for example, is just the symbolic expression of this reality. The fact that humanity uses nuclear weapons against itself is no less brutal than cannibalism. While the real task of social science should be to prevent this dismemberment and preserve wholeness, it has itself become increasingly fragmented, thereby becoming the main source of danger. The result is innumerable local, regional, and global wars, nationalism, fascism, and every imaginable form of violence. I have, therefore, tried in this book to integrate religion, mythology, philosophy, science, and literature into a harmonic state of mind. A defense of the people,[3] a defense of human essence, can only be developed on this basis. Ultimately, the strength of such a defense will depend on the degree to which the imposed civilizational paradigm is successfully analyzed and resisted.

The Middle East Today

The reality behind the chaotic situation of Middle East is to be found in the region's roots in a millennia-old civilization. These roots and the influence of European culture over the last two hundred years has produced a deadlock instead of a solution. While European civilization has been developing habitable systems in all geocultures, it has been unsuccessful in the geoculture of the Middle East, and this problem is by no means merely regional. Huntington's concept of the "clash of civilizations" has been roundly criticized, but it is actually realistic in some respects.[4] There *is* a clash of civilizations, but it is not a struggle between Islamic and Western civilizations. The problem is deeper and more far-reaching. Even if Islam disappeared from the scene, the foundations of the conflict would continue to exist. The evil that escaped Pandora's Box in Iraq in particular shows that the roots of this conflict run deep. A careful analyst would immediately recognize that all sorts of contemporary and historical figures have appeared on the scene of the Iraqi quagmire to peddle their various "solutions," which might well lead to a historical solution but are just as likely to go nowhere at all. The parties to the conflict are not the caricatured Saddam and Bush but, rather, the numerous intertwined systems. The systems that have emerged since the Neolithic Age, with their ethnic, religious, and sexist shadings, are either trying to secure a place for themselves in the US-led empire of chaos or are attempting to exit the chaos.

In military conflicts, it is understandable that parties try to achieve a balance of power. But in conflicts and struggles between civilizations, the existing balance of power is difficult to determine. The substance of the conflict is complex. The use of military weapons in the conflict only plays a small part. The truly decisive factors are experienced at the level of the mentality and political and social structures, and it can take centuries for a conclusion to be reached.

Solutions can range from restoration to radical change. In a confrontation between two systems, the time factor must be taken into account. Even though the Middle East resists through the last Islamic civilization, this resistance is nothing beyond symbolic. Islam had its most productive period from the eighth to the twelfth centuries CE. Everything else is just a shell; it has nothing to offer beyond the grandeur of its past. Islam is so out of touch that it cannot even be reformed. The resurgence of Islam in the last thirty years is entirely artificial. Its resurgence within a Western civilizational environment is itself because of the West. It has no originality. Opposition in the name of Islam means accepting defeat right from the start.

What model should the Middle East follow? Adopting the innovations of European civilization cannot be anything but artificial. The contributions made by European civilization to politics, society, and economy don't really provide a solution but, rather, lead to stagnation. There is no place that people could migrate to in the way that Jews migrated to Israel. It is also impossible to imitate Africa. African culture may struggle within itself, but it can only try to replicate European civilization. A conflict wouldn't make much sense and could only have limited success. Asian and Pacific systems, such as those in China, India, and Japan, could achieve results by skillfully transmitting the European system. Their cultures enable harmony, not resistance, to be more meaningful and successful. The cultural framework of Latin America has lived with the European system for five hundred years. This cultural framework can achieve a sustainable life by being a little more creative, although it is difficult. But the culture of the Middle East does not resemble that of any of these regions. From its regimes to its understanding of individuality, from its mentality to its economic structures, unsustainability and chaos are on the agenda.

Today, the mentality of the Middle East is in complete disarray. It is very far removed from the revolution in mentality that took place in Europe. There is no apparent desire for a Renaissance, Reformation, and Enlightenment adapted to the specific conditions of the region, although there is no inhibition to mimicking the latest trends or drawing upon the practical advances the European Renaissance, Reformation, and Enlightenment have given rise to. There is also no great understanding of the historical roots and development of the mentality of the Middle East that people in the region think of as their own. For all groups, interpreting history is nothing more than trite self-adulation. For mentality communities, examining history is nothing but an opportunity for self-praise and for declaring their opponents to be enemies. There is no other, no third, side.

Even the question of how objective or subjective these interpretations are never arises; there is neither a synthesis of the templates of mentality nor a habit of thinking in terms of opposites, i.e., thesis and antithesis. Rather, the thinking is paradigmatically closer to viewing things as black-and-white. Nature is not seen as something animate and ebullient, as it was during the Renaissance or the Neolithic Age, but is portrayed in a hopeless, worn-out, and pessimistic way. The way society is viewed not only lacks utopia, but the magnificent elements of tradition—mythology, religion, and wisdom—are also entirely lost. Neither what lays behind nor what is to come are approached with any hope or excitement, and without hope and excitement there can be no creativity. The scientific, philosophical, and the artistic fruits of mentality have dried up. It does not have much of an assertion anymore. Instead, a spiritual atmosphere that is worse than insanity is a constant. Pride in the past and hope for the future are long gone. Any thought as to the meaning of life is vague and distant, and no one feels confident about anything they do. The desire to understand has withered away. People devote all of their energy to just getting through the day.

Even people who are generally regarded as particularly socially skilled are unable to develop relationships that go beyond cliques and cronyism. Their commitment to an organization or party is based on a deep-seated egocentrism. As such, they are very insidious and exploit existing values. Their last refuge is a symbolic familialism that has long since lost its original meaning and is now perhaps one of the most reactionary spheres of life. There is no longer a profound love for human beings, no humanism. There can be no love if there is no definition of what it means to be a human. Even the greatest nationalists have a self-interest that is tightly knit with expediency. In short, what is left of the historical mentality of the Middle East is little more than obliviousness, an embrace of it in ignorance, and illusions so totally devoid of creativity that they cannot even be called fantasy. At the same time, however, pride prevents the adoption of the mentality of Europe and the Far East—the strength is simply lacking.

Regardless of the phenomenon, event, or process these definitions of the mindset, which could be further developed, were applied to they would not allow for an enlightening analytical result. The blockage lies with the mentality. When patterns of mentality, including religion, nationalism, and socialism, combine with the existing mentality in the Middle East, they are denatured and turn into blunt tools with nothing to offer. The nature of the existing mentality prevents it from solving any problem. Furthermore, because of the nature of this mentality, no synthesis with other mentalities is possible. As a result, all proposed solutions are doomed to failure before they even get off the ground. The give and take necessary for meaningful development is lacking. There is not even a mentality that, as was once the case in Europe, could be the target of a *Praise of Folly*.[5] In the mentality reflected in the medieval epic Layla and Majnun, there is at least *blind* love. Today, however, there is nothing left of *that* love, even if it is blind. The result is nihilism—suicide. The final stage in the loss of meaning in human existence. Beyond this, all manner of madness is possible, and this is exactly what we find. Where else in the world is there as much madness as we find in the area stretching from Afghanistan to Morocco, and how much longer can this go on?

To describe the situation only in narrow economic, political, and military terms is insufficient. The malady is in the mentality. The only way to overcome this is by waging a substantive struggle for meaning. There is a need for contemporary figures like Mawlana and his dancing dervishes, Mani and his synthesis of religions, Suhrawardi with his *Philosophy of*

Illumination,[6] examples of which are common in the history of the Middle East. Today's scene is dominated by a fake sectarianism with a diseased mentality that must be overcome if these respectable historical values are to once again give us strength. The other mentalities of our time are in deep crisis. What contribution can they make? This is why grasping the meaning and importance of the struggle for a suitable mentality and making an effort to that end is one of the fundamental tasks at present.

Obviously, a general understanding of the essence of history and a familiarity with contemporary science and philosophy are prerequisites for a successful process of mentality enlightenment. Without absorbing Western science and philosophy, it will be impossible to connect with history and to create the necessary synthesis. This is not something that can be carried out with Islamism or Buddhism. While, in my books, I am also in conflict with Western mentality, this is not a blind conflict. I want an honest and genuine rapprochement, but Western mentality does not in and of itself seem satisfactory to me. It has immense moral shortcomings, but it nonetheless possesses enormous scientific knowledge. The aspect of Western thought that I envy and respect the most is the ability to success-fully achieve this scientific knowledge. At the same time, I'm sure that a huge malady or deficiency stems from this very fact. I am convinced that with regard to moral and ethical questions, Western scientists are no more than a contemporary version of the Sumerian priests. Moreover, I don't believe they can overcome this flaw. The mercilessness of their approach to nature and society—almost devouring them–is frightening. They should have created ethical values that kept pace with their scientific knowledge.

How do these scientists reconcile letting the system be unethical with their consciences and their enlightened minds? Who or what has caused them to do so? Perhaps the ruling power bought them off long ago. The situation of the class of scientists may well be one of greater dependency than that of the working class. This is the basis of my despair. That said, during the Renaissance, scientists displayed a fierce resistance. Can we revitalize the spirit of people like Giordano Bruno in the present? Will we succeed in letting the voice of a Socrates ring out anew? Nobody can claim that the mindsets of these great men have perished forever. Rather, their spirits, along with those of Mawlana, Mansur al-Hallaj, Mani, and Suhrawardi must be revived. The soul and the essence of things that are prophetic also need a contemporary form. It is necessary that we live with the understanding that, in a certain sense, these figures have not died and must be genuinely represented. Doing so, these links, could bring us closer to the mindset that we need today. This does not mean that I do not appreciate the values of our age, and it would not be very creative to do nothing more than revive these past forces who were defeated long ago and from whom alone no positive impulses will emerge.

I am aware that when there is a need to defend a people, the Kurdish people, and with them, all of the people of the Middle East, the greatest power would be a new or transformative power. I fully understand that taking refuge under the wings of this or that political power will only continue the current deadlock. In the same way, I am also aware that any help received in that context might well foster weakness rather than conferring strength. The refusal to seek refuge under the wing of a guardian angel may provide the opportunity to develop the intellect. Solitude, if one can cope with it, may even give rise to the mentality that is required for our time. The whole world system piled on top of me when I was in the Middle East. It does not really matter whether it was intentional or spontaneous. But if NATO, the system's largest military power, and the US, the United Kingdom, Israel, and the scheming Greek state consciously participated in putting me in this enormous solitude, having had many reasons to be made enormous and terrible, what I must do is wage a war of morality and the intellect, a war that will be the greatest war of all. Such a war could perhaps bring them to their senses and, thereby, possibly contribute to successfully ending the real war that has begun in the Middle East.

State Power

State power in the Middle East is an imposing obstacle to development in mentality and is far from paving the way for civilian initiatives to open up the society. A historical definition would illuminate what it is today. Its despotic character has hardly changed, even though attempts have been made to refurbish it with the contemporary polish of nationalism, republicanism, or socialism. Its posture over the last two hundred years is not based on its own power. Internal conflicts within the West have played a fundamental role. Then, in the twentieth century, it could only sustain itself by creating a balance of power between fascism and real socialism. In fact, at the moment, it is experiencing an extremely fragile balance of power with the world's leading power blocs, which is why some states are now being described as "rogue states." After the disintegration of the Soviet Union this fragility gave way to precarious blocs of power and government blocs that resemble icebergs floating in the ocean, which makes them dangerous. The winners and losers of wars can find a place of some sort within a new balance of power. Ruling powers in the Middle East, however, see sealing themselves off from a solution to be the highest art of power—likely adopting this position in the service of the most despotic of interests. Of course, they hide this very efficiently, using pretexts like "elevated national interests," the "unity and integrity of state and fatherland," or "the well-being of society." That the people suffer, that their country is in ruins, and that the society is far from being healthy doesn't matter to these ruling powers in the least. For them, demagoguery is the most effective approach to politics and the subtlest forms of populism have been developed, all putatively in the name of democracy. Disguising the state's true machinations with shameless lies is seen to be mastery in the art of politics. Kicking the people from one political corner to the other, as if they were a soccer ball, is called "effective leadership."

Politics is the art of solving the vital problems of society, but in the current reality in Middle East it has become the mastery of occlusion. It does not even have as much value as *conservative* politics. Under certain circumstances, fascism presents itself as a solution. The Middle East, however, is ruled by archaic forms that go beyond fascism. It is most unfortunate that at the very moment when this system was on the verge of collapse and should have been destroyed, the balance of power unnecessarily prolonged its life for two hundred years. When modern military technology was added to this, it became a true Leviathan.

Theocracy as the Foundation of Every State

The foundation of the state is theocracy. This has never changed no matter what form it has taken. One should see the theocratic state as essence rather than form. It is important to see the ideological essence in the ferment of this institution that arose around the priest's temple in the Middle East. Without establishing a bond of credibility in the mindset it would be difficult to make thousands of people work for a very long time in the service of the temple with naked force alone.[7] The divine, or "sacred," quality of the state arises from this need. The state construct cannot be made solid and long-lasting without relying on the dominant mentality and ensuring legitimacy, whether based on mythological or religious belief.

The leitmotif of the Old Testament is the need of the Hebrew tribe— which played a huge role in the formation of monotheistic religion—to become an authority and to establish a state distinct from the Egyptian and Sumerian states, which, in all their grandeur, stood on either side of it. In this sense, the Holy Scripture forms a kind of ideological foundation for the kingdom of the Hebrews. The First and Second Books of Samuel in particular are close to being a foundational manifesto for the state of Judah—a god-state. While Zoroastrianism was the decisive religious factor at the base of the Median-Persian Empire, Christianity became the common gene of all post-Roman European states. The Islamic state, for its part, was religion in and of itself at its very birth. All medieval Islamic states necessarily regarded themselves as religious states. In Iran, Shiite Islam, which replaced Zoroastrianism, is still the state's official ideology. Islam is the religion of the state and the official ideology in all Arab countries. The Republic of Turkey, which has declared itself to be secular, has the largest staff for religious affairs—the official ideology and official state religion being Sunni Islam. Islam is the official state religion. Pakistan and Afghanistan are officially Islamic states, and Israel is also a theocratic state.

Without a radical revolution in thought, the idea of a secular state will remain utopian. However, we can speak of implicitly or explicitly religious states. Unless the state transforms itself into a transparent institution that serves general security and the necessary common good, it cannot liberate itself from its religious structures and attain a truly secular character.

Society in the Middle East is dominated by the state to a degree unparalleled in any contemporary regime. The more the state grows in opposition to society, the more powerful it feels itself to be. It sees the totalitarian state as its ultimate guarantor and the source of its strength. Thus, attributes of the state, such as traditional, sacred, motherly, and fatherly, are never lacking. The state feeding the people has become a classic expression of this. But *first* the state steals from the people, then it playacts the role of the bighearted philanthropist distributing alms to beggars. Thus, it is more dangerous than the worst criminal, because it can legitimate any misdeeds by invoking its authority. We indeed have many reasons to say that the real Leviathan is the modern-day state. The bitter irony is that to the people this state appears to be the guarantor of work and bread. The very state that drained everything is now expected to provide the services that will bring about everything.

Without an analysis of the state in the Middle East, we will not be able to overcome any economic or social problem. That today's state in the Middle East can neither be like the state the West favors, with its developed democratic sensitivity, nor an openly—as opposed to implicitly—fascist state is the source of all of the problems. It must be restructured. The problem cannot be resolved, as if often claimed, by solutions based on concepts like "unitary," "local," or "federal." Above all, there is a need for a state that is open to finding a solution. At the very least, the state must cease to be an obstacle to the freedom of the individual and the democratization of society. It not only has to downsize; most of all, it has to become more functional. Except for those devoted to reasonable general security and true common good, it must abandon all other unnecessary institutions and rules. Without that sort of reform, seeking to resolve any problem will end in a deadlock because of this inert and cumbersome nature of the state.

Today, the problem of state power poses itself more urgently than ever before. Without falling into the malady of the real socialist, social democratic, and national liberation states of the recent past or, indeed, falling for delusions of conquering the state through compromises or by destroying it and erecting a new one in its place, our fundamental task must be to create the possibility of a principled democratic compromise or solution. This task must become the goal of all political activity.

The social fabric of the Middle East is where the crisis is experienced most intensely. All social establishments, such as the family, aşiret, city, the peasantry, the unemployed, religious communities, intellectuals, and popular health and education institutions, are experiencing their most nihilistic and crisis-ridden period. The social body resembles an obese patient cordoned off by power and the dominant ideology from above and squeezed by an economy characterized by scarcity from below. However, it is not the obesity we come across in the US or the EU, but, rather, calls to mind the swollen bellies of the starving children in Africa. The people, as the social fabric in these institutions, no longer play any real role. The institutions themselves do not generally play any meaningful role. Reality is only found in the cafés and tea houses. The institutional reality that should be an instrument for socialization of the individual has turned into a trap that ensnares people,[8] leading to a further degeneration of the already compromised health and socialization, exacerbating the existing crisis. The arabesque music, with its wailing tone and its resignation to fate, is the sick artistic reflex in the face of this reality. Moreover, the social fabric that comes from the outside is inadequate and hasn't even developed defense mechanisms against attacks, because it lacks the necessary mentality and moral wherewithal to do so. Since the social structure is determined by the political structure, the social revolution reflexes have also largely been blunted. Only very rarely do we find spontaneous social dynamism that does not originate from within the state or result from some demagogic policy. Sociality is unable to function as anything other than the ballyhooing of the state and its politicization, because it is not accustomed to having any other role. This is how the principle works: it is squeezed by the economy and drawn out by the state, and the greater the economic problems become, the louder the cry goes out to the state, which exploits this to the maximum. Civil society's search for solutions and its efforts to this end, on the basis of its own interests, are limited.

The Situation of Women

The social tragedy generated by the mercilessness and hopelessness of politics in the Middle East shows itself the most in the reality of women. As the prisoner of a five-thousand-year-old hierarchy and state tradition, no other life is harder than that of today's woman. The difficulty does not merely arise from the tradition. The feminine values produced by European civilization are at least as destructive as the dogmatic traditions. Women are horrified at being caught between a culture that embraces pornography and the culture of the pitch-black veil—they are entirely disoriented.

The woman of the Middle East is an artificial figure who is even older than the state. All the virtues of being a woman have been flipped on their head. Everything about herself that she can be proud of and that can be shared is dominated by the moral law. The only activity open to a woman in a situation where religious tradition has deprived her of herself and turned her into a man's most valuable property is absolute compliance with the wishes of her man. What an emperor is for the state, men in general and husbands in particular are for women. In the vocabulary of masculinity, a joint decision or a compromise made with a woman is seen as shameful. Absolute and unconditional commitment—with no principles—to her husband is regarded as the highest virtue of a woman within this morality. She is far from being able to freely claim that she has a body and soul. The political, economic, and social structures have weakened and excluded her to the degree that she eagerly searches for a man she can slavishly devote herself to. She is lonesome, and her situation appears to be worse than death.

Since all other women are in a similar situation, there is hardly anyone who is in a position to understand them and give them hope for a truly humane life. The reality of being culturally besieged forces women to constantly surrender. No matter how much they resist—unless they consider suicide—they will be broken. Thereafter, all the excessive modes of femininity are taken on. Each part of her body is marked with a sign from these modes. Womanhood is truly the most difficult craft. The period when a woman is single can be compared to being an appetizer at the table of hungry wolves, while the period of motherhood is filled with the endless pain of many births. Raising each and every child becomes true torture. Furthermore, women are permanently disappointed by a world that offers no hope for her offspring. One pain is added to another. The social status of women in the Middle East is the cruelest of practices. The slavery of women resembles the slavery of the people, the difference being that the slavery of women is even older.

The proposition that women's reality largely determines social reality is certainly correct. In the Middle East, the extreme masculinity and extreme femininity represent a dialectical contradiction. The resultant negative features for men from this relationship is the hollowness of the dominant masculinity. The rule of the powerful over men is projected onto women by men and then onto children by women. Therefore, the permeation of domination from top downward to the bottom is all-encompassing. The level of woman's slavery constantly reproduces the most unfavorable of conditions, thus further deepening the level of slavery in society. The power at the top can easily rule the feminine society born in this manner. As well as suffering the greatest cruelty against their will, women are also turned into means that allow society to live even more cruelly. The Middle East is forced to capitulate by outside forces, and it has internal difficulties because of the relationships it has imposed upon women.

For these reasons, the chance of any movement that is not based on women's freedom leading to a genuinely and permanently free society is limited. This is also why attempts at targeting power first, for example, socialism and national liberation, did not lead to the longed for results. The work to achieve women's freedom goes far beyond the question of equality of the sexes; it is the essential substance of democracy, human rights, environmentalism, and social equality.

The first step to be taken toward women's freedom is to avoid treating them like property and to make sure they become forces for action in their own interests. The currently fashionable concept of "love," overloaded with feelings of property ownership, is rife with danger at its very core.

In a society with hierarchical and statist traditions, love is the greatest of all deceptions. It is a construct meant to cover up the crime committed. Respect for women and support for their freedom means, above all, admitting the existing reality and working honestly and sincerely to overcome it in the pursuit of freedom. A man who lives out his dominant masculinity, however he may perceive it, to the detriment of women cannot himself be considered a sound value for freedom. Achieving a physical, mental, and intellectual strengthening of women is perhaps the most valuable of all revolutionary efforts. In the Middle East culture, which was once the center of the mother-goddess cult, a true heroism of freedom is required to make a contribution to reenable women to have the power to make independent decisions and make their own choices, alongside their other advanced social values.

The Economy
The role of economy within the overall mentality, power, and social status is one that complements social integrity. Liberal economy has no place within traditions or at present. The biggest monopoly is the state, which makes it possible to run the economy in the interests of political power. While, in Western civilization, the economy partially determines ruling power, in the Middle East mainly it is the ruling power that determines the economy. The presumed economic laws are barely valid in the geoculture of the region. On the one hand, there are small household and family economies—a remnant of the Neolithic period, and, on the other hand, there is the state economy. In between, there are shopkeepers and merchants who are dependent on the state. The middle class has limited prospects for influencing the state and its policies based on its economic power. The state, on the other hand, can't function without the economy, because it is the indispensable source of its rule. Only when the state in the Middle East is completely restructured on the basis of the Western model will its influence on the economy recede.

This economic structure explains why the state in the Middle East has often in the course of history been called a "merchant state." Its economic character serves to explain the many wars that have flared up around trading routes and why states have collapsed when cut off from these routes. While the Western states mainly developed by capital accumulation and industrialization, the Eastern states did so through trade, confiscation, and unearned income. Instead of relying on capital accumulation and industry, they used the values they amassed in this way to run the state. It is part of ancient political craftiness to regard everything that belongs to the society, the homeland and all its resources, including the human being, as the private property of the state and to try to sell everything. The state's behavior resembles that of a thief distributing stolen goods.

Therefore, any economic development in the Middle East requires that the present status quo within society be disentangled. The present structure of the states impedes their integration into the global economy. With its current economic framework, the chaotic and crisis-ridden system will be unable to prevent the accelerating process of society's dissolution. That states find it necessary to resort to heavy-handed despotic methods is best understood as an attempt to prevent this dissolution.

The Western system has long supported despotism for exactly this reason. This support mainly served to open access to a larger share of the oil wealth and to prevent movements that could create problems for the system. Today, the harm caused by these methods outstrips the profits they bring in. The system has rendered itself superfluous, as further impoverishing the masses decreases the population's purchasing power. The events around the regime in Iraq illustrate this very clearly. As the falling purchasing power makes it more difficult to control the masses, the despotic state structure begins to obstruct the global system. Being squeezed from both sides is the material basis for the Greater Middle East Initiative.

In short, in today's Middle East, the status quo can no longer be sustained. It took advantage of the balance of power created by fascist Germany and Soviet Russia to extend its lifetime for a hundred years. The demise of both of those systems substantially limits its new policy of achieving a balance of power. The contradictions between the US and the EU, on the one hand, and between the US and China, on the other hand, do not allow for a new balance of power ploy. For similar reasons, Turkey's attempt to lead a new solidarity alliance does not have much potential of success. Power blocs that do not integrate into the system to an acceptable degree create the most dangerous but also the most dynamic region in today's world. Power blocs that deny individual freedom and prevent the democratization of society are becoming increasingly unacceptable to the global system. In much the way they entered into World War I and World War II, the bloc made up of the US, the leading power in the empire of chaos, and its allies has now, in a certain sense, begun World War III with the invasion of Afghanistan and Iraq. While NATO steered to the region, other important powers, including Russia, China, and India, are neutralized. With the Greater Middle East Initiative, they are attempting to find a way out of the chaos and toward a solution. In response, people too can formulate an option, thereby putting more democratic, free, and egalitarian solutions on the agenda.

We are quite obviously going through a period of chaos. There were similar phases during World War I and World War II. The emergence of the Soviet Union during World War I and the defeat of fascist Germany during World War II led to the formation of power blocs that, having come out of chaos, were unstable. All the states that emerged out of the remnants of two big empires—the Ottoman and the Persian Empires—proved unable to adopt either the Soviet system or the classic Western system, but they were able to extend their lifetime into the 1990s by taking advantage of the balance of power between these two systems. When the balance of power was destroyed by the collapse of the Soviet Union, parts of power in the Middle East increasingly became "rogue states." It was impossible to live with the new global system, so the US-led coalitions entered the region. The system's partial crisis situation has the traits of a complete chaos in the Middle East. Under these peculiar circumstances, the analogy of a World War III cannot easily be dismissed. In fact, this is a consolidation of unsettled accounts from World War I and World War II. Allowing new despotic regimes to rise would not make sense within the logic of globalization.

The system must open up to the demanding masses of people, not to those of the state blocs, and this will require getting a share of the wealth and democracy.

Can we speak of a new stage in the imperialism phase? To what extent does the talk about "democratic imperialism"—according to the system's standards, of course—correspond to reality? Are other options possible? What are we to understand by the concept of "moderate Islam," i.e., the Turkish model? To what degree can Western democratic models be modified to suit the requirements of the Middle East?

What, on the other hand, can the social democratic globalization, even if weak, which has begun to raise its voice with the World Social Forum–Porto Alegre, mean for the region? Can a Democratic Middle East Federation be developed as a realistic utopia? Can a Democratic Iraq Federation be the prototype for such a tendency? For an idea like this to have a chance in this historical period, there is much work to be done by social science and morality. A social science that escapes the monopoly of power-knowledge and dares to build its own science would be vital to finding fruitful solutions for exiting the chaos. To arrive at a societal structure that is more democratic, favors woman's freedom, and is ecological, we first need a new social science framework. What follows is an attempt to sketch a draft for this noble and exciting undertaking.

Scenarios

If September 11, 2001, is to be truly considered a turning point, it should not be seen as the beginning of World War III but as the beginning of a strategic stage of the war that followed the Cold War—we could call it the "postmodern war."

To what extent did the plot that led to my abduction play a role in this? Was it a provocation by the global system? Compared to the objective developments, the answers to these questions are mere details. Many thinkers, groups, and political forces find the US offensive senseless and regard it as a violation of international law and ethics. There have been many negative reactions. But despite all obstacles, the system's dominant power carried out a strategic offensive.

In light of our social and historical analysis to this point, it appears that the US is acting as an empire within the chaos. Just because we find this immoral and illegal does not make it any less true. At the moment, many nation-states, particularly the nation-states in the democratic republics of the EU, are very concerned, maybe rightly so. All the same, they are not being realistic. The globality of systems and their tendency to turn into empires has existed since Sargon of Akkad (c. 2400 BCE). Should we be surprised that the US carries forward these world empires, handed over by the British and the Soviets practically without a fight, by unifying them into a single empire, hundreds of links having been added along the way?

We can discuss the third big global offensive of capitalism and the depth of its crisis. Its chaotic features can be listed. All of which would confirm that this period requires a regime with imperial qualities. As civilization advances, many people insistently point out that states don't accept lacunae and politics can't tolerate a vacuum. It is, therefore, inevitable that the US, site of the most recent scientific and technological revolution, has established its leadership and created immense military and economic power and continues to expand, as the system's structure dictates. This is the nature of politics and the state. Noting this, as we said above, does not mean that we think that the US is in the right.

Similarly, saying that the age of nation-states is over is not tantamount to approval of global imperialism. The truth is that the forces behind the global economy and the military and political reality no longer regard this nation-state model as fruitful but see it as a hindrance. Contrary to what nationalist discourse suggests, a nation-state is not a completely independent state. There is no such concept as complete independence in the world of any phenomenon. The actual universal reality is interdependence. There is no object and subject that are not mutually dependent. The fetishized independent nation-state is a petite bourgeois utopia. Neither the independence of states nor the independence of nations is real.

States and nations depend on one another because they have different properties. The form of dependence imposed by the US imperial tendency is the most flexible. It doesn't rely on outdated methods like rigid colonialism, ethnic cleansing, or religious fanaticism. Rather, it experiments with forms of dependency that are even more postmodern than neocolonialism. In any case, because of the structure of their rule, a large number of nation-states perceive dependence on the US as rewarding. The nation-state has not been abolished, but it is also not permitted to behave as recklessly (i.e., as a "rogue state") as was previously the case. In this new phase of globalization, nation-states will inevitably have to reorient, a process that is taking place right now everywhere from Europe to China. This is not about a new war but about either bringing the ongoing war to an end or making it profitable for the system. When and where necessary, the US imposes the system's chaos regime, using economic and military means to preserve the status quo, to prevent further decline, or to renew structures and make them more expedient. It tries to realize its own alternative plans by developing far-reaching solutions and exiting the existing chaos. If this reality in the Middle East is our starting point, what possible developments can we predict?

We must always be aware that the US worldview is based both on the scientific revolution and its own interpretation of religious and philosophical reality. It develops its own models, projects, and plans by putting hundreds of thinktanks into action, constantly checking data, rarely slipping into dogmatism, and making frequent corrections. In all of this, historical developments are not ignored. The US tries to meaningfully develop its own models by finding a historical basis for them. All of this provides the US with the opportunity to flexibly plan new nuanced projects.

The Greater Middle East Initiative, as it has come to be called, targets the post-1990s with an analysis of recent imperialism and of attempts to solve current problems. It finds the order established by France and England after World War I flawed and inadequate. It even includes a self-critical reflection that after World War II its own practices strengthened despotism in the name of security and stability. The extreme impoverishment of the people of the Middle East is regarded as detrimental and dangerous to the system. Therefore, they seem to want to address economic development, individual freedom, democratization, and security simultaneously. In an attempt to prevent new explosions, it hopes to use this model to solve chronic problems like Israel-Palestine, Kurds-Arabs, and Turkey-Iran and to find a solution to the social fabric that has been shredded by despotism. In a way, this is a new Marshall Plan, like that once realized in Europe and similar to the approach taken to Japan but adapted to the Middle East. When a region so extremely important to the system—and this one certainly is—undergoes a period of chaos, a project like this is both necessary and realistic. It is actually surprising that it took so long. But now the system's project is taking shape step by step and picking up speed.

But the big problem standing in the way of such a project is the fact that the Middle East is in a totally different position than post-collapse Europe and Japan were. The Middle East has never experienced an Enlightenment or an Industrial Revolution. Democratization was never on the agenda. Without destroying the despotic political systems based on denominations and ethnic groups that are weighed down with nationalism and religionism, which are worse than fascism, there can be no renewal of the kind that occurred in Europe or Japan. The existing regimes are constantly producing crises. The local state blocs, which are very crafty, are masters at securing their existence at any cost. Those who masquerade as the opponents of the system are nothing but despotism's spare tires. The main goal is advocacy of the state, and the remnants of the god-state are stronger than presumed. The current states are merely empty shells with no historical role. In a way, they are the strongest of all the religious communities. The individuals produce them, and they, in turn, produce the individuals. Even the opposition considered the most revolutionary does not have any goal other than determining how it could better run the state.

On the other hand, historically, the region has a federative character. It cannot endure so many nation-states. The number of existing states itself breeds a deadlock. Under such conditions, denominations, ethnic structure, sects (tariqat), and other religious community–like groups bind the states to themselves and enter a period of mutual bolstering. This structure itself is the dead end, and it is this structure that the Western states have always supported. If their project is to have the desired effect, the first thing they will have to do is discard these regimes.

The US finds itself at an impasse in the truest sense of the word. After September 11, 2001, it took steps that may well have more serious consequences than the decision to enter World War I or World War II. For the US, the consequences of World War I were not too profound and did not reach a threshold where they affected the fate of the system. The war did, however, demonstrate the importance of the US. Even had it been defeated in the war, it could simply have retreated to its own continent and carried on without any problems. Then, after World War II, it succeeded in encircling the Soviet system. Even though the US lost some wars, as well as control over some territory, it succeeded in retaining, even expanding, its power. In both world wars, it was dealing with more modern state structures that it shared a Christian culture with. Under these circumstances, there were only a limited number of factors that could have deepened any clash of civilizations. Although the parameters of a certain chaos became apparent, they were not significant enough to threaten the system.

But in the Middle East, we find very different and clearly distinct factors. The US must either risk war with this despotic system, which has been becoming increasingly conservative since 1250 CE, or retreat. Wars such as the ones in Afghanistan and Iraq are insufficient. Without breaking up the power blocs in the region, each step taken will mean even more serious failure. Relying on one despotic state to defeat another is certainly not an effective tactic. The culture of the Middle East is skilled at reproducing despotism in situations like that. But should the US decide to take the whole thing down, it will be faced with the problem of controlling the masses. The deadlock in Iraq provides numerous lessons that could explain not only what is happening now but also what could happen. The US was a long-time supporter of the regime, which just made the problems worse. The regime is now ravaged, but both the general cultural milieu and various power blocs stand ready to foster new structures that are either identical or very similar. It is very unlikely that the cultural milieu can be overcome simply by introducing Western individualism. Dismantling the power blocs would be a truly revolutionary step. Such are the dialectics of the current impasse.

It seems inevitable that the UN and NATO will enter the picture. But this can't happen in a superficial way, as it did in Afghanistan or Somalia. The situation requires a lasting and comprehensive effort. It is only gradually becoming clear how important it is to actually analyze the Middle East. The problems that accompany its dissolution will be many times more complex than the difficulties raised by the collapse of the Soviet Union. The consequences we can anticipate from breaking the molds of power and the mentality in the region, which have become increasingly conservative over the last eight hundred years, have no parallel anywhere in the world. The unfettered sociality of individuals, tribes, and religious communities would be a powder keg that could be set alight at any point.

What revolution in mentality or economic revolution could dismantle these little despotic blocs and establish a new mentality and economic structures in their place? With what and how will the gulf between the European individual, that product of deep-seated traditions created by the Renaissance, the Reformation, and the Enlightenment, and the individual in the Middle East, as defined here, be overcome? Even though East European culture is not all that different from the culture of the rest of Europe, it has taken a quarter of a century for the transition from a highly modernizing system like real socialism to a liberal system and this is only now beginning to show some success, even though this is a system-immanent solution. Whether or not a similar dissolution in the Middle East could result in a system-immanent solution is a subject for extensive discussion. Clearly, a future rife with problems awaits us.

On the other hand, a failure on the part of the US-led coalition would create even more strategic problems. For the US, it would be a blow of global proportions that would serve to hasten the decline of the empire. Should the US suffer a defeat in the Middle East, it would set in motion a period of US defeats in Asia, Europe, and Africa. It might even be unable to retain its positions vis-à-vis South America, Mexico, and Canada, finding itself in a position similar to that of Russia. But given the current balance of power, for the US to accept such a drastic outcome is against the reality of being a ruling power. Therefore, the US will proceed strategically. Whatever it may cost and whatever the worldwide objections may be, it has to remain in the Middle East and produce some results and some solutions.

If we were to put the short-term, medium-term, and long-term problems that the Western capitalist system will have to solve into a hypothetical order, Afghanistan and Iraq would be the first in line in the short-term. In both cases, the idea of a democratic federation is being discussed, and federate structures are thought of as the new model countries for the region. Their draft constitutions envisage democratic federal systems, at least on paper. This is clearly an approach that involves innovations and ideals. The practical outcome is awaited with much anticipation. The encounter between cultures that include many ethnic and religious groups, on the one hand, and democratic federalism, on the other, could lead to a major civilizational transformation. In a way, it would have an impact comparable to the French and Russian Revolutions. Be all that as it may, the restoration of the old despotic regimes certainly seems very unlikely.

Democratic federalism is a structure that could only function with great difficulty in the empire of chaos. Where would the forces that could lead such a structure be found? The aspirants to power, which are at least as despotic as past regimes, are far removed from the mental and political structures that would be required to bring the ethnic and denominational character to a positive synthesis. The liberal free individual has still only developed a little in the Middle East. Democratic and socialist idealists are practically nonexistent. The nostalgists are so shallow that they are unable to assume any responsibility even for themselves. So trust is displaced onto the UN, NATO, the EU, and the coalition forces. The democratic federalism of an externally dependent structure would be highly questionable.

The most important medium-term problems are the Arab-Israeli conflict and Kurdish-Arab, Kurdish-Iranian, and Kurdish-Turkish relations. No doubt, the new distinct efforts of the UN, NATO, the EU, and the coalition could accelerate solutions to these historical problems. These problems are complex and have historical roots that reach far back into the depths of civilization and a relationship to modernity that is rife with contradictions and tensions. The solution to the Arab-Israeli problem largely depends on peace and strengthening democratization in the region. Contrary to popular belief, saying that the Israel-Palestine problem must be solved first creates the risk of deferring a solution for another fifty years. At the root of the problem lies Arab society and states that are not democratizing. A democratization of state and society in the Arab world would create the conditions for Israel-Palestine peace. If this democratization is not achieved, the conflict will further strengthen the conservative mentality and structures in Arab society and states that are far from democratic or orientated toward freedom and egalitarianism, as has been the case to this day.

The Kurdish question is even more complex and multifaceted. Kurds have deep-seated problems with the Arab, Iranian, and Turkish states and social structures. Kurds are denied even the most basic civil rights, and their political and economic rights are not even on the agenda. They are subjected to cultural genocide. The recent impositions of the US might lead to a few tentative steps and may result in some limited developments. The Iraqi federal state of Kurdistan is particularly open to provocation. Under the influence of the UN, NATO, and the coalition, further flare-ups can be expected. The current status of the Kurds effectively forces them to revolt. If a sustainable and a meaningful democratic solution proves impossible, we can expect a bloody geography that is even worse than what we see in the Israel-Palestine conflict. A conflict with a Kurdish population of forty to fifty million in the most inaccessible geography would further aggravate the problems of the region and would leave the region open to all sorts of possible developments.

A long-term solution will only be possible through advances in human rights, democratization, and economic development in Iran, Pakistan, the Turkic republics, and the Arab states and societies. Conservatism and the powerful interest blocs within states and social structures will fiercely resist any such development. However, there can be a limited system-immanent transformation if the dominant system succeeds in reaching out to the people and offering them feasible, constructive alternatives and the pressure put is never absent.

In the short, medium, and the long run an extensive use of military and economic power will be necessary. The execution of the Greater Middle East Initiative will require continuous military and political operations. Furthermore, the oft-referenced women's freedom and the development of liberal individuals will be indispensable. Without an awakening of women and minimal freedoms, no other efforts can bear fruit. Without the liberation of individuals—both women and men—being generally ensured no social group can achieve liberation.

To summarize, we can sketch three scenarios for ways out of the chaos of the Middle East. In the first scenario, the forces that want to preserve the old status quo, namely, the states created after the world wars, will insist on the nation-state model politically and economically. But since the balance of power between the Soviet Union and the US has been disrupted, and because the US approaches the region in an imperial manner, it has become increasingly difficult to maintain the former nation-state model.

Its economic, political, and cultural transformation appears inevitable. The old-fashioned political and economic structures that are statist, nationalist, and religious now represent an obstacle to the new globalization offensive in every respect. It is expected that they will reintegrate into the system, because the era of national capitalism is long since obsolete, and there is very little likelihood of the sort of balancing act seen in the twentieth century at this point. In this context, the states want to push up their price at least a little bit before they reintegrate. They will attempt to achieve this by presenting themselves as nationalist, conservative, or social and by using the media and various PR ploys to try to win the support of "their" masses. Although these shallow and inefficient efforts—we cannot even call them developments—are already being forcefully projected as politics, they are pure deception and demagoguery. These interest groups that are traditionally statist—it is unimportant whether they are republics or kingdoms—religious, and denominational primarily aim at securing their economic and political rentier rights. It is unlikely that the prominent capitalist centers, i.e., the US, the EU, Japan, and even China, that are promoting a restructuring in keeping with the information age will cooperate with these rentier-based economic and political structures, whose representatives will, thus, have to accept that the days of classic comprador capitalism are over. The status quo that Turkey, Egypt, Pakistan, and Iran in particular are trying to prop up will face significant difficulties as the system ramps up its engagement in the region. They can no longer maintain themselves with new alliances either among themselves or with the outside, as was once the case. However reluctantly, they will have to accept that there are no obvious rational options to reintegrating into the system under the leadership of the US and into the framework of its project for the region.

The second scenario is a restructuring brought about by US influence. There are plans for a process similar to the one carried out by France and England after World War I. We can imagine this as creating a status somewhere in between the nation-state and neocolonialism. Continuing to use the new NATO—enlarged and more dependent on the US—to target the regional status quo, with the involvement of the UN, would be the US's preferred scenario. As we previously said, this is a restructuring similar to the reconstruction of Europe in the framework of the Marshall Plan and of Japan after World War II. We can add to this the US's immediate neighbors Mexico and Canada. But it is quite obvious that a restructuring in the Middle East has to unfold very differently than was the case in these examples. Since the states characterized as Arab, in particular Egypt, as well as Iran, Afghanistan, Pakistan, and the Turkic states, including Turkey itself, cannot be sustained as before, they will, therefore, have to do their homework seriously in restructuring.

The main logic behind this restructuring is related to economic liberalization, freedom in the social sphere, particularly for women, and democratization of politics within the framework of the system itself—i.e., bourgeois democracy. The US will secure the support of Europe and Japan, procure legitimacy with the UN, and bring out the new NATO stick when necessary to ensure short-, medium-, and long-term transformation of these countries. Those who oppose this will be forced into line by a whole range of military, political, diplomatic, and economic (IMF and World Bank) measures. This scenario is not so much about changing the borders, as in the examples of Afghanistan and Iraq, as well as Georgia and the Balkans, as it is about a more democratic political structure that can make the transition from a rigid, centralized bureaucratic structure to a federation with more flexible and stronger local governments. Alongside this, statist economies will be dissolved, priority will be given to an economic structure based on privatization and a mixture of foreign and multinational corporations. The media sector in general will be restructured so that it is at the service of this project, and there will be investment in cultural and artistic work, especially to promote individual rights and women's freedom. It is possible that Afghanistan and Iraq are envisaged as prototypes for this scenario.

The weakness in this plan is that it will not work if it is only accepted by one side, namely, the system. Resistance on the part of the nation-states that defend the old status quo and the increasing demands of the social opposition will force concessions. Since it is impossible for a one-sided integration by the system to succeed, it will have to be open to mixed structures.

The third scenario will be developed in response to this necessity. The US will impose a compromise on the nation-states and the social opposition, premised on the US becoming the dominant hegemonic power. Under today's conditions, what we used to call subjugation will be transformed into compromise. Neither self-sufficient nation-states with wasteful and inefficient economies nor widespread uprisings or protracted national liberation struggles on the part of the people will be tolerated. The option will be rapid compromise or being crushed. The current status of Western European and former Eastern European countries can perhaps be seen as a concrete example of this scenario. They will not become Canada or Mexico but also will not remain like Turkey, Egypt, or Pakistan. The goal will be more toward a developed bourgeois democracy. We can also expect that people's forces will gain more influence, while the influence of nation-state forces that are pro–status quo will steadily decline. Perhaps we will see an interesting experiment involving both popular democracy and bourgeois state–based democracy.

In coming out of the chaos, the balance of forces necessitates that such options are not ignored. The main issue when addressing the restructuring of the system is to neither mount a blind resistance nor enter into an unprincipled compromise. It is important not to lose everything by trying to win it all.

It is likely that over the next quarter of a century there will various attempts to exit the chaos of the Middle East, with solutions developed toward this end, which will doubtless increase the number of available options, as different scenarios intermix. What will be even more important is how the scenario or utopia of the people, laborers, and social forces—evident at the Porto Alegre meetings—develop. History has never been determined by the unilateral will of the ruling powers alone. A lasting result has always been determined by the communal and democratic stance of societies.

The Future of the Region

We can draw a number of parallels between the situation in the Middle East today and the situation in the Roman Empire in the fourth century, when, with the exception of the areas east of the Tigris, the region consisted of Roman provinces. Christianity expanded quickly and conquered Rome from within, while "barbarians," comparable to the national movements of our time, attacked and attempted to defeat it from the outside. The imperial system reacted to this by absorbing both movements. Throughout the second and third centuries CE Rome tried to brutally crush the ethnic and social movements. Later, it used a policy of concessions to integrate the upper echelons of these movements into the system. This latter undertaking didn't work out particularly well. In fact, it set the stage for greater decay and growing signs of collapse. In 263 CE, Emperor Julianus II attempted to revive ancient paganism, to emulate and become the second

Alexander the Great, and to wage war against the Persians. This campaign came to a sad end on the shores of the Tigris. The current president of the United States, George W. Bush, who is apparently now trying to become the next Alexander the Great, is also driven by religious belief. But, as is well known, his goal may not be the dissemination of paganism but, rather, of Evangelical Christianity—a denomination that mixes Judaism, Christianity, and in some respects even Islam. Evangelicalism is a form of paganism that opposes scientism—which is, in a sense, today's religion. The similarity lies in the rejection of the dominant mentality in the name of something even older. After Julian II, the Roman Empire declined rapidly, splitting in two in 395 CE.

There are other remarkable parallels as well. At the time, Christianity was much more of a movement of the poor than real socialism ever was. The communal order was maintained with great care. The monasteries were genuine communist institutions. The Christians resisted Rome for three hundred years before being integrated in a compromise engineered by Constantine the Great. The indigent base, however, continued to resist, one of its forms being Arianism.[9] In a certain way, the people of the Migration Period who were called "barbarians," particularly Teutonic and Hunnish ethnic groups, were comparable to today's national liberation movements, and they resisted and attacked the empire for centuries before their upper echelons were assimilated, a process that hastened the integration of the ethnic groups as a whole. Even though the Roman Empire appeared to grow and become stronger through new alliances, it was essentially shrinking and falling apart. This became increasingly clear over time. It finally fragmented and disintegrated, because the values that had defined Rome had been lost, and the empire no longer met the needs of the people.

There are similarities between Rome and today's US Empire. Both reached their zenith as world empires. The US becoming a world empire is what lies behind the third great globalization offensive. When Rome was at the zenith of its power, it had already begun to decay, disintegrate, and fragment. The US empire of chaos is itself now showing a number of signs of disintegration, and the extreme geographical extension of its power is one factor contributing to this. It is in the case of the EU that we see fragmentation. We can perhaps compare the emergence of the EU as a second power bloc with the partitioning of the Roman Empire into Eastern and Western Rome.

A more profound parallel is the absorption of real socialism—the Christianity of its time—by the capitalist system. To this degree, the similarity of 1990 and 312 is striking.[10] Led by Soviet real socialism and after a long period of resistance, the "modern form" of Christianity struck a compromise with the main system, with the bureaucratic upper class betraying the poor. Another similarity can be found in the regimes that emerged from the broader national liberation movements. They too have entered into compromises with the US Empire. One after the other, the chiefs of the national liberation movements—the Teutons and the Huns of our day—became the US's provincial governors.

Today, in the 2000s, we are at the pinnacle of this process of dissolution and fragmentation. However you look at it, the offensive after September 11, 2001, was not an expansion of the system but a move to stop the disintegration, fragmentation, and decline. It is important to understand the difference.

Of course, such similarities do not mean that the developments will follow a similar course. The US is extremely pragmatic. Rather than eventually leading the system to the kind of collapse suffered by the historical empires, it may transform itself and make a smooth transition based on a policy of far-reaching concessions. This possibility must also be taken seriously. The US's growth so far is closely linked to an approach based on pragmatism and compromise. The key to the success of the capitalist system is its ability to simultaneously use repression and compromise, using its military, intelligence, economic, cultural, media, artistic, advertising, and scientific-technological power. It is also possible for the peoples and the laborers to avoid being integrated into the ruling system, which was the fate of Christianity and the barbarians. To do so, they will have to combine their intellectual power with a democratic and communal stance. While they should not ignore the possibility of principled compromises, renewing their offensive for democratic civilization and obliging the ruling system to accept it could allow them to elude integration.

Just as the historical development of the dominant forces in its totality needs to be seen as links in a chain, much the same is true of the freedom forces. Even though the shape of each may be different, they have all been links in the ongoing demand for freedom throughout the ages and into the present. Once again, the role of each distinct shape becomes clear: to preserve the essence of the demand for freedom and allow it to be carried forward. Essence, however, has the capacity to gain richness and depth.

The richness of the historical chain was determined by the particular shape of each of its links. In the language of society, these links are called structuring and organizing.

Because of domination, the need for freedom is universal. The need for freedom and the form that freedom will take for various people depend on the kind of domination they face. As long as domination is universal, whether individually or socially, both the need for freedom and the struggle to achieve it will continue. The need and desire for freedom is essential for development. Nonexistence would only be possible if the need and desire for freedom were obliterated. As long as nonexistence is not actualized, when necessary, the will of freedom—like that of the plants that shatter rocks—will pierce through every wall of repression and, like a river, will seek its bed and flow ceaselessly forward.

To arrive at a holistic perspective on the problem of freedom for the people of the Middle East, we have to evaluate it in connection with historical tradition. The struggle for freedom has an everlasting history; the important thing is to determine the particularities of this history at given points. One of the dominant power's important achievements has been leading people to believe that there is no problem of freedom for society and the people, neither at a collective nor at an individual level. The only valid, universal, and absolute history is the dominant power's own history, full of gods, sumptuousness, heroic acts, and sacredness. They are masters at negating the extraordinarily rich history of society with abstract and meaningless figurative values of this sort and presenting this fictional and bloody beyond brutal exploitative history as if it has been a godlike march.

One of the crucial reasons for the defeats of social libertarians is that they succumb to these dominant historical discourses. The very first thing they need to do if they are to succeed is to have the strength to live their own history. They must continue to affirm their own history of freedom, or at least its tradition, as a moral attitude. As long as there is repression, there will also always be the desire for freedom.

These abstract elaborations are meant to give meaning to society in the Middle East, which appears so static on the surface. There is a history of social freedom in the Middle East, and it is very powerful and profound. It is the primary duty of freedom fighters to discern this history and bring it back into daylight. Every plant needs its roots to blossom. Our present-day freedom struggle can only grow and flourish if it is based on the roots and traditions of freedom.

We live within the borders of the contemporary Roman Empire and are besieged by the various provincial powers. The provincial governors, who today are embodied by the regional states, are cruel, as has so often been the case throughout history. Jesus was crucified by the proconsul of Judea, Pontius Pilate. Therein lies the symbolism of Jesus. The history of Christianity is the history of thousands of similar events flowing together to become a great flood. On the other hand, provincial governors have also frequently plotted uprisings and have sometimes been successful. After a while, they either become emperors themselves, give in to the system, or are buried under their own rebellion. This is something that takes place within the system that has no value regarding freedom and in social terms, or, when it does, only indirectly. This kind of resistance on the part of provincial governors must not be confused with that of societal freedom movements. If our understanding doesn't rise above the reality of the contemporary empire, the struggle against it either has no chance of winning, or even if, by chance, we are victorious, it can't be worth much. The restructuring of the provinces in the Middle East is, however, due to the current chaos.

We often talk about the unique reality of the chaotic situation. Because chaos is a short time interval when the possibility of freedom and formation is at its greatest. In this short time interval, what is most needed from the freedom front is the necessary power of meaning—and knowledge of its history and its era. It is a fact that the system is exploding at just such a chaos interval, after an approximately five-thousand-year period of hegemony, and, more recently, the last 260 years of capitalist hegemony. This situation must be rigorously evaluated. We have highlighted the main scenarios with which the US-led contemporary empire might try to address the chaos, which we did to make a realistic description of the situation and the options available to the people and to societal freedom forces. The reaction of these social forces cannot be the same as that of the Christians in the Roman Empire or the barbarians on the outside. We can learn from them but should not imitate them. Nor would reproducing real socialism or the national liberation movements be useful at present, because, as a result of their fundamental flaws, whenever they were successful they failed to avoid being integrated into the system or even actively pursued integration. Our response must reflect our way of knowing.

What the term "mentality revolution" implies is a consciousness of and belief in a free society. Consciousness means more than knowledge of *what is*. It also means knowledge of *how to*. Belief, on the other hand, means trusting what you know and doing what is necessary. This denotes the capacity and the determination to act on your beliefs. To correctly and skillfully lead an ideological struggle in the Middle East requires a true understanding of the structures of the mentality that dominates society. It is necessary to distinguish between the aspects of society that need to be overcome and those that need to be preserved. Similarly, a thorough knowledge of the mentality molds that must be struggled against is also necessary. To gain a new mentality requires an immense labor and moral attitude to attain the necessary social consciousness and belief. Those who cannot expand their mental world cannot wage a long-term freedom struggle.

Degeneration begins where and when the mentality is drained and exhausted. Essentially, all of the wise people and prophets of the Middle East have led struggles around mentality. Mentality, in and of itself, is worthless if it is not linked to morality. Morality is the strength to continue to walk on the path illuminated by one's consciousness despite all obstacles and errors. It is the insistence on society's indispensable values of conscience. Breaking the bond between consciousness and morality casts the door open to hooliganism and irresponsible idleness.

We must also understand our opponent's mentality and, as much as needed, nurture ourselves upon it. The mentality of state power has always been very well organized and should never be underestimated. If we don't succeed in hemming it in, there will be no successful advance and solution. Politics and action, including military action, detached from our mentality and morality can always backfire like a rogue mine. Our politics and actions must always be clear-minded and morally exacting. Otherwise, there can be no escape from being an instrument of the political offensives of counter-mentalities. I have consistently pointed out the drawbacks of embarking on political offensives without waging successful struggles for the mentality, as outlined here.

History's great ascetics have tried to gain the necessary mental capacity by retreating into great hermitages, trying to find a way to prevent the repetition of these errors, as well as a way to teach humanity a bit of a lesson.

It is not an accident that, although an imperial power, the US works with hundreds of think tanks, i.e., organizations of mentality and thought. It knows from historical experience that the better it understands the areas where it operates, the more successful it will be in securing its interests.

The revival of Islam and the tariqat in the region arises from the desire of certain social groups to achieve the mentality necessary to serve their interests.

Without understanding and disentangling the tariqat and, more generally, without researching the effects of revived Islamism on society, a correct mentality struggle cannot be waged. The same is true for the various forms of nationalism. Without understanding how the nationalist mentality, which is in a way contemporary ethnic mentality, was born and organized and how it gained validity within society, the ideological and practical struggle in the Middle East cannot be skillfully led. The still prevalent mentality of ethnic power, including familialism and tribalism, must also be well understood and countered. It is essential that all of these mentalities are understood, hemmed in, and those concerned are given the true mentality values they need. This is much more difficult than carrying out practical struggles but must be recognized as an essential task.

When entering a mentality struggle in the Middle East it is necessary to be like Moses leading the Hebrew tribe, like David fighting Goliath, like Jesus mobilizing his apostles, and like Mohammad motivating his faithful to work. Moreover, we must know how to say "know thyself!" with the excitement of Socrates, "value democracy" with the enthusiasm of Pericles, and "make way for Alexander" with the science of Aristotle. What we mean by acquiring a new mentality in the Middle East is to turn to nature with the excitement of the Renaissance, to love humans, and to thirst for knowledge. It is to pierce through religious dogma with a Reformation, acquiring the necessary belief that exists in our essence, to take science, philosophy, and the arts to the people through an Enlightenment, and to mobilize movement of intellectuals for freedom.

In the Middle East, walking while thinking and thinking while walking only become meaningful if accompanied by such a definable mentality. When this is the case, we will once more attain the natural liveliness of the Neolithic Age and the power to approach all things with sacred enthusiasm. The mythological thought of the civilizational eras abounds with lessons, and the books of wisdom will open themselves up to us one after another. Then the history of humanity and civilization will reveal itself, this terrible and sacred, numbing and exciting history that denigrates and exalts life. The true meaning of the Holy Scripture and the great prophetic experiences will come alive. The revival of the dried-up streams of civilization, the urbanization of the ruins, and the awakening pure peasantry of the *höyük* will, each in turn, appear to us.[11] The cruelest to the richest, from Nimrod to Croesus, and the resistance fighters, from Job to Mazlum Doğan, Ferhat Kurtay, and Kemal Pir,[12] the black and white values, will step forward into the light of day. The mentality struggle is how these values express themselves, how they blossom in our hearts and souls. Under these conditions, no force and no mere necessity of life will hold us back. We will resolve and transcend all obstacles with a consciousness as deep as the sea and a will roaring with the excitement of a flood. Then we will ingeniously review all issues, whether political or military, and act in an epic manner.

In today's Middle East, we can't make headway with classic left, right, religious, or nationalist positions; in prophetic terms, we cannot be free of impiety. We also can't make any headway with the New Left, a civil society with its head in the clouds, and a women's movement that is unaware of history and of labor. One could at best have a picnic with the urban petite bourgeoisie, which is being tightly squeezed and has simply withered or engages in mindless activities with no real conviction. Those who are convinced rentiers or who are primarily committed to attaining a higher social status make for even worse companions when it comes to advancing any idea or belief. None of these options would do justice to the individuals and peoples of the Middle East, who have already gone through so much and been hurt a thousand times.

As we begin to take action in response to social reality of the Middle East, embracing and walking with a mentality defined as such will lead us to the region's buried history and unite us with its faded heart and its reality that seeks the light. Only then will we be able to begin a noble struggle worthy of the region's true history and its freedom lovers. This struggle will always rise anew and continue the march toward its goal—it can never be stopped, even when it is distorted, betrayed, or destroyed. Then history will be ours, and our hearts will always beat in unison. And when this happens our social reality will become a creative divinity. Our people, the people of the Middle East, will finally achieve the freedom that they have longed for and deserved for millennia.

The Middle East's political option for exiting the chaos must be one that addresses the question of freedom not only on a regional level but also on a universal level. The fate of the global offensive will be determined in this region, because the success or failure of the US-led system will have a determinant influence on the future of the entire world. The attempt to carry on with the power blocs that were pieced together from the twentieth-century feudal powers without being transformed is the most difficult option to implement. This is why the broad base of society, which has traditionally been dominated in the extreme, has to some degree come into play. The global capitalist powers that want to restructure the region also understand that this is necessary. It is very doubtful, however, that it will be possible to limit the masses to the particular wishes of the capitalist powers once they have been awakened. Nonetheless, it is unclear what will actually emerge from Pandora's Box. This uncertainty can only be resolved by creative and liberating efforts during the current interval of chaos.

There will be a period of practical change that can't be compared to anything that has happened at any other point in history. A historical time for restructuring society that bears certain similarities to the founding of new cities has come. This reality underlies the difficulties in the Middle East. This restructuring will give rise to a complicated mélange of relations and contradictions between the dominant system, on one hand, and the struggles by the freedom forces of the people and society, on the other.

Democratic Politics

Before we turn to the blocs to be restructured, we need to define the concept of "politics" in a way that is specific to the region. We can define *politics* as *the practical management of society* in both the short term and the long term. Politics is conservative if it hampers social change and progressive if it leads to leaps forward. A third dimension of the definition concerns content. We can define *politics* as *statist* when it is centered on the state bloc and as *democratic* when it concerns the masses separate from the state. It can also be defined relative to areas like the economy, culture, social affairs, or the arts. We can call it *high politics* if it is about far-reaching changes to society and *basic* or *limited* politics when it has a narrower focus. The common point in all the definitions is that *politics* is defined as *the art of societal guidance, change, and transformation*. Political activity is society's construction work.

If efforts around mentality mean working on utopias, projects, plans, and programs, the political undertaking is the work of education, organizing, and action. It is important not to confuse the efforts around mentality with the political undertaking, and even more importantly the opposite is also true. The work of the architect, the foreman, and the construction worker all require particular expertise and much more care when it comes to the social realm and can be defined as an art, the art of politics.

This means that political activity requires a special preparation in the field of mentality. In the practical realm, however, it requires the ability to educate, organize, and act to guide, change, and transform society. It is not for nothing that politics is regarded as a "divine art." When talking about god-kings, the sultan as the "shadow of God," and the state as the incarnation of God, the emphasis is actually on divine art. If we want to disentangle and analyze religion and mythology, we need a certain competence in sociology and social science.

The US and its prominent partners are now carrying out an intense military and political restructuring of the Middle East. We should not see military practice as separate from politics. In an environment where there is a fierce armed conflict, *war* is just another word for *politics*. In such an environment, militancy is decisive. Politics as an extension of military practice comes to the fore once the weapons fall silent. This is the inverse of Clausewitz's famous formula: "war is simply a continuation of political intercourse, with the addition of other means."[13] It is not politics that determines war, but war that determines politics. This can be seen very clearly in Iraq. What paves the way for politics—a new politics—in Iraq is the state-of-the-art technological war conducted by the US. In any case, in the entire history of Mesopotamia, war has always stood at the crossroads of politics. This latest war faithfully reflects this historical truth.

Once the war is low-intensity or stops altogether, political activity, as its extension, gains momentum. Which is to say, politics is the part of war not executed with arms. It is the part that is carried out with education, organizing, and action without resorting to arms but based on the same mentality. In this sense, with massive military support, the US and its partners are conducting, adjusting, and continuing political restructuring, especially in Afghanistan, Iraq, and throughout the Middle East, based on the mentality of their Greater Middle East Initiative.

In the previous section, we presented three scenarios that summarize these efforts. Now it is important to clarify the kind of political struggle based on the defense of people and society that the freedom forces opposing domination must adopt. We have already defined our priorities: developing both the necessary mentality and our concept of "politics."

Turning to concrete policies, our first task is to carry out, develop, and qualitatively improve a process of democratization that emanates from the non-statist communal society and the democratic stance of the people. Not focusing on the state must be a point of principle. Societal freedom stands in contradiction to the state-focused work. State-focused work can only be carried out on behalf of the dominant power. For social forces whose goal is freedom, it is entirely obvious that their focus must be on democracy as a "non-state" policy, because they have a fundamental duty to oppose domination rather than be associated with it.

We distinguish our definition of *democracy* from democracy as a bourgeois veil for the state. Even when addressing Athens and the first Sumerian urban democracies, we must carefully differentiate between true democracy and the state. One cannot be an extension of the other; the proliferation of one decreases the other, and the end of one represents the complete victory of the other. The kind of democracy the US and its partners impose is the bourgeois-feudal democracy of a very small group that relies on the extensive military-ruling power apparatus. On the other hand, although relying on a society's minimal defense forces, the forces of societal freedom regard democratic politics as their main work. Democratic politics subsumes all the activities, including education, organization, and action, of all individuals and social groups suffering at the hands of the dominating power. The means used to achieve political, legal, and economic goals can range from demonstrations, rallies, protests, and uprisings to war, should it become necessary. These activities are generally necessary daily tasks or ongoing undertakings meant to achieve reform or change. When they include major qualitative change, they can be considered revolutionary. The more the dominant system strives for power and control over democracy, the more intertwined and confrontational the freedom forces efforts for democracy will become.

It is also important not to repeat the mistakes made in the English, French, and Russian Revolutions. This means ensuring that care is taken so that the democratic efforts of any one side don't end up being absorbed, negated, or destroyed by the other, as this would be a catastrophe and a grave historical mistake, which could also be called a forced correctness. There will likely be both a relationship and contradictions between the two democracies. They can either coexist in harmony or confront each other as opponents. The main thing to avoid is the danger of one side becoming the only one by being absorbed by the tendency to negate and destroy the other. The rules, conditions, and principles of either coexistence or confrontation must be clearly defined. Singularity is always dangerous in democracies, because it leads to the negation of democracy. Being attentive to the distinct democratic option of each group, both internally and externally, is the superior aspect of democratic genius. The opposite would be the politics of Plato's philosopher kings or the mythological god-kings—the politics of fascism and totalitarianism, hierarchy, despotism, and dictatorship of all kinds. This is, after all, the antidemocratic character of all dominant systems.

The democracy that will develop in the Middle East will probably be of a mixed nature. It will need to address both feudal bourgeois demands and the demands of the social groups and working classes in an intertwined way. We are past the point where an exclusively bourgeois democracy is an option. In any case, it has never existed in a pure form, and the same is true for a pure democracy of the societal and people's forces. This does not mean that a societal and people's democracy and a bourgeois democracy can never exist independently. Each group of people will profoundly experience its own form of democracy, and that is a good thing. The more a group internalizes its own democracy, the more able it will be to carry out, change, and transform the common democracy together with other groups and classes based on shared principles and experiences.

In light of this analysis, let's take a closer look at the relationship between democracy and social reality in the Middle East. We have seen that democratizing the state is not something that can be done. Instead, what is necessary is that the state be receptive to democracy. Being receptive means accepting democratic mentality and structures and their practices. One might object that this would limit the power and size of the state, and that is correct. After all, the existence of democracy is tantamount to constraining and downsizing the state. In countries where democracy functions effectively, the state has to be redefined as the organization and institutionalization of the mandatory overall security and related needs within the common public sphere. In democracies, there is no place for the classic dominant state.

The state and democracy can only coexist within this basic framework. Under the present conditions, neither the classic state nor a democratic leadership can exist exclusive of the other. In this sense, we could see the current period as an era of transition from the state to democracy. Generally, in times of transition, the fundamental institutions of the past and the future coexist, as was the case during the period when feudalism and capitalism coexisted.

Religion and ethnicity must also change during the democratization phase. Religion and ethnic groups can be represented by modern political and nongovernmental organizations. Democratic and political structures could take the place of the classic religious and tribal structures. Neither states and democracies based on religion or ethnicity nor formations that totally ignore and negate the two have much chance of success. The key reason for the failure of European-style liberal and left tendencies to gain a base is that they fail to correctly analyze and connect with religion and ethnicity. However, the social fabric is largely the product of these two phenomena. It is unlikely that politics, particularly democratic politics, will succeed without developing radical approaches to religion and ethnicity and the related structures. If this is not done, success would only be possible with an extremely violent revolutionary or counterrevolutionary dictatorship, but whether this could endure is another question altogether.

In this connection, we must also take a look at the denominations and brotherhoods. In both cases, we can see a kind of monastic order reminiscent of the Middle Ages. They resemble medieval forms of civil society. Genuine efforts must be made to orient these still existing institutions toward democracy. It would be best if they were neither negated nor repressed but were accepted as sociological phenomena and integrated into the tendency working for freedom. Women's rights and freedom are also indispensable components of a democratization process and will thus play an important role, a point we will return to.

In the concrete case of the Middle East, the development of democracy has been very limited. Democratic thought and its reflexes are not yet fully awakened. Despite the deep longing of many groups, the millennia of brutal state repression have put these longings to sleep. Even though these longings manifest in the form of outbursts and rebellions from time to time, the brutal despotic character of the state has repeatedly buried them. However, the radical contradiction between the reality of our age and this state structure is awakening the longing for democracy, freedom, and equality. The twentieth century showed us many signs of this development. In the twenty-first century, however, a development from longing to realization seems increasingly likely.

The Arab states are lagging behind. The subordination of the religious and ethnic structures to the state, as well as the statist character of their upper layers, which are bound to the state through strong ties of interest, hampers the awakening of democratic reflexes and the drive to take action. An intervention from the outside is needed.

Although the development of the state of Israel in the midst of the Arab states has strengthened Arab nationalism and religionism up until now, it is now at a point where it will have a reverse effect. Everyone has now realized that the chronic Arab-Israeli conflict cannot be solved by nationalism and religionism. Overcoming the nationalist and religious leadership and the emergence of a group of democratic leaders is the only thing that can overcome the current deadlock. As we can see in the case of Cyprus, internal and external conditions provide a strong opportunity for a democratic solution tendency. This is also why the Greater Middle East Initiative comes into play with more concrete plans. The democratization of Saudi Arabia and Egypt are seen as particularly important. The other smaller Arab states have begun perforce to take an interest in democracy, as if they have learned their lesson from the example of Iraq. On the outside international public opinion and on the inside the longing of communal society and a democratic stance that has been suppressed and distorted for thousands of years are about to awaken. It is unlikely that the despotic Arab states can hold out for long against these two developments and totally close the door to democracy. In terms of democratization, it is unimportant whether the states in question call themselves kingdoms or republics—both are inclined to despotism. The important thing is that they are receptive to democracy and are ready to allow for the restriction and downsizing of the state.

We have established that the existence of these states was dependent on the traditional balance of power between systems. Since 1990, the situation has become more difficult for these states. The hegemonic presence of the US in the region has increasingly reduced them to a provincial status and will continue to do so. To survive as states, they will most likely move toward a democracy that suits US principles. It will be increasingly difficult to sustain their power based on blocs that previously relied on the US, and before that on England, France, and even the Ottomans. The Greater Middle East Initiative is the result of this difficulty. Though democratic structures may look different in every country, there will also be commonalities. Human rights, nongovernmental organizations, elections, multiparty systems, pluralist media, stronger parliaments, and greater individualization are commonalities that will increasingly be on the agenda. We can also expect constitutional and legal improvements. The emerging democracies will be neither entirely feudal bourgeois democracies nor entirely people's democracies. Democracy might initially express itself in limited advances against the state but will eventually spread to the rest of society.

In the Arab region, Israel and Syria are two strategic elements that are key to democratization. Israel has a well-established democracy, which is not a weakness for Israel but an important factor of its strength. It is difficult to say the same thing about Syria. Syria is at a serious crossroads. If it doesn't accelerate its steps toward democratization with serious reforms and resolve its problems with Israel, it might become a second Iraq. Syria's democratization and peace with Israel could enable the transformation of the regime in Syria without resorting to force. The presence of powerful intellectuals, its diverse ethnic and denominational structure, and middle and poor classes could all lead to a more fruitful process of development in a joint democracy. The role of the Kurds in Syria is not like that of the Kurds in Iraq; in Syria, there is more likely to be an opportunity for liberal democratic transformation. The receptive approach by the state will be decisive. Berbers, for example, could play a similar role in North Africa.

Iraq is a candidate for being a democracy laboratory for the Arabs, or even for the entire Middle East, a feature that is further strengthened because it contains almost all of the region's ethnic, religious, denominational, political, and social elements. The increasing efforts of the US and its allies, on the one hand, and the increasing democratic initiatives from below of the various ethnic, denominational, and social groups, on the other hand, put this country in a strategic position in terms of democracy. A rich history and its oil, if used correctly, could give democracy a chance. The insistence of the Kurds on democratic federalism will have important regional consequences beyond the areas where they can be found. A Democratic Federation of Iraq could serve as a prototype for a Democratic Federation of the Middle East, a factor that will become increasingly evident in the future. The reason that developments in Iraq are so important is that solutions there could spread to the entire Middle East.

The democratization of Iran is also becoming an increasingly timely issue. The classic state finds it more and more difficult to bring its powerful tradition in step with the present. Iranian people increasingly and enthusiastically long for democracy. After Iraq, democratic federalism could also be on the agenda for Iran. Iran is more inclined to federalism than division. Elements similar to federalism have prevailed in Iran's 2,500-year state tradition. If the intensifying longing of the people is coupled with a contemporary federalism, Iran could become the strongest democratic federation in the region, a kind of second Russia. Instead of engaging in resistance to the increasing pressure from the US à la Saddam Hussein, moving toward democratic federalism could be a realistic and sustainable option for Iran. The extreme politicization of religion negatively affects democratization. Religious ideology may become increasingly ineffective and could easily backfire. Iranian culture is particularly susceptible to democratization. Its historic traditions of resistance and its personalities, from Zoroaster, Mazdak, and Babak to Hassan Sabah and others,[14] provide the basis for democratic culture. The recent experience of highly colorful opposition could help to create a coherent democracy if the Iranians can free themselves from their various maladies. Communication technology could serve to speed up this process. If the state leadership shows the necessary flexibility, we might see democratization in Iran similar to that in Spain.

In Pakistan, religion plays an even more negative role. Religionism, fostered by anti-Hinduism and tribalism, has literally taken both the state and society prisoner. However, the end of US support for religion and the experience in Afghanistan might weaken the religious fabric and could lead to a secular democracy. Otherwise, Pakistan cannot compete with India, Iran, and Afghanistan. The Pakistani model needs to be rapidly transformed. Afghanistan could be a template for the entire Central Asian area, similar to Iraq for the Middle East. A democratization of Afghanistan would exert massive pressure on Central Asia to change. The democratization of the Turkic republics, however, depends more on Russia. But it is possible that the influence of elements in their immediate environment could trigger distinct developments.

Because of its fragmented mentality and states, the political structure of the Middle East does not easily turn toward EU-like developments, but the region's historical base makes cooperation more rational. Today's Islamic Conference is not particularly functional. On the other hand, a Democratic Federation of the Middle East can be an idealized concept. The fact that the US and its allies find democratization more appropriate for their interests increases the likelihood of such a development. Before 1990, antidemocratic and despotic forces were generally supported, but in this new phase the opposite approach is increasingly on the agenda. The accelerating tendency toward democracy in our age cannot tolerate the region being ruled with outdated state structures for very long. The fifty- to sixty-year-old nation-states that once based themselves on the balance of power between the Soviet Union and the US have become unproductive, crisis-ridden models that can no longer be tolerated by globalization. A downsized and restricted state that listens to the people at the bottom as much as it does to the system and that is receptive to democracy as a result is a strong possibility. These factors mean that the transition of the Middle East into a democratic civilization could also make an important contribution to the transformation of the world.

These predictions about developments in the Middle East in the near future obviously do not provide the ideal for the democratic and communal system of the people; it is an ideal like the past socialist utopia, but a more realistic ideal. It is important that those who campaign for social freedom and equality do not sacrifice their principles for state-focused solutions—or, rather, non-solutions. They must never give up their principled position in exchange for certain concessions, as was the case with real socialism, social democracy, and the national liberation movements. Insistence on and depth in democracy is the surest way to gain freedom and equality. As Lenin once noted, even if too late, our goal can only be achieved through the tenacious pursuit of the broadest possible long-running democratization.

The Freedom of Women

In the civilization of the Middle East, the situation of women is central to solving all social problems. We won't repeat our earlier brief historical elaboration here. In the coming period, our fundamental objective must be achieving the third great sexual rupture, this time to the *dis*advantage of men. Without the social equality of the sexes, any demand for freedom and equality is meaningless and out of reach. Woman's freedom is the most enduring and encompassing part of any democratization process. The question of women's freedom is the weakest point of the system that first turned women into a property and now horrendously commodifies them in every possible way. The role once played by the working class must now be played at its best by the lineage of women. The analysis of the lineage of women must take precedence over any class analysis if class division and the division into nations is to be better grasped, analyzed, and resolved. Genuine freedom for women requires the removal of feelings and will that enslave them, that of their husbands, fathers, lovers, brothers, friends, and so on. Under such feelings and will, the greatest love has actually become the most dangerous property relation. The identity of the free woman can only be illuminated by a rigorous criticism of all the molds of thought, religion, science, and the arts produced by the dominant male world as they relate to women. The woman must first and foremost belong to herself if she is to cease being a "commodity." When a woman becomes a commodity or property, it also prevents a man from behaving morally. Living with that sort of a woman is also an obstacle to being a free man. A woman debased in that manner is a debased man, but in reverse.

It is correct to say that the level of freedom in any society depends on the level of women's freedom. If we look at the issue in terms of aesthetics, we will see that those who are not free cannot have anything that is aesthetic about them. A life that is aesthetically empty borders on the life of a primate. It may make more sense and be more critical to view the phenomenon of the woman as an artistic phenomenon, rather than viewing her as a commodity or as property, or in the way a worker or peasant is viewed. For an aesthetic life, women must be understood to be the most functional and receptive aspect of nature, even sacred in a certain sense. Furthermore, they should not be addressed using male-dominated language, but an understanding the language of the woman that is laden with secrets is important. The worst imaginable social practice is imposing male domination and male selfishness upon women. Nothing seals the fate of a woman who has been deprived of all her options more than the vulgar male attitude. In my view, the democratic man, i.e., a man who is strong, mature, and receptive and who understands something about freedom and equality and the corresponding society can only come in to being by creatively adhering to the criteria we have outlined here and the implementation thereof. A society where slavery runs the deepest is a society that looks down on the woman the most. A society that has no understanding of how to live life is a society that has accepted living with the woman aimlessly. Additionally, the worst and emptiest possible life, a life devoid of enthusiasm and meaning, is a life lived with an enslaved woman.

If we look at society in the Middle East in this light, we will begin to understand why a backward, senseless, cruel, ugly, and intolerant life prevails. It is so clear that a male society that treats women in such a crude and unaesthetic manner, as if a worthless commodity, possibly even a problem to dispose of if incorrigible, can only live in strife, deprived of peace and surrounded by ugliness. Male societies of that sort cannot create the sacredness of life, the eminence of a homeland, true virtue, or a sensible approach to animate nature. When they fail in this way, they often find their pretext by pointing at the "demon woman." The woman that is called "demonic and deficient" is the vilest lie told by a male society that has suffered a huge loss. Free life cannot be attained without an intense struggle against the dominant male ideology, morality, and social forces and the adherent individuals. Without this struggle it will also be impossible to create a genuinely democratic society or, concomitantly, socialism with equality. The people's political option is not simply a democratic society; it is a society that is democratic *and* that promotes woman's freedom.

Concretely, the women's freedom struggle has to be carried out in conjunction with the establishment of a women's political party, building a broad-based mass women's movement, setting up nongovernmental organizations, and establishing structures that advance democratic politics. The more women can rid themselves of male domination and male-dominated society and gains strength by acting on their own initiative, the more women can develop free personalities and identities. Marrying women off at an early age is the cruelest kind of slavery; the noblest behavior is not to marry women off but to free their minds.[15] The abject practices imposed upon women by the male hand—ranging from the burka and hijab to pornography—are eviler than any class- or nation-based cruelty. Therefore, the highest expression of comradeship and humanism on the part of men would be to support women's rage and struggle for freedom and consciousness, as well as women's movements. The Middle East is more than familiar with civilization and is the site of both the strongest goddess cult and the deepest enslavement of women. To bring about a third great sexual rupture, the space must be created for a great march forward to the advantage of women that is worthy of the region's history. Sharp declines are followed by breathtaking ascents. On this basis, if we proceed as if we are the believers in a new goddess religion, we may well reach the well-deserved sacredness of the mother and the womanhood of love.

Economy

I don't find questions concerning economy, class, and socialization in the alternative society of the Middle East very meaningful. In my view, the issues that need to be resolved are those raised above. Recognizing the workers or the unemployed and the peasantry is not revolutionary but *not recognizing them* truly is. Imagining these class divisions to represent the servants of an aga or a chief might well bring us closer to reality. Freedom is achieved to the extent that we *overcome* being workers or peasants, if not economically, at least in our mentality and in the realm of democratic politics. It is out of necessity that one becomes a worker or a peasant. If freedom means the transcendence of necessity, then being a worker or a peasant must also be surpassed. If a genuine class struggle is carried out with this mentality and in a democratic manner, socialism begins to acquire its real meaning as equality.

Unemployment is the result of a lack of democracy. A democratic society can never have unemployment. The greater the level of unemployment, the lower the level of democracy. Unemployment is a disorder, a disease of class civilization in general. People and communities who know how to oppose it will never end up with unemployment. Since the greatest work is the work for democracy, if no other work can be found, there still remains the best work for all. Be a good democrat, and fight for freedom; you will soon discover that you will never in your life have an idle hour. People and communities unable to wage a struggle for democracy will always remain idle, unskilled, and unemployed. Thus, the struggle against unemployment, idleness, inebriation, and laziness can be won if individuals and society are educated and organized as part of the struggle for democracy and begin to take action.

If the people of the Middle East do not stand up for democracy, they will also be unable to free themselves from the centuries of indolence, idleness, and unemployment. Societies that know how to be democratic can also enjoy their homeland, their resources, their achievements, and their cultures and make human labor productive in the process. When this labor is combined with today's science and technology, there should be no trace of hunger and unemployment. Unemployment and idleness are products of a lack of democracy and a habituation to slavery. Those who want to put an end to this situation will get the best results by establishing democratic organization and democratic action not by begging at the feet of the state and the boss—the two main sources of unemployment and every sort of debasement. As such, the real economic struggle is intimately intertwined with democratic action. All other labor disputes are stage-managed by the yellow unions and the bosses' agents.[16] With cheap concessions they see to it that people remain slaves their entire lives, either as workers or as peasants. Countries and societies that have understood and embraced democracy have always been prosperous and successful, from Athens in its day to Switzerland or England today.

Ecology
The history of the Middle East is also the history of the death of ecology. Since class society–based civilization has become alienated from nature,

the permanent destruction of the environment has continued day by day, year by year, century by century. All the forests and the soil that were once humanity's fertile lifelines are now almost deserts. These forests and this soil, along with animals and plants, provided the original basis for civilization. At the point that some humans put other humans in servitude, they set about destroying nature with their cruel axe, transforming areas that had sparked dreams of paradise into wastelands. Soon after the forest disappeared, the land was spent, and as the land was lost, so too were the plants and animals, leaving humans hungry and thirsty, so they left. In the end, the most fertile land became the most depleted, and this led to massive migration. The land that people had flooded from all four directions became steppes and deserts, and the people fled from it in all four directions. Like the history of women, the history of ecology in the Middle East also remains unwritten. Just as to be free a woman must know her history, to have an ecological society we must know the history of the region's ecology. A democracy and a society that promotes women's freedom that is not based on environmental awareness, and action is not a real option for the people.

A movement for democracy and women's freedom can be no different from any dominant male world if it is not based on something as basic as a major commitment to reforestation and to protecting the land from erosion. An ecological movement is one of the indispensable components of the new society we hope to build. Ecology cannot simply be reduced to economy. It is a mentality in its own right, the return to a lost conception of animate and sacred nature. Living a life in the absence of an awareness of nature that is animated, that talks to us, that comes into being with us, that calls us into being, instead of seeing a nature that is inanimate and has lost its sacredness. A tainted land that is as black as death amounts to a life that has largely eroded. Environmental consciousness means more than addressing water and air pollution; it means being completely at one with nature, turning back from a nature divided into plots to a nature that is a whole. This would be to arrive at a democratic and socialist society. The interconnection really is, in fact, this profound. It is, after all, respect for the chain of evolution that has brought about the human being.

Today, with the help of science and technology, we are able to recreate the natural society that was once brought about spontaneously by primordial communal society. Compared to the bloody problems of the Middle East, ecological problems might sound like imaginary problems. We must not forget that these problems of bloodshed, hunger, and unemployment are the result of betraying ecology. Just as there can be no sound treatment for a disease without an understanding of healing, there can be no sound society that is not based on ecology, which means that without sound ecology no society that is democratic and pro–women's freedom can be established.

The Middle East and all of its people are at a crossroads. US hegemonic power, with its imperial tendency, has little in the way of solutions to offer. But it's not realistic to fight the US by calling for new Vietnams or attempting to repeat the experience of 1920s Turkey.[17] Since there is no longer a Soviet Union to provide a balance of power and, more importantly, imperialism no longer takes the form that it previously did, national liberation like that of Turkey or even that of Vietnam is no longer an option. Every historical stage has its own conditions and goals, which is why organized struggles are also different. The most meaningful response to the US and its allies is to mobilize society and all of the people's freedom forces around a coherent and implementable democratic, libertarian, and ecological program and integrate them into extensive organizational networks. This might be a way to wage a very conscious and effective but less bloody war.

When necessary this can be done through principled compromise. Where that is not possible, we can set up our own democracies in villages and towns in the mountains and deserts supported by our self-defense forces. People who fail to democratize themselves have no chance of success. The people will see that there is no social cause that they cannot accomplish if, broadly speaking, they set to work based on congresses and act through all sorts of nongovernmental organizations, cooperatives, and communal working groups. When the people rise up in this way in the new historical period of the Middle East, they will not only thwart encroachments similar to the former imperialist interventions but, with meaningful and principled compromise, will even be able to guide efforts toward peaceful democratization. Rising up in this way would be worthy of the Middle East's historical civilizations.

One might ask what role remains for revolutionaries. First and foremost, they must act in a way that is consistent with the social science conclusions outlined above. Revolutions or social transformations lacking social science can inadvertently clear the way for treachery and crime. This can only be prevented by taking our social science out of the hands of the ruling powers and forces that have a monopoly over knowledge and by restructuring it. Given that the mentality underlying our politics must be based on social science, it is essential that we create our own social science schools and academies.

Perhaps even more importantly, we must prioritize social morality. An appropriate moral policy requires the aspiration, belief, and patience to pursue the path one has chosen to its end. We must not back down, betray our principles, or find excuses to retreat or sell out. Morality means being in tune at each and every moment guided by our mentality, which has been shaped by science, and always means living consciously. When science, politics, and morality all join hands, there will be no social cause that we cannot tackle and successfully address in the service of humanity in general and the people of our region in particular. More than ever before, our morality, as the conscience of history and society, demands that we implement a policy that is loaded with such consciousness, so as to bring about the social changes and transformations we anticipate and desire.

In the age of the transition to democratic civilization, the people of the Middle East have three main options. First, carrying on with the existing status quo remaining unchanged. However, the system that profited from the twentieth-century balance of power is now coming to its end. The dissolution of real socialism accelerated the current crisis and led to an increasingly unipolar world. I described above how US hegemony and its empire of chaos are trying to overcome this crisis. At the same time, the third major offensive of capitalist globalization is occurring. The surplus of supply, which has grown enormously with the revolution in science and technology, encounters the poor masses as an obstacle. Globalization cannot reach its goal without resolving this contradiction. The nation-state structures, which are pro–status quo, are the main barrier. The goal is to overcome these structures on the basis of individualization, liberalization, and democratization, and this restructuring is gradually gaining traction.

This development harbors both positive and negative aspects for the people. It can be seen as an objective factor in accelerating democratic awakening and mobilization. Therefore, both the system's hegemonic power and the increasing awakening and mobilization of people from below make the status quo more and more unsustainable. The status quo tries to turn this impasse into a way of life and, when the pressure mounts, polishes things up a bit or, on other occasions, uses provocations to extend its life but is now increasingly isolated. This system, which no longer has the backing of the US or Soviet systems, has become more aggressive and is trying to win some time by treading water.

It also seems that, unlike in the past, the status quo is no longer succeeding in its efforts to use pseudo-left-wing or pseudo-right-wing demagoguery. The control of the state and of society with fascism or totalitarianism no longer enjoys the support it once did. As it increasingly loses the support of the people, the status quo nation-state is disintegrating, with the upper layers integrating into the new hegemonic structure. However, the popular masses' grassroots search for a democratic system stands to sideline this option based on force.

Even if this intense process, which is unfolding daily in the Middle East, does not lead to an all-embracing solution of the profound problems, it can contribute to a situation in which the status quo forces are no longer an obstacle. The Arab states, particularly Egypt, vacillate between the status quo and change, as do Pakistan, Turkey, and Iran. They are unable to make clear decisions about the process ahead. However, influenced by the Greater Middle East Initiative from above and under pressure from the democratic, pro–women's freedom, and ecological society project of the people from below, there is a strong possibility that they will embark on a process of change.

The second option is a mixed democratic system, which is limited and more practical. The time when imperialism could unilaterally build an order at will is over. It is unlikely that the US, as the new hegemonic power, will establish and maintain a similarly one-sided system. On the other hand, the nation-states created by various national communities in the recent past can no longer solve problems and have become problems themselves, both at home and abroad. In this intermediary stage between systems, where there is an equilibrium, fully independent positions are becoming increasingly more difficult to maintain.

The age we are in emphasizes interdependence, and the third great offensive of globalization accelerates this process. The era of international relationships is being replaced by an era of corporate relationships. The nation-state is transforming itself into a corporate state. National capital is being replaced by inter-corporate capital. On the other hand, local cultures are awakening and showing a great deal of dynamism. The concept of "local" is an increasingly important value. In this light, we can define our time as one when both the global and the local are moving to center stage.

The political system that corresponds with this cannot be either an advanced national-bourgeois democracy or fascism, nor can it be the underdeveloped nations' real socialism or the national liberation totalitarianisms. Perhaps democracies of a mixed character based on the coexistence of the two systems will emerge. The soundest approach would be democratic alliances of national and local social groups. Both the one-party models of the left and of the right, with their internal and state administrations, are being replaced by multiparty systems and effective democratic administrations. Any group capable of self-representation will be in a position to enter into more direct and flexible contact with the global system and increase the ebb and flow of surplus supply.

It is becoming increasingly likely that this global process will affect the countries of the Middle East. The necessity to overcome the very old structures of the status quo puts this option on the agenda, which is what underlies the US's Greater Middle East Initiative. The people of the Middle East, on the other hand, lack the consciousness and the necessary level of organization to develop their own democracy. The fact that their will is fragmented and they are only just now awakening and beginning to act means that it will be difficult for them to unilaterally formulate a democratic option, making it no more than a future utopia. Nevertheless, it is indispensable and essential that we diligently and skillfully develop our own internal democracy to lay the groundwork for principled compromises. It is the possibility of freedom and creativity in the interval of chaos that makes this age of transition so important and provides an opening for the people to play a major role in mixed democracies.

The third option is to a large extent a utopic vision of the future: a democratic, pro–women's freedom, and ecological society that prioritizes morality and is not state-centered. The fact that it's a primarily utopic vision doesn't mean that nothing about it can be lived today. Quite the contrary, it is our current task, always and everywhere, to carry forward this noble cause with modest steps. Sometimes only a little of it will come alive, but sometimes and in some places great progress can be made. We can draw a little closer to this society and this democracy every day by learning to live in a way that improves the internal democracy practiced by the people and by various free communities, ensuring woman's freedom and meeting the needs of an ecological society. Communities that cannot govern themselves without relying on a state can never attain the freedom and equality they long for. To expect democracy and socialism from the state amounts to the very negation of democracy and socialism. There are hundreds of historical examples of this approach, and every time it has further strengthened the oppressive and exploiting powers. In nonstate-oriented democracies, communities must provide their own self-defense. The people's defense militias must be able to protect all of the people's essential values, in particular the people's democracy, against usurpers, tyrants, and thieves wherever necessary, be it in the village, the city, the mountains, or the desert.

With communes, cooperatives, and various other working groups, it is possible to develop an economy that is not based on commodification, does not threaten people's health, and does not harm the environment. Unemployment is a structural feature of exploitative systems and, therefore, cannot be a problem in a people's democratic and ecological society. This society, one in which morality not law plays an essential role, whose passion for life and creative education is highly developed, with no room for internal war, and where fraternal and amicable relations prevail, is the best way to make the transition to a highly egalitarian socialism. A synthesis of communal society and ethnic groups, with their high level of equality, that has been experienced in the longue durée of history in the Middle East combined with today's scientific and technological potential will finally facilitate a more developed democratic, pro–women's freedom and ecological society, and this will become meaningful as the most noble of values.

NINE

The Kurdish Phenomenon and the Kurdish Question in the Chaos of the Middle East

Introduction

A realistic approach to the Kurdish phenomenon is more important than ever before. A significant part of the chaos in Iraq was due to the Kurdish question. How this chaos, which is very high on the world's agenda today, can be overcome is as yet unclear. Western civilization does not have the ability to achieve a solution. Once again, the powerful are trying to find a way out of the situation with major international projects specific to the post–world wars situation. There is great anxiety in the region. None of the established regimes is feeling confident. It is not clear what tomorrow will bring. On the other hand, there is an increase in what is called the phenomenon of "terror," with no real effort to reveal the nature of the actual terror. Ominous developments are lurking in the fog of chaos. Despite everything, however, there is hope for the dawn of freedom.

We have reached a point where the Kurds cannot be ruled as before. An inert continuation of the old cursed life would be impossible to reconcile with our age, even if the Kurds themselves wanted to pursue that course. Internal and external influences will accelerate the dissolution of the present Kurdish reality. What a solution will look like and what direction it will take will depend on the nature of the forces that arise and the pace at which they actively intervene. It seems as if the Kurds will play a disruptive role for the whole Middle East not unlike that played by Israel for the Arab states. The establishment of a Kurdish federal state in Iraq will contribute to the erosion of the rigidly centralized nation-state model in the region. Although involuntarily, this might also accelerate a tendency toward a general federation, which would correspond much better with the history of the Middle East. At present, the burning question is whether this will lead to a conflict of two nationalisms or to a solution through a democratic compromise.

Since emerging as the only world power after 1990, the US has intervened in the Middle East at a level never previously seen. Its Greater Middle East Initiative is the subject of daily query, with one of the most important topics being the place of the Kurds within the project. It is possible that the relationship between the Kurds, the US, and Israel could become increasingly strategic. The consequences for the region must be carefully evaluated. It is worth considering whether the current period will be rife with betrayal or will be a period in which the Kurds become the rising stars of the region. It is the first time that the relations of the Kurds among themselves and with the neighboring peoples and states are such that that they will profoundly influence strategies for the region. Kurdish-Arabic, Kurdish-Iranian, and Kurdish-Turkish relations will, from this point on, be permanently on the agenda.

On the other hand, do the Kurdish parties and movements that are responsible for coming up with ideas, action, and the restructuring of the Kurdish reality have the necessary competence for the tasks they now face? Would primitive nationalist, real socialist, and liberal approaches be suitable for responding to the challenges of our time? Questions as to how the necessary ideological renewal and intellectual capacity are to be attained are also very important. Does the leadership of Iraqi Kurdistan act with sufficient responsibility when taking steps that concern not only all Kurds but also all other peoples and states in the region? Can they transcend their character, which has been defined, above all else, by their traditional narrow interests and exploitation for their own personal gain? What measures can be adopted so that they do not cause a new disaster, and who should take responsibility for this? These questions will certainly be of continuing importance. The existing problems are also back on the agenda in all parts of Kurdistan and require realistic solutions. Effective democratic grassroots work will be particularly important to prevent inordinate suffering. Possible solutions that are reassuring and a renewed political approach that does not threaten borders will be increasingly important. As such, the search for solutions in all parts of Kurdistan is on the agenda and can no longer be postponed.

As the leading force of the last thirty years, the PKK has gone through important changes that continue to have an impact today. The problems experienced by the left around the world in the aftermath of 1968 and 1990 would find their reflection within the PKK. The party line, which was somewhere between real socialism and national liberation, was insufficient for actualizing and organizing the party's true potential, and this was aggravated both by external pressures and by internal weaknesses. This resulted in a praxis that was half-insurgent and half-guerrilla, leading to unnecessary casualties. The gang-like and vagrant insurgent group praxis increasingly exhausted values that had been built with much effort and imposed a de facto liquidationism. Despite all efforts, after 1995, the PKK broke with its true essence. The KADEK and Kongra Gel undertakings,[1] along with theoretical, strategic, and tactical changes led to the restructuring of the movement. The old cadres were not able to keep up. They displayed their innate inertness through actual splits among themselves. To protect the positive legacy, PKK-Reconstruction was considered as a step against both right-wing and left-wing liquidationism. With Kurdistan now entering a period that is new in every respect, all of this requires a comprehensive analysis, accompanied by critique and self-critique and a reformulation of our responsibilities.

Some Distinctive Lines in the Kurdish Society
A Short Sketch of the History and Concepts of "Kurds" and "Kurdistan"
There are difficulties associated with defining Kurdistan as a country and the Kurds and other minorities as societies. In the Middle East, the concept of "country" has a number of diverse definitions. If we start with the Middle Ages, the dominant definition of *country* was based on religion, such as *diyar-i islam, country of Islam,* or *diyar-i küffar, country of the infidels.* Even though various kavim and ethnic groups can be distinguished, there are no clear territorial boundaries. If clarification of the territorial borders of any given kavim or ethnic group is requested, the answer given will be far from certain. In general, the settlement areas of the kavim and aşiret communities are specified. But these do not correspond to any particular political formation. Political structures are mostly city-based and their territory is also the city's area of activity. The boundaries of aşiret's spread may change from summer to winter. The estate boundaries of the powerful dynasties are also far from being politically significant. In general, the borders of Arab, Turkish, Kurdish, and Persian territories,

as well as those of smaller kavim, are roughly determined by language and culture.

The term "Kurdistan" goes back to the Sumerian word *kur*, which means *mountain*.[2] The suffix -*ti* refers to an affiliation. As such, *Kurti* means *inhabitant(s) of the mountains*, or *mountain people*. The term can be found in writings from the third millennium BCE. We also know of other designations. The Luwians, a people who resided in West Anatolia more than three thousand years ago (around 1000 BCE), called Kurdistan *gondwana*, i.e., *country of villages*. In today's Kurdish language, *gond* still means *village*. During Assyrian rule, the word *nairi*, *people of the river*, was used. We even know of a Nairi Federation, which was founded in the area between the Tigris and Zap rivers. A larger region was called a *madain* or *med*, which probably means something like *country of metal*. These names were widely used during the Middle to Neo-Assyrian Empire era, from 1300 to 600 BCE.

The word *urartu* also stems from Sumerian. *Ur* means *hill* or *peak*; *urartu* could thus mean *highlands*.[3] Because the Sumerians lived in Lower Mesopotamia, they always gave Kurdistan, which was located on the plateaus to the north and east of them, names that expressed this comparative height. The word *hurri* very probably also comes from that source and, thus, also means *people of the highlands* or *mountain people*.[4] *Commagene* is a name that comes from Greek. The Kingdom of Commagene, with Samosata, near today's Adıyaman, as its capital, existed from 250 to 100 BCE. In Kurdish, *kom* is still used, in the form of *zom*, for semi-nomadic communities and their settlement areas. *Gene* means *lineage*, *tribe*, or *aşiret*. Thus, *Commagene* means the *country of semi-nomadic aşiret*.

In the Middle Ages, during the rule of the Arab sultans, the term "*balad ekrad*," to mean area of the Kurds, was used. The Persian-speaking Seljuk sultans, however, were the first statesmen to officially use the word *Kurdistan* in its present meaning, *land/country of the Kurds*. The Persian speaking Seljuk sultans were the first state officials to use *Kurdistan, land/country of the Kurds*, in the way it is used today. Later, the Ottoman sultans, especially Selim I, used *Kurdistan* to denote the governments and provinces (*eyalet*) of Kurdistan. The land laws (*arazi kanunnamesi*) of 1848 and 1867, formally established the provinces of Kurdistan. During periods of constitutional monarchy in the Ottoman Empire,[5] deputies (*mebusluk*) of Kurdistan were set up. In the 1920s, many of Mustafa Kemal Atatürk's written orders and statements used the words *Kurds* and *Kurdistan*. The official denial of the Kurds and Kurdistan only began with the intense assimilation policies that followed the suppression of the uprisings. Thus, *Kurdistan*, meaning *land/country of the Kurds*, has the distinction of being one of the oldest historical names for a people and their country. More recently, it has been used more in a geographical and cultural than political sense. The foundation of a federal state in Iraqi Kurdistan means that in the future we will also frequently encounter a political version of the word *Kurdistan*. Most certainly, as a consequence of political developments related to the PKK, *Kurdistan* has become widely known both regionally and internationally, not just as a word but as a social and political concept.

Kurdistan is located between the regions settled by the Persians, the Azeris, the Arabs, and the Anatolian Turks and comprises an area of about 450,000 square kilometers [approximately 280,000 square miles]. It is the most fertile region in the Middle East, with the highest mountains, the vastest forests, fertile plains, and the richest water resources. The flora and its soil are suitable both for animal husbandry and growing all kinds of fruit, vegetables, and grains. Between 11000 and 4000 BCE, it was the center of the Neolithic agricultural revolution, the most important revolution in history. It was the source and transit area of numerous civilizations. While this strategic position allowed the Kurds as a *qawm* to protect themselves in the face of the continuous transitions and occupations, in terms of civilization they lagged behind.

Comparatively, Kurdish society is easier to define. The Kurdish people are almost synonymous with mountains, agriculture, and animal husbandry. Urbanism is alien to the Kurds; village life is central to their society. It is possible that the Kurds' ancestors were the first in history to actualize this most fundamental social phenomenon.

The Kurds are primarily *gundî* (villagers) and nomadic and regard city life as alien. As the notion of "Commagene" suggests, the Kurds have cultivated a way of life that has been half-centered around the village and half-nomadic for thousands of years. As for the cities, they were mostly built or inhabited by the conquerors. That, of course, doesn't mean that the ancestors of the Kurds never founded cities or civilizations. A number of urban civilizations, particularly the Urartian, Median, and Mitanni states, testify to the contrary. In the Middle Ages, they also established a number of city or provincial governments. However, because these city or provincial governments were mostly short-lived, the cities generally represented strongholds or bridgeheads for the occupying forces and surrounding society. In antiquity, the cities and the written culture had a

Sumerian, Assyrian, Aramaic, Persian, or Hellenic character. In the Middle Ages, the Arab and Persian languages and cultures left their traces, and many intellectuals, statesmen, and commanders played a role with these neighboring languages and cultures. Even though the cultural roots of the Kurdish language reach very far back, the fact that it was not so much a written language and never became a state language meant that it was not documented, which prevented its further development. Despite all of this, Kurdish culture has been able to display its existence indirectly, both by the perseverance of the Kurds as an ethnic group and through historical vestiges.

According to many archeologists, it is very likely that the direct predecessors of the Kurdish language and culture—as the language and culture of the Neolithic Age that emerged on the slopes of the Zagros and the Taurus—constituted the basis for all later Indo-European languages and cultures. It is assumed that since the ninth century, the expansion into the Indo-European region was more cultural than physical. We can assume that this culture itself emerged sometime between 15000 and 10000 BCE. The culture and the language very probably emerged following the fourth Ice Age (20000 to 15000 BCE) as one of the most autochthonous—i.e., native—of cultures and languages in the area. The Kurds as an ethnic group differentiated themselves beginning in the seventh millennium BCE. On the historical stage, the Kurds first appeared as the Hurrians in the third millennium BCE. The Sumerian and Hurrian tribes attacked each other and defended themselves for millennia, because the Sumerians wanted wood and metals and the Hurrians were keen on the treasures of civilization. This historical dialectic continued with Babylon, Assur, the Hittites, the Scythians, the Persians, and the Hellenes. The Kurds might be the people who have practiced the mutual movements of sedentarism and nomadism for the longest time.

The role of the Hurrians and Medes as the predecessors of the Kurds was decisive for the transmission of Sumerian civilization to the Hittites, Luwians, Ionians, and Persians. The fact that these peoples belong to the Indo-European linguistic and cultural group is closely related to this reality.

The ancient *Histories* written by Herodotus make it pretty clear that from the tenth to the fifth centuries BCE, the Greeks were strongly influenced by the Median culture and language. It was during this period that they adopted elements of both material and immaterial culture from

Urartian, Median, and Persian sources, enriching them with their own synthesis. It is assumed that the ancestors of the Kurds, the Hurrians (2500–1500 BCE), the Mittanni (1500–1250 BCE) who were descendants of the Hurrians, the Nairi (1200–900 BCE), the Urartians (900–600 BCE), and the Medes (700–550 BCE) all lived in aşiret confederations and kingdoms. During this period, Kurdish society underwent a transition to hierarchy and the state, after which we can observe a strongly developed patriarchy. In the Neolithic agrarian age, women were more functional and played a far more central role in the Kurdish society, so it is very likely that they had used their power over an extended period. The predominantly feminine elements in the language and the cult of the goddess Star support this conjecture.[6]

Zoroastrianism, the teachings of Zoroaster, developed between 700 and 550 BCE as a mentality revolution among the Kurds. The Zoroastrian mentality was based on agriculture, a love of animals, equality of women and men, and a doctrine of free morality. This culture, which emerged at the border separating the West from the East, strongly influenced Eastern culture through the Persians and Western culture through the Greeks. Its profound influence on both has meant that it was at least as important a source as Judaism and Christianity in shaping the civilization.[7] Persian civilization was actually founded by the Medes, who later governed it together with the Persian tribes, so one should actually speak of a Persian-Median civilization,[8] as Herodotus's *Histories* makes clear.[9] The Medes were one of two ethnic group to play a role in the Achaemenid Empire over the course of its existence. The same situation continued in the Sasanian dynasty. In this light, it makes sense to consider the Kurds as having played a secondary role in all Iranian civilizations.

While a developed patriarchy clearly existed among the predecessors of the Kurds, at this point, there was not yet any clear class differentiation. The influence of aşiret nomadism and primarily living in the mountains meant that classes were barely visible. Because of their mutual kinship relations, aşiret and tribal communities did not allow slavery, which was, in any case, largely a product of urban civilization, to develop in their midst.

Kurdish folklore mainly consists of epics. Since these epics give voice to heroic deeds, it is quite likely that they go back to the hierarchical period. The roots of epic melodies such as "Mem û Zîn," "Memê Alan," and "Derweşê Evdî" have their origins in the Sumerian music. They are probably Hurrian creations from the fourth millennium BCE that have been transmitted by the Sumerians to our time. Kurdish music and dance are among the most expressive in the Middle East and possess great artistic value. The historic existence of the Kurds is most strongly expressed in music, dance, and clothing.

Summarizing, we can say that the lineage and dignity of the Kurds reaches back into protohistory. The harsh nature of the mountains, a historical background that dates even further back, and resistance against continuous ruthless occupations played an important role in the development of their dignity.

The Hellenic period left its traces during the transition to the Middle Ages. From the fourth century BCE, there were the kingdoms of Abgar, with Urfa as its center, of Commagene, with Adıyaman/Samosata as its center, and of Syria, with Palmyra as its center; they all had similar characteristics and a strong Hellenic influence—or, more precisely, they represented splendid examples of this first historical Western-Eastern synthesis. Until the conquest by Rome—Palmyra fell in 269 CE—these civilizations represented important regional developmental stages. The historical artifacts in Urfa, at Mount Nemrut, and in Palmyra are from this period. These civilizations had an extensive exchange with the Kurds. At that time, Aramaic and Greek were the predominant and competing languages. While these civilizations dominated the trade routes, the Kurds, mostly as cultivators and nomads, represented the periphery. Even today, remnants of this framework remain. The alienage of urban centers and the Kurdishness of the village and nomads at the periphery constitute a dialectical relationship.

Zoroastrianism was the ideological foundation of the Sasanian Empire at the beginning of the third century CE and the influence of the Kurds stayed unchanged. The prophet Mani (210–276 CE) introduced an important innovation. He created a synthesis of all of the religions of his time and tried to turn this synthesis into the basic mentality of the Roman and the Sasanian Empires,[10] with the goal of creating peace and a Renaissance. Instead, he attracted the ire of the conservative Zoroastrian priests and was killed. Even so, his powerful line of mentality left its mark, with traces that reach down to the present day.

The expansion of Christianity also occurred during this period. Urfa, in particular, which at the time was called Edessa, and Nusaybin, at the time Nisibis, functioned as strongholds of Christianity and, as such, also exercised an influence on the Kurds. Some Kurds even converted to Christianity. But Zoroastrianism, especially in the Sasanian Empire, posed a barrier to the quick expansion of Christianity further East.

In retrospect, Manichaeism appears, in a certain sense, to be an earlier version of Islam, and Mani an earlier incarnation of the Prophet Mohammad.

The destructive wars between the Roman and Sasanian Empires would continue to wreak great havoc for many years, particularly in the region between Diyarbakır and Nusaybin. Unlike during the Hellenic period, society was unable to develop in peace. There was a competition between Christianity and Zoroastrianism; then, under Sasanian influence, Nestorianism emerged as a competing Christian current. The Assyrians were one of the first people to adopt Christianity, and they went on to play an important role in the culture and science of the time. Their contribution to the dissemination of Christianity throughout East Asia was greater than that of the Greeks. Many important bishops came from their ranks, and they created a huge number of literary works. They founded well-equipped academies in Urfa, Nusaybin, and Siirt. They also played a decisive role in the establishment of the academy of Gundishapur, the scientific center of the Sasanians. Their Aramaic language continued to be the lingua franca in the East for trade, literature, and religion, while Greek expanded in the West, which is to say, in the Byzantine sphere of influence.

We can safely assume that the feudal social structure among the Kurds emerged during the Sasanian Empire (250–650 CE), with the Kurds gradually undergoing a social transformation to adjust to this structure. The development of feudalism demonstrates a differentiation in ethnic structures. The Islamic revolution broke out during the developmental phase of feudal civilization. Islam essentially transformed both the rigid slavery relations and ethnic bonds that were an obstacle to development based on urbanization, and, thus, was the mentality revolution that created the ideological framework feudal society required, which, compared to slavery, was a progressive system. It represents the revolutionary development that took a more evolutionary path in Europe, India, and China. Islam was the last great revolution in civilization in the Middle East.[11] Until the twelfth century, Islam's ideological and political framework was central to the development of feudal society.

Islam rapidly developed among the Kurds after the fall of the Sasanians in 650 CE, creating a feudal aristocracy in the process. The hierarchical and statist Kurdish forces that underwent a transformation under the influence of a strong Arabization were among the strongest social and political groups. The Kurdish Ayyubid dynasty (1175–1250 CE) became the most powerful dynasty in the Middle East,[12] playing a very influential role among the Kurds. Of equal importance, the Seljuk sultanate, which inherited the Abbasids in 1055 CE, coexisted with the Kurds. This coexistence primarily took the form of partnership rather than conflict, as is also basically the case in Kirkuk today. Other important feudal states founded by dynasties with Kurdish roots, including the Shaddadids, the Buyids, and the Marwanids (990–1090 CE), also rose at this time, as did a number of Kurdish princedoms and governments. The Şerefhanoğulları principality,[13] with Bitlis as its center, proved the most durable until the time of Suleiman the Magnificent, well into the sixteenth century. The feudal social characteristics led to an important transformation in the mentality of Kurdish society. The remnants of Zoroastrianism were erased, except among the Yazidis. This transformation probably played a counterrevolutionary role in the development of collaborationism among the Kurds.

While Arabic became predominant in the Islamized cities, there was no decline in the Kurdish language and cultural presence. It was also at this point that we see the first textualization of the Kurdish epics by Ahmad Khani, among others. As with all ethnic groups, a culture overlaid with Islamic motifs took roots among the Kurds. Nonetheless, there were always conflicts with the expansionist Arab tribes in South Kurdistan, and these continue to this very day, particularly with the Shammar tribe.[14] The epic Derweşê Evdî testifies to these conflicts. It is assumed that the events described in this epic took place in the eighteenth century. This is an epic that insists on having Zoroastrian roots and carries strong traces of Kurdish culture. It seems that under the influence of the Islamic environment, Zoroastrianism was a sort of cultural resistance, the noble resistance of Kurdish culture to alienation. Kurdish Alevism, with its partisanship for Ali, which actually has a fairly thin Islamic cover and represents the Kurdish version of Shiism, is, next to Zoroastrianism, the strongest expression of Kurdish cultural resistance. In contrast, Sunni Islam, especially the version found among the South Kurds who are close to the plains developed an extremely reactionary and collaborationist character. In Urfa, Mardin, and Siirt in particular, these representatives of the feudal merchant mindset, who deny their cultural descent, are not only deep into betrayal but are also incredibly collaborationist and driven by self-interest. Among the Kurds under Iranian influence, the degeneration has been less pronounced, and they preserve their cultural essence with more authentic structures.

The relationships between ethnic Kurdish and ethnic Turkish tribes and their states was important at the time. There were very few conflicts; instead, relations were friendly and based on solidarity and on a common opposition to Byzantine influence. The fact that the Armenians and Assyrians were Christians also played an important role in this approach. The victory of Sultan Alp Arslan in the battle of Manzikert in 1071 CE was basically the result of a Kurdish-Turkish alliance. Without the support of the Kurds, the sultan could certainly not have been victorious. At that time, there was substantial assimilation of the Turkmen tribes by the strong local Kurdish culture and the Kurdish tribes, a process that continued until the end of the nineteenth century and only began to reverse direction with the advent of the Turkish republic.

The Kurds, who were under the overall cultural influence of the Middle Ages, experienced a decline in free life to the extent that they underwent feudal class division. Feudal serfdom constantly developed in opposition to tribal freedom and constituted an important phase in the shift in the mentality, with the accompanying alienation. Even though the Kurds gave rise to a number of Islamic scholars, their tendency to collaborate with the states in the region meant they never had a lasting influence. The most interesting example of collaboration with the state and flattery for a sultan is that of İdris of Bitlis.[15] Sunni brotherhoods like the Naqshbandi also deserve a mention in this connection. During the 2004 local elections in Bingöl, it was interesting to watch a group with its roots in this brotherhood chant "İdris of Bitlis is here, where is Yavuz Selim?" This would suggest that they expected Erdoğan to fill Yavuz Selim's shoes. Unless the Naqshbandi betrayal in Kurdistan is evaluated in its entirety, a revolutionary enlightenment will remain impossible.[16] On the other hand, the enlightenment of the Alawite Kurds has been more positive. Examining the striking influence of historical dynamics on the present, particularly in connection with these brotherhoods and denominations, could provide important lessons. These brotherhoods think that by denouncing the republic's enlightenment as "Kemalist" they can disguise their ugly faces from the Kurdish people. Without analyzing and exposing the latent reactionary nature and self-interest of many brotherhoods of Sunni origin, a consistent Kurdish patriotism and democracy cannot be developed.

When adjudication through the discussion of precedents (*iğtihād*) ceased in Islamic civilization after the thirteenth century, at a point when this civilization was being simultaneously attacked by the Mongols and the crusaders, a phase of stagnation (1200–1500 CE) and decay (1500–1918 CE) set in that it was never able to recover from. Until the thirteenth century, it contributed to the civilizational development that took its first steps in Europe on behalf of the Eastern civilization, but the Ottoman Empire found it difficult to continue this tradition during its period of stagnation and decay. Even though the Ottoman Empire led the last defensive battle of the East against rising Western civilization, the backwardness of the ideological, political, and economic system prevented its success and could not stave off its collapse.

After the time of Sultan Selim I, in the early sixteenth century, the Kurdish ruling classes generally enjoyed a high degree of autonomy and, as a result, were the most assiduous supporters of the Ottoman rulers. This state of affairs continued until the beginning of the nineteenth century, finally collapsing with the first forays of European colonialism. The decisive factor was the weakened central government exacting enormous taxes, while simultaneously drafting numerous men as soldiers. Uprisings replaced friendship and solidarity.

The nineteenth century marked a new stage in Kurdish history and Kurdish society. When worsening relations with the Ottomans led to uprisings, and English and French missionaries stoked separatism among the Armenian and Assyrian Churches, the situation got more complicated. Relations among the Armenians, Assyrians, and Kurds also deteriorated. The deterioration of relations among themselves and with the Ottoman rule led to one of the most painful periods of their common history. By the end of that period, after World War I, the Armenians and Assyrians, bearers of millennia-old cultures, had been largely annihilated, both physically and culturally. Even though relations between Kurds and Turks had also been seriously damaged, there was not a complete rupture, as was the case with the Armenians and Assyrians. Therefore, in the 1920s, the Kurds participated in the national liberation struggle alongside the Turks. After Alp Arslan and Selim I, this was a third instance of this strategic and structural partnership. Without the support of the Kurds in Alp Arslan's 1071 victory and in the 1514 victory of Selim I against the Iranian ruling house of the Safavids, as well as his 1516–1517 victory against the Mamluks in Egypt, neither the conquest of Anatolia by the Turkish tribes nor the expansion of the Ottoman Empire to the east and south would have been possible.

This historical trend continued in the 1920s. This third strategic partnership prevented the envisaged imperial expansion and aided in the success of the republican revolution. But the traditional collaborationist feudal upper class incorrectly assessed the situation in the republic, was easily deceived about imperialism's intentions, and, as a result, rebelled, leading, among other things, to the founders of the republic changing their policies. The consequence was the abandonment of the joint Kurdish-Turkish liberation project that led to one of the most negative phases of Kurdish-Turkish common history. This strategic deterioration in Kurdish-Turkish relations led to the existence of the Kurds being denied, and they were kept in a state of enforced underdevelopment, were forcibly assimilated, and were increasingly entirely excluded from the system. The fact that Kurds could only hope to be accepted to the degree that they allowed themselves to be Turkified further deepened these policies. The great worldwide enlightenment of the 1970s led to resistance to the policies that obscured the Kurds and Kurdistan and gave rise to a new Kurdish intellectual movement, which was followed by a period of political and military resistance in the form of the PKK. Although with much conflict and sorrow, a more dignified period in Kurdish-Turkish relations had begun.

The Struggle Over Kurdistan, War, and Terror

Kurdistan's geocultural and strategic reality has made it into a country that has experienced more struggle, war, and terror in its history than most, by which I mean the use of violence and fear to rule over the people. The present-day Kurdish region roughly covers the area where, about twenty thousand years ago, after the fourth Ice Age, Mesolithic culture arose, followed by the Neolithic Age, about twelve thousand years ago, during which the cultivation of the land and domestication of animals first developed. We have already discussed the reasons for this. As the most highly developed center of Mesolithic and Neolithic culture, this area attracted many migrants from all directions who were still living in Paleolithic conditions. We can safely assume that the increase in productivity during the transition from hunting and gathering to agriculture led to the concentration of population at that time and in that area, as is proven by archeological and paleontological findings. The people became sedentary and founded villages, which in turn accelerated the development of a culture based on cultivation of fields, vineyards, and gardens. It is very likely that this is how social and economic conflicts around fertile soil, land, and grazing grounds first developed. There are village ruins dating back to this time that offer a certain support for this assumption. That, for obvious reasons, the first major social and economic struggles in history took place in Kurdistan is food for thought.

To the degree that it is possible to reconstruct migratory movements, there appears to have been immigration from various communities in today's Arabia and North Africa, as well as from Iran and areas still further east, the Caucasus in the north, and Anatolia in the west. Just as people today emigrate to Europe or North America, the first major socially and economically motivated migrations were to today's Kurdistan, which was a "land of the sun" for all of humanity for about fifteen thousand years. Of course, playing the role of the land of the sun for such a long time gave rise to major disputes and conflicts. After Neolithic culture was generally established, around nine thousand years ago, there was migration in the opposite direction. Based on what we know today, around seven thousand years ago Neolithic culture expanded both physically, as a result of migration, and culturally, through interaction with areas stretching from the Atlantic to the Chinese Pacific coast, from Siberia in the north to North Africa in the south and, thus, the population concentration decreased considerably in its original center.

Researchers believe that after that, between seven and five thousand years ago, the Aryan cultural and linguistic group took form in Kurdistan, and the transition was made from a clan and tribal society to an aşiret society. Aşiret society was characterized by a tighter organization of a larger human community and the related increased capacity to act. While clan and tribal societies consisted of twenty to fifty people, aşiret societies allowed for the organization of several hundred people. This meant that if there was an increase in social and economic problems, conflicts between the aşiret communities might grow more intense. Archeological findings of some completely destroyed villages from that time show that social conflicts did indeed get worse, mostly for internal reasons. The economic causes of the conflicts included the growing population on fertile land and along watercourses and the greed of neighbors. This probably led various aşiret to draw their own borders. It is, therefore, not unlikely that aşiret areas were geographically fixed for the first time around 4000 BCE, making it possible to distinguish the harvesting and grazing areas constituting the collective property of various aşiret. We can also assume that these aşiret created their own language and dialect groups, as well as undergoing other cultural differentiations. This allowed for the development of musical and folkloric motifs, as well as giving rise to cults of worship. The discovery of several female figure artifacts points to the significance of the domestic culture of the mother, but, overall, we can characterize this time as a period of struggle around social content and economic goals.

Between 3000 and 2330 BCE, Sumerian civilization was born and firmly established in Lower Mesopotamia, and the struggles just mentioned reached the level where they became wars. The tradition of seizing and pillaging economic values using organized military force and violence arose for the first time in history. This was the birth of a very long tradition. The force of warrior ruling power is essentially the force of plunder. Attributes like divinity, sacredness, and heroism only serve to obscure the extortion and plunder hidden within.

Kurdistan is one of the main birthplaces of this civilization. The Gilgamesh epic, the first written epic of Sumerian civilization and, indeed, all humanity, narrates the story of a foray into Kurdistan. Gilgamesh, the first half-heroic human, half-divine king of Uruk, seduced a barbarian named Enkidu with the aid of a woman forced into prostitution, the symbol of urban civilization. His incursion into Kurdistan with Enkidu is the main topic of the epic.[17] In a way, Enkidu is the first example of a highlander, a "Kurti," who comes down from the mountains into the city and collaborates with the dominant powers. He leads those occupying his own country. In return, he gains access to a different life and is given a place at the king's table and rewarded with women. Perhaps Gilgamesh himself came from the mountains, because, in Kurdish, *Gilgamesh* means *big buffalo* or *man like a bull*. It is no accident that the history of Kurdistan is overrun with traitors of this sort. The Sumerians had already waged wars for resources and often had to undertake expeditions to the north, because they urgently needed wood, stone, and different ores. Wars like the recent Iraq war are nothing but a brief, summary repetition of this history.

Forces of civilization participating in the occupation, invasion, and plunder of Kurdistan for the first time was a qualitative development. The powers that had become states undertook expeditionary campaigns against ethnic communities, including aşiret, tribes, and clans, to plunder and enslave. While the struggles had previously been about self-protection, access to watercourses, and possession of fertile land, in the period of civilization everything was primarily about enslavement and plunder. The premeditated killing and capturing of humans was central to these operations.

The migration and cultural exchange in all directions probably also continued as before. Archeological findings from the time of the Hurrians highlight social struggles and wars. The defensive facilities and heroic sagas are testimony to the battles and wars. In the third millennium BCE, various expeditionary groups came through Iran, the Caucasus, Anatolia, and Arabia. The high ramparts around Sumerian cities and Hurrian fortresses were designed for defense. People took refuge in the mountains, which, functioning as natural fortresses, offered some defense. The mountains have always provided a base for safeguarding Kurdish people's ethnic existence. The Kurds' ancestors tried for millennia to protect themselves against the evils of invasion, occupation, and plunder that flooded in from all directions by retreating to the peaks of the mountains. This is one key historical reason for the lack of developed urban civilization on the plains.

Between 2000 and 1000 BCE, new elements participated in the invasions in Kurdistan. The Middle Anatolian Kingdom of the Hittites and the barbarian communities called the Scythians from the Caucasus joined the invasions of Hurrian-Mitanni civilization and the rich cities of Babylon and Assur further to the south. Once again, ancestral groups of today's Kurds were among the most pressed. While Kurdistan had previously only been attacked by the southern Sumerian, Babylonian, and Assyrian states, at this point, the Hittite state and the militarily skilled Scythian barbarians, in particular, joined in from the north, as did other groups, including the Persian tribes from Iran and Luwian ethnic groups from the west.

The dilemma of the Kurds and Kurdistan was that Kurdistan was a wealth-producing area located in the transition zone between the newly established civilizations. To survive, the Kurds resorted to both resistance and collaboration. The simultaneity of resistance and collaboration is a pattern that has been repeated quite frequently throughout history. While the hierarchical upper class has always relied on collaboration, the underclass had to continually resist.

In a written document from around 1600 BCE, a Kurdish principality—probably in the region of today's Elbistan[18]—addressed Prince Anitta, the founder of the Hittite Empire: "You miscreant, we have raised you, we have made you a prince there. But we did not do so for you to come to our border with the whole mob of your warriors to harass us. Try to prove yourself worthy of the promises you made." This document shows that the Hittite kingdom was at first strongly influenced by the Hurrians, but, as it steadily grew, it slowly began to threaten the Hurrian and Mitanni tribes. Around 1300 BCE, the famous Hittite king Šuppiluliumaš I wrote to the Mittani king Šattiwaza: "I am giving you my daughter for your wife. You are now considered a son. Don't rebel again. Don't stir up unrest. Try to live comfortably in your beautiful country. You have my support." Here we see the two trying to establish kinship and peace, despite existing conflicts, through a political marriage.

When the terrible power of Assur appeared on the scene during this period, the Hittite-Mitanni alliance became necessary. Interestingly, the well-known Egyptian queen Nefertiti was a Mitanni who married into the Egyptian dynasty. The troubled time around 1500 BCE was witness to many diplomatic and political agreements, as well as many wars. The Great King Hammurabi of Babylon, who is famous for his legislation, lived around 1750 BCE. In 1596 BCE, Babylon was occupied by an alliance of Hittites and Hurrians. The flight of Abraham from Urfa to escape the ruling Nimrod is alleged to have happened around 1650 BCE, and the flight of Moses from the pharaoh is said to have taken place at the beginning of the fourteenth century BCE. The famous Battle of Kadesh, with the ensuing peace treaty,[19] took place in 1285 BCE. In these centuries of war and peace, Kurdistan was a central area where the events took place. Kurdistan is a country where there was never a lack of wars.

The period from 1000 to 330 BCE marked the final major stage of the Mesopotamian-centered civilizations. The Assyrian Empire, with its capital in Nineveh, had come onto the scene as the decisive power of the time. Nineveh even surpassed its rival, Babylon. The Assyrians were notorious for using terror against their neighbors. The Assyrian emperors were known for piling up hills and building ramparts and towers out of human skulls. Many war scenes on reliefs and elsewhere convey a vivid impression of what happened. At the time, it was common to display the severed heads of victims. The most merciless bellicose expeditions were undertaken against Kurdistan, Syria, and Egypt. These succeeded in extending Assyrian influence to West Anatolia.

Around 1200 BCE, the Hittite Empire was fragmented by the Phrygians, who came from today's Thrace, south of the Taurus Mountains, and was replaced by small city kingdoms. In Kurdistan, the Nairi confederation was founded in the area of today's Bohtan sometime between 1200 and 900 BCE. After its collapse, it was replaced by the state of Urartu, which existed from 875 to 606 BCE. The Assyrians engaged in merciless warfare against all of the states and principalities that had emerged after the collapse of the Hittite Empire. Once again, these expeditions were driven by the desire for resources, in this case wood and various ores and metals, and control over trade routes. The Urartians, who were famous for their defensive tactics, managed to bring an end to these attacks.

During this period, the Medes strengthened their presence further to the east, in today's Iranian Kurdistan, benefiting from the Urartian model, grasping the need for a political structure, and gathering strength by staving off the Assyrian's eastern expeditions. The famous three hundred years of resisting and laying the groundwork represents the Urartu period and their increasing strength. Defeating Assyria was something like today's Iraq managing to defeat the US would be. Therefore, it required intense preparation and tactical innovation. In the end, the famous Median commander Cyaxares and his Babylonian ally Nebuchadnezzar destroyed Nineveh in 612 BCE, definitively ending the Assyrian Empire. The Medes were successful in creating a political framework quite similar to an empire, which existed from 715 to 550 BCE and had Ekbatan, today's Hamadan, as its capital. This formation had a strong Kurdish character. The attacks by the Scythes from the north and their relatives, the Persian tribes, from the south and east prevented the Medes from growing even stronger. Because of the treason of the famous commander Harpagus, who collaborated with the Persians, ruling power fell into the hands of Cyrus, the nephew of the Median king, and, thus, also into the hands of the Persian tribal hierarchy.[20]

The Persian Empire was the continuation of the Median Empire. In fact, it was a sort of joint state. And, once again, the main theater of war was Kurdistan, which was mostly the site of the Scythes incursions. It was during a battle against the Scythes that Cyrus was killed. As a result of barbarian attacks from the north, the empire relocated to the safe southeastern region of Media. The great expedition against the Scythes, led by Darius the Great (520–485 BCE), tried to strike at the roots of this evil. For two centuries, from 530–330 BCE, Anatolia was shaped by the Median-Persian Empire. One after another, it ended the political existence of Phrygia, Lydia, and Lycia and brought all cities on the Aegean Coast under its control. We can say that this was a time of quiescence for

Kurdistan (Media) on the road to becoming civilized. The strengthening of the patriarchal family and the strong Median aşiret structures granted the Medians a special position in the Persian army. After the conquest of Egypt in 525, the Median-Persian regions became the main center of civilization. In contrast, Babylon had a semi-dependent status but still remained the cultural capital of civilization.

From Greek sources, we know that the Greek and Macedonian aristocracies made a zealous effort to conquer Anatolia, to remove the threat of the Medes and the Persians, and to appropriate their unparalleled treasures. Day and night, they discussed this and dreamed of it coming to pass. Actually, they believed that achieving this was their greatest divine task. The great thinker Aristotle (385–320 BCE) inculcated his pupil Alexander the Great, the son of the Macedonian king Philip, with this belief. It was probably also Aristotle who taught Alexander to regard the people of the East as animals to be squashed like vermin. Alexander grew up in this atmosphere and under Aristotle's strict education. After his father was killed, while still young, Alexander united the Greek cities and then the tribes living around Macedonia, before beginning his expedition to the east, which changed the course of history. In a way, Alexander the Great was the answer to Darius the Great. With his blitzkrieg-like expeditions, he destroyed all his opponents and advanced to the banks of Ganges. He conquered everything in his path.

The famous decisive Battle of Gaugamela, with which Alexander set in motion the fall of the Persian Empire, took place in 331 BCE, near Arbela, today's Erbil/Hewlêr, in Kurdistan. As a symbol of east-west synthesis, Alexander married ten thousand warriors from the Balkans to ten thousand daughters from the Medoc and the Persian nobility when he returned to the then cultural capital of Babylon. He himself married the daughter of King Darius III, the last king he defeated. During preparations for an expedition to the west against the up-and-coming Roman republic, Alexander died, at the early age of thirty-three, of an infection he had contracted in a swamp region.

There are still many traces of Alexander in Kurdistan. For example, the city of Bitlis is said to be named after one of his commanders. It is said that he crossed the Zagros Mountains like a guerrilla. In terms of his military skills, he could be called a demigod. For Kurdistan, his expeditions entailed a new dilemma. From then on, it was to become the center of the famous conflict between the East and the West. The conflicts between the

THE KURDISH PHENOMENON AND THE KURDISH QUESTION

Parthian Empire (250–216 BCE), which replaced the Persian Empire in Iran, and the Hellenic kingdoms of the Diadochi, the kingdoms that followed Alexander, were mainly fought in Kurdistan. At this time, the Armenian kingdoms also came into play. The right to conquest as the basis of all rights passed from one to another. Fortresses were erected on the shores of the Euphrates and the Tigris, and all cities adopted a defensive position, erecting ramparts and towers.

Under Hellenic rule, Commagene, with Samosata as its capital, and Abgar, with Urfa as its capital, became particularly important, as did Palmyra. They created the most outstanding work of the East-West synthesis. The mentality of their epoch was different from both the preceding and subsequent epochs. This could be considered as civilization's most splendid period. Iranian (Parthian) and Hellenic influences were interwoven and cultural exchange was as lively as commercial exchange.

At that time, another power entered the scene in the form of Rome. Bit by bit, the Roman Empire conquered the Hellenic kingdoms, advancing all the way to the borders of the Parthian Empire. Then, in 53 BCE, the famous Roman commander Crassus was defeated and killed in battle at Ctesiphon on the Tigris.[21] During their victory celebration, the Parthians and Armenians put his head on display for several days. This took place in a city in Kurdistan, Ctesiphon.

Jesus's apostles, who fled from the Roman terror after his crucifixion, also first made a stopover in the border regions of Kurdistan, namely, in Antioch (today's Antakya), Edessa (Urfa), and Nisibis (Nusaybin). A period in which political and religious terror slowly emerged. By 50 CE, the Roman Empire had conquered all of Anatolia, Syria, today's Israel, and Lebanon and had crossed the Euphrates. The new Christian communities retreated to the mountains, caves, subterranean catacombs, or the desert. They began to live semi-secretly, going underground. Political terror on a mass scale was perhaps used for the first time during the persecution of the Christian believers. Thus, the mountains of Kurdistan became the first refuge of the Christians.

From the third century BCE on, there were further conflicts between the Roman and the Sasanian Empires. Once again, the major battles took place in Kurdistan. Sometimes, the boundary was at the Euphrates, sometimes, it was at the Tigris. Towns such as Diyarbakır and Nusaybin were destroyed several times and repeatedly changed hands. Kurdistan was frequently divided.

Progress was barely possible in this area, which civilization inundated with violence and looting. While life continued in the nomadic tribes called kom in the mountains of Kurdistan, the cities became the headquarters of the invaders. This process led to the development of a clear separation between ethnic society and military society. The merchants formed the intermediary link between the invaders and the ethnic groups.

Because of the continuous wars between these two empires, the fourth and fifth centuries went down in history as a dark period. In an environment of fear and terror, the propaganda activities of the Christian and Manichean groups were the only serious social activity. The destruction of Palmyra, Abgar, and Commagene could be said to mark the beginning of this dark age. Be that as it may, classical slavery was in its final throes.

Christianity began to herald the new era, conveying the belief that after the darkness, there would be light, and the divine kingdom would come. It pronounced an ideology of liberation. A social liberation army was established. Both former great empires, the Roman and the Sasanian, were collapsing internally. Increasing harsh external attacks by ethnic groups led to the Roman Empire splitting, and then to the destruction of its western part. Thereafter, the Byzantine Empire, donning the mantle of a second Rome, claimed Mesopotamia for itself. Additionally, there were all the various conflicts between different Christian denominations, giving rise to dividing lines that were quite similar to those among the Sunnis and the Alevi today. Political conflicts were compounded by religious and denominational conflicts. While social struggles were being fought in religious guise, ethnic conflicts began to resemble qawm struggles. The Assyrian priests, particularly the Nestorians, were very well educated. They were, so to speak, "warriors of knowledge." Confessional and religious conflicts were a reflection of and parallel to political and military conflicts. A time of anticipation of a Messiah, a Mahdi, or the prophet of the Last Judgment who would return to the world set in.

Mohammad had an excellent intuitive sense of his time. The belief that he might be the expected prophet increasingly grew. In the context of the darkness of the *dschahiliyye*, the time of ignorance and disunity of the Arab tribes, he rose like the sun. Mohammad heralded the age of blessedness (*asr-i saadet*). Islam emerged and rapidly expanded during the seventh and eighth centuries. God arrived, and superstition departed. The sun rose, and the darkness was lifted. Then the conquests came, one after another, and Kurdistan was again threatened, this time from the south. War was no longer only on the agenda for establishing dynasties and empires but now also on behalf of a religion, Islam.

After the defeat of the Sasanian Empire by the Arabs at the Battle of al-Qadisiyyah in 638 CE, the Islamic campaigns of conquest intensified in Kurdistan. One village after another was Islamized. While the Iranians tried to preserve their distinction by adopting Shiism, the Kurds tried to retain their ethnic and qawmi existence by their continuing adherence to Zoroastrianism and the Alevi faith, which is only superficially Islamic. Sunni Kurdishness is actually a defeated Kurdishness, a Kurdishness characterized by betrayal.

As much as one may want to etymologically associate peace with the word *Islam*, it is nonetheless an effective ideology of Arab national war. Just like today's globalization, it aimed at a worldwide expansion. Conducting the jihad, holy war, was regarded as the greatest service to God. Everything conquered during the jihad, or holy war, was yours to keep. You could turn the defeated into slaves. You could take all of the women as booty. Islam was not content with military conquests alone, like present day rulers aren't. Control and domination was established over the social, economic, and faith-related values of those conquered. The domination of the mentality was experienced most intensely. Islam, as the ideology of feudalism, claimed that it would entirely reshape society in the Middle East. The concept of a single and convinced community of believers, the umma, prepared the social basis of the Islamic Empire that was soon to follow. The ideology of the one and only God that was created with great skill was actually the ideological foundation for the sultanate as the only authorized authority. Islam, which so masterfully built a social edifice, with the believers as its base and the sultan at the top, was perhaps the most brilliant theoretical formulation of centralist feudalism that has ever existed.

With Islam, the Arab ethnic group, which had not managed to move beyond the confines of the Arab Peninsula since the time of the Sumerians, experienced one of the biggest upsurges history has ever seen. It quenched its millennia-old thirst for power by crushing the Byzantines and the Sasanians and creating a splendid feudal civilization. The Arab Empire reached its climax under the Umayyad (650–750 CE) and Abbasid (750–1258 CE) dynasties. Its expansion and influence penetrated deep into Kurdistan, all the way to the foothills of the Taurus and Zagros Mountains, a process accompanied by huge massacres. One of those infamous for cruelty that paralleled Alexander's, was Al-Hajjāj ibn Yūsuf, the Umayyad governor of Baghdad.

The Arabs expanded their territory to the Caucasus, the Hindukush, the Pyrenees, and the borders of Constantinople. Islam reached its peak around 1000 CE, unifying the splintered tribes behind a single religion, much as the Hebrews had around 1000 BCE. It was only later that the Seljuks and Ottomans, who were of Turkish-Oghusian descent, made their appearance. The last major expeditions were led by sultans with Turkish roots in the name of Islam and Sunnism.

During the time of the Abbasids and the Seljuks, the line of conflict once again ran through Kurdistan. A major consequences of the wars between the Byzantine Empire and the sultan's armed forces was the alternating conquest and reconquest of cities in the regions of Kurdistan. With the Seljuk sultan Alp Arslan's Battle of Manzikert in 1071, the Byzantine troops were driven out of Kurdistan. Even though there were conflicts at the time of the Ayyubid sultans and the Turkish principalities, Islamic civilization continued to expand, gaining the upper hand in Urfa, Mardin, Diyarbakır, Siirt, Malatya, and Elazığ. Islamic culture pushed Christian Assyrian and Armenian existence into the background. By that point, the Islamization of Kurdistan was complete.

Then, in the twelfth and the thirteen centuries, crusaders and Mongols descended upon the region like a plague of locusts, devastating it once more, and, once again, whoever was able to do so took refuge in the mountains.

At the beginning of the sixteenth century, the region was once more shaken by fighting. While Byzantium and the Sasanians had once faced off against each other, the dividing line was now between the Iranian Safavids and the Ottomans, who had already undertaken conquests in the Balkans from their home base in Anatolia. With his victory over the Safavids at Chaldiran in 1514, achieved with the help of the Sunni Kurds, Sultan Selim I pushed the classical border further east than ever before, laying the foundation for the division of Kurdistan that persists to this day. Despite various frequent internal attacks at the border lines, in 1639, the still existing division of Kurdistan between an Anatolian and an Iranian power was officially drawn up and cemented in the Treaty of Qasr-e Shirin. Mesopotamia and most of the Kurds remained within the borders of the Ottoman Empire.

The balance established between the Ottomans and the Kurdish principalities and governments led to a period of relative calm that lasted until the beginning of the nineteenth century. While Islamic civilization developed along Sunni lines, the Zoroastrian and Alevi Kurds were in semi-rebellion and compelled to live on the mountain peaks and out of sight. That Sultan Selim I, fearing the Safavids, had his grand vizier Murat Pascha (called "Murat the Well-Digger") throw forty thousand Alevi into wells alive and execute Pir Sultan Abdal was the most incisive and lasting testimony to the use of terror.[22] The previous massacre of the movement of Sheikh Bedrettin, who strove for a communal system and the execution of the sheikh himself were also expressions of this terror.[23] The Celali rebellions,[24] which were directed against poverty, as well as the draft and the duty to pay taxes, and their suppression also clearly show to what extent the Islamic nobility drowned the country in terror. The Turkmen tribes in the mountains were also subjected to terror campaigns. The terror of the Ottomans in the interior of the empire was at least as merciless as the war against external enemies. Apart from all that, the murder of heirs to the throne by their siblings and the execution of grand viziers was a widespread practice. As such, it is obvious that the Ottoman era was marked by widespread terror guided by Sunnism, the official interpretation of Islam.

In Kurdistan, the whole nineteenth century and the period up to the collapse of the Ottoman Empire, following World War II, were characterized by numerous uprisings and expeditions to suppress them. There were also the increasing suppression of the Armenians and the Assyrians, whose relations with the Empire had worsened under the influence of English and French missionaries. At the end of the nineteenth and the beginning of the twentieth century, these ancient people came close to being annihilated. The nationalism incited by capitalism bore increasingly deadly fruits. The Kurds, however, did not suffer the same fate as the Armenians and the Assyrians, because they had a different religion and mounted a broader resistance.

The religious and denominational conflicts of the Middle Ages wrought at least as much destruction as the conflicts and wars of antiquity. It was clear that civilization could not develop in Kurdistan due to these conflicts and wars. A dialectical relationship could not have been established between the ethnic groups, which continually tried to safeguard their existence by retreating into inaccessible mountain regions and the towns, which were the bridgeheads of invasion and occupation. Both locations remained reactionary in their own way and were literally suffocated by their isolation.

Once one scratches the surface of a "redeeming" Islam even a little bit, the repressive and exploitative power of millennia comes to the fore. The sultan and his underlings ran a regime of tyranny and exploitation that hid behind a number of divine attributes, Koranic verses, and prophetic quotes. While in previous periods, the outlaws who roamed the mountains had been coarse and direct, the rulers in the town were just as tyrannical and exploitative but attired themselves in robes and turbans—in this case, with the consent of God. The difference was not in essence but only in form.

As such, the war, terror, and struggles in and for Kurdistan began with the social struggles of the Neolithic Age and were intensified by the wars during the time of ancient slavery, becoming even more acute throughout the wars and terror of the feudal Middle Ages. That the Kurdish people were able to preserve their existence in this atmosphere of struggles, war, and terror at all is remarkable in and of itself. Despite all its flaws, ethnic resistance was essential to the Kurds' continued existence throughout this relentless historical process, although things might have turned out differently under strong and advanced civilizations.

After the fall of the Ottoman Empire, Kurdistan was even further divided and drawn deeper into a constellation of violence. On the new map of the Middle East drawn by the imperialist colonial powers of Great Britain and France, Kurdistan was placed under the rule of the Republic of Turkey, the shah's Iranian monarchy, the Iraqi monarchy, and the Syrian-French government—or, rather, it was forced to become part of these states. Rebellious movements based on the limited zeal of the formerly autonomous Kurdish collaborationist upper strata whose interests were further narrowed under the new regimes arose but were mostly restricted to provocation and led to an intensification of the terror. These uprisings were far from making any national or democratic demands. They were the expression of the struggle of the feudal Kurdish collaborators who longed for their old privileges and demanded their share in the new regimes. However, these new regimes relied on capitalism and were influenced by its nationalist ideology. For the Kurds, the fanatical advocacy of a unitary state under the principle of "one nation, one state" of the new regimes meant the denial of their existence grew even worse, that the repression intensified, and that every attempt at rebellion ended in massacre and forced assimilation. They were thrown back into the darkness of the Middle Ages and found themselves in a vice-like chokehold. It can be said that after the Jews, the Kurds, as a people, an ethnic group, and existing beings experienced the most extreme terror on a regional scale at the hands of chauvinist nationalism. What the Kurds experienced as a result of being abandoned to feudal backwardness by their own collaborationist traitors, who failed to understand the contemporary democratic national movements, is among the ugliest tragedies of the twentieth century.

The policy implemented in the part of Kurdistan annexed by Turkey was officially called the "flood." It was considered a "good thing" that it buried and leveled everything it flowed over. The pain of the loss of the Ottoman Empire also played a role in this. The goal was to weld together at least the remaining parts. The Turkish regime went as far as banning the use of Kurdish—a measure that was unprecedented anywhere in the world. After millennia of social struggles, merciless conquests, and wars of occupation and colonization, all social values, all manifestations that might serve to express the people's Kurdishness, were forcibly hidden behind an impenetrable black veil. Only intense efforts in the field of social science and literature concerning the life of the Kurds under the Republic of Turkey might possibly bring the truth to daylight.

The practices of the new Pahlavi dynasty of the shahs in Iran were in no way different from those in republican Turkey. The Kurdish mobilization, beginning with the uprising under the leadership of Ismail Agha Simko and expressed in the short-lived Kurdish Republic of Mahabad, were easily similarly eliminated for reasons that were primarily ideological and class-related.[25] What followed was a backward terror regime that brought the fascistic nationalist methods of the twentieth century to the fore. The practice of Britain and the France in Iraqi and Syrian Kurdistan was very similar; they put in place a comparable oppressive and colonial regime, which relied on the collaborationist Arab dynasties.

In the twentieth century, the Kurds were indeed confronted with a policy unparalleled in the rest of the world—being caged and domesticated like wild animals. There is no indication that the Kurds, as a social phenomenon, were even considered human. They weren't even considered worthy of a colonial policy like that used in Africa. The usual forms of modern oppression in ethnic, national, or colonial form, with political, social, legal, and military means, were considered too great an honor to be applied to the Kurds. Recently, the new Turkish prime minister Recep Tayyip Erdoğan publicly declared: "If you don't describe yourselves as Kurds, there is no Kurdish question."[26] With this, he only repeated the credo of the "deep state." The denial of the existence of an entire ethnic group and the acceptance of its individual members as a quid pro quo for their self-denial and their affirmation that they belong to the ruling nation and denomination is quite simply one of the most dangerous forms of fascism. The form of fascist terror against the Jews was open and clear. Denial, by contrast, is hidden and takes place in the dark. Therefore, we could call the terror against the Kurds "covert terror."

Since the end of the twentieth century, a dangerous and contradictory policy is being pursued in the region and in Kurdistan, which have been opened up to US activity. The current effects of this policy, namely, the emergence of a Kurdish federal state, on the one hand, and the attempted liquidation—the implemented war and its results—of the PKK and the Kurds in Turkey, the largest part of Kurdistan, on the other hand, would be unthinkable without the US and the EU. It is quite possible that the Israel-Palestine drama will repeat itself with Kurdistan and its neighbors, only in an even worse way. The epithet *horror* can be added to the ongoing policy of struggle, war, and terror. It is difficult to find historical examples of policies against any human community that are as horrific, with all of the far-reaching decisions based on these policies accompanied by such planned and insidious violence.

At this point, I must note that it is not at all sufficient to try to explain these bellicose policies as an expression of "colonialism, denial, and anni-hilation by the Turkish, Arab, and Persian nations," as we previously did. This only leads to erroneous conclusions. Actually, the phenomenon has to do with complex historical and social systems. It would also be too abstract and reductionist to simply blame the Turkish, Arab, or Persian states for the praxis in Kurdistan. That wouldn't explain the real origin of the phenomenon. In spite of what many people assume, there is no such thing as a Turkish, Arab, or Persian "nation-state" or "national interest." The nation-state is an epithet, an ideological description, but not reality itself. Nations don't have states. Even classes, in the narrow sense, can't have states. The state has a tradition stretching back at least five millen-nia. It has snowballed and split into many varieties. Ethnic groups have exploited it to a greater or lesser degree, but no ethnic group as a whole has ever used the state, only certain hierarchical and class-based groups have.

Perhaps the Turkish, Arabic, and Persian nations and ethnic groups have experienced as much oppression and exploitation from the state phenomenon as the Kurds. It would be misleading to claim that what the Turkmens suffered, what the Bedouins went through, and the Mamluks' truth are less than what the Kurds suffered and endured. Besides, the question "which Kurds?" is extremely important. The Kurdish feudal lords, who liked to play the roles of the bey, the emir, the haji, and the *hodja* were primarily responsible for this bellicose policy.[27] Had it not been for those who always did great harm to the poor and laboring Kurdish people and their provocative uprisings, which had no serious purpose or method, and which were followed by despicable surrenders, no Turkish, Arab, or Persian nationalist or statist would have been able to devise the present practices. Thus, if the Kurds want to determine the strategic factor that played the most negative role, they will be right on target if they look for traitors in their own ranks—at all times and all places, using every possible method and approach. These traitors set the Kurdish people and the rulers against each other in the service of their selfish interests and, with their own machinations, going beyond even the Israel-Palestine tragedy, and after doing so they fled the scene. In return for their treason, they were permitted to keep their property, allowing them to build rural mansions and summer residences for themselves in the metropolises and holiday centers and to continue to seamlessly play the established, cursed, and very ancient game.

I have tried here to elucidate the history of this policy that is at least five thousand years old and is even addressed in the guise of the epic of Gilgamesh and Enkidu. I believe that 99 percent of the Turks, Arabs, and Persians have no real interest in the policies being implemented by the power blocs, either in the form of the state or the nation.

It is not just that they don't gain any advantage from these policies; their backwardness, their hostilities, their misdirected hatred, the mutual violence, the squandering of resources, and the undeserved meaningless life that result from this are also terribly damaging. Social science offers us the best remedy to uncover this vicious circle, this magical game full of secrets. By this, however, I mean a true social science that disentangles power, the wars on which this power depends, and which it gives rise to, and the underlying social structures. I am not talking about the social science that refuses to see the whole, the soul, and life and knows of neither love nor respect. Such "cadaver science" leads to an even worse outcome than the Sumerian priest's "science of fate" that focused on the movement of the stars.

I believe that the most important contribution I have made in this book is to unmask this science, thereby helping to move us closer to the truth. Is nationalism a science? Is religionism a science? Is the reification of social-ism/liberalism/conservatism a science? Perhaps all of these edifices are just idolatry, that is, actually more backward than the idolatry of antiquity, i.e., paganism. The damage of this latter idolatry was quite limited, but who can calculate the harm that the idolatry of these infinite concepts has done over the course of history? Any believer in the holy scripture of any religion—and I have tried to interpret some of these scriptures sociolog-ically—will remain firmly committed to the values therein. But just how faithfully do the idolaters of the cadavers and these concepts stand by their alleged insights? Do they really believe they are useful? In the following chapters I will deal with these topics in a self-critical manner, but for now let us come back to the issue at hand.

I insist that if we do not properly disentangle and analyze the reality of power in Kurdistan and the war upon which this power is based, it will do great harm to every person, every state, and every social and political group that intervenes in the Kurdish question. Questioning themselves and abandoning their major mistakes, missteps, and madness and focus-ing on the many possible humane solutions would probably be the most meaningful approach for all involved. The wars of the twentieth century have, at the price of infinite suffering and horrendous loss of human life, certainly shown that no fanatical nationalist, religious, or leftist approach—whether in the name of the oppressors or the oppressed, the exploiter or the exploited—can provide a solution.

As should be clear from our admittedly very rough sketch, the prac-tice of struggle, fighting, war, and terror in Kurdistan has created a very particular sort of power bloc. These power blocs, based on war and mili-tary power, have not only continued to grow more effective in all of the major systems throughout history but knead and shape every inch of the social fabric like a dough. There is no structure that can be called Kurdish society or a Kurdish nation that has emanated from its own specific dynam-ics. What is truly decisive here are the traditions of force that have become ruling power and its institutional expression since the very beginning of time. There is no hidden corner of society that has not been penetrated and determined by these instruments of force, which have attempted to legitimize themselves, first through mythology, later through an alleg-edly supreme religion, and today in the name of "our nation" and "our class," our "nationalism" and our "socialism." The real Kurdish question arises from the way in which these phenomena came to be. Because of this historic enmeshment and formation, the Kurdish question is truly a maze of problems.

The most painful and dire thing is that the Kurds have largely lost their ability to solve these problems, which instead have them in a choke-hold. The Kurdish social fabric looks like an organism riddled with cancer or a tree afflicted by woodworms. As a result, such Kurdish identity and individuals are abundant. Whether we talk about the Kurdish language or Kurdish parties, insofar as they exist, or about women or the oh so well-known leaders or villagers or townspeople or intellectuals or religious scholars, whether we talk about religion or nationalism, about patriots or traitors, about diplomats or politicians: How many of those addressed have even the slightest understanding of what they are doing? How many are helpless, fake, crafty, horrific, and traitorous? How many are good, beautiful, and honest? These are questions that are very difficult to answer. Who is responsible? The existing and historically shaped components of power about which there is no clarity as to who they serve, how they do so, and to what degree. Ultimately, though, they are held in this situation by the coercive apparatuses of yesterday and today and the wars and the terror brought about by these apparatuses. These are the determinants of the phenomenon of Kurdish society, keeping it culpable and helpless in its present modes of being.

Whenever there is an insurrection or guerrilla-like resistance against these apparatuses the result is a conflict similar to the Israel-Palestine conflict. This situation has not yet fully unfolded, but should that happen the result might well be worse than that of its progenitor. Is it possible for the parties to the conflict, whatever their self-interests might be, to posi-tively address any social problem using this model? Fighting fire with fire seems unrealistic. Therefore, the methods of warrior ruling power cliques for solving social problems must be abandoned. This includes apparatuses of the insurgents. A new way of addressing the problem must be found and a new approach adopted.

We should not expect a method for resolving the enormous distortions in the Kurdish phenomenon from the apparatus of war—particularly not from ruling powers that can dominate with force. If the opponent does not intend to use force but seeks a peaceful democratic political solution and for clear and sincere reasons, the dominant power should immediately respond in kind, beginning with deactivating the military apparatus.[28] Leaving the means of discussion and solution to a dialogue involving civil and democratic instruments would not only be more humane and make more economic sense but would also be in the interests of the overwhelming majority of society's members.

In 1982, I compiled the book *Kürdistan'da Zorun Rolü* (The Role of Force in Kurdistan).[29] At the time, I believed I had disentangled and analyzed force. Our later practice showed that, my self-confidence notwithstanding, my thinking was fraught with major flaws. I can say that I now return to the role of force in Kurdistan a little more realistically prepared. I am profoundly aware that the path to a solution will not be "sacred violence," as many people thought, in a similar way, was necessary to achieve socialism. The contrary is true. All forms of force, with the exception of necessary and obligatory self-defense, must be condemned. Therefore, I am trying to proceed responsibly as I analyze the Kurdish phenomenon and the Kurdish question.

The Policy of Forced Assimilation Targeting the Culture of Kurdistan

One of the most popular social policies of warrior and power blocs is assimilation. The main purpose of assimilation policies, which, in general terms, amount to cultural dissolution, is to deprive those subjected to domination of their capacity to resist. Therefore, such policies repress the local language—the basic tool of mentality—and intensely enforce the use of the dominant language. Enforcing an official language diminishes and reduces the local language and culture to the point where they no longer play a role. The dominant language and culture become the route to a career or studying, the language of politics and the economy, and provide advantages and success to those who embrace them. Embracing the suppressed language and culture causes harm to the user. Caught in this dilemma, the local language is increasingly unable to hold its ground against the language of power. This is even truer in the case of a language without a pronounced written culture or a primary dialect. For such languages and dialects, the future looks grim. However, assimilation does not take place in the realm of language alone but in all social institutions shaped by power. An adaptation to the institutional reality of the dominant nation, religion, or group occurs on all levels. As soon as the political, social, and economic realms, and even the realm of mentality are officially defined and put under the protection of the law, the next step is forced or voluntary assimilation of the equivalent institutions of minorities and the vanquished, which are modeled after the dominant institutions so that they can take their place in the formalities of the dominant institutions. The more repression used and the more economic and political interests come into play, the more profound the assimilation.

Forced assimilation has been at least as destructive to the cultural existence of Kurdistan as war and terror. We can apply the same historical method and trace this back to antiquity. It is perhaps not an exaggeration to call Sumerian the first and most important assimilationist language and culture. Both etymological and syntactic investigations support this conclusion. The languages of the Hurrians, the Mitanni, the Urartu, the Medes, and the Persians were influenced first by Sumerian and then, in this order, by Akkadian, Babylonian, Assyrian, and Aramaic. This can be seen in the written artifacts of these languages. These are, as such, the major languages that assimilated other languages in the ancient Middle East. The local languages were communication tools used by ordinary people who could neither read nor write. The aristocrats, as collaborators, probably spoke the official languages of the various states they lived in—at least the written artifacts of the Urartians seem to indicate this. This is quite similar to the situation in today's dependent countries, whose leading personnel generally speak English or French.

As with English today, in late antiquity, Aramaic was the language of diplomacy and trade everywhere in the Middle East, the lingua franca, a general instrument of communication, a kind of "interethnic" language. The nobility and the state bureaucracy often used Aramaic as one of their written languages, alongside the local language, particularly in official communication. Historians assume that Jesus spoke Aramaic, and Aramaic is even found on Persian tombstones.

As the documents in these areas show, there was also an intense assimilation process in the realms of architecture, governance, literature, and the law. Neo-Assyrian, a "more national" form of Aramaic, was widely used as an assimilation tool. While Hebrew had only a relatively limited reach at the time of Hellenism, Greek became increasingly important in the Middle East. Greek and Neo-Assyrian competed, as English and French do today. Both struggled for influence in Kurdistan, particularly in the cities. A typical example was Urfa, where Aramaic, Armenian, Neo-Assyrian, Arabic, and Kurdish still had firm cultural roots. Later, Turkish was added to the mix. But extreme assimilation also leads to extreme cosmopolitanism, as a look at Urfa today makes clear.

The Neo-Assyrian language played a more progressive role in Kurdish culture than Arabic subsequently did. We call it a language of enlightenment, because the Assyrians mainly lived in cities. The Kurds were a Commagene people, and the nomads and peasantry generally spoke Kurdish dialects. There are barely any written sources, but this does not mean that such sources do not exist at all. Numerous written documents from the Mitanni capital of Washukanni, today's Hoşpınar, near the cities Resulain and Ceylanpınar on the Syrian-Turkish border, in particular show that around 1500 BCE some sort of proto-Kurdish was in use as a written language.[30]

The presence of a population with Hellenic roots in Kurdistan at the time of the Hellenic kingdoms (300 BCE–250 CE), and their influence, particularly in the cities, meant that Greek was also used for quite a long time. It functioned as a kind of colonial language. Then, as today, the urban population in Kurdistan was dominated by a foreign language and culture, while the rural population lived with its own local language and culture.

With Islam, Arabic moved to center stage. The rise of urbanization and Islam resulted in Arabic, previously the language of the Bedouins, becoming the most prestigious language in the Middle East and the language of literature and science. As the official language of war and power, Arabic acquired a status far superior to other languages. It took the place of the weaker African-based languages and became the dominant language from North Africa to the south of the Taurus-Zagros system. Speaking Arabic came with privileges. Those who mastered it could hope for posts in the bureaucracy, become religious scholars, or practice science. Therefore, Arabic was the language of advancement, including advancing personal interests. It owes its current significance to such material realities. In terms of influence, Persian was second to Arabic at this time. It mainly spread because it was the official language in Iran during the rule of the Seljuks. When the Seljuks conquered Anatolia and founded a state, with Konya as its capital, they also made Persian the official language. The famous mystic Jalāl ad-Dīn Mohammad Rumi, also known as Mawlana, wrote his most famous work, *Masnavi-ye-Ma'navi*, in Persian. At that time, Turkish like Kurdish was the spoken language and the languages of oral tradition in rural areas.

Arabic became very dominant in Kurdistan, because prayer leaders and mullahs were required to use it as the language of worship. Furthermore, in the cities, it became fashionable to live an Arab lifestyle—including adopting the dress and even Arabizing the family lineage. It was also thought to be a good idea to insert an Arab into your family's ancestral history. The dominance of all things Arab and Arabic in education, fashion, politics, diplomacy, the arts, and science did not even leave Persian, which had a very strong state tradition, untouched. It was, in fact, "conquered" by Arabic to a considerable degree. Everyone in the Middle East took on Arabic names and nicknames. This superiority continued intensely until the emergence of nation-states and national consciousness.

The expansion of the capitalist system and the formation of the "nation-state" further intensified the process of the linguistic and cultural assimilation of the Kurds. The pressure of Arabic and Persian was supplemented by the rising pressure of another language, Turkish. Kurdish language and culture, which could still be maintained within the ethnic group during antiquity and the Middle Ages, was now largely crushed and assimilated under the influence of three dominant languages and cultures that had at their disposal the improved tools provided by science and technology. The Kurdish language and culture, which, in the Middle Ages, had produced a number of literary works like Ehmedê Xanî's Mem û Zîn (Mem and Zin) increasingly shriveled under the political pressure. Doubts were seeded as to whether a Kurdish culture and language had ever existed. Speaking the language or practicing the culture were criminalized. In fact, just being a Kurd was increasingly criminalized. Kurds faced the most extreme form of bourgeoisie's crime and prison practices. The Kurdish phenomenon and the problematic it gave rise to were eventually categorized as the most dangerous of crimes. In the Turkish, Persian, and Arab nation-states, the campaign to assimilate Kurds, to alienate them from their own culture and language and bind them to the dominant language and culture, was carried out with full violence, not just against the Kurdish language and culture but against Kurdish existence as a whole. Access to schools, particularly to education in Kurdish, was forbidden. While those who had the material wherewithal were able to learn about "modernity" in the schools of the dominant nation.

The Kurds and all things Kurdish remained locked out of "modernity." The mere act of diffusing Kurdish music, newspapers, or books was regarded as "Kurdish nationalism" and "separatism" and fell under the rubric of political crime. Meanwhile, the respective nation-states propagated their own languages with a kind of nationalism that resembled the fascism of Hitler. Rhetoric about being the "most elevated nation" was ubiquitous. The Arabs were regarded as a "noble nation." To be a Turk was a "cause for happiness." Being a Persian was proof of the "greatest historic nobility." The nationalist sentiments awakened by capitalism had become an opiate used to mask any kind of backwardness.

However, the third major capitalist globalization offensive, and with it the growing esteem for all things local, combined with technology like radio and television, made the ban on a language meaningless. That and the increased capacity to act from beyond borders have contributed to a little space for Kurdish and the Kurds to recover. Of course, the contemporary resistance played a decisive role. The national democratic resistance enabled the Kurds to regain their identity, language, culture, and self-confidence. Defensive resistance against the force of warrior ruling power that created the enforced assimilation became the midwife to the rebirth of the Kurdish language and culture.

Ethnicity, Class, and Nation in Kurdistan

Identifying the ethnic, class, and national aspects within a society's way of life is important if we want to understand it in its totality. As far as their essence is concerned, societies are all the same. Their differences show themselves in their form—e.g., ethnic, class, and national characteristics. Ethnicity, which is the overcoming of forms such as the clan and the tribe,[31] becomes something real once differences in lineage become more pronounced and interest groups become conscious of themselves. For most of its existence, humanity lived in clans and tribes, the latter representing a somewhat more developed form. Within these scarcely differentiated migratory groups, consciousness about lineage barely existed, because the contradictions that would later lead to this consciousness were not yet present. It is assumed that during the long Paleolithic Age, the Old Stone Age preceding the Neolithic Age, the form of human cohabitation did not surpass the clan way of life. Tribes becoming ethnic groups required an area to which they were bonded by self-interest, within which they could organize their way of life and gain a certain feeling of belonging. Their joint productive activities and their shared language increasingly bound these groups together. Because of factors like attacks from the outside and food shortages the importance of these associations grew over time, raising the need for governance and defense structures. The emerging social hierarchy also brought about the domination of one sex, i.e., patriarchy.

All these developments led to the lineage form called ethnicity. The influence of time and place led to a differentiation into cultural groups that later had to defend themselves from each other or synthesize. The fact that certain lineages gained prominence over others led to the establishment of hierarchy among ethnic groups, followed by the emergence of federations of ethnic groups or aşiret. As the process accelerated, it led to confederations, but when these structures dissolved and there was no simultaneous relapse to older structures, the result was the emergence of states and classes. The fact that this process took place under the Neolithic mode of production has often been noted and is easily understood when considered rationally.

The age when aşiret emerged and developed, their golden age, was the Neolithic period. The first agrarian revolution, the domestication of animals, and the transition to the village order were all closely connected to the aşiret system. Patriarchy developed in the later stages of this period. There is strong evidence that the domestic mother order was initially predominant, but with the increasing development of hierarchy the heyday of patriarchy began.

Even though the emergence of classes was connected to the development of hierarchy, the real beginning of class division was with the privileged groups that the military coterie assembled. In these groups, personal skills rather than kinship bonds were decisive. The association of the ablest defenders and hunters under the leadership of the strongest male created unprecedented privilege in its early days. At this point, rule by force developed. Gathering under the rule of a strong chieftain led to relations that transcended aşiret relations. Class was the form of the new relationship. A class might consist of professional groups and smaller entities that either separated from the aşiret or had never been part of one in the first place. Aşiret, however, resisted the emergence of classes because of their kinship relations. It is difficult for class to develop within an aşiret. Due to its very nature, it doesn't recognize class relations and strongly opposes and constantly resists them. This is why aşiret societies, called "barbarians" by the system of slavery, constituted a permanent threat to the system.

The expansion of class division was accompanied by economic productivity. Where slave labor offered productive advantage, a class division based on slaves intensified. With the emergence of states, this process accelerated even more. The state is essentially an organized administrative system of slavery. It would be futile to look for its essence in some divine thought, some national interest, or in questions of security. In this sense, the link between the state and classes is undeniable.

The division of the main aşiret led to formations called people or kavim, which represented linguistic and cultural groups. When we talk about a kavim or a people, we mean social groups within which there were only loose relations but which more or less shared the same language and culture. In that sense, it is accurate to draw a connection between ethnic groups, peoples, and kavim. Kavim represented one of the most important social categories of late antiquity and the Middle Ages. As a union of lineages, they played an important role in the birth of the Middle Ages. The fact that Teutonic tribes were able to conquer Rome, that Arab tribes could overrun Byzantium, and that the Turks and Mongols were able to sweep through the Islamic world was to a large extent due to their character as kavim.

In the kavim form, settlement on a given land and cultural differentiation was more evident. The key classes were the aristocracy and serfs. Urbanism fell within this general category, representing limited independence and cosmopolitism. We should regard the city as an autonomous unit pretty much beyond the bonds of ethnicity and kavim, in which class relations were more pronounced.[32] With feudalism, although the ruling and the ruled classes came from the same ethnic group, their relationship was nevertheless characterized by profound alienation. Under slavery, the master and the slave only rarely belonged to the same aşiret.

Nationhood and the phenomenon of the nation appear to be the continuation and extension of kavim relations. One aspect of nationhood is the dissolution of economic structures that were separated by feudal boundaries and the creation of a more developed common market. As much as the common market is associated with capitalism, it is still by no means coterminous with it. There was a common market even in precapitalist social systems, and it could also exist in postcapitalist social systems. The market is a general category of social development, and it is natural and useful for it to also exist in socialist systems.

The common language and culture around developed markets led to the development of national bonds and relations. More precisely perhaps, language and culture developed to the point that they became the nation's central bond and relationship. On that basis, the capitalist system could develop, but the same would also have been possible for noncapitalist, communal, democratic, and socialist systems. If capitalist class domination is prevalent within the nation, it might make sense to talk about a bourgeois or capitalist nation. But still, it would not be correct to identify capitalism with the nation. If ties of exploitation are weak, and democratic and communal relations prevail, a nation can be called democratic and socialist.

Within nations, the complexity of the ties among ethnicity, sex, and class increased. Even though the bourgeoisie and the working class constitute the fundamental classes, many other strata, including the peasantry, also emerged anew. It is possible to find a large number of kavim and classes, as well as the oppressed sex, within the nation, making the concepts of the ruling nation, the ruling class, and the ruling sex more transparent. The next stage is the formation of an official language, national privileges, and oppressed ethnic and cultural groups. Even though the notion of the "nation-state" refers to the state that emerges within the phenomenon of the nation, it is more of a nationalist concept. If the ideology of the state is nationalism, it is called a nation-state because of the dominant nationality. There are also multinational states, to which a concept different from "nation-state" should probably be applied.

One of the most dangerous aspects of nationalism is the practice of identifying each nation with a state and each state with a nation. Characterizing the state as a common specialized organization, without intermixing the categories of "state" and "nation," would provide a much better way for nations to be free, equal, and democratic.

Best, however, would be to understand *transnational* to be the synthesis of groups of nations with close and common interests. A focus on the syntheses of nations that don't deny but, rather, enrich each other might lead to extremely productive results that are effective in problem-solving. Neither national nihilism—denial of the nation—nor national fanaticism can be the solution. On the contrary, the best and the most correct way to dispose of the present-day nationalist hodgepodge might be to strive for the syntheses of various nation's values.

These fundamental conceptual definitions will better facilitate our investigation of the reality of ethnicity, class, and nation in Kurdistan. It might be realistic to identify Kurdistan as the main site of the origin of ethnicity. Being one of the most developed and oldest centers of the Neolithic Revolution goes some distance to explaining the ethnic structures that are still in effect. Kurdish society is perhaps the oldest and most intensely experienced mosaic of ethnic communities, primarily because for millennia the Kurdish region served as a center for the flow of migration from all four cardinal points. The productivity of the agrarian revolution played a fundamental role in this. While conditions in Lower Mesopotamia and Egypt were more suitable to a more rapid development of class-based civilization, in Upper Mesopotamia and its periphery ethnic communities were more advantageous. The conditions in that area required a seminomadic lifestyle and defensive structure, as well as seasonal migratory movements between the mountains and the plains, creating ideal conditions for ethnicity. The Neolithic Revolution was the result of precisely these conditions. The rapid population growth led to a struggle over settlement sites and productive areas early on, leading to aşiret-like organizations that were the most fundamental organizational units for defense, settlement, and production.

Back then, the state as an organizational form could be torn down at any time through various forms of attack. The conditions in the Kurdish area were unsuitable to early statehood. The chances of survival in smaller units, such as villages or extended families, where the aşiret had not yet appeared were limited. The options for these units was either to join another more influential tribe, to emigrate, or to resist to the very last. This thesis is supported by the fact that it was mostly small, rebellious groups that took refuge in areas where conditions were difficult. The sedentary inhabitants of the plains, on the other hand, mostly fell more easily under the influence of a state. If we compare the mountain aşiret with those on the plains, we will see that the primordial and largely untouched ones were located in the mountainous regions, while the inhabitants of the plains underwent a fairly intense process of assimilation, which is why Kurdishness in the mountains and Kurdishness on the plains have serious differences.

Scholars assume that Proto-Indo-European, the first predecessor of the Kurdish linguistic group, developed about twelve thousand years ago. Because this was the language of agriculture and animal husbandry, it constituted the origin of the languages of those with a similar order of life. Thus, we should see the expansion from Kurdistan less as a physical but primarily as a cultural process. The strength of the Indo-European language family comes from the foundation they rely upon—their speakers launched an agricultural revolution that lasted for thousands of years, which explains why certain basic words are so widely encountered in such a large geographic region. Some very old Kurdish words found in a similar form in many languages of the Indo-European language group, such as *murd*, meaning *death*, *jin*, meaning *woman* and *life*, *ro*, meaning *sun*, and *star*, meaning *star*, illustrate this fact.

There is clear evidence of the existence of linguistically and culturally different groups is around 4000 BC. One of the first historically identifiable proto-Kurdish groups was the Hurrians. Some of the words that the Kurdish aşiret hailing from the mountains used were also found among the Hurrians. There are also striking similarities in their mythological systems and the world of their gods.

Their geographical location as a passageway between the Sumerian and the Hittite civilizations created an even stronger incentive for these ancestors of the Kurds to strengthen their aşiret presence. Because their early statehood would have accelerated their elimination, they opted for a seminomadic lifestyle, a kind of semi-guerrilla life. With a growing number of states in their environment, strengthening the aşiret structures became increasingly necessary. Even today, aşiret among the Kurds live a semi-guerrilla way of life. If we take a closer look at the families within these aşiret organizations, we will see that matri-power and -freedom come to the forefront. Women were very influential and had a high degree of freedom. Again, all of this means that the tenacity and persistence of the aşiret developed in the form of a semi-guerrilla lifestyle. Once again, we see that the degree of the women's freedom determines the general degree of freedom within society. The traditionally agile, strong, and brave Kurdish women stem from an ancient historical tradition. The negative side of an aşiret-like life, however, was that the possibility of transformation into a more developed society was limited.

The city was born from class society. With the emergence of the city there was an accelerated development of writing, the arts, and science. The founding of the state greatly extended the scope of thought and action. Because of enhanced economic productivity, a larger population was able to live together in a smaller space. Nonetheless, the insistence of the Kurds on a free life in their own country is not evidence of any particular shortcoming but, rather, of their actual quality, which may very well have prevented them from developing a slaveholding civilization along similar lines. It is also due to this resistance and their insistence on freedom that they have been able ensure their existence to this very day.

If we were to apply freedom as the criterion for "development," the Kurds are perhaps the most advanced people, or ethnic group, in history. The proto-Kurdish aşiret was important for the Mesopotamia-centered civilizations to survive until around 330 BCE, as it had the most respected and sought-after characteristics in the region. The best source for this is

Herodotus's *Histories*. The author mentions the Medes quite often and points to the tendencies that, even at that time, considered the highly developed Greek society to be collaborating with the Medes. The Medes, as the Kurds of their time, owed their desirable qualities to their freedom-loving identity.

Zoroastrianism is a religion characterized by a powerful freedom-loving morality that comes close to equality and freedom in relations between women and men, advocating for a system of ideal partnerships between the sexes. To be a good partner was regarded as a virtue of good morality. Attention was given to the upbringing of children, and commitment to the truth was the first principle of education. It was very important not to lie. Zoroastrianism was also very attentive to animals and the environment. The impact of Zoroastrianism is obvious in terms of the strength of the Kurdish family, with a similar tradition still alive among the Yazidi and Alevi Kurds.

With the impact of civilizations, both the Kurd's moral and aşiret structures gradually deteriorated. With the invasion of Hellenism, a new synthesis of East and West provided a new stage on the way to civilization, as is demonstrated by the inscriptions on the ruins on Mount Nemrut, the monuments of the Commagene kingdom. Until the emergence of Islam, the mountains remained significant in Kurdish social life. It's safe to assume that at that point a Kurdish aristocracy class established itself, first in the Persian Empire, and then in the Parthian and Sasanian Empires. An aristocracy that has dissociated itself from ethnicity was far from constituting a class in its own right, although it may well have been able to do so before the founding of the Persian Empire. Available sources indicate that after becoming the collaborators of the empire, Kurdish aristocrats were generally expected to display servant- and serf-like loyalty. The more the Kurdish ethnic group was characterized by a spirit of freedom, the more its aristocracy was colorless and eager to collaborate. The emergence of classes on this basis among the Kurds was distorted and was accompanied by an aristocracy that denied its lineage. However, no aristocracy arose in Kurdish society that could equal the Greek, Roman, or Persian aristocracies. Instead, in each case, the Kurdish aristocracy constituted a subordinate element within the ruling aristocracy, which it always tried to emulate. One might say that the Kurdish collaborators always acted "more Catholic than the pope." Had there been an aristocracy like the one that developed in Rome, or even a state-aligned class similar to those in Sumer and Egypt, social development in Kurdistan would have undoubtedly taken a different path. The Kurdish aristocrats, however, did not create any cities of their own, preferring to become the servants in cities founded by others. When we look at the cities founded by the Hellenes in Asia, the glaring difference is obvious.

Throughout these various periods, the distinction between the village and the city was accompanied by deep social division. While the cities had played the role of centers for alien rulers since Persian rule, the kom and the nomadic way of life had long functioned to preserve local culture, a reality that continued for a very long time. The first cities were shaped by the Sumerians, then—in order—by the Babylonians, the Assyrians, the Persians, the Hellenes, the Romans, the Byzantines, and the Ottomans and, finally, by the nation-states. On the other hand, the village and the kom sustained and represented Kurdishness. The Kurds remaining a village and kom society was not arbitrary but, in key ways, was the result of merciless conquests and occupations and the establishment of alien urbanization. The city meant alienation, enslavement, and collaboration.

Islam had a multifaceted influence on the Kurdish ethnic group and its aristocracy. The ethnic collaborators and the urban aristocracy were the first to render homage to it. Their capitulation was deep-rooted. Their role in the emergence of medieval classes constituted the basis of their treason, which persists to this very day. They perceived themselves as somehow better than the Kurds from rural areas and organized themselves within the ruling power groups.

We can analyze this better if we look at the topic objectively. The area was organized as the area of civilization thousands of years ago. To the ancestors of the Kurds, however, the cities were completely alien, never giving them the opportunity to build their own cities. They did not descend from the mountains as conquerors. Collaborators had long paved the way. It fell to their successors to continue on this path. Whether Sumerian or Hellenic, Persian or Arab—there was no ruling aristocracy that the collabo-rators could not disappear into. It is little wonder that an ethnic group that lost its elite in this way, or, rather, whose elite had this particular character, was unable to further develop its own language and culture.

Even though there were some Kurdish dynasties in the Middle Ages, they could never liberate themselves from Arab and Persian influence and were unable to become national dynasties. The rule of the two most famous among them, the Marwanids (990–1090 CE) and the Ayyubids

(1175–1250 CE), was scarcely different from the rule of the Arab dynasties. They did not seriously care about the Kurdish language but simply carried on with the classical line. The fact that the people were divided into different Islamic *mezheb* and tariqat helped preserve at least a modicum of Kurdish essence. Despite its negative impact, the feudalism of the Middle Ages did not succeed in annihilating all particularities of the Kurds as a kavim. On the contrary, they managed to manifest their existence through some real political, intellectual, and literary achievements, albeit only to a limited degree. The chronicle Sharafnama (1596 CE) and the epic Mem û Zîn (c. 1690 CE) show the degree of development of the Kurdish language and Kurdish kavim characteristics. From these works, we also learn that there was separation from the aşiret groups for the first time.

This separation is what we call the *Kurmanj*,[33] which describes a group of people outside of the aşiret.[34] This group either developed because of the dissolution of the aşiret order or because people broke away from the aşiret. The population of the first peripheral urban settlements were made up of the Kurmanj. This process accelerated after the nineteenth century, in a way comparable to the process of proletarianization under capitalism. There is a difference between the Kurd of the aşiret and the Kurd of the Kurmanj, and the Kurmanj represents genuine Kurdishness. The aşiret is unthinkable without hierarchy, but the Kurmanj have a family structure. They are a sort of Kurdish working class. The notion of "karker" (worker) correctly refers to this group.[35]

The Kurdish serf, or *xulam*, was the servant of the aga, the big landowner. The institution of the aga, which developed in the Middle Ages, has a particular position within the Kurdish aristocracy. The agas managed to create serfs from the aşiret. Agahood developed in villages offering the option of agriculture, particularly under the Ottoman Empire. When an ethnicity settled in an agrarian village, its hierarchy began to transform and center around the agas. Agas were known for their harshness, quite different from the *reïs* (aşiret leader). They were quick to use the rod. The reïs, on the other hand, led on the basis of kinship bonds. The institution of sheikhdom, however, has its origins in the Arab tradition and developed under the influence of religion.[36] It also had an economic basis,[37] but it primarily represented medieval intellectualism. The sheikh had a function similar to that of the head of a tariqa. We can thus describe the reïs, i.e., the head of the aşiret, the village aga, and the sheikhs of the religious tariqat as the Kurdish ruling class of the Middle Ages. From that perspective, there is a certain development in class division.

The collaboration of the Ottomans with the house of Şerefhan, whose intellectual leader was Emir İdris Bitlisi, served the interests of this ruling upper class. In the nineteenth century, this Kurdish upper class began to lose its privilege. The central state demanded more taxes and soldiers than it previously had, triggering a number of uprisings. But none of these rebellions ever reached the level of Kurdish nationalism, not even the level of the Western bourgeois revolt or of the Armenian and Assyrian nationalism that emerged simultaneously. The defeat of the Kurdish rebellions had negative consequences for the population, curtailing its freedom. The attempt to transform the Kurdish kavim into a national movement also failed, and the old Kurdish elites never succeeded in rising above their traditional role.

We can pinpoint the beginning of this development and the accompanying deterioration that so negatively impacted the Kurds with the nineteenth-century uprisings. For the first time in history, the status of the Kurds was rescinded, and from then on they ceased to play any particular political role. When the Ottoman sultanate collapsed after World War I, the Kurdish collaborators found themselves in a difficult situation. Once they understood that the purpose of the national liberation war was not the salvation of the caliph but, rather, the creation of a republic, they withdrew their original support and rebelled. After the uprisings were suppressed, they contributed to a situation characterized by new heights of denial and collaboration. As they largely lost their Kurdish traits, they didn't hesitate to function as a clique of agents within the state. In order to be accepted as minority groups, they did not shy away from pandering to the ruling nation by acting like the most ardent of nationalists.[38] Their variety of nationalism was just as dangerous to any people and any nation as their variety of religionism.

The development of Kurdish nationhood followed an unusual and contradictory course. The Kurds never had the opportunity to develop within their own language and cultural boundaries around a common market. The uprisings and the subsequent harsh crackdowns prevented that. The breaking of the resistances, and the inability to create a contemporary national movement seriously undermined Kurds' level of nationhood. They were unable to build any contemporary national parties and movements, and there was no significant Kurdish enlightenment.

Even though the Kurds founded the republic with the Turks, their longing for the old order and failure to recognize the republic meant that they wasted the opportunity available and set the stage for the ensuing uprisings to end badly for the Kurds. The way Kurdish collaborators subsequently facilitated assimilation and made headway within the ruling nation's politics in an unprincipled and treacherous way played a decisive role in making the twentieth century—the age of national liberation—the worst century ever for the Kurds. To the extent that the collaborators corrupted their own nation, they also corrupted the nation or nations in which they attempted to play some role.

It seems unlikely that Kurdish nationhood will develop around a common market or as a bourgeois national movement. It is also questionable to what extent the US's offensive in the Middle East will serve the interests of Kurdish collaborators and their bourgeois nationalism, because rather than being allies based on principles they very much pursue their own interests.

Nonetheless, the activities of democratic communal society in a Kurmanj-like formation could possibly achieve results. The development of Kurdish nationhood around a democratic, communal, and civil society would perhaps be among the healthiest and most timely possible approaches. A departure from the classic state-oriented national movement that prioritizes effective civil society and democratization activities rather than relying on the protracted national liberation war and its means could clear the way for a democratic national formation. The importance of this formation in particular is women's participation based on freedom, leading to a form of nationhood that is free from nationalism, does not accommodate religious radicalism and is based on the independent development of local culture, woman's freedom, and an ecological and environmentally conscious course of action, which would be the healthiest road to a democratic nation that eschews separatism or the use of violent methods.

In this way Kurdish nationhood could perhaps provide a model for resolving the conflicts in the Middle East, the region where slaughtering one another for ethnic, religious, denominational, and nationalist reasons is most common. New methods are inevitable, especially given the seemingly insurmountable impasse of the nationalist approach in Israel–Palestine, for example. It is time to finally accept that it is unrealistic to attempt to solve problems with violence and separation, which simply cannot resolve the existing problems. Likewise, it is impossible to extinguish national realities with state terror. More importantly, we should finally understand that living and intermingling with different national, ethnic, and religious cultures can provide an enriching and vibrant way of life and need not be a source of anxiety or of a sense of loss. As soon as we realize that people from different nations and cultures do not need different states but, rather, full democracy, it will also be clear that there is no such thing as a national question that can't be resolved.

At the moment, the Kurds are trying to become a nation using two different approaches together and intertwined. First, the path of the primitive nationalist feudal bourgeois Kurdish ruling strata supported by the Western capitalist system that at this juncture has embodied its program in the Kurdish federal state in Iraq. Second, the path of the toiling Kurdish people whose goal is to become a democratic and libertarian nation that relies on its own strength. While the first approach is guided by feudal, religious, and aşiret tics that at this point are reactionary and driven by self-interest, the second is based on democratic, libertarian, and egalitarian ties that transcend narrow aşiret relations and are not based on feudal and religious tendencies.

While the representatives of the first method have primarily focused on taking the lead under the US occupation in Iraqi Kurdistan, adherents of the second path have tried to be self-reliant and to contribute to the establishment of a new understanding of Kurdistan as the driving force for the democratization of Turkey rather than an obstacle.

Given the worsening problems of democracy and the various national questions throughout the Middle East, the significance and the role of these two distinct methods will be better understood. Whether Kurdistan will become a more comprehensive new Israel-Palestine or a country with peaceful democratic solutions will depend on which of the two approaches prevails. The more the narrower ethnic, kavim-based, religious, and nationalist methods are sidelined and the military methods laid aside, the more likely that the complicated social problems in Kurdistan will be resolved using democratic, freedom-loving, and egalitarian means based on a democratic nation.

Official Ideology and Power in Kurdistan

If tales of ideology and power were to be written it would probably be a very important step forward in the modern theory of social reality. Quite obviously, sociology hasn't yet succeeded in disentangling the phenomena of ideology and power. As long as the role of ideology and the execution of power as the common way of thinking and dominating, as well as in molding the rest of the social fabric, have not been entirely clarified, economic, social, and political analyses will ultimately lead to extremely dangerous forms of social ignorance. The failure to understand the difference between the application of the scientific method to society and to everything that lies outside of society will only make the problem of knowing and doing even more complex. A certain self-knowledge on the part of society must be considered part of that reality. The capacity to self-define is perhaps the most basic property of any society.

It is difficult to even talk about the existence of a society that cannot self-define. One might even see this as society becoming a corpse. Another name for self-definition is *social ideology*. Ideology, for its part, can also be defined as a set of common ideas expressing themselves through will. This, in turn, we can call social morality. The main task of social morality is to ensure social existence. Social existence is possible only if one stakes a claim, i.e., if one becomes an ideological force, thereby closing the final connecting link in the circle.

Even though power is very closely connected to ideology, it is a quite distinct and decisive phenomenon, particularly in societies that are under domination. Power itself is the institutionalization of violence in society, a means to disguise the violence. Therefore, it is perhaps impossible to define power in and of itself. Defining a mask is only possible if we know what it is supposed to be hiding. Masks cannot be defined on their own. Violence is only comprehensible when it explodes. Then the mask falls, and it becomes clear that power is not something that exists on its own, that it is a complement of violence, its beguiling face. There can be no normal condition of being for societies determined by violence, only a state of explosion. But, as in nature, a state of continuous explosion in society is very rare. Besides, far-reaching cooperation of emotional and analytical intelligence has the ability that could prevent social explosions, such as wars, revolutions, counterrevolutions, uprisings, and other struggles. Even in the most problematic situations, solutions without explosions are always possible. The claim that there is no solution without violence and military action is simply not reasonable.

This brief outline has been necessary to lay the groundwork for a proper evaluation of official ideology and power in Kurdistan. The official ideology is an instrument for legitimizing and defending the status quo that state power has established in society. It's the mindset created by state power and implemented to unilaterally ensure approval and secure its power. A few examples would include mythology among the Sumerians, philosophy among the Greeks, religion in the Middle Ages, and science in modern Europe, all of which essentially functioned or function as ideological instruments. Practice, in terms of prayers and/or rituals is a secondary function. What is decisive is that these ideological instruments be paradigmatically established as society's mentality.

The official ideology in Kurdistan consists of a whole chain of theses: there is no such phenomenon as the "Kurds"; were Kurds to exist, it would be of no importance; were the Kurds to actually turn out to be important, it would be very dangerous to acknowledge the fact. The justifications for these ideas are extremely far-fetched. Some of them freeze you while others burn you. These ideas are repeated ad nauseum until the rulers of the day and everything related to them is fully accepted and seen as valid. The main reason for this approach is that Kurdistan was conquered long ago, and as a result the Kurds have capitulated. Oddly enough, the Kurds do not recognize any of this. Any Turkish, Arab, or Persian ruler will wallow in the tales of the spectacular wars in which they conquered and subjugated the Kurds and will revel in heroic tales of the conquest. The Kurds, for their part—presuming they can muster the courage to insist on their own existence—are foolish enough to listen to these shameful stories. They are barely capable of posing simple questions about who and what was conquered in the process. They find themselves at the point where social mentality and, therefore, social morality ends.

The official ideologies have continued to have an effect in different forms across the centuries until today. They are like unbroken rings in a chain. For example, the Arabs pointed to the Islamic conquests as fundamental proof of divine legitimation and said, "We conquered, and, therefore, it is ours." Can there be a greater right than to conquer in the name of God? This is the underlying idea, and claims based on this argument are still insistently advanced. The Persians go a step further and claim to believe that the Kurds are relatives of a lower order, that the Persians already own everything that was theirs and know with a certainty that the Kurds agreed to all of this a long time ago. They find it unnecessary to present any further justification. They seem to ask: "Can Kurdishness even be an idea in the face of our great state ideology and state power?"

The Turks invoke the same scenario of conquest. They argue that they conquered Kurdistan as part of Anatolia a thousand years ago and see no need for any further discussion, speaking confidently about the unquestionable fact that conquest grants the conqueror absolute rights.

The facts squarely contradict all of this. While it is true that the conquest of the Balkans and of Constantinople by the Ottomans may have had a certain significance, even mention of the simple fact that Diyarbakır was never conquered or that ever since the Seljuks the Kurds have acted on the basis of common policies, and that this is the key course of history, is regarded as an attack on the right of conquest and its ideology. We have, however, clearly shown that the Kurds created a culture, have called this land home for more than fifteen thousand years, and, thus, have rights that are a thousandfold more valid than any right based on the conquest of the Kurds. Given that, as a basic source of their rights, the Kurds seeded the land summer and winter, transforming it into the fields that provided the basis for the villages and cities where they sweated, resisted, and died, a land, every acre of which they have treasured, in short, a land they have tended to in every possible way, so at a minimum the question arises: How could a land that they lived on in this way, a land onto which they embroidered their very existence like a pattern on a tambour, become the property of the Arabs, Turks, or Persians at a single stroke? The Kurds might rightly suggest that while the land has been illegitimately occupied at some point, we have conquered it every day with the sweat and toil of hundreds of generations.

The official ideology also asserts that *Kurds* and *Kurdistan*, while unimportant, are dangerous concepts that give rise to separatism accompanied by terror. But we have proven that the words *Kurds* and *Kurdistan* existed thousands of years ago, at a time when no one had yet heard of Arabs, Persians, or Turks. We have also shown that the Kurds are by no means unimportant but actually represent the oldest of the primary sources of civilization. The claim that simply saying this could be the source of separatism and violence is contradictory in and of itself. Anyone who makes this argument is acting like a thief who expels the owner from the house—and is, therefore, the actual separatist. Why should the Kurds separate, that is, divide, the land they have worked to create over thousands of years? The Kurds are the ones who are constantly shot and killed, and it is their land that is under permanent occupation. The actual sources of violence come from the outside. Why would the Kurds use violence?

Why would the necessary resort to legitimate self-defense be regarded as separatist violence?

The official ideology doesn't really say all of this openly, but what I sketched above is its actual content. The corresponding ideas are expressed in mocking verses about the Kurds like "wheel and deal and send the Kurdish Mehmet to keep guard" or "Kurds don't know how to feast but only how to drink ayran aplenty."[39] Official ideologies and those who implement them consider it an essential duty to present these basic ideas in public schools as the scientific framework behind all aspects of history, economics, politics, literature, law, the arts, the military, and even religion and morality. They firmly believe that this will gain them social legitimacy. In this sense, ideology plays an even more dangerous role than massacres. Denying the very existence of a society's people because they have been weakened or defeated is not just a violation of that people's rights but an effective denial of all religious, philosophical, and scientific facts. No social problem could be more dangerous than this. From such denial, it is a short step to annihilation.

It is not my intention to discuss how these ideas are articulated in the Arab, Persian, and Turkish states here, but only to define their ideological function.

I will address, however, the issue of ideological instruments. To establish their legitimacy, such ideological concepts were repeated as if they were a fundamental truth thousands of times a day by wandering hodja, dervish, and *sayyid* in the past, then, subsequently, they were propounded through books, and, today, they are spread by newspapers, radio, television, the official educational system, and the mosques. Anyone who dares to put forward a contradictory thesis will be severely punished; they will face the immediate intervention of the security forces and the judicial apparatus, will be prosecuted, tried, and convicted, and their sentence be executed with extreme prejudice. If one of the most fundamental privileges of a society and its people is to freely express themselves, but obstacles of this sort prevent them from doing so, can there be any good outcome for members of that society whether they are the rulers or the oppressed?

It is clear that the official ideology creates a serious problem. Its primary function is to legitimize and justify the violent essence of power as an accepted commonplace and create a status for itself. Whether addressing the rulers or the oppressed, ideology attempts to create a fundamental paradigm that make a one-sided perspective dominant within society, thereby obscuring reality and preventing the development of a sound approach. This drains away the real essence of any possible social peace and solidarity. In the final analysis, it ultimately has the contrary effect, laying the base for the potential emergence of opposing ideas at any moment, thus encouraging an atmosphere of struggle and violence. It is always the illegitimate claims of an ideology that prevent social peace and provide the pretext for war by inevitably provoking countervailing ideologies and structures and leading to a situation where the society is in a persistently tense and conflict-ridden state.

Freedom of speech opens the way to genuine peace in the ideological realm. Following centuries of intense ideological conflict, Europeans recognized the importance of the freedom of speech, making it a basic right. Freedom of speech brings the flaws or weaknesses implicit in an ideological approach into the open, causing it to more closely reflect reality, which encourages intellectual production. Ending the ideological siege on the Kurds in Kurdistan and allowing free speech in books, newspapers, the cinema, and on the radio and television is not, however, only necessary for democracy and human rights; it will, in fact, make a key contribution to clearing the way for society to recognize reality and in bringing society into contact with scientific knowledge, thereby facilitating the development of an information society. Getting correct information is a better and sounder way to achieve the most rational and peaceful possible solution to the problems we face. That Europe recognizes this as the basis for the dignified approach it feels its societies deserve is the source of its international esteem.

As long as the present official ideology concerning Kurds and Kurdistan continues to exist, it will pose a real danger, because it sustains an atmosphere of tension that can be easily exploited from the outside. The events in Iraq are a clear example. Those who carry the official ideology like a hump in their back will fall far behind on the road they take in becoming contemporary. Therefore, regardless of the claims of its supporters, the operational official ideology creates a situation where separatism and violence are always possible, thereby posing a real threat to the integrity of the country and the state. This is why history has so often seen societies, states, and countries start mindless wars that lead to division and major losses.

If we look more concretely at the official ideology that is influential in Kurdistan, we see that it is dominated by nationalism and religionism.

In all four parts of Kurdistan, Islam functions as a state ideology. Even though there is a lot of talk about secularism, Islam continues to play a political role in all of these discussions and to determine the relationship between the individual and Allah—essentially, the relationship between the individual, on the one hand, and power and the state, on the other—and, in any case, these discussions are nothing but a deception. Some countries, Iran among them, do this quite explicitly, while others do it implicitly. The Diyanet İşleri Başkanlığı (Office for Religious Affairs) in Turkey has more than one hundred thousand cadres.[40] It is possible that not even Iran has an army that size in the service of religion. The imam hatip schools in Turkey have a status similar to that of the state secondary schools.[41] If one adds Koran courses, religious institutes, and theological faculties, the aggregate number of cadres is close to half a million. Secularization, or worldliness, cannot be achieved by applying a thin laic polish to the educational system. Only a sociological analysis of religious thought and overcoming it through literature can bring about genuine worldliness. In the countries we are concerned with here, there is a toxic mix of religiosity and science, a mix that leads to a deadlock in the mentality and is the foremost obstacle to the creative thinking and philosophical development that could provide the basis for a high-quality literary paradigm. These countries actually have not considered what the impact of Islamic ideology might be. In the daily calculations around their rule, they see it as a means to control women and society overall. They don't even realize what being prevented from developing a scientific paradigm has cost them.

In addition, when this mentality is organized around tariqat and parties directly playing a role in politics, a situation that can't easily be resolved is created. Whether an individual is religious or not is of no particular importance in and of itself. A religious person can play an important role in society, just as an absolutely nonreligious person can. But for this to be true, a sociological analysis of religion is essential. Religious tradition should not be belittled and disrespected. Its significance must definitely be grasped. If such an approach is adopted, religion is valuable in terms of defining society's identity. If, however, it is reduced to the rote learning of meaningless rituals, forms of worship, and prayers, religion will only numb and neutralize the mind and emotions, shutting down access to knowledge. This is why the power structure clings to religion, particularly as arbitrary rule, or despotism, grows harsher. This is an attempt to weaken the consciousness and will of society.

Just as in Iran, religion is a central tool of choice in Iraq and Syria, as well as in Turkey. There was sociological content in Mustafa Kemal Atatürk's religious policy.[42] His preference for a scientific mindset was clear. He undeniably waged a struggle to change the mentality. But, in the long run, the lack of an in-depth interpretation of the religious tradition, the failure to surpass religion with philosophy, and controlling the religious tradition with the Office for Religious Affairs had a counterproductive impact. As such, laicism in the European sense was never achieved.

After Atatürk's death, the religious paradigm degenerated further and was politically instrumentalized, with the result that the republic's previous achievements were largely lost. Under the rule of Demokrat Parti (DP: Democrat Party) and the Adalet Partisi (AP: Justice Party),[43] the politicization of religion was more explicit. With the military coups of March 12, 1971, and September 12, 1980, this practice became official ideology as the so-called "Turkish-Islamic synthesis." After 1980, Turkey resorted to becoming another Iran of a sort. With the ascension of the AKP to the government in 2002,[44] Islamic ideology officially took power. The rule of political Islam, contrary to popular belief, was not a choice but was, in fact, the result of a long-standing state religious policy. This transformation was achieved by, of all possible forces, the Sunni Naqshbandi current, adherents of an extremely conservative Islamic denomination. The contradiction with the Islam represented by Iran is not one of substance but of form. The conflict is between the Shiite denomination, which has a more predominant focus on the social, and the Sunni Naqshibandi, whose interpretation is largely conservative and statist in nature.

Today, the US wants the Islamic movement, which they once founded as a bulwark against communism as part of its so-called "green belt,"[45] to act as a force of "moderate Islam" against "radical Islam." The US is currently testing this approach in Turkey, in order to eventually carry out a far-reaching Islamic reform project under the leadership of Fethullah Gülen in particular,[46] both in the region and around the world. In both the political and social roles, Islamic ideology is ultimately negative, because it prevents societies from being transparent. It is far from being an accurate interpretation of social tradition.

The predominant form of political Islam in Kurdistan and among the Kurds is the Sunni Naqshbandi tariqat. Kurdish sheiks and tariqa leaders played a major role in the development of the Naqshibandi Brotherhood in the Middle East, which has a long history. In a way, this was an attempt to use the Naqshbandi current to fill an ideological void that had opened up. After the uprisings of the princes, ideological leadership fell into the hands of Naqshbandi sheikhs. The Nehri uprising of 1878, the Bitlis Mutki uprising of 1914, the uprisings led by Sheikh Said in 1925 and by Sheikh Ahmet Barzani in 1931, and the movements led by Masoud Barzani and Jalal Talabani beginning in the 1960s all shared prominent Naqshbandi ideological motifs. The Naqshbandi tariqa has also been prominent in Turkish-Islamic synthesis since 1980. With Turgut Özal, it made a significant move within the Anavatan Partisi (ANAP: Motherland Party).[47] The tariqat had already been influential within the DP and the AP, but after the coup of 1980, under the protection of the state, they created parties, foundations, schools, associations, media conglomerates, and other holdings, thereby institutionalizing themselves in all of these areas.

There is no question that there has been an ideological counterrevolution against the Kemalist republican ideology. However, it was not an open counterrevolution but, rather, was executed quietly and covertly. The details of this counterrevolution remain hazy. Although the US played a role, the internal official dimensions remain unclear.

One of the key figures is Fethullah (Gülen) Hodja. Some say that, Fethullah Hodja has modernized the teachings of Said Nursî, the most important Naqshbandi leader in the transitional phase from the foundation of the republic until 1960. Gülen, whom one might call the leader of an Islamic version of evangelism, is an ally of the US. The former prime ministers (Necmettin) Erbakan Hodja and Bülent Ecevit failed to sufficiently adapt to the US and the state bureaucracy, and, as a consequence, we saw that a new wave rose under the leadership of Recep Tayyip Erdoğan, with his AKP. This can be described as a political victory for the Naqshbandi.

The role of the Kurdish Naqshbandi leaders is also important. After the parliamentary elections of 2002 and the municipal elections of 2004, a number of leading Naqshbandis became deeply involved in the state and in official politics, including Abdülmelik Fırat, today the chairman of the Hak ve Özgürlükler Partisi (HAK-PAR: Party for Rights and Freedoms), Cüneyd Zapsu, Erdoğan's top counselor, Minister of Education Hüseyin Çelik, and Zeki Ergezen, AKP MP and former minister—all heirs to Sheikh Said and Said Nursî.[48] Jalal Talabani, chairman of the Patriotic Union of Kurdistan and Masoud Barzani, leader of the Democratic Party of Kurdistan, are both also Naqshbandi sheikhs who support the Naqshbandi tradition in Turkey.[49]

Since the rule of Özal, they have carried out numerous joint operations in collaboration with the Turkish state against the Kurdish workers' and the democratic movement.

Because the Kurdish Naqshbandi operate semi-secretly, it is impossible to say much about their ongoing organizing in Europe and the United States or in the Middle East. It is clear, however, that they are at least as influential as the Shiites. Their relationship with the US is strategic and without a doubt plays an important ideological and political role in the Greater Middle East Initiative. Moderate Islam is basically Naqshbandi Islam. At this point, it is becoming clearer that their alliance with the US also extends to a program for Central Asia. Thus, a renewed moderate Islam and the old Ba'athist Arab nationalism, as well as the Kemalist nationalism of the Cumhuriyet Halk Partisi (CHP: Republican People's Party),[50] Saudi-Arabia's Wahhabi sectarianism,[51] and Egypt's Muslim Brotherhood are emerging as an alternative to Iran's Hezbollah.

The second major version of the official ideology is bourgeois nationalism. These tendencies—the favorite ideologies of the nineteenth and the twentieth centuries—were meticulously instilled by the bourgeoisie as state ideology to weaken the working class inside and the real socialist currents abroad. This is a natural consequence of the nation-state understanding; nationalism is, in a way, a contemporary religion. It is the most recent version of ethnicity (aşiret nationalism). It was the most influential official ideology in Europe in the nineteenth century and outside of Europe in the twentieth century. It played an important role in subduing social contradictions, in carrying the nascent bourgeoisie to the pinnacle of the state, in procuring a common market for them, and in attacking other nations and ethnic groups.

Turkish nationalism, which took its earliest form in the middle of the twentieth century with the dramatist and poet Namık Kemal and the *Tanzimat* reforms,[52] originally focused on preventing the collapse of the Ottoman Empire. Its primary focus was the demand for a constitutional monarchy. After 1876, it became even more radical in its opposition to the reign of Abdul Hamid II. The nationalism of the Young Turks in the form of the İttihat ve Terraki Cemiyeti (İTC: Committee of Unity and Progress) continued to attempt both to declare a constitutional monarchy and to take total control of political power to prevent further disintegration. The German policy of opening up to the Middle East and Central Asia added an ingredient of racism to Turkish nationalism.[53] The result was the liquidation of the Armenians, the Greeks, the Assyrians, and, to a lesser degree, the Kurds.

The nationalism of the republican period, with its rigid concept of the "nation-state," encased the society like an armor. With the deepening of the doctrine "one language, one nation, one state," lineage was literally elevated to the rank of a religion. Even though classical sharia had been pushed back, a new cult was created in its place that almost functioned like a religious denomination. The centuries-old dynastic regime and the occupation and isolation following World War I were the main factors in these developments. To safeguard unity, the republic took its cues from the French Revolution, ramping up the latter's nationalist influences in the process. Though a nation without classes and privilege was a worthy goal, the means to realize it were lacking. Because this remained abstract, it risked falling into ideological bigotry. Nationalism had undertaken the mission of covering up all of the government's weaknesses. Society was expected to swallow anything under the exaggerated slogan of "supreme Turkishness."

Mustafa Kemal's nationalism was more patriotic in nature. It was not entirely unscientific and was not guided by adventurism. Nevertheless, its essence was rapidly lost, and it was transformed into political power's instrument for numbing the masses. After 1980, an attempt was made to mix this nationalism with elements of the Sunni Naqshbandi current and to present this as a new "Turkish-Islamic synthesis." This project pursued two primary goals: internally, extreme Turkish nationalism, the so-called "idealism" of the Milliyetçi Hareket Partisi (MHP: Nationalist Movement Party),[54] was to be contained and, even more importantly, the continued growth of the Kurdish movement that was rising at the time was to be prevented. The section of the Kurdish upper class that came from the Naqshbandi tradition was to be integrated into the system to prevent it from joining the Kurdish resistance movement. The corollary abroad was support for the Naqshbandis Masoud Barzani and Jalal Talabani to broaden the front against the PKK. The price for this was a clear departure from the revolutionary ideology of the republic. All of this resulted in the AKP government in Turkey and the Kurdish federal state in Iraq.

Although they cannot exactly be called official ideology, other related ideological tendencies also appeared. Neither liberalism, as a bourgeois tendency, nor the efforts of social democracy were able to significantly influence the state. Even though the various left ideologies claim to be radically opposed to the power structure, they lacked the depth necessary to overcome statism. The actual role these ideologies played in power relations demonstrated their true character.

While ideologies, which act as the common mentality framework of societies, obfuscate the power structures, it is necessary to analyze how power itself obfuscates a social reality based on violence. As long as the triad of ideology-power-violence is not disentangled, *no* social phenomenon or question can be truly illuminated. Social coercion and exploitation are not easily carried out if not embedded in mechanisms of ideology and power. Literally, since the time of the Sumerian priest state, the main task of politics has been to carefully develop the ideological structure and the institutions of power—state forms and regimes—necessary for coercion and exploitation. The question of whether ideology produces politics or vice versa is linked to deeper social conditions. Enforcing coercion and exploitation within a society is more difficult than people tend to believe. This is where ideology and politics come into play. The true function of ideology and politics is to establish the basis for involuntary and undemocratic material and immaterial relations that would otherwise trigger a fierce reaction. The formal ideology and politics prevalent in Kurdistan that play this role must be constantly taken into account or analyzing the Kurdish phenomenon and the search for a solution to the Kurdish question will not only be very difficult but will arrive at a depressing and tangled outcome.

In this historical sketch, we have tried to trace the development of force and power. When we analyze today's rulers in light of this information, we find that all current regimes rely on fetishizing a crude right to conquest to justify and defend their existence. The reality, however, is that at some point in the past some of their ancestors seized the Kurds and Kurdistan by force through war. Since that time, this right to conquest has allegedly passed to each new generation down to today. Some people may embrace the belief that war and force are the original source of all rights, and that the right to conquest is sacred and legitimizes all other alleged rights, but, from a sociological point of view, this only proves that the proponents of these views *interpret* the source of rights to be naked force, war, and power.

This may be a realistic perspective, but it falls short of explaining why this is the only source of rights. The Europeans fought devastating wars and finally came to the conclusion that basic human rights and democracy are actually the best sources of legitimacy. The right to conquest has increasingly been left behind, while the scope of human rights and democracy has continuously grown. The view that this is the best way to guarantee both individual and collective rights is being turned into the foundation of all laws and constitutions.

Let us now put the Middle East at large to one side for a moment and focus on the rulers of the states that have a status in Kurdistan. Since Sargon of Akkad, the first expansionist, they all assert that they are the absolute conquerors of this land, with the idea that people cannot even think of picking up a pebble without their approval.[55] The practice of power in Kurdistan shows in a striking way that no more explicit definition of power, with violence as its base, would be possible. Kurds can't receive an education in their own language and are not allowed to use modern communication technologies. They are not permitted to make their own political decisions. They are denied the right to any economic planning. They cannot develop their own domestic or foreign political relations. They are not allowed to form national and democratic institutions.

These facts prove that it is violence that determines the right to conquest and power, and that this power, in turn—regardless of how it originally came to be—determines all public, social, economic, and intellectual institutions. Even though this may violate a sense of justice, the structure of the mentality and institutions of power make it perfectly clear that power relations are decisive.

To put it even more concretely, the state powers in Kurdistan do not entertain the slightest doubt that they have the right to shape this land and its people as they wish, including the right to kill them—on the contrary, they embrace it as a divine national duty. They alone decide what to exploit and how, who to teach what and how, how much in taxes and how many soldiers to collect, who will have a job, who to ban from what, and who to charge with something. Similarly, officials alone determine the political social and economic institutions, as well as science and the arts.

The Turkish, Arab, and Persian ruling classes and forces are not even theoretically open to and respectful of the notions of "Kurds" and "Kurdistan." On the contrary, they consistently consider the criminalization of these very notions to be one of the most important and serious focuses of the state. That all of this is classified as "top secret" is presented as evidence of the importance they assign to national security. It would not occur to them that another understanding of security would recognize the Kurds as a society and consider them as subjects with some rights. The fundamental task of the armed forces is to design detailed plans and projects aimed at denying the phenomena and problematics of the Kurds and Kurdistan in minute detail, to destroy any Kurdish essence that shows a potential for Kurdish resurrection, and to crush all possible uprisings. The military regards doing this and supervising the other institutions to ensure that they do the same as its essential task.

The military leaves issues it considers secondary for the government, parliament, and the bureaucracy to take care of by complementing the military's activities with laws, regulations, and decrees, which only serve to exacerbate the problem. They adhere to the maxim that politics is an area that produces "solutions" that exclude the Kurdish question. They have no doubt that the only method for resolving the Kurdish question is violence—to crush the snake's head while it is still small. Otherwise, they are sure that their rule will suffer a serious blow. Traditional politics has actually become a reflex. The approach taken resembles that of whips who agitate against the opposing team at a soccer game.

Political parties and related semi-political associations are the propaganda arm of this mechanism and are tasked with influencing the people. Any inclusion of the people's demands and any structuring of policy accordingly is seen as a bothersome and superfluous task that occasionally comes to mind. The best party is the party that best represents the state. The idea that parties shouldn't be institutions that represent the will of the state but should represent the will of society never even arises. Being the party of the state is considered honorable, while any party of society is seen as a hindrance. The fact that state parties deteriorate into state propaganda bureaus goes unnoticed even by themselves. This is seen as national commitment to the fatherland and the state. In this context, "politics" means simply playing dumb and ignoring the snowballing social and economic problems, as if these problems were entirely natural and had absolutely nothing to do with this structure.

Even the civil society institutions whose definitional task should be to limit state power always depend on the state. They often see to it that the demands of individuals and society are relegated to second place. Here we can see how powerful the understanding of the traditional sacred state, the god-state, still is.

The economy is also affected by this way of exercising power. It is also regarded as a realm that must be completely adjusted to the interests of those in power. They determine the economy with no concern for economic laws. What are economic laws compared to their impact? Hunger and unemployment are structural products of this system, and they regard taking advantage of these phenomena in the name of the rulers as a fundamental policy. The hungry and the unemployed are consistently hammered with the message that their value rests on their degree of loyalty to state power and its parties. The economy is unscrupulously used against the Kurds to deliver the message: the satisfaction of your essential needs will depend on your support for state power.

During the last municipal elections in Turkey, all state parties and the entire bureaucracy stood together wherever there was the slightest possibility that patriotic Kurdish democrats might win.[56] And that is not all: millions were pumped into every city to once again buy the votes of the pauperized masses, those Kurds who are historically for sale, thus supposedly fully safeguarding the system. Once more, the Kurdish provinces were conquered, although this time it happened by stealth and with the AKP as the main player. Historical records show that when Yavuz Selim took control of Bitlis, he also sent saddlebags of gold. I guess when, in Bingöl, they chanted, "İdris-i Bitlis—the Ottoman spy Kurd—is here, where is Yavuz?" they were hoping to repeat history. As such, nothing has changed on the eastern front! The practices of the other countries are even cruder. In Turkey, market mechanisms function, at least to a limited degree.

The three S's, the numbing effect of "sports, sex, and the arts" [Turkish: sanat], is an integral part of this general mechanism of power. Whatever may be left of the individual is hollowed out by the three S's, and the person is tossed aside like completely useless residue. This approach was the most popular policy of the twentieth century and was generally applied to all social and national problems, giving rise to a world overrun with fascism, war, and terror. The supposed "security policy" created the most insecure possible world. Finally, US president Bush affirmed the effectiveness of this policy in the twentieth century, more or less saying: "In the name of stability, our policies produced despotism and created an atmosphere of terror. Democracy is how we liberate ourselves from this, which is why we bank on it." Acting on these insights would represent an important political reversal.

The US was behind Turkey's post-1950 policies. Its strategic goal was to support Turkish nationalism against the Soviet Union. To this end, the nationalists were given the green light to organize themselves as a counter-guerrilla, thereby creating the fascist terror of the 1970s. Instead of the

İttihad nationalism fueled by the Germans, which led to the collapse of the Ottoman Empire, this brought the fascist nationalist republic supported by the US to the brink of an explosion. The situation compelled the Kurds to revolt. When the social opposition was crushed with the most brutal policies during the coups of March 12, 1971, and September 12, 1980, this only proved that in the final analysis, yet again, violence is the main determinant. After 1980, all of Kurdistan was subjected to a reign of violence. The military and semi-military organizations of all classes and the classic use of Kurdish treachery tried to crush the patriotic democratic movement. Similar regimes were maintained in Iran in the name of the Islamic Revolution and among the Arabs through Ba'athist nationalism. There were massacres like the one in Halabja.[57] In Kurdistan, thousands of villages were evacuated and tens of thousands of murders were committed.[58] None of the regimes in power changed in the slightest.

The judiciary has been one of the institutions most used against the essence of the law. Hundreds of thousands of people were criminalized, questioned, charged, and tried. Extremely one-sided verdicts and prefabricated schemas made for a highly questionable form of justice that calls to mind "executions without a verdict."[59] The judiciary proved to be the most unjust institution of power, actually playing an enforcement role that was purely fascist. To be accused, it was sufficient to be a Kurd, and if you carried your Kurdish identity with dignity, that would certainly be more than enough. Being either Kurdish or from Kurdistan were declared completely illegal.

The system benefited from the use of civil society, the arts, sports, and lust and sexuality, especially when their general policies deemed it useful to do so. In suppressing the resistance of the Kurds and Kurdistan, the family—the private house—and the brothel—the public house—unavoidably became fundamental elements in the counterinsurgency policy in Kurdistan.

What led to such extremely negative applications of power in Kurdistan was the rulers' fear that the concealed policy of violence that lies at their core might lose even a fraction of its effectiveness. The system was built on unlimited force applied without any consideration of contemporary standards. The goal was to make sure that the phenomena of Kurds and Kurdistan remained outside of history and society, and the perpetrators behind these official ideologies did not shrink from proclaiming their nationalism and religionism in the most extreme of forms.

The main policy approach of the official rulers currently is to defame the Kurdish resistance as a whole as "terrorist" and to attempt to convince the rest of the world to adopt the same line. To this end, they have marketed all of the strategic and military assets and especially Turkey's economy to the relevant states, primarily the US. No concession to the EU states was too big, as long as they declared the PKK terrorist. A similar policy was promoted anywhere that the PKK had so much as a single office. According to the official rulers this was what a total war looked like. When necessary, Europe was also subjected to threats, as were many other countries. A carrot-and-stick approach was used. When Syria was threatened with war, I was forced to leave the country. With İmralı, a new stage in the big hunt began.

The US international and Middle East policies sketched in the previous sections destabilized these power policies in Kurdistan and in all its base and superstructural institutions. The emergence of a federal state of Kurdistan necessitated a complete revision. The trilateral meetings between Iran, Turkey, and Syria resumed. For the first time, these states began to seriously fear that they would not be able to maintain their power in the usual way. The effect of this configuration and the implementation of power on Kurdish individuals and Kurdish society will be addressed later. Fully besieged by power, individual citizens of the dominant nation-state lacked the strength and skills necessary to seriously propose a humane and democratic solution. They have allowed themselves to be fooled and have swallowed everything that the state dangled in front of them hook, line, and sinker. Civil society and self-defined left groups have also shown no hesitation about listening to the "word of the elder," as though in the grip of a patriarchal mindset, and have spontaneously displayed the required reflex. In return, they got an intense economic crisis, a mounting domestic and foreign debt, an exponential growth in unemployment, the attrition of politics, and four countries—Turkey, Iran, Iraq, and Syria—that were no longer able to stand on their own feet without foreign support, with their level of self-confidence falling lower than ever before. As always, it is inevitable that miscalculations of this sort will be understood sooner or later, and that is the case in this instance too.

In closing, I want to emphasize the importance of being clear about one point. We must not confuse the state and power with one another. Our analysis has conclusively shown that the state represents an ongoing consolidation of society that has existed since the emergence of hierarchical society. It is the most comprehensive official institution based on tradition in which all social relations are concentrated and the pinnacle of social existence, with the most advanced analytical logic. Most definitions of the state regard it merely as a certain class's tool for domination and exploitation. These definitions have significant inadequacies and flaws. Furthermore, definitions of the state as an ethnic or national entity only capture certain aspects but fail to define its essence. Power, on the other hand, denotes the transient forces of implementation and is embedded in this state tradition, with its dominant aspect almost always being domination and exploitation. There can certainly be no state without power. But the idea that the state consists of nothing but power falls short of reality and leads to many inconsistencies and much confusion about reality and relations.

The distinction between the state tradition in Kurdistan and the power that is executing that tradition at any particular time is very important, and just as important is the distinction between being against the state and being against power at a particular point. This is one of the core points I am making in this book, which is why I have returned to it several times. In the age of democratic civilization, the state needs to be reformed into a body responsible for general security—agreed upon by the society—and the public good—issues of common good, again, agreed upon by the society—and to continue to exist as a smaller but more effective and functional body.

On the other hand, we must unequivocally reject the formation of various state powers, which was evaluated briefly above, including their practice in Kurdistan, which is corrupted to the core by embezzlement and considers state-supported murders by unidentified assailants to be politics, with the rule of law and social democratic aspects existing only in name. If we are unable to understand the difference between the two definitions, a coherent legal, social, and democratic struggle will hardly be possible. Within the Kurdish movement, there are currents that strive for a separate state, and there are currents that want to create a state that is democratic and social and adopts the rule of law in line with these precepts, and which, to this end, struggles to establish a democratic society anchored in democratic politics. It is essential to clearly understand the difference between the two currents and to adapt one's theory and practice accordingly.

Self-Awareness and Resistance in Kurdistan

Political revolutions in Europe began when the people first conceived of themselves as independent of the royal regime. Initially, this awareness concerned their own history, which was different from the history of the kingdoms. Previously, all historiography had been uniform. History was the stories of the emergence and the maintenance of kingdoms and empires. This approach to history is particularly marked in the Middle East. The king or the emperor represented either a god or an omnipotent force as the "shadow of God" responsible for all decisions about society. Any existence apart from him, any separate body, was unthinkable. Subordinate individuals only had meaning as part of the body of the kingdom. A separate identity, human rights, and democracy in particular were all cursed topics that people were not even allowed to think about, because they expressed the "cursed truth" as opposed to the sacredness of the rulers.

This approach to history was questioned by some intellectuals and historians before the 1640 English Revolution in England and at the beginning of the eighteenth century in France. Eventually, insight that a people and a nation possess an identity and a history separate from the king and the kingdom's history took hold. Later on, the demands of the different classes began to emerge under the rubric of national rights. Each class began to identify itself with the nation. First came an immense wave of nationalism in Europe, followed one after another by the class movements.

In the Middle East and Turkey, the initial consciousness of a people and a nation separate from the sultan began after the Tanzimat reforms of 1840, with the Young Ottomans and Young Turks movements.[60] The intellectuals of the First and the Second Constitutional Eras slowly began to talk about the difference between the sultanate and the nation.[61] The advent of the republic was accompanied by an extremely radical discourse in the Turkish nation. Patriarchal attributes notwithstanding, Atatürk took a huge step in developing a new concept and practice of the nation distinct from that of the Ottoman Empire. He was massively influenced by the French conception of "the nation." That a form of ultranationalism emerged under the occupation conditions after World War I is hardly a surprise. After the war of liberation and to some degree influenced by the existing political situation, this ultranationalism ended up suppressing social reality. As such, its revolutionary value was limited. The nationalism after the 1950s was even more fascism-laden. The concept of the "Turkish-Islamic synthesis" in the aftermath the 1980s mixed the concepts of "nation" and "umma," effectively, further degenerating the class contradiction. Neo-Islamism can be seen as the inverse of this general trend. Similar developments also took place in Iran and the Arab countries.

Becoming aware of yourself anew and resistance are phenomena that go hand in hand. Today, social awareness continues to grow and has become more profound in the areas of ecology, feminism, and subcultures.

Understanding difference is closely related to freedom. If difference is not understood, the enslaving and stupefying effect of totalities cannot be overcome. Identities based on difference, however, lead to freer and more creative societies.

It wasn't until much later that the Kurds in Kurdistan became aware of themselves as a nation and a people. The uprisings of the nineteenth century awakened a certain sense of Kurdishness, but this sentiment did not go beyond concepts of "the sultanate" and "the kingdom." Any distinct Kurdishness was thought of in royalist terms. At that time, a rupture with the medieval understanding of the sultanate was still unthinkable. As a result, the consciousness of a Kurdish nation and people had not yet awakened and was almost indiscernible in the nineteenth century and the first half of the twentieth century.

In the second half of the twentieth century, the reality of the Kurdish people began to be exposed through the debates among intellectuals, a development that to all intents and purposes occurred within the left tradition in Turkey. The Kurdishness in South Kurdistan, which was heavily influenced by the tribes and sheikhs, was not strong enough to break with the classic concept but was satisfied with the demand for a Kurdish king to replace the Turkish, Arab, or Persian king. The communist parties, which took their orientation from real socialism, and the bourgeois and feudal parties also failed to develop a concept of a distinct "Kurdish nation" or "Kurdish people." They were content with the occasional tactical mention of these notions but never did any serious work around history or policy. But the left tradition in Turkey made a significant contribution to the modernization of Kurdish consciousness, particularly with its offensive in the 1970s. The fact that even from the gallows Deniz Gezmiş and his comrades shouted slogans defending the freedom and fraternity of Turks and Kurds was of historic significance.[62] The efforts of many other revolutionaries, particularly Mahir Çayan and Ibrahim Kaypakkaya,[63] to promote the fraternity of peoples were just as important. But slogans alone do not constitute action and resistance. Resistance requires a new phase of its own.

Kurdish people becoming distinct began with two intertwined developments: a clean break with the Turkish chauvinist understanding of the nation and the dissociation from any primitive Kurdish nationalism. It was far from easy for the movement to break away from this harsh oppressive environment in two directions. There was the stifling ideological hegemony, which also had a revolutionary left mask, and state power and the dominant local forces that collaborated with it. To stand up to this ideological and practical dominance necessitated both intellectual ability and organizational skill. This, of course, soon led to resistance. The combined political and legal atmosphere made any work on a sound mentality impossible. This latter task required a movement that was to some degree a combination of Mohammad in Mecca, Christ in Jerusalem, and Galileo Galilei and Giordano Bruno in Renaissance Europe.

Perhaps the reality at the time will be better understood if I try to narrate what happened as someone who experienced it first-hand. In primary school I began to feel that my difference as a Kurd was going to cause me a lot of problems. During primary school and high school, I was not capable of untangling the mentality at play, but it was a fact that followed me wherever I went like a shackle around my ankle. However much as I tried to evade it and to flee, it clung to me like my shadow. The official ideology that the teachers hammered into us at school did not help me address this in any way. Even if we had totally accepted the imposed Turkishness, the old Kurdish traditions in families and in the clearly Kurdish local communities screamed: "I exist." As a result, individuals lived with enormous hypocrisy.

Breaking with tradition produced a kind of phoniness, a deceitful avoidance of a greater part of the truth. This is a process that erodes the personality. Breaking with one's own identity in this situation meant falling into a deep void like a leaf falling from a tree. For an individual's personality, it also meant a loss of society's moral structure. Denying your society, your past, and your tradition leaves you with a pathologically disordered personality—that much became increasingly clear to me every day. Turkishness—and the same is true in the Iranian and Arab areas—was instilled in ways that went far beyond natural assimilation, ways that were similar to the rote learning of religious rites in a language that you don't understand.

Whether you adopt Islam, using Arabic, which you don't understand, or learn to be a Turk through an official ceremony, the effects on your personality will be the same; you will say "yes" and "amen" to prayers you do not comprehend! The Kurdish personality had already been forced to wallow in shallowness and ignorance in the name of Islam for centuries, and then an extreme Turkification through what is effectively a religion with a contemporary appearance further eroded the personality. The reality is that the decision of an older person to turn to Islam and Turkishness makes a certain amount of sense. Social needs can make this sort of integration reasonable. Nonetheless, Pan-Islamism and -Turkism as a form of daily worship have no place in a mainstream contemporary educational system.

I wanted to make sense of both. In primary school I aspired to be faithful and Turkish. But how far would that go? My determination to embrace my Kurdishness began to develop in the left intellectual environment of the 1970s, which was characterized by an intense discussion that included the "Kurdish question." The many years of religious and Turkist practice could not compete with the attractiveness of the left. That my peers courageously advocated for independence and freedom and for equality for both peoples, without in any way distinguishing between Kurds and Turks, evinced the true colors of the choice I made for my life. My bereavement for these leaders, each of whom was a hero to me, made it a question of honor to continue on their path and to carry on the fight for the cause. To fully embrace "being a Kurd" despite the impositions from both sides constituted a historical step forward.

Researching the Kurds, a typical undertaking of this period, was carried out with limited resources. The primitive nationalist interpretations that were overwhelmingly emotional and the dogmatic real socialist interpretations of the "right to self-determination" were out of touch with reality. The discussions was constrained by questions like "Do the Kurds, in fact, exist?" and "Is Kurdistan a colony?" There was a lack of sufficient data, documentation, and the necessary in-depth and objective sociological interpretations for historical and socialist approaches to the problematic. Judgments were made but we were in the dark about most things.

Furthermore, the political atmosphere grew constantly tenser, and the state's traditional fear of the Kurds led to overhasty reactions. Both sides tried to achieve results as quickly as possible. Despite limited information and a weak understanding of the time we were living in, it was nonetheless clear that the existing status quo would not accept anything and was itself totally unacceptable. This status quo not only refused to think about reform, mere statements of fact were sufficient for people to be immediately criminalized and convicted. The prospect of achieving anything by legal means was essentially zero. On the other hand, what we had learned from our left-wing activities and from Kurdish reality made resistance a conditio sine qua non, as if not resisting would be tantamount to abandoning our humanity. A genuine sense of honor required us to defend our cause under any circumstances and above all else.

In this situation, we, a small group of adolescents, could do no more than form limited regional groups of sympathizers. Though we had thoroughly acquainted ourselves with the national liberation struggles and were convinced that we would be able to make history using guerrilla methods, this was mere utopia and did not stand a chance of being more than that. If it worked, wonderful, if not, God is merciful, and tomorrow will take care of itself!

Once more, we have a parallel to the hijra, the exodus of Mohammad from Mecca, the wandering of the apostles, and the ordeal of the pioneers of science. The first protests could have taken place, the first shots could have been fired then. At any time, any member of the group of "believers" could have become a martyr or been sent to prison. As for so many social movements, these horrors were on the agenda for the Kurds, and everything was pushing events toward a tragedy. The cause demanded people with an absolute willingness to sacrifice, or, from the perspective of our opponents, their gods wanted sacrifices.

No account of the environment in which Kurds began to differentiate and develop has yet been written, but that absolutely needs to be done. To describe this period would require employing the power of literature and every possible means, including utopias, tragedies, drama, narratives, and films. The issue is: a seed was planted. Once this was done, questions remained: Is it rotten? Will it blossom? We had nothing but hope, as in the saying: "Hope is the bread of the poor." Thus, we bowed our heads to this time we found ourselves living in, just as one bows to one's head before fate.

More than thirty years have passed since we set out on the path of Kurdish differentiation and resistance in the early 1970s. The most important result has been not only a growing awareness of the Kurdish phenomenon and an understanding of the options for a solution, but, in fact, this amounts to the destruction of an anomaly that has made the neighboring people and states captive along with the Kurds: a type of national oppression that is hollow and meaningless. It has also proven that a regime that cages all of the social groups involved, a system where the ruled hold the ruler captive and the ruler holds the ruled captive, cannot survive. Another lesson to be drawn from all this is that a people cannot develop if it does not fight for social dignity. Social dignity means staking your claim and self-reliance; it is the strength to know thyself and to develop. Societies that lack the strength for this have nothing to offer, even to the powerful—this is another lesson. Those who cannot do good for themselves cannot do good for others. If the Kurds were that destitute, what of worth could they offer their neighbors? Even if one is a colony, to constitute some kind of a value the path must be left open to possess a value. As we embarked on this path, the Kurds were stuck in a deep, dark dead end, a terrible directionlessness with no exit.

One could object and ask: Are these few lessons worth all the suffering and all of the losses? This is a question best countered with a different question that applies to societies as well as individuals: Can a society or an individual live without dignity? Can life have a meaning and worth if you cannot hold on to your identity and express it freely, something that everyone throughout history and in modernity has regarded and regards as indispensable? Can those who lose their meaning and worth offer anything to others?

The leading elites, including the Turkish, Arab, and Persian elites, are mistaken if they regard a situation in which the Kurds are mute, depleted, and helpless as ideal. If Kurds made a contribution during the most critical phases of the history of Turkey, this is only because the Kurds themselves had value. If they did not have any value, would the Kurds have been able to participate in the War of Independence? At that time, there was no great abyss between the Kurds and the Turks; they both shared the hope of developing a common future.

If there were a war today, could the Kurds and the Turks possibly stand side by side as before? The best answer to this is given by the Iraqi Kurds. Had Saddam's regime managed to maintain a fraternal alliance with the Iraqi Kurds, would Iraq have descended into the current tragic situation?

We have to understand that Kurdish-Turkish relations and, for the same reason, Kurdish-Arabic and Kurdish-Persian relations, especially during the twentieth century, became extremely aberrant.

Historiography tells us that none of the Ottoman sultans were as violent as Selim I, also called "Selim the Grim." But it is reported that when he was formulating his policy for Kurdistan he sent an empty sheet of paper comparable to a blank check and said, "Write what you like on it; it will have the force of law."[64] The blank sheet came with his signature already on it. Today's ruling elite, who remain completely obstinate and insensitive, particularly need to understand the lesson that this story teaches.

The ruling elite always purports to remember Atatürk with the utmost respect. Atatürk also had a certain way of approaching problems. For him, the social significance of a problem was the decisive factor. If something absolutely needed to be crushed, he crushed it. If some other approach was necessary, he spent sleepless nights wrestling with himself and then made the necessary decisions. As such, he would probably not have permitted a state of affairs in which a single problem led to so many difficulties, debts, and dangers for the country and the state. Moreover, a personality of his stature, having said "freedom is my character trait" would hardly have shared the state with the tariqat under the pretext of saving it. He was, in the grandest sense, a Turkish nationalist, but he would have tried to understand the Kurds. He would have found a solution in keeping with his freedom-loving character. Is it really possible to doubt this, particularly given that he specifically talked about it several times before the uprisings? Even when he crushed the Kurdish uprisings, he did not try to impede Kurdishness or curtail the liberty of the Kurds. Did he not, on the contrary, know very well that imperialist intrigues would spell the end of both Kurdishness and freedom? For how long will people conceal these facts and continuously provoke renewed Kurdish resistance?

The resistance of the 1970s was very dogmatic. This was, of course, also true of all its actions. The formation of parties, fronts, and armies unfolded under the heavy influence of this dogmatic mindset. Despite all its honest efforts, it was unrealistic to expect a very young and inexperienced movement rid itself of the dogmatism that had characterized society for so long. The movement tried to practice what it believed socialism, national liberation, and guerrilla struggle to be. Confronted with reality, the limits of this approach became clear. Life didn't work the way the theory said it would, so the theory had to be adjusted to life. The same was also true of the national system of repression. The system was also firmly rooted in dogma, which always leads to the incorrect belief that it is prepared for any eventuality.

In a later chapter, I will evaluate the lessons of thirty years of political practice. This does not only include the lessons of the resistance but also of the transformation the world has gone through since then. There have been significant developments in Kurdistan and among the Kurds, but, essentially, the chaotic situation continues. Both the political and military approaches to finding a solution could lead to a development not only in the Middle East in general but also in Kurdistan—it is up to the parties involved which approach will be used. The biggest lesson from history is that finding democratic solutions to all the problems should be at the top of the agenda. For this, peace and the bilateral abandonment of violence are decisive. If this necessity continues to be stubbornly ignored and a military path is pursued, the active military resistance necessary to bring the historical and social reality out of the chaos will then be on the agenda.

In the 1970s, there was not really a choice between the military and the political. The path of resistance was akin to destiny. But here, in these writings, I have tried to prove that this is no longer true in the third millennium. It would be most useful to evaluate the stormy developments of the last thirty years in all their dimensions to determine more precisely just where the possibilities and problems of both paths to a solution, the military and the political, lie.

TEN

The PKK Movement: Critique, Self-Critique, and Its Reconstruction

Section A—Historical Sketch of the PKK

First Phase: Emergence

We began in April 1973 as a group that it would be too much to even call amateurs. At the shore of the Çubuk Dam in Ankara, this group of six talked about acting as an autonomous Kurdish group for the first time, reasoning mainly that Kurdistan was a classic colony. We began by disclosing this reasoning collectively in this group of six like a secret. Transforming the way I explained the truth from one-on-one conversations into a collective way of doing this could be considered the actual beginning. This method had a quality that led us to organize. From 1974 to 1975, the group developed under the umbrella of the Ankara Demokratik Yüksek Öğrenim Derneği (ADYÖD: Democratic University Association Ankara). In March 1977, I traveled from Ankara to Kurdistan to attend meetings in Ağrı, Doğubeyazıt, Digor (near Kars), Dersim, Bingöl, Elazığ, Diyarbakır, Urfa, and Antep. That trip and those meetings were an attempt to bring the group to Kurdistan. After the journey, I returned to Ankara. The martyrdom of Haki Karer "three days after the meeting" in Antep came as a serious shock to us.[1] Our response was to take the step and begin to build a party. At the end of the same year, I wrote a draft program in Antep. As the summer of 1978 approached, we headed for the center of Kurdistan, for Diyarbakır, which had seen much betrayal, with a troublesome marriage. On November 27, 1978, in the village of Fis, our group of twenty-two amateurs swore to found a party. Because we knew that we would not survive for long as a party in the cities, we had to make use of the two options available, namely, the mountains and the Middle East. Just as Abraham made his exodus, on July 1, 1979, I set out from Urfa to Syria in search of freedom, and from there to the land of the old Canaan.

I now want to take a closer look at this phase, which lasted for ten years—until August 15, 1984—and the ideological and political environment at the time.

The 1970s was the beginning of a period in the capitalist system's history when a significant rupture became apparent. The system came out of World War II having recuperated, and the US leadership had grown more self-assured. Europe was once again on its feet, and in the Far East Japan emerged as a giant. The real socialist system was at the apex of its influence, and the national liberation movements were at their strongest. At this exact point, the 1968 youth movement launched a new revolution in mentality.

It may appear surprising that a historical social system that has reached such a zenith would enter into a period of chaos. But we should remember that it is always just one step beyond the peak that the descent begins. Today, an increasing number of scholars agree that a period of chaos has begun, with effects that are accelerating.[2] In retrospect, it will be seen that the main factor underlying this is the realization that even though the state-oriented movements of real socialism, social democracy, and national liberation seemed to have achieved their goals over the course of the previous 150 years, they were all far from able to keep their promises to the masses. This calls to mind the question of whether Christianity conquered Rome or Rome conquered Christianity. Perhaps both are partially correct. Christianity entered into a synthesis with the imperial cult, a synthesis from which the feudalism of the Middle Ages emerged, giving rise to a different social system, although not an egalitarian or peaceful one. On the other hand, Christianity also largely lost its freedom-loving and egalitarian qualities in the process.

The socialist, social democratic, and national liberation currents sparked by the capitalist system during its "brutal" years did not succeed in breaking away from the system. Actually, they were born of it. It would no doubt be unrealistic to say that they were entirely poised to act as auxiliary currents of the system, but today we can confidently say that they never really sought to overcome the rational basis of the system and its way of life. Wherever such attempts were made, they generally amounted to nothing but empty phrases and slogans. The roots of egalitarian and freedom-loving ideas lie outside of the hierarchical and class society. They are born of the longing for a communal and democratic life. Unfortunately, we know of numerous historical examples where they constantly degenerated to such an extent that their essence was finally lost in return for concessions or they were constantly suppressed through coercion. If we look at the collapse and dissolution of the real socialist countries, the crises of many states after successful national liberation struggles, and the dwindling distinctions between social democratic and conservative governments, we can safely conclude that all these currents are no more than denominations of the system itself. The crisis of the 1970s had to do with the increasingly obvious fact that the system would no longer be able to adequately utilize these auxiliary denominations. The 1968 youth movement was essentially an expression of this fact. What had been hoped for had not arrived. All three currents had come to power and been unable to keep their promises. Moreover, a new capitalist class and bureaucracy had emerged from their midst that was even more backward than that of classic capitalism. The crises of these models and the lack of freedom and equality within them led the people to almost long for the system they had once so bitterly criticized.

This reality represented a serious threat to the legitimacy of the capitalist state. It was soon to lose its capacity to impress the masses. The opposition would turn to currents that were not state-oriented. Even though the 1968 revolution had many shortcomings, it still paved the way for this development. With the New Left, feminism, the ecological movement, and local cultural currents, a broad new form of opposition to the state developed. This was the main factor that initiated the chaos within the system. On the other hand, growing environmental problems, a rise in wages, as a result of policy of concessions, and a deficit in demand, triggered by the poverty of the masses, led to an increase in costs accompanied by an excess in supply. The internal contradictions of the system had increased along the US-EU-Japan axis. Beginning in the 1980s, neoliberalism was seen as a remedy to this new chaotic situation. The dissolution of the Soviet Union in the 1990s was not a success for the system but a factor that served to deepen the crisis. The new neoliberal "global offensive" took place against this background. Under heavy bombardment by the media, which were increasingly becoming monopolies, an attempt was made to manufacture fraudulent paradigms. They worked feverishly on theoretical constructs that were meant to define a new goal for the system. The thesis of the "clash of civilizations" that was to replace the struggle against communism was well-received. Thus, the incompatibility of the regimes in the areas designated as "Islamic" with the interests of the system was highlighted much more than had previously been the case.

In the early 1970s, when such far-reaching developments were taking place around the world, the left-wing movement in Turkey and Kurdish movement in Turkey, which saw itself as committed to both the left and the resolution of the Kurdish national question, had not succeeded in over-coming the classic left and nationalist tendencies. Thus, it lagged quite a bit behind the world. While the left in Turkey oriented itself around the Soviet Union, China, Albania, and European communism, the Kurdish left, an intellectually weak movement, embraced a hodgepodge of primitive Kurdish nationalism and Turkish leftism. At the time, I was interested in both of these currents. I tried to become active as a sympathizer. Even though my sympathy was primarily with the Türkiye Halk Kurtuluş Partisi-Cephesi (THKP-C: The People's Liberation Party-Front of Turkey) that had come out of the Türkiye Devrimci Gençlik Federasyonu (Dev-Genç: Revolutionary Youth Federation of Turkey), the Türkiye İhtilâlci İşçi Köylü Partisi (TİİKP: Revolutionary Workers' and Peasants' Party of Turkey) that took a more comprehensive approach to the Kurdish question continued to attract my attention. The fact that Deniz Gezmiş, the leader of the Türkiye Halk Kurtuluş Ordusu (THKO: People's Liberation Army of Turkey), and his friends used their last words before execution to emphasize the frater-nity of Kurds and Turks based on freedom was a message that we had to be committed to. At the same time, in 1970, I became a member of the Devrimci Doğu Kültür Ocakları (DDKO: Revolutionary Eastern Culture Centers) in İstanbul. In the turmoil after the coup of March 12, 1971, and the compli-cated organizational situation that ensued, I faced potentially being driven underground at any moment. And, indeed, after Mahir Çayan and nine of his friends' martyrdom in March 1972, I was arrested following an occu-pation of the Faculty of Political Science at University of Ankara and only released for lack of evidence after seven months in prison. I experienced firsthand the disheartening situation of the organizations in which I had invested my hopes and concluded that a new organization was necessary.

The decision taken in Ankara, in the spring of 1973, to organize inde-pendently proved important, not because of the opportunities we had but because of what it signified. We neither wanted to be a primitive Kurdish nationalist current nor to resemble the left currents that were essentially

Turkish nationalist, which we called social chauvinist, but to start with a distinct historical interpretation and assessment of existing conditions. At first, we called ourselves "Revolutionaries of Kurdistan." This was a clear change in line that separated us from other organizations, and the significance of that became clearer by the day. In ideological terms, it meant we should neither dissolve into the currents of the dominant nation nor into the primitive nationalism of the Kurdish collaborationist currents that merely represented an extension of the dominant nation's power. Taking political initiative was enabling us to attain a free identity. I still believe that this was the right choice. It carried within it the seed of a development that, to the extent of their contribution, would make Kurds and other people conscious that they were free people. Striving for the identity of a free people without succumbing to the nationalism of the oppressor or the oppressed nation was the right decision. It was also a timely and appropriate safeguard against the aberrations of real socialism, social democracy, and the national liberation movements, which had, worldwide, all become denominations of capitalism. It had the quality of a path that would lead both to the development of a correct mentality and to democratic politics. An exaggerated emphasis on national liberation could have easily led us astray. Here, the dogmatic interpretation of the principle of the right of the people to self-determination played an influential role. At the time, "a state for every nation" was regarded as the only correct interpretation of that principle. This situation, which also stemmed from real socialism's understanding of power, was an obstacle to the creativity of the line. The founding declaration of the PKK in 1978 prevented this aberration from developing further.[3] Instead of taking the approach of a typical African national liberation movement, the PKK's line based on the freedom of the people was further reinforced. Even though we were not conscious of it at the time, this corresponded to the transformation that the left subsequently underwent all over the world, which meant our line had a chance at a real future.

Even though the ideological dimension of our line was not yet entirely clear nor particularly deep, it was open to further development and, thus, prevented major and permanent aberrations. Our insistence on calling the socialism we advocated "scientific socialism" may explain our interest in social science. We tried to be cautious of the plague of losing touch with reality that can result from ideological rigidity. Furthermore, the fact that social science also faced severe problems and had only begun to take an interest in the problematics of local cultures, ecology, and women only proved the importance of our line. Our line kept us clear of the hodge-podge of social science, which in turn rendered the ideal of freedom and equality more vivid and apparent. At the very least, it allowed us to limit the destructive effects of the crises of socialism and social science. The lines of other left-wing organizations in Turkey didn't allow them to do this, and they were unable to prevent their own marginalization as they vacillated between dogmatism and a hollow individualist liberalism. The factional strife among these organizations deprived them of the chance to become politicized from the outset. The same process went on among the groups described as the "Kurdish left," the only difference being that these groups experienced this process less significantly.

The successful politicization of the PKK line was closely linked to its ideological aspect, as was proven by the speed at which it was accepted by the people who constituted its potential base. Had we been infected by the disease of narrow nationalism or the emphasis on a particular class, we would have been just as marginalized as many other groups.

It is known that a process of deep politicization was not experienced. This has to be seen in connection with the "question of becoming a cadre." Because of their existing form, the cadres themselves were obstacles. Without a solution to the question of the cadres, one of the main factors that led to the collapse of real socialism, no political proposition and organizational undertaking could avoid becoming dysfunctional. Like the political line, the organizational model was also open to developments. Because of conditions at that time, legitimate armed defense, understood as self-defense, was entirely justifiable. But the lack of cadres who wanted to take this on constantly disrupted the line. We wanted to overcome these problems, which can be also seen as an organizational crisis. That some limited developments were achieved was primarily the consequence of the popular support of the movement, but to bring about bigger changes in accord with our line required professionalism.

The most important question the PKK needed to clarify about its political line was whether or not we sought an independent state. Even though we often used the slogan "independent Kurdistan," it is difficult to say whether or not this was synonymous with the call for an independent state. As one of those intimately involved in the events, I can say that we neither reflected upon nor discussed the question of the state in general or the concept of a state of Kurdistan in particular all that deeply. Although

there was a tendency in that direction in a utopian sense, we were realistic, so we were not overly interested in it. I think this had little to do
with whether or not we wanted or did not want such a state but, rather,
with the fact that we had no clarity about the degree to which having a
state might offer a solution. That it had anything to offer was by no means
certain. And we knew that this problem was also theoretically contentious.
The question of whether to adopt "democratic socialism" or the "dictatorship of the proletariat" was a consistent source of disorientation. What
was clear from all of the examples was that the problems of laborers and
peoples had not been resolved, even though they had acquired states, and
that shaped our thinking. All of this led us to intuitively feel that even
though focusing on a separate state might be attractive, it would probably only create irresoluble problems for us. Moreover, the difficulties of
founding a Kurdish state under the conditions in Turkey and the Middle
East, combined with the new problems that would then ensue, made the
issue even more delicate. As a result, instead of the "state," we preferred
the concept of Kurdistan as the "homeland"—although its status was not
all that clear. Even the main slogan we chose, an "independent, democratic,
and socialist Kurdistan," included no direct reference to or preference for
a state. It made perfect sense that in the end it would be concretized in the
more realistic and revolutionary concept of a "free Kurdistan." It would
perhaps be better to interpret "Revolutionaries of Kurdistan" as "advocates
of a Free Kurdistan."

The real significance of this problematic would become apparent later
on. After the "Federal State of Kurdistan" was proclaimed in 1992 and the
establishment of "free areas" by the PKK, we had to think about state power
in a more focused way.[4]

The fact that the problem of the state could not be completely resolved
by socialist ideology made things even more unclear. This problem was
further exacerbated by an interpretation of the right of the people to
self-determination to mean that every nation should have its own state.

When we speak of the state, we must automatically speak of force
and war. Another important problem at the time was that war was not
simply considered as a necessity for legitimate self-defense but also as
a permissible means of achieving political goals. The strategic position
adopted was that without war, a protracted war at that, nations could not
be liberated, and without the liberation of nations the liberation of classes
was also impossible. The questions of war and power that had led to such

far-reaching aberrations in the history of all freedom movements would now increasingly also be on the PKK's agenda.

That the state attacked us at that time was due to us being a part of the general left and Kurdish groups. There was also nothing about us that would have required the state to react against us in particular. Nobody could have thought that we could become a distinct and long-term epicenter of resistance. All signs indicated a potential military coup on the horizon, so we had two options: we could either choose to head for the mountains or retreat abroad, to another location in the Middle East. In fact, we ended up doing both. In late 1979, the movement had the means to retreat in both directions without serious losses. But it was happening very slowly. Apart from a few regrettable arrests, like the arrests of Mazlum Doğan and Mehmet Hayri Durmuş, we suffered no serious losses in the process.

We had become a movement, we had launched a party, and the positions necessary to secure its existence were in place. Consequently, we managed to act presciently with regard to the coup of September 12, 1980, and to put in place the necessary provisions. In the beginning, expanding abroad was not considered in the long-term. We thought the "law of revolution" was that we would go through military training with a few dozen cadres and then carry out a protracted guerrilla war until liberation. We believed that everything would go according to plan.

As we had envisaged, in the beginning of 1980, groups trained in the Middle East and then returned home. Together with other organizations, we formed a political front under the name Faşizme Karşı Birleşik Direniş Cephesi (FKBDC: United Resistance Front against Fascism). The fact that this did *not* work as planned necessitated a fair amount of theoretical work. To this end, beginning in 1981, a number of speeches were recorded, transcribed, and published in book form. The first, "The Question of Personality in Kurdistan, Life in the Party, and the Characteristics of Revolutionary Militant" was soon followed by "The Role of Force in Kurdistan" and "On Organizing." The first PKK conference, aiming at a more fundamental and lasting orientation to Kurdistan, was held in 1981, followed by the second in 1982. The Israel-Palestine war of 1982 further accelerated this process.

In fact, the revolution in Iran had created favorable conditions in East and South Kurdistan, and it became apparent that it would be more appropriate to build our bases in those areas and work from there. This is something we had already considered. Mehmet Karasungur, who had gained experience in the conflict in Siverek,[5] was there at the time and was capable of making the necessary preparations. It was a great misfortune that he fell victim to his righteousness and amateurishness and became a martyr in May 1983.

Duran Kalkan and Ali Haydar Kaytan were sent to South Kurdistan in 1982 to fill the void, and they were expected to oversee things and implement the line in that area. Earlier, in 1980, our general perspective was that we should build a line of resistance that extended from Botan to Dersim under the leadership of Kemal Pir and Mahsum Korkmaz.[6] The unfortunate arrest of Kemal Pir in July 1980 was a serious loss. The situation of the group around Duran Kalkan, which was actually the group we expected would make a breakthrough, was the first to trigger concerns about tampering with the line. If I remember correctly, at the time, I said something like: "To repeat what has already been done in the Middle East would be like painting a donkey and selling it back to its owner."[7] When the planned breakthrough didn't materialize, Mazlum Doğan took action in the Diyarbakır prison, on Newroz 1982,[8] the group around Ferhat Kurtay subsequently carried out a self-immolation,[9] and Kemal Pir, Mehmet Hayri Durmuş, Akıf Yılmaz, and Ali Çiçek became martyrs on hunger strike. This caused me great concern, and I felt responsible. This subsequently turned into anger and rage about the expected but not materializing breakthrough. In January 1984, to address this, for the first time there was a small assembly of a limited number of central committee cadres, and the posture of some friends—primarily Duran Kalkan and Cemil Bayık—was openly and profoundly criticized.

Second Phase

We had reached a point, a forked road, at which we could either develop into an exile movement or a contemporary national liberation movement, that is, a movement for the people's freedom. Our historical responsibility for the long silence of the freedom movement weighed heavily on us. The martyrs in prison and the torture were the primary factors that made it necessary for us to act. Otherwise we would inevitably be stigmatized with betrayal.

In that sense, the offensive of August 15, 1984, could be described as both belated and insufficient. The answer of the state—Özal had just become prime minister—was once more inadequate, in that its representatives always spoke about a "handful of bandits," an approach that left no hope for any political initiative. In its boundless trust in classic military strength, the state presumed it could quickly crush us and launched its campaign with loud and rumbling propaganda. However, until late 1984, our opponents were utterly unsuccessful. The road was paved for a guerrilla war. But when, apart from the internal stumbling blocks mentioned above, the KDP (Kurdistan Democratic Party) created additional obstacles, the expected powerful offensive did not take place, even though it had the support of the people. What was missing was a cadre of real commanders capable of leading and organizing the movement. This was a decisive problem, and it was to become characteristic of all negative developments.

Kemal Pir and Mahsum Korkmaz had realistically criticized our approach to armed struggle. They were two comrades that could have led it correctly. The loss of Kemal Pir in 1982 and of Mahsum Korkmaz in 1986 were heavy blows to our ability to effectively develop the war according to its rules. We had to partially withdraw, and that same year we held our third congress, which further deepened the crisis. The problem did not lie in a lack of means but in an excessive satisfaction with what we had already achieved with great difficulty. Our nerves were stretched to the breaking point by Kesire Yıldırım's provocations, discussed further below. Despite all the problems, however, in 1987, we developed a broader perspective and prepared the material conditions for a new and crucial foray. But gang culture had already sunk its roots in the movement and was being organized in an increasingly conscious manner. The problem was made worse by the irresponsibility of the central cadres. Thus, work of great value, the result of many precious people's extraordinary sacrifices, was blocked, hampered, and neutralized.

In response to this almost inexplicable situation, general leadership, which was becoming more and more difficult, increasingly fell to me. This required me to carry out more comprehensive analyses and to deepen the education of the cadres. Despite the weight of it, I was able to fulfill my responsibility successfully. Almost every prospective cadre got the support she or he needed to participate in the revolution with dignity. But instead of respecting this and contributing, some people launched an internal power struggle that poisoned all of our activities. What we called the gang of four, Şahin Baliç, Şemdin Sakık, Kör Cemal, and Hogir, set in motion a veritable massacre of cadres.[10] We still don't know how many precious cadres they murdered and claimed had "fallen in battle." The deaths of many comrades remain "unclarified." Many civilians, ordinary people, women, and children, who should never have been targeted, were killed. The central committee no longer had any influence, and I still don't know how accurate the information I received from afar was.

I only woke up when Hasan Bindal, my childhood friend, was killed in the most horrible and wicked way said to be "accidentally shot in a military exercise" right before my eyes, on January 25, 1990. My unshakable belief in patriotism and socialism notwithstanding, these disgraceful and inexcusable murders gradually led to an emotional blunting within the movement. By that point, a large number of people who were quite likely innocent had already been murdered as alleged agents. If those responsible dared to act like this when I was there, the scale of such practices in faraway places had to have been all the more horrifying. These treacherous activities were followed by Talabani's rapprochement and the KDP's previous and continuing collaboration with Turkey in relation to the PKK. Together they clamped down on the movement. With the only option being "capitulation or annihilation," we couldn't find our way out of the crisis we were in despite numerous efforts, many heroic deeds, and popular support.

The decisions taken at the 1990 congress and in some conferences were thrown to the wind. Nevertheless, all these adverse circumstances did not prevent probing analyses, all of which are well-documented, and the education of several thousand cadres each year—or the participation of the population, which was joining our movement en masse.

For the first time, there were serious developments on the part of the state. President Turgut Özal showed an openness to discussing the problem and addressing the ceasefire we had declared in 1993. The prime minister at the time, Süleyman Demirel, said, "We recognize Kurdish identity." This inspired hope but did not guarantee anything. The ceasefire could perhaps have led to a lasting peace if Turgut Özal had not died in spring 1993, or, as many claim, had not been killed, and if Şemdin Sakık had not shot thirty-three unarmed soldiers in reaction to the unnecessary and senseless guerrilla losses.[11] But the internal nature of the state, the gang culture that took the initiative within the PKK, and the treachery of Talabani and Barzani all combined to prevent this opportunity from being seized. As a result, things got even more complicated and slid totally out of control. Between 1994 and 1998, the same approach was stubbornly repeated, leading to tremendous exhaustion on both sides. However, the unilateral ceasefire declared in 1998 in response to the events of February 28, 1997, changed the tune,[12] and we hoped that the state would not remain indifferent. In the end, no solution was forthcoming, as I was forced to leave Syria as a result of the pressure exerted on the country. The state continued with its massive attacks, feeling that it could use the opportunity that had arisen to end the problem once and for all by military means. My well-known "odyssey through Europe,"[13] followed by my imprisonment on the island of İmralı, marked the end of the second phase of the PKK's evolution and the beginning of a new phase.

This fifteen-year phase, from August 15, 1984, to February 15, 1999, which could also be described as a period of low-intensity warfare, can be evaluated from various perspectives and a variety of directions. Assessments based on leadership and political-military administrative practices or from the perspective of the art of war and the art of power games are certainly possible, or we could focus on which approaches were basically correct and which were erroneous, as well as which actions were clearly acceptable and which should absolutely never have been carried out. It is also possible to examine things from the perspective of changes in the world in the 1990s, including the dissolution of the Soviet Union, the election of Bill Clinton as US president, the Iraq crisis, and the need to profoundly analyze the new globalization offensive. In connection with all of these we could reevaluate theoretical concepts: transcending the old left, what a new left should look like, and revolutionary utopia itself among them. Having done so would have enabled us to see the flaws in the existing assessments and recognize and correct our errors.

Some Thoughts on the PKK

I have tried to briefly summarize the history of the PKK, because this could be helpful when carrying out particular analyses. I had earlier said: "It is not the moment that is analyzed but history, not the person but society." Applied to the PKK, this maxim becomes even clearer. What is being analyzed and disentangled within the PKK with all its positive and negative aspects is both Kurdish history and Kurdish society. We only need to read them correctly and draw the appropriate lessons.

I have never doubted that the formation of the PKK represented a contemporary milestone, a "birth," for the Kurds. What I did not fully foresee was that individuals who are called "Kurds" could be so contradictory, meaningless, and weak, on the one hand, and so straightforward, consistent, willing to make sacrifices, and brave, on the other hand.

I had analyzed the personality many times, but still cannot claim that I completely grasped and analyzed what a Kurd is. They were thoroughly alienated from themselves. Even though they looked Kurdish from the outside, at their core they had become something else. They didn't even realize the extent of this treachery. To them, laws regarding neither humans nor animals applied,[14] as if they were some third lifeform.

The actual role I wanted to play in building the PKK clearly related to mentality. But despite all my efforts, the attempt to analyze the Kurds as individuals and as a product of their society through the lens of the existing social theories proved deficient and rife with shortcomings. As early as 1975, I had started to present the outline of my thoughts on imperialism and colonialism to Mehmet Hayri Durmuş. My conceptual paper (which I believe still exists) has lost none of its validity and would be as useful today as it was then. It was a good outline of ideas that left their mark on the revolutionary activities of the time and had the potential to make a serious contribution to the mentality struggle of the "Revolutionaries of Kurdistan," as we referred to ourselves then.

The journey I took through Kurdistan on the basis of this outline proved to be remarkable. It began with a speech at the Chamber of Architects in Ankara, in March 1976. Thereafter, I traveled to Ağrı, Doğubeyazıt, Kars-Digor, Dersim, Bingöl, Elazığ, Diyarbakır, Urfa, Antep, and then, in May, back to Ankara. This march ended on May 15, and on May 18, 1977, came the response to it: Haki Karer was murdered in a plot orchestrated by Alaattin Kapan, who belonged to a dubious group called Stêrka Sor (Red Star). This was a shock, as if someone had poured boiling water on our heads. This was an event that changed the course of history. The possibility that this group had connections with the KDP, some remnants of Turkish groups, and several groups under the control of the state turned the development of the struggle for a different mentality against this dubious hodgepodge of a group into an absolute priority. There was, however, the danger that the struggle for a different mentality would prematurely turn into crude means of physical battle.

This was around the time of when thirty-seven people were killed at an International Workers' Day demonstration in Istanbul on May 1, 1977, and the attempted assassination of Prime Minister Bülent Ecevit. It was a time when images of a dirty civil war were being displayed in Turkey. It was under these conditions that we decided to turn our group into a party as quickly as possible. In autumn of that year, I authored the draft program. I did so in memory of Haki Karer, while staying in Antep, where he had been murdered. From there, I traveled once more to Ankara and then, after my curious marriage to Kesire Yıldırım, we left for Diyarbakır in the early summer of 1978.

Our marriage can be seen as a great struggle of mentality, as well as a political and emotional struggle. Kesire's personality was character- ized by her Alevi and Kurdish identity and shaped by the state, making it highly provocative due to the struggle I had begun in terms of mentality. When, as a woman, she joined the group, she should have opened up new circles and pushed us all forward. But when she instead behaved like still and deep-running water, she became a dangerous vortex that mercilessly dragged everything around it under. There were only two possibilities: to totally move away from her or to take the necessary steps to prevent this danger from becoming an overwhelming threat. Totally moving away would have been too simple and would have amounted to a defeat. I offered to marry her because I hoped to reestablish calm in the group and thought that it would be better if she settled her scores with me. It was quite obviously a political, emotional, and intellectual relationship. Had she actually turned out to be a Kurdish socialist, good. On the other hand, had she been working for the state, which was a possibility, the question of who was using whom would be a matter worthy of serious thought. In that regard, I had self-confidence, however limitedly. The fact, however, is that my pride would not allow me to believe that a woman who appeared so very Kurdish was in the camp of the state. Even if that were the case, one could still wage a struggle against the state on behalf of a single woman, if necessary. Perhaps this struggle could have led not just to fierce wars but also to reconciliation and peace. That is how I felt at the time.

That she was an Alevi also encouraged me to build a relationship with her, as I didn't take my Sunni background particularly seriously. I thought that this relationship might contribute to the unity of Kurdish Sunnis and Alevis. Her family had been on the side of the Kemalists during the Dersim genocide and later continued with the CHP, which followed this tradition and experimented with social democracy, and I saw this as creating an opportunity. Social democracy could be a gateway to reconciliation and peace. We would eventually come to better understand that the CHP's social democracy was, in fact, only a thin layer of varnish in the service of the state, and later it would also become clear that Kesire's left and social democratic stance was a similar thin layer of varnish. During this fierce mentality struggle that lasted for more than ten years, I never found a way to reconcile myself with this woman's Kurdishness, Aleviness, and left-wing statism. I disapproved of the suggestion of some people in the organization that she be killed. Curiously, in the end, she was spirited away with the help of the same Greek secret service that would later participate in me being kidnapped in such a shameful manner. After her departure in 1987, she was never seen again.

Some perfidious persons within and outside of the organization have not hesitated to disseminate malicious slander, doubt, and rumors about me because of this relationship. In reality, this great struggle between different mentalities was extremely difficult and literally required a superhuman effort to endure. Perhaps the most important part of this struggle was that it led to the formation of the free Kurdish individual and in particular the free woman. This great struggle between different mentalities was a struggle for patriotism, freedom, and love.

Here, the question arises as to whether or not, in response to provocations of this sort, we should mix struggles between different mentalities with political or even violent actions. The nature of the politics of domination leaves little room for such questions. Nonetheless, it became increasingly apparent that we too were in the process of contracting these sorts of political diseases.

Once in Diyarbakır, in July 1978, I penned my handwritten theoretical piece, the manifesto titled "The Path of Revolution in Kurdistan,"[15] which was my second major leap forward in terms of mapping out a different mentality. It is perhaps of interest and to some degree illuminating to know that this work was written in the war-like atmosphere of my then recent problematic "marriage." There are those who say that when Mehmet Hayri Durmuş and Cemil Bayık (and another friend, possibly Kemal Pir) came to the house where I was living at the time and saw the state of my relationship they became extremely angry. "How can this woman treat our leader—a designation that began to develop at that time—this way?" purportedly suggesting, "Let's kill her without him knowing about it and deliver him from this problem." But Kemal Pir, who never lost his bearings, reacted very maturely: "Our friend probably knows what he is doing. We should not interfere." It is also said that when he was on hunger strike to the death in Diyarbakır, in reference to this episode, he stressed, as a kind of legacy, that "the party must always be particularly cautious and never forget about it."

"The Path of Revolution in Kurdistan" became the founding manifesto of the party, whose existence we were planning to announce at the time, and it was published in the first issue of the newspaper *Serxwebûn*, a publication that had been in the works for some time. When we look back at the manifesto, it can be seen as the culmination and concentrated expression of the assembly of 1973, the declaration of 1975, and the series of speeches in 1977. It obviously alluded to the *Communist Manifesto*. It tried to address not only the people of Kurdistan but also, indirectly, all societies in the Middle East. Its style and content point more to social freedom than to national character. It neither accepted a nation without freedom nor envisaged liberty that did not address national issues. This manifesto inevitably accelerated the founding of the party. All that was missing was a few not so important details, such as what to call the party and who would be its founding members.

At that time, founding a party was a question of honor. There was no way for us to bring about an immediate response, but with each step we took an enormous void of honor was evident. Wherever I looked, I could almost feel the debasement—as if everything had been betrayed. All dichotomies whether mountain-plain, village-city, history-present, individual-society, the state-citizen, woman-man, child-parent, the road-the traveler, in short each and every dichotomy, was blinding and treacherous. Something had to be done, that was certain. A party might be able to give meaning to these dichotomies and put them on the path to a solution. We were not founding a party in a narrow sense but, rather, as a new way of life. The transformation of identity was imposed on all of us. Such a level of discord with our country and history, as well as the contemporary world, could not be explained through any rationale. We felt obliged to intervene in this situation, irrespective of our actual weakness and rationalizations. In a sense, it was suicidal to found a party under these conditions. This was certainly not a conscious individual suicide action but simply a reaction to the unbearable situation in society and an effort to seize even the slightest opportunity to struggle for a dignified life. From that perspective, the founding of our party represented an attempt to save our honor. It was, in a certain sense, the opposite of an "honor killing." Personally, instead of sacrificing myself to a narrow conception of "honor," which I had refused since I was a child, I preferred an honorable act of historical and social significance. It is difficult to explain our course of action solely on the basis of class, national, ethnic, religious, or familial interests. It would be closer to the truth to see the main factor as the action of ordinary people who had educated themselves with great difficulty and gained a certain degree of clarity. We could perhaps best be compared with the Russian *narodniki* (friends of the people). If we look back at the impact of the PKK, we can say that the particular way that we became a party certainly played its role, and the subsequent developments showed that this decision satisfied an overall need, as well as that of honor.

The intellectual efforts made around the mindset at the beginning of the 1980s served to better clarify the relationships around and between politics and force. The speeches "The Role of Force in Kurdistan," "The Problem of National Liberation and the Road Map to its Resolution," "The Question of Personality in Kurdistan, Life in the Party and the Characteristics of the Revolutionary Militant," and "On Organizing," which were printed in book form, aimed to address more concrete problems. The experiences of the Middle East and the Israel-Palestine conflict also influenced us. Despite the many years of intellectual effort around the mentality, we had only succeeded in awakening a very small number of young people. But it seemed an overall and deep-seated shake-up of society would depend on politico-military steps that would affect everyone. Genuinely becoming a party and that party's coming of age would be determined by taking these steps. Otherwise, it would be as if the party had died of some infantile disorder. The combination of the prison resistance and the work taken up in the Middle East made a guerrilla offensive inevitable. There hadn't even been the smallest positive development on the opposing side to prevent this. Total denial and all-encompassing repression were the state's modus operandi. The two realities were absolutely and irreconcilably opposed. It was futile to seek grounds for a compromise. Only later did we address the question of whether or not the very odd behavior by Kesire and the lawyer Hüseyin Yıldırım, who popped up at around this time, in Europe might actually have been directed by the state. But it was difficult to find evidence that supported that scenario. Moreover, it would have been difficult to even dare to do such a thing. The later behavior of Mehmet Şener and Selim Çürükkaya raised similar suspicions. But even if these suspicions had proven accurate, these people didn't have the potential to be anything more than low-level agents. Therefore, we didn't take them particularly seriously at the time.

The discussions after the offensive of August 15, 1984, basically rotated around the question of why it had remained so limited and insufficient, but not around why it had been carried out in the first place. We had not used a particularly creative military approach. It resembled anything but the guerrilla. The question we always asked ourselves was why we

failed to develop an effective guerrilla line. Even the minimum requirements of becoming a party could not be mirrored inside the guerrilla. I am
convinced that two factors played a role in this. First, from the beginning,
the personalities involved were not ready to truly commit to either this
struggle between mentalities or to the corresponding practical efforts
with a deep-rooted belief and consciousness, and, second, my stubborn
commitment and extraordinary efforts to keeping these people going
despite their personal weaknesses. As with the Turkish left, their structures predisposed them to throw themselves blitz-like into the battle and
sacrifice themselves, with not much headway being made. I, for my part,
wanted them to stay alive and succeed.

At the same time, some individuals who were locals had rapidly risen
to prominence and were quick to detect and fill gaps in the command structure. This tendency, which later became more tangible as the "gang of four,"
didn't respect even the most minimal requirements of being a society, let
alone the requirements of being a party. These figures were to be a source
of devastation that went far beyond banditry, or even anything the most
sordid agent could not have brought about. This happened because a local
banditry of sorts collided with influence of a party that was still weak, a
situation that continued until it precipitated the failure of the second leap
forward on our route to becoming a party.

The first leap forward to becoming a party was almost brought to a
standstill by Kesire, Şahin Dönmez, and others while we were still determining our mentality. Our second leap forward almost perished at the
hands of the gangsterism mentioned above. Every attempt to undertake
countermeasures was rendered ineffective by the deep-rooted gang structures, and, as a result, these measures came to nothing. This was neither
because of the inadequacies of the movement leadership nor the attacks by
the state and its collaborators. It is more realistic to say that the real reason
was that we underestimated the power of the gang culture and didn't
succeed in countering it effectively. Neither the movement leadership
nor the state prevailed in this particular struggle—victory went to gang
culture.[16] The current situation of the village guards who are beholden to
the state and the gang chiefs, most of whom became "*itirafçı*" defectors,[17]
better explains this phenomenon. But this weapon, which was maximally
used by the state, would later have an obvious boomerang effect. The state's
decision in the 1990s to support the tribal leaders in South Kurdistan, who
can be rightfully thought of as more capable gang chiefs, would later lead

to the Kurdish federal state. In the north, the collaborators as village guards and tariqat established themselves so firmly within both the political and the military state structures that they could no longer be easily taken on.

I am convinced that during this period the leadership fulfilled its task, addressing ideological problems and problems with the political and military lines, providing basic education to the cadres, building relationships with the community, and organizing logistics and armaments. One might, however, criticize my choice of location.[18] However, this criticism loses its edge if you factor in the possibility of doing activities safely. The most important point here is that some of the leadership responsible for implementing the line on a daily basis didn't live up to its role—neither politically nor militarily—despite the painstakingly arranged resources at its disposal. Actually, all of the conditions for success were present. From arms to money, from bases to external relations, from relationships with the community to relations with states, with a large number of trained military and political cadres drawn from a pool of potential members, everything was in place and only needed to be properly shaped by an honest military, political, and organizational command structure. Had that happened, developments would have been very different.

We probably couldn't have attained state power, but that wasn't really something we had planned for. But we could easily have reached a democratic solution, and we could have done so without very many losses or much suffering on either side. The main factor in the failure to reach a conclusion was the development of gang culture both within the PKK and within the state—the central committee of the PKK, which should be held responsible, failed to address its tasks. It is clear that neither the state nor the PKK won. In fact, both suffered heavy losses, while the insidious and collaborationist feudal Kurdish upper class managed to feather its nest.

To protect their own key interests, the traditional tribal leadership in South Kurdistan dared to act in an entirely treasonous way at the most critical point of Turkey's war with the PKK.[19] An overall appraisal of this kind of treachery and the treachery in the prisons and the war zones indicates that it was planned in an extremely devious, precise, and secret fashion, and that it encouraged Turkey to rely on its policy of supporting the gang culture to an even greater degree. While the politicians by their very nature were quite open to this, the fact that the army also felt compelled to take this approach turned out to be the first step on the road that culminated in today's federal state. Undoubtedly, the Turkish leaders hadn't expected this outcome but had seen the relationship with the South Kurdish leaders as tactical. They were certain that this would end with the liquidation of the PKK. Moreover, they didn't have a clear picture of the actual dimensions of the US plans for Iraq. The collaborationist Kurdish leadership was much more methodical and conscious in the pursuit of its goals. It made masterful use of its relations with both the PKK and Turkey, whereas both the PKK and Republic of Turkey's command structures addressed the issue in a superficial and oversimplified manner. A careful evaluation of this phase would doubtless lead to a number of important insights. Of particular importance would be clarifying what the relationship between the classic state and the gang state approaches looked like within the Turkish state and what contradictions existed between the two.

Which politicians and state institutions were responsible for the true devastation of the state must be clearly established and exposed, as it was not just the work of the PKK. We need to understand how a completely different state, entirely detached from the republic's revolutionary principles, began to be built under the rubric of "Turkish-Islamic synthesis." What role did the war in Kurdistan play in this? We also need to understand how Kurdish tribalism, the village guard system, and the tariqa of the traditional feudal and religious circles could converge and lead to anti-republican developments and how it could lead to further developments similar to the Kurdish federal state in the future.

We must also recognize the part international developments played in this situation. None of this can be sufficiently understood if you only look at the developments within the PKK and the Turkish republic and don't consider other developments. The dissolution of the Soviet Union beginning in 1990, globalization, and the Clinton administration policies had extensive direct and indirect effects in the Middle East, Turkey, and Kurdistan. The collapse of the Soviet Union weakened Syria's resolve, leading to my well-known departure from that country in October 1998. Diplomatic support had weakened, and we were bereft of any potential comprehensive support.

Globalization and the enforced changes it is likely to cause in the Middle East oblige us to plan more precisely for the future, because, otherwise, the impact of developments in many countries, Iraq in particular, will be incalculable. Insistence on the old paradigms leads to conservativism and prevents an appropriate assessment of the coming challenges. We should have foreseen that following the arrival of Bill Clinton the tactics used in the region would change. If we had developed a comprehensive understanding of US policy for the region, Turkey, and Kurdistan, my departure from Syria would perhaps not have been followed by the well-known developments. Superficial and belated assessments lead to an inability to act in a timely fashion and to a loss of initiative.

The fact that the theoretical and paradigmatic shift was not carried out in time also contributed to the current blockage. We had not followed the situation of the left, the cultural movements, feminism, and the new ecological initiatives over the last quarter of the twentieth century very well. We also did not have the necessary depth of understanding of the importance of civil society and the struggle for human rights. The program, organization, strategy, and tactics of the PKK had been strongly influenced by real socialism and the national liberation movements. The corrections that we carried out at our congresses never went beyond being tactical changes. The basic paradigms remained unchanged. Even though the *çözümleme*, or analyses, were more in depth, the lack of a new paradigm made a radical transformation impossible.[20] We still looked at social development in a schematic way. A dogmatic mentality affected our perspective on nature and society. We had overcome the mentality of the Middle Ages, but the real socialist schematic way of thinking did not lead to a creative theory of nature and society. Approaching things using these established patterns prevented us from perceiving the rich world of phenomena and the abundance of transformation and change. More importantly, an extreme concentration on the political and the military reduced the personality to single dimension. This, in turn, imposed a hierarchy within relationships. The malady of power spread rapidly, like an epidemic. The fact that the revolution was supposed to be for the freedom and equality of the people and that democratization was a necessary station on that road increasingly became of secondary importance. The political and military approach determined all relations. It was one of the basic maladies of real socialism to mirror such behavior, which might make sense in a military environment, to the people as a whole.

In reality, there was no interest in new theoretical models or in a paradigm shift. Perhaps this can be explained by the fear that our views might prove incorrect and a certain hesitation in the face of the consequences that this could have.

However, the dissolution of the Soviet Union made a fresh look at socialism inevitable. Even though our interest in the women's question and environmental problems had increased, our theoretical depth remained limited. A more realistic approach to the question of ethnicity could have led to a break with the economist and narrowly class-oriented tendencies and to a rich communal and democratic perspective. Although over time there was more interest in that direction, this interest was not sufficiently deep to overcome the existing blockage. In reality, the PKK carried on with the 1970s paradigm until 2000. Even though that paradigm had not completely collapsed, it had lost significant functionality.

No phenomenon is ever exclusively negative. The history of the PKK is also the story of major changes and transformations in the history and social structure of the Kurds and Kurdistan. We can safely say that the last quarter of the twentieth century in Kurdistan bears the mark of the PKK. The transformation of the mentality and the political and social upheavals that this brought about have made history.

Despite all the damage it has suffered, the organization still asserts its existence to a great extent. In Turkey, abroad, and in all parts of Kurdistan, there are logistical possibilities, cadres, and numerous groups and civil society organizations that represent a potential base for organizing in various ways. The political consciousness of the people is highly developed. The PKK has a mass base that is prevalent throughout Kurdistan. In addition, it has the support of millions of sympathizers abroad and in the neighboring metropoles. There has been an enormous awakening and a remarkable organizing process among women. A new world is emerging with women at its center. The essential elements of the new theoretical approach and paradigm is anchored in women's freedom. The youth is in a similar situation. A youth that has not lost interest and enthusiasm is the most determined driving force for achieving the ideal of a free society. The slogan "a free life or no life" has become a banner that the youth will not surrender.

As such, founding the party was not completely in vain. Based on its enormous experience, its thousands of cadres, its tens of thousands of sympathizers, and its hundreds and thousands of supporters, the party can easily reconstruct itself both in essence and in form as it sees fit. The guerrilla maintains its presence, with thousands of fighters in the center of Kurdistan and at all the strategic points, despite the undeserved losses and the gang culture. As it frees itself from the severe maladies of the past, that, together with the wealth of experience that it has acquired and a more realistic program, mean it is readier than ever to be successful. Despite being regularly besieged by its opponents, the PKK has friends all over the world and continues to build upon this network. Thousands of martyrs count on comrades who can represent them correctly in terms of mentality and practice. Efforts undertaken in the name of freedom will never be a source of regret. The pain we feel is due only to senseless losses, blind obstinacy, and tasks not fulfilled on time. But for all who know its value, such pain has always been the best teacher. This time, valuable lessons can be learned from this teacher: deserved lessons of goodness, truth and beauty in the best way possible.

Section B—Critique and Self-Critique in the Name of the PKK

According to the sages and prophets, the greatest struggle is the struggle of humans with their *nefs*, or ego-oriented impulses. A story about Alexander the Great is instructive: the wise Brahman Calanus had come from India and voluntarily accompanied Alexander. He wanted to self-immolate in a ceremony. When Alexander the Great was unable to persuade him to drop the plan, he said of Calanus: "This man has defeated bigger enemies than I have," even though he was perhaps the greatest warrior of all time. Even he knew and accorded greater significance to being a warrior for wisdom.

The Prophet Mohammad felt the same way. He called the struggle between armies the *jihad sughra*, the little war, but termed the struggle of the human being with her or his "nefs" or ego-oriented impulses—a form of inner mentality struggle—the *jihad akbar*, the big war. A consistent and truly transforming self-critique is actually the greatest struggle any individual can be engaged in. Self-critique is the struggle against one's own weaknesses, errors, and flaws. In scientific terms, it is the struggle of analytical intelligence to overcome the false impulsive traces of emotional intelligence in order to correctly orient this intelligence. This is the development of reason. In effect, the difference between humans and animals is rooted in a development of analytical intelligence into wisdom.

It is perfectly obvious that Kurdish identity cannot be defined as something extremely different from the identities of other human communities. Even though we can identify particularities, in the final analysis we can divide the history of the Kurds into the same phases as that of other human communities. The particularities constitute differences, but a great deal of overall similarity is apparent. The specific traits of the Kurdish identity are determined by the way it was historically and socially shaped. I devoted a large part of my defense writings to these traits. The extreme oppression and being shaped at the hands of the ruling power have incalculably crippled the Kurd's freedom and the unfolding of particularities to a great extent. The result is a society that we could describe as crippled, even pathological, rather than as marginal.

In the past, I tried to identify these pathological traits by analyzing the personality and developed far-reaching educational and practical measures to remedy them. In that sense, the PKK represents a normalization that has contributed to the formation of a contemporary human being—the transformation of the Kurds into contemporary human beings. To what extent this has been successful is an open question, but that undoubtedly has been one of the ways the PKK has proven to be socially significant.

If transformation has been particularly painful in the concrete example of the PKK, the main factor is the social base on which it must rely. If the organizational structure has democratic characteristics, one can expect many of the negative elements from that social base will permeate the organization and influence the newly emerging individual, making that individual an extension of that social base. If this occurs, the organization will have no impact on social characteristics and will remain indifferent, and the isolation of the organization from the society will be inevitable. Alternately, at the other extreme, members of the organization might be completely unable to extricate themselves from social influences, in which case the organization will directly mirror society, i.e., it will be nothing more than an appendix. In that case, the organization would either be rife with diseases, or there would be no difference between it and the society it wants to change. The desirable and balanced situation is to synthesize the influences coming from the social base with the organization's revolutionary aspects and influences for change and to make a dialectical leap to a richer and higher level of development. This is the framework in which the dialectical development between a revolutionary organization and the society it wants to change takes place.

The concept of "critique" is related to the dialectical nature of the development. The purpose of critique is to reveal and eliminate factors that don't contribute to this dialectical mode of operation. Criticism should correspond to the course and nature of development. On the other hand, self-critique expresses the opinion of the agent of development—the person who is in a position to actively bring about development—in terms various situations, events and processes that do not correspond to what should be achieved and desired or help accomplish one's goals. In other words, it means putting an end to unsuccessful thoughts, concepts, behaviors, and actions that do not correspond to dialectical development and committing to correct ways of thinking and developing an appropriate practice.

We can hardly claim that the PKK's attempt to achieve a normalization appropriate to our own time was a total success. On the contrary, the analysis presented here shows that not only were there important flaws and errors, but that there were also far-reaching cases of treachery, both within and outside of the organization.

The conclusion to be drawn is that comprehensive critique and self-critique are always necessary. If critique and self-critique don't lead to the desired result in practice, then what the sages called the "struggle against the nefs or the ego-oriented impulses" has not really taken place. Thus, people deceive themselves and those around them knowingly or unknowingly—in the name of what the sages called "keeping up appearances." This puts the person in question in an even more difficult situation—the position of being guilty, hypocritical, and a liar.

If this is the case, resorting to more severe sanctions may be necessary. These take many different forms, including acknowledgment, exposure, isolation, imprisonment, and being given various practical tasks. Until the goal is reached, such corrective approaches will continue. If a given organization fails to do this, it will come into conflict with its essence and be disrespectful of its goals and its practice. If the person goes much further that will exacerbate the situation, and the person will be considered a traitor. Being a traitor is the worst and most dangerous state one can find oneself in in terms of society or the organization one belongs to. If an insistence on betrayal does not end with desertion, the result will be open warfare, which in turn means physical or intellectual killing and death.

Defining the reality of critique and self-critique in this way and applying it to the PKK leads to some conclusions of historical consequence. We should say in advance that persons or organizations who dare to carry out critique and self-critique in a consistent way are by no means weak but, rather, will find themselves in a stronger position. Only organizations and individuals who are weak and lack self-confidence try to evade critique and self-critique. For them, critique means destruction, and self-critique is tantamount to total collapse. Those with self-confidence will be strengthened by critique and self-critique and will be able to pursue their goals much more successfully—overcoming whatever is blocking their success and achieving their goals through decisive and increasingly effective steps.

In the following critique and self-critique, which I make in the name of the PKK, I will refrain from addressing certain secondary topics that I have repeatedly elaborated upon elsewhere.[21]

The Concept of "the Party"

We must begin with our concept of "the party." Contemporary parties as we know them generally emerged in the capitalist societies that developed in the nineteenth and the twentieth centuries. They based themselves on the classes and social categories of these societies. Most of all, they focused on the bourgeoisie and the workers as the fundamental contrasting classes. In addition, there was often talk about the petit bourgeois parties representing the intermediate class. The main goal of all these parties is to arrive at the state. Whether by revolutionary means or through elections, the ability of each party to gain the exalted position of state power and secure a position in parliament or government represents success. This is true for all states, both existing ones and those yet to come. To become part of the state or even the state itself is seen as tantamount to being exalted, to sharing in the state's blessings, and to control the rudder of progress. This holds equally true for all classes.

We can say that this tendency to "become the state" was among the motives that led to the founding of the PKK. Although this was not explicit, there was a basic unspoken assumption that all our hopes would be fulfilled by the state, either through accessing the already existing state or by building a new one of our own design. All activities in all dimensions, including ideology, politics, the military, organization, and propaganda, were ultimately state-centered and had the goal of arriving at the state. Even though the theoretical emphasis was on a classless communist society without exploitation, the preconceived assumption was always that without the state that is called the long-term "dictatorship of the proletariat" this could not be attained. Therefore, gaining state power was one of the PKK's key objectives, just as it was for all of the twentieth-century parties. It can hardly be denied that like all other parties the PKK had an interest in the state and wanted to attain state power and represent the state.

We can discuss the degree of consciousness and skill with which the PKK fought for that goal and whether or not it could have reached this goal. One could also evaluate whether the PKK is closer to a "bourgeois state" pole or to a "proletarian state" pole—but claiming that the PKK never aimed at a state would simply not be true. The question of whether or not "becoming a state" meant a Kurdish state or a state under the name of another nation or country changes nothing essential. The decisive question is whether or not we were state-oriented. And since this quite likely was the case, it was only natural that the personality of the people involved, of the organization, and of the modus operandi of "becoming a state" left its mark on the PKK's practice and its secondary goals. Given this situation, the main focus of theory inevitably became politics and the state, and the main strategic and tactical issues addressed how to position classes in the short- and long-term, how to pick friends and allies, and what forms of organization and action to choose to conquer or arrive at the heights of the state. Thus, all daily work was carried out on the basis of these theoretical, strategic, and tactical guidelines.

Because all other parties and fronts in the nineteenth and twentieth centuries shared this orientation, the question that arises is whether or not these goals were achieved by becoming this sort of party. Now that parties built in the name of classes or nations succeeded in founding states and have had sufficient time being in power, we cannot claim that they achieved their goals. In fact, it is not necessary to provide much evidence to prove that they didn't.

In the nineteenth and twentieth centuries, wars, inequality, oppression, and destruction were more extreme than ever before. The use of atomic bomb posed a huge threat to humanity. Assimilation, oppression, and massacres took numerous forms. As a result, at the beginning of the third millennium we see a civilization overrun with increasing inequality, war, lack of freedom, environmental destruction, and sexism and an ever growing abyss between the rich and the poor. In spite of all the lofty ideals that inspired their founding, the proletarian parties share at least equal responsibility with the so-called bourgeois parties for this outcome. As is well known, the real socialist experiments bore fruit that was far inferior to that produced by the bourgeois experiments. It only makes sense for the communist parties, as vanguard organizations, to accept responsibility for this outcome.

Thus, the party itself, as the expression of a state-oriented will, runs contrary to the ideal of freedom and equality, which we can call socialism—it squarely contradicts that goal. Parties that aim to become a state cannot be expected to reach the ideal of freedom and equality. On the contrary, that they are actually leading us even further away from that goal can be considered proven by the practices experienced. To resolve this contradiction, we must, at long last, renounce this orientation toward a state. In other words, if we definitionally agree that the state stands for inequality and unfreedom, we can finally go beyond being the state-oriented party, at least in principle. *Being* a party in the name of a state or *founding* a party to create a state must be seen as fundamental errors. Honest self-critique and the renunciation of parties of this sort would be the best way to deal with these insights.

The goal of becoming a state and the ideal of freedom and equality are mutually exclusive. Each requires that the other be overcome. Please note that I am not talking about demolishing the state or disrupting it. The concept of "overcoming" is related to the concept of the "withering away of the state" that Engels developed at the end of the nineteenth century.[22] For socialism, the state is like a ball of fire that must slowly be extinguished. I call this "the snowball theory or the pomegranate ball theory." This snowball—the state—has not only greatly extended its sphere of influence for millennia, without in any way bringing about liberty and equality but, rather, further developing inequality and unfreedom for those under its domination. The state cannot be chosen as a means to achieve freedom and equality, because it is the oldest tradition of hierarchical and class society.

Opting to use the state to implement socialism and any ideal of equality and freedom has proven to be the gravest of errors. When we look back into the depths of history, we see even more serious errors to this end. Even Christianity, which fought the Roman Empire for three centuries, diverged from the ideal of freedom and equality for the poor once it became the state, becoming an empire with a class-based society in the process. The people of the Migration Period, who were organized communally and democratically, also quickly departed from freedom and equality once they became states. The great nomadic societies of the Teutons, Arabs, and Turks gradually lost their communal, democratic, and egalitarian structure after their upper classes transformed themselves into states. There is no shortage of historical examples of freedom and equality lost in this way. The answer to the question of why opting for the state continues to prevail is related to the essence of state power.

Power and Violence

It's necessary that we untangle power.[23] What is power? It is the concrete realization of the state institution. Power is the state at a given point. It is the construction of the state from the respective classes, from the social strata of a given period, as well as from the upper strata of ethnic, religious, and tribal groups. It is the domination of state institutions by organized groups from a new class, an ethnic group, a dynasty, a denomination, or a nation. The emergence of the relations, organization, and action of any of these categories as domination and exploitative force implies the state. The state is neither God himself nor the "shadow of God," as statist ideologies claim; it is neither the holy mother nor the holy father, neither a god-king nor the supreme embodiment of reason. It is the activity of tyrannical and dishonest groups seizing the laboriously accumulated values of societies, especially their surplus value and products and has been ever since the first hierarchical and class-based society in history. The state is the aggregation of institutions and rules where these activities are carried out. Power underlies the action of such groups, which permeate and manage the existing institutions and rules at their whim.

Since we have discussed the general definition of power extensively in the section on societies, I will only briefly touch upon it here. Power is attractive and advantageous because of the extent of control over the accumulated social values it permits. Being in power means being in possession of the accumulated wealth, with the institutions, rules, might, and methods to further expand them, which is to use fancy words to say that claiming to use this power to achieve freedom, equality, and development is to deceive and hinder not only ourselves, but also our immediate environment and the society we rely upon, knowingly or otherwise. You cannot bring about revolution or achieve any change through power. The only thing power can do is usurp and divide values among the rulers. Furthermore, power consumes value rather than producing it. Whether in the form of taxes or by force, it takes from society and distributes what it has taken among its members. When it invests and produces, that is, when it runs a state economy, this is little more than a way to plunder and confiscate values.

We can, of course, ask: Why was a working-class politician like Lenin unable to recognize this reality? A detailed explanation is in order. In this connection, we should briefly note that the 150-year history of socialism was built on the paradigm of coming to power. Lenin's contribution was to apply this paradigm with no further ado and to determine the right ways and means to succeed. Even though in *The State and Revolution* he stressed that the road to socialism goes through the most advanced form of democracy, he and his party regarded establishing socialism by the shortcut of the dictatorship of the proletariat as a basic tactical approach. One of their most fundamental convictions was that under the conditions of imperialism it would not be possible to survive without a party and being in power. History, however, has disproven this—even if it took seventy years to do so.

This does not mean that everything about Marxism-Leninism was wrong. It only shows that the theses about power and the party were false, and that socialism cannot be achieved in this way. It is impossible to say precisely how Marx and Engels understood this issue, because they basically acted solely as theorists. But they also talked about the necessity to use the state as a tool of domination against the bourgeoisie at least for a short period. Apart from them, there were the anarchists, who were not statist, and a number of utopists. Non-statist democracies have, of course, existed at various times in various places, and after the Russian Revolution, many socialists were critical of the socialist state and demanded that it wither away posthaste.

As a result, we can conclude that using the state and state power to achieve freedom, self-determination, and equality does not work but, rather, takes us further away from our goal. If there is a commitment to these aims and their success are desired, it is essential that we work out new political models for parties and coalitions as fundamental tools of struggle and develop them into the necessary theoretical and paradigmatic view. New parties will only make sense if they provide a meaningful response to this problem.

Thus, we must pose the following questions regarding power: Where do the political power holders get their enormous strength? How do they succeed in confiscating and commanding so much value? These questions lead us to force as the foundation of power, and to the fact that force is determined in war. We must not forget that the basis of the state and, therefore, of power is not social reason but force and war. The state and power do not emerge as instruments for the solution of social problems. If we don't distinguish between the public sphere as the source of problem-solving and the state and its power as the force for domination and exploitation, we will tumble into utter confusion.

There is no social activity that power doesn't meddle in. Even the family is not spared state interference. The stage reached by global capitalism, has turned the state into both the most intensely applied and the most superfluous instrument of all. The fact that it has become superfluous does not, however, mean that it has grown weaker. On the contrary, it still strives with full force to secure its influence—when necessary, using policies that

offer the most concessions. We can describe such state power as totalitarianism. It can perhaps be said that the time of the earlier fascist variety of
totalitarianism and its real socialist variation is in the past. Nevertheless,
the state as such is totalitarian. This is true of all states that exist today.
This is a response to the needs of capitalism, its current crisis, and the
emergence of alternatives.

Essentially, the force that the state has been based on since its establishment, i.e., the phenomenon of war, continues to this date. War is the
foundation of power. Being in power means shaping society on all levels
based on the culture of war and maintaining the status quo. Most of all,
however, state power is incongruent with the ideals of freedom and equality, which if realized would mean its negation. Its practices do not serve
these ideals. To carry on operating, it must ensure just the opposite in
its starkest form. That is why, regardless of good intentions, the ideals of
freedom and equality promoted by the parties come to nothing once they
constitute the state.

Democracy

If the new parties acting for freedom and equality want to be consistent,
they will have to orient their program around political and social forms
that are not state-centered. The alternative to the state is democracy. So far,
all attempts to challenge the state with nondemocratic alternatives have
failed. In addition, no regime other than democracy limits, restricts, legally
constrains, and minimizes the state. Destroying a state in no way equates
with transcending state culture. In its place, a new state will immediately
be set up or another state will fill the void. Only democracy can share the
field with the state and extend society's realm of freedom by constraining
the state. Only democracy can reduce the state's seizure of values and bring
society a little closer to equality.

Democracy is not a form of the capitalist state, as one might think. I
define democracy as the self-governance of a non-state society. Democracy
means governance that does not become the state—the capacity of communities to govern themselves without a state. Contrary to popular belief,
since the emergence of human society, states have been far less common
than democracies. It may well be that up to now no complete democracy
has ever existed in any country or nation, but, even so, the way in which
society exists is communal and democratic. Without communality and
democratic reflexes, it is impossible to manage a society using the state

alone. The state can only rule by growing at the expense of communality and democracy. The ground from which it emerged and upon which it maintains itself is society's communality—the need for coexistence—and a democratic stance. There is a dialectical relationship between the state and democracy. Therefore, when society and civilization coalesce, the fundamental contradiction is between the state and democracy. The less there is of one, the more there is of the other. Full democracy is a condition of statelessness, whereas total state sovereignty means a complete lack of democracy. As a result, we can say that the relationship between the state and democracy is not based on destruction but on democracy transcending the state.

Only a state can destroy a state. Democracy doesn't destroy the state, because this can only lead, as in the case of real socialism, to a new state. Thus, only democracy, by constraining the state and making it smaller, by limiting its excesses in society, and by cutting off its tentacles, can further increase the possibilities for freedom and equality. The basic function of democracy thus emerges. When all is said and done, the state may perhaps become superfluous and wither away. Engels, and also Lenin, to some degree, thought that would be the case, but, unfortunately, they didn't develop this theory completely.

In states where there is democracy, there are certainly also important changes in the state's form. The state is gradually forced to give up all unnecessary institutions and rules, retaining only those that serve the "general security" of society and the "public sphere," i.e., areas of the common good of society. In the EU countries in particular, this relationship between the state and democracy has been acknowledged and implemented, if only belatedly and very slowly. Thus, in a sense, on behalf of all humanity, Europe has performed a sort of self-critique with regard to state and democracy.

With this brief assessment, we hoped to show that being a state-oriented party constituted a fundamental error in our worldview from the very beginning. Regardless of whether or not such a party founds or arrives at a state, it cannot achieve democracy, freedom, and equality by using the state. Unless it rejects this option, it cannot become a libertarian and egalitarian party of a new type. The path to a democratic and socialist party is to ensure renewal by transforming state-oriented theories, programs, strategies, and tactics. We need democratic and socialist theories, programs, strategies, and tactics that are not state-oriented.

Self-critique makes sense if developed on this basis. Otherwise, a relapse into the old in the name of renewal is inevitable. The situation the parties of real socialism, social democracy, and national liberation find themselves in clearly demonstrates this.

Self-critique of the PKK

Restructuring the PKK will be meaningful if the party carries out a comprehensive self-critique along the lines elaborated above and shows the strength to then apply its conclusions in practice. Looking back at the past once more, we can see that what was behind all of the PKK's mistakes and shortcomings was the classic statist understanding of what a party is. If we imagine Kurdistan either as a separate state or as part of a common, federal state, accept this state as the actual goal, and direct all efforts toward that goal, we predetermine how the cadres and the organization will work and what actions and propaganda will look like. The PKK cadres were faced with the oldest historical state traditions. The power relations they entered into without a particularly deep understanding of political science very soon led them to use their power ruthlessly. I have frequently and publicly criticized this.

Today, we have a better understanding of why even after seventy years Soviet socialism slipped back into brutal capitalism: it lacked a democratic education. An overhasty statism sowed the spirit of totalitarianism within society. When that repression was removed, the previous backwardness sprang back to life. It was the backwardness of Czarist Russia that had not been democratized and continued to surreptitiously exist—the gloss of state capitalism only succeeded in hiding this for seventy years. That being the case, we, the PKK, should have known and anticipated that if the cadres are put in a relationship of power, arms, and politics, the possibility always exists that they might lose themselves and become ruthless despots, especially within a society that is constantly on the brink of a massacre—I have frequently strongly criticized the practices of Şemdin Sakık for exactly this. The cadres who took part in the institutions we created were either completely unaware or turned into little despots. The primary underlying reason for this was a lack of political education and, above all, absolutely no familiarity with democracy. These cadres did not even want to know anything about how democratic institutions worked or about their rules and processes. Because of the traditional culture, shirking democracy was a habit that facilitated an easy life. However, democracy requires social consciousness, knowledge of political science, a scientific approach, and experience in social guidance. These virtues cannot be attained easily but require rigorous education and experience.

Because they were based on the state tradition, the politburo and the central committee turned themselves into a hierarchy and made themselves inaccessible and untouchable. Becoming a state starts with having authority, which requires an approach whereby one deals with the people harshly and coldly. One of the first acts of the Median chief Deioces when he had created the first Median Confederation was to break off all past humanitarian relationships and refuse to meet with anyone.[24] Then he had the newly erected capital of Ekbatan encircled by seven city walls—a truly strange situation. It proves, however, that identifying with the state means that you must curtain yourself and embrace a mask. The Ottoman sultans continued that tradition, appearing only behind a curtain. Essentially, the socialist parties, starting with their senior leadership, were forced to do the same thing, because this is a necessary corollary of the state.

I must admit that this was the issue that I found the most difficult as a person who played a role in the practice of this movement from the beginning. I was never able to make my peace with the state form and its protocol. I wavered between my democratic composition and a composition that was becoming statist. I was torn between the two. As the PKK grew, I began to understand the power play better, and I have to say that I didn't like it. At the core, the biggest battle I fought rotated around the question of whether or not I should conduct myself like a statesman. The greatest challenge to maintaining my enthusiasm as we approached 1995 was an increasing awareness that I was drifting away from my goals. I realized that even if I was becoming a statesman, there was not much good in it, as it was reducing the stature of the people around me. They would behave servilely around me, but I knew that they were not being sincere. I also presumed that they could be dangerous if the opportunity arose. This was a development that bothered me. It did not at all correspond to my ideal for relationships. For the first time, I became convinced that this approach could not be successful, that any successes we scored would correspond to entirely undesirable goals. This basic truth is the core of the difficulties that have haunted the PKK since 1995.

A flimsy "civil servantism" emerged in all of the relationships and structures of the cadres and the institutions.[25] Having a utopia, being very enthusiastic, pursuing and creating new things every day was no longer an issue. Everybody was carried away by the desire for a mediocre life based on the revolutionary values that had been acquired with so much difficulty. This was one of the most dangerous maladies. The fact that the revolutionary PKK had developed a degenerate gang culture and ruthless despots, on the one hand, and was behaving like a civil servant, on the other hand, also meant its end. All of the immeasurable effort I had put in produced nothing but stunted people.

I have devoted a lot of energy to untangling this phenomenon. My analyses since 1990 indicate how intense these efforts were. I made extensive use of critique as a weapon. If the disorder was not correctly diagnosed, there was no reason to expect a successful treatment. Under the conditions that Kurdistan was in, that the cadres of a party, which from the central committee down to our base, idealized statehood would deteriorate into brutal gangs if they were of peasant background and into despotic civil servant–like posture if they were semi-intellectuals was only to be expected. This type of deformity was inherent in the party's very goal.

This is what I mean when I say that the second phase of building the PKK failed. It is not a question of whether or not this leap forward was foiled militarily or technically. These are secondary questions. If the PKK had transformed itself even ever so slightly into a state, it would have drawn to a close, that is, its revolutionary essence would have been extinguished. It would inevitably have turned into a formation like the KDP and the PUK. From 1995 to 2000, I did not have the capacity to fully address this problem. Until 1995, the PKK was primarily a utopian movement, with a lot of enthusiasm and profound beliefs. As we approached the end of that phase, we realized that something was seriously wrong, that things were repeating themselves endlessly, and that we were unable to see what the remedy was, so we simply held on to our existing positions, adding a few new ones. We had fallen into a situation of trying to keep up appearances.

The process up to and including my time on İmralı Island has contributed to me finding a solution to this problem. This is the result of having had the opportunity to look at the nature of the sciences and, therefore, social reality more realistically. Moreover, it proved advantageous to be cut off from intense practical work. Had I too been profoundly afflicted by the malady of dogmatism, like most of the cadres, I would probably not have mustered the later strength to untangle problems and resolve them. I have come to untangle not only Marxism but also all utopias addressing freedom and equality and, in addition, the phenomena of state and democracy. Moreover, I also deciphered the relationship between power and war.

The malady of wanting to conquer power and the state is particularly likely to result in an extremely dangerous despotism in individuals from a reactionary social background who have not enjoyed a serious scientific and humanitarian education. To satisfy their desire for power, they will try to solve even simple problems with armed violence. This was explicitly clear in the case of some individuals. During the process of becoming gangs in particular, some brutal characters emerged. Their style of leadership and command consisted of treacherously shooting the most precious comrades they were annoyed with in the back like they were killing particularly annoying bugs. This was the biggest horror. Sending friends they wanted to get rid of on suicide missions, or even doing so simply to meet their simplest of needs, became common practice. Of course, this form of decay was only understood much later. Being in power, being a commander, became very attractive. There was total recklessness. Because these people could get anything they wanted with this kind of power, the eternal malady of power played its evil hand once again. The game of power was their favorite game, and they masterfully played it against each other with plots and counterplots. This was the most dangerous form of decay within the PKK. The effect on the people was much worse. Even loyal people who were invaluable to us were overwhelmed. Actions were accompanied by activities that never should have taken place. People forgot that women and children are entitled to particular protection. Even animals were squandered. All of this was clearly inhumane and unacceptable. On the other hand, we must not forget that the practices of the ruling power often included the total removal of villages and cities from the map—they were simply leveled.

Becoming civil servant–like was no less common a malady. Taking refuge in a civil servant–like career in the midst of a life and death struggle was one of the worst forms of deterioration. The others wasted time in inadequacies that included cronyism, minding one's own business when that was not what was needed, and making do with what had already been achieved. Thus, an era in the history of becoming the PKK came to an end.

Obviously, the reason for all these negative developments was the fundamentally statist nature of the party. Advocating freedom and equality but taking the state as the means for getting there made this aberration inevitable. One way out of this situation is to abandon being a party based on this fundamental quality and to surpass it, and this is the path that we have chosen for the reconstruction of the party.

National Liberation

A second significant error on the part of the PKK was its definition of the nation and the national liberation struggle. Like a quasi-religious prayer, we had learned by heart that the path to becoming a nation was via a national liberation war. After all, both the classics of socialism and the examples of contemporary wars seemed to dictate this. Without becoming a nation, we could achieve neither freedom nor equality, and the path to being contemporary human beings would remain closed to us. The road to achieving this passed through a national liberation struggle fought with full force, a struggle that had three strategies: defense, equilibrium, and offensive. With this goal in front of us, we went everywhere: abroad, into the mountains, to prison, to the villages, to the towns. Because we approached our task with a dogmatism that has become integral to the people in the Middle East, we felt that we had to carry out a national liberation war. There was no other path to becoming a dignified nation. By this point, "war" had become a sacred concept. Fighting for national liberation was even more important to us than the concept of "jihad" is to Muslims. Clearly, just as in our approach to other phenomena, we had relapsed into the illness of dogmatism.

If we analyze the phenomenon of war, we can only conclude that it is a malady that should not be compatible with human society. Apart from mandatory self-defense, no form of war is acceptable. It is extortion and rapaciousness at its very essence. Irrespective of the ways in which its traits may be hidden behind masks, thievery, domination of others, and plunder are an inseparable part of its nature. War is based on the belief that conquest confers upon you every right. Therefore, war is the biggest disaster and the worst evil of human society. We had not fully grasped that war only makes sense if there is no other way to protect and ensure our existence, freedom, and dignity. What we understood by national liberation war involved conquering everything anew. It could easily go beyond legitimate self-defense and become a retaliation campaign and a mutual attempt at conquest. At the time, we did not worry about any of this. If we had thought more about the war of legitimate self-defense and distinguished between the theory, strategy, and tactics of such a war and all other kinds of war, we could undoubtedly have avoided many mistakes and losses, as well as much suffering. Investing all our hopes in winning a national liberation war had major drawbacks given the actual reality.

Given the international situation, the deployment and organization of forces, and factors like logistics, winning a foolhardy national liberation war would require luck. Because we failed to recognize this, we engaged in low-intensity warfare for more than fifteen years, which could maintain its existence after 1995 only by excessively repeating itself. It would be incorrect to argue that this war didn't produce anything positive, but it is still the case that conceiving of it as the only possible option and acting accordingly led to many senseless losses and to failing to gain the results we might have had if we tried other approaches. Our three-stage strategy was a typical example of dogmatism. Although a more realistically organized defensive war with support bases and tactics appropriate to the geographic conditions of Kurdistan and our relations with the people might not have led to a state, it could, nonetheless, have led to a coherent democratic solution.

Personally, I believed in the leading cadres in the country and thought they could achieve this. I was very supportive and made numerous sacrifices. But the same malady of power had emerged even more dangerously in the inlands where they were. The gang culture had reached a level of vileness and decay that cleared the way to easily eliminating even the most precious comrades. The decisive issues were not whether or not there were intentional provocateurs in our ranks, the treachery of collaborators or betrayal in our midst. The fact that the art of war was a dirty art in general and that in particular national liberation was understood dogmatically engendered such an outcome. The danger arose that all sorts of nationalism would be stirred up, that tendencies toward separatism and blind violence would increase and would, as a result, further deepen the social chaos.

If we had refrained from fetishizing the concept of "the nation" and instead defined it as a loose form of society and concentrated on the much more important point of living as a democratic, egalitarian, and free national community, we could have achieved results that would have demonstrated a greater understanding of reality. Possessing a unified nation and an all-encompassing state of our own should not have been seen as a nation's best, most beautiful, and most fitting ideal. In addition, the important thing was not being under the roof of a state but being democratic. That would have meant that the path to achieving our goal was not a war with any manner or method, but if war were to be necessary, only a defensive war would make sense. From that perspective, efforts toward a democratic society and the most varied kinds of organizing and solidarity that served that goal would have been possible, and we could have developed freedom and equality without falling into the nationalism of either the oppressor or the oppressed nation and without allowing for separatism or excessive violence. But a dogmatic approach based on an interpretation of the right of the people to self-determination prevented us from recognizing the numerous possible alternate solutions. It also prevented us from paving the road to the democratization of Turkey. The flames of oligarchic nationalism were fanned in a truly horrible way, and those doing so regarded this as a wonderful opportunity to profit both economically and politically.

If through our policies and actions we had proven how much of a strategic and indispensable element the Kurds were for the unity of the country and for the nation-state of Turkey, namely, as a free national community in a common homeland and under the roof of the same state, there might have been a positive solution for both sides. That this sort of rich path to a solution was never actually considered has to do with the understanding of the party, power, the state, the nation, and the war to achieve all these that I talked about above.

I hope I have largely overcome dogmatism, and in doing so have contributed more realistic dimensions to definitions of the state, power, war, the nation, and the nation-state today, thereby paving the way for a solution based on a renewed foundation of the party for a democratic society that is also open to a comprehensive and legitimate war of self-defense, if necessary. This is not just a strategic and tactical transformation. Behind it lies paradigmatic and theoretical considerations solidly rooted in a scientific mindset that enable richer political thought and a different approach to party building. Integral to this radical transformation is overcoming the malady of statism that has characterized socialism for 150 years, turning away from the bourgeois understanding of the nation, accepting the communal and democratic approach to sociality that has been seen throughout history as our fundamental reference point and, correspondingly, linking the ideal of freedom and equality to these radical shifts.

This critique and self-critique in the name of the PKK inevitably raises the question of the reconstruction of the party. We face burning problems and tasks that must be resolved urgently: a renewed foundation of the party based on a brief summary of the current situation, legitimate self-defense, and the foundation of a congress as a fundamental organizational form for the people.

Section C—The Questions in the Restructuring of the PKK

In the early 2000s, I had already said that the PKK's stagnation was primarily due to internal problems and that carrying on with the existing framework would not lead to a solution but would, on the contrary, prevent it. I suggested that it would, therefore, be better to dissolve the PKK and to continue to pursue its legacy under another name with a different framework. In my submissions to various courts, I evaluated the new situation, as well analyzing both history and the age we are in, to elucidate what the form and content of the possible new structures might look like. On the basis of these analyses the KADEK was founded, followed by the Kongra Gel. The extremely limited information I received in prison suggested that a sincere a self-critical examination of the past had taken place, and that as a result these new formations offered a way forward. At the same time, I tried to act in a sensitive manner during the İmralı process so as to contribute to the ceasefire that we had been trying to implement unilaterally since 1998 and if possible transform it into a permanent and meaningful armistice.[26] Through various letters and dialogues that represented an indirect continuation of the dialogue that began during my interrogation, I made proposals for a responsible course of action to both sides. Until the events of September 11, 2001, I did my best to remain hopeful of a solution. But, apparently, the leadership of Turkey regarded the US's new "anti-terror" offensive as a golden opportunity and bet on the option of annihilating us, ending the phase of indirect dialogue at that point.[27]

Meanwhile, the November 2002 parliamentary election came onto the agenda. Before determining the new orientation of the movement we wanted to see the election results. The AKP won an absolute majority, enabling it to govern alone. I wrote a letter to the AKP government and the new prime minister requesting that the Kurdish question be resolved through dialogue. Their response would determine our course of action. At least, I would be able to give clear responses to the expectations PKK members had in me. Even though I extended the deadline several times, I never received a response. Finally, I stated that our declaration for a "democracy and peace reconciliation" would end on September 1, 2003. After that, the KADEK was to decide for itself how to proceed. The KADEK announced a new initiative for November 1. Prior to this, I had suggested a unification of the Kongreya Neteweyî ya Kurdistanê (KNK: Kurdistan National Congress) and the KADEK so that there would not be two separate centers but instead the creation of a Kongra Gel. The proposal was well received, and, in autumn 2003, the Kongra Gel was founded.[28] But then, instead of the anticipated new initiative, there was a split.[29]

To be honest, I had not expected anything like this, but because I knew the organization and the cadres, it was not difficult for me to assess the situation. The cadres who had been members of the leading PKK group since its official founding proved unable to take on the necessary personal renewal and development, even though, in the direst of conditions, we always made theoretical and practical support available to them. Their training in the Middle East, together with the new possibilities and circumstances and the experiences they had gained were supposed to enable them to advance, but instead of undertaking the leap forward expected of them, their lack of clarity about their own intentions led them to scuttle all plans. The fact that they delayed offensives similar to that of August 15, 1984, and when they did implement them they did so in quite a different way than intended, steadily increased my concerns.

Since 1981, I had tried at numerous conferences, congresses, and educational meetings and with many instructive speeches to induce them to base their practice on the party line. I have also made harsh criticisms. More often than not, they chose to force me to take up their ways. They insisted on the modes of behavior I described earlier, when I tried to briefly explain how this behavior eventually led to the liquidation of the PKK.

The way that the split came about clearly shows that their self-critique of the early 2000s had not been sincere. Their new initiative for the people and the fighters was nothing more than irresponsible, ugly, and liquidationist wrangling (I am trying to avoid the word *treason* here) that in no way corresponded to history, society, companionship, the martyrs, our morals, or the crucial political developments. According to the press—my lawyers, for whatever reason, didn't deliver the expected explanations to me on time—these horrible developments were instigated in late 2003 and early 2004, and this ugly conduct was fueled and spread without me becoming aware of it. I should note that at the time I had been cut off from the outside world for extended periods.[30] I was subjected to an even greater isolation within the already imposed isolation. From the limited information available to me, I concluded that there were certain far-reaching calculations being made about me. They (I do not want to talk about a "faction") assumed that I did not have much control over developments, and that I was unlikely to get out of prison alive, so they had already written me off. They did, perhaps with the best of intentions, what the gangs had previously done within the guerrilla. But this time, they expanded into all areas: the political, military, and ideological realms, as well as the grassroots level.

I am not in a position to know the intentions and the true roles of the friends who took part in this process. I also consider this of relatively minor relevance. For me, it is obvious that these friends regard themselves as standing above the historical, social, ideological, political, and organizational line and its implementation.

They did not participate wholeheartedly in the existing organizations nor in the restructured ones, or muster the necessary intellectual power or willpower this requires. They have not participated with passion in the people's sacred cause for democracy, freedom and equality. They have either let themselves go and, thus, given in to objective defeat or have, with their extremely egocentric behavior, sacrificed or tied the cause to their personal whims. They have exploited the possibilities offered by the movement to puff themselves up. But, most of all, they have failed to understand the true value of my efforts in Turkey and the Middle East and, finally, throughout the İmralı process, and, thus, haven't acted accordingly. They haven't behaved like true comrades. They haven't understood that becoming a party requires devotion and self-sacrifice in the implementation. They have never really come to know the world of true politics, organization, and thought. And they have never appreciated the value of women and women's freedom.

Can there be any explanation other than that they consider my extraordinary efforts a weakness and have behaved accordingly? Can I still stand by idly while they, as they recently did, not only act against the party but also against the democratization efforts of the population? It is well known that our electoral potential in Turkey is certainly not less than 10 percent of the vote. The fact that the results stagnate at around 5 percent because of their machinations is less a quantitative than a qualitative problem. It proves that they have no interest in what democratization entails. Just as they didn't want to understand war or how to become a party, they now do not want to understand that with their unfounded impositions from the outside they leave the people—who came together with great effort—in the difficult situation of having to abandon the struggle. Even the ablest provocateurs could not have achieved what they did during the last municipal elections. Apparently, they really have internalized their role as little despots. I eventually grasped that some of these scoundrels were actually angry about my contributions to the democratization efforts of the people over the last six years, even when it meant neglecting my own legal defense.

It is known that there are one or two volumes of my speeches in which I have criticized and condemned Osman Öcalan. Before my mother died, I didn't phone her even once to ask how she was doing, because that might have harmed the people's cause. It is well known that I have been acting very responsibly and sensitively in terms of family cronyism. Nevertheless, recently there has been a slanderous campaign targeting me. Of course, there is more behind this than the usual behavior. It is not understandable that some of these wretches display the sort of crude behavior that even the state shies away from. There have even been incidents in which some of my sick family members have been treated badly that could be described as being terrorized. I cannot understand what the perpetrators expect to achieve by this. If this is about gaining more influence, the connection with me is clear. But, actually, I didn't criticize them because they became leaders but because they failed to become leaders! What then do they want revenge for? What was it that they wanted from me but failed to get?

Within a movement, there may be fools, idiots, scoundrels, conspirators, traitors, and provocateurs, just as there are heroes, sages, and honorable, honest, and dedicated people. But I absolutely don't understand what we have seen here recently. I think it is akin to political gangsterism. This wouldn't matter much if the effects were limited to these people themselves. But if these extend to military, political, and ideological issues, there will be extremely dangerous consequences. At the same time, these people are too dimwitted to realize that they are even stupider than Abu Jahl.[31] How can they approach the values that nurture their own honor, dignity and everything else? I don't intend to elaborate by providing a list of issues.

The most recent situation goes beyond factionalization, aberration, flight, or similar issues. We need another way to understand this situation. They denounce Osman to obfuscate the real situation. In my opinion, Osman is a donkey who has been ridden into a minefield. They are all allowing themselves to be used by others in the worst way, none of this has any other meaning. I also won't keep my opinion to myself about another matter. How can we explain that people like Cemil Bayık and Duran Kalkan were repeatedly unable to stop some of the most useless people from fleeing the organization, when all the while under their rule many honest people committed suicide, fled, or were arrested and punished by them merely because they had ignored orders? How long can the constant division that is causing people to flee and getting them killed go on? I will refrain from providing the names or elaborating on the actions of those they were responsible for bringing to the forefront. Do they not know how much damage they have done to us?

I don't intend to discuss the good intentions of these two friends and the sacrifices they have made in their own way. But how can they reconcile their consciences with the price of their actions done in the name of the people and thousands of values ? Can our political and organizational standards tolerate such things? If they have any concerns, however slight, for the development of the struggle and the war, do they think it can survive the negative impact of their actions? My point here is not the degree of anyone's responsibility. Political reason demands that we avoid such situations. What is meant by leadership is not only openly exposing such attempts with extraordinary foresight but making sure that they never actually materialize. Could this be the result of the oaths you have taken? How could engaging in consistent self-critique about political and organizational topics, as well as the actions undertaken, end in such developments? I'm not asking who is right and to what degree. No one who is not a provocateur, a scoundrel, or totally vacuous would tolerate such things, let alone become an instrument in such developments. Our movement, our people, and all the values we are fighting for deserve better. I want to remind the comrades and our friends and enemies once more that I have given my word before history, the people, and my comrades that I will never allow anything like this to happen on their behalf.

Given my circumstances, all that can be expected of me is that I draw my red lines very clearly. These red lines will above all else clearly determine what my opinion about party building, organization, action, and grassroots work is to the friends who have been following their own line in party building, war, and grassroots work for more than twenty years. Someone like me cannot be expected to capitulate to them. How can they dare do something that even the state has not dared to do? They should at least approach the matter with the same degree of seriousness as the state. Even if they see me as their enemy, they should at least show the seriousness that this requires. But if they, as they claim, want to be friends and comrades, given their age, they must at least fulfill the minimal requirements for this. I am sincerely ready to accept them as a tendency within the congress. And if they are in any way sincere, they should at least be able to take steps in a manner that allows them to live up to their tasks in the congress. An overwhelmingly awakened majority of our people want me to contribute to the cause to my last breath. If these people can't help in that process, I demand that they at least cease being an obstacle.

In conclusion, I respect the right of those who see themselves as a side in a conflict to organize themselves as a tendency. They can express themselves on ideological, political, military, and social issues and implement them. They can even found their own party. But the minimal precondition for this is that the statutes of the congress are respected. Everybody should respect the will of the congress and embrace their tasks in that spirit.

Of course, it follows that I too have the right and responsibility to continue on my own path. To retain my human dignity, I consider it necessary to make use of my right to free speech and to tackle my responsibility and, most of all, to enter the discussion about the reconstruction of the PKK based on intellectual foundations that I have been pondering for a long time. The best path to reconstruction would be for the existing tendencies to get to know themselves better, so they are in a position to reunite should the opportunity arise. Because of the high expectations of thousands of comrades, millions of our people, and the many thousands of martyrs have in me, I think this is the right attitude to adopt.

To repeat what I have said above, I want to ask these friends not to become inordinately emotional in the face of the problems but to prove themselves worthy of the people and of humanity through not only displaying wisdom but a true political, military, and organizational personality. It is never too late. Let us be successful in fulfilling the historical obligations of the moment. Unity and success through big truths and big deeds is more valuable than accidental achievements gained by fragmented attitudes and personalities in their thousands. Everyone, including those in the former gangs, should know that I regret the position they have slid into even more than they do. Even though our social reality imposes its cursed features, trust in people is essential. Moreover, if my friends, who have endured the most difficult circumstances for such a long time, really know and respect themselves, it is unthinkable that they won't be able to develop a political, organizational, and practical approach suitable to the situation. I hope that they will have much future success and declare that if they pursue the right path they can count on our support.

Kurdish-Turkish Relations

The key to resolving the Kurdish question lies in Kurdish-Turkish relations within Turkey. The Kurds in Iran, Iraq, and Syria only have a limited potential to achieve a durable solution on their own. That they can only play a secondary role in achieving a resolution, has been proven by the various phases of the Kurdish question in Iraq. The current Kurdish federal state is a formation that emerged in exchange for the US and its allies declaring the PKK "terrorist," at Turkey's behest. If Turkey hadn't accepted it, this solution would not have been possible. The result has been the endless chaos in which Iraq finds itself today, with the final outcome being entirely unpredictable. In this connection, the long-term course of the federal state of Kurdistan, with its feudal-bourgeois character and, in particular, its affect not only on Iraq but also on Iran, Turkey, and Syria, is unforeseeable. There is a danger that an Israel-Palestine-like conflict will develop and become more entrenched throughout the region. If a Kurdish nationalism is developed as an ideological derivative within the capitalist system, it could potentially amplify the region's Arab, Persian, and Turkish nationalisms, creating a deadlock that would prevent the resolution of problems. On the other hand, a solution that accepted the political borders as an established fact, would be based on the legal recognition of Kurdish status accompanied by a deep commitment to cultural freedom and democratization. This distinctive approach to a solution could find its place on the agenda as a fresh non-nationalist model for a solution. Since this could be realized peacefully, while respecting the integrity of the states and nations of the countries involved, it is more compatible with historical and social realities. A comprehensive presentation of the bases and consequences of both approaches to a solution would contribute to our understanding of probable developments in the near future.

The history of Turks and their relations with the Kurds and the Greater Middle East Initiative that the US dusted off and put back on the agenda compels the Republic of Turkey to adopt a more practical approach to the reality of the Kurds and their relationship with the Turks. In this context, the historical dimension of Kurdish-Turkish relations also gains importance. We can now clearly see that the denial policies of the recent past are giving out distress signals. If, hereafter, we want to avoid experiencing a Kurdish-Turkish tragedy similar to the Israel-Palestine tragedy, then we must approach the problem with a historical and social perspective in a creative and democratic manner. However, despite some recent token statements about democratization, the practice of denial still binds together the entire system of the state and society—everyone from the right to the left—and not only in terms of discourse but also intrinsically. This gives rise to a tremendous concern and an atmosphere in which even bigger conflicts might once again arise. Based on our experience, it is of great importance that we offer ideas and suggestions so that these concerns can be convincingly dispelled, leading to an atmosphere that promises a genuine solution.

First Contacts

Between 9000 and 7000 BCE, some of the South Siberian tribes, among them proto-Turkish tribes, moved south into today's China, Korea, Japan, Mongolia, and Central Asia, as well as going further west. Others migrated across the Bering Straits that connected Asia to the American continent. There is convincing scientific evidence for this migration, including the results of etymological and genetic investigations. At the same time, the Neolithic Revolution reached the coast of the Pacific and the South China Sea. It is assumed that the productiveness of the Neolithic revolution set these tribes in motion. The long-term population increase that accompanied this new system was a causal factor for this ongoing migration.

The first known urban civilizations in China emerged in the third century BCE. The Yellow River played the same role as the Nile, the Euphrates, the Tigris, and the Punjab did elsewhere in these tribes creating civilizations.

As civilization developed along the Yellow River, the attacks by the tribes in the surrounding area likely became a chronic threat. Indeed, the first written Chinese sources, from the third century BCE, report attacks by the Uighurs, a tribe from the surrounding area that is generally regarded as the ancestor of the Turks. The official chronology of Turkish historiography begins with Metehan, in 209 BCE.[32] A number of sources document a major migration of proto-Turks to the south: to China, Afghanistan, and India, as well as to the west, today's Kazakhstan, and from there to Europe. For the most part, these people are now concentrated in today's Kyrgyzstan, Kazakhstan, Uzbekistan, Turkmenistan, and the autonomous Uighur region of Xinjiang, in China.

The fourth century CE saw a major migration of the Huns to Europe, when many of those migrating were unable to make it to China and changed course. Apart from this expansion north of the Caspian and the Black Seas, there was an increase in the expansion to the Aral Lake region and south of the Caspian Sea in the direction of Afghanistan. Population increase and droughts accelerated migration, and in the sixth century this pattern of migration exerted pressure on the Iranian border. This kind of pressure goes back to the times of the Persian Safavid Empire. The stories about Afrasiab and Turan date from this time.[33]

With the expansion of Islam into Central Asia toward the end of the seventh century, a new stage in the history of the Turks began. Since the Göktürk states and the later Uighur state were more like confederations, it can be assumed that they lacked the experience of a strong centralized state. At that point, there had not been a centralized state in Central Asia for long durations. The confederations that emerged under the influence of China and India never lasted for more than one or two generations. Even the world empire of the Mongols only endured for about half a century.

The Turks adopted Islam for political rather than religious reasons. Had they not converted to Islam, they would not have been able to continue with their traditional pattern of migration. Their increasing Islamization beginning in the ninth century further accelerated with their first political formations. After the princedom of the Karahan, the earliest state of the Turkish tribal aristocracy emerged with the first Seljuk princedom in Merv, in today's Turkmenistan. The victory in the Battle of Dandanaqan, near Merv, in 1040 CE, led to the foundation of a Seljuk dynasty in the Iranian state tradition. After the Islamic caliph in Baghdad declared the Seljuk prince the sultan, the dynasty's borders expanded from the Mediterranean to Afghanistan.

It was at this point that, for the first time, the Turkish migratory tribes saw the far-reaching emergence of feudal class division. While the aristocrats became the state and founded a large number of princedoms that spread to the Middle East, most Turkmens, who were the poorer part of the population, continued their independent migratory life at the bottom. The tenth to the fifteenth centuries saw the intertwined development of urbanization and class divisions within the growing Turkish population in the Middle East, on the one hand, and of the state, on the other hand. After the sultanate of the Great Seljuks, which lasted for about a hundred years, they founded princedoms called *beylik* and *atabek* in its place. Among them, the princedoms in Anatolia unified and established the Anatolian Seljuk state, with Konya as its capital. As a result, in 1076, the first Islamic state in Anatolia was founded.

Around two hundred years later, in 1308, the Ottoman princedom emerged further to the west on the foundations of the Byzantine Empire. Later on, this became the largest feudal center, the empire of the Turkish Ottoman dynasty. This empire ended up in a position to defend the East against the West in the era of capitalism's development and rise. The nineteenth and twentieth centuries saw the development of Turkish bourgeois nationalism. In 1839, the Tanzimat reforms were introduced. These were followed by the first and second constitutional reforms, in 1876 and 1908 respectively. Later, with the war of national liberation in 1920, Turks exited the ruins of World War I and founded a state. Thus the era of the Turkish nation-state had begun. This republican era was a historical phase during which the Turks took an enduring form as a nation in Anatolia and made the transformation from a feudal society system to a capitalist society system. This approximately millennium-long Middle East adventure allowed the Turks to consolidate and build a state, primarily in Anatolia, while transforming themselves from tribes into the nation of Turkey. Their relationship with the Kurds played a strategic role in all of this.

Relations between Kurds and Turks can be traced back to the legendary discourses of Zoroaster and Turan. The military campaigns of the Persian-Median Empire against the pro-Turkish provinces brought a legendary dimension to the relations with the Scythes. At the time of the Parthians and the Sasanians, the Turkish tribes, primarily concentrated in the Khorasan province in the northeast of Iran, forged relations with the Kurds who had also migrated to the area for various reasons. But the significant contact took place during the rule of the Great Seljuk sultans. From the tenth to the fifteenth centuries, Turkish and Kurdish tribes lived side by side in today's Iraq, Azerbaijan, Armenia, and Mesopotamia, with a complex web of relationships and contradictions.

After the Great Seljuks, many Turkish princedoms, including the Aq Qoyunlu, the Kara Koyunlu, the Artuqids, and the Atabeqs of Mosul, lived side by side with the Kurdish princedoms. The shared Islamic religion, the fact that they faced the Christian states of Byzantium and Armenia, and the later crusades played a strategic role in all of this. Sultan Sancar, the last great Seljuk sultan, used the word *Kurdistan* to refer to an administrative unit in 1155.

Historians agree that the Kurds supplied the second largest army in the victory of the Battle of Manzikert, in which Sultan Alp Arslan defeated the Byzantine emperor Romanus, a victory that definitively cleared

Arslan's path to Anatolia. On May 15, 1071, before the battle, Alp Arslan went to Silvan, then the capital of the Kurdish Marwanid state, and, in addition to the almost ten thousand ready forces, he gathered an equal number of tribal forces. What does this tell us? Without the support of the Kurdish political formations, Turkish existence in Anatolia would have been impossible, or, if possible, it would not have avoided very serious threats. We must remember that whatever equilibrium a society is founded on, it will continue to exist by relying on that equilibrium into the future. Whenever this balance is disturbed, it will face ongoing serious threats to its existence until a new equilibrium is established.

Beginning in 1071, there were two different dimensions to the relationship between Kurds and Turks. First, the political and state dimension, meaning the relations and contradictions between the Kurdish and the Turkish princedoms. Those relations and contradictions began around 1050 and continued until the collapse of the Anatolian Seljuks in 1308. The second dimension concerned the social and cultural realm. The tribes intermingled and underwent a natural assimilation, primarily into Kurdish sociality and culture. It was a peaceful and culturally enriching period. With the founding of the republic, the result of intense Turkish nationalist political pressure, a period of forced assimilation of the Kurds into the Turkish nation began. Kurds experienced tremendous social dissolution in the face of the political, social, economic, military, educational, and artistic policies implemented during this period.

The Strategic Alliance

The second phase of Kurdish-Turkish relations began in the sixteenth century as a strategic political relationship, when, during the rule of Sultan Selim I, the Ottoman Empire turned to the East. To be able to cope with the Safavid Empire in Iran and the Mamluks in Egypt, Sultan Selim needed the firm support of the Kurdish princedoms, which were in a strategically important position. Historians report that he sent baskets full of gold and blank sheets of paper bearing his signature to create an alliance. He concluded separate alliances with twenty-three Kurdish princedoms. Selim would have preferred for all Kurdish princedoms to unite under a *beylerbeylik*—a primary Ottoman administrative division—but internal contradictions made this impossible, so he appointed a *beylerbey*—a lord of lords—based in Diyarbakır. This relationship and the participation of all of the Kurdish princes guaranteed Selim I victory against the Safavids at the

Battle of Chaldiran, near Van, in 1514, and the Battle of Marj Dabiq, north of the Syrian town of Aleppo, in 1516, as well as against the Mamluks at the Battle of Ridaniya, in Egypt, in 1517, thereby establishing the largest empire in the Middle East. Without this strategic relationship not only would the victories over the Iranian and the Egyptian states have been unlikely, but it would, in fact, have been almost impossible for him to have moved an inch beyond central Anatolia. Had the Iranian and Egyptian states allied with the Kurdish princedoms instead of choosing confrontation, that might well have spelled the end of the Ottoman state. Indeed, in 1402, the Turkmen sultan Timur the Lame delivered a crushing defeat to the Ottoman state in the Battle of Ankara, because he had nurtured exactly these relations.

Until the beginning of the nineteenth century, the Kurds always maintained privileged relations with the Ottoman sultans. The Kurdish princedoms in which many local governments, principalities, and *sanjaks*—districts—had a privileged system in place, with power transferred from father to son. This privilege was not granted to any other group of subordinates within the Ottoman Empire. They enjoyed complete autonomy in terms of their domestic affairs, and any limitations regarding language, cultural existence, or the arts were simply unthinkable. Kurdish language and culture produced much of its literary work during this period, for example, the epic Mem û Zîn. The social and cultural superiority of the Kurds remained a reality at the time. They sent the Sultan gifts or participated in his military expeditions only if the Sultan asked and of their own free will. The Sunni Kurdish princedoms had good relationships with the sultanate. These Kurdish princedoms, whose relations with the state remain good today, were, largely part of the Naqshbandi tariqa system. On the other hand, the Alevi Kurds, who wanted to defend their cultural autonomy, turned to the Shiite Iranian-Safavid state. This, but even more so their strong devotion to their freedom, made them a permanent target of the Ottomans. During the rule of Selim I, who was called "Selim the Grim" because of his cruelty, his general Murat Pasha, also known as "Murat the Well-Digger," had forty thousand Alevi thrown into wells, in the hope of destroying a strategic threat root and branch.

The beginning of the nineteenth century marked a new stage in Kurdish-Turkish relations. The growing demand of the Ottomans—who were being pushed into a corner by the West—for taxes and soldiers led to a radical course of action against the Kurds. The result was a period of bloody uprisings led by the Kurdish princes, who had a significant amount

BEYOND STATE, POWER, AND VIOLENCE

of autonomy. The first of these uprisings started with the Baban principality's uprising in Süleymaniye, in 1806.

The uprisings continued in 1878, this time under the leadership of the sheikhs. With the suppression of the uprisings led by Sheikh Said in 1925 and Seyid Rıza in 1937, this stage ended in defeat. At no point had all Kurds participated in any of these uprisings. They all began as local uprisings, and none sparked a national uprising. The feudal structure proved to be an obstacle to such a development. Nonetheless, the uprisings led by Prince Bedirhan in 1846 and by Mahmud Barzanji in 1923 might have been successful if the British had not supported the respective ruling states. Today the leadership of Barzani and Talabani, the most recent representatives of this line, have roots in both sheikh leadership and tribal chiefdoms. The fact that they underwent a bourgeois transformation and enjoy the strategic support by the Western countries provides them with a final highly risk-fraught opening.

During this long political phase from 1071 to the end of the Ottoman Empire, Kurdish-Turkish relations essentially consisted of a strategic alliance based on mutual needs. If they abandoned this relationship, a strategic loss for both sides was inevitable. With the Ottomans wedged into Istanbul and Central Anatolia, the Kurdish princedoms would have lost most of their existing autonomy and ceased to represent a meaningful political and social force. Thus, this strategic alliance has a strong historical and social foundation.

No social or cultural relations were prohibited; in that sense the atmosphere was free in a way unimaginable today. The forced dissolution of ethnic groups is the result of biopower policies of the capitalist age.[34] Even though we rightfully reject feudal regimes today, they were not a source of cultural assimilation, which would have been considered unethical. This is reflected in all forms of political organization in the Middle Ages. The dissolution and annihilation of peoples' languages and cultures is an immoral practice of the capitalist system, facilitated by capitalism's lack of ethics. This is why, prior to the influence of capitalism, Turks did not interfere with the linguistic, religious, and cultural life of any people.

As soon as the nationalist ideology of capitalism was adopted, the devious policy of forced dissolution began. Natural assimilation, however, has always led to an enrichment on the basis of a mutual synthesis of cultures. In terms of respect for the religion, language, and culture of others, the Ottoman Empire was more advanced, free, and humane than any Arab,

Persian, or Turkish nationalist state today. It would, therefore, be a major error and distortion to think of capitalism as superior to and more liberating than the Middle Ages in every way. On this issue, capitalism is actually modern barbarism.

Capitalism in Turkey

There were several phases to the process of becoming capitalist and bourgeoisification in Turkey. The Ottoman Empire, with its centralized feudalism, was perhaps one of the last of the great precapitalist civilizations in history. It was a regime that fiercely resisted the transition to capitalism, thereby slowing capitalist development in the Middle East for several centuries. As a consequence, the Middle East was not completely colonized; it retained its Islamic identity, and the worsening problems of modernization were held at bay until the present. Now, however, problems are escalating, with no solution in sight.

The Greek, Armenian, and Aramean bourgeoisification and adoption of capitalism occurred more easily because of their Christian identity. This also led to an early nationalism, which, given the extreme power imbalance at the time, quickly resulted in conflict and, finally, in their liquidation. The real cause of this process must be sought in capitalism's propensity for profit and accumulation.

At the end of the nineteenth century, the İttihat ve Terakki Cemiyeti (İTC: Committee of Union and Progress) began the actual state capitalist transformation.[35] Using its Pan-Islamist identity, this party first tried to force this transformation on all Muslim subjects of the empire, but because of the growing nationalism among the different Muslim peoples they failed, which only served to accelerate the disintegration of the empire.

We can divide the capitalist transformation in the era of the republic that rose on the ruins of the Ottoman Empire into three phases. The first phase primarily focused on building the necessary superstructure and developing the mentality of capitalism. Mustafa Kemal Atatürk's republic and all its institutions were inspired by the French Revolution and based on what was fundamentally a Western mentality. Although quite belatedly, he attempted to use revolutionary methods to jumpstart a process of Renaissance, Reformation, and Enlightenment. While the attempt to very rapidly replicate a development that had taken several centuries in Europe and to do so within a narrow nationalist framework produced significant results, it did not succeed in creating a revolutionary bourgeoisie. This first phase basically resulted in a bureaucratic capitalism largely concentrated in the hands of the state. Until the 1950s, this bureaucratic and collective state capitalism continued to develop, but when faced with the balance of power between the East and the West it turned toward the West and, as a result, went through a phase dominated by private capitalism.

In this second phase, the era of the Demokrat Parti, private capitalism gained momentum. The military coup of May 27, 1960, was an attempt to restrain this monopolistic private capitalism, which initially developed in some of the big cities, primarily Istanbul, İzmir, and Adana. This coup was basically a product of the contradiction between state capitalism and private capitalist transformation. Even though the transition from authoritarian state capitalism to oligarchic private capitalism was painful and conflicted, it continued to accelerate. During the era of the Demokrat Parti, it was primarily exponents of trade and agrarian capitalism who were represented in the oligarchy, while the industrial sector dominated during the rule of the Adalet Partisi, from 1960 to 1980. Then the financial capital sector grew much more powerful from 1980 to 2000, under the governments dominated by the ANAP. Within the state, the influence of the army increased and civil forces gradually grew weaker. From 1995 to 2000, the Kurdish upper class, which had been suppressed during the first phase of the republic, secured its place within the oligarchy, albeit through quite varied and different groups, and then sought to defend it. Those who best proved their loyalty to state ideology could count on special privileges.

While the ideology of the first two phases was primarily characterized by nationalism, beginning in the 1950s, the Turkish-Islamic synthesis, chauvinist-fascist circles, and tariqa-type Islamism gradually gained influence within the state. While the national consciousness during the times of Mustafa Kemal Atatürk and İsmet Inönü was primarily fueled by Western culture, after 1950, due to the anticommunist policies of the US, it relied increasingly on nationalism, fascism, and reactionary religious ideologies. The Kurdish upper class could only survive by transforming itself into a tool for mediating this intense denial and assimilation.

At that time, the classes excluded from both state and private capitalism were unable to overcome their traditional resignation to fate. A push for democracy could not be developed. The classic left-wing attempts were crushed without gaining much resonance among the people. After the Kurdish uprisings, the cultural erosion of the Kurdish people accelerated to a point where Kurds almost ceased to be themselves. The PKK was the most pronounced reaction to this development. But it would be too narrow to regard the PKK as nothing but a Kurdish movement. Essentially, it emerged as a countermovement against all statist, political, and ideological forces in Turkey and the other parts of Kurdistan.

We can characterize the third phase of capitalism in Turkey primarily as "Anatolian capitalism." It was distinguished by the development of small and medium-size enterprises and medium-size capital. One could also speak of an "Anatolian capitalist revolution." This is a third-generation Turkish way of becoming capitalist. The first generation was a bureaucratic collective Turkish capitalism, the second generation was the monopolist private capitalism in the big cities, and, finally, with the generation of Turkish "Anatolian capitalism," the system is complete. The AKP aspired to be the main boss of this Anatolian capitalism. Even though Anatolian capital also developed during the time of the DP, AP, and ANAP-RP, it is trying to consolidate itself as the true master of the political center through the AKP, acting as an independent political movement. In the process, it is also making a considerable effort to integrate the developing Kurdish bourgeoisie into the overall scheme.

The Era of the Republic
The most critical phase of Kurdish-Turkish relations began during the republican era. The traditional Islamic ideology was replaced by nationalism as the mindset for relations. Turkish nationalism was fed by two external sources: first, the historical and social knowledge acquired from the intellectuals among the Kazan Turks, who were subjected to the repression of Czarist Russia, via Europe. They, for the first time, tried to show that there was a Turkish history outside the history of the Ottoman dynasty. The second source was the German Empire, which was a latecomer in the colonization process. Germany wanted to use the Turkish communities to expand east toward Central Asia, and, therefore, tried to entice both Pan-Islamist and Pan-Turkish currents, including supporting their respective doctrines. The idea was to use both of these ideological currents to foster Islamist and Turkish chauvinist uprisings against Czarist Russia to create opportunities for expansion. Beginning in the 1880s, Germany dislodged England and France from their place at the side of the Ottoman Empire and continuously expanded its influence. As a result, the defeat of Germany in World War I also destroyed the Ottoman Empire.

Feeding on German and expatriate Turkish sources and inspired by German nationalism, the nationalism of the İttihat ve Terakkiperver Fırkası (İTF: Party of Unity and Progress) had a racist character. At that time, German historians pursued and held in high esteem ideas like "purity of race." The İttihadist nationalism aimed to rally the whole Turkish world around a similar racist nationalist flag, clearly befitting the intended route of German expansionism. The fact that this approach was detached from historical and social reality would later cost the Ottoman Empire dearly.

The nationalism of the movement led by Mustafa Kemal Atatürk, who led a national liberation war, founding the Republic of Turkey on the ruins of the empire, had a different orientation. We can describe his nationalism, which referred back to the cultures and civilizations of Anatolia, beginning with the Sumerians and the Hittites, as cultural nationalism or Anatolian patriotism. Mustafa Kemal Atatürk understood the difference between these nationalist concepts. He openly rejected the frequent suggestion to call the newly founded republic Türk Cumhuriyeti, i.e., Turkish Republic, or Republic of the Turks, preferring the name Türkiye Cumhuriyeti, that is, Republic of Turkey—a name that refers to the *country* and not to any race or ethnic group. Nationalism or patriotism of this sort cannot be called racist.

But some intellectuals in the tradition of the İttihat continued and elaborated upon the racist discourse. Most extremely, the nationalism of Nihal Atsız ominously pointed to the Jewish *dönme* and the *devşirme* from among other peoples,[36] defining them as the most dangerous groups, alleging that they had undermined the state and Turkishness during both the Ottoman and the republican eras.[37] This position was advocated by the Millet Partisi (MP: Nation Party), founded in 1948, and, since 1960, has been the position of the Milliyetçi Hareket Partisi (MHP: Nationalist Movement Party).

Anatolian nationalism, for its part, was first very rigid within the Cumhuriyet Halk Fırkası (CHF: People's Party),[38] and, since 1960, although accompanied by a social democratic discourse, has not lost its essence or undergone any transformation. Nationalist ideology continues to be used to various degrees by all left, right, and Islamic parties. As capitalism developed in Turkey, nationalism continued to develop and spread from the state to the society to become a prevalent mentality, even replacing the dynastic mindset within the Turkish patriarchy.

Turkish nationalism has, in fact, taken on a highly patriarchal character. Being a backward capitalist country played a clear role in this development. Of equal importance, Islamic ideology was never entirely abandoned. For example, the Office for Religious Affairs was established as a ministry during the republican era. The Office exercises control over Islam, Sunni Islam in particular, and works to control society, using an alleged laicism. This laicisim is not a sociological phenomenon but is part of the official state ideology. In a way, this ensures that religion becomes compatible with modernism in a controlled manner. Other ideological variations of the republican era are represented by the not so well developed statist (all left- and right-wing parties of the Republic of Turkey are statist) liberal and socialist currents. Alongside this, there are the Islamic tariqat, whose sociological character is more closed and semisecret. Mustafa Kemal Atatürk made a great personal effort to give the republic's ideology a firm scientific base, but he was not particularly successful. The end result was a blurry mix of left- and right-wing capitalist discourses of doubtful scientific value, intertwined with the feudal Islamist tradition.

The military and political foundation of the republic was based on an interesting balance of power, both internally and externally. Externally it found support from the still lively backdrop of the Bolshevik Revolution of 1917, the first revolution against capitalism. Internally, Mustafa Kemal Atatürk united the Kurdish and Turkish popular masses, who feared a complete fragmentation and annihilation at the hands of the victorious powers led by England, behind the Misak-ı Millî (National Pact) strategy.[39] In this way, Kemal Atatürk organized the liberation movement both on the local and the national levels. Using these external and internal balances of power he achieved both a political and military victory. He put an end to the sultanate and the caliphate, and adopted the French Republic as his model. This was clearly a serious political revolution. Smashing a state structure based on dynasties and religion, with roots reaching back thousands of years, and declaring a republic was a serious revolutionary step and an unprecedented event in an underdeveloped and occupied country.

From the 1920s to 1945, the republic developed by taking advantage of the struggle between the capitalist and socialist systems. When capitalism, under the leadership of the US, gained predominance after 1945, Turkey adapted to these external developments and tried first to militarily integrate into NATO and then economically, socially, and politically into the system in general, a process that accelerated during the DP's rule.

The political development from authoritarian republicanism to an oligarchic republic was accompanied by the development of industrial and financial capitalism. With the global neoliberal offensive that took place around the world after 1980, it reached a new stage as a result of external dynamics and a departure from the nation-state model. Subsequently, Turkey was entirely drawn into the chaotic period of the world capitalist system under the leadership of the US in the aftermath of the Soviet dissolution. Integration into the system seems to be complete in the military, economic, political, media, and cultural areas. Previously Turkey played the role in NATO's anti-Soviet section. Now it is a frontline state in the Greater Middle East Initiative and must once again confront its historical and social foundations "on the basis of the clash of civilizations theory," as it tries to emerge from the chaos with a new structure by revitalizing its relationships and contradictions.

Kurdish-Turkish relations can be divided into three phases in connection with the developments in the republican era.

1920–1940
The first phase lasted from the war of national liberation until 1940. When the national liberation phase began, the main body of Kurdish society was still under the spell of the classic understanding of the umma and loyal to state culture. There was a joint reflex of resistance among Kurds and Turks against English and French occupation in the south. The resistance in Urfa, Antep, and Maraş is a typical example of this joint resistance, the continuation of a historical tradition. Both felt connected to the other religiously and nationally in terms of kavim.

Nationalist ideology was not openly articulated during the war of liberation.[40] Based on a certain understanding of the umma, the Islamic brotherhood played a more prominent role. When parliament, the Türkiye Büyük Millet Meclisi (TBMM: Grand National Assembly of Turkey) convened in 1920, it was regarded as the common assembly of both peoples. The Kurdish deputies were officially called People's Representatives of Kurdistan. There was no national (kavim) contradiction between the two peoples. In this spirit of fellowship, there was even an attempt to end the Kurdish Koçgiri rebellion that erupted during that period.

The strategic role of the Kurds in founding and proclaiming the republic was at least as clear and pronounced as their role in the strategic victories at Malazgirt in 1071, Çaldıran in 1514, and Mercidabık in 1516. The strategic and tactical thinking of Mustafa Kemal Atatürk played a decisive role in this. In his view, a division between Kurds and Turks and especially hostility between them would lead to catastrophic consequences for both. Thus, he argued that both people had to act together. Apart from a few limited provocations, the Kurds reacted positively to this call, both the population at large and the aristocratic upper class. However, various factors led to a deterioration of the situation by 1925. First, it became clear that the republic would be based on Turkish nationalism, that the abolition of the caliphate and the sultanate were permanent, and that the umma would, therefore, not be returning. Second, Kurdish collaborators lost their former privileges, and it became increasingly clear with every passing day that there would be no place for them as Kurds in the Turkish nation-state. Third, there was incitement from various sides, be it from the English because of the Mosul-Kirkuk question or from remnants of the Ottoman dynasty around the idea of a return of the sultanate and caliphate. In the case of the uprisings, the Kürt Teali Cemiyetleri (Society for the Rise of Kurdistan) founded by some Kurdish intellectuals played a part. After the second constitutional period, at the end of the nineteenth century, a primitive Kurdish nationalism emerged that led to the founding of several associations and journals; the hope was to win a few reforms in support of the Kurds.

Objectively, these uprisings could be understood as a continuation of the internal uprisings in the conflict between the understanding of the umma, based on the feudal remnants of the Ottoman Empire, and the republican version of Turkish nationalism—the Aznavur and the Yozgat uprisings are examples.[41] The conflict between Ottomanism and republicanism was projected in this manner onto the Kurds lasting until around 1940.

The Kurdish uprisings of the time can also be divided into three phases. The first was the uprising led by Sheikh Said, which broke out in 1925 in the region of Hani and Genç. It continued until 1928 as a local conflict. It was strongly influenced by the late Ottoman understanding of umma, and the influence of the Sunni Naqshbandi tariqa was evident. The loss of privileges from the Ottoman period also played a role. Rather than making the establishment of Kurdistan their goal, the stronger objective was the return of the Ottoman caliphate and sultanate. There was a clear tendency to strive for a state based on religious belief. Because its leading members were arrested, the Azadi Cemiyeti (Freedom Society) founded by Kurdish intellectuals under the leadership of Xalîd Beg Cibranî in 1924 was unable to play a vanguard role. The British influence, for its part, was indirect. The British used the uprising as a trump card in an extortionist manner during negotiations in Lausanne, telling the Kemalists they would support the Kurdish rebellion unless the Kemalists withdraw from the cities of Mosul and Kirkuk, in today's Iraq. This was an important factor in the deterioration of Kurdish-Turkish relations, even though Mustafa Kemal Atatürk had declared only shortly before, in early 1924, that he recognized the problem of Kurdish freedom and had said at a press conference in İzmit later that year that efforts were being made to find a solution.

The uprising destroyed any possible attempt at a solution. From this point on, the tendency toward a complete liquidation and assimilation of the Kurds prevailed. Mustafa Kemal Atatürk saw a serious danger that the caliph, the British, and the advocates of the umma would use this uprising to pool their efforts to abolish the republic. This was the main reason for his very violent suppression of the uprising. Rather than seeing it as an expression of the Kurdish question, he saw it as an attempt to destroy the republic and replace it with a sultanate collaborating with imperialism. All the uprisings that followed was seen through the prism of this perceived threat, a mindset that has continued until today, acquiring an almost paranoid quality along the way.

This was the most fundamental rupture in the history of the republic in terms of the negative approach toward the Kurds, whereas the Kurds were a primary constituent in the founding of the republic. That this deep-seated rupture led to exaggerated and aberrant repression has much to do with the perception of threat described above, which was turned into a political line aimed at making it impossible for the Kurds to breath. Even when seeking their basic rights, Kurds were silenced to the point that they could not even say who they were. The role of the British was extremely destructive, in that it provoked both sides. The same was true of the other big Western states, which played a decisive role in the liquidation of the Armenians and the Arameans. Had it not been for the interventions of those powers, the catastrophes these people suffered would have been unthinkable.

The uprising of the second phase was the Ararat uprising of 1928–1932, under the leadership of Ihsan Nuri Pasha, with the organization of intellectuals, the Xoybûn, jointly founded by Armenians and Kurds in 1928, exercising ideological influence over the movement. This uprising was triggered by factors similar to those that had sparked the previous uprising, but it had a more nationalist character. However, it failed to develop beyond the local level.

The third phase was the Dersim uprising. The Dersim region had largely been able to preserve its freedom until that point. The central authority of the republic was seen as an end to this freedom. While there had always been uprisings of varying magnitudes in the region, the final uprising in 1937–1938 represented a climax with effects that continue until today. The region is distinguished by its Kurdish Alawi tradition. Kurds in this region had not joined the Sheikh Said uprising in 1925, because it was a Sunni Naqshbandi uprising. This is a fundamental division between Kurds. Because of the Hatay problem, in 1936, the French began to exert an influence similar that exerted by the English in 1925,[42] one of the factors that contributed to the brutal suppression of the Dersim uprising.

Mustafa Kemal Atatürk and İsmet İnönü were well aware that the problem of the uprisings could not be solved by military suppression alone. In his memoirs, İnönü writes that executions in particular went too far. They fully understood that this had seriously hurt the republic. Nevertheless, they opted for a cover-up rather than a genuine solution. At any rate, it was unthinkable that the nationalism of the dominant nation's state, a form of nationalism that had just reached its climax around the world, would allow for any other solution. Moreover, the pain of the losses engendered by the demise of the empire lingered in the background, and it seemed that the only remaining option was simply to swallow the Kurds and Kurdistan whole, even though this exact approach had been one of the main reasons for the downfall of the Ottoman Empire. Great Britain, for its part, reacted with liberal solutions to the loss of its empire and has, therefore, been able to maintain its influence around the world to this day. We can see the uprisings and their suppression as two historically mistaken actions that mutually promoted and provoked each other because of their ideological character and class structure. The most important factor was undoubtedly the framework of the capitalist system, which produces nationalism, fascism, and colonialism.

1940–1970

The second phase of Kurdish-Turkish relations during the republic was the phase of the great silence from 1940 to 1970. Under the difficult conditions of World War II, one could hardly expect any movement. But under the rule of the DP, things developed in a different direction. When the aristocracy regained power, with the takeover of the government by the DP, the Kurdish nobility was not forgotten. The Kurdish feudal, religious, and tribal leaders offered a great opportunity to organize an intense reaction against the CHP. The DP used this potential as an important force to create and develop the oligarchy. The Kurdish upper class was all too willing to shed its Kurdish character to take their place within the state. To rid themselves of the scourge of Kurdishness and become a good example of Turkishness suited their historical character perfectly. Contrary to similar examples in other countries, they did not even play the role of bearers of the Kurdish language and culture. Since the time of the Sumerians, it has practically become second nature for them to live using the language and culture of the dominant ruling power of the day. Even their role in the various uprisings, was never anything but a trump card that allowed them to expand their share of power through blackmail.

Apart from a few weak intellectual voices, in this phase, there was no activity on the part of the Kurds. There was only indirect influence from the Kurdish uprising in Iraqi Kurdistan, as well as from some Kurdish radio programs broadcasting from abroad.[43] Without them, the Kurds would have scarcely been aware of themselves. On the other hand, the state pursued an intense assimilation policy, with the maxim "Citizens, speak Turkish!" that reached the level of thinly veiled threats. It was impossible to publish even a single Kurdish newspaper, magazine, or book. It was presumed that this would be enough to have the issue resolve itself by simply fading away. In the 1970s, this policy eventually backfired. Nonetheless, examining all these policies with all of their subtleties at some point would doubtless prove enormously enlightening.

1970 to Today

The third phase, which continues to this day, began with the youth movement of 1968. The influence of the movement of '68 on Kurdish youth came primarily through the Turkish left. At that time, the Marxist position on the national question was intensely discussed. At the end of the 1960s, Kurdish intellectuals and youth created the Devrimci Doğu Kültür Ocakları (DDKO: Revolutionary Eastern Culture Centers), which later split into different factions that proved influential. The PKK emerged stronger from the intense ideological struggle between 1970 and 1980 and left its mark on the later developments throughout Kurdistan with the breakthrough that August 15, 1984, constituted. For the first time, there was an attempt to develop a Kurdish freedom movement based on the ideological and political perspective of working-class Kurds. This movement continues to act effectively, both in terms of the problems that it has raised and the solutions that it has proposed.

Section D—Reform and Social Transformation in Turkey
This short summary of Kurdish-Turkish relations in the era of the republic exposes what lies behind the fundamental stagnation and introverted nature of the state and society. The state, for its part, sees all social problems as security issues. For a better understanding of how such a situation came about it would be useful to conduct a more detailed evaluation under the heading "Turks and the State."

Since their departure from Central Asia, the Turks have fully understood that they can only protect themselves by being warriors. Furthermore, they have also led a life of constant tribal conflict among themselves. In every step the Turks took toward the Middle East, they needed to find allies and fight foes. This was necessary if they were to make any headway, or even to retreat, and any progress was determined by the laws of war. War seemed to be the only way to assert your existence, because the Middle East is one of the key areas that has been ruled by war and power since the Sumerian era. To control even an inch of land required war and power. When the Turkish tribes advanced into this region for the first time, this law proved more severe than ever before. The war-based expansion of the Seljuks differed from the previous, more limited tribal social migrations. Beginning with the Seljuks, the Turkish tribes were advancing by becoming a state. This is how they advanced from Merv, where they first intensified their political and military power, to the most western outpost, the Székesfehérvár castle in Hungary. Retreating was also only possible through warfare. During every retreat from the second siege of Vienna in 1683 to the Second Balkan War of 1913, the rules of war were in force. Not only was internal Turkish rule primarily based on military authority, the same was also true for the communities they ruled over. Political power had not developed. The sultan was a soldier emperor who directed the state and society with daily orders called *ferman*.

The era of the republic is also primarily characterized by military leadership. After all, the republic was founded in war, and all the subsequent basic political and social institutions were realized under strict military supervision. This plays a more important role in the relationship of the Turks to the state than is the case for other countries, peoples, or nations. It is as if statism had become ingrained in their genes. Statism not only became central for the class of state leaders and bureaucrats. It is a phenomenon that no group in society seems to be able to do without anymore. Just as one is unable to live without Allah, one is also unable to live without the state—or at least that seems to be the common conviction. The stronger and more violent the state, the more secure people feel. The weakness or collapse of the state would be tantamount to their own annihilation and death. This might be an exaggerated approach on their part, but there are very obvious historical social reasons that necessitated such an approach. Since Turkish rule was never established within Turkish structures but was always wrested from others, it was also always feared that it could, in turn, be wrested from them by others. Therefore, there could be all kinds of danger lurking, including annihilation and death. This should clarify for the reader why we present this relationship as a historical and dialectical reality for Turks.

Because the republic was built on this culture and emerged as a consequence of a war against the "powerful nations of the world," security will always be the highest priority for both the republic and society. Turkish development is in many ways different from that of Western societies. In the West, many societies have asserted their existence not through war but by resisting and constantly attempting to constrain the warrior ruling power bloc. The existence of such a culture facilitates the emergence of a civil society and democracy and gives priority to human rights. Nonetheless, the tradition of war and power is decisive for all social relations. The difference lies in its intensity and how it is philosophically understood.

Among the Turks, the state is experienced in an intense manner, with the most sacred philosophical and religious interpretations. Therefore, anything that could put limits on the state—civil society, human rights, or even universal legal and political norms—is regarded as a threat. Trust and faith in democracy are still very weak. It is feared that democracy could weaken the state and lead to its collapse. Since 1945, there has even been an effort to exercise complete control over the pseudo-democratic interplay between the two oligarchic parties. Because democracy is seen as a trap for the state, very strict controls are all but omnipresent.

This state-oriented social perspective is palpable in every institution. Progress and personal advancement are believed only to be possible through a state position, particularly in the military. Therefore, working for a state institution is both an honor and the best way to make a decent living. It is clear that in a state-oriented society like this, there is little room for the development of self-confidence and creativity. A society that literally discounts itself in the name of the state and regards itself as unworthy will, of course, be unable to develop civil society, the rule of the law, economic power, and creative political institutions. This attitude of the Turks in relation to the state has its worst consequences during times of crisis. Whenever the state enters into crisis, it is seen as catastrophic. Because there is no alternate solution that will come into play, a crisis like this is considered a life-or-death moment. For both the state and society, it is a criterium of modernity *not* to expect everything from the state and to curb the state in ways that would prevent it from becoming a burden. Europe has been able to establish an efficient position for the state by arriving at an understanding of state within this framework.

We must treat the problem of the relationship between the state and the political parties separately, because it runs even deeper. All parties without exception have a subjective or objective fixation on the state. Just as is the case for society, by conceding priority to the state, political parties lose their purpose from the outset. Parties are the foremost institutions that are there to create a balance between the demands of the society and the state, and, thus, should always give priority to society and are responsible for raising its awareness and increasing its level of organization. Instead, they are always either expecting revolution from the state or seeking to gain the state's political support. First and foremost, however, like rentiers, they regard the state as a source of unearned income. Even though parties are indispensable to democracy, this particular approach gives the parties an antidemocratic character from the outset, turning them into secondary shadow states. As if one state were not enough, each party represents a mini-state, with every politician regarding himself as a "statesman." By nourishing themselves and their environment on the state, they weigh down the state and make the damage it does even worse. There is perhaps no other country where the tradition of "state parties" is as strongly internalized as in Turkey, and even if there is another country, it is probably not as widespread and wholehearted. Putting the state at the center of all values blunts the ability of the parties to generate politics, develop economic policies, promote and strengthen democracy, or provide society analytical tools—to at least the same degree as is the case for the state. As a result, they become useless to both the state and society. Because the people understand this, all parties hoping to rescue the state are delivered a sound beating at polling booths.

The parties have become instruments for developing crises not solving them. This has been a fundamental factor in the failure of democracy to develop to contemporary standards in Turkey after World War II. This has in turn led to the failure to cultivate a democratic culture in society and to a belief that it falls to the state to address everything. The statism of the parties, which they shed only when they are in the opposition, is the main cause for today's political and economic crises. The CHP—the founding party of the republic—is the main source of the contraction in the political arena and the inability to develop an effective oppositional policy. This is because it has voluntarily defended all state policies, especially against the PKK, and, before that, against the revolutionary left movements. Instead of coming up with a policy for addressing problems it has preferred to function as a state propaganda and agitation squad. This led both the state and the CHP into a dead end and allowed for a mountain of problems to accumulate.

The clearest consequences of the way the state emerged and functions among the Turks reveal themselves with regard to Kurds and the Kurdish question. Anyone who wants to understand the Turkish state can gain insight from this situation, because it is both one of the most hidden and one of the most obvious symptomatic features. The Turkish state perceives any distinction, any articulation of the problematic of the Kurds, as a security problem. On the one hand, the state claims there are no Kurds, while, on the other hand, when the Kurds make even the smallest possible demand for freedom, it perceives them as a terrifying threat that must be immediately crushed.

This approach is the result of the impasse of nationalist ideology. If the state were not so infected by nationalism, it would not feel obliged to confront Kurdish reality as it does. As we saw in our historical reflection, there is a strong preference for a close association on both sides. Even though their attitude toward the state differs from that of the Turks, the Kurds are inclined to accept the state as a joint tool for defense against external threats. We saw this during the Ottoman era and in the early years of the republic. The one history, one language, one nation, and one state understanding based on nationalism—and the influence of rebellions— meant that forced assimilation became the Kurds lot, resulting in them being excluded from the economic, social, and political development of the system. At this point, the Kurds have been declared an overarching source of danger. "The best Kurd is a dead Kurd." Even a solution that was

100 percent favorable to the Turks would be insufficient for them to stop seeing the Kurds as a grave danger. The smallest stirring among the Kurds, every social and political demand, is labeled "separatism." This approach has nothing to do with science or modernity and would have been an anachronism even in the Middle Ages. It is pure nationalism, which considers even the smallest difference as a threat and/or a reason for eradication. Therefore, the state cannot imagine any solution other than a full-on military, political, economic, social, and cultural assault.

During the time of the Kurdish freedom movement under the leadership of the PKK, this policy was embraced as a sacred goal by both the state and society across the spectrum of left- and right-wing politics. Under the slogan of "national unity and national integrity," even the most democratic initiatives and demands were stigmatized as separatism. To this was added the policy of denouncing everything as "terrorism." In the last quarter of the twentieth century, foreign policy and all available state means were mobilized to have the PKK declared "terrorist." The result was the crisis and chaos that began in the 1990s. A total mobilization was declared. As a result, the area of law totally collapsed, the economy was bogged down in a quagmire of debt, and politics in general was reduced to nothing more than an instrument of security policies. The build-up of a structure of village guards and the fostering of the tariqat led to a renewed and strengthened tribalism among the Kurds.[44] The primitive nationalist groups were supported in South Kurdistan, which led to a Kurdish federal state. At the same time, Kurdish Naqshbandi sheikhs were carried over into the Turkish state. The republic's most important institutions were handed over to its opponents. This cannot even be called a pyrrhic victory but is a declaration of the bankruptcy of blind nationalist policy. With the US's Greater Middle East Initiative, we're back to square one: either cooperate with the Kurds or you will be stopped. Under the new conditions in the world today, it is impossible to make headway in any other way.

There is no need to present further observations about what is happening; if there is no immediate reform of the republic, not only progress but even the preservation of the existing structures will be impossible. The last couple of years have clearly shown this. The state initiated some supposed reforms. However, since these reforms do not address the most necessary central reform, they cannot avoid losing value as long as the fundamental obstructions to reform remain in place. In fact, the society, which is on the verge of a great development, cannot free itself from the constrictions imposed by the Kurdish question. Society is thereby forced to veer steadily to the right, which prevents the necessary historical transformation. Again, because of this question, the state-fixated parties are also constantly liquidated one after another, and rather than being democratic instruments they become obstacles to a real democratization. The point has been reached where the stagnation prevailing in the republic and in society is now shaping individual mentality, including that of children. It has still not been grasped that right-wing conservatism cannot be the fate of the republican revolutionarism. We are experiencing the pain and loss that comes with making changes to Mustafa Kemal Atatürk's policy, which might have been reasonable at the time, being entirely taboo. The lack of meaningful policies and leadership has brought the rage percolating within society to a boiling point. Clearly, if a real democratization is desired and reform of the state and transformation of society are to make sense at this historical stage, it must be understood that we will only get there if the Kurds, who represent one of the founding elements of the republic, gain their freedom.

There remains a historical necessity for an initiative based on the free union of Turks and Kurds that is concurrent with the strategic periods seen in the past. The most realistic model in overcoming the chaotic situation in the Middle East is based on a free union of Kurds and Turks. Any solution engineered by the US-led global coalition would very probably become the source of new problems. The situation of the Arabs is closer to producing a deadlock than a solution. Thus, the current political and economic status quo can lead to nothing but deepening contradictions. It is also clear that the policies around Israel, which have become a knot are unlikely to be resolved in the near future. Iran, for its part, has its own conflict with the dominant world system, which will very probably grow more intense.

This leaves us with Turkey. As long as Turkey fails to positively overcome its "Kurdish obsession," it will repeatedly and unavoidably slide into crisis. The result is the deepening of US policy based on the Kurds, which could lead to a situation that will be no less problematic than that of Israel-Palestine. Both history, including the most recent history, and the present show that the most immediate option for the democratic transformation of the region necessitates the establishment of a new Kurdish-Turkish relationship that could lead to a democratic solution to the Kurdish question. If this option is approached scientifically and sociologically, it should be obvious that it wouldn't pose any danger to a genuine national integrity and state unity in Turkey but would make a lasting contribution. This is why a "reform of the republic" that frees the state from useless ballast and limits its purview to general security and the maintenance of public space, with an understanding of "Turkey" that is free of national chauvinism and that views differences as enriching, and a "social transformation" based on a democratic society and democratic politics that includes women's freedom and an ecological society is a key objective. With a transformation of mentality in these core areas, it would be entirely possible for political reform and social transformation to provide the best and most moral solution and help us to exit the chaos in the Middle East.

The Kurdish question will be central to any process of reform in the Republic of Turkey and Turkish society. There are three tendencies that will try to establish a long-lasting presence through the struggle around the relations and conflicts of the different parties to the conflict. Which will gain the upper hand and become permanent will be determined by the intellectual, moral, and political—education, organization, and action—struggle among the parties.

Nationalists

The first tendency is determined by the nationalist paradigm and practices and defends the status quo. This particular tendency, which was dominant in the recent past and continues to be very influential, brings with it insularity, secession, and violence. On the Turkish side, this means a hardline conservatism overrun with racist nationalism and rigid statism on both the left and the right. The state and the nation, as well as society itself, share a certain paranoid and schizophrenic apprehension that the last bastion of Turkishness is about to fall, and that everything will soon be lost. Drowning Turks in round-the-clock Turkish propaganda is seen as a primary responsibility. In addition, the requirements of Islam are not neglected, in the hope that that particular mentality will bring with it salvation. On some occasions, Mustafa Kemal Atatürk and Kemalism are unhesitatingly embraced, in spite of the role of Kemalism in the most important twentieth-century projects for change. However, this essential aspect of Kemalism is overlooked, because a fetishized variety of Kemalism is seen as preferable. Although it starkly contradicts many facets of genuine Kemalism, particularly its modernism and its position on women, science, and republicanism, this use of Kemalism is key to this current's particular approach. Alleged Kemalist platitudes that actually have nothing to do with the true essence of Kemalism are widespread, both in state institutions and in the social arena.

This tendency has become even more conservative in the parties from both wings, in the CHP and DP tradition, that have been playing a role in the political arena. Since the 1990s, with the rise of the Kurdish freedom movement, these parties have become political extensions of the counter-guerrilla campaign. They have tried to cover up a number of extralegal attacks. The idea that politics should be carried out in the name of society has been completely lost, and, instead, they have committed themselves to "saving" the state. The result has been an even deeper crisis of the state and society. The wave of crises spelled the end of the previous representatives of this tendency, primarily the CHP, the DYP,[45] and the MHP. However, some capitalist circles that assessed the situation more realistically started a new process with the AKP.

Finally, the exponents of this tendency were strategically abandoned and left to their fate by the US, in which they invested so much trust. The US had supported this tendency's fascist escalation since 1950. This was true for the AP, the MHP, and a whole number of anticommunist institutions. But with the new global offensive in the 1980s, their extreme conservatism and statism were seen as obstacles, and support for this tendency was withdrawn, first partially, and then entirely. The US updated its approach, initially by supporting the ANAP and, since 2000, the AKP. The statist ruling circles remained the most conservative bloc in the republic. They opposed reforms of either the state or society, and one might call them "republican conservatives." Most recently, the fashionable name "Red Apple Alliance" has been coined for them.[46] They have effectively turned the once revolutionary republic into a national chauvinist, state capitalist, and conservative bloc that is anti-people. Thus, much like the authoritarian republic of the Atatürk era before it, the oligarchic republic with its two-bloc power structure came to an end.

Regarding the Kurds, this tendency had a policy of denial and eradication, complete systemic marginalization, and immediate suppression of any stirrings of dissent. An important element of this policy was the use of traditional collaborators who had betrayed their Kurdishness to gain control over the people. This system, from the left to the right, carried out concerted action against the Kurdish freedom movement the PKK was trying to develop. Speaking as one voice in domestic and foreign policy was adopted as "sacred politics." The judiciary, the economy, politics, sports, and the arts became aspects of a general military mobilization. The whole society was turned into an aggressive national chauvinist bloc. The result was an era, path, and tendency in Turkish and Kurdish relations like none before. None of this had anything to do with the frequently invoked Kemalism. Mustafa Kemal Atatürk's Kurdish policy was a product of his anti-imperialist stance. Furthermore, he left no documents that suggest any hostility toward free Kurdishness, although he may have overestimated the role that the Kurds might have been able to play in the destruction of the republic and the restoration of the sultanate and caliphate were they instrumentalized by imperialism. There can be no doubt that this is what underpinned his Kurdish policy.

The overall policy of these conservative national chauvinists who posed as republicans contradicted Atatürk's attitude. Their attempts to secure foreign support against the freedom struggle of the Kurds in order to quash it increased their dependency on the US and the EU in particular, with their economic, political, diplomatic, and military dependency developing to a great extent as a consequence of their opposition to the PKK. Finally, they turned the leadership of Turkey into the midwife of the Iraqi federal state of Kurdistan, which was founded by the primitive nationalist and feudal Kurdish circles in Iraq in cooperation with the US and Israel. They also gave the followers of the tariqat the opportunity to organize themselves within the Turkish state. All these practices are very clearly anti-Kemalist.

The Liberal Bourgeoisie

The second tendency emerged from the first. It could be described as the weak bourgeois liberal path. It mainly developed after 1980, during the global capitalist offensive. The ANAP, led by Turgut Özal, was the first version of this tendency.

While the status quo can be summed up as insular, ultranationalist state capitalism, this new opposing tendency is characterized by an openness to the outside, liberalism, and a tolerance of differences and seeks a place in the transnational global tendency. It superseded the DP and the AP but acted as their contemporary version, insofar as it was no more anti-oligarchic than they were. It is by no means completely open to democracy but is, nonetheless, more solution-oriented and readier to take a contemporary approach to problems than the conservative republican defenders of the status quo. Although it is mainly the tendency of the industrial circles of

Turkish capitalism, it is capable of bringing together other circles of capital on common ground. The entrepreneurs' association Türk Sanayicileri ve İş İnsanları Derneği (TÜSIAD: Turkish Industrial and Business Association) is among the most important advocates of this tendency. With the support of the US, the EU, and Japan, the AKP is well on its way to becoming the second version of this tendency. But even though it is still aligned with these powers, it is, nonetheless, still far from making a serious start to tackling the reform of the state or launching the projects necessary for social transformation. It recoils in the face of the state's most important power centers and cannot overcome the bureaucratic apparatuses. It is possible that the AKP will prove to be just as effective as Turgut Özal was in his time, but this is far from certain. Recep Tayyip Erdoğan displays neither Özal's courage nor his sophistication. It is by no means unlikely that Erdoğan will capitulate to the bureaucracy, especially in relation to his approach to the Kurdish question. Nonetheless, he can't put off addressing the Kurdish question indefinitely, and his mask will very probably slip.

This tendency's Kurdish policy offers only a limited possibility of a solution. Turgut Özal in particular intended to take some steps, motivated by an attitude that was unusually liberal in the history of the republic. This promptly brought about his end. The chaos Turkey experienced after his death is the result of this contradiction. This process and the related crisis, which have long been described as a conflict between representatives of the "First Republic" and representatives of the "Second Republic," have grown more intense since my incarceration on İmralı. The policy of the DSP-ANAP-MHP government under Bülent Ecevit,[47] which relied on the traditional denial approach, only succeeded in inciting the opposition of society in its entirety. As a result, our unilateral ceasefire was not put to good use. It became apparent that the state was far from grasping what was happening. The status quo tendency had to absorb yet another heavy blow when it was buried at the polling booth in November 2002.[48]

There are no clues as yet about the Kurdish policy of the AKP, which replaced it. Even though it strives for harmony with the US, it does not have the strength on its own to develop and implement a Kurdish policy. It hangs its hat on the US acting against the PKK and the Koma Gel.[49] In addition, the fact that a number of Kurdish collaborators are members of the same tariqa (Naqshbandi) as AKP politicians and have considerable weight in the federal state in South Kurdistan and could snap up influential positions in the Turkish state, as could collaborators in North Kurdistan, might make the AKP receptive to a US-sponsored solution. In the meantime, it's becoming increasingly obvious that the AKP is trying to effect some developments based on a semisecret and *taqiyyah* logic.[50] Due to the extreme sensitivity of the Kurdish question, they can be expected to act under economic, social, and religious cover to keep their plans secret both from the Kurdish revolutionary popular forces and the Turkish conservative-statist institutions. The tacit alliance between the AKP and the Kurdish collaborators was to some degree visible in the municipal elections of March 2004, when Talabani and Barzani openly supported the AKP. It is very unlikely that the Kurdish question can be resolved by such an underhanded and obscure foray. Rather, this approach could lead to violent eruptions at any moment.

The most dangerous aspect of this tendency, which is receiving massive financial and diplomatic support from the US and the EU, is that it wants to impose the model of the federal state of Kurdistan in North Iraq, to Syria, Iran, and Turkey by fueling primitive Kurdish nationalism. Just as the US and the EU declared the PKK terrorist, they also try to defame the Koma Gel as terrorist, presumably to assuage Turkey. They make various pronouncements and give various guarantees in this regard, but in so doing they are actually increasing the danger twofold. On the one hand, this will give primitive nationalism a major boost, and, on the other hand, the PKK and the Koma Gel will benefit from the current contradictions, leading to major new developments. The result of this path could well be the development of a second much feared Israel-Palestine-style confrontation that implicates Turkey, Iran, Iraq, and Syria. The potential for the nationalist tendencies to become stronger on all sides only increases the likelihood of such a development.

Democrats

The third tendency is society-oriented, based on the people's quest for freedom and equality within a shared democracy. The notion of a "Nation of Turkey" as a superordinate identity could break through the chauvinist and racist understanding of nations and function as a common denominator for all cultures. In many countries of the world, there is a territorial rather than lineage-based understanding of "the nation." Even though the large majority of nations are multilingual and multicultural, the different language groups and cultures are able to unite under the shared umbrella of a single nation-state, e.g., the US, Switzerland, and Great Britain. In these cases, it is not a problem that the most commonly used language is also the official language. However, not restricting the right to use other languages either in daily life or in any kind of education is the common contemporary practice around the world.

The basis of state reform would have to be its transformation from an ideological instrument into a technical service tool. The understanding of a historical redeemer and conqueror serves as an obstacle to the self-confidence and creativity of society. This understanding leads to the expectation that the state will take care of everything, like a god might. Therefore, radical reform requires the state to withdraw from all areas apart from general external security and the necessary public services required by all segments of society.

The bloated state in Turkey lags very far behind society and plays a hugely conservative role. But because of the generally exaggerated expectations in the state, a bureaucratic and social conservatism has developed that can only be overcome by radical reform. This reform must abolish the discrimination against any group of citizens. It must give all individuals the opportunity to freely express and live their cultural identity, as is guaranteed in international treaties. The state must not define itself in terms of a specific ethnic group and must not discriminate against any religion or denomination. It is essential that any reforms are undergirded by amendments to the constitution, as well as by the necessary changes and additions to the law.

An essential element of social transformation would be dropping sexist social attitudes and women becoming free and equal. Artificial discussions like the one about the hijab must stop. What is instead necessary are effective measures against attitudes and practices that treat women like property. Women's centers must not merely be "shelters" but should be developed extensively as the cultural centers that are necessary for women's freedom.

Another increasingly important topic is the ecological transformation of society. A free society is only possible if it is also an ecological society. In the light of the latest scientific insights, a society that is compatible with ecology should be included in the constitution as a goal.[51] An economic system based on the healthy sustenance of society with natural foodstuffs must also be a priority. We have to make a transition from a profit-based economic system to an economy based on use value, one that sustains health and a contemporary life, with a gradual decrease in commodification. A free society will put an end to phenomena like unemployment, the impoverishment of entire regions due to a lack of investment, and a massive income gap.

The tendency of state reform and social transformation that I have outlined here, is closely connected to resolving the Kurdish question. The projection of this tendency onto the Kurdish question would mean the acceptance of peace and a democratic solution. The first thing necessary for peace is a bilateral ceasefire. As to a democratic solution, we must look at two possible options.

The democratization of Turkey would clear the way for one possible approach to a solution, as it would require the sort of state reform I attempted to outline above. There would need to be an end to both the open and hidden roadblocks to Kurdish democratization, including the removal of all legal obstacles. The fact that it is still forbidden to use the Kurdish language when demonstrating is one indication of the degree of legal obstruction. There are, however, more serious de facto obstacles. In particular, the practice of recruiting cadres for the state from the traditional denialists and collaborationists of Kurdish, Arabic, Aramaic, Armenian, Greek, and Caucasian descent must stop. Recruiting from the dönme and devşirme cadres, contemporary Janissaries of a sort, fuels a racist nationalism mindset that is conceptually similar to being more Catholic than the pope. Furthermore, this practice also fosters nationalism among minorities. In this way, true patriotism, the free and democratic unity of the people, is destroyed. The contribution made by individuals of a similar character to the dissolution of the Ottoman Empire and the current contribution to the degeneration of the republic cannot be underestimated. With cadres like this, no democratic solution will be possible. Democratization is incompatible with cadres that have a tariqat identity. This form of sectarianism makes use of democracy but rejects its virtues. Thus, much has to change for Turkish and Kurdish people to come together around a common democratic platform, and in this context, minorities must be protected.

The second approach to a democratic solution would be for the Kurds to establish a democracy of their own. If the first approach continues to be blocked, it is only natural that the Kurds will choose to develop their own criteria and the institutions necessary to pursue their own democratization. The most recent parliamentary and municipal elections again showed that even when Kurds elect their own candidates, the state's antidemocratic laws and financial obstacles, as well as its coercive measures, ensure that election results are not respected and implemented.[52] Should these restrictions remain in place in the coming period, the self-democracy experiments of the Kurds will gain momentum. The process that began with the foundation of the Koma Gel will take shape a step at a time. Methodically establishing their own local governments, with the Koma Gel as their overall coordination tool will constitute the core of Kurdish democratization. This democratic movement bears no resemblance to the Kurdish federal parliament in Iraq. Its federalism is based on a feudal-bourgeois concept of "the state". The Koma Gel rejects statism on principle. There is a dialectical contradiction between democratization and becoming a state. The theories and institutions emerging from the Koma Gel initiative will constitute not a federal but a democratic Kurdistan.

A democratic Kurdistan would not challenge the integrity of Turkey, Iran, Iraq, and Syria as states and countries. Those states are only being asked to enable a unity based on democratic reconciliation. Therefore, a democratic Kurdistan would mean a democratic Turkey, a democratic Iran, a democratic Iraq, and a democratic Syria. This is the only way we can prevent a slaughter based on various nationalisms and the creation of new Israels and Palestines. Any approach besides the democratic approach will mean oppression and denial and, in reaction, revolt and war. History provides ample instructive lessons on this matter.

Even though voices calling for democratization and a democratic solution are increasing in Turkey, they have not yet gained a sufficient place on the political agenda, whereas, many European countries, and even many countries in Asia, Africa, and the Americas, have applied the democratic model to solve the question of people and culture. This is always the course of the world. The latest example of this general trend is Cyprus. A problem that has been festering for many years is approaching a solution in the form of a democracy with two partners. This could be highly instructive for the democratic solution of the Kurdish question. The models found in the Basque Country, Northern Ireland, Scotland, Switzerland, and Belgium could also contribute to the solution.

The Turkish administration must finally comprehend that it cannot continue to rule over the Kurds as it previously has. If they do not want a second Iraq, they must seriously consider peace and a democratic solution. It must be clear that such a solution in no way contradicts a realistic implementation of Mustafa Kemal Atatürk's approach to freedom. Any claim that Atatürk was an enemy of free citizenship for the Kurds and joint or separate democratic organs, so as to assert that Kemalism was hostile to the Kurds, would be tantamount to falling into the nationalist trap. A democratic and free Kurdistan is a permanent, fraternal, and genuine guarantee of the unity of the state and the territory of Turkey. It is a strategic pillar in the present, just as it was historically. A continued denial of the Kurds and Kurdistan, however, will inevitably create an ongoing problem and a constant danger of rebellion and external intervention. It would mean squandering all of the material and immaterial resources of Turkey and its society and drifting into crisis. It would mean a loss of prestige and power in the Middle East, in Europe, and worldwide. Amid the chaos in the Middle East, an initiative based on the joint democratization of Turks and Kurds would be at least as important as any comparable strategic initiative over the course of history. Those refusing to see and implement this are either enemies of the people or traitors of the homeland. All the developments in the world, in the region, in Turkey, and in Kurdistan urgently call for peace and a democratic solution.

There is a great desire to push forward the new capitalist process in Turkey that has gained momentum since the 2000s by maximizing relations with the EU and the US. It is considered necessary to take refuge in a token democratic drive similar to the one seen when the DP was in office. This tepid democracy is the veneer necessary both for gaining the sympathy of the EU and for acting against the army. The AKP is not equipped—either intellectually or substantively—to implement a coherent democratic line. Presenting adherents of Islamic ideology as "conservative democrats" falls far short of being completely free from the influence of taqiyya, which have attained a great deal of weight within the state as a result of the rupture caused by extended periods of internal and external struggle. In the upcoming period, the AKP will clarify its social and political bearing and find its true place.

In the face of Turkish capitalism's latest move, all the people in Turkey, especially the Kurds, need to think and act in a highly sensitive way. As the continuous losers in the first two stages, this third stage opens the way for a process that could at least allow for partial success and offer the only way out of an avalanche of unemployment and poverty.

The main item on the agenda for the people of Turkey is to transform their democratic stance into an organized movement capable of acting. In all three phases described above the left nationalist and real socialist currents, such as the TKP, proved unable to go beyond their state orientation and play an objective role other than strengthening the capitalist process. But, on the other hand, there is, in fact, a strong freedom-loving and egalitarian legacy. The challenge is to use this legacy to build a coherent democratic, free, and egalitarian grassroots movement. A democratic Kurdish movement that is active and moving forward would be in a position to make the greatest possible contribution to this process. What is really necessary, however, is for left-wing groups in Turkey to cease being state-oriented, develop a coherent understanding of democracy, and create unity on this basis.

Seen from that perspective, the Demokratik Güçler Birliği (Unity of the Democratic Forces) recently formed by the five parties, the Sosyaldemokrat Halk Partisi (SHP: Social Democratic People's Party), the Demokratik Halk Partisi (DEHAP: Democratic People's Party), the Emek Partisi (EMEP: Labor Party), the Sosyalist Demokrasi Partisi (SDP: Social Democratic Party), and the Özgürlük ve Dayanışma Partisi (ÖDP: Freedom and Solidarity Party), was a step in the right direction.[53] However, they were not successful because they could not rid themselves of the negative aspects of contents and structure they inherited and make a radical break with statist ideology and bureaucratism. The correct starting point would have been a radical break with bureaucratism and the creation of an umbrella organization relying on a broad base of the poor and unemployed, particularly those in rural areas and the suburbs, and launching something new based on the diverse grassroots civil society, human rights, and feminist and ecological movements. Given the dynamism of the Kurdish democratic movement, a new departure of this sort could provide a real response to the democratic, free, and egalitarian aspirations of our people and ensure their victory against the oligarchic rulers complemented by Anatolian capitalism.

ELEVEN

Contribution to the Debate about the Refoundation of the PKK

Introduction

In the previous sections, we tried to present the historical, social, and theoretical approach necessary for a reconstruction of the PKK.[1] We analyzed some properties of capitalism—the dominant social system of our age—under global and regional conditions, as well as under the conditions in our country. At the same time, intertwined with this, we have tried to delineate the democratic social development and its course throughout history. We have stressed that one must regard the historical development of projects for freedom and equality as a chain with many links. We have also tried to show how the ideals of freedom and equality get distorted, drained of their content, and integrated into tyrannical and exploitative orders. We attempted to present the reality of civilization in the Middle East within the same paradigm. We used a similar framework to discuss the phenomenon of Kurdistan and the Kurdish question, as well as how to theoretically approach a resolution. We analyzed the formation and development of the PKK as a movement, showed how it stagnated due to internal factors, and argued for the necessity of a renewal through critique and self-critique. Moreover, we analyzed some of the new theoretical elements and political currents found in ecological, cultural, and feminist movements. We also consistently emphasized that a reconstruction of the party will only be meaningful if it embodies all these developments.

Therefore, based on our conjectures regarding all these issues, the rebuilding of the PKK first and foremost requires a concrete analysis of the situation in the world, the region, and Kurdistan. Drawing upon the assessments in the relevant sections above, we hope to briefly summarize the connection between various topics.

Today, US-led global capitalism has neither the option to turn to new colonies, as in the nineteenth century, nor the conditions for the redistribution of the world through war, as was the case in the twentieth century. Whatever the similarities, the new conditions of globalization are different from the old in specific ways. The scientific and technological revolution provides the capitalist system with different ways to make a profit. I refer here to the profit accumulation of the transnational corporations that emerged with globalization. These transnational corporations are the world's new ruling powers, directing policy at their whim to create legal conditions suitable to their interests. These corporations allow for maximum profits. Nation-states that stand in the way are reshaped and political structures that function smoothly are created. In this way, the system attempts to maximize profits even in a chaotic environment.

All of this is the basis for the intense interest the US-led system has had in the Middle East since the early 2000s. The current political, military, economic, and intellectual structures of the region pose the most fundamental obstacle for the system. A hairball of problems makes the region the system's weak spot: the Israel-Palestine conflict, oil, the Kurdish question, a radicalizing Islam, a despotic political structure, an economy that produces unemployment and poverty—and, not least, the lack of women's freedom. The ruling system cannot tolerate this situation, which is the political reality that the political powers in the Middle East refuse to comprehend. They think they can sustain themselves with their classic political thinking and their theory of the nation-state. The US, as the system's imperial power, feels it must act to meet its responsibilities, while the opposition of the other powers is only meant to keep up appearances for their own people and is, thus, illusory. It is merely their way of saying that they want a larger slice of the pie of power. In the near future, all of the system's leading powers and institutions will solidify their coalition and act against the region, with the coordination of the UN, NATO, the EU, and the G8 taking shape. Sometimes military campaigns will be carried out against countries like Afghanistan and Iraq, while other countries will face threats, and economic means will be used to force yet others to integrate into the system.

To ensure results, countries and political structures that resist will be driven into bankruptcy with expanding embargos. Ineffectual economies will be hammered with a number of reconstruction measures and will be forced to reform and liberalize. The region will be effectively integrated into the system within the next twenty-five years, give or take. A complete break with the system cannot be expected, because the economic, military, scientific, and technical bases are lacking. Even rebellious "rogue states" will be unable to exist for very long. These ineffectual political and economic structures cannot be sustained by either the ruling system at the top or the broad mass of people below. Under these circumstances, individuals, particularly women, will need to engage in an offensive to gain their freedom.

The system will behave according to its own logic and institutional framework, but the key question will be how will the society, the people's forces, behave? The people of the region do not have to accept the system as it is. It is becoming evident that they must seek solutions in line with their own goals of democracy, freedom, and equality and not continue on as an auxiliary of the nation-state. The people's non-state-oriented democratization efforts, encompassing environmental, feminist, and cultural movements that have ties with human rights organizations and civil society, have a transnational significance that is at least as important as the system's limited democratization efforts and its globalization.

The situation in the world and in the Middle East was discussed in detail in the previous sections, so what follows will only be a short summary. We will, however, examine in some detail the concrete conditions in Turkey and Kurdistan. The critique and self-critique delivered above and my assessment of the problems of reconstruction have already to some degree pointed to the tasks ahead. The following elaborations on a democratic solution will hopefully contribute to a better understanding of the Koma Gel.

Tasks in Reconstructing the PKK and the Time of Koma Gel

If the PKK is to be reconstructed, we must first have a clear understanding of why the old framework ceased to function. We critiqued the old framework in three main areas. First, we understood the concept of "the party" as an extension of the concept of "the state" and as a means that would carry us to the state, even though there is a dialectical contradiction between being a state-oriented party and developing democracy, freedom, and equality, both in terms of essence and of form. The PKK was unable to completely free itself from this concept.

The second issue was the way power was perceived. A party attempting to take power will always hamper rather than nurture social democratization. Cadres formed in this context will not rely on the people but on the authorities, or they will try to be the authorities, because what appeals to them is the life of unearned income that comes with power. Historically, this is what transformed three important revolutionary currents into denominations of capitalism. Real socialism, social democracy, and national liberation movements focused on quickly gaining power rather than on broadening democracy. This resulted in the corruption of all three currents and their transformation into auxiliary forces of the capitalist system.

My third self-critique related to war. Without understanding the actual nature of war—no matter what sort—we regarded it as a sacred means for the purpose at hand. In reality, except for vital and necessary self-defense every act of war was murder. War was the basis of every exploitative power in history. Their laws and social institutions were linked to and arranged in accordance with war, and all rights accrued from victory in war. This sort of thinking is obviously neither democratic nor socialist. A socialist party should not be state-oriented, strive for power, or embrace war as the determinant that underlies everything.

It has been emphasized that unless the PKK redefines itself, it is entirely possible that it will make significant mistakes and its refoundation will be marred by serious flaws. Our definition of what a party is must correspond to the self-critique presented in this book. It must not be state-oriented and cannot place power and war at the center of this new social transformation. Because power and war are the basis of capitalism, the most recent form of class society, a party hoping to overcome capitalism must exclude power and war as the foundations of society, which will only be possible if communal existence and the democratic stance of society are transformed into a democratic, free, and egalitarian society.

Considering these factors, we can define the party as follows: it has a program seeking a democratic, free, and egalitarian transformation of society, with a common strategy for all social groups that have an interest in this program and based on a broad organization and on forms of action adopted by environmentalist, feminist, and cultural movements, as well as civil society organizations, without neglecting the tactical necessity of legitimate self-defense. In this sense, the party is the leading organization of this sort of social movement.

Theory

Theory is indispensable for a party or a movement. Just as the body is unthinkable without a spirit, a party cannot exist without a theory. The name we give to our theory—the fundamental worldview that guides the content of our definition of the party—can still be *scientific socialism*, provided that it is in the context elaborated here. We could also call it *democratic socialism* to refer to the triad: philosophy as the most comprehensive generalization of social science; morality as society's sense of freedom; politics expressing the society's will for transformation. More important than the name, however, is the content. Theory must embody the paramount generalization of scientific development, and at the same time grasp politics, the will to transform morality and society, as an art. As long as we live under the capitalist system and until the social transformation becomes a natural phenomenon through the continuous concurrent application of social science, morality, and politics, we will need the mentality of the party.

Mentality is the party's capacity to render meaning, and it is quite clear that the mentality of the party requires a good grasp of social science. Social science, the most recent defining science, which encompasses the whole of scientific development, serves as an enlightening force within a society searching for transformation. While it previously fell to mythological, religious, and philosophical schools to try to cast light on social phenomena, today, following a long march, we are closer to a social and scientific explanation, albeit a limited one. A scientific understanding of society is a great source of strength. In this sense, even a limited understanding of sociology is the strongest aspect of social transformation. But this alone is insufficient. In the final analysis, all mythological, religious, philosophical, and scientific efforts in the history of humanity originated in society and were undertaken in order to understand society, to find and realize solutions to its problems. They do not exist abstractly and at a remove from the society. Without understanding society, we cannot properly understand individuals, material objects, or nature. Ignorance and tyranny lie at the roots of the catastrophes created by the human hand—the state, rulers, and war. We can only overcome these tyrannical and ignorant institutions by gaining an understanding of society. Thus, if the state, power, and war are indeed perverted products of analytical intelligence, overcoming them will only be possible using both analytical and emotional intelligence. Those who occupy themselves with the problematic of the

465

state, power, and war, and, thus, also with peace, must give priority to making the society competent and capable.

Morality must also be an integral part of our party mentality. Morality is actually the traditional form of social freedom. In the final analysis, morality is consciousness. A society whose moral foundation has disintegrated has also lost its freedom. A society without morality is a society in tatters. Therefore, recognizing morality as a basis in any effort to transform society is indispensable. Social currents that make no room for morality cannot be expected to endure. Those who are determined to transform society must never lose their ties to the morality of freedom.

Practice

The relationship between the mentality and political willpower is all about practice. Comprehension and morality are only valuable when they become integral to practice and contribute to solving problems. Being moral and scientific in the absence of politics is rife with deception and tantamount to capitulating before the ruling dominant powers or selling out to them. It means becoming part of the power-knowledge structures and official morality. The neglect of this connection contributes to many scientists playing an ineffective or even counterproductive role that is contrary to society's interests and to numerous reasonable appeals for greater responsibility going unheeded. There is an increasingly widespread and dangerous tendency in our age for individuals to occupy themselves solely with morality or with science or with politics, which opens the door for all sorts of catastrophes. Today, perhaps we need nothing more urgently than an approach that overcomes this disconnection.

This is exactly why our definition above of the mentality of the party matters. If we don't base ourselves on a mentality of this sort and find a way to act upon it, we will be unable to avoid the same dead end that real socialism, social democracy, and the national liberation movements ended up in, and, like them, will become the system's auxiliary force. That is why we attach primary importance during the reconstruction process to mentality—an essential component in defining what a party is. The more developed the party's mentality, the easier it will be for the organization to effectively put its program into practice strategically and tactically. If it fails to do so the loss of what has already been achieved will be unavoidable. Even after successful revolutions, it is rarely possible to prevent the dissolution of the structures they build, as the experience of Soviet socialism makes perfectly clear. It is not, however, simply a matter of the unity of theory and practice. The theoretical content and the mentality orienting the party are also important. An insufficiently coherent theory and mentality that are not clearly in line with our goals will, in the end, lead to a distorted practice. Therefore, we must put the unity of theory and practice on a solid foundation.

Program

For theoretical soundness to be meaningful it must be reflected in the program. The program of a party expresses its fundamental criteria for social transformation. A community that lacks the ability to work out a program or works one out but fails to internalize it can barely be called a party.

What, in fact, is a party?

Etymologically, the word *party* means *part, division, section,* and *portion.* The party, as such, has undergone a long historical development. It is possible to regard the first experienced guiding group in a society as a party. The hierarchy's first ruling group was also a party. When states were first founded, the ruling clique, the group that organized things ideologically and practically, also constituted the ruling party. The lower society that it fettered to itself mentally and used for production was left without a party. The respective totemic beliefs of clans and tribes were also tantamount to parties. Even community traditions are parties in a primordial sense. To the degree that we are able reconstruct this aspect of history, Abraham's tribe represented the first serious freedom-loving party of the poor tribes, opposing both the Nimrods of Babylon and Assur and the pharaohs of Egypt. It was both a popular party and a rebellious party that can quite rightly be regarded as an insurgent people's party. Jesus, on the other hand, divided the Jewish tribe for the first time and initiated a party-like movement of the poor, or, rather, he took an already existing small party, the Essenes, to a new level. Christianity fought the Roman Empire as a party of the poor for three centuries. Mohammad likewise started a revolt against the nobility of Mecca with a small group of poor people. Within Islam, we can regard the Kharijites, the Qarmatians, and the Alevi as party-like movements representing a similar poor tribal stratum and the proletarian elements. The denominations of the Middle Ages were also like parties. Depending on class affiliation or mindset, they each represented certain social groups. And, finally, everyone is familiar with the capitalist party system.

Throughout history, the belief systems and structures of all these traditional movements were actually the same as party programs and organizations. The program is a social creed that is clearly understood, abided by, and realizable. In other words, it is the molding of thoughts and beliefs into principles. Those who are most committed to these principles act accordingly in every aspect of their lives. Without principles or a program, there can be no goal, leaving everyone trimming sails to the wind and following their own weaknesses and desires. Those who base themselves on a theoretical, moral, and political mentality acquired with great effort and concretize it in a program, thereby sketching the concrete principles for social transformation, have already taken the most important step toward building the party. Without these steps, party building will be crippled and will never go beyond a circle of sympathizers. Party building is a serious matter. Sometimes it requires decades of personal contemplation and self-discipline to acquire the necessary virtues and abilities. In the history of religions and denominations we encounter holy men and women who discipline themselves by living an ascetic life as eremites for decades. There are many historical examples of this in the three great monotheistic religions and in Buddhism. We should not hesitate to situate our considerations about the mentality and the program of our party within this historical context.

There are legendary examples of outstanding mentality and commitment to principles among PKK members. Haki Karer, Mazlum Doğan, Kemal Pir, Mehmet Hayri Durmuş, Ferhat Kurtay, Mahsum Korkmaz, Taylan Özgür, Berzan Öztürk, Zîlan (Zeynep Kınacı), Bêrîtan (Gülnaz Karataş), Bermal (Güler Otaç), and many more than we can mention here are exemplary examples of comrades who succeeded in embodying the principles of the party. There is much to learn from each and every one of them. On the other hand, we can also find many examples of treachery, apostasy, corruption, negligence, wretchedness, and superficiality, as well as many who worked very hard but never developed a particularly noteworthy mentality or embraced sound programmatic values.

Programs do not represent unalterable or unrenewable principles and views. Since change is continuous, it is only reasonable to make changes to the program when significant shifts in the situation occur. What should not change, however, is the ongoing serious effort to recognize the fundamental needs of society, to solve society's problems, and to continue far-reaching party-building efforts. It is the ability to successfully live by these ideas and pursue these goals until one's last breath. Contrary to what some people believe, rebuilding neither means liquidating everything that exists nor sinking to the level of a mere club. When the task of crafting a new program for the PKK is undertaken, it is important to keep this framework in mind.

In different parts of the submissions before you I have tried to expand on our theoretical views, which are the main pillar of our mentality and will determine the restructuring of the PKK. We have often referred to the features of our theory as systematic views reached in relation to the universe, nature, physics, chemistry, biology, humans, and society. Our theoretical approach, at least at the level of definitions, has been illuminated from the cosmos to the quantum, and from the first formation of the universe to human thought. Instead of repeating these, we will continue to reflect on these issues when necessary. Thus, as we proceed, we must always be accompanied by theory. Those without a theoretical basis cannot easily lead a party movement. The more we ensure theoretical strengthening, the more we can develop our practical skills in problem solving. In turn, restructuring will be successfully achieved.

We will now continue elaborating on the program. In what follows, I will present some proposals that address four core programmatic areas: politics, social affairs, economics, and individual rights.

Political Objectives

The problems of states and regimes must be examined at the political level, and as a result the political reorganization necessary to replace the old regimes must, first and foremost, be determined by principles. Up to this point, we have tried to lay out the political approach to our new party building in the concrete cases of Turkey and Kurdistan. A sociological approach to the state and politics has been developed, and we have pointed out the oligarchic and antidemocratic properties of the state, with democracy existing in discourse, but with no development in practice. The Kurdish question proves this. The political realm is far from being democratic. A particular feature of this situation is that all of the parties work as propaganda and agitation wings of the state. Even though society's longing for democratization is strong, the profound influence of the statist tradition makes it difficult to begin the process of democratization toward civil society, human rights, the environment, or women's freedom. Despite all efforts at reform, the army's traditional influence on the Turkish political system is still strong enough for it to remain the decisive political force in the country.

The main demands of our program in relation to the political sphere should include reform that enables the state to be receptive to democracy that goes beyond empty promises. The old PKK program completely rejected the state, meaning that we intended to completely abolish it. In its place, we imagined—albeit not in very concrete terms—something like a Kurdish state. I now think this was wrong, not because it would be difficult to implement, but because as a matter of principle being statist does not concur with our worldview. The immediate complete abolition of any state whatsoever is certainly unrealistic and rings of nihilism and outdated anarchism, but rejecting the Turkish state and demanding a Kurdish state in its place is too simplistic, even more so since neither a Turkish nor a Kurdish state actually exists, as such. The state, as a historical and weighty tradition, always prioritizes the interests of a small minority, with its service in the public realm extremely limited and generally a matter of appearances. Because public realm and general security are important issues that cannot be neglected, I am suggesting a new understanding of the state that dominates in Turkey and in all of Kurdistan, neither calling for its immediate abolition, which would be scientifically unrealistic, nor allowing for its continued existence. The reduction of the concept of "the state" to its classic form, and particularly to the current despotic practices of the rulers, is unacceptable. A better approach would be to reach a compromise on a much more limited and much smaller political institution that is not considered a state in the old sense but is a general public authority that provides public services and ensures general security.

Working with this description, it would be possible to call such an institution a "republic." *Res publica* originally meant *public affairs*, and this comes close to the definition of democracy as the rule of the people. The current state, however, cannot be identified with democracy but must be defined as no more than a state that is receptive to democracy and accepts it, because the representatives of state authority are not elected but are appointed.[2]

For the Kurds, a Republic of Turkey as we've defined the *republic* represents or should represent a citizenship based on civil rights and freedom and legally recognize the Kurds (including constitutionally). Making the Kurds a legal entity means an official recognition of the Kurdish identity in both a general way and a specific way. To get the Kurds as a people and as a culture to recognize the republic, the republic must recognize *them* as a cultural entity and a people with political rights. This recognition must be mutual and must be based on legal guarantees.

The Republic of Turkey in general needs reform and a Renaissance Turkey-wide, but particularly in terms of Kurds because of their predominant position. Although there are currently some legal and constitutional amendments being made, they can hardly be described as reforms. As long as the dishonest approach toward the Kurdish question and the denial of the Kurds as a people are maintained, it will be difficult to find a compromise on which to base a new constitution. For the PKK, as a force that regards itself as first and foremost responsible for Kurdistan, achieving compromises between democracy and state rule in all four countries it is divided among is the highest priority. If the states—and this is also true of the Kurdish federal state in Iraq—want to continue to exist in Kurdistan, the criterion must be the provision of the services and ensuring general security that are not directed against the people. The task of the Kurdish representatives is to address these criteria with the responsible state authorities and reach the necessary compromises. A unilateral and unlimited measure by the state is naturally unacceptable if it does not have the consent of the people. If such measures are forcibly executed, the people have the right to resist. Therefore, what is needed is a compromise between the state, as the general public authority, and the delegates of the people who have demonstrated their democratic will.

We could summarize this most important point of the program under the heading "The People's Democratic Self-Governance in Kurdistan + the State as General Public Authority." A Kurdistan with this status would come close to democracy, on the one hand, and freedom and equality, on the other hand. In the current historical phase, demanding an entirely stateless democracy would be nothing more than self-deception and adventurism. What we need is a compromise on a state entity whose boundaries are defined and downsized. In fact, we insistently emphasize that this authority cannot be called a state in the classic sense but is a general social institution that is more contemporary and adheres to democracy in substance and in form.

On the other hand, democracy in Kurdistan means electing and supervising the delegates of the people who are tasked with finding answers to their common social needs, particularly their economic, social, and political needs, both locally and in general and at regular intervals. Democracy is not the state's business; it is the people's own affair. All the state can do is respect the democratic will of the people. It is only responsible for delivering services, when necessary. In brief, for Kurdistan, a well-defined and agreed upon formula of "democracy + the states of Turkey, Iran, Iraq, and Syria as a general public authority" could become a fundamental component of the program.

The democratization of Kurdistan is not merely a question of laws; it is a comprehensive social project. On the one hand, it includes resistance against the circles that prevent the people from determining their own identity and fate. On the other hand, it includes all other groups when developing its economic, social, and political objectives and building, directing, and controlling the corresponding institutions. This is an ongoing process. Elections are only one of the instruments used to articulate this will. However, it essentially requires the effective organization and action of the people. It is a democratic process that extends from local village and small-town communes through city councils and municipalities to a general People's Congress and signifies a dynamic political life. Depending on the circumstances, this can be jointly organized as a democracy with the neighboring people or, if this is not possible, it can form its own democratic system.

Democratization is also an important task in the sphere of politics. Democratic politics requires democratic parties. As long as there are no parties and subsidiary institutions that are not state-oriented and prioritize the demands of society, we cannot expect the democratization of political life. The parties in Turkey are the propaganda arm of the state and when they take over the state are nothing but instruments designed to serve rentiers. The transition to parties that focus on social problems and have an appropriate legal status is an important part of any political reform. It is still forbidden to form a party for and with the word *Kurdistan* in its name. Non-state parties don't have much of a chance of success, and clearly this must change. The ability to form parties and alliances in the name of Kurdistan is pertinent to the essence of democratization, as long as they don't advocate secession or resort to violent means.

An understanding of democratic politics and democratic society and efforts for transformation are of particular importance in Kurdistan. Given the despotic character of political phenomena in Kurdistan, understanding and developing democratic criteria is particularly vital. It is not just the center-right that has state-oriented policies that are despotic and rentier-oriented, the same is also true of most left-wing policies. These basic features explain why the people of the Middle East hate politics so much. Once the role attributed to politics is reduced to fraud and repression, it becomes inevitable that society will remain outside of politics, or, rather, that it be the object of politics that dominates. The best method for overcoming this alienation of politics is the art of democratic politics, which has as its goal a democratic civil society and is centered around it. Without a theory and practice built on democratic politics, any effort within social groups will inevitably run the risk of being deceptive. Good will alone doesn't count for very much. Instead, we must carefully examine the commonalities and differences between platonic loyalty to the people and the art of democratic politics.

Essentially, my submissions to the court give the utmost priority to clearing the way for democratic politics in Kurdistan. Only with the implementation of the universal criteria of democracy can we overcome the culture of submission and subjugation that is prevalent among individuals and institutions. Of late, we have witnessed the use of the PKK's legacy in the service of extraordinarily undemocratic practices. The fact that the DEHAP did not achieve the desired results in the 2004 municipal elections was primarily because democratic theory and practice have not been adopted and developed as a way to solve the problems of leadership and cadres and how they function. In the other parts of Kurdistan, a despotic style of politics is even more prevalent. What is essential for a free Kurdistan in the upcoming period is the creation of political establishments centered on democratic society and politics that do justice to the concrete historical and social conditions of each part of Kurdistan. In this light, all existing parties, associations, and nongovernmental institutions must be transformed. There is no more valuable work than recognizing, believing in, and implementing democratic politics to the best of our ability.

We are faced with the main task of establishing a democratic means of functioning in all organizations, all manner of work, and all activities in every part of Kurdistan, neighboring metropoles with large Kurdish communities, areas with Kurdish minorities, and, finally, abroad, especially in Europe. At the same time, our people must prove adaptable enough to include the minorities in Kurdistan that they live with and their friends who are willing, as well as prioritizing grassroots organization and activism before all else. The PKK should organize and implement its own democracy. It should follow the existing democratic laws, and in the absence of democratic laws organize its life and struggle around its own democratic rules and statutes. All democratic institutions from the communes to the Koma Gel should elect their leadership annually in regional congresses based on candidates' success and their capacity to resolve the problems we face. Appropriate methods should be adopted to prepare a system for holding elections and electing office holders from among the candidates. Member of a leadership body should not be elected for more than two consecutive mandates, and they should only be able to run again after a gap of two elections, and then only if they propose fresh projects.

Our people must ensure that they operate a democracy of their own making in ways they see fit in all parts of Kurdistan, in the metropoles, especially in Europe, and should elect the candidates they find the most promising to all levels (from the local commune to the Koma Gel), demand regular reports, and oversee them accordingly. If the states respect the people's democracy, they will agree to compromises, but, otherwise, democratic resistance using the appropriate means must continue. It is essential to grasp self-democracy—the best path to freedom and equality for our people—and to practice it until victory.

We also require free media in the political sphere. Without free media, the state's receptiveness to democracy and the democratizing of the political sphere will prove impossible. The demand for legal amendments in relation to the media in Kurdistan should not be based on individual rights but on public rights. Linguistic discrimination in any form must be barred.

Feudal institutions represent an obstacle to democracy. That is why appropriate means must be found to democratically transform the relics of the Middle Ages, such as *agaluk*,[3] sheikhdoms, tribalism, and sectarianism. These institutions are parasitic, numb the mind, and raise obstacles to the development of free morality, preventing democratization as much as the classic state institutions do.

Social Objectives

The program for the social sphere should primarily seek to determine and address the problems facing women and the family and the difficulties to be addressed around health care, education, morality, religion, and the arts. The social sphere can be treated as a separate issue for convenience, even though, together with the political and economic sphere, it forms an integral part of a whole. Although the social sphere should be thought of as the truly decisive sphere, it experiences the extreme pressure of being caught between the domination found in the political sphere and economic exploitation. It has come to resemble a disease-ridden body. Increasingly strengthening and defending the social sphere should be considered central to the program. Which is to say, the focus should shift from economics and politics to the social sphere.

Key to the liberation of society is moving away from the time-honored practice of stripping society of its economic means and then giving tiny morsels back to create dependency and establish control. This is how state systems control society. Using the economy to condition society must come to an end. The relentless use of this strategy against Kurdish society has turned our people into beggars. First and foremost, this trap must be eliminated from the social sphere, which means recognizing the right of society not the state to control society's economic resources.

The women, men, and children within the family are the most stifled parts of the system. The system has literally turned the family into dross, an institution that is suffocated by all of the system's contradictions. Marriage, the wife, the husband, and the children have not yet overcome the old feudal relationships, yet find themselves besieged by merciless capitalist relationships, and, thus, live in absolutely prison-like conditions. While the family is considered sacred in Kurdistan, it has also been totally subdued, by the lack of freedom and financial resources in particular, as well as by problems related to education and health care. The situation of the women and children is a complete disaster. The murder of female family members, a phenomenon known as "honor killings," is actually a symbolic expression of the predicament of life in general. The women are made to take the brunt of society's diminished honor. A destitute masculinity revenges itself on women. Under the existing circumstances, the crisis of the family can only be resolved with the overall democratization of the society. Education, publications, and broadcasts in the mother tongue could make at least a partial contribution to this end by reassembling the deteriorated identities of any people affected. Furthermore, special economic support could help the poor families, at least temporarily.

Apart from the state and a small group of collaborators, there is yet the *Other* form of humanity in Kurdistan about which no one dares to write or speak. Without solving the problem of the identity, freedom, and equality of these Others, it is nonsensical to talk about having overcome the consequences of the dirty war. A unilateral tragic war rages within Kurdish society, its families, and its women, men, and children. The program should seek to clearly, forthrightly, and intensively address this problem and offer creative solutions.

There must be freedom of education both in the official language and in one's mother tongue. Even if such instruction is not supported by the state, efforts on the part of the people to build educational institutions with their own resources to promote their language and culture must not be impeded. The state and the civil society must also guarantee a functioning health care system as a public service, and artistic activities must be free from constraint, so that artistic movements able to nurture society can develop.

No task can be mastered successfully as long as society is not guided by morality. Acquiring a free morality has to do with society becoming conscious. Therefore, the far-reaching formation of society's consciousness must not be obstructed. A free society is a moral society, and this should be reflected in all the work taken up within society. The place of religion in social life should also be discussed, and religion should be freed from its ball and chain. Since it represents the oldest social tradition and the conscience of society, it must undergo the necessary reform and be brought into harmony with contemporary science and philosophy. Developing a common language of religion, philosophy, science, and even mythology is key to breaking out of today's crisis around the nature of the individual. Religion must play its role primarily as part of the new morality of freedom and must consider it a duty to reinterpret the relationship between science and society from its own perspective and present its conclusion to society. This is essentially the role that prophets played. Religion today is more corrupt and dysfunctional than ever before. The main goal of a religious reform must be to help religion regain its functionality.

Another primary concern is restoring the significance the social realm once had. The small minority that controls the state and the economy must cease gnawing on and plundering a society that has survived to date despite the great pain it has experienced and the thousands of years spent trying to destroy it. This minority must accept a basic social policy that shows society the respect and esteem that is due. Protecting society from both this state minority and individual plunder, theft, and assault should be understood as the fundamental task of the program in the social realm.

Women
Freedom in a society can be measured by the freedom of women, and the level of freedom in society determines the overall level of democracy

and of the social state that is receptive to it. The centrality of the freedom of women makes it absolutely essential that the issue be addressed as a distinct programmatic point. Our analysis of the women's question indicates that it is the fundamental reference point for social transformation. Alongside the question of power and war, the question of women is the second key area where real socialism failed. Women and power are two phenomena that are highly contradictory. Women are the first oppressed class, sex, and nation. Without an evaluation of women's freedom and equality within historical and social development and a corresponding theory, sound practical progress is impossible.

Elements remaining from the Neolithic Age continue to have influence over women in Kurdish society. That being said, women have suffered during every phase of civilization. They have a resilient composition. Clearly, our own age has betrayed them. Were this awareness merged with the universal achievements of feminism, a separate women's party could play a huge role in the struggle for freedom, equality, and democratization. The founding of the Partiya Azadiya Jin a Kurdistan (PAJK: Women's Freedom Party of Kurdistan) could be a step toward addressing this need.[4] Even though it cannot easily get rid of the dominant masculine mindset, insistence on freedom is of utmost importance. The combined use of emotional and analytical intelligence by women themselves would be the best way to attain the liberation of the women's world. Mythology, philosophy, religion, and science must all be examined anew from the perspective of women and must be interpreted through free and distinct women's intelligence and put into practice. Approaching theory and practice with women's intelligence could more meaningfully lead to a world that is peaceful, freedom-loving, egalitarian, and close to nature, as well as to a life that is charged with beauty. The persistence on PAJK in Kurdistan and the headway that could be made thereby might well facilitate the achievement of the virtues of goddesses, the truthfulness of angels, and the beauty of Aphrodite.

There is no male culture this sort of women's synthesis could not disentangle, no life force it could not attract, and no action it could not carry out. Unless a female virtue equivalent to the sacredness of the goddess prevalent in mythology is developed—against housewifization and the despotic masculinity that has constantly deepened as a culture of slavery throughout the history of civilization[5]—grandeur, freedom, and equality in life cannot be achieved. If these values are not reclaimed, life cannot evade being a lost value. This is the framework that the program must articulate on the question of women.

Ecology and Economics

The basic programmatic position in the economic realm should include the transition from an economy based on commodification and profits to an economy rooted in use value and sharing. The economy ramped up by profit has not only destroyed society but has also destroyed nature. We are moving toward an uninhabitable environment. If bourgeois economic policy is not stopped, it will lead the world into a true hell. As a result of the rise of those sections of the bourgeoisie that pursue the goal of maximum profit, particularly the circles profiteering from financial speculation, humanity experiences the most negative sides of globalization. Never before in history has any class pocketed such enormous profits and value. Key to the decadence of society is the level of financial speculation the economy has reached. On the other hand, industry and trade, driven by financial capital, have brought about continuous production and marketing of the most profitable and most superfluous commodities. This, in turn, has led to the formation of the other human who is shaped by the alleged overabundance that the society can neither buy or consume, a human who lives with hunger and poverty that has reached breathtaking proportions. Humanity can no longer live with this political economy. Addressing this problem is, in fact, the true task of socialism.

We can define this task as bringing about the gradual transition from a commodity-based society to a society that produces for use value, from a profit-oriented production to a production based on sharing. This is the political economy of socialism, and the economic principles of the program must be based on this economic policy. Once this economic policy is implemented, unemployment, poverty in the midst of abundance, hunger alongside overproduction, and environmental destruction for profit will cease to be fate.

Ecological society is essentially socialist society. All the talk about ecological equilibrium and ecological society only begins to make sense with the transition from the society that is alienated from nature and the environment and permeated by power since the onset of civilization to a socialist society. The liberation of the environment under the capitalist system is an illusion. This system destroys ecological equilibrium to an unprecedented extent. The environmental question will be radically solved to the degree that the current system becomes ineffective and a socialist society system develops. This does not mean that nothing can be done for the environment right now. On the contrary, this emphasizes the necessity to wage the struggle for the environment intertwined with the struggle for a general social transformation in order to more actively advance the environmental struggle.

The program should emphasize that unemployment and increasing prices, poverty and hunger, environmental destruction and extreme commodification, overproduction and the lack of use value are all rooted in the dominant capitalist system and should make people aware that this is not fate, and that these problems can be solved by turning toward a socialist economy. These issues should be directly addressed in articles in the program.

Another issue that should be carefully addressed in the program is the issue of choice between the commodity value and the use value of the goods. The commodification of goods leads to the regime of profit, which in turn leads to the development of divisions, including overwork accompanied by high levels of unemployment, overabundance alongside scarcity, luxury alongside pollution, oppressors and oppressed, exploiters and exploited, masters and the doomed, the oppressor and the oppressed sex, and many other such dichotomies. On the other hand, the production of goods as use value does not lead to these dichotomies but, rather, to developments in society that are socialist in nature. Let me clarify this point with a simple example, the planting of oaks. An oak tree doesn't have much commodity value, but it does have high use value. Its acorns are valuable, its wood is solid, and the shade it provides is quite delightful. Furthermore, planting trees contributes to solving environmental problems. As well as being incredibly ecological, planting oak trees could reforest the Middle East, which has become barren. A sustainable reforestation program would also create work for many people. Planting and nurturing oaks doesn't require any complicated professional training. Thus, this simple measure could have positive economic and environmental effects, while simultaneously demonstrating an alternative to the ubiquitous profit-oriented way of thinking.

Internationalist Aspect
The internationalist aspect of the program should be elaborated in both its regional and global dimensions. Concretely, Kurdistan is inseparably

interwoven into the history, geography, and people of the Middle East, so the need to exclude nationalism is even more obvious. The basis for the catastrophe and dead ends in Israel-Palestine relations and contradictions lies in nationalism. The fact that nationalism based on the nation has been added to religious nationalism has only exacerbated the catastrophe. If, instead, the possibilities for a democratic solution had been taken as the basis, there would probably have been less suffering, and an order that would be more favorable than the current one might have been created. The ultranationalist statist approach has clearly proved itself not to be a solution but to be a policy of terror. Should such nationalist statist currents gain the upper hand in Kurdistan, the result will not be just a single Israel-Palestine-like conflict but four of them. There are a number of conclusions to be drawn from this. The many negative consequences of the conflicts around Chechnya, Nagorno-Karabakh, Kosovo, and Cyprus, as well as those between the Ottoman Empire and the Armenians or between the Ottomans and the Arabs, are as well known as those resulting from the conflict between the Kurds and Turkey and Iraq.

The best way to prevent the rise of new catastrophes is mustering the courage to comprehensively resolve the Kurdish question through a consistent and sincere peace and democratic reform rather than denial and annihilation or allowing Kurdistan to fade away and fall into mendicancy. We have already presented a concrete formula for this with the example of Turkey, i.e., "the state + democracy in Kurdistan," in effect, a partnership based on general security and attention to the public sphere, an approach that could be applied to the Middle East in general. Concretely, this would mean "democratization in the Middle East + the openness of the state to democracy = freedom for Kurdistan." A free Kurdistan is a democratic Kurdistan. In the general global context, one of our tasks is to transform the World Social Forum into a supranational platform for local democracies, into a "Global Democracy Congress" of the people, one that is not fixated on states. The supranational slogans for the coming period may well be a "Democratic Kurdistan," a "Democratic Middle East Federation," and a "Global Democracy Congress."

Individual Rights

Individual rights should be included in the program as human rights, and the individual's freedom of thought, speech, and will must be preserved under all circumstances. No country, state, or society can deprive individuals of the right to freely think, speak, or express their will in their own interests. The primary goal should be to attain the optimal equilibrium between sociality and individuality. In the final analysis, social freedom not based on individual freedom is as doomed to failure as individual freedom not based on social freedom. Fundamental human rights can attain more value without attacking the right to be a society, knowing that they can only exist with a society and by not succumbing to extremely individualistic, irresponsible, and antisocial tendencies.

All this should be based not on the international solidarity of the sort seen in the past but on a supranational approach; solidarity should not be international but, rather, supranational or transnational. People should be able to embrace a solidarity that transcends religion, nation, and class identity. This would make the solidarity of both labor and humanism more meaningful.

The program must clearly explain the relationship between democracy and socialism. Socialism is generally defined by "equality," and achieving this goal is often equated with the collectivization of property, but its link with democracy and freedom has never been explicitly elaborated. It even got to the point where the idea arose that it did not matter how and with what system socialism was established. Real socialism ultimately degenerated into state capitalism. Both theoretical developments and the results of practice have clearly shown that it is impossible to arrive at socialism without a full implementation of democracy and thriving of the above-mentioned freedoms. Socialism cannot be established by the state. Since the time of the Sumerians, the state has engaged in many intense collectivization processes. In fact, states were the agents of the most far-reaching examples of socialization. That being the case, it follows that the state could be called the largest socialist institution. The Soviet experiment was the continuation of this historical tendency. In this sense, it is entirely appropriate to describe the expropriation by the state and such movements for equality as generalized systems of patronage. Instead of an effendi, an aga, or a capitalist, this system essentially plays the same role as the common identity that subsumes them all. It will only be possible to talk about true socialism once democracy means a *minimal* state and equality is achieved through democratic development. As a condition, it is necessary to determine that this is something that cannot occur without freedom. Equality can only be conceptualized as socialism when equality—as the absence of domination—is combined with freedom. Equality based on coercion can never be socialism. Therefore, only an egalitarian society that is brought about in the context of the freedoms experienced as part of the most extensive democratic practice can be socialist.

This concludes, in rough, my thoughts about a draft program and its theoretical structure. What we envisage is a program that is free from statist and nationalist influences and aims for a social transformation that is democratic and in the direction of freedom and equality. It is not a liberal program, but it concedes a realistic role to individual initiative. It is a program that adopts the line of democratic authority instead of power, freedom instead of social control, use value and sharing instead of liberal commodity exchange and a profit-oriented market, as well as providing the optimal balance between the individual and society. Of course, these are just sketchy propositions presented for discussion and open to change and development.

Organizing

While the program embodies the essence of the reconstruction of the PKK, organizing determines its form. Just as theory determines the program, the program determines organization. Organization can be compared to a skeleton. Just as the body without a skeleton would merely be a mass of meat, a party without organization would be an equally empty mass unable to implement its will. On the other hand, the appropriate organization of cadres provides a foundation and scaffold upon which society can rise and build. There are, thus, two aspects to organizing: the organization of the cadres and the organization at the base.

Cadres

Throughout history all formations that resemble parties have had firmly committed and determined cadres. Many groups lacking such cadres have inevitably disappeared into the depths of history and fallen into oblivion. A cause is taken seriously when it is represented by parties and strong cadres.

As we have frequently emphasized, cadres are the militants who have best internalized the mentality and the programmatic principles of the party and enthusiastically try to put them into practice. They are the organizational staff of transformation. They are characterized by their capacity to make the connection between theory and practice and effectively play leadership roles, bringing together mass organizations and activism. Moreover, such an identity should artfully combine social morality and the creativity of politics at a personal level. When we look at the history and the reorganization of the PKK in this light, we can make out many intertwined positive and negative elements. That the PKK is still alive today is primarily due to its brilliant cadres who have provided an example of humanity. At the same time, serious problems with the cadres have prevented the party from achieving complete success. Both the successes and the failures are due to the cadres. A giant hairball of social contradictions has been uncovered in the personalities of the cadres. There were those who were broken when these contradictions were uncovered and others who drew strength from addressing the contradictions. A cadre tragedy, heroism, and betrayal have always been experienced intertwinedly. Despite our educational efforts and attempts to guarantee a good practice, we never fully succeeded in generating cadres who could take the lead and implement the line in an exemplary manner. Our party-building process stalled because of the inadequacy of our cadres, and the most fundamental problem of the upcoming reconstruction process is becoming sufficiently strong cadres.

Solving this problem would facilitate the successful implementation of the program. If we fail to achieve this, new blockages will arise. To be a cadre is a matter of love and passion. It is to devote yourself to your goals with full conviction, determination, and acuteness of mind. Those who don't possess these qualities and want to reach the top for careerist reasons and to fulfill a passing desire will always deliver negative results. Becoming a cadre requires more than a passing desire; it requires theoretical foresight, a deep commitment to the program, and a dedication to constructing the party structure. Obviously, in this new phase, the organization of cadres must serve to develop these qualities. All serious social, political, and economic organization requires a similar understanding of what a cadre is and the art of leadership. To be successful, this is an essential component.

I have already stressed above that in our determination to reconstruct the PKK we must focus on the serious problems before us. While the most precious comrades became martyrs, and many who survived worked with devotion, there were also those who were opportunistic, careerist, and gang-like, who gnawed away at our values from within. It was as if social reality was almost reborn within the party. Although we were living through some of the most critical moments in our history, there was never a shortage of people who shamelessly hoped to satisfy their personal ambition and craving for power. There were also quite a few who weren't even as productive as the average worker and lazed around while a lot of work simply remained undone. They hoped to reach high positions in the organization without doing anything. They even tried to instigate an infantile and dangerous power struggle over the legacy of the party.

They lacked the sense of responsibility necessary to realize that while making some arrangements on behalf of the party, we tried to protect the cadres, and in doing so we risked our own well-being. Conscious of the potential tragedy that awaited us, I was, in fact, only trying to act as a worthy comrade. The heavy criticism they received was an invitation for them to take responsibility. That they had to prove themselves worthy of the memory of the martyrs in their thousands and live up to the expectations of the people, because history would not pardon those who failed to do so, was constantly emphasized. Nevertheless, these people lacked the creativity necessary to develop a successful approach. The most calamitous event was the power struggle over the legacy of the party that began with the "İmralı phase."

On the one hand, comrades immolated themselves and the people wept bitter tears, and, on the other hand, a power struggle began between various groups that was both in essence and form unworthy of our tradition. This was an enormous contradiction, and it must be resolved with the refounding of the party. If the question of cadres is to be addressed as outlined immediately above, there is no room for assessments based on the balance of power or other similar calculations. There is, however, little likelihood that those who have organized themselves as groups within the party will abandon their thinking and participate in the renewal of the party. Therefore, it would be best to present our theoretical and programmatic understanding and claim our legacy together with those who consciously say, with conviction and determination, "I'm on board," and in this way reshape our essence.

It is well known that our legacy includes potential cadres whose number and quality would be sufficient to found several parties. We took responsibility for facilitating a voluntary convergence of all these cadres in our effort to build the party based on a far-reaching freedom of thought and free will. The proposal to form a twelve-person preparatory committee for reconstruction was a further step in that direction.[6] The problem is not one that can be resolved through speedy appointments. Repeating the past is also out of the question. Our goal is to work with astute cadres who will overcome the errors of the past, show the skill necessary to meet the requirements of the moment, and secure the future, and who never hide behind any inadequacy. After having sufficient successful practice with these qualified aspiring cadres, we will know if they can play a lasting role as permanent members. We can make a decision about those who have taken sides and the various groups that have emerged after in-depth discussion and evaluation, as well as the necessary critique, self-critique, and practical effort. It should, of course, be clear that people cannot work together and form a party as long as old scores remain unsettled.

What is decisive here is not good intentions but clear criteria. We are not, however, entirely breaking all contact with these groups. We will continue to work with them under the umbrella of the Koma Gel. This will prove that a democratic party, above all else, maintains internal democracy.

I don't think that a large number of people is necessary or helpful in a cadre organization. I am quite sure that three to five hundred cadres would be sufficient to carry out the program, to mobilize the masses, and to be represented in all areas of work.

It is only natural that the cadres prefer a productive organization rather than organizing according to mechanical schemes. Appointments should not be made to fill areas and staff positions but should be organized around directly addressing and successfully accomplishing pending tasks. The criterion is the pending tasks and the cadres who can successfully accomplish them. Representative bodies or committees can be created according to need, individually or by the dozens, but because collectivism is essential, at least two representatives for each committee would always be preferable. This promises greater functionality than the classic central committee, political bureau, and branch organizations. However, we should not get caught up in problems of form but strive for solutions suitable to the essence. People who feel they can solve a problem can volunteer for tasks at hand, or there may be assignments by appointment. However, coercion is never appropriate.

In the coming months, the focus could be on assigning sufficient cadres to areas where there is an urgent need. It should be easy to organize one hundred cadres within a period not exceeding six months. Depending on need, however, that number could be smaller or bigger. Both collectivism and individual initiative should be made use of in an intertwined manner. As is generally known, a successful working style requires speed, consistent reflection on actions taken, and determination. The right approach to getting work done in a timely manner is no less important than theoretical and practical competence.

As is well known, everyone—the grassroots, the defense units, those who work in the legal spheres, and those underground—is branded a "terrorist," making it necessary to work in particularly creative and original ways. Our demeanor and lifestyle should radiate enthusiasm and be attractive. Repugnant behavior is just as dangerous as a provocation.

In brief, you should all get down to practical work after sorting out the cadre policy and its minimal organizing. Exemplary discipline in work is just as important as voluntarism. With a legacy of heroic deeds, we march alongside a people that has risen and is passionately fighting for freedom. Turning to new tasks after a great experience and thoroughly analyzing past practice is not only exciting but also requires productivity and an attitude that does not tolerate failure. Successfully carrying out a task is the clearest criterion for what a sworn oath is really worth and shows us the true substance of a person.

The party's statutes are another key organizational issue. The general nature of such statutes is well known. They can include sections about the regular congresses, chairpersons elected at these congresses, and a central committee or a party council, as well as a small executive body elected from this body's members, a general secretary and deputies, central bodies, regional, local, and communal committees and subunits, grassroots branch organizations, sectional organizations for different countries and different parts of Kurdistan, etc. I am not in the position to make an assessment for or against this model. However, we know from experience that this model was always used in a state-oriented manner, served to increase authoritarianism, and did not allow for the operation of the democratic aspect that much. It is difficult to say if this model necessarily produces these results. If people act with an awareness that theory and practice are decisive and that the statutes are unimportant in and of themselves but are only a means for implementing the program, then the statutes could easily lead to democratization. This also depends on the quality of the cadres. Theory, the program, cadres, the statutes, and operations are of a whole cloth.

Each part of Kurdistan may need its own organizational section. The party in each part must neither be completely independent from nor completely dependent on the central headquarters. Organizing as sections may be a more appropriate approach to this semi-dependency. Centralized institutions could include, for example, media and an editorial board, an academic board for the sciences and the arts, and a board for legal and disciplinary issues, while mass organizations could include free women's units, a union of democratic youth, labor unions, cooperatives, and associations for migrants, farmers, craftspeople, and entrepreneurs, among others. To ensure the sound functioning of such bodies, more specific statutes and a fruitful combination of collectivism and individual initiative would be necessary. There are, of course, other models of statutes as guidelines for internal processes. Here, I just wanted to present a few thoughts on some points I consider important.

I also want to address a few points with regard to the PAJK, which requires a particular approach, particularly in terms of cadre policy, because I think this is important. I believe that the PAJK should have a core group of cadres. The centrality of women's freedom to the solution of all problems of democratization, freedom, equality, and even ecology is often underestimated. Since we can't immediately liberate all women, it seems clear that this process needs to start with a small group of cadres. If a core group from the PAJK can't liberate itself, how can it succeed in liberating the women and men who are perhaps the world's most problem-ridden? I have made much effort to this end myself.

What we are confronted with is the reality of women as the first slave class, the first slave sex, and the first slave nation in the history of civilization. The confinement of women in private and "public" houses is the practical implementation of this slavery. The source of this repression is social rather than biological. Housewifery and husbandry, in terms of their forms within civilization, are institutions that operate against women and against society in general. The husband is a projection of the political imperator in the domestic sphere, always playing the role of the little despot when it comes to the woman. This has nothing to do with individual intention but must be understood as a reality of civilization.

When we talk about the freedom of women, it is perhaps best to begin with the domestic culture of the mother or of the mother-goddess culture that made great progress with the agricultural revolution. This is why I have chosen the trinity "Goddess-Angel-Aphrodite" as a mythological blueprint. Without tearing down the image of the "simple wife" and the "simple girl," we can't develop any feeling for the grandeur, prestige, and beauty of women. According to the criteria of civilization, men are of divine origin, while women are deprived of all criteria that are divine, sacred, angelic, and beautiful.

There is an old, and established concept of "honor" that may be valid in a certain sense—for both the men and women among us. But this concept of "honor" and this culture of husbandry and housewifery is incompatible with my revolutionary aesthetic understanding of life.

I have already tried to explain my concept of "the mother." In my opinion women continue to be more sensitive to the natural world than men. Men are a kind of extension of women, not, contrary to what is believed, at the center of things. The scientific data clearly indicates this.

The enormous oppression and exploitation imposed on women have led to a situation where they have to conceal and differentiate their true nature to an incredible degree. The fashionable masculine discourse applied to women has led to the most unbelievable narratives, definitions, and language in the name of religion, philosophy, and even science and the arts. In this malicious and degenerate manner, women have even been forced to worship the very things they most disbelieve in. I am fighting for real freedom and an equitable balance of power and, therefore, no one should expect me to participate in or approve of this civilization game. I don't like the world of the male gods, but at the same time I have a good grasp of its penetralia. It should also be clear that I will not take part in the rituals surrounding the divinities of this world. These divinities, which project themselves as the state, religion, politics, the arts, and science, are only relevant—at least to me—when analyzed, untangled, and understood. I do find the divinity of women interesting and attractive, but at the same time I know that it requires courage and is difficult to achieve. I also don't believe that a more peaceful, more beautiful, more sentient life, in short, a life worth living, is possible if it is not built on women's freedom and the strength that makes it possible. On the other hand, a masculinity based on women's slavery still disgusts me as much as it did when I was a child. I can't be expected to approve of this abomination.

The phenomenon that we call "love" can determine everything else. By this point, the reader presumably understands that I am insistent on love when it comes to our women cadre policy. In fact, we have tried to develop this approach intertwinedly within a significant cultural and political framework and with a concept of "freedom" and "equality" beyond the dimension of sexuality. This requires a definition of love that can be attained by women breaking away from the culture of slavery, which includes breaking away from the mostly domination-based male culture and assuming a free and equal position within an overall democratic equilibrium in the political realm. This approach rejects the fatal relationship that develops between dominant masculinity, which is superficial and based on sexual passion, and feminine slavery.

This requires an understanding of the divinity that should exist in the relationship between a man and a woman, which is very hard to experience in class civilization in general and in the capitalist system in particular. What we mean by divinity is the great and exciting power of meaning that realizes itself in the emotional and analytical intelligence of human beings over the course of the universal story that, according to the latest scientific data, has lasted fourteen million years. Humans are nature that become aware of itself. Women are closer to this universality than men, as scientific data indicate. When I say women are universal and divine, I mean it in this sense. When this meaning, which makes itself felt in the world of the arts, politics, and science, and during revolutions from time to time, is reflected in the relationships between women and men, it is possible to talk about the divinity of the relationship. This is how it should be. The various religions understand this, but because they are predominantly male ideological and social identities, they have done great harm to the divinity they express by excluding women. We are making an effort to bring about this divinity between the sexes in a balanced, democratic, free, and egalitarian manner. I will leave it at that for now, as this is not the place for further elaboration.

If we accept this premise, the questions are: Do prevailing relationships correspond to this definition of divinity? Are we not, on the contrary, witnessing a massacre of women in their relationships, sometimes physically, executed with murderous weapons, including axes, and—even worse—beaten down with treacherous and empty expressions of love? Is this not the materialization of men's swinishness? The attempt to legitimize present-day relationship between men and women is perhaps one of the most abominable forms of disguised slavery ever.

Thus, we can talk about the core group of the PAJK consisting of about three hundred women who consider themselves to meet the definitions of goddesses, angels, and afreets (fairy-like creatures, the name comes from Aphrodite) as outlined above. Thus, a woman is a goddess to the degree that she is conscious of her universality, takes her place in the democratic balance of power, is free, and ensures equality in her social relationships. It is clear that a man would not even try to housewifize and dominate such a woman. He can only show his respect and express his affection but cannot expect forced love and obligatory respect or, most particularly, sexist relations from her. A man can only expect love and respect when he has become free and equal within the framework of a democratic balance of power with a woman of similar principles. This should be understood as our fundamental moral principle. If this moral principle is respected, it might just be that the phenomenon called love will emerge. This, in turn, is only possible through the heroism of the struggle for democracy, freedom, and equality. Any other approach is a betrayal of love, and when love is betrayed, creativity and success become impossible. True love in the ranks of the PKK is only possible through heroism that proves itself with success.

But what can we say about the many women and men who leave the organization together? We can regard them as evidence of the extent to which the Kurdish identity has been broken. It is a painful tragedy that while, at forty or fifty years of age, many of our friends do not live in typical slavery relationships, they, nonetheless, have not been able to integrate the kind of love we are discussing here into their thinking and actions. In fact, comedy and tragedy are intertwined. It is as if some of them have gone mad. Others are satisfied with coming together as a man and a woman, and yet others are satisfied only in their dreams. Some of them made marriage a political issue in the organization. Others objectively resorted to "protest" and neglected their revolutionary tasks, because they were prevented from satisfying their urges. In brief, they insisted that their expectations, which were typical for the system, be satisfied. I can understand these friends, but we, as men and women, promised each other that we would achieve freedom and equality when we faced the fiercest tests of our lives. We understood that this promise could only be fulfilled in a free country with a democratic society and avowed to make it so. There is no denying that I have made every effort to honor that oath and our determination.

My recommendation is to carry out the struggle for love as it is outlined immediately above. One must trust women's sense of justice. Men generally suspect women of all sorts of evil deeds when they are left unsupervised, a suspicion obviously based on millennia of oppression and cruelty. I advocate an approach that is the opposite of the ruling masculinity. Justice, freedom, and equality make up a large part of women's nature. Or, to be more precise, the essence of women's sociality is based on justice, freedom, and equality. Moreover, this sociality is peaceful in the extreme. Women are very well aware that a meaningful life requires justice, freedom, equality, and peace. They are also sensitive to beauty, with a superior conception of what it is. When making a choice or taking a decision, they do not resort to war and repression or impose inequality, because all of this runs counter to their nature and their manner of socialization. These issues will be understood to the degree that women are able to act freely. The freer they are, the greater the opportunity to make more beautiful, just, and equal choices. As such, the vitality of the concepts of "beauty," "justice," and "equality" in society is firmly rooted in women's liberation.

A self-confident man should not be an obstacle to women's liberation in this manner; but he should know that it would require unselfish support. Such a man would not say, "She is my woman," but would prioritize saying, "She is a woman who must be free." Only then will we be able to determine the conditions of the phenomenon of love. To begin with, for women to fully exercise their right to make a choice, the first condition is for women to access equivalent power with men in terms of freedom and equality. To this end, the other prerequisite is the complete democratization of society. The second condition is that men, both within themselves and within the male-dominated society, overcome the principles of domination of women that they have acquired over thousands of years, thereby accepting to arrive at an equivalent power with women. Obviously, a democratic struggle for freedom and equality waged to establish these conditions will bring the individual closer to the phenomenon of love. To begin with, of course, the kinds of love that exist in the current system must be neutralized.

Real bravery can mean something in this context. Such people's interest in and tendency to love will garner respect. Our brave women and men who consciously risk their lives are also a warning for us not to betray love. They embody the principles and are both the practitioners of the sacred rules of love and its abiding heroes, not only for us but also for our country and our people. At the very least, we should show our respect for these heroes. I know that the above criteria are very difficult to live by, but then what could be more difficult than being fiercely scorched by love! Love is the extraordinary essence of the veracity that drives us to struggle on. Some of those in the PAJK may well hope to be among these heroes—I say this, because I have seen signs of it. At a minimum, we should not put obstacles in the path of those who make this leap and hope to lead a life with a greater purpose. They should discuss this among themselves, and they should educate themselves and make the leap from a cursed history to a history of freedom. They should outline the guidelines for a life overflowing with love, affection, and respect. They should make their own decisions about their own organization and their own practice. They should create their own system with their own regular meetings and congresses. They should work to attain the strength necessary for true love. Could anything be more valuable? For a PAJK that attained this kind of strength, there would no longer be insoluble problems or impossible tasks.

Perhaps many, including those among us, will say that the reality of the Kurds and Kurdistan doesn't allow for this understanding of love. Such a thought is unworthy of the history of our people. The legends of our tradition suit the views presented above. The legends of Memê Alan, Mem and Zîn, and Derwêşê Evdî, all of which take place along the Botan and in the Süphan and Sinjar Mountains, come pretty close to this kind of divinity. It may be difficult to transpose these love epics to our time, but our martyrs and I valiantly shouldered the work required for progress on the path of love. If those who allegedly desire love still do not recognize our efforts, they are blind, troublemakers, or possibly even traitors. What more work in the pursuit of love could you possibly expect from us?

At the same time as you are unable to carry out your revolutionary tasks, you still clearly and shamelessly say, "I want a relationship!" Love in Kurdistan is not like love in a Hollywood film, or in a Yeşilçam film, the Turkish corollary to Hollywood. The love we are talking about requires victorious gods and goddesses as much as wisdom. Even birds build their nests in unspoiled places. Can a love nest be built in a place and or a heart that is completely occupied? Any power under whose wings they seek refuge will, first and foremost, attack the lovers. My own experience clearly shows that it is impossible to live with a woman from the system without betraying your revolutionary duties. There may well be totally typical marriages within our ranks. I see them as servile relationships that seek to maintain physical existence. If we are not to call the friends in these marriages traitors, they must at least properly complete their revolutionary assignments. Furthermore, it is treason when they put their revolutionary assignments at the service of their relationships. Kurdish history wades ankle-deep in treason and treachery, which is generally the result of this sort of relationship. I would further argue that these typical marriages take place at the expense of love. I, for one, still favor an approach that fights for love. There cannot be any limit, age or otherwise, on this. As I have emphasized elsewhere: anyone who reduces love to sexual desire betrays love.

Under the conditions in which we struggle, love is hope, the precondition for success in addressing our duties. It is also passion, will, the power of reason, the quest for beauty, courage, a willingness to sacrifice, and belief that is necessary until a dignified end is reached in peace or war. The strength necessary for success in the struggle for patriotism, freedom, and dignified peace, which is also the struggle for love, will be found in the reality of PAJK; the free man will be created from the free woman.

The People's Congress

As an organizing tool, the Koma Gel (People's Congress) is at least as significant as the party, maybe even more so. The People's Congress, as the people's basic organizational framework, requires a specific definition for the concrete case of Kurdistan. First, a People's Congress is different than a party. In parties, the ideological aspect predominates, while the People's Congress prioritizes the political aspect. It is an expression of the identity of an awakened people demanding its rights and striving for its freedom. It is the shared decision-making and supervisory body for those who desire freedom for the country and democracy for the people, regardless of ideology, class, sex, nationality, opinion, or belief. It is not a parliament or a classic law-making body, but it is the force that can make decisions that enable the people to live free and equal and that can monitor the implementation of laws. It is both a legal and political organ, the supreme non-state-oriented organ of the people. It is not a state organ nor does it represent an alternative to the state. It is, however, one of the most important institutions among those that treat democratic criteria as the yardstick for addressing all of the social problems of our time. It is responsible for making the necessary decisions in the economic, social, political, juridical, ecological, media, and self-defense fields—areas where the state normally aggravates problems rather than solving them—and monitors their implementation. The People's Congress is the most important interlocutor of the people, both domestically and abroad.

We must be aware of the historical and political circumstances that have led to the founding of the People's Congress in Kurdistan. A weak and undemocratic bourgeois nationalism, on the one hand, and the existence of repressive nation-states that are not receptive to democracy, on the other hand, made a governing body in the form of a congress necessary. There is no people's state, but a congress that is the democratic decision-making body of the people is, nonetheless, essential. More clearly: since the national state cannot be the people's instrument for resolving the national question in Kurdistan but only risks deepening the deadlock, and because the people will not accept the former life of slavery under any circumstances, a People's Congress is the most appropriate instrument for a democratic solution.

As a result, we are confronted with the fundamental question of whether the nation-state and a people's democracy can coexist. We can find examples in many European countries, as well as within the federative structure of the United States, proving that it is possible. Even though the bourgeois nationalist state seriously constrains democracy, a certain amount of democratic space remains for the people. Because of their extremely unitary structure, Turkey and the other states that rule over Kurdistan leave very little lawful space for the people to articulate their democratic will. Exclusion is the main principle of the domestic policy. This engenders constant rebellion and suppression. In order to untie this critical Gordian knot, the authority of the People's Congress, i.e., its decision-making power, must be improved. Until the ruling states enter into a democratic compromise, it will be necessary to continuously develop people's non-state democratic institutions. That we have not adopted nationalism and the formation of a competing state is not our goal does not mean we are compelled to submit to the current status quo. On the contrary, what is required is the constant development of civil society and democratic institutions to prevent reciprocal nationalist strife. Leaving the ever-increasing problems of society to existing or yet to be founded states will only aggravate problems. A new state cannot be easily established, and if established could not solve the existing problems, in any case. Twenty-two Arab states have been founded, and their problems have only become more serious. The same is true of Africa, with almost fifty states. The EU is only slowly resolving the problems created by Europe's nation-states. The US is an expression of the *unity* of fifty states. In other words, an abundance of states tends to increase problems, not solve them. Since the existing states have lost their capacity to find solutions, the People's Congress, as a non-state democratic body, is the key instrument available to us for addressing problems.

Following a long experience with war, the developed countries have worked out a model along these lines. Other countries, however, are still far from even grasping this sort of solution. As unitary states, they always mistake it for a concession. For them, patriotism and sacred loyalty to their states means sticking by their national unitary state to the point that it decays. In Yugoslavia, in Iraq, and even on the small island of Cyprus, this led to unanticipated results. The Republic of Turkey, for its part, is still far from understanding the function of democracies, regarding them as rivals.

Even though the Kurds were a founding people of the republic, the authorities think they can rid themselves of the Kurdish question by simply denying its existence. They refuse to understand and recognize the strategic role that the Kurds have played in the past and continue to play today. They insist on going the way of Yugoslavia and Iraq, simply relying on military power and the size of the country. The role of the Kurds can be better understood if one compares it to the situation in the United Kingdom, where one small part of Ireland, Northern Ireland, posed a major problem, or to the case for Russia, with Chechnya. If it were to recognize that military solutions can never be lasting, and, in fact, tend to spiral out of control, as well as their enormous cost, the Turkish state would understand how important it is to find a solution. The situation in Cyprus was left unresolved for forty years—to whose benefit? There certainly were numerous losses.

As we move toward a solution by way of the congress, the state and society of Turkey need to be clearly and effectively reminded of the strategic role of the Kurds and Kurdistan. Kurdistan acquiring a status that can be used against Turkey would mean constant problems, economic losses, and political and military threats. Since the formation of the nationalist and tribalist Kurdish federal state in South Kurdistan, it has become clear that its influence will be lasting. Thus, given its current status, Kurdistan has very quickly arrived at a place where it can cause Turkey problems. If democratic solutions are not implemented, nationalist movements will inevitably arise, and a new Israel-Palestine-like conflict that could easily last for fifty years will emerge. What has already happened in Iraq will come into more widespread play, particularly seriously in Turkey, with the PKK. We know the initial conflict between the Turkish state and the PKK was not a pleasant experience, and this time around there will be more comprehensive preparations and planning. The state may choose to rely on its traditional policy of oppression, but it is not yet clear what the Greater Middle East Initiative might bring with it. It is open to all sorts of dangers. The Kurds becoming a strategic element opposing Turkey would have far-reaching consequences, including starting numerous discussions and providing the basis for making new demands of Turkey.

Once it is understood that the use of quick crushing and lulling tactics have not worked and will not work, a renewed round of conflict, whether short- or long-term, will be the most dangerous development.

There's no overlooking the fact that the Kurds could use their strategic role to ally with any state or power, first among them the US and Israel. Hoping to simply persuade the whole world that the PKK is a terrorist organization is nothing but self-deception. This situation would, on the contrary, awaken the world and create the opportunity to make additional demands of Turkey. Hasn't Turkey already made quite a few economic and political concessions? It is obvious that this would be the wrong approach, and the Kurds do not ever deserve such treatment. The fact that the Kurdish tribalist forces in South Kurdistan were gifted a federal state to induce them to act against the PKK-led freedom movement has also had catastrophic consequences, and more will come. Not only does the Turkish state employ and pay almost one hundred thousand village guards to prevent the Kurds from supporting and turning to the PKK in North Kurdistan, it has also given the reactionary primitive nationalist tariqa chiefs numerous positions within the state. It is these forces that will enable the creation of a second Iraq. In addition, all of this contradicts the principles of republicanism and democracy. What could a Kurdistan that is economically paralyzed do but explode in the face of all these developments?

During my time on İmralı Island, I have made every effort to overcome this senseless imposition. I am not sure to what extent this is clear. The new AKP government keeps its silence more persistently than any government before it. It apparently thinks it can neutralize the Kurdish question by creating positions within the state for a great number of Naqshbandi tariqat forces. During the elections, these elements received all kinds of state support to ensure their election. A strategic error is being made, and when the consequences quickly become apparent, those responsible will be unable to rectify it.

Significant state-rooted obstacles have been created to block our quest for a shared democratic solution in Turkey. Both internal and external obstacles have been thrown up to hinder the Demokratik Güçler Birliği (DGB: Union of Democratic Forces).[7] The exclusion of Kurdish democrats was regarded as essential to national security. All of this is a huge mistake; this is an insistence on the status quo and a deadlock. It is presumed that the Kurdish people cannot go their own way. Complete surrender brought about by hunger and repression is the anticipated outcome, with social policies, combined with diplomacy and internal security, as well as economic and political initiatives, still strictly implemented to this end. All of this is based on a single strategy of confronting the people with a clear dilemma:

"surrender or die!" The AKP government has added another component to this policy; the power of religion and the tariqat. The current phase is incredibly provocative, with Turkey insistently creating an impasse. All calls for a "peaceful and democratic solution" remain unanswered and studiously ignored, an approach that could not be expected from any similar movement and that could benefit everyone. We have seen none of the efforts that were made for a comparatively smaller problem, i.e., Cyprus, with the Kurdish question instead being deemed nonexistent. At the same time, hopes were pinned on both a split within the PKK, and US troops in Iraq. If it proves impossible to develop a joint democratic solution, the most positive resolution would be to develop our own democracy based on our own resources. Thus, from now on a congress solution will be on the agenda.

The people of Kurdistan must mobilize for a congress solution in all parts of the country and abroad. In the framework defined here, an extraordinary congress of the Koma Gel should take place in response to the group that recently emerged.[8] This congress should thoroughly evaluate current internal and external developments. Necessary decisions should be taken regarding economic, social, political, judicial, and ecological issues, as well as the media and self-defense. An executive council should be appointed. All those who are dreaming of a split and fragmentation will be disappointed.

People should commit all of their energy to a congress solution in all parts of Kurdistan. Because parties are excluded from national parliaments by electoral thresholds, bans, and similar mechanisms, local democratic governments should be mobilized. Self-government units should be elected and take responsibility in every village and neighborhood. Democratic solutions should lead to enlightenment in all realms of people's lives. Ways to achieve lasting solutions should be proposed. Wherever the appropriate conditions exist, the decisions of the congress should be implemented. An education that meets the needs of the people should be implemented to the degree possible. The people should not be abandoned to beg from the state. There will be no opportunity for the game of preying on the people by keeping them at the edge of starvation. Wherever there are attacks on human rights and cultural freedoms, the people should defend themselves. The evacuation of new villages should be prevented, and the old villages should be resettled. Numerous forms of solidarity should be used to act against hunger. A plethora of new forms of organizing should be developed. Civil society should be extensively organized. Democratic schools should be developed in every residential area to educate the people about their own democracy.

The congress solution will be ready for a democratic solution with any state. It will persistently push for democratic options based on peace and community solidarity and free from secessionism and violence, rather than nationalist oppression and denial.

Moreover, it will make clear that it is capable of defending itself from attack. This isn't about seceding but, on the contrary, a guarantee of genuine unity. It will be persistently emphasized that this is the most responsible way to prevent further tragedies. Should the states try to crush these efforts, the response will only grow stronger. The people, living under unbearable conditions, will step up their democratic action in a more organized and conscious way. They will not be seduced by nationalist and conspiratorial efforts but will also not refrain from all kinds of activities in the social, political, judicial, and artistic realms and in the realms of media and self-defense. In defining the essentials of this new phase, which we call the "congress solution," we believe it is our historical duty to call upon everyone to be more attentive and to contribute to a solution before new tragedies arise.

As part of this brief explanation of the definition and orientation of the People's Congress, we must address some topics in even greater detail. First, we must mention the internal power struggles that began at the first meeting of the Koma Gel. This fractious behavior, which was displayed at a moment of a major theoretical, political, and practical sea change toward a democratic solution, is clear evidence that some people have not understood the essence of democratic politics or what politicization means within the PKK in general—or they have dared to deliberately ignore it. I have already emphasized that such a behavior toward this political experience, which has lasted a quarter of a lifetime, must be subjected to serious analysis and dealt with thorough critique and self-critique. All of this has demonstrated how strong is the tendency to ignore rules, to pay no attention to circumstances, and to fail to evaluate consequences, which, in essence, is unpolitical, as well as being amateurish and failing to overcome cronyism when it comes to matters of power. It also reflects personality traits that aren't centered on successful work but are either bogged down in ideological templates or caught up in primitive drives.

Actually, I'm very familiar with these attitudes. They existed during the initial formation phase of the PKK as a group and persisted after the party was founded. These attitudes gave rise to extremely arbitrary practices and behavior when the armed struggle began on August 15, 1984, that have still not been adequately addressed. Thus, all this can be seen as the continuation of approaches imposed by those who have not been able to take on any real responsibility over the course of fifteen years of war. My mistake was choosing to treat these people very amicably instead of insisting they behave as our institutions and rules demanded, because my goal was to save them. I always approached them thinking and believing that they would gain experience and improve. The end result of my approach is my current situation.

The fact that I have been unjustifiably instrumentalized once more since I've been on İmralı Island is not as painful and devaluing for me as it is for those who have behaved this way and become the playthings of others. They chose this course even though I warned them and provided numerous examples to illustrate my point. I said, "There are some things that you can do when I've returned to dust, other things you cannot do even once I'm in my grave, and some things you can never do as long as I am still breathing." The mountains have an effect that is both liberating and bestializing. Obviously, the liberating aspect has been incorrectly internalized. I warned both the PKK and the relevant states that no one would profit from trying to manipulate me. Let there be no doubt that I am unshakably and entirely committed to doing what is right. I want everyone to understand that even though I may appear helpless and miserable, that is not, in fact, the case. Although I'm not doing splendidly, I wanted everyone to know that I cannot be considered completely devoid of dignity. However, the friends I speak of are apparently thrilled with their way of life and their way of waging war. It turns out that despite everything, I acted and must continue to act maturely.

Regardless of how difficult and important or how simple and unimportant any particular work may be, one must accept it as sacred and do it well. My question is: Do those who triggered this situation have the courage to just once appreciate what I have done to salvage their revolutionary honor? I can barely breathe through a tiny vent, but I continue trying to live by the values of our people's struggle for dignity, values that should never be underestimated. The situation here on İmralı Island is such that any ordinary person would commit suicide within three days. I am striving for unity and prudence and am trying to stay focused, which is very difficult. Will these friends prove by mature, successful efforts that they are capable of holding on to their dignity?

To this end, I have reflected and made proposals. I truly believed and expected that these friends would successfully renew themselves through an institution like the Koma Gel, thereby salvaging their honor. I also want to remind the friends of something else: this sort of power struggle ends in an ignominious death. They should not deceive themselves. How can people waste time on these "Byzantine intrigues," given the enormous tasks they have before them? Let's not debate who is right and who is wrong or use notions like "agent provocateur" or "coup plotter" to escape our responsibilities. Even if this were actually the case, our method of resolving the situation at hand cannot be allowed to put the fate of a people at risk. I have experienced hundreds of examples of this, but I have never neglected the tasks of the moment. You don't deliberately begin a battle that no one can win. What did the parties to the conflict hope for when they started a fight that would not only hurt them but everyone, all of our people? Even if one side were to win, how would they sell this victory, which would be worse than treason, and to whom?

What is even stranger is that they acted in my name, placing me in a sort of isolation within an isolation, which I find hard to comprehend. These people should acknowledge and explain what they have done. How can someone who is nurtured by their mother every day want her to be unable to any longer provide milk? I have recounted the story of the struggle with my mother. There were obvious historical reasons for it. But what reasons do these friends have? Neither the friends nor our enemy have ever claimed that I have nothing to offer. Why, therefore, do they devalue me? What are the reasons, and who is encouraging it? The answers to these questions are essential for further development.

I want to remind everybody, both those who participated in this and those who could, consciously or subconsciously, end up in a similar situation that participating in the struggle for the dignity of the people requires honorable and determined human beings acting willingly. Those who can't do this should not join our organization to begin with and should certainly never hold a rank within it. They should not forget that chasing after a rank is the enemy of democracy. But they should not shy away from holding a position, because that often means the absence of any aspirations and goals. Can they actually deny that they have behaved in an undemocratic fashion? I was able to follow some of the developments and must say that even the sultans wouldn't have employed their methods. How do they intend to justify violating the will of the people who are ready? How can it be that people opposed to democracy to such an extent are still living in our midst? They must at long last understand democracy. If even the most astute of the Turkish politicians have not managed to gain much with demagoguery and despotism, what could these beardless greenhorns possibly imagine achieving? I find writing all of this down quite difficult, and I hope I don't have to make similar comments in the future.

I am sure that had my friends held my position in the organization, they would have liquidated me a hundred times. And, even so, I continue to march alongside them. But I must add: don't play games with me. It will not end well for you.

The Koma Gel will work, even though the states attempted to paralyze it from the outside and various factional groups have tried to do the same from within. Let's talk about the states later. The groups that see themselves as conflicting parties should not forget for even a second that there is only one thing that can save them, successfully addressing the tasks they face.

I'm not in a position to say anything about the substance and the number of people that should be involved in the congress. In addition to what I have already said, I want to repeat my proposal that the board of the congress be elected annually, and that no one be allowed to run for two years following a second mandate. I see this as an important statutory democratic stipulation that should apply to all offices in the people's organization that require special skills but are non-ideological in nature. If one doesn't want to specifically focus on one-year terms, one could contextualize it as two office terms. In parties and institutions requiring specialization, the limitation on the term of office should depend on the particular situations of the people involved.

Annual plenary sessions in April that may last several weeks would also correspond to historical tradition. Now or in the future, a particular city could be selected as the site for the congress. This would show the strength and seriousness of the congress. It should be part of the general by-laws of the organization that the congress elects an executive, a disciplinary commission, and a chairperson. It is important that only people with sufficient principles and determination are elected to the executive. I have previously suggested that the executive should work as seven committees whose members could be elected from the executive or from the general ranks. In addition, the congress could elect seven corresponding preparatory commissions to make necessary decisions between terms. These commissions could make proposals and contribute to decision-making and supervision based on research. Depending on the particularities of the respective committees, offices, schools, or associations could be connected to them. Units of each of these offices, schools, or associations could be established in regions, towns, districts, and villages down to the lowest levels. Neighborhood and village communes are a basic requirement for any democracy. Based on this organizational template, no group in the population would be excluded from or uninfluenced by congress activities.

A legal or an illegal approach can be taken, depending on the situation, but legality should be the standard course of action. The party resolve can only reach the grassroots through the congress organization. The defense units can also be described as units that adhere to the decisions of the congress, as well as developing and protecting democracy. Relationships with legal parties should take place at the sympathizer level. It would be wrong to run legal institutions by giving orders. The congress should organize the geographical distribution of its members in line with the tasks at hand and the security situation. All these disparate points could be broadly discussed on the basis of practical needs that could be reinforced with sound evaluations and decisions.

The second important issue is how relationships between congress forces and state forces in Kurdistan can be maintained and contradictions resolved. I want to stress in particular that up to this point the maxim "all or nothing" has always been the approach to all power struggles. There has rarely been any room for dual power and democratic authority. The more natural and ordinary occurrence is for the forces of power and democracy to live together with all their contradictions and relations. In spite of constant denial, to a very large extent this is the prevalent reality in society. Concisely expressing this point and drawing lessons from it would be extremely fruitful for a solution. When launching our August 15, 1984, offensive, we acted on the basis of the maxim "all or nothing." Today, it is better understood by both sides that this is not the right approach. Our current circumstances mean that both state forces and congress forces cohabit the same country.

States cannot disappear in a day or even a decade nor can the democratic stance of the people simply be uprooted and tossed aside. Since permanent war brings massive destruction to both sides, the appropriate middle course should be based on living together and going to war only if it is unavoidable. In the coming period, we should organize our lives and our wars in all of the regions of Kurdistan based on this principle. The states will undoubtedly initially continue to pursue the principle of "all or nothing," but their attacks can be neutralized by democratic resistance and self-defense. It should be the core task of the democratic struggle and the art of the war of self-defense to find the right way to do this.

In the past, there was a similar phase. But neither side really tried to behave democratically, and both waged war without respecting the rules. Another example of this is Israel-Palestine situation today. Preventing a similar situation from arising elsewhere is of the utmost importance. During the İmralı court process, I proposed a dialogue for bilateral cease-fire and a democratic reconciliation. This was persistently ignored. Our friends could not grasp the importance of the issue either. They saw it as a tactic and nothing more, in spite of the fact that the chaos in the Middle East clearly shows that there is no other meaningful way out.

It is well known that we had some expectations of the AKP government, and that I even wrote a letter to them. But it is becoming increasingly clear that the nationalist and tribal forces want to play the same role in Turkey that they have played in South Kurdistan, this time using the AKP. The traditional and collaborator minority leaders and Kurds in Kurdistan promptly turned away from the CHP, MHP, DYP, and MSP,[9] throwing their support behind the AKP, a process directed and guided by the state. A lot of money was spent to eradicate the Demokratik Halk Partisi (DEHAP: Democratic People's Party). The AKP became the new home address of the gangs and of Hezbollah, which formed in the 1990s. Under the cloak of the Naqshbandi tariqa, they became the state's new class of guards. This is a very dangerous development that could eviscerate the substance of democratic solution for both Turkey and the people of Kurdistan. The fact that the tariqat and the village guards have been offered an opportunity to influence the people with the support of the state amounts to a new declaration of special warfare.[10] In fact, a tacit second Iraq is being created. The integration of the Kurdish collaborators into the state began in the 1950s, making them economically powerful and increasing their separation from the people. More precisely this social stratum was given economic privilege so that it could be used as a gatekeeper against the people. The Kurds partially rallying around the ANAP, and to an even greater degree around the AKP, is on the basis of primitive Kurdish nationalism and the Naqshbandi tariqa.

This is also the nature of the social base of the federal state in Iraq. The Kurdish feudal lords are being seamlessly transformed into a Kurdish bourgeoisie. Every day, it becomes clearer that the US is investing significant energy to bring this about. Kurdish nationalism could well cause major problems for everyone in the region, particularly the Kurds. Some of the traditional collaborationist minorities are also being integrated in this way, allegedly "helping the state." In this way, ideological gatekeepers are added to the armed guards, and they will constantly harm the people and stand in the way of democratic development to protect their own class interests. In many towns, they have been assisted in carrying out antidemocratic counterrevolutions. In numerous provinces and counties, particularly Van, Urfa, Mardin, Ağrı, Bingöl, Siirt, Bitlis, Muş, Adıyaman, and Antep, state-sponsored counterrevolutions resulted from intense efforts on the part of the government under the protection of the state around municipal elections. We know how much money changed hands and what kind of political manipulation took place. First, the people were pushed to the brink of starvation, and then fake "saviors" were provided. Hunger is not the only means used to discipline the people. They are made to take part in this sort of counterrevolution. Much of the AKP's behavior has already raised major doubts about its commitment to democracy, particularly with regard to the Kurdish question. The US and the EU listing the Koma Gel as "terrorist" is pure sophistry. The objective is to bolster the traditional collaborators among the Kurds and the minorities to induce them to continue acting as state agents. The events in Iraq are also extremely instructive in this regard.

Of course, the Koma Gel forces will try to forestall this game, but if the states insist on these traditional collaborators, they will deepen the conflicts. The states, particularly Turkey, must develop an approach that enables them to secure a lasting peace and the unity of their countries by turning away from a policy based on these new collaborators, relying instead on the people and their democratic character. An insistence on working with the Kurdish collaborators will only deepen the war and encourage secessionism.

The people of Kurdistan will not allow their country to go from being under the rule of the feudal lords to being ruled over by bourgeois collaborators. I want to once more stress that this would be tantamount to creating a second Iraq or a second Israel-Palestine. In the process of creating an artificial Kurdish bourgeoisie, there was a particular focus on Diyarbakır. Our people in Diyarbakır, having conducted a major struggle for democracy and having prevented the rise of fascism, will not tolerate a green Kurdish fascism either.[11] The example of Hezbollah has allowed the people to recognize fascists with a Kurdish mask, like the village guards and the confessors before them. The people will not be fooled just because these people are wearing modern disguises. The state is making a dangerous choice in this matter. In the near future, there will be calls made to the Turkish democrats and efforts to form an alliance, and the Koma Gel will insist on a democratic solution. The workers and people of Kurdistan will not fall for the game being played but will continue to insistently play their historical democratic role.

In the time ahead, there will probably be a dual presence of the congress forces and those of the state. Whether this dual presence becomes confrontational to a large extent depend on the behavior of the state.

If the state attacks the people's struggle for democratization or the entirely necessary and legitimate self-defense forces, there will be war. If attempts to achieve a democratic reconciliation on all levels are taken seriously by the state, the integrity of the country and the toiling population will benefit the most. The congress forces should be very cautious to avoid being dragged into dead-end war games like those of the past. That said, if the usurpation of their rights is not enough and the state forces attack, the people have the right to defend themselves by any means, a right they will exercise. No state forces, including the Kurdish federal state, should prohibit legal democratic institutions and legal political parties; they should permit their free activity. Finally, there should be a bilateral ceasefire. The Koma Gel forces will undoubtedly be supportive and respond positively to any decision in favor of the path to peace and democratic reconciliation. If the opposite turns out to be the case, the Kurds will respond to these liquidationist and annihilationist efforts in each part of Kurdistan, further consolidating their own democratic position with the most appropriate methods. The Koma Gel's policies and leadership in the new phase shall deem taking up the struggle based on self-critique and adhering to the requirements of their oaths of determination as the only way to hold on to their humanity and dignity.

A third point concerns Turkey's efforts to get others to label the PKK and the Koma Gel terrorist, a fundamental aspect of its policy. As we have frequently said, this policy, which is being pursued jointly with the US, is rife with pitfalls. One should never lose sight of the possibility that it will backfire against the state. Powers that appear to support the "terrorist" label but then collaborate politically with anyone they deem suitable are probably more ambitious and skillful in their policy. People ought to be aware that these forces always work to fuel the tension between the PKK and Turkey, hoping in this way to keep Turkey powerless. The long-term consequences of the terrorism charge need to be carefully weighed, keeping in mind what has become of some of those who were once described as "terrorists" by the US. Moreover, it would amount to falling into a trap of one's own doing if one gets obsessed with the "PKK" name. The reality of Northern Iraq is very instructive in this regard.

Within the Koma Gel solution, the Kurds' place in Turkish history, as well as in the Iranian and Arab civilizations, must be constantly addressed. The strategic role of the Kurds must be understood and made practical. The Kurds' neighbors need them to play this strategic role even more than the Kurds themselves do. The decisive factor in the downfall of Saddam's regime was that Saddam failed to accurately calculate the role of the Kurds. The neighboring states face the same danger. The Kurds in all parts of Kurdistan could unite and develop a joint strategy. If they did so, those who express the greatest hostility would suffer the biggest loss. It is the task of the Koma Gel to understand and play this strategic Kurdish role. That this has not yet happened is due to the treachery of the Kurdish collaborators. Under the new conditions, it will be difficult for them to carry on as before. The Kurds will develop an increasingly clear strategy and move closer to the point at which they can act upon it. The historical examples we have provided of Kurds and Turks living together as tribes and peoples and acting jointly at certain strategic junctures should be well understood. The Kurds did not behave this way to be eradicated from history, but because they recognized it as a political necessity. Important Turkish statesmen have also understood this. If this strategy is not implemented with the Turks but with another power—and there are many contenders, including Iran, the Arabs, Israel, the EU, Russia, Armenia, and Greece—the Turkish nation will obviously be the biggest loser. This outcome shouldn't be encouraged with simplistic charges of terrorism. The liquidation of the PKK and the Koma Gel is impossible. Moreover, their legacy might be picked up by others in a very negative way at any moment. The Kurds must also understand that opposition, even hostility, toward the Turks is not in their best interest. Kurdish-Turkish hostility is a "lose-lose" proposition. We have a relationship in which a gain made by one side is not tantamount to a loss for the other side. Once the anachronistic thinking about this relationship has been overcome, we will have a permanent "win-win" situation. But, unfortunately, at present, the policy is "the Turks are everything, the Kurds nothing."

The opposite is, of course, also possible, i.e., a policy of "the Kurds are everything, the Turks nothing." The current policy encourages that. The insistence on the terrorism accusation and the attacks against the congress forces will obviously get the wheels of the "lose-lose" situation rapidly spinning. It should be well understood that we have gone to great lengths not to take this path. The reasons we adopted this attitude are far from simple. As should be clear, I have taken the historical social reasons into account to arrive at my opinion. A solution based on the Koma Gel is the way to achieve the free unity, democratic reconciliation, and peace that is the most appropriate way to preserve the integrity of the country, the state, and the nation. It is necessary to understand who benefits the most from a policy that takes any approach to a solution out of the hands of the Kurds and gives it to collaborators and anti-republican and antidemocratic tariqa forces. By this point, the genuinely democratic forces in Turkey have probably figured out why they have been excluded by making a thorough analysis of their own Kurdish policy. They have probably learned that no policy, let alone a social democratic policy, is possible if one plays the game of the "three wise monkeys."

At its extraordinary general assembly, starting from a correct evaluation of the current situation, the Koma Gel should be able to overcome the old parochial character that offers no solution and instead embrace democratic power and prove that the criterion for being a true democrat is successfully carrying out your duties in the context of an institutional reality. This would make clear that nothing short of success in addressing the coming historical tasks will be acceptable. It can play its role successfully by foiling the efforts of the nationalists and feudalists and by doing justice to the requirements for a truly democratic struggle and the necessity for self-defense.

The People's Defense Forces
The Hêzên Parastina Gel (HPG: People's Defense Forces) will also continue to play an important role in resolving the Kurdish question. Its role in the democratic struggle as an organization separate from the party and the congress, its relationship with the party and the congress, and how war is to be carried out are all points that need to be clarified.

As people know, our perspective on war when we launched the offensive on August 15, 1984, was based on ideas that we had learned by rote: the national question could only be solved by war and, therefore, war must be endlessly praised, and we seek shelter from the god of war. This was understood to be the highest principle, and people needed to act accordingly, because that was what socialism required. This approach was obviously dogmatic and entirely failed to take historical and social conditions into account. It stated a general principle and nothing more. Marxism didn't include any analysis of the theoretical problems of war. Marx had borrowed from feudal-bourgeois French historians, and Engels's limited work on the topic was not particularly clarifying. For the most part, the role that the theory of violence plays for power and the social order was left unexamined. Even though the ruling colonial powers overwhelmingly came from bourgeois societies, national wars were treated like a separate socialist category—a socialist had to wage the national liberation struggle. Because I have already analyzed war in the relevant section of this book, I will not repeat myself here. I have explained that both power and the state are exclusively determined by war and force, that every social order is founded on war to some degree, and that without an analysis of war, we cannot fully analyze either power or society; we can't even analyze the economy. This is not to say that we see war as sheer evil; the goal here is to examine the place of war and violence in sociality. I hope to explain what and how much can be won and what can be lost in war. In brief, my goal is a sociological analysis of war.

I have always said that the offensive of August 15, 1984, was necessary, although its execution was full of flaws and inadequacies. I have consistently engaged in serious critique and self-critique about this phase of the war, a phase of both great heroic deeds and major perfidy, achievements, and losses. Undoubtedly, the HPG, as a continuation of this great legacy, cannot continue in the old style, but this does not mean that it has no role to play and is going to be dysfunctional. Neither a permanent ceasefire nor peace has been concluded, so we must continue to attend to the problems faced by the HPG, its tasks, and its quantitative and qualitative situation.

To prevent any misunderstanding, I will provide a brief evaluation of the role of violence in Kurdistan. The situation in Kurdistan as a country and in Kurdish society is determined by the law of conquest. From the Sumerians to today, this tradition of conquest is based on the idea that "whatever you rule, you own." Thus, rule and force are seen to be the basis of all rights. The land and the people belong to those who most recently conquered them. Islam in particular combines this with a supreme religious injunction. Bourgeois nationalism also frantically clings to the principle of conquest. The role of the people is to submit to the conquerors and do what they are told. However, revolutionary principles define war very differently.

The legitimacy of war that leads to oppression and exploitation and, thus, to the right of conquest, is a deception that reflects the will of the oppressors. Not submitting to this but resisting it is a sacred duty. The humiliation caused by war can only be overcome by ending submission. War against oppression is sacred for oppressed people and is the fundamental instrument of liberation and must be resorted to, if necessary, to end the debasement they are subjected to.

State rulers in present-day Kurdistan regard themselves as the "once upon a time" conquerors of this place. They use the right of conquest to justify the permanence of their rule. They don't see themselves as responsible for the backwardness of the people, for its close to nonexistence, or for the complete lack of freedom and equality. Obviously, there is a big problem here, and the essence of that problem is rooted in force. The people we call "Kurds," who have worked this land for centuries have never said, "Please, come and subjugate me." Knowing the nature of our time, how can we overcome this status based on force? There are two ways: democratic reconciliation or, if that proves impossible, using force against force. Living in any other way runs contrary to the time we are in and would mean hunger, unemployment, and lack of culture and language. Had there been fully functioning democracies in the countries where the parts of Kurdistan are located, there might not have been an opening for the principle of force.

Funneling the people's democratic stance and practice into the wrong channels within the gears and levers of the state, thereby ensuring that they come to nothing, ultimately leads to the loss of their essence. Turning the state into a temple and inviting the people to make a pilgrimage to the ballot box every four or five years, as is the case today, has nothing to do with democracy. Irrespective of the number of parties, elections only legitimize the state and transform the public administration of the people into a deceptive game. That this kind of game is called democracy has to do with the capitalist system's enormous advertising power. It is the product of a misleading campaign, similar to the insistent attempt to convince a mentally stable person that they are mad, until they begin to believe it.

The people's democratic stance and practice are primarily about embracing their identity, committing themselves to their freedom, and attaining self-governance. Consciousness of their own identity is based on their history and social reality. When this consciousness is organized, it creates strength, and strength leads to freedom. People cannot liberate themselves without getting organized and growing strong. Once they liberate themselves, the next necessary step is to attain self-governance. It is irrational and immoral to attain freedom but not to be able to govern yourself. Our definition of democracy within this framework is based on a process that creates lasting consciousness of identity, as well as organizational work on all levels among the people. Overall our definition of democracy could also be called democratic action. It could also be understood as the transition from a democratic stance to a democratic practice. Instead of using electoral rituals to bind the people to the state, democratic action means encouraging the people to take responsibility for their own existence and to strive for freedom and self-governance. Running after positions within the state structure and attempting to gain approval from the people in order to rule deal severe blows to true democracy. This is exactly what happened in the nineteenth and twentieth centuries, and it constituted the betrayal of democracy, a deeper and more far-reaching betrayal than that which Jean-Jacques Rousseau drew attention to in the eighteenth century.

A meaningful democratic struggle in Kurdistan must occur within the framework outlined here. Otherwise, all we have is the game of choosing our own masters, which is nothing but an occasional assembly of the slaves so they can confirm their masters. A true democratic endeavor can only take place if it is based on the social identity, freedom, and self-governance of the people. There must be a continuous effort to raise consciousness and improve organization. Thus, a true act of democracy would be to assemble with the people and make decisions about how to address their fundamental problems and determine who will be responsible for implementing these decisions. That left, right, religious, and nationalist parties all serve to legitimize the state, entirely lack prestige among the people, and routinely lose at the ballot box is closely related to the facts we have outlined here. The system's parties can play no role in Kurdistan other than legitimizing the system in the basest of ways. They are dishonest, deceitful, and exploitative instruments similar to the religious tariqat of the past.

Being a democratic party and carrying out democratic action is noble. It was democracy that allowed Athens, which I have heavily criticized elsewhere,[12] to put an end to both the Spartan monarchy and the Persian Empire and experience a "golden age." When democracy is actually realized, it is both a virtuous regime and a school for creating conscious and free citizens who can protect the country and the people from any despot or occupying power. No endeavor in politics is more valuable than democratic action. In that sense, the best guarantee for the people is having sons and daughters who love and nurture democracy. Any state-oriented effort in Kurdistan, regardless of who undertakes it and under what rubric, can only mean the negation of democracy. In today's Kurdistan, there is no endeavor that is more valuable—that will resolve issues and lead to peace and freedom—than carrying out a genuine democratic effort and building a democratic movement.

However, Kurdistan is still quite far from being a contemporary democracy. The Middle East is experiencing pre-democracy, wars, and chaos. Kurdistan is at the center of this chaos and these wars. Regardless of the angle you approach from, the people's self-defense challenges are grave and must be addressed. The inability to even use our language—the most basic communication tool—under the contemporary standards is evidence of the depth of people's self-defense problems. On the other hand, the absence of many of the conditions and means necessary for a generalized war of resistance makes it necessary to narrow and limit the struggle. In resisting the political and military forces of the ruling states, the armed struggle can take the form of low- or medium-intensity warfare or could even be further narrowed down to war waged by small cells. Not resisting at all makes submission eternal. Not eradicating state sovereignty through resistance but making it accommodate democratic reconciliation seems to be the best way forward under the current conditions. The role of the HPG can be defined as promoting and protecting the people's democracy until a democratic reconciliation can be reached. Paving the way for democratization means that the indirect obstacles posed by the forces collaborating with the antidemocratic state power must be removed.

Another acceptable condition for war would be a war of defense against attacks directly targeting the HPG. As such the HPG must use guerrilla warfare to the fullest possible extent. The tasks of the HPG include solving problems ranging from its own deployment to its relationship with the population, from logistics to training and education, from command structures to political contacts. There may even be times when this is the basic form around which the people and all organized forces revolve, and the HPG will face the task of protecting and developing all democratic efforts.

The HPG has to provide the necessary political and organizational capacity. It also has to make its own quantitative and qualitative situation compatible with the tasks it has to fulfill and determine the required tactics and strategies. It will be responsible for the safety of the whole party, the congress, and particularly civilians who are in danger. While executing its difficult but important tasks, it will be faced with a well-trained military and other security forces.

Another important topic is my role in our armed struggle. The great efforts I made in this area before and after the offensive of August 15, 1984, are well known. Nevertheless, there was an enormous difference between my understanding of war and what occurred in the first fifteen years of that period. Since I have already carried out extensive critique and self-critique about this earlier in this book, I will not repeat it here. Had I known at the time that the deviation was as great as it was, I would have relocated to Kurdistan in the 1980s, certainly by the beginning of the 1990s, at the latest. That many of groups that took on tasks at the time failed miserably had a lot to do with the fact that they either knew nothing about the nature of war, its political foundations, and its ideological background or that their level of consciousness and training was too low. The main reason for defeats and losses was that the commanders didn't live up to their tasks. The root cause of the situation that I am in should be sought in the same place. My abilities only allowed me to lead the war, both theoretically and practically, in the way I did. It was enough to enact some things, but not enough to achieve what was desired. I must quite openly say that after 1995, it might have been better had I chosen to reflect on the situation more profoundly, rather than endless repetition of what we had already done. Expecting success from the command cadres in 1993 was unrealistic. The offensive from 1993 to 1995 was important, but the insistence on carrying it out with seasoned but unsuccessful cadres led to the well-known repetitiveness. It is now well-established that offensives before that also lacked serious commanders.

That was the context in which my departure from Syria in 1998 took place. I could have gone to our country but didn't, because I was worried that that might result in our total annihilation. Up until September 11, 2001, I favored an end to the armed struggle in the event of an agreement on a minimum democratic reconciliation, but after 9/11 there was no apparent intention for reconciliation on the part of the Turkish leadership. In my view, we could have launched a legitimate war of defense immediately after the parliamentary elections of November 2002, when it became clear that the government would not respond to any proposal for a solution, but that decision was not mine to make. The conditions of my incarceration are not conducive to such decision-making. It would be wrong to expect orders from me. It is the task of the confident and responsible cadres to make decisions about the way to wage war and the corresponding tactics and strategies based on a comprehensive analysis of the new phase. I have given them completely free reign in that regard. That said, I would not consider it morally acceptable to use war as a coercive factor. War is an act that must only be engaged in to meet the historical and indispensable demands of the people. That is why I said, "Discuss it with the people and make your own decision." This remains my view today.

I have made some of my theoretical considerations about war clear in the past and have tried to dig deeper in the work before you. I have formulated some fundamental positions about the role of force in our country and the nature of the war of resistance. It should be obvious that these are not in any way orders but just attempts to illuminate the topic at hand.

I have also made some recommendations regarding the state of the women's units, the creation of autonomous democratic regions, and the specific features of people's defensive wars. These thoughts and proposals might be worth considering, given that the conditions of war can change in twenty-four hours, and it might be necessary to adapt tactics at any moment. In situations like this, everything can change; I, therefore, repeat that my proposals should in no way be understood as orders. In war, the decisive factor is the will of the fighters themselves. They must arrive at and carry out decisions based on their theoretical and practical knowledge. They themselves are responsible for any successes and defeats, and they must understand this. It is their responsibility to choose or to avoid war based on the circumstances, their strength, their experience, and their theory.

Until now, I have made some remarks that included, albeit indirectly, warnings to the state and our congress forces. When I recently noted behavior that aimed at undermining the decision-making power of the congress, historical responsibility obliged me to suggest the reconstruction of the PKK and, out of commitment to the congress, an extraordinary general assembly. I had to convey my opinions whatever the cost, even if it was the last thing I ever did. Even though the inadequate communication angered me quite a bit, I tried to do the best I could. Finally, I have had the opportunity to succinctly present my opinions on a number of issues in the submissions before you.

I assume that the congress will meet by summer at the latest and hope that there will be no abnormalities. The friends in positions of responsibility face even more important tasks than was the case in preparation for August 15, 1984. Those who accept a position in the name of the party, the congress, or the HPG must proceed with confidence and rely on their own strength. Given the situation, it would be beyond nonsensical to have any expectations of me. No matter how unfit my health may be, I will of course try to show the strength to take things to a dignified end. I must, however, also point out that if they were genuine comrades they wouldn't have behaved as they have under the current circumstances.

When Kemal Pir heard about the action of Ferhat Kurtay and his comrades, he is said to have said, "It should have been us who carried out this action." As we know, after that the fast to the death began. I strictly oppose suicidal acts and consider them wrong, but I don't regard the actions of Kemal Pir, Mehmet Hayri Durmuş, Mazlum Doğan, and Ferhat Kurtay as suicidal acts. They said, "If there were the slightest possibility to live with dignity, we would pursue it and live our lives with dignity to the end." These words set out the necessary criteria for how life should be lived. In this situation, there was only one thing left that could be done to uphold human dignity. They went ahead with that act of resistance. We know that Hayri Durmuş expressed his determination with the words *we succeeded*. Their maxim was "human dignity shall prevail!" This is the tradition of our war of resistance, and it must be understood and implemented correctly.

Many friends who were released from prison are now at your side. It would be worth asking what they understand about life. Nobody expects you to carry out suicidal acts—there was enough of that in the period that began on August 15, 1984—that would simply be unacceptable. Nevertheless, there are numerous options for democratic action and a war of self-defense. There is room to move freely without complaining about the spatial and temporal conditions, and, thus, it is undeniable that for your dignity and that of the people the conditions and possibilities exist for experimenting with any imaginable option. We took your self-critiques in the early 2000s seriously and believed that you would develop a successful practice. In the end, however, in spite of our expectations of you, you reduced our legacy to a cadaver, torn in two, and sent it to me. Clearly, this is not what a war for dignity looks like. You are among our people and free humanity, but, most of all, you are in the mountains, which, as the result of tireless effort, hold the promise of freedom.

Let's not forget that I have made enormous effort to get each one of you to this point, for which I don't expect any personal repayment. On the other hand, I will never accept behavior that violates the dignity of our people in this way, and not just the dignity of the people; you must realize what you are doing to your own dignity. I, or we, have not done anything or made any mistake that forgives your behavior. I will continue to try to correctly understand humanity's war for dignity and meet its requirements.

In the last part of this section, I tried to clarify Kurdish phenomenon and the Kurdish question in the light of comprehensive analyses and assessments and to make some proposals for a solution. All of this can also be understood as my response to the concerned circles. Now it is the task of each concerned group to accept their responsibility and respond as they see fit.

As a result of all these discussions, I have indicated some of my own errors and shortcomings with regard to the phase that began on August 15, 1984. The most important thing to note is that in the beginning we were not really clear about what we wanted. I certainly acknowledge that I was not sufficiently clear and could not develop adequate solutions and analyses in the early 1980s. I believe I have made the necessary self-critique in these writings. My second mistake and failure was to be unclear about the actions that had to be carried out. I think I have since gained a better clarity in this regard and have shared my thoughts with the circles I'm concerned with here. At this point, there are two possible courses of action.

Options for Democratic Action and a Democratic Solution
It is obvious that I prefer democratic action and a democratic solution. I have consistently and comprehensively presented my position. That I failed to achieve this clarity in the early 1990s was a serious flaw.

Even though these insights were late in arriving, and even though I am the one who made a great effort but also suffered the most as a result, today, on the eve of important developments and historical circumstances, it is very important that I have been able to present a clear and viable proposal for democratic action and a democratic solution. Thousands of activists say that they are determined to carry out the democratic struggle, and millions of people have stood up for freedom. This is the capacity of the militants and people to offer a variety of approaches to problems that can be resolved without a resort to arms. The historical responsibility for the failure to use this opportunity will weigh especially heavily on those who are in leadership positions and others in charge. Freedom for the country and democracy for the people can be achieved by the millions who demand their rights through a variety of civil society and democratic forms of organizing. All that is needed is some time and a democratic political leadership that has internalized democracy, believes in its goals, and is able to build close ties with the people.

Wherever necessary, this could take the form of fighting for law that overcomes undemocratic legality and clears the way of democratic rights and freedom.

No one should insist on squandering the hopes of the people in favor of the remnants of the Middle Ages, while still carrying the traces of their alleged left and social democratic identity. Regardless of anyone's nationality, sex, religion, or denomination, by keeping to the minimum requirements of being a democrat, there is nothing that cannot be achieved; whether it is peace, camaraderie, freedom, or equality in present-day Turkey and Kurdistan.

The Second Path

If all our calls and warnings go unheeded, if all the hopes and efforts of our people for freedom, equality, and democracy continue to be suppressed by insidious special warfare methods, if practices that are incompatible with the revolutionary principles of the republic, the integrity of the country, and contemporary forms of the state and the nation persist, then the answer will have to be the comprehensive implementation of a war of self-defense. As should be generally understood, this is not our preference. But the games that are being played require that we be well-prepared and not hesitate to launch a war of self-defense, if and when necessary. It is obvious that I could not be responsible for its execution or direction, even if I wanted to. I can neither prevent nor prohibit it. The historical responsibility lies with the states and the people's defense forces. In their interplay, they will determine the strategies and tactics, with their greater or lesser implementation dependent on their respective forces and capacities. Each side should know the other side well and act accordingly.

Nonetheless, I have to point out that a bilateral ceasefire can be formulated on the basis of extensive items.[13] Even the rules to be followed in the event of war can be publicly declared before hostilities commence and be presented to the relevant international authorities.[14] A document on conditions for a ceasefire could also be presented. Should we arrive at this situation, we will be at a point where the two forces—the state forces and the congress forces—will be in a situation where one is trying to annihilate Kurdistan and the other is trying to survive under the existing conditions in Kurdistan. It is possible that those caught between the two will be very quickly liquidated. There could be a call made out to them as well. At the very least, civilians, those who are indifferent, children, women, and the elderly should not be harmed. If both sides respect the rules of war, it will keep the door open for a more humane course of events, which might, in turn, lead to a ceasefire and a democratic reconciliation. Quite obviously, logistics and human beings are necessary for survival. The guerrilla's fundamental pillars are the mountains and the people.

War can develop in the mountains, the city, or the villages. Roadblocks and confiscations are a common practice on both sides. Recruiting and levying of duties are also a common practice. In order to live, everyone must understand how they can determine and implement their goals.

I don't think it's necessary to expand any further on these topics. It is my sincere hope that this scenario will never arise. I wanted to point to the possibility of this scenario as a warning to both sides. It is, of course, entirely possible that things will develop in a much worse way. If we think of the tragedies in Israel-Palestine and Iraq, it is obvious that this is by no means empty conjecture. My analysis of the conspiracy against me obliges me to point these things out. In my opinion, there are no problems with Turkey, including the framework of the democratic integrity of the country, that cannot be solved if the state makes a genuine commitment to democracy. What makes the most sense to me and is in accordance with the requirements of my belief is to strengthen the historical cooperation between our peoples not only through contemporary and democratic principles but also through freedom and equality. There is no question that I'm prepared to make any sacrifice necessary to bring this about. Nothing is closer to my heart than trying to prevent the shedding of a drop of blood of one single person or anyone having a painful moment. Equally clear, however, is that the significance of all of this can't be detached from my humanitarian, social, and popular identity, which I have discussed here in detail. At any rate, outside of these issues there can neither be an aspect of life that can be understood nor a possibility to live it.

One might perhaps ask what the topics I have dealt with up to now have to do with my lawsuit before the European Court of Human Rights (ECtHR). The developments occurring every day under the aegis of the Greater Middle East Initiative show how closely connected all these topics actually are. Without an analysis and understanding of Western civilization, neither my trial nor Turkey's relations with the EU and the US can be properly understood. In turn, without analyzing these relationships correctly, we cannot respond in the appropriate way to the problems of life that have now turned into a chaos or hell faced by the Turks, the Kurds, and all of the other peoples of the Middle East. Despite the claims made, the fact that the EU and the ECtHR separate lawsuits from their social context and individualize them indicates how far this whole process is from one that favors human rights and democratization. This reflects the disorder of extreme individualism and the selfishness of European civilization. I will devote the concluding chapter of my defense submissions to an analysis of this point, to show that justice for the individual is only possible if it accompanies justice for that individual's society. I will prove that our individual freedom passes through the freedom of the society to which we belong.

TWELVE

The Role of the ECtHR and the EU in the Lawsuit against Abdullah Öcalan

An analysis of the story of the crucifixion of Jesus, a very important event for European civilization, will throw further light on my case. In looking at it, we are less interested in the formal process than in the essence of what occurred. Sociological analyses of the Bible and other texts concerning the events generally concede that the cult and the culture that were symbolically expressed through Jesus were rooted in the rapidly developing social segregation of the time. On the one hand, we have the traditional aristocratic and bureaucratic circles, which were converging around the rapid spread of the Roman Empire in the region, and, on the other hand, we find the poor of all peoples and cultures, whose numbers were increasing at an equally rapid rate. Jerusalem, in the eastern Mediterranean, was one of the most important centers at the time. The Hebrew tribes, with their history reaching back far into the past, had also undergone social segregation. Judaea was a small Hebrew kingdom, with Jerusalem as its center. As the social segregation grew, the clergy also split. The kingdom and the upper layer of the clergy united closely. Following a period of significant resistance, they began to collaborate with the Roman Empire.

While this was unfolding, there were several periods when the threat of a major uprising arose. A whole series of oppositional foci developed. The Essenes, a sect led by John the Baptist, may have been the most important of them. John staunchly opposed the Judaean collaborators, but he fell victim to the intrigues of Herod Antipas's wife Herodias. His head was presented on a tray to those whose interests he had dared to threaten. Even before John's death, Jesus had already established himself as a kind of successor, and it was now up to him to lead the social unrest. Essentially, he waged a class struggle in the form of a religious tariqa of the poor, which took shape as an important link in the widespread prophetic tradition of the day. What distinguished this movement was that Jesus, for the first time, broke with the Jewish community and emerged as the spokesperson of *all* people. In a way, he represented internationalism as opposed to Jewish nationalism. The cosmopolitan Roman Empire had established the objective basis for this process. The people of the Middle East were being rearranged and intermingled anew under the rule of the Romans. Two parties emerged, one of the rich and the other of the poor. In the Hellenistic era, there had been a similar split in Judaea, namely, between the Sadducees and the Pharisees. With Jesus, this tradition overcame the boundaries of the Jewish people and addressed the poor of all peoples for the first time. This triggered panic among the prominent priests in Judaea, and they demanded that the Roman prefect Pilate punish Jesus. Even though Pilate did not wish to do so, the Jewish collaborators succeeded in pressuring him, and to preserve the common interest he agreed to the crucifixion.

The narratives of the Apostles and holy men and women tell us what kind of religion later emerged. In particular, the new religion was most extensively adopted by the Greeks, who were dissatisfied with Roman rule. They developed a religious-tribal resistance, particularly in Anatolia and on the Greek peninsula, making inroads into the Empire via the new religion and becoming well established. Under Emperor Constantine, they become partners in the state and, as the "Byzantines," left their mark on the East Roman Empire. Under the influence of the new religion, the Assyrians, as one of the most powerful and cultured people of the time, also underwent a far-reaching cultural reform, achieving a similarly influential position in both the Byzantine and the Sasanian Empires. In the three centuries after Jesus, due to the efforts of great bishops, the religion of the poor turned into the official ideology and the popular base of the state. Later on, Christianity, the fundamental ideological fabric of medieval European feudalism, along with the Reformation, would become one of the leading ideologies accompanying the birth of the new age of capitalism.

The answer to the question of who spilled the blood of Jesus of Nazareth, drank it like wine, and got wealthy off of it is: Western civilization itself. It was the Roman Empire as the worldly kingdom of European civilization that shed the blood of Jesus. The papacy, in its turn, made wine of his blood, drank it, became the spiritual otherworldly kingdom, and created the fundamental moral values of European civilization.

The fate of Jesus and his poor, ascetic successors, however, was to be persecuted, tortured, and killed. When we analyze these formative developments of Western civilization, we recognize how the system murders its victims, while simultaneously heralding and praising them.

This is the most important contradiction in Western civilization. In his novels, the famous Russian writer Fyodor Dostoyevsky describes in impressive depth how bishops who are completely alienated from the essence of Jesus proceed to crucify him a second time. Sometimes the victims of a massacre worship the murderers, but in Western civilization the murderers worship the victims. It would, however, be incorrect to ascribe this fact to Western civilization alone. All systems based on domination and exploitation nurture themselves from the blood and sweat of their victims. All the stories told about the struggle of the people are stories of them liberating themselves from exactly that situation. But, in the end, even these stories cannot help but to ennoble their masters.

Two thousand years after the events surrounding Jesus of Nazareth, I—among others—suffered a similar fate in a location and culture close to his. This time, instead of Rome, the United States is Western civilization's imperial power. While Rome was the power that gave birth to Western civilization, the US is likely to be the power that buries it. Just like Rome in its time, it must expand rapidly in the Middle East, and to do so it urgently needs collaborators.

Once again, the chasm between the rich and the poor is getting wider in the Middle East. Apart from the collaborationist parties of the rich, the poor have also given rise to a number of parties. This time around, the poorest people in the region are the Kurds. They are subjected to numerous kinds of oppression. I am not saying this because I want to emulate those past events, but because the way that I came to be, grew up, entered the system, my opposition to it, and the way I was finally captured bears a certain resemblance with the story of the prophet Jesus in both form and content. It is well known that our movement is also based on the poorest of the poor in the Middle East. The search for a new ideology, a new mentality, is also central. Communities characterized by extreme commitment have sprung up, and the US, i.e., the new Roman Empire, and its collaborators are quite alarmed. The state of Judea is, once again, a firm collaborator. Among the Greeks, there are also strong supporters. This time, the deadly treason of Judas Iscariot was carried out by the Greek Savvas Kalenteridis,[1] who pretended to be a close sympathizer of mine. Even the kinglets of Kurdish Judaea intensely fear the rise of the Kurdish poor. All the collaborators feel the need to consolidate their positions in the region. My ideological and political position is anathema to all of them. Their interests have converged to favor the making of a conspiracy, so long as they can further entrench their despotism!

Paul, one of the greatest of the apostles, was sacrificed after a few major expeditions—Rome was the tiniest bit tolerant—whereas I was kidnapped and caught on my first European expedition. There is no need to elaborate on this particular story. I have traveled to the centers of all of the denominations. When I officially called on the Greek capitol of Athens, followed by the Russian capitol in Moscow, and finally the Rome of the Latins, I realized that there was no place for me in their ice-cold calculations of interests. There is no avoiding the heavy price of engaging in politics based on states—although my engagement was only in form and not in essence. They were quite clear that ideology and friendship have little value in the face of naked interest. The thoughts and beliefs of these forces have long been shaped by money. They are masters at promoting their material interests, using conspiracies and other similar means; for that, they have the necessary experience. In the final analysis, Rome was the crucial authority in the case of Jesus. Without the authority of Rome, Jesus would never have been arrested and crucified. When I was apprehended, the United States was the decisive authority. Without the US, my arrest would have been unthinkable. The Turkish leadership was consigned to the role of guards and executioners, while the EU, as one of Western civilization's key juridical powers, got the last word in the adjudication of my case.

We could describe the relationships we have just sketched more concretely. The Byzantine Empire was closer to the empires of the East than those of the West. However, because of the balance of power during feudal civilization, the crusaders were unable to hold their ground in the East. Like the post-Alexandrian Hellenic civilization, they were condemned to be absorbed. The first major attack on the part of rising capitalism was undertaken by Napoleon in 1798. The obstacle he faced was the Ottoman Empire.

Europe would become the center of civilization, as the capitalist system secured its place as the new dominant force of civilization. Europe clearly had the upper hand. While Eastern civilization in the form of the Arab sultans was expelled from Spain once and for all during the late fifteenth-century Reconquista, the period of rapid decline of the Ottomans began after a major defeat following the second siege of Vienna in 1683. Neither could hold their ground against the rising European civilization any longer; their time had long since passed. With the defeat of Napoleon, Great Britain became the leading power of the civilization. Because the representatives of the British Empire were well aware that the road to world power ran through the Middle East, they began to turn toward this region in the early nineteenth century. Although caught between Czarist Russia in the north and the British Empire in the south, drawing upon its well-known policy of maintaining the equilibrium, the Ottoman Empire managed to survive for another century. But what happened to the victims of this policy of equilibrium is what is important. Three historically preem-inent peoples, the Ionians (Greeks) of Anatolia, the Armenians of Cilicia and Eastern Anatolia, and the Assyrians of Mesopotamia, were largely liquidated in this balancing ploy, and the Kurds were only able to preserve their physical existence.

England, France, and Russia all sought to assert a new rule over the region and to use the peoples just mentioned as a threat to extract conces-sions from the Ottomans. Capitalism's calculations of its material interest were treated as far more important than the millennia-old culture of these peoples. For every step backward the Ottoman Turks had to take, they blamed these peoples, and each time they throttled them a little more. With the beginning of World War I, the alarm bells of history began to ring loudly. The Ionians, Armenians, and Assyrians were at death's door under the ruins of the empire, while the Kurds were only barely able to retain their physical existence by retreating deep into the mountains.

The eight-hundred-year struggle between the Turkish sultans and the feudal and capitalist European state powers ended with Europe on top, a process that left many unfortunate victims in its wake. Historians don't generally discuss the actual reasons for and consequences of the woeful story of the victims, because the mirror of reality would reflect their own ugly, murderous faces. Decisive responsibility for what happened in the Middle East over the last two hundred years lies with the major European states. The same peoples—the Ionians, Armenians, Assyrians, Kurds, and others—were still there. Because of the balance of power that they created within the Ottoman Empire, at least economically, they were doing well and could comfortably live according to their cultures. Politically too, they were not so far behind the Turks. Because they trusted Europe and harbored the unrealistic hope of founding their own states, they bet everything on one card, or, rather, were *pushed* to do so. In the end, they lost everything. Those of their children who survived the massacres became immigrants in the West; they set out for Europe or the United States. They tried to live with the utopia of a "promised holy land."

In 1896, the Jews launched an offensive by holding the first Zionist Congress. We can see similar initiatives picking up speed in the US and Europe today. They are likely pinning their hopes on the US's Greater Middle East Initiative. The occupation of Iraq opened a new and exciting phase for them. The Kurds are the most likely candidate to be a solid ally in the context of this project. The goal is to change the economic basis and the intellectual and political superstructure in the region, which poses an obstacle to the expansion of the capitalist system and to the continued existence of Israel. For this, the system's two organized forces—the UN and NATO—must be appointed the project's active diplomatic and military forces. The G8 will certainly contribute their share of economic power.

The actual problem is how the Republic of Turkey, as heir to the Ottoman Empire, will react to this phase. Both the external and internal conditions for a renewed national liberation initiative are lacking. If Turkey tries to resist the system, it will be no more successful than Iraq, Yugoslavia, or even Russia. However, total capitulation also would not be in their interest. Furthermore, the conditions of alliance formed after the 1950s cannot continue as they are. The only remaining possibility is reform, but there is no real will for it. Instead, misery is the preferred policy. There is an attempt to protect Turkey with an extremely conservative mentality that considers every day spent under the present status quo a victory. In this sense, Turkey today bears a striking resemblance to the Ottoman Empire in its final days.

It was under these conditions that the plot against me was hatched. Without a precise understanding of the background of the plot and the participants, it is impossible to address any of these problems or to accurately assess what the future holds for Turkey.

Despite some serious inadequacies and errors on my part, it is nonetheless the case that I undeniably represent the democratic awakening of people in general and the people of Kurdistan in particular. Before the actions of August 15, 1984, I tried to organize a certain mentality, but I have to admit that it never went beyond a mix of real socialism and national liberation, and I failed to achieve a more advanced stage. The fifteen years between August 15, 1984, and February 15, 1999, was the phase where this organized mentality embodied action, a phase where action came to the forefront. It has been said that nothing clarifies things like practice. A consequence of this phase was that I was able to better define myself. It could be said that I truly tested the reality I represent, its problems, and my ability to solve them. Of course, that fact that I use "I" in this connection is no cause for exaggeration. I am no more than a mediator of the social reality of an honorable people who have been suppressed for thousands of years. Even though I have extensively analyzed divinity in these pages, the terminology I use is much closer to scientific.

That the reality of the people of Kurdistan has come to light greatly annoys the conquerors and those who have been collaborating with them for thousands of years—including Gilgamesh and Enkidu and others who have been exposed since. Under the protection of the US, the imperial power of our day, they began the 1998 Ankara and Washington processes. They agreed to a political program that would amount to envisaging a federal state of Kurdistan. This program was to be carried out under the auspices of the leadership in Ankara. In return, a joint decision would be taken for Abdullah Öcalan's abduction and the PKK being condemned as terrorists, an outcome that objectively meant "annihilation and liquidation." Even though the Ankara-Washington agreement concluded on September 17, 1998, was meant to remain secret, an attentive political observer would notice the agreement's many contradictions. All parties to the agreement were trying to deceive one another, and the agreement itself was nothing more than tactics. As a result, the great pincer movement and the hunt for Abdullah Öcalan picked up speed on a world scale, with at least one faction in the US showing particular zeal. There was also pressure and comprehensive support from the Israeli right. The United Kingdom planned things well, with Israel's secret service agency, the Mossad, also participating and providing intelligence. A military and economic pact between Israel and Turkey was concluded in 1996. On May 6, 1996, an attempt to assassinate me failed; a vehicle carrying a ton of explosives blew up the compound where I was staying. Prime Minister Tansu Çiller paid fifty million dollars to finance this attempt. When it failed, the final plot was launched. The next step was the September 17, 1998, speech by the commander of the Turkish army, which was tantamount to an ultimatum for Syria. With war against

Syria looming, the Syrian government did not resist and told me to "go wherever you want to go, but go!"

After a call, the background of which is still not entirely clear, but which could be described as a semi-official invitation, I decided to go ahead with the "Athens adventure." It would in fact have been ideal for me to head to the mountains of my country, but, out of moral concern, I postponed this expedition, which might have led to the deaths of thousands of people. I decided it would be more appropriate to take the opportunity to achieve a political solution in Europe. Beginning in 1997, I had received several messages through our European organization that I believed came from military circles. These messages reinforced my thinking. However, in Athens, I was not received by true friends but by the mythological goddess of war Athene, a creature who sprung from the forehead of the male god Zeus and lured the famous Trojan hero Hector into the wrong battle.[2] For political gain, they forced me to fight all the profit-minded civilizational forces in a deadly arena in the hope of taking Troy, i.e., Anatolia, and Cyprus or at least the loom of such a political possibility. The real socialist and national liberationist ideological lines that nourished me and so many others were not suitable tools for seeing through this subterfuge. The famous skullduggery of Athene, about which both Alexander and Napoleon spoke, lives on in the Greek state tradition. What could the wisdom and bravery of the Middle East have hoped to achieve against this?

Critique of the ECtHR
One of the most important criticisms of the proceedings against me before the ECtHR concerns the relationship between the individual and society. As I have already extensively detailed in the first part of my defenses to the court, sociality has an extraordinary significance—a precedence in the development of the human species. All descriptions of the individual that fail to refer to sociality are nothing more than deception. In societies in the East, the dominant factor is always sociality. This is the result of the age and development of society. Whereas in the birth of Western civilization, individualism predominated. There was no lack of individual awakening in the Greek and Roman phase of the Western civilization or, thereafter, in the interpretation of Christianity during the medieval period. But during the Renaissance and afterward, there was a historical revolution of individualism. In the movements of the Renaissance, the Reformation, the Scientific Revolution, and the Enlightenment, which

followed one after the other, the sociality that had proliferated in the extreme in the societies of the East for centuries, suffocating individuals, was shattered. At first, this led to an equilibrium between the individual and society but, ultimately, in the nineteenth and twentieth centuries led to the extreme rise of the individual. Our age is marked by individualism, and this time around the extreme malady that eats into society stems from individualism.

The balance between a healthy society and a healthy individual has now tilted in favor of the individual in a way that is quite literally absurd. Sociality is perceived as slavery. In fact, this kind of individualism is a form of bestiality, the ultimate return to the way of the primates at a more advanced level and under new conditions.

The fact that the ECtHR only accords an "individual right of appeal" is the legal reflection of this malady. Individuals are, in fact, entirely social and manifest themselves as such in every respect. To regard them even hypothetically as separated from their society and the will of the people is nothing but a legal ruse. This approach also contradicts any feeling for justice, which is the basis of all law. It also consciously or unconsciously serves to hide an important political reality. It keeps the free political movement of the Kurdish people beyond the law. The fact that the legality and legitimacy of the Kurdish freedom movement are kept off the agenda creates a situation that obscures the responsibility of the EU for the Kurdish people. This reality became glaringly apparent in the case of Leyla Zana and her friends.[3] She received superficial support, but the "protection" of her human rights separated her from both Kurdish people in prison and those on the outside—in any case, the "outside" is nothing but an open-air prison. This is how they salvage "human rights." As a consequence of my case, it is impossible to accept this subterfuge that stems from European civilization. My expectation is a decision that respects the equilibrium between the individual and society.

In its May 6, 2003, decision, the ECtHR rejected the verdict of the Turkish state security court, arguing that the court was not independent and that I did not receive a fair trial. On the other hand, it accepted the legality of bringing me before a court that is not independent and can't rule justly, as a consequence of one of the most momentous plots of the twentieth century. In reality, this opinion and ruling are entirely political and, thus, only continue the plot. They had already been fixed beforehand as part of a larger plan.

My abduction totally contradicted article 5, paragraph 2 of the European Convention on Human Rights, according to which I should have been returned to where I was seized. The fact that I was not even heard demonstrates that the decision had already been made beforehand. There is a lot of evidence regarding my abduction. Even more important is the fact that I was kidnapped in a place that must be seen as European territory.[4] If the Grand Chamber of the ECtHR wants to respect the truth, then it must hear my testimony. If it doesn't see this as necessary, then it must at least hear the testimony of Şemsi Kılıç,[5] Savvas Kalenteridis, and others who witnessed the events. Moreover, my lawyers' well-founded and extensive arguments must be taken into account. I have no fear of standing trial. However, it is my right to be tried before an independent and just court in accordance with the spirit of the conventions to which Turkey is a party. The ECtHR's most important task is to ensure such a trial. This would be the first step toward fairness. The court's decision failed to take that step. On the contrary, it prevented my execution but accepted my rotting away in prison for the rest of my life with no possibility of parole—cajoling me into accepting the lesser of two evils. I am not blind to the fact that this artifice has been used by the dominant powers for thousands of years. If the Grand Chamber of the ECtHR really wants to clear the way for a fair trial, it must consider the following:

> First, I have been recognized as a political refugee by a decision of the Roman Appellate Court. The court is in the possession of the relevant documents.
>
> Second, legally and on the basis of the decision of the Athens Criminal Court I should still be on Greek territory. The fact that I am in a one-person prison on İmralı Island is unlawful. This is completely obvious. The question that the Grand Chamber must answer is: Why am I being held in a solitary cell as a prisoner with a life sentence with no possibility for parole, even though legally I should be within Greek borders? If the Grand Chamber confirms the decision of the First Chamber without answering that question, it will prove that its actions are entirely politically motivated.
>
> If the court wants to understand the details of my abduction without prejudice, it must hear my testimony, briefly summarized here, in full and summon all of the witnesses to the events. Any legitimate ruling must see me as being within the territorial borders

of the EU. As a consequence, both Turkey's claims and those of the Kurdish side should be heard by an independent court, and a juridical and just verdict should be delivered. Turkey routinely accuses me of being responsible for the deaths of thirty to forty thousand people, but the fact that almost four thousand Kurdish villages and hamlets have been depopulated, that there have been more than ten thousand murders by unknown perpetrators, that almost thirty thousand guerrillas have been martyred and several hundred thousand people have been arrested, that exile, flight, and torture have become chronic, abrogating all human rights and trampling democracy underfoot—all of this is only a small part of the other side of the balance sheet. How can the ECtHR rule without taking any of it into account?

This is, in fact, the balance sheet of a war. There has never been an individual terrorist in history who could kill thirty to forty thousand people. If the fact that this was an asymmetrical war fought against the Kurdish people is accepted, then the best path to a just trial for me and the other parties would be the establishment of a process like the Nuremberg trials after World War II, the trials in Den Haag after the war in Bosnia, or the trials conducted by the UN courts that were created after the massacres in Rwanda and Liberia. There are thousands of complaints from Kurdish victims before the ECtHR. Should these not call to mind the balance sheet of the war? Historically, the Kurds have always been cheated. Shall we continue to be cheated even in Europe, a region that has developed a very high degree of transparency? How can humanity reconcile this with its conscience? At my trial, a thousand intrigues were used to judge a people for whom the ban on the use of its mother tongue has still not been completely lifted. How can the ECtHR dare participate in the crime of making all of this "compatible" with European norms?

The answer to these and hundreds of similar legal questions will show whether or not the court is independent of political influence and will allow for a fair trial. If the path to a fair trial is not opened up and I and thousands of other comrades, including Leyla Zana and her friends, are left to rot in prison for eternity (the question of being released is a secondary issue), we will have no other option but to state quite openly that it is actually the EU that is trying us, using the Turkish administration as a cat's-paw. We will also have to openly and with great anger say that the leading European states bear the primary responsibility for the asymmetrical war that has been carried out against the Kurdish people for the last two hundred years, that the US has participated in it since the 1950s, that it is apparently not enough for them that the Armenians, Ionians, and Assyrians were liquidated, and that it is now apparently the Kurds' turn.

In brief, if one looks at the whole picture, the main parties to my trial are the EU countries, the Kurds, and me. That the trial was subcontracted to Turkey was merely a sleight of hand.

The efforts of the EU countries, with the support of the US and Israel, to push me out of the jurisdiction of European law took place openly. The Italian government did what it could to secure this result. It exerted enormous psychological pressure and even mobilized financial resources. Even though I hadn't entered either the UK or Switzerland, both declared me to be persona non grata, an undesirable person. Official litigation against me was instigated in Germany and France. In some other countries, my request for asylum was preemptively and unfairly rejected, even though I had the right to asylum. A general campaign was undertaken to psychologically wear me down. Behind all of this are the quiet and secret agreements that Turkey concluded following the August 15, 1984, offensive, agreements that are based on ugly financial interests. We know very well that the various Turkish governments have literally given half of Turkey to European countries to induce them to take their distance from the PKK and accept the idea that the Kurdish freedom struggle is "terrorism." Had it not been for these self-serving relationships of the sort that the European governments generally try to hide, but which have become obvious in my case, legally I would have been granted asylum immediately. Because of these interests, European law in the form of the European Convention on Human Rights (ECHR) was glaringly contravened.

Abducting and removing me from Europe was meant to remove me from the purview of European law. Being banished to Kenya was the result of these disgusting relationships of interest. If it actually intends to respect European legal norms and conventions, the ECtHR must reject this unlawfulness. Even though the decisions of the Roman Appellate Court and the Athens Criminal Court have no practical relevance, their positive rulings are binding on the ECtHR. These decisions recognize me as a political refugee who should be free on European soil. Based on these decisions, it must be recognized that the judicial and execution processes on İmralı Island completely contradict European law and should not have occurred. What we expect from the Grand Chamber of the ECtHR is that it acknowledge my right of free movement on European soil in accord with European law and the rulings in Athens and Rome, that it reject the injustice of İmralı Island prison, and that if a retrial is necessary the court ensures that it be fair and impartial—in accordance with the First Chamber ruling of the ECtHR. The conditions of the ECHR will only be satisfied if I receive a positive decision on that basis. Otherwise, the ECtHR will inevitably become nothing more than an instrument in a far-reaching political plot.

This is why I have devoted the largest part of my court defenses to explaining European civilization. This civilization is destroying us. When executing their schemes to secure their temporary power or their masters' profits, the politicians never particularly worry about the eradication of this or that people. We already know that. But if there is still a tiny spark of justice, then an institution like the ECtHR should lay the sleight of hand of an "individual trial" to one side and address the essence of the case. With its ruling, it should at least show what an objective, realistic, and timely judgment looks like. If Turkey is a war party—and the whole world knows that it is; it even says so itself—and has declared me and my organization to be the greatest threat and the key enemy, how can it guarantee a fair and impartial administration of justice? How can the ECtHR assume it would? Are there other schemes that we do not even know about? If so, why has the ECtHR accepted my lawsuit? If these questions are not answered in a convincing manner, do we not have to conclude that this is just another well-played act in a political game that has been in the works for a long time? If that is the case, I have no other option than to do what my reason and my consciousness tell me to do to prevent myself and my people from becoming the plaything of others.

All of this indicates why my submission to the court has to be developed politically more than legally. The Kurds as a people are not treated in accordance with either national or international law. The fact that European law stubbornly insists on the individual dimension and ignores the underlying historical social reality means that the problem cannot be resolved by legal means. This approach has prevailed ever since the Treaty of Lausanne, in which the existence of the Republic of Turkey was accepted without recognizing the Kurds.[6] In return, the Brits were handed the cities of Mosul and Kirkuk. The Republic of Turkey adopted capitalism, and the Treaty of Lausanne was its reward. While the Western states regarded the Armenians, Ionians, and Assyrians as minorities worthy of protection, they could not give any guarantees to the Kurds. This meant turning a blind eye to the cultural and political—though not yet physical—annihilation of the Kurds. The consequences of relationships, contradictions, and conflicts between the Western imperialist states and the Turkish rulers over the last two hundred years should be examined closely. The backwardness of the Middle East today, its lack of freedom and democracy, are essentially the result of relations during these years. The Greater Middle East Initiative must be seen as an inevitable result of the last two hundred years, and its content should be carefully examined. The Kurds, as the most strategic element of this project, have a special obligation to examine and evaluate themselves in this regard, which is one of the main goals of my present defenses before the court.

The connection between my imprisonment on İmralı Island and the formation of the Kurdish federal state in North Iraq is quite obvious. The Turkish authorities must understand the following very well: you have handed the Kurdish federal state to the feudal-bourgeois Kurdish forces in return for the liquidation of me and the PKK, and you will be held responsible for the consequences.

This amounts to laying the foundation of a conflict that resembles today's Israel-Palestine conflict. With this, not only is the foundation of the revolutionary republic being eroded, but an atmosphere suitable for all kinds of nationalist provocation is also being created. Nationalist sentiments are to be inflamed to set the people against each other so that those in power are able to continue their systems of rule in new forms. The Israel-Palestine conflict has almost been turned into a problem of the last century and has become a justification for the worst administrative practices among the Arab people. The rulers are now trying to extend the same game to the Kurds.

It is at this point that the plot against me gained an international dimension, because the mere existence of my person and the movement I represent did not fit into the game and even had the potential to thwart it. It appeared strategically important to strip our movement of its influence over the Kurds and place it in the hands of the imperial powers, with the goal of disciplining the Arab, Persian, and Turkish nation-states. Tens of thousands of Kurds in Europe and the US were being prepared to this end. They insistently tried to create a Kurdishness that suited their own mentality. In fact, the process that Israel had begun after World War II with the Barzani family was gradually extended, which is why the Kurds slowly gained importance as the new favorites of the West. The states in the Middle East, with their tradition of conquest, also redefined their own Kurds. They formed a Kurdish army of intelligence operatives and village guards under the command of the security forces. The third group of Kurds, namely, the poor and the laborers, was shaped by the PKK's patriotic and democratic line. Thus, three groups of Kurds emerged. First, the Kurds affiliated with the US, the EU, and Israel—the old feudal and tribalist upper-class circles that are on their way to becoming a bourgeoisie, and who are trying to gain influence by exploiting tribal loyalties, with the financial support of the states. At the moment, their basic political program is the Kurdish federal state. Second, the Kurds who serve the conquerors' security forces—the Arab, Turkish, and Persian nation-states—for money and out of tribal loyalty, whose goal does not go beyond money and local authority. The third group is made up of the PKK and the Kurds who feel connected to it by their patriotic and democratic sentiments and consciousness. This force seeks to achieve democratization and a free Kurdistan. Various possible structures could emerge in the future from these three groups and the interactions and contradictions among them.

Kurdistan, which has awoken from its deep thousands of years of slumber and is in a dynamic process, will inevitably be one of the most important actors in the emergence of a new equilibrium in the Middle East and can certainly play various roles in different scenarios.

In its founding phase, the Turkish republic saw the Kurds as a fundamental element, but after the uprisings it denied them any access to law and politics as Kurds. From the perspective of the political juncture at the time, this might have made a certain amount of sense, but turning it into a permanent principle was one of the most disastrous errors made. I believe that the imperial powers pursued the goal of exploiting the contradictions resulting from this error to the advantage of the Kurdish structures closest to them and to bind the Turkish, Iranian, and Arab leaderships that they have a conflict of interest with more closely to them or otherwise curb their influence. To do so, they consciously tried to liquidate the option of freedom for poor and working-class Kurds linked to me. The first product of these contradictions is the Kurdish federal state in Northern Iraq, and that is just the beginning. Should the leadership of Turkey proceed against the Kurds in an alliance with Iran and some of the Arab forces from Syria and Iraq, it will fall into the real trap. The historical allergy the Iranians and the Arabs have to the Turks should not be overlooked. If the project of inciting the Kurds against the Turks succeeds, some historical problems will certainly flare up again. Among these, the historical claims of the Anatolian Greeks, the Armenians, the Georgians, the Iranians, and even the Arabs, claims that reach to the Taurus Mountains, will be reinvigorated, reducing the Turks to the status they had in the sixteenth century.

At that time, Selim I deflected this danger with his Kurdish policy. The fact that Mustafa Kemal Atatürk also succeeded in doing so in the 1920s was the result of his alliance with the Kurds in a freedom-based relationship. The Anatolian history of the Turks was based on a very close dialectical relationship with the Kurds. The disintegration of this relationship and turning Kurds into complete enemies would be the gravest strategic loss on the part of the Turks, whether they know it or not. The blame for the uprisings must be sought on both sides. Neither the primitive chauvinist nationalist tradition nor the religious feudal tradition were capable of understanding and acting upon this strategic connection. This strategic relationship is on the brink of being destroyed by the extremely violent liquidation of the Kurds. Both Mustafa Kemal Atatürk and İsmet İnönü realized this toward the end of their time in office, but the situation was irreversible. Since 1950, the revitalization and strengthening of the Kurdish feudal class in return for the denial of their lineage has led to a further disintegration of this strategic relationship, which has become increasingly meaningless.

After the 1980s, the Turkish-Islamist current, which is a synthesis of extreme religionism and Turkish nationalism, completely ignored this strategic relationship. In this situation, the Western powers and the states in the region expressed their traditional indignation by turning a blind eye toward the PKK. But all of them, with the firm support of Iran and Syria, played a role in the formation of the Kurdish federal state, which represented a singularly important step in putting the historical games back on the agenda. The Kurdish movement linked to nationalism will totally sever the traditional strategic relationship with the Turks. We see examples of this process in the separation between Israel and Palestine or Russia and Chechnya and in the Balkans, with the dissolution of Yugoslavia. These random and self-deceptive policies are a far cry from showing any understanding of the importance of the historical relationship. They have all been blinded by nationalism and religionism, and short-term rentier economics and politics have made them incapable of seeing beyond the next day. I have tried very hard to prevent myself and the PKK from being used in this game.

The developments within the scope of the US Greater Middle East Initiative will continue to accelerate in the near future. Although it is allegedly the strongest partner, it is, in fact, unclear whether Turkey will be a partner or a target of this project. In the 1990s, there was also a lot of talk about strategic partnership. The results speak for themselves and may have been instructive. Whether Turkey is a partner or a target, it will be unable to maintain the old status quo. To insist on the old status quo would turn Turkey into a second Iraq or a second Yugoslavia—even though Iraq and Yugoslavia had conceded their own nationalities a number of rights to varying degrees. Comparatively, the Turkish chauvinist thought templates are much stronger, and the people have been forced to adopt these chauvinist templates for years. If this continues, a rupture is inevitable. The conflict with the PKK alone makes this obvious. Kurdish-Turkish structures characterized by nationalism will shatter the historic and strategic relationship completely. In my opinion, this has been the conscious and deliberate goal since the 1950s. First, Turkish nationalism was ramped up to the point of fascism and religionism, a process exacerbated from the outside, just as Pan-Turkism and Pan-Islamism had been before World War I. At the time, Mustafa Kemal Atatürk understood this better than anyone else. He thwarted these two ideological currents and propagated a patriotism that was open to freedom.

The above-mentioned provocative factors within the Kurdish uprisings disrupted this policy and the strategic relationship between the two sides. In reality, extreme nationalism ran straight into a trap, because it believed it could obliterate the Kurds. Even someone like Ziya Gökalp, who is regarded as the father of Turkish nationalism, could still say, "The Turks cannot do without the Kurds, and the Kurds cannot do without the Turks." In this light, it is very important to reinterpret the development of the attitude toward the Kurds after 1950. Since the turn of the millennium, Kurdish nationalism, again encouraged by outside influence, has accelerated. Despite all its flaws, the PKK and its internationalist position on the people of the region has been the main factor in thwarting this game. The US decision to immediately dub the PKK "terrorist" was not due to its great love for the Turks but, rather, to deepen the conflict. Had the US and the EU done only 0.1 percent of what they did in Cyprus to address the Kurdish question, they would have strengthened Turkey enormously. But they carefully refrained from doing so. Instead, they executed a policy that could be described as: "To the hare: run! To the greyhound: attack!" The political and economic war profiteers also enthusiastically jumped on the bandwagon, bringing Turkey to the brink of demise.

This was the point at which the forces at work thought that if they handed me over I would undertake a crude resistance and die, which set in motion the total collapse of Turkish-Kurdish relations. All the ropes of the Kurdish movement would be centralized in one place. Today we have a better understanding of these plans. Even in the best-case scenario, the US and the EU would not have refrained from supporting Kurdish nationalism. Israel also urgently needs Kurdish nationalism in the Middle East. Without Kurdish nationalism, the West will not be able to bring the Arab, Iranian, and Turkish lethargy to a position that suits its goals. The way in which they hoped to use the PKK was a trap for both sides. With a policy based on the greyhound attacking and the hare running away, both sides are losers. This is exactly what happened after 1925, and once the Kurdish nationalists gain access to modern armaments in the 2000s, it will be hard to openly confront them. Perhaps neither side can score a strategic win, but they will certainly both lose big, and, as always, the real winners will be the imperial forces. Should this situation come about, Kurdish nationalism and those who deny the existence of the Kurds and deprive them of their rights will be equally responsible. The question arises: What has the Republic of Turkey gained by leaving the Kurdish question unresolved for seventy-five years?

Moreover, one would really have to be blind to overlook the fact that given today's technological development a policy of denial is not only condemned to failure but will also engender a Kurdish-Turkish conflict that might flare up at any time. The Soviet Union and Iraq are sad examples of the result of relying on military power. Already, the military expeditions to Kurdistan are synonymous with economic crises. Continuing to block a resolution of the Kurdish question, refusing to end the conflict, and provoking a period of potential new war would amount to the total destruction of one of the main pillars of the strategy that has been vital in keeping Turks alive in Anatolia for a thousand years. I repeat: to fail to see this, you have to be either a traitor or an enemy of the people.

Nobody should expect that a movement that is the product of unbelievable hardship and effort will simply surrender. Since 1998, I have patiently mapped out a comprehensive ideological and political position, both for myself and for my organization, and have asked everyone to adopt it. My proposal was the most prudent possible and would have been to the advantage of all concerned parties, the country, and our people. At the time, I received positive reactions from my friends. While I can't say that there had been no reaction whatsoever on the part of the state, I must say that the state is still a long way from acting constructively to bring about a solution. Continuing to wait risks destroying the process completely.

The PKK will neither relinquish Kurdistan to reactionary state policy and the representatives of the status quo nor to primitive Kurdish nationalism. The PKK has not insisted that the Kurds have a state of their own, but it has also never turned its back on the project of democracy and freedom for the Kurds and Kurdistan, and it never will. There can be no doubt that a democratic dialogue is the most constructive and solution-oriented relationship possible. A careful investigation of the history of the Turks, Iranians, and Arabs will show that conditions in the Middle East have always resembled a federation, and only full democracy can prevent nonproductive disputes from arising within a federation. So far, history hasn't found any solution that is more effective than that.

In all of this, Turkey is in the best position to prevent a situation in which the Kurds as a whole, but particularly the PKK and its initiative, become the focus of new regional intrigues. This would also best suit Turkey's history and it's particular common strategic roots with the Kurds. For the Turks, it is neither possible nor useful to try to eradicate the Kurds from history. On the contrary, it is undeniable that mutual dependency is a vital factor for both peoples. Continuing to wait at this point would mean heading toward decay and further squandering the potential basis for positive relationships. If they are denied a democratic dialogue, the Kurds will choose a major offensive to win their freedom. And as for how the war will develop, the approach of the parties involved and the foreign powers will be decisive.

We must carefully analyze what will happen if Turkey fully throws itself into the chaos in the Middle East without addressing the Kurdish question. It is becoming clear that three groups will compete for Kurdistan. The first one is the US, Israel, and the collaborationist Kurds. The second is the Turkish, Iranian, and Arab representatives of the status quo, along with a small section of the Kurdish militias, collaborators, and tribes, as well as the comprador bourgeoisie. The third group is weightier and comprised of the impoverished laborers and the patriotic and democratic population. This type of separation is new. It is highly likely that the collaborationist Kurds willing to make common cause with the representatives of the status quo will decline in number over time. This can be deduced from the situation of the Kurds in Iraq. If the Turkish, Iranian, and Arab leaderships do not make reforms to their Kurdish policies, the most diverse possible alliances could develop between patriotic and democratic Kurds and the Kurds who collaborate with imperialism at all levels. In the end, all Kurds might even take part in a coalition under the leadership of the US. If there is no option for a compromise with the Turkish, Iranian, and Arab leaderships, we should expect even the Kurds under the leadership of the PKK to enter into relations with the coalition forces on the basis of a ceasefire and democratic solution. The Arab leadership of Iraq has already taken a strategic blow because of such a relationship. It was the US, Israel, and Kurdish alliance that destroyed Iraq. If Turkey stubbornly continues to defer a solution of the Kurdish question, the consequences could be many times more severe than in Cyprus. Neither the capitulation offered to the Western states as hush money nor investments can continue to be effective in this new phase.[7] Even though the Greater Middle East Initiative doesn't envisage the same things for Turkey as the Treaty of Sèvres after World War I, the republic as a nation-state produced by the domestic and external balance of power at that time can no longer be sustained in its pro–status quo mode of being.

Turkey is definitely in a transitional period, and how it will emerge from the chaos will depend on the extent to which it defines its new condition correctly. Should it expand the war with the Kurds instead of seeking a reconciliation, the result will probably be a situation somewhere between Sèvres and Lausanne.

A democratic solution to the Kurdish question will enable Turkey to assume a leading role along with the Kurds in a democratic Middle East a strong possibility. If the opposite proves to be the case, the strategic bond would be completely broken, and Turkey would run the risk of being squeezed into Central Anatolia. All these options will be on Turkey's agenda both in the short and long run, with things sometimes moving slowly and at other times quickly. A renewal of the post–World War I Kurdish-Turkish compromise on a democratic basis would lead to a situation where both sides emerge from the chaos in the Middle East stronger. This time, this must happen in a historically appropriate way through democratic and free unity. The road to this goal is rife with dangers posed by feudal and bourgeois nationalism. Should the project fail, the formation of a Kurdistan that resembles Israel would be inevitable.

To conclude, the Grand Chamber of the ECtHR is faced with delivering a historical judgment that could pave the way for a just and impartial trial. If there is a role for the law in enabling a democratic solution to the Kurdish question, it must include the attempt to thwart this political plot. This would show the face of European law that is oriented toward peace. I was tried under such harsh conditions as a result of the non-application of European law. My abduction served to remove me from Europe's jurisdiction. The significance of my kidnapping, a story that could be the subject of a novel, goes far beyond me as an individual. In the last quarter century, there has been extensive bargaining between the Western states and Turkey about the Kurdish people's freedom struggle. Because of the capitalist system's greed for profit, the struggle of our people, which takes place amid terrible poverty and suffering, is simplistically and entirely unjustly reduced to a mere violation of my individual rights. This is yet another example of the EU and Turkey trying to reach a compromise. But, actually, it is not only me who loses; the Kurdish people will be the ones to really lose. It is important that the ECtHR does not allow itself to be instrumentalized in this way. It is obvious certain forces are putting significant energy into trying to manipulate my will. Even guinea pigs are treated better. What, therefore, is the legal justification for the EU demanding that Turkey provide a fair and independent trial?

It is common knowledge that in Turkey trials of the Kurds in particular are carried out on orders from above. The judicial institution is at the forefront of the fascist centers. In the way it deals with the Kurds, it does not have the slightest legal feature. To expect a fair and independent trial from such an institution is an insult to me and to our people. Our name, culture, and existence are not recognized. The law deems the Kurds and Kurdishness nonexistent. How can anyone expect a fair and impartial trial as long as this is the judicial reality in Turkey?

I was not apprehended in accordance with international law. Did I surrender to Turkey of my own free will while I was still physically under the jurisdiction of European law? How is it possible that the First Chamber of the ECtHR is unable to establish the fact that I was abducted using the most despicable methods, which is, after all, very easy to see? There remains only one explanation: during the more than twenty years of asymmetrical warfare against the Kurdish people, European capital has squeezed a lot of profit out of Turkey. The ECtHR is now paying the system's debt. Actually, it is the decision of the First Chamber of the ECtHR that prevents a fair and impartial trial. The Grand Chamber should now act in accord with the ECHR and reverse the previous decision. That would pave the way for a truly fair and impartial trial, which would create the possibility to compensate the Kurdish people in some small way for the great pain and the major losses they have suffered. Then, in the context of its path into the EU, Turkey would actually have the opportunity to become a country that applies the rule of law. As a country conforming to European law, Turkey would become a fundamental guarantor of peace. All of this would prove that the EU, which itself emerged from self-critique of Europe's war-ridden past and where peace and human rights are accepted as supreme virtues, is indeed an unshakable bastion of law and democracy.

THIRTEEN

An Identity That Must Be
Accurately Defined

It would be an important shortcoming if I were not to redefine my own identity in this defense. Instead of repeating the self-definition I have provided elsewhere, I will add a few things that supplement and complement what I have already said.

While working on this part of the book, I thought a lot about Enkidu's identity. When I tried to understand the Enkidu of the Gilgamesh epic, the oldest known written epic and the oldest of our narratives, I noticed that he actually represents all those who long for the state and the city. Uruk was the first city and first city-state in history to have a written chronicle that is still extant today. The famous hero Gilgamesh is one of the demigod kings of Uruk.[1] He is possibly the founder of the city. From the epic, we learn that the city of Uruk was often attacked by savage tribes and wild animals. As a result, Uruk was the first city in history to be protected by imposing ramparts and to engage in fierce defensive wars.

It is not rare in history to encounter situations where warriors needed for the city are found among the uncivilized "savage" societies. King Gilgamesh tried to recruit strong warriors from the tribespeople living in the mountainous forest regions in the north of today's Iraq. His approach to this is extremely interesting. The city-state of Uruk had discovered a new way of life, and the glamor of city life was very attractive. One of the key things that made the city attractive was the prostitution of women. To put it more precisely, it was highly attractive for men to have a pleasant life ruling over women, who were the remnants of the mother-goddess and

541

gradually imprisoned in private homes and "public houses." Men's new slaves gave them access to a life of unlimited pleasure.

It is not without reason that Innana, the goddess of Uruk, went to battle against the crafty male god Enki.[2] Inanna was a later incarnation of Ninhursag, meaning the "goddess of the mountain regions." She represented the domestic mother who developed the Neolithic civilization. This is how the society that emerged around the mother became a divine symbol. Probably one of the issues that she resisted most was women being offered as sexual commodities in private and public houses. This is what was behind the major struggle she waged for the dignity of the goddess. The epic names a well-known pleasure woman as the most important factor binding Enkidu to Uruk, which is entirely credible. It is this woman who seduces the wild Enkidu near the water and captures him. As he becomes bound to the woman from the city, Enkidu finally becomes a great military commander in the service of Gilgamesh. Thereafter, the further adventures of Gilgamesh and Enkidu are immortalized in this oldest surviving epic of humanity.

When I compared the history of Enkidu with my own first contact with elementary school and the city, it did not take me long to realize that this story was actually also telling my story. Let me recount an incident that might be of interest. I encouraged the children of our village to go to the elementary school in the neighboring village of Cibin. Among these kids, there was a boy named Şevket, the little brother of Cumo, against whom I carried out my first "guerrilla action." His mother was one of the poorest and most uncultivated women in the village, but what she said when Şevket was first sent to school was literally worthy of a professor. I remember it exactly; she said, in Kurdish: "*Şevketê me buye hukûmet*" (our Şevket has become the government). It was only after working on this court defense that I understood what she meant.

Each one of us was now an Enkidu who was coaxed into running toward the city, which is to say, the state. We were breaking away from the mother-based society. Bit by bit, we began to feel contempt for the village. Against the background of the superiority of the city, the village increasingly faded away. Our mothers were increasingly losing their importance. We began to disdain our bond to tribe and family. The city and the state hidden within it pulled on us like a magnet. Thereafter, it would not be easy to escape its influence. The city and the state in it objectively functioned as tremendous propaganda tools in their own right. Everything about the city was presented as perfect. It would have been impossible to refuse the prostitute who paraded in such beautiful garments and exquisite makeup. The city exploited everything to demonstrate its superiority, and we totally lost sight of our own little village. The most ordinary state official was now our new deity. His every word and the very garments he wore constituted the new divinity. Everything was designed for effect. On top of it all, the Kurds were given the epithet "those with tails." The formula for shedding this epithet as quickly as possible was to rapidly become urbanized, that is to become part of the state and to become Turkish. Not only did we begin to despise our village and our family but also our Kurdishness. These felt like shackles on our feet. Our whole world unfolded within this triad: the more urbanized you became, the more you became part of the state, and the more you became part of the state, the more Turkish you were, and the more Turkish you were, the greater your chances of advancement. This was our new societal custom. Religion and knowledge were only meaningful on that basis. For us, a whole new socialization took place in the context of this triad.

I conclude from this that urbanization and statization have priority over the formation of class and the nation. Contrary to popular opinion, this identification with the city and the state was the most fundamental and primeval factor of socialization. Being a proletarian or socialist are nothing more than a product of this urbanization and internalization of the state, resembling the attributes of the state-god. Sociology has yet to fully analyze the formation of the personality by the city and the state. The communal and rural personality and the urban and state-fixated personality are starkly different sociological phenomena. Without dissecting them, no analysis of class, socialism, and democracy can ever be complete or coherent. There are fundamental contradictions and differences between a society shaped by the city and the state and a rural communal society. Rural society is communal, i.e., egalitarian and democratic, which is to say, free to the same degree that the society shaped by the city and the state is statist and authoritarian. In that sense, the most important contradiction in history is between urban statist society and rural communal society, and the real struggle takes place between urban statist authoritarianism and rural communal democracy. But I only understood this much later.

Our journey toward the city and the state was cemented by our passion for attending military school and the political faculty. Authority attracts authority. We wanted to achieve political and military authority not at a measured step but at a run. When I was confronted with obstacles, I was extremely saddened, and when I could not attend military school, I considered myself very unlucky indeed. At that time, the attraction of urban woman was a separate draw but an attractive force in the same vein. Under these circumstances, being a revolutionary meant to be the best practitioner of statism. Socialism was understood as the smoothest functioning state, and we felt it would provide us with the greatest possible progress. For us, the state was like our new, modern flying vehicle. Our rebelliousness was perceived as yearning for the past and as a reaction against the new. Kurdishness, however, was always experienced as a problem struggling to articulate itself.

When our statism appeared to be something that was even more accessible in the Middle East, we firmly believed that we could achieve our goals using this instrument. Although it did not give us much reassurance, combining the possibilities opened up by being state-oriented with our revolutionary goals allowed us to advance quickly. Let me just be clear in saying that this was the first time that I felt that my personality was experiencing an erosion of meaning. The sacredness of life was losing its value a bit at a time. I came to understand that we would not win with a state but would, in fact, lose. I began to doubt that we could reach our goal by jumping on the state bandwagon. But since we had already made a good deal of headway, I was far from ready to reverse direction and analyze how it would be possible to change tracks. While my personality that was aboard the state bandwagon was breaking down, the path I would search for and find with my new identity was full of uncertainties. The socialist state in which I had placed my trust had ceased to be real, but it would have been beneath me to take refuge in the capitalist state. The fact that my relationship with the Syrian state had been tactical from the outset made it possible for me to endure it. It was too late to go to the mountains in Kurdistan, and I couldn't really see the results of my efforts. In a way, I felt I had been betrayed. With a heavy heart due to these thoughts and feelings, I was feeling aggrieved as I set out on the twisted road of my Athens and Europe adventure.

When I first ran toward the state, I was excited. I had learned by rote. It was all about developing a rank and file. Religion and faith had turned into rank and money. A revolutionary attitude allowed me to overcome this personality. But even my revolutionary attitude worked in tandem with a statist personality. An authority that was more precise and led by me made that attractive. In fact, I did not run toward a state that was so far away that I could never reach it but toward my own state, a state close to me. It was, in a way, kind of like a search and a struggle for a new religion, a new nationality. My flight to Diyarbakır and my march to Syria and to Lebanon stoked my passion for our own national state. The inspiration I drew from this was enough to keep me going.

Despite my enormous efforts, I felt that deep down inside I had lost something important. The statist mentality had deprived me of myself. The degeneration that state-centered socialism in particular and revolutionary expression in general experienced at that time also showed up at my front door. My own contradictions would come out into the open when I was faced with the world of ice-cold European calculations of the Athens-Moscow-Rome triad. I could never really be a part of this world, would never fit into the calculations of capitalism, would never get used to Western life. The journey was over. A fairly shallow and grey utopia seemed to be coming to an end. Even as the betrayal was becoming visible on the horizon, I felt numbed. An attentive observer would have been able to detect the Greek intrigue, but I continued to believe in friendship; I had to believe in it. The recent years of my life had been based on this friendship, and I felt that that would be the case until the end. Even if betrayal had come calling and said, "Here I am!" I would have responded, "You are a friend."

It had been the same with Kesire; actually, this woman revealed herself loudly and clearly. She had sent a message from every fiber of her body: "My name is treason, don't come near to me." I responded: "If you are to stay with me, you must be in love with me." When my love and my friends joined forces and sang the same betrayal songs, I would say, even had to say, "What beautiful, revolutionary, and patriotic songs my lover and my friends are singing." When the Greek driver on the island of Corfu brought me to the airport in a jeep, he bumped deliberately into the airplane that was about to take me to Kenya.[3] I still continued to believe in friendship and was smitten with blindness.

Actually, it was the inevitable bankruptcy of the personality traits that had led me to run toward elementary school, the city, and the state. Everything related to the city and the state in the values that made me who I am needed to crumble and fall. The state had decided to eradicate the state within me. This was the real state, the big state. It was the US and EU state. The capitalist state wanted to be rid of me, even sell me for a profit, were I to reject becoming one of its conventional servants. Given the circumstances, escaping this true master wizard was very difficult. If I managed to get away unscathed—great! However, the Leviathan had surfaced from the sea and shown its teeth.

The Greek state was one of the foremost of the Leviathans. However, I still think that I was correct to act in the spirit of friendship right to the end. This was the most important remaining aspect of my personality, and I wanted to keep it unscathed. Let them have betrayal—friendship would still be mine! Being taken to Kenya was like being thrown into Tartarus, the mythological Greek well of hell. The modern bastards of Zeus did not shy away from committing this sin. And the Africans also nicely followed their orders in this well of hell. I found myself at the border between dream and reality. When I emerged from hell and was chained like Prometheus on the rock of İmralı, I was like a creature that is half human, without it being clear what the other half might be. Enkidu fought great battles but died a terrible death. Hegel took the state for the incarnation of God. The fact that all the gods of the world homed in on me seemed to bind me to the lineage of Prometheus, the half-god, half-human. Even if my heart was eaten a thousand times every day, I had to find the strength to renew it. Even if the ravens were to peck at my brain every day, I still had to find a way to make it work. The society shaped by the city and the state had chewed me up and swallowed me, only to regurgitate me. I, however, had not succeeded in destroying their stomachs. After all, how can the urban statist society and the rural communal society, or, in modern terms, the ecological socialist society, coexist, not in a feigned peace but as a dialectical contradiction? This was the problem I focused on. In my court defense, I have tried to present some results for serious consideration. They offer possible lessons, because they are the fruit of an unsparing life and honest and nondeceptive reasoning.

One of the differences between my mother and me concerned my concept of "friendship." She said that I was deluding myself. She probably found my intense, passionate search for friendship unusual. As she saw it, it did not suit the existing social values. She thought that I might end up alone, while my friends pursued their own interests. This was something that I only belatedly recognized as true. The problem was: How far was it possible to go with friends, including the best and the most devoted? What could we do together? As I saw it, there was no work that we couldn't complete together, no goal that couldn't be achieved by our joint efforts. These deeply rooted relationships were another reminder of the relationship between Gilgamesh and Enkidu. Such relationships are repeatedly found in history—this is perhaps a requirement of universal dualism. Anyone who wants to achieve great things will need deep friendships. I was already looking for these friendships as a child in the village, and the result was Hasan Bindal. How did the cursed gang get wind of this and work him into their larger conspiracy? I still don't know the answer to this question. Had they pursued the plot they undertook with my friend with any consistency, they could have shot me dead then. My friend seems to have been a truly great friend after all.[4]

Kemal Pir was also one of the most important among our friends. It would probably be difficult to find another who was equally attentive and sensitive. However much people may praise him and tell stories about him, it still cannot approach the truth. I think that people still haven't really understood him or acted upon his legacy. What is important in people like him is not just how they kept themselves alive but also how they cherished and kept their friends alive. I was thus able to make friends. Thousands of them are still alive. But there were also those among them who used and exploited us. Events would show that our friendships were abused in the most sordid way and that this phenomenon was more widespread than we thought. I have always believed in the greatness of my friends. I always thought their greatness would allow them to play a role, because, on the one hand, I had excessive self-confidence, and, on the other hand, I stepped back to give them space, in total disregard of myself. I was not yet able to analyze what the race toward class society, the city, and the state could do to the individual. It seemed so straightforward to simply generalize my own development. I wanted to achieve a community by imagining that the others were like me, thereby ending up being closer to them than they were to themselves. I was very effective at creating unity, even though it is now difficult for me to admit that my mother was right, and I went too far. I should have understood that the world works differently than I thought. The result was that I slid into dogmatism. My absolute belief in principles and in the idea that everything would turn out alright, even though things were not going well, had long since crossed the line into dogma. This mentality also led to black-and-white thinking: either the perfectly good or the infinitely evil. That also probably had to do with remnants of traditional Zoroastrian belief.

On the one hand, this deep-rooted understanding was attractive and helped to organize people. On the other hand, it led me astray by preventing me from seeing the facts as they were. The stagnation in the PKK must also be partly seen as the result of this understanding of mine. Assuming pure black-and-white opposites is not a particularly productive dialectal approach. It leads to a superficial and mechanical way of thinking.

In the end, I also fell victim to this superficial and mechanical way of thinking and departed from a colorful and vivid reasoning that would have been more productive. Superficial dialectics actually amount to dialectical dogmatism. I too was now in the throes of this kind of idealism, which was widespread in real socialism. As a result, a contrast developed between the values of the PKK, which were laden with greatness, heroism, goodness, trueness, and beauty, and everything that was the opposite. It is generally the system's hollow personalities who profit from contrasting dialectical pairs of this sort. People who had not really become "PKK" in their hearts, but who *thought* they had, used all its virtues crudely. People who couldn't even tend to a handful of goats became leaders or guerrilla commanders within the organization, which had never been the intention. Initially, the reason for this was the conviction that friends would handle everything successfully and in the best manner. Later, it became obvious that it was impossible to be more successful than we were with this approach. But we had not yet determined how to develop and reach a new organizational understanding.

The problem runs even deeper. Since the early 1980s, to the best of my abilities I have made a great effort to analyze and transform the individual in a profound way by dissecting Kurdish social reality, but there were individuals with an insistent personality who responded to my attempts by saying, "we are extremely obstinate." They were not going to give up these traits. Even when their personalities were entirely sucked into the slime of betrayal, infamy, overindulgence, and decadence and were wasted, defeated, and useless, they remained incredibly narcissistic. This was the human reality, but it was an inverted humanity that was totally used up. I literally ground myself like wheat into flour, made bread, and fed them, but still they did not come around to reason. They insisted on their own lives and their so-called way of fighting, but, in reality, they could not really do much. If they were let be, they would literally be like gunpowder that was only sufficient for a single shot.

Even those who were considered excellent militants wouldn't have been able to survive for more than a year. But I was also extremely obstinate. I wanted to keep them alive at all costs. I put everything else aside and took up the struggle for the lives of this human rubble. I even deceived myself into believing that I was dealing with the finest possible material. This was exactly what my mother had so vehemently criticized me for. She had noticed how I deceived myself at a very young age.

Two unspoiled sons of the Black Sea, Kemal Pir and Haki Karer, threw themselves into my kind of friendship with great enthusiasm. To prevent me from hardship, the two of them headed to Kurdistan before the rest of us, even though they neither knew its language or customs. Unfortunately, it would turn out to be wrong to expect the children of a society that had been the victim of betrayal to have the same psychic sensitivity. None of them worked voluntarily, linking their hearts and minds. For these people, it was as if they were literally caught up in a "matter of honor." Perhaps they believed they could salvage their honor by doing things in the way they considered correct. Their insistent understanding of honor was worthless. I tried to convey values to them that their family and the state never would. I presented them with everything that would enable them to *really* preserve their honor. Herein, not working in the way that genuine honor would have demanded was put in front of me as a huge problem. I successfully placed before them the first offensive meant to build the PKK. Any of them could have been a good party member, but they did not condescend to do so. As a consequence, I placed before them the second great offensive meant to build the PKK everywhere, namely, in the mountains and all four parts of Kurdistan, in villages and the cities and abroad. Their heads were aswirl with the possibilities, but they didn't really want to understand. In the Middle East, in Syria, I never ate or slept comfortably, not even once. Instead, I nurtured more than ten thousand sons and daughters.

I put up with their unbearable insistence on some things so that they could remain free and begin to mature, with their dignity intact. It was only later that I understood that even this incomparable willingness to sacrifice could be misinterpreted. Quite a few fell prey to the delusion that I was living like a king. I still remember this well. Duran Kalkan, who was very self-confident and tried to be a good speaker, was suddenly searching for a telephone to speak with a particular person. The way he talked and handled this relationship could have destroyed all the relationships we had established where we were located in just a few minutes. He probably felt like he was talking "like a revolutionary." Later on, I observed the same thing about his practice. As much as he genuinely tried and was selfless as he did so, he liquidated everything in sight, and he didn't even know it.

Watching him made clear the way in which the Turkish left destroys itself.[5] And Duran is regarded as one the best among us. As for the others, if they were left to their own devices, they would not even be able to feed themselves. That they even stayed alive with a weapon at hand was a miracle. Again, I had to endure the sorrow they caused, but I continued to defy my mother's observation and hoped to prove that my friends were good people.

If you look a bit deeper into this phenomenon, you will recognize the personality traits of a despotic society that have solidified over the millennia. The subservient personality turns into a slave when at the bottom and a despot when at the top. A large part of the effort I made to analyze this personality type and to motivate it to action would essentially backfire. What these people understood a commander to be reflected the saying, "Give a beggar a horse, and he'll ride it to death." They were best at liquidating each other and destroying one another's work. I know for a fact that, either by design or by deliberate negligence, they were responsible for the loss of hundreds of wonderful comrades.

Their mentality was so base and their hearts were so hardened that it had become routine for them to send comrades they wanted to get rid of to their deaths without even batting an eye. In their activities within the organization, these scheming individuals even went as far as to try to liquidate me. Some of them—the trio of Şahin Baliç, Mehmet Şener, and Cihangir Hazır[6]—who murdered my childhood friend and neighbor Hasan Bindal as a dry run for assassinating me,[7] maliciously camouflaging the affair as an accident, very probably formed certain relationships in the early 1990s, the actual character of which is still unclear. They formed a gang of some sort, but I don't believe that they were all conscious agents. They probably resorted to conspiratorial methods to seize control of the organization and to act like the beggar in the idiom just mentioned. It was only later that I understood that this was a very widespread practice in the areas where we waged a struggle. Contrary to common belief, the Turkish army did not defeat the guerrilla; it was the treachery of those just described that paralyzed it from within.

I am hesitant to name names, as I have not done the required research sufficiently, but we have lost hundreds of my most heroic friends as martyrs in this way, beginning with Mahsum Korkmaz (Agit). One of the most infamous persons of the sort just mentioned was Şemdin Sakık, who wasn't simply satisfied with a system of subservience but was one of those best at playing the role of the beggar. Cemil Bayık, one of our most honest leading members, of whom we had high expectations, beyond not being able to hold them accountable, wasn't even able to prevent the flight of Mehmet Şener, Cihangır Hazır, and Şemdin Sakık. Had it not been for me, these people would have destroyed everyone else with just a few blows. They didn't even realize what was actually happening. True to the saying "If you can't kick the master, kick the dog," they mercilessly held to account those unfortunates they could get a hold of.

Quite frequently, the unscrupulous types who were destroying the organization and the guerrilla were given free reign, while very young adolescents, including Saime Aşkın, who were having difficulty adapting to guerrilla life were punished for disciplinary infractions. She had been a teacher in Urfa and was one of the first to join our group. She was willing to make sacrifices. She was sent abroad and educated. When I heard that she had been sentenced to death in our first camp in Kurdistan, a camp Duran Kalkan and Ali Haydar Kaytan were responsible for, I was very surprised. The explanation was: "She totally upset the whole military discipline and sabotaged everything, so we had to punish her." I had no choice but to believe what was said—that too was part of discipline. But it was an incident that I placed somewhere in my heart. In my opinion, she should not have been liquidated in this manner, no matter how severe her crime might have been. But I couldn't do anything to prevent it. My heart had also been frozen by dogmatism (in the real socialist sense). In Russia too statist socialism had murdered its most valuable comrades, including Nikolai Bukharin and Grigory Zinoviev, among others, in just this way.[8] Millions of peasants had been killed, and the whole country had been thrown into chaos.

Later, it would become clear that this was not socialism but a barbaric form of capitalism with Russian characteristics. This was actually the mode of being of the Great October Revolution that was betrayed, which had given rise to such high hopes. Just as in many previous great revolutions, the traitors generally got away with murder. History is full of examples, ranging from the followers of Mohammad to those of Jesus. But I think that with this court defense I am presenting a theoretically developed perspective that shows that this must not be treated as fate. I believe I have succeeded in analyzing the personality traits, including my own, that were responsible for this, which provides consolation to certain extent.

Quite obviously, the PKK brought about its own liquidation. Despite all of the heroic deeds, despite courage and a willingness to sacrifice, and despite the pain and the losses we have inevitably suffered in our recent history, this cursed history of ours and the wizards of the capitalist system did not easily allow us to make any real headway in overcoming ourselves and achieving freedom. Even though we applied the methods of national and social liberation of the last two hundred years, our achievements were limited. We did not arrive at an honorable peace. The method I had wanted to try was an offensive under the heading "a democratic solution and peace," which I hoped would cause at least as much excitement as we had experienced in the mid-1970s. I had expected that those I addressed would react with a high level of understanding and contribute, but because they regarded me as utterly defeated they didn't take me or my project seriously. They probably even considered it a humiliating undertaking. How painful it is to say that even among those still in the organization, there were quite a few who agreed with this assessment. Some openly accused me of "surrendering to the bourgeoisie." Most of the other comrades concluded that I had reluctantly reached this point and prepared for the new phase in their own way. Again, sadly but gradually, I realized that there were quite a few who aspired to use the new phase to appropriate our legacy, even though they didn't know what this legacy was and failed to realize that they were attempting to take advantage of it like degenerate heirs. There was something that each group could take that would secure their survival. I sensed this.

The model I suggested to replace the PKK, which had dissolved itself, was an entity that corresponded to the democratic essence I have sketched. Thus, the KADEK was founded, and after it, the Kongra Gel. I wholeheartedly wanted to develop the content of my defenses to the various courts during my time on İmralı based on the theory and practice of democracy. This is their actual essence, even though I may have only succeeded superficially. With this approach, I hoped to analyze and dissolve the remnants of slavery and despotism in our personalities. A meaningful offensive for democracy among the people could contribute to both a political solution and peace. This period could have provided a favorable opportunity.

While the well-known US post-9/11 offensive stopped the steps that could have been expected from Turkey, at the same time it turned out that the behavior displayed in the name of the KADEK was not oriented toward a solution. The people involved didn't understand that the struggle for democracy and peace is harder than a "hot" military battle. They proved utterly unable to understand that peace was a lot more difficult than war, required a focused effort, and could only work if accompanied by a massive democratic organization and action.

When the DSP-ANAP-MHP coalition government under the leadership of Prime Minister Bülent Ecevit, a man who was living in his own dream world, was overthrown,[9] the coalition working under the collective name AKP shrewdly profited from the historical vacuum and took the road to becoming the government. Leftists and social democrats proved unable to understand and interpret what was happening. Unfortunately, the KADEK and later the Kongra Gel didn't fare any better. Even worse, I came to recognize that they had their own calculations about the democratic efforts I was making amid great difficulty. Then one day, under aggravated isolation conditions, I learned with great difficulty that the Kongra Gel had two opposing groups, led by Osman Öcalan and Cemil Bayık respectively, and had completely paralyzed itself before it could even take its first steps. Factions within a movement are only legitimate to the extent that they can concretely develop things. Otherwise, regardless of how well-meaning those involved may be, they cannot avoid their activities being evaluated as mischief and scheming intrigue. They—including these recent factional groups—are illegitimate, because they have once again blocked the general struggle and led to its liquidation. Our history has already shown us this reality.

While those who encompassed the remnants of the Middle Ages within the Turkish state were trying to go on the offensive using dubious pretensions of democracy, the representatives of the remnants of the Middle Ages in the PKK didn't even deem a "simulated democracy" necessary. In the pasha tradition, they went straight for the conquest of power. There were tendencies on both sides that were not simply undemocratic but were far more backward than the population in general and destroyed all of our democratic efforts by insisting on acting on their reactionary passions. To be honest, after seeing the games played by both sides during the municipal elections, I felt violated and made it clear that I would resist.[10] I openly declared that I would not tolerate the distortion of my democratic offensive, and that to at least safeguard my honor I would thwart any such effort and those acting recklessly. When I began to work on this defense, it became clear that the EU was also part of this game, and that I had to provide an exhaustive response. When the US-instigated Iraq War was launched, it became even more pressing to write a historical "Democratic Defense."

The People's Congress model was in many ways solution-oriented. It was meant to simultaneously solve the state question by democratization and to offer suitable solutions for approaching the problems of the freedom and the equality of the people in the framework of this democratization process. At the same time, it might have been able to solve the problems of personality with education and an exemplary democratic practice. The democratic people's congress was clearly a more suitable way to overcome the dead end of modern revolutions. It may appear simple, but a truly democratic behavior can be defined as the most important virtue, both historically and in our day. Instead of "solving" problems with advanced technology and war, leading to mass destruction, democracy—with its highly educational aspect—could bring about the most humane solution possible, thereby achieving peace and improving the quality of life for people in all of their diversity. The criticism that this is not tough enough, because no blood is shed, or that this doesn't correspond to the military balance of power, is not particularly ethical and, therefore, has no human value.

Even though these profound democratic efforts around the question of Kurdistan may appear like simple steps, they are necessary if we hope to bring about more durable and definitive long-term solutions and to dissuade the states from resorting to the meaningless practice of force. They could contribute much to the offensive for democracy that the Middle East so urgently needs. I have explained the historical basis for this both here and in other works. Beyond that, this course would not have excluded armed self-defense until a durable peace was reached. Those under attack could have exerted their legitimate right of self-defense when necessary in all fields and against antidemocratic practices, ensuring the quantitative and qualitative reinforcements necessary for the purpose. By overcoming the narrow, authoritarian, state-oriented party culture, they could have acquired the qualities necessary for the democratic action of the people. In this way, the transformation of the personality and the democratic formation of society could have become a mutually interwoven process. The potential cadres had been given the theoretical and practical resources, as well as methods and schemata. Had they comprehended their essence and been gripped and moved by love for democracy, every activist would have had work to accomplish. When the expected development doesn't occur, dialectics favor its opposite. At critical moments, politics doesn't tolerate a vacuum. At a time when the collaborationist Kurds are undertaking important forays in an alliance with the US, those who were supposed to succeed on behalf of the people have turned their historical shortcomings and their apolitical perspective and intentions, based on narrow grouping and individualistic horizons, into a problem.

Their peasantism meant that they were unaware that they had become entangled in a false power game. Those who cannot muster the strength for historical steps will turn to family disputes instead. Even though the accumulated problems should have been solved in a way that would have brought about positive external developments, the calculation of who was to get what from the family estate would be made at critical moments. The dangerous situation I am in at the moment makes these calculations even more important. Those who are unable to organize a real political and military army relied on forming their own coteries. They controlled a significant amount of material and talent. Did they care about all of the historical labor that went into this, the pain and the blood that has been shed, the hunger used to discipline the people in incredible ways, and the imprisonment of thousands of comrades? None of this seemed all that important to them; they provided a cheap pretext to "explain" why there had been no progress. This is how the first phase of the Kongra Gel unfolded. Of course, this situation came naturally to those who hadn't been living up to their task for years, but they were unable to understand that the legacy of the PKK would not tolerate their approach, thereby reminding them once again of the reality they found themselves in.

It was against this backdrop that I issued my warning. From the outset, I have never enjoyed exercising power and authority, but I have been very sensitive when it comes to doing good work. For me, it has been a question of belief and the conviction that I must not under any circumstances distance myself from certain very central tasks essential for the people. I have often warned: "the Kurdish people have a few values that they will be able to protect as long as they follow my line." Anyone who ignored this warning would sooner or later have their efforts end in utter failure. It is time that some inside and outside the organization understand that this is their situation.

Whether or not there are groups around Osman Öcalan and Cemil Bayık is not something I take particularly seriously. I would even pray for the emergence of groups that are strong enough to be able to liquidate me first. I wish they had strong groups that aspired to come to power. I would congratulate them if they hit their enemies really hard, and me even harder! On the other hand, if such groups really exist it is also inevitable that they will all, knowingly or unknowingly, lead to flight and liquidation, and that makes whether one of them is bigger than another fairly unimportant, because such a phase is itself a setback, a waste of time and energy, and an affront to dignity.

For me, the more interesting thing is that in their dispute the contention between them is superficial, while they are not aware that I am their actual target—regardless of whether the alleged issue is Osman's surname or the behavior of the other group—based on their demeanor that has reached me even here. More precisely, as we have experienced in many similar cases, they showed their reaction against me by forming two bogus groups with some phony praxis. It is impossible to act directly against me at the present stage. To do so would require them to flee, and that is not in their interest. So they have had to carry out their struggle with me indirectly, albeit passionately. Because they have swallowed the anger that has been building up within them for years, which they would have liked to unleash upon me, it was necessary for them to find a way to blow off steam. It was a simple peasant-like settlement of scores. They need to concede that my understanding of what is going on is not mistaken. If all this is not true and they are sincere, they can only prove that by taking on their historical responsibilities despite all of internal and external provocations and intrigue. If their ambition and rage are rooted in noble motives, it will probably be the primary attitude of each and every comrade claiming to be sincere to successfully complete their duties as the people and comrades expect of them. I want to stress once more that we recognize that this is their right, and if both sides do not fully understand the depth of what is happening, I'd be happy to explain it again.

I must once again note that, for me, both groups are basically the same and the formal differences between them are not very important. Now I want to say a few things about that. Should there be mistakes in my interpretation due to a serious lack of knowledge of the situation, I will, of course, not hesitate to correct them to prevent a shadow from being cast on the reputation of my friends. I am, after all, someone who constantly engages in self-critique.

I have thought much about these groups and similar deviations, which appear to reflect adverse reactions against each other, even though these reactions are actually directed against genuine leadership. The history of our movement is the history of our social reality, which is characterized by an inability to achieve unity and to establish self-management, with sense-less and toxic disputes between various tendencies being routine. These events are nurtured by this culture. Forming groups is the first reflex of those whose individualism and self-interest have gained the upper hand. They try to bring some part of the movement under their control. The historical success of our organizational efforts is linked to overcoming the effects of this culture. This kind of behavior dovetails with the tendency in our society to make small talk devoid of content and to display primitive caprice and unpolitical behavior. We could talk at length about the objective basis for this behavior, and I have already analyzed these issues in detail.

I still remember that many of those who have left the organization complained, "The PKK is stealing our lives." Both in prison and outside, those who made attempts at liquidation made such claims. Of course, a leadership that wants to save its people and liberate its land must steer clear of egotistical and narrow social aims and utilize the life of the comrades-in-arms responsibly toward elevated and liberating goals. Any other kind of organization and leadership is simply impossible. In this connection, their talk about "social life" is a means to an end.[11]

We have to understand that those who fail in the political and military aspects of their lives will also be unable to organize their social lives, and that even if they could theirs would be lives of alienation. If we are to analyze our life and work based on genuine heroism and the dignity of freedom, I am not sure whether having a social life, a family, a partner, and children will be truly meaningful for those who cannot attain a minimum level of success in their struggle. Committed fighters must never forget this. If they do, they must find another way to define themselves.

It is well known that as a leader I have always put a lot of energy into avoiding familism. It was me who most thoroughly criticized and stood against Osman Öcalan's recognized tendencies. It is, therefore, quite interesting that some are making the effort to get rid of what they call "Öcalanism," both within and outside the organization, on the pretext of even the slightest mistake I make or by using Osman against me to this end. For example, one person wrote in a newspaper: "The left will not be able to advance if it doesn't liberate itself from Kemalism and Öcalanism." Those who have written such things are also those who live their lives in the most egotistical way. They are hoodlums and heedless. If they had the strength to live like I do for even a single day, I would willingly and immediately hand my entire legacy over to these crooks. They are so myopic and heedless that they do not even see that without us they would be deprived of their right to life.

It is well known that Osman Öcalan, with all his flaws, has created major difficulties for both the movement and myself for a long time now. Since the 1980s, he has been unable to keep up with the developments. He has stagnated at an emotional level and has never really deepened his theoretical knowledge. What he tried to achieve by the rule of thumb was anything but successful. He was superficial and easily duped. What he experienced in the traitorous war of the South Kurdish forces in 1992 was the result of his helplessness.[12] If countermeasures had not been taken, he would have become Talabani's plaything. In objective terms, what he did saved Cemil Bayık and Murat Karayılan's groups from destruction. My thinking was that rather than lose everything, it would better to salvage those values that could be saved.

The result of Osman's trial is well known.[13] At the time, I tried to address the problem of familism in a thoroughgoing manner. He regained his composure and began to make some progress. He had an understanding of politics in the narrower sense, but since he possessed no theoretical depth, there was always a likelihood that he would provoke dangerous situations—as could be expected, given his personality. He could have played a very beneficial role if the central committee had dealt with him intelligently. This would have required a very political and cautious approach. I would imagine that the relationship with the US that he entered into recently is quite similar to his previous relationship with Talabani. This was an area in which one is prone to making errors. He could have been useful in these relationships if he had been under tighter control. Of course, he should never have been given full authority in any of this. That, in any case, is how I would have handled the matter. I don't think he entered into a relationship with the US entirely on his own.[14] I think it is inevitable that he had direct and indirect associates.

The second thing we know is that he wanted "to lead a contemporary life, marry, engage in politics, give the greatest weight to the South," etc. I know these inclinations well. While he may not have had bad intentions, just as in 1992, he failed by a long shot to achieve anything, as the behavior of Turkey and the US indicates. In 1992, I had no faith in a diplomatic process. When Özal showed tendencies in this direction in 1993, I said, "childish mistakes." We know what became of him.[15] A decade later, I was asking myself how a dialogue that failed to produce any progress on

İmralı Island would proceed in Iraq. That said, I am not opposed to using any opportunity that offers itself. Politics requires that we always try to establish diplomatic and political relationships with Iran, Syria, the US, the PUK (Yekîtiya Nîştimanî ya Kurdistanê: Patriotic Union of Kurdistan), and the PDK (Partiya Demokrat a Kurdistanê: Kurdistan Democratic Party) whenever possible, as long as these relations don't result in capitulation or seeking shelter under their roof. The fundamental precondition, however, is reliable and viable bases in the country itself.[16]

If I am to express my opinions in this way, it is also necessary for me to elaborate on the topics of "contemporary life and marriage." If this were just a social or biological question, I would not expand upon it very much. It has, however, serious political consequences, as well as implications for our actions. Therefore, it is also a question that I am personally interested in.

I perceived an approach that frames my position regarding the questions of social life and women as inadequate and faulty. That is an extremely ignorant position that risks overlooking a far-reaching struggle that is currently unfolding, as well as being egocentric in a lowbrow way. In order to respond to perceptions that might arise, as I embarked on writing this court defense, I reminded everyone that I have struggled for sociality in my environment since the age of seven—only a lack of knowledge or and unjustified rejection could be behind the inability to evaluate this properly. To speak of a "contemporary social life" is, in fact, a war against me, because I demonstrated the courage to struggle against the sociality of my mother since the age of seven. This is a war that isn't simply social in nature; it is also political. To demonstrate what I mean, I discussed the example of Kesire in detail. Not understanding my approach to women's freedom struggle is a loss not only for the PKK but for our times. I see myself as a person that wages the greatest struggle for women's freedom in our time. In this regard, I am very confident. I don't think that anyone has analyzed the social, political, and military relations surrounding women as profoundly as I have. This is true for sociologists but also for lovers, soldiers, and politicians. I must admit that I have hindered the first love and affection of my very brave young men and women comrades, but as a result I have brought about incredible practical achievements and theoretical breakthroughs. I will elaborate on the formula for this.

Let me add a few things to what I have already addressed in detail in other chapters. My struggle with my mother was the traditional struggle about "honor" that is specific to the Middle East. I have shown how to separate this concept of "honor" from its vulgar and simple sexual context and how to give it a new meaning in the context of society, politics, and war. The result of this is that women were the first class, first sex, and first nation ever oppressed and exploited. It is perfectly clear that no democratic socialist struggle can achieve its goal if it is not predicated on the freedom of women as a sex, a class, and a nation. Marriage, sexuality, and romantic relationships in Kurdish society will be without value if they are not based on the freedom and equality of women and do not theoretically and practically lead to a development. I will repeat as often as necessary that without this these relationships are no different from "prostitution in private and public homes." For me, the promise made to a woman and the friendship offered implies a deep philosophical, historical, and social understanding and entails a practical commitment to freedom, equality, and patriotism. What a pity that you do not realize that I have not only worked out a true theory of love but am waging a great battle for it!

I consider it an indispensable requirement of freedom, war, equality, and democracy to leave the environment open to love within our ranks. Democracy, freedom, equality, and patriotism cannot develop in an environment that is not open to love. No honorable cause of the people can be achieved in the absence of the great advancement of women. Freedom of women is our movement's foremost value. Furthermore, the women's movement is one of the most fundamental aspects of the social revolutions that are experiencing new developments everywhere in the world. Women's revolution is a revolution within the revolution. To understand women who are becoming free is to understand history, society, and life anew. One of our main tasks is to end women's position as objects of extreme commodification not only by religious-feudal reaction but by capitalism as well. Moreover, one of our fundamental tasks is to free ourselves from dominant male morality and marriages laden with feudal and capitalist values.

I don't think it's necessary to elaborate any further. Women must play their role by making use of the PAJK. My use of mythology in my analyses above, with references to goddesses, angels, and Aphrodites, essentially expresses their rebellion against the five-thousand-year-old dominant male culture. This culture has placed women in a terrible position. One of the worst threats women face is the institution of marriage, which is a relationship that turns women into property. Without women's freedom, we will be unable to develop a truly meaningful and valuable free life worth living. Women must lead a far-reaching struggle. Without this struggle, patriotism and equality cannot be developed. Contrary to popular opinion, love absolutely requires a sociological theory and practice of its own and cannot simply be reduced to passion between two individuals.

Love calls for great bravery, victory, and affection. Those who can't achieve victory will also be unable to love. The face of love is always turned toward the victorious struggle for freedom. This is how I would define being the laborer of love that I strive to be.

Of course, I know that humans as individuals are divided into two sexes, but we are at war, and the conquerors have taken everything from us, and as a result there are no women left who we could call "our women." The existing women have been turned into commodities, little more than cheap household articles. Men having relationships with these women while fighting for freedom is essentially contradictory. For women striving for freedom, a relationship with this type of men represents even more of a contradiction. Ever since Plato it has been said that the important thing is to perpetuate oneself through ideas. The perpetuation of physical existence is based on sexual instinct. I know of this sexual instinct—it is the only way left for our people to perpetuate itself, and that has caused huge problems. What matters is the perpetuation of the lineage of ideas, but that requires major social and philosophical struggles. Consequently, those who do not succeed in developing revolutionary love can always turn to women with head scarfs—something that is also widely discussed in Turkey. Servile marriages with women who stay in their homes are permissible as long as the men do not betray their duties and these attitudes are not carried over to the political and military areas. I repeat: these marriages are like marriages within the system and must not be allowed to encroach on the political and military areas. If that were to happen it would throw the door wide open to the enslaving effects of the feudal and capitalist ways of life. This does not happen even in the system's armies.

What happens in our revolution is even more important, in fact, it is historic. The concept of becoming goddesses, angels, and Aphrodites, which I suggested to a group of female comrades, is part of the battle against the horrific culture of women's enslavement in the Middle East.

At this point in history, we need women of such lineage. Hundreds of them have already proven this with their heroic demeanor and their martyrdom. Our memory of them is very important to us. I believe there are still many brave women among us. Personalities of great courage, justice, and love are just beginning to emerge. Women are re-creating their own personalities by providing excellent examples of the connection between emotional and analytical intelligence. This is a very meaningful historical turning point. Even I did not and could not dare to be in possession of women with such an essence, let alone to housewifize them with a system-like attitude. We can never do enough to facilitate women becoming stronger. They already represent collective love. There are many highly qualified male and female comrades we can be proud of, but, even so, I don't think that privatized affection will be very helpful at this stage. Once peace is achieved, there will undoubtedly be free marriages, but the marriages of many comrades, myself included, have shown in practice how difficult it is to live free relationships under the current conditions, particularly in war zones.

I do not know the background of Osman's marriage to a woman from Iran.[17] Perhaps it is politically significant, or perhaps it is a marriage of simple passions, but presenting and promoting this sort of marriage within our troops as a requirement of contemporary life is extremely dangerous. The fact that he has even dared to do such a thing is in itself dangerous. In the past, the spread of such tendencies literally destroyed some groups on the Turkish left. Therefore, I repeat: anyone who wants to be married like a peasant, an urbanite, or a petit bourgeois, can do so with the permission of the organization provided that they remain duly committed to their tasks and do not turn it into a political issue. But this cannot be an arbitrary or individual decision. This is not the time for the mere physical continuation of one's lineage but is, above all, the time to carry our intellectual, political, and patriotic ideals to victory. As long as the minimal conditions for this have not been realized, being a husband or a wife, having children, and love will just lead to trouble. I have nothing but the highest respect for love, but I'm clearly saying "no" to self-deception that lacks the necessary philosophy and practice. I think that practical developments within the framework of these concepts will lead to greater freedom and pave the way for the true affection and love we all long for.

Theories based on "contemporary life" and becoming refugees in South Kurdistan are not meaningful. Life in extraordinary times is called a revolutionary life. Becoming refugees is dangerous in every respect. For children, the elderly, and some women, it makes sense to talk about a life as ordinary refugees, and the Makhmur encampment could be called a refugee camp. But being absorbed by the Kurds in Iraq will not serve either those who are engaged in private relationships or the general movement. Had we accepted life as refugees in Syria, what happened to us in the end would not have happened. I don't know whether or not these issues have been discussed, but the movement's views and practice in similar cases are well known. For Osman Öcalan and the group around him, the only honorable path is to respect the discipline of the Kongra Gel. If, however, they are preparing to sell out and desert the noble values of the movement, we know full well how that will end. It is vital that they take all the steps necessary to be successful.[18] Neither suicidal outbursts nor fleeing and taking shelter with any particular power are acceptable conduct. If I had more detailed information, I could say something more precise about these matters.

I don't know to which extent Cemil Bayık, Duran Kalkan, and Rıza Altun have formed a group. It seems Rıza's activities in Europe weren't terribly productive. I don't know whether he has intervened in the DEHAP, but it doesn't look as if he has contributed much to democratization. I don't take the claims about a coup seriously,[19] but the objective situation creates the impression that they have been acting as a group for some time now. In the end, having two such groups in the leadership must have been very unproductive and worn everyone out. Where would it have led had they simply been left to themselves? At this critical point, it would have probably been the most correct and expected attitude if a collective intensity had formed in the committees of the congress and in the executive leadership to take care of the most important tasks. Time was squandered as a result of backward positions, and that had a negative effect on our people and on us. They did not behave in a way worthy of the promises they made during critique and self-critique. Most probably there will be a correct evaluation of events that took place in the congress, and an example of their steadiness will be shown by giving their critique and self-critique.[20]

I want to emphasize the need for sincere and consistent self-critique. This is how a true PKK member evolves. My attitude on this topic is well known. The best thing to do would be to reconstruct the PKK. Overcoming the behavior that brought the PKK to a standstill and those impeding its renewal will be tantamount to a rebirth. With historical phases comes historical tasks. Those who see them through earn a well-deserved place of honor in the memory of the people and of humanity.

It is important to correctly understand the most recent period of my life well. Generally, the misinterpretation of my life by my friends causes them to make major errors and to squander opportunities. Such superficial behavior should be abandoned at all costs, because it does not contribute in any way to one's own person. Let's think of Kemal Pir's approach once again. Keeping the memory of Kemal Pir alive is particularly a task for those who have been released from prison. Of course, he is also a symbol for all his friends. There are thousands of others with similar noble values. For those who are even one-tenth worthy of them, there is no task that will prove too difficult. Nothing in the world other than meaningful achievements can absolve those friends who are in conditions of freedom. It is time to think big, to act nobly, and to achieve meaningful results.

As you know, I have spent just as much time preparing for peace as I spent preparing for the phase that began on August 15, 1984. Peace requires at least as much endurance and theoretical knowledge as war. It is definitely not a task that should be taken lightly. In reality, there are more difficulties associated with peace than with war. I was very careful to take a balanced approach to the various states, as well as to our movement. I hope that necessary lessons are learned from what is taking place in Syria right now.[21] What has become of our relationships, which we built despite all odds and with the proverbial care of a goldsmith! The same can be said about the activities in Europe, and even about the democratic peace efforts in Turkey. That people behave as if defeat were their fate is, in fact, the result of the actions of the formerly discussed diseased personalities. When we began, we were at point zero, but we passed the flag to you after we had run half the race and victory was in sight. Your response to this is effectively: "we stumbled and fell." It is not a dismal life that is the problem. The remorse of people who don't understand anything doesn't mean very much. What is important are the noble successes of a dismal life. If that does not happen, even if you have grown old, what good is it? What shall befit you is to find a way to gain some reward for your labor, that you take what you feel entitled to from your competitors, your friends, and even your comrades. The most befitting and expected attitude from all of you is for you to shake off my enchanting aura and attain a successful breakthrough in the areas of freedom. Let me very clearly say that it was a comradely gesture on your part to stand behind my past peace efforts with Turkey under the most favorable conditions. However, the conditions I find myself in now and the fact that the state hasn't taken the historical steps that it should have represent a great loss. Since 9/11, the state has fallen silent. I think the developments in South Kurdistan came as a shock; it is still unclear what the outcome will be. The state simply can't seem to get past its policy of cooperating with the US when addressing anything. The loyalty to the US is just incredible. Since 1950, everything the state has done has been with US sponsorship. The US gave the green light, and the blackest forms of fascism were implemented. Nowadays, a system is being created in which black is replaced by green, but the character of that "green" is not yet clear. It is inevitable that Turkey will move toward a new balance of power. Without a solution to the Kurdish question, Turkey will find it even more difficult than was the case after the World War I to turn the balance of power to its advantage. It is very likely that if it continues to devote all of its energy to a discourse centered on the concept of "PKK terrorists," this policy will backfire just as its South Kurdistan policy did. As you know, we have persistently insisted that for Turkey to come out of the chaos of the Middle East stronger requires a democratic resolution of the Kurdish question. But this was perceived as a sign of weakness or was considered a tactical ploy. The state placed its bets on the US support and on splitting our movement. For some reason, these forces can't free themselves from the idea that the military path is sacred. I do not yet know how, together with the US, they plan to clamp down on you, but we do know how they clamped down on me, and I hope that you continue to draw the necessary conclusions from this. I'm not saying that there shouldn't be any relationship with the US, but it has become clear that the kind of relationship that is accredited to Osman is not meaningful.

After the congress, in keeping with the necessary decisions that you will have taken, you will probably engage with Turkey with one voice, reminding it of its responsibilities. Turkey prefers this approach.

At this point, I'd like to once again say a few words about my situation. Unfortunately, I must say in advance that if things continue as they are, we will be faced with wars that absolutely outdo the one that followed August 15, 1984. My sentience will not be sufficient to prevent this from happening. The powers that be do not want me to play a role. Perhaps there is even a plan for a war that will totally destroy you. That is to say, the state might simply insist on war. The atmosphere spread by the AKP government is no better than that promoted by Tansu Çiller's government. It is extremely negative and callous. The prime minister said, "If you don't describe yourselves as Kurds, there is no Kurdish question." The provocations in Siirt are intolerable. This government is doing everything the MHP could not do. We must really ask ourselves what plans it may have made with a handful of primitive Kurdish nationalist traitors.

If a coherent, democratic, and peaceful step is not openly taken, you will be faced with a comprehensive war calculated to liquidate you. I have warned the prime minister with letters and messages, but these have not been taken at all seriously. I have mustered all my strength, and in the court defense before you have presented the line we must adopt to achieve a peaceful and democratic unity advantageous to all. I am perfectly well aware that I am presenting it not just to you but to the state authorities as well. This is not because I am tired and battle-weary, but because the situation does not make sense; it appears that you and the state will have to settle accounts once again. Neither side should count on me continuing to take responsibility for all of this, because that wears me down in the extreme.

If I wasn't strong-willed, I could engage in all kinds of provocation. I have been patient and hoped for developments to resolve things, not because I was afraid but because of the incomprehension I was faced with. At this point, it doesn't make any sense to carry on under the threat of death, although I don't think it would be meaningful to sacrifice myself before exploring all potential avenues. The important thing is to understand what the task is. I do not shrink from death for even a second. Death is only bitter if it isn't timely. Timely deaths are invaluable. I don't mean to suggest that I'm ready to sacrifice myself. Many scoundrels did not believe I would be able to persevere for so many years. Given their political interests, some political camps have long been waiting for my end. Perhaps the state also wanted to test how I would hold up under the circumstances. The former secretary of the National Security Council, Tuncer Kılınç, said something like, "We implement a system against him that cannot be remedied. We didn't kill him once; we kill him every day." But I have endured. And, if necessary, I will endure another six years. But that is not terribly relevant. I was able to endure it pretty well—not just in terms of the length of time but also in terms of meaning and content. I am extraordinarily aware of how to act responsibly. If anything more befalls me, I will do so again. More than that is simply impossible.

I want to tell you about a deep-seated conviction of mine regarding all of you. The overall goal of my cadre policy was to prioritize that you have long lives. I truly believed that the conditions you would find yourselves in would teach you many things, a belief that you know very well turned out not to be very realistic. There was too much irresponsible behavior. You neither achieved my objectives nor your own. And my role in this has always been decisive. Most of you are pretty old by now. In my opinion, you haven't developed your talents to their actual potential. You should ask yourselves why that is. Here too my excessive support and the fact that I handed you so many things on a silver platter played a huge role. But what was really dangerous was the fact that you completely lost all direction, relinquished many values, and deserted the people at your side, particularly the young people and the comrades, to annihilation, degeneration, and ineffectiveness. It has always angered me that you did not adequately embrace the efforts that were undertaken to achieve a dignified life. I demanded that you and our people would behave in a truly disciplined way on the road to a contemporary and free life, instead of making yourselves comfortable in the existing situation, living shabby lives and losing easily. That kind of discipline was necessary, but your reactions, which I find difficult to explain, have been very conservative and have pulled us backward.

In reality, I didn't actually expect total ideological and political agreement, but I did expect and longed for you to engage in a practice that would at least save your own dignity. You know perfectly well how you reacted, particularly the top leadership. The young people also failed to survive and achieve the successes they had promised they would. You know that this undercut the effectiveness of my work. I should have immediately moved to the mountains when I began to sense this. Had I known how you would develop, I would have been the first to move to the mountainous areas of our land in the early 1980s. Most of the facts had come to the light by the early 1990s, and I should have come to the mountains at that point. Today I see it as a major error that I didn't. I didn't because I wanted protect you, whom I regarded as my friends, and nurture your talents in a sustained way. Even if I wanted to, at this point, I can no longer help you in the way I previously did, keeping you alive and providing you with direction. That would make no sense. If you really understood dignity in the way Kemal Pir did, your long experience and your deep understanding of things would leave you free to settle the historical accounts with the elements and structures that insist on incomprehension, injustice, and a situation offering no solution. This is your right and duty. We must absolve all that we owe to one another. But, even so, the most important thing in war and peace is the attainment of the right to a free life. We must never pursue a senseless practice of "kill or be killed," although it can make sense to die or to kill in pursuit of great historical achievements. As Kemal Pir noted, even that kind of death and killing takes place only because you love a dignified life and to earn it.[22]

Some of you may be brave warriors. I tried to slow those of you who are. Some of you could have easily died, but I held you back. I opposed any undertaking that didn't have a chance of succeeding. You, on the other hand, prevented many things I wanted. In short, neither of us has been as successful as we deserved to be. Most of you have grey hair now. You have gathered a lot of experience. If you seriously turn all of this into a question of honor, you still have a great chance of success. At the very least, you could avoid becoming refugees. However, after tens of thousands have already become martyrs, it seems unlikely that you will leave, preferring a degenerate life. Even if I were to demand it, you would curse all forms of degeneration and insist on a free life—even if only partially—on your own land. Nobody, including me, can enforce such decisions from the outside. They depend on your free will and your determination. Because I presumed this to be the case, I have used this court defense to develop the unequivocal formula "one state + one democracy" to be developed in each part of Kurdistan. On August 15, 1984, we said that none of the states should remain standing. That was unrealistic and did not correspond to our true nature. Even if the conquering states had actually disappeared, they would simply have been replaced by a Kurdish state that would have exercised its own domination, and the formula "one state + one democracy" would still have been necessary. Just as a state has no religion, I also believe that it doesn't have a nationality. It is always a coalition of minority interests.

An Arab, Iranian, or Turkish state is only a matter of appearance or a conjunctural approach. Its essence is quite different, and it has the character I have addressed in detail in this court defense. Regardless of nationality, as long as they exist through the organization they call the state, we will exist by virtue of our democracy. In particular local democracies need to be our most fundamental areas of existence. When necessary, we will defend those areas from our mountains. Wherever our people are, our democratic units will also be. If accepted, they will be legal, if not, semi-legal or illegal. At this point, the question arises: Is this even possible? It must be possible, because there is no other option. Put another way, other than death or the realization of our democracy there are no other options.

If states really want reconciliation, they will do what is necessary. If not, a struggle to the very end is also a way to improve life. We must approach our work with conviction and the knowledge that building democracy is foundational work. I have written about the theory and practice of all this in considerable detail. It is possible for us to strengthen ourselves both quantitatively and qualitatively, at least in those areas in the country where you can establish a base, protect yourselves, and successfully sustain your defense. The people also no longer have any other option. The absolute authority understanding of the states necessitates the democratic authority of the people. The powers that be do not even want to understand the era we are living in. All they understand is the blind application of the formula: "the ruling state and the ruling nation are everything, and the Kurds are nothing." As I just pointed out, it is inevitable this formula will be proven wrong and replaced with the correct formula. You can certainly under-stand that this offensive will bring with it a whole series of innovations, and that you are in a position to develop your tactics and strategies accordingly.

This constitutes a summary of my thoughts about the new phase. I do not know what position you and the states concerned will adopt. What matters is that I have comprehensively responded to all of the expecta-tions people might have in me. I have no doubt that I have done so in a very mature way. With any other approach than the one outlined here, all of the states will find themselves in the same situation as Iraq under Saddam Hussein in the long run. We really have to understand the role of the Kurds organized by Saddam. It must be understood that there are also other possible options. Turkey, Syria, and Iran believe they are in a very strong position in their dealings with the Kurds. This may be so. However, it doesn't remove the danger; it actually provokes it. Saddam's stubbornness was not helpful, and the stubbornness of these three states is even greater than his. They refuse to learn anything from the chaos in the Middle East. They venerate positions and power in the extreme. They put an enormous amount of trust in the weakness of the Kurds. This makes me really angry, because it is not in the genuine interest of any people or any country. Moreover, it is simply stupid of them to indulge in the oppression of the Kurds. To regard you as a rogue mob or as terrorists is a catastrophic error. A wounded snake is bound to bite. I really do not understand what they think they are doing.

Some of you will not capitulate but will flourish at war. After all, you won't act like dunces forever. If you manage to use your extensive expe-rience and perseverance, you only need three hundred guerrillas to deal with any state. This needs to be well thought through and must be explained to the states concerned. Before waging a comprehensive war, you should establish everything from the criteria for a bilateral ceasefire to the rules of war. You should work out statutes for local government and establish their link to yourselves, prepare guidelines for mutual retaliation and grounds for arrests, and these war and peace rules should be presented to both sides and announced to the people. This was something that was missing on August 15, 1984. I would very much have liked to resolve the problems through a process of democratic action, but at the moment democracy and its operating principles count for nothing. So the burden of doing all of this again falls on the mountains.

I am tempted to once more say that history and the gods prefer this course, but this would smack too much of the old belief in fate. I also do not know whether you will kill or be immediately killed. History has arrived at a juncture where a decision must be made between a democratic and peaceful step or a comprehensive democratic and combative step. You can also warn the US and Iran about the situation. They are major states, and perhaps they will suggest a way forward. But if they insist on war, you must demonstrate your decisive moves one after another and believe that you are strong enough to bear the consequences.

As a result, in the coming period there are three options with a variety of complex forms that will fight for dominance in the chaos of the Middle East.

First is the conqueror's state tradition related to the policies regarding Kurdistan, which aim at maintaining the status quo. The existing system will resist the aspects of this new phase that bring about change, regardless of whether they are the result of internal or external dynamics. They will try to deny the existence of the Kurds, and if this doesn't work to fob them off with miniscule concessions. But most of all, they will also make ample use of the stick to beat the Kurds over the head. The Arab, Iranian, and Turkish representatives of the status quo will probably try to strengthen their alliance.

For their part, the US, the EU, and Israel will support primitive Kurdish nationalism in all parts of Kurdistan and insist on a federal status. Cyprus is the trial run for this approach, and Palestine and Kurdistan will have their turn. They will gradually try to establish this model all over the Middle East. The regional states representing the status quo will resist this and may well make use of their traditional influence and arm the collaborationist Kurdish militia to an even greater degree. There is a possibility that the Turkish Republic will further extend the policy that it has already used with Barzani and Talabani.[23] Within the AKP, primitive Kurdish nationalism in North Kurdistan has been ceded a role behind a Naqshbandi mask.

This is how we must understand people like Cüneyd Zapsu, Abdülmelik Fırat, Hüseyin Çelik, Zeki Ergezen, Mücahit Can, Mustafa Zeydan, Zülfikar İzol from Siverek, and others. They will turn out to be covert, semifeudal, and semicomprador primitive Kurdish nationalists. The local elections made this clear. Those who shouted the slogan "İdris Bitlisi is here, where is Yavuz?" summarized this quite succinctly.[24] New Islamic Kurdish figures for the Middle East in general are probably already being prepared abroad, particularly in the US. What Fethullah Gülen is for the Turks, Cüneyd Zapsu and Abdülmelik Fırat are for the Kurds. They represent the Kurdish-Islamic synthesis. They are striving to become a pro-Western form of the Middle East's Hezbollah. They are the Kurdish version of the "Idealists."[25]

Turkey has come under the influence of two currents of the Naqshbandi order. When Prime Minister Erdoğan said, "If you don't describe yourselves as Kurds, there is no Kurdish question," it called to mind their deceptive policies, which he also uses in other areas, including in the way he deals with the hijab.

It is still not clear whether or not the AKP are conservative democrats. The reality that emerged during the local elections makes it seem likely that it is a controlled, right-wing "state party." The discussion around the hijab and secularism could well be a staged theater piece meant to divert attention from the real agenda. The void left by the bankrupt and despised DSP, ANAP, and MHP coalition, the completely statist CHP, which tries to pose as a "guardian of the republic," and the DYP, as the party of the counter-guerrilla and the mafia gangs, had to be filled quickly. It appears that in a joint initiative of the monopolistic and medium-size corporations and a section of the state, the AKP was pushed onto the stage. It may be more correct to interpret their conservative "democratism" mixed with moderate Islam as ideological camouflage or as a superficial veneer. It is even further to the right than the ANAP and calls to mind a corporate syndicate. It appears to be a coalition with a Turkish-Islamic synthesis that was cobbled together specifically to gain the support of the US and the EU. If social developments accelerate, it could fall apart even quicker than the ANAP did. But if there is no consistent democratic opposition, it could become an enduring phenomenon, possibly in the form of a center-right party. The collaborationist Kurds, with their weak primitive nationalism and Naqshbandi-Sunni understanding of religion, might also gather under the roof of the AKP. Talabani and Barzani's support for the AKP is certainly no accident.[26]

The broad Naqshbandi and general Sunni alliance with primitive nationalism, which includes Barzani and Talabani, being developed inside the Turkish Republic is based on hostility toward the PKK and needs to be well-understood. This US-engineered policy approach, which began in the 1990s with Özal, has—for now—led to substantial unease within the Turkish Republic. Whether the Kurdish feudal-bourgeois bloc will side with the US, the EU, and Israel or with Turkey is currently among the most controversial and conflicting of issues and could lead to new cleavages and compromises at any point. The line on democratic resistance and patriotism under PKK leadership in the new phase must continue to resist the insistence on the status quo since the early 1990s, because the status quo alliance is based on an anti-PKK stance.

Second, in response to possible developments, new policies and positions may come into play. Primitive Kurdish nationalism may hope to emerge from the deepening chaos in the Middle East by strengthening a greater partiality for a separate state. Adding the Kurds in Iran, Turkey, and Syria to the Kurdish federal state in Iraq might also become part of the agenda, in which case it will extend its alliance with the US, the EU, and Israel and try to get the PKK on board. This plan can be detected at the core of the factionalization that emerged when the Kongra Gel was being established. The same thing was attempted in 1991. If the PKK does not become a well-rounded organizational force, the participation of individuals in something like this will lead to absorption and inevitably to liquidation and there will be a surge in Kurdish nationalism. It is possible that there will be several developments that resemble those in Israel-Palestine, Iraq, Cyprus, Chechnya, and Kosovo. In return, Turkey, Iran, and Syria would try to counter this with a joint policy. The PKK, however, must preserve its line in favor of a "free and democratic Kurdistan" as the basis of its reconstruction. At the same time as the PKK strives to enhance the democratic authority of the people, it will diligently preserve the firm and farsighted theoretical, programmatic, strategic, and tactical principles underlying this line. It will insist on the formula "one state + one democracy" and implement it creatively.

The third possible option would be a democratic solution and peace. The newly reconstructed PKK and the Koma Gel are the most important forces in this process. As the policies of the state tradition based on conquest and the US-backed Kurdish policies based on primitive nationalism deepen the deadlock, the option of a democratic solution and peace may develop. For this to occur, it is important that democratic left policies emerge and develop as the source of hope, replacing the right-wing nationalist and religious policies, especially in Turkey. The status quo that insists on a deadlock needs to decline among the Turks in Turkey, as has been the case with Cypriot Turks. In fact, the AKP came to power by using the "left option," even though it is not yet a permanent factor on the Turkish agenda. The crisis of the Turkish left and its inability to come up with solutions are the decisive factors for the AKP's success. Furthermore, the AKP was able to surge in Kurdistan because of DEHAP's inability to implement the democratic line. Once again, it has become clear that there can be no vacuum in politics. Rigorous work for the democratization in Turkey and all parts of Kurdistan and the establishment of democratic authority could transform this line from fantasy to reality. The fact is that this is the tendency of our time, but both in Turkey and in Kurdistan the cadres, the leadership, the creative work necessary to understand and internalize this line as a concept, and the actual attempt to achieve it is, as yet, lacking. However, successfully pursuing this goal could, in the end, lead to historical leadership throughout the Middle East. I have always said that this line is the most likely political option for the Middle East, because the area's historical and social foundations suit a democratic federation quite well. In fact, the culture, geography, and demographics necessitate this option.

In practice, this will probably mean that all three of these options will be on the agenda in a variety of mixed forms. There is no black-and-white distinction to be made between these options. There will be an admixture, with sometimes one and sometimes another aspect coming to the fore. They will realize themselves in a dynamic and mutable framework. Because the status quo and primitive nationalist forces are unlikely to achieve a solution in the long run, the option of a democratic solution and peace in Kurdistan will be the most discussed option on the agenda in the future. This option must develop and be successful under the leadership of the reconstructed PKK and the Koma Gel as the hope of all people of the Middle East. Everything depends on the degree to which this line is internalized and creatively realized.

Some of the later practical developments make it clear that there were some serious inconsistencies within the Demokratik Güçler Birliği (DGB: Union of Democratic Forces),[27] which had been expected to provide a model for the democratic option. The position adopted by the SHP and probably the ÖDP, along with some members of the DEHAP, was aimed at the liquidation of the DEHAP.[28] In particular their discomfort with Abdullah Öcalan, who is embraced by the people, as is reflected in numerous slogans and the efforts to isolate him, made this evident. Objectively, it is clear that a position similar to that of the CHP and Deniz Baykal was adopted. The reaction of the people could be read in the election results. Whether the DGB has a chance depends on whether it can credibly prove that it has overcome the extremely statist influence of the CHP and convincingly evince that it is a society-focused option not just in theory but also in practice. But if it directly or indirectly continues the "anti-Apoism," it will simply dissipate. The "unionist forces" must understand that the Kurdish people's democratic reality is not state-oriented, that they are highly organized and conscious and, thus, will not relinquish their party and its fundamental policies.

AFTERWORD

My personal and political life can be divided into three phases. The first phase began with the conflict with my mother on the basis of my claim that I should be able to establish my own sociality and continued with my first adverse reactions against my family and my village, followed by my enrollment in primary school. Primary school was where my interest in the state first began to seriously develop: the personality of anyone who attends school takes a transformative step away from communal society in the direction of statist society.

This was accompanied by a process of urbanization, in which the values of the city are regarded as superior to rural communal values. Intermediate school, high school, my time as a civil servant, and studies in my final year at the university were all preparatory steps for statesmanship. It is around the age I was at the time that the personality of the city and the state clearly becomes dominant for people. On the other hand, belonging to an oppressed nation and being intentionally underdeveloped turns into a reaction against the state. At the end of the day, even sympathizing with the left amounts to nothing more than the search for a state that is more just, equitable, and pro-development. During this phase, people's personalities are largely detached from traditional society, with the mother-based, communal, rural, and lineage-based society largely being denied. Instead, a rather marginal personality emerges; one that denies and despises its own past but venerates the grandness of the city and the state and unflinchingly conforms to the official order. It is indeed a very tragic massacre of the personality that takes place during this phase.

In all underdeveloped countries, this new "parvenu" personality that despises the old society, mothers and fathers, siblings, neighbors, relatives, the village, the elderly, the children, the women, as well as its own origin and class has turned into a disaster. In the grips of a modernism devoid of content, this personality experiences a deep alienation from the fundamental social values of humans. Developed under the overwhelming superiority of the capitalist system, this personality remains marginal, even if it superficially rejects the conditions and turns to "the left." This only further deepens its detachment from society. School, working in the city, and being a civil servant within the state have detached this personality from history and tradition and turned it into a "tin" personality. Everything that comes with this sort of personality, a personality that has become an insensitive, salaried denier that submits to the whoredom of the city, will inevitably go bankrupt in the face of capitalism and the values of the society that is an obstacle for this personality. There is a close connection between this sort of personality and the inability of real socialism, social democracy, and national liberation to effect a genuine social transformation. All sorts of anomalous, fascist, and totalitarian ideologies and practices of our age are socially based in the formation of this personality. However, after making a great leap forward with the French Revolution, in the 1990s, this type of individual lost its old charm, resulting in a new normalization process.

The second phase began with my attempt to form an independent ideological group with the aim of breaking away from bourgeois society and the bourgeois state and establishing our own contemporary social and political system. Whereas the first stage of my socialization began in praying together with the other children and our shared walk to primary school, my second socialization developed with university students on the basis of left and national liberation ideology. Although we made an effort to once again seek out our own society in opposition to the values propagated by capitalism and the chauvinism of the ruling nation, these attempts fell far short of their goal, because the existing left and national liberationist currents lacked the power to overcome the norms of capitalist life. During this phase, which could also be qualified as the beginning of becoming the PKK, I was blown here and there like a leaf in the stormy world of the 1970s. I broke with the traditional world but also refused to make peace with capitalist values. It was a typical process of sectarianism and marginalization. There were innumerable groups founded in a similar way that disappeared just as quickly. A struggle against the state began that resembled the battle of an ant against an elephant. While to some degree we hoped to rediscover our own society and country through our theoretical and practical quests, in general, we were simply following the left-wing trend that was sweeping the world at that time.

We eventually had an idea of our own, with which we tried to seed something new in the old society that we hoped would blossom in time. The group developed and grew larger. We started to see ourselves as something special. It seemed very likely that the seed would actually grow. When I left the country like a caterpillar slipping out of its cocoon, a phase of self-confidence and youthful bravado had begun. Hope that our utopia would become reality was in the air. When the support of the people for our group developed into a mass movement, our self-confidence grew further. We had also gotten to know the power of arms. The guerrilla group of the contemporary national liberation movement had been trained and armed, and they had reached the difficult and elusive peaks of our mountainous land. The time for a new historical departure had arrived.

The initial stage of this phase, which lasted from 1972 to 1984, can be evaluated in a number of ways. You might call it the awakening of the destitute Kurdish people, who were now catching up to the era they lived in. You could describe it as a first uprising, the first shot fired against blind fate. You could interpret it as an outcry for honor and dignity. Alternately, it might also make sense if it were compared to David's first successful act against Goliath. Or it could be considered as one of the initial steps toward mustering the courage necessary for freedom of thought. It could also be seen as a rupture with norms of slavery, with its millennia-old roots. Altogether, this phase can be defined as something like a second birth, which was meaningful and necessary, and as a bit of luck and a lot labor and faith. It was, in fact, a phase where we developed our own paradigm once again.

The subsequent part of this second phase of my life covers the years from August 15, 1984, to February 15, 1999. Those fifteen years marked the second stage in the development of the PKK, an amazing period in which the armed struggle was prevalent. In the context of the history of the Middle East, comparisons could be drawn with the Babak Khorramdin's group, the Kharijites, the Qarmatians, or Hassan-i Sabbāh's fedayeen. While the first part of this second period was dominated by a situation that can be likened to Jesus-like sermons, the second part, with its exodus and armed return, more resembles a mixture of movements forming around

Moses and Mohammad. Leading a group of exiles barely able to get its act together "into the Promised Land" requires a great deal of effort and ability. While our wandering evokes associations with Moses, our acts of war were reminiscent of Mohammad in Medina. There was a strong prevailing atmosphere of spiritual belief and conviction. Like true believers, we devoted ourselves completely to our convictions. We practiced scientific socialism like believers powered by the strength of faith and regarded our war as a sacred activity. The human being, the individual, slowly became nothing, and from that point on, the goal was everything. It was very difficult for me to even understand that I had fallen prey to the historically typical malady of power. The weak personality from a rural area that has been bombarded by the state and the city for years barely knows how to do anything but to cling to power and isn't able to grow beyond its own one-dimensionality. When able to create a system of its own, as a countertendency, the personality that has been horribly isolated by capitalism can experience a magnificent sociality. The most typical expression is a willingness to sacrifice everything to the belief that action is the most sacred thing of all.

Our task should have been to say that *life itself* is the most sacred value of all. Instead, a fanatic personality came to the fore, which, on the contrary, believed that the goal was everything and life itself was nothing. We can define the fatalism in this type of dogmatism as a commitment to a set of principles or a kind of religionization. The paradigm we acquired was, in any case, both pure and abstract.

Analytical intelligence shone. Emotional intelligence was suppressed. Dying and killing were reduced to a purely technical matter. In the final analysis, in reality, we acted as ideological satellites of capitalism under the influence of its profit-oriented work ethic. We complied with the general character of the time, even though, in the final analysis, it took the form of a divergent denomination, we also lived and swam in a sea of capitalism. We absorbed the knowledge of a capitalist tendency on the most abstract level by adopting real-socialist and national liberation generalizations, while frantically striving to form the related political and military entities. To us, this seemed to be the only way to catch up with the times.

Of course, that chase did not take place in a vacuum. The system has its masters, and they have their own rules and act in accordance with the needs of their sovereign world. February 15, 1999, can be considered as the day on which the power of the capitalist world that has become like the angel of death Azrael grabbed me by the throat, using 1,001 machinations to do so. In this connection, I must mention some of the strategic mistakes I made in this period of my life. In 1982, I should have trained cadres who were actually capable of leading an armed group, and I should have sent them into the country only once I had completed that task. Perhaps it would have been more appropriate and led to a far-reaching development if we had sent Kemal Pir and others into the North via South and East Kurdistan with a larger group in 1982 and not in 1980. Having Duran Kalkan, Ali Haydar Kaytan, and Mehmet Karasungur as the most important cadres in charge of that area led to inadequacies and proved to be a strategic error. The root of this error was that they simply replicated the general process taking place in the Middle East, and even lagged behind doing that. Tailgating the KDP, being estranged from the people, not being worthy friends, doing superfluous work, repeating work that had already been completed, unnecessary involvement in the conflicts between the PUK and the KDP, failing to see the potential before them and the situation brought about by the Iran-Iraq war—all of this represented a continuation of that strategic error. The failure to live up to the historical moment and to work accordingly, along with arbitrary and meaningless analyses, resulted in a strategic blow to our efforts. In this situation, good intentions and much effort paved the road to hell.

My second major strategic error was failing to recognize the emerging tendency to form gangs early enough and to take adequate measures. A further consequence of dogmatism was that I left this task to reliable friends. I should have noticed that they were squandering so much noble value and stopped them. These developments were heavy blows against all of the PKK's noble efforts. It is difficult for me to explain the incredible way in which some people with almost monstrous personalities became so capable. Even more incomprehensible was that our structures that had been trained so carefully capitulated to these persons so easily. Because of my concept of "friendship," I kept telling myself that they would do their best, that they were the most honest, that they could accomplish anything, and that they were contemporary apostles. This belief actually bordered on dogmatism and was an important factor in all of these developments. When I finally woke up, much too late, and realized what was happening, young fighters, first and foremost, but also significant popular support and many other material and spiritual values that had been strategically developed over a long period with a great deal of effort were already lost.

I should have also drawn more far-reaching lessons from the events of 1992–1993. It would have been better had I been with the groups in the country in 1992 and during the Iraq-Kuwait crisis. What I hadn't done in 1982, I should have done then. I should have put the activities in the Middle East on the back burner. But taking my usual approach, I was convinced that the situation could be successfully dealt with by simply sending massive reinforcements.

I had always believed that there would be some among the thousands of highly qualified cadres who would emerge to live up to the requirements of the period. But the gang culture at the heart of the movement and the irresponsible approach of the central committee rendered all contributions in vain. Our struggle was blatantly failing right before our eyes. Discipline and a willingness to sacrifice alone were not sufficient to secure our values and allow us to successfully accomplish our tasks. In late 1992, by happenstance, Osman Öcalan's fortuitous agreement with the PUK, which resembled capitulation, and the suicidal undertakings of Murat Karayılan and Cemil Bayık coalesced to prevent even greater losses.[1] This was the point at which I should have really internalized the lessons in all of this. The time had come for a radical analysis of the key cadres, without, however, neglecting the day-to-day management of elements within the country. The attempt to correct this from Syria by establishing new schools and the repetitive character of the work I had to do completely sapped my energy.[2] This kind of effort had become largely meaningless. I had failed to personally intervene on time. I could not bring myself to move to the guerrilla zone after such major losses. To me, it made more sense to try to break through the stagnation by political rather than military means, because a military orientation might have proven to be total suicide, while political work could possibly lead to conduct with greater potential. Monotony in our ranks continued until the period of the Koma Gel. The current internal crisis has its roots in the continuation of the way that the cadres entered the country and established bases and the way they worked and developed an understanding of tactics. Self-critique had not been done in a meaningful way. People persisted with their old personalities and their established way of working. This could only lead to senseless losses, unaccomplished tasks, suffering, and ultimately the collapse of whole areas of work, always and everywhere.

The second phase of my life was contradictory, because it was state-oriented, but I still had not lost the qualities of the communal democratic approach. My struggle between the two poles of this contradiction would determine the outcome. Among other things, February 15, 1999, dealt a death blow to my state-oriented march. If state-oriented partisanship and statism were maladies, then the blow that all the states of the capitalist world dealt me on February 15, 1999, would at the same time play the role of a midwife and the necessary medicine for my third birth.

The third phase of my life, if what I am experiencing can be called "life" either in name or in essence, began on February 15, 1999, and might well last to the end of my life. The defining feature of this phase is the beginning of a break from state-oriented life in general and from modern capitalist life in particular. I am not, however, reverting to "wildlife." I won't be going back to the times of ten thousand years ago. Nonetheless, it is certain that some of the fundamental values of humanity are secreted away in those very years. The real liberation and freedom of human beings is not possible unless the humanity that marked that period, which was cut short via 1001 machinations and by tyranny, is integrated with the present level of science and technology.

The rupture with civilization and state-oriented life is not a regression. On the contrary, an end to the deadly rupture from nature and surrendering the overblown power-rooted personality based on blood and lies could offer us the opportunity to recover our health at the most fundamental level. This is about turning away from a diseased society toward a healthy society and about the departure from an absurdly urbanized society—which is in a way cancerous, completely alienated from nature, and a suffocating weight upon ecological society. It is also about turning away from a thoroughly authoritarian and totalitarian statist society toward a communal, democratic, free, and egalitarian society. Ending and eliminating the links in a chain that led from hunter culture and the slaughter of animals to civilization's massacre of human beings, bringing an end to capitalism, which leads to the destruction of nature could push the door open the tiniest bit for the development of a new humanity. A moral and political personality that cultivates friendship with animals and is at peace with nature is based on a balance of power with women, is peaceful, free, and equal, and provides a life full of love, putting an end to the power of science and technology being the plaything of rulers and wars, attracts me at least as much as the attraction that bound Enkidu to the city and the state and gives this desire its meaning. I assure you that I'm not simply expressing a longing that arises from being held in isolation in a one-person prison! I am talking about a significant intellectual and spiritual paradigm. I am really sick of and hate the categorical approach, the worshiping of far-reaching power, the glittering life of our age, and, indeed, everything about civilization that shines through the bloodstains.

As a child, I had totally internalized hunting culture. I cunningly hunted and decapitated birds and killed animals without batting an eye. I want to begin this new phase of my life by asking all those animals for forgiveness.

I believe that the greatest felicity is not found in splendid palaces but in simple huts surrounded by nature. I believe that the virtue of life can be achieved by perceiving nature in all its colors, voices, and meanings and by becoming one with it. I believe that real progress has nothing to do with huge cities and ruling authorities. These are, on the contrary, the greatest source of affliction. I actually believe that life in a place that overcomes both the old village and the new city and that combines ecological settlement with the latest insights of science and technology is the real revolution. I believe that the huge buildings of civilization are the mausoleums of humanity. If there is a path to the future, I believe that it will be meaningful and worth following only if based on these realities.

The break with the hierarchical, statist class civilization represents the strongest self-critique imaginable, and I believe I will be successful. The childhood of humanity, the forcefully forgotten history of the laborers and the people, the worlds of freedom and equality in the utopias of the women, the children, and the elderly who have managed to remain children—I want to participate in all this, and this is where I hope to attain success.

All of this is utopian. But sometimes utopias are the only life-saving inspiration of a life that is buried in buildings that are worse than mausoleums. Without a doubt we can only come out of these structures that are worse than tombs by having utopias. My situation does not resemble that of any other person, and I don't want it to. Now that I understand and feel all this better I am probably on the right track. A person filled with meaning and feeling is the strongest of all human beings. I will certainly never again commit the sin of trying to be like the "mighty ones." Anyway, I never really wanted or managed to be like them. The humanity's past is more real. I will be respectful of it, will look for and find life there, and will start it anew. The future will be nothing but the active form of these efforts.

Do I always only think of myself? By no means. My defense is a message to all of humanity. The newly reconstructed PKK can unite all my noble friends, comrades who have the power of meaning and will to understand. The people of Kurdistan and their friends can gather under the democratic roof of the Koma Gel. The HPG can provide able defensive war against any attacks on our life, our country, or our society, and it can call the transgressors, the tyrants, and the immoral to account. The women with the highest aspirations can unite under the PAJK, which brings together the mature wisdom of the goddesses, their understanding, the purity and saintliness of the angels, and the beauty of Aphrodite.

With this defense, I present my fundamental understanding and ideal of humanity to the European Court of Human Rights, the judicial organ of Europe—the ultimate representative of a civilization that is proud and generally self-confident. But let me just say that rather than having positive expectations, I regretfully expect the court to play no other role than that of a tool in the service of the system's mastery of profit.

I respectfully offer my hope for a more democratic, free, and just society.

April 27, 2004
one-person prison
İmralı Island,
Mudanya, Bursa

APPENDIX

Letter[1]

1

It seems my incarceration on İmralı has caused many of the friends in key roles to begin to ponder what should happen in the time "after me." Normally, one would have to regard this as a responsible way to proceed, but, unfortunately, these calculations stand on the wrong foundation. These friends, to all intents and purposes, have failed to build mutually supportive relations with the institution they call "leadership." The traits that had always characterized them again clearly came to the fore when I found myself in an extremely critical situation. They bided their time to see whether or not I would survive and whether or not I would squeal. One of the first things to happen, unbeknownst to me, was a power struggle concerning the guerrilla, support of our people, political organization, the media, the women's organization, and quite likely the distribution of financial and other resources as well. This was, in fact, a continuation of the tendencies we saw at each critical point, such as the runup to August 15, 1984, in 1992, and even in 1986 and 1987. The details of these important events in the history of our movement are well known. It is also clear that I noticed these tendencies and tried to overcome them by continuously providing comradely critiques. Another important point that has once again become clear is the fact that this comradely approach was never honestly appreciated.

Even though I don't regard it as particularly meaningful to name names regarding the most recent splits, I will name three names for each group to enable the different sides to know themselves a little better. This can be extended should that become necessary. The first group consists of Cemil Bayık, Duran Kalkan, and Rıza Altun, while the second group emerged on the instigation and through the alignment of Osman Öcalan, Nizamettin Taş (Botan), and Hıdır Yalçın (Serhat).[2] One can hardly describe this second group as an organized faction but should rather refer to it as an initiative. In addition, there are also those in between. Whether there are people who are loyal to me in form and content and, if so, who they are, I do not know. The actual loyalty of the twelve individuals nominated for the preparation group for the reconstruction of the PKK can only be demonstrated in practice. I don't have any personal objections to them, but the extent to which they are able to represent my line in form and content will only be seen in practice. Therefore, I do not want to impose any particular course of action on them.

To say that the mentality and the style of dispute of both factions sharply goes against our valuable traditions, against our theoretical perspectives, and also against me (may I remind you that I am still alive?) is probably the mildest way to put it. I never anticipated people compromising the well-being of our people and our struggle through such a greed for power and such squandering of our legacy or that they would demonstrate such a lack of respect for me. Once again, I have had an opportunity to gain a better understanding of the true nature of human beings. I now understand that none of my warnings was taken seriously, that not a single thought was given to questions of class, society, and ethnicity, and that all our values were nihilistically denied. I am also struggling to understand whether or not my friends have lost all self-control and whether or not they are involved in things that I have yet no knowledge of. That they have acted against each other so mercilessly also makes me think that external factors may have played a role. I want to add immediately that I am not judging these friends in any subjective or emotional manner. I find the situation into which they have put themselves even more poignant than the one I find myself in. I wonder how they got into this situation, even though there was no pressing need for it.

Nevertheless, I will never insult these friends. Though I am well aware that both sides are instrumentalizing me, I will not resort to expressing myself in this way. I just want to draw attention the following facts:

a

It doesn't matter to me whether people regard me as their comrade, their friend, or their enemy—but they should be open and honest about it. After all, we have personally met each other more than once, and they didn't seem to lack respect for me then. At this point, I'm asking myself: Why did they want to exclude me in this way, when in fact I made an enormous effort to preserve the honor of every single one of them? I'm not, of course, saying that I alone created all of our values.

These are values that, with great effort, I have tried to assemble and deepen after the people, the destitute masses, had shed tears, suffered hunger, felt fear, and experienced treason. They are *their* values and the values of their country—the values of my people and its country, from whom I have never been so audacious as to ask for a personal weapon, a house, or a life partner. They are the values for which I have sacrificed myself beyond measure to prove myself worthy of them, values for which I have toiled and struggled, and that I hoped to see grow, prosper, and succeed.

b

In this situation, I found the behavior of some people very astonishing and extremely ungrateful. They were essentially saying: "I have seven thousand guerrilla fighters behind me; whoever dares to even frown at me will get their eyes gouged out." It is common knowledge that the friends who said such things were the same ones who treated these many guerrillas in the worst way, in that they either rebuffed them or deployed them in battles using the wrong tactics. The fact is that some other friends were unbothered when before their very eyes thousands of young people, each of them as valuable as gold, died as martyrs. That these friends were capable of such an egotistical behavior is equally horrible and shows the same level of ingratitude. What can we even say when, in spite of these facts, they continue to discuss whether or not they should accept tasks? Perhaps by this point you understand what it was like for me before prison, and that I had no sense of taste and could not even taste bread. During the five years in the sea climate of İmralı, where I have been trying, against the odds in spite of my breathing problems, to sustain my biological existence with nothing but a miniscule air gap, I have never even for a moment prioritized myself. I haven't indulged in self-pity. Out of respect for the people, I did not accept being stabbed in the back. Even though all the powers of the world have left me without a single spark of hope, I have produced good thoughts and perspectives for the comrades, the people, and humanity. I accomplished the impossible. You on the outside should at least have worked hard enough to prove worthy of these efforts. I must say that it is a great misfortune that you haven't even proven yourself as serious as Turkey, a state you really don't like, and that you have not drawn the necessary conclusions for yourselves from my situation or even learned anything from the political changes.

c

Your calculations don't add up. Perhaps you are not even aware of that. You speculate on power and you engage in a power struggle, but in terms of your approach to power your personalities are less stable than mush. As soon as someone tries to lean on you, you immediately collapse. I have repeatedly tried to call you to reason, because no one else would help you and act as your friend. Just as for many people before you, what is waiting for you is either repugnant treason, an unworthy death, or becoming a constant problem. None of these alternatives is the right path to take.

It has often been claimed that I was robbing you of your youth, and, yes, I have indeed done so. That was my historical task; I had to steal your youth and devote it to the cause of the freedom of the people and their land. This angered you terribly. The congress decisions about marriage and other things are your attempt to take revenge. Your slick maneuvers have played no small role in creating a situation in which Osman became the donkey sent to clear the minefield. As I have already said, you don't understand anything about either love or partnership. Anything you have done in this regard merely amounts to the traditional "mutual sullying." This is what I intended to prevent you from doing. I was always in favor of producing a love in the service of our cause and based on freedom. I assure you that I led beautiful and brave young women and men into these sacred mountains once regarded as the "throne of the gods and goddesses" to enable them to get to know true love at least for one day. Do you have the hearts and minds necessary to understand this? You have buried a large number of them in unknown graves long before they were able to achieve any success. You should treasure the memory of these young people on a daily basis, but instead you impose on me such things. Instead of just talking about your memories each and every day, had you been in my shoes, how would you have reacted in the face of all of this?

d

Don't present me your arguments. I know what you are to each other. I fail to see any difference between you. The initiatives of both sides are directed against me. I will not bother to delve into it in detail here, but the way you carry on fighting is wrong. I blame myself, because I was unable to dissuade you from your way of struggling. But you shouldn't see me as powerless; there is still much I can do and will continue to do, even from my grave. For the sake of your own well-being, I'm begging you to stop employing these methods in our movement. Doing so would prove your courage for once. I don't want to have to organize a separate force against you. I don't even want to reveal your names. I will ask the people and the members of the organization to forgive you. You should by all means accept this amnesty and to compensate this by living a long time. This is the first alternative.

The second alternative: you may have a certain part of the guerrilla within the organization behind you, certainly fewer than seven thousand, and you are free to preserve them and to fight with whatever these numbers are. You could even form a separate tendency with its own name. But don't use this force against me, because I would then have to defend myself. If that were to happen, you never know who might lose. In addition, you should also openly explain to both friends and foes just how you want to wage war and conclude peace and what exactly your goals and demands are. Who are you, what are you against, and how do you intend to fight? This is what everyone must know if they are to join you. Only then would it be obvious how much actual value you have. If you do this in accord with the general principles, I too will support you. The criteria in my most recent court submissions are clear. If you succeed in organizing a resistance, a defensive struggle, I will regard that as a positive development. I will muster the kind of understanding for you that you didn't summon up for me. This would, as such, be an example of exemplary support.

You know my stance with regard to the gang culture of the recent past. Briefly stated, such power games are useful only if they serve the legitimate demands of the people. That is why it is wrong for you to engage in reciprocal accusations. The struggle in which you have been engaged for years reminds one of vultures fighting each other. You have to stop this. You are the spitting image of each other. You have no choice but to team up and satisfy the demands of the people. It is quite obvious that rendering the movement dysfunctional on television and in the newspapers can only be regarded as an effort by rivals to destroy the movement. You should, however, know that our people are not so destitute. The people, and I guess the values that you are basing your calculations upon, are stronger and more precious than all of us. If we prove ourselves worthy of the people, they will embrace us, but, otherwise, they will jettison us without batting an eye. Don't forget for even a moment that it is on account of the strength and values of this people, which I still represent, that you are able to live and breathe.

Everything invites you to engage in honest, humble, and serious self-critique. If you are honest, you will certainly not hesitate to do the right thing. Everything clse will prove that your road is the road of the Gang of Four, the road of Mehmet Şener and Selim Çürükkaya, and that some of you are competent agents provocateurs. No one will prevent our people, the guerrilla, and our ideological leadership from protecting themselves and from continuing to walk the road for the cause of a free life.

2

For those who believe in self-critique, harmony, real mutual cooperation, and the necessity of reconstruction, and who consciously and resolutely want to shoulder responsibility for this, my court submission will be very helpful. The need for self-critique is not to save the day but to act in response to history and to the people, and to do so successfully. This is of great importance for those who want to achieve intellectual strength. In any event, it is clear that those who cannot transform their mentality are unable to pursue a revolutionary cause. If you have kept a vital problem on the agenda for years and have been unable to solve it, you have to look for the root cause of this within yourselves. Problems cannot be solved by forming factions, blaming others or by accusing another faction; this will only make the problems worse.

My latest court submission contains elements that are part of a paradigmatic shift. Every sentence in it is worth internalizing. At the very least, it can contribute a lot to promoting competence by deepening understanding. It cannot be read like any random book. It presents a powerful perspective for the utopia of the people, for democratic civilization, and for socialism in the twenty-first century. I am convinced of both its theoretical and practical value. More precisely, it provides an opening to the process in this direction. There is an urgent need to internalize this work. We can achieve great practical successes only on the basis of powerful utopias and democratic and socialist thought and conviction. Without these, there will be no safeguard against decay, marginalization, and the risk of becoming the plaything of other forces.

Those of you who should feel historical responsibility should give your self-critique with a deep awareness that you have broken with the 150-year-old state-oriented socialist and national liberation denominations of capitalism and are trying to return to the historical option of the peoples, with enthusiasm and mental power. With this court submission, my defenses, I have shown the point I have reached on this road. Even more than I, you, my friends, are in need of this transformation in this direction and the focus it requires. You have seen for yourselves that otherwise you will not be able to advance. The need to subject yourselves to self-critique has nothing to do with whether your own group is in the right or not but, rather, with the fundamental problems that I have raised in this book. This is how you should address the issue. If you do so, you will feel as if you are reborn, and I'm sure you will overflow with enthusiasm. No dam will be powerful enough to stem this tide. You know very well how urgently you need this. Why, then, do you insist on a situation that suffocates you and those around you, instead of living and winning in a great way?

Recently I got a letter from a German intellectual. He describes his enthusiasm for my writings in an impressive manner. I hope and am certain that all our friends will profit from the comradely support they receive with profound sincerity and deep understanding and will no longer be a source of problems but will, instead, prove themselves able to address all tasks and problems masterfully and with ease and, thus, shoulder every task and become forces for success.

3

There are indeed some points about my person that require elaboration. It is important to note that even though my messages are able to overcome the roadblocks erected by the state, they are, on orders from above our organization, not allowed to reach the prisons.

It is clear that there have been fierce reactions to my writings. I have not received any information from outside and, at the same time, some of the perspectives that I wanted to point out were ignored for years. I know that this was already the practice long before Osman's behavior. The task is not to reveal some supposed plot against Osman but to reveal the plot directed against *me*, which had already begun when I was first brought to İmralı, and which Ahmet Zeki Okçuoğlu talked about.[3] This cannot simply be explained with provocative statements such as "Osman has taken a wife and run away."

People can reject my behavior in prison and condemn it as not sufficiently revolutionary or patriotic. Every current can declare this openly. They are the ones in control of the organization. That they do not do this openly could only be because they are afraid of the loyalty that the people have to me. It is obvious that they are using me for their own purposes but want to neutralize me by isolating me completely.

There have also been other indications, but I don't think it makes much sense to elaborate on them here. What I want to know is the following:

a) Was an organizational model used? Why were my messages not passed on to the prisons and not reported in the media?

b) If it is not true that people tried to strike me by striking Osman, what are the counter-responses? There was an attempt to isolate almost everyone from Urfa. This was done even though it is well known that I am not at all in favor of family cliques and local coteries.

c) What is the explanation for the fact that probably all those who are loyal and respect me were about to be dismissed from influential positions?

d) What did you want to do after you had taken complete control of the organization? There were those who were worried that there would be a serious attempt at liquidation. It is obvious that not all of the members of the group that went away together with Osman were simply trying to get married. A significant number of these people are individuals with dignity. They are probably, even if insufficiently, also loyal to me. Could it be that this was the actual point in all this? These friends are afraid. How did these friends, who were not afraid of war, come to be like this?

e) Even though these friends have serious flaws and are guilty of serious crimes, shouldn't there have been an effort to win them back? Why were they suddenly pushed into a position where they felt like they were being chased away? All the more so since it is known that for many years we have done our very best to win over every single individual? What kind of humanism, what kind of patriotism, what kind of revolutionary attitude can explain the fact that the efforts of so many years were discarded in the blink of an eye? Had these friends put up resistance, a thousand or more comrades might have died. Who could possibly have taken the responsibility for that?

f) Recently old-style armed groups' movements have been seen. I don't understand that. How can it be explained that even though I proposed democratic action, this is ignored?

g) The fact that DEHAP withdrew from the municipal elections without me even being told about it and the fact that all candidates were imposed from up above negates democracy.[4] This alone shows that the organization has been stripped of its revolutionary democratic content. How is it possible to explain the antidemocratic stance that was implemented everywhere? Is it not clear that this is deadly for becoming organized?

h) Such an attempt to take control, not just against Osman but of the entire heritage of the PKK might well be carried out with good intentions, but why did people want to neutralize me? Perhaps they wanted to liquidate me altogether, or maybe there were other reasons that I am ignorant of. Wouldn't it have been better to explain these reasons, publish your manifesto, and take this approach to seizing control of the organization? Instead, you attempted to use a secret, mafia-like model. How could you reconcile this with your own understandings?

i) Suppose you had succeeded in taking control of the organization. Would it not then have been necessary to decide on a strategy and tactics and mobilize the almost ten thousand troops? Since this was not the move you made, how and where did you hope to link our forces to? If our forces are not functional they will either decay, disintegrate, or collapse. Have you ever thought of your responsibility in this? Would it not result in chaos to simply apply the old methods to launch an offensive? Would that not be ten times more dangerous than the gang tendency that developed after August 15, 1984?

One could pose even more questions of this sort. The friends may have acted with entirely good intentions, but all the same, each of these questions is necessary. They show the pronounced or potential presence of events independent of your own willpower. Hopefully, you now recognize with horror the kind of catastrophic situation that was brought about by the power struggle within the organization. You probably now understand that this is not as simple as it may seem.

4

It may be that a power struggle within an organization can be necessary under certain conditions. The fact that I was exposed to a process of elimination may have necessitated this sort of safeguard. At the beginning, both groups may have been acting with good intentions. Therefore, I do not regard you as conspirators with bad intentions. But, hopefully, you understand that your style of political and military struggle is worthless, both within the organization and when it comes to influencing things on the outside. You are setting yourselves, our people, and me up for defeat in a meaningless and negative manner. Well-intentioned as you may be, the fact that you cannot transform your personality toward a military, political, and organizational identity is, above all, devastating to you. Nonetheless, you have many positive qualities, although you seem committed to taking them to the grave with you. Was there anything you wanted but could not get from me? What have you ever asked for in the name of friendship and comradeship that I did not give you or prepare for you? As far as that goes, there are numerous leadership positions, more than you could ever share. Why, then, this obstinacy, this self-destructive behavior?

Once you prepare for your self-critique, you will probably consider these issues. Don't be afraid to renew yourselves. You should, instead, be afraid of maintaining your current personalities. I have been patient with these traits for the last twenty years. I don't want any of you to be hurt in any way. You should carry out a genuine self-critique without fear of what the future will hold. Accept every task you can fulfill and don't belittle it as beneath you. You should neither sulk nor be hostile. Shoulder your tasks with determination, with wise serenity, and with a promise to the sacred memory of Kemal Pir, Mazlum Doğan, and thousands of others, as this is the only thing that befits you.

5

You have obviously started a struggle over leadership. This is wrong, both in terms of timing and approach. First of all, you haven't understood my sociological function. That is why you are making so many mistakes. Recently, some circles talked about me derogatorily as a representative of "Kurdish Kemalism." Supposedly, overcoming "Kemalism" and "Öcalanism" is necessary for the left to develop. I have analyzed Kemalism a number of times. Mustafa Kemal Atatürk clearly wanted to replicate the French Revolution. Therefore, Kemalism is generally viewed in the category of nineteenth- and twentieth-century revolutions. I have often said that Kemal's revolution remained incomplete due to local conditions. I have often discussed "updating" it. Only recently, the British author Andrew

Mango has also talked about the necessity to update Kemalism. It is important to note that the relationship of the Turks with the Kurds also played a key role, not just after Kemalism, but during the whole process of the Turks becoming a nation, beginning when they first settled in the Middle East. Although this relationship was correctly and strategically established in 1071, in 1515, and in the 1920s, today this strategic bond is in danger of breaking. Therefore, an update must be primarily about a realistic and sincere reform of Turkish-Kurdish relations. Otherwise, it will be impossible to prevent the development of a model characterized by a strategic conflict between Kurds and Turks.

My role may partially evoke a Kurdish Kemalism, but there are also many differences. The decisive difference is that my stance is not statist but democratic. What is essential to me and is my highest priority is that I achieve a situation in which the Kurds gain their own dynamism and authority based not on the model of the national state but on the model of a democratic people. Kemalism inaugurated the era of nationality in the Middle East; it is our task to initiate and represent the era of democracy. Between the two, there is no insurmountable mountaintop, but they also should not be simplistically equated. What I actually mean by "updating" is to explore the possibilities of a synthesis or a reconciliation of Kemalist Turkish nationalism and Kurdish democratism. This is of the utmost importance. This is a key issue in resolving both the Kurdish question and the Turkish question. It is also a cornerstone for a way out of the chaos of the Middle East. The historic, geopolitical, and social conditions all point to the possibility of such a synthesis playing a very significant historical role. Other ideologies, such as the chauvinist Turkish nationalism of the left or the right, Kurdish primitive nationalism, and Islamism are either far removed from offering solutions or are unable to avoid relying on hegemony and acting independently. The popular base for these ideologies is very weak, and they are essentially externally driven.

Thus, if you want to surpass me, first you need to clarify your ideological orientation. The attempt to achieve something by distorting and using me is futile. Even if I were to die, this would prove difficult. Dozens of people have tried, and they fared very badly. You probably have the ability to learn from these examples. I don't know to what extent you want to confront me, openly or secretly. Be that as it may, I must be frank with you, if you have a meaningful political line and do not act with hostile intentions, in keeping with my democratic identity, I see that as your right.

The minimum criterion is to agree on the definition of patriotism and freedom. But if, once again, your approach is dishonest and conspiratorial, I will have the right to defend myself. In other words, taking advantage of the heavy blow dealt to me in an attempt to take control of the organization without a coherent ideological justification and by exaggerating very minor issues falls into the category "coups and plots." I am not in a position to determine whether or not events unfolded in this manner. I am merely providing an assessment. Such methods are employed all too often in Turkish political culture, and I definitely warn you against them. These methods are entirely detrimental.

The situation of "isolation within isolation," which I recently mentioned, along with what I have been hearing, although it is not completely reliable information, suggests that an image of me is being created, as if I have established a "dynasty," which some others want to destroy. I cannot know who, i.e., which institution, is disseminating all this or to what extent, but it is an objective reality that such an atmosphere was created. It may be that the emergence of the problem with Osman and the way it was used played a role, but this was not decisive. It is more likely that it is driven by a tendency with connections both outside of and within the organization, whose roots are to be found in the past. Kurdish primitive nationalists and the Turkish left are making maximal use of this discourse, as are many renegades who have left the organization. The worst aspect of the most recent faction formation is that people haven't learned from all the past experiences and are objectively speculating on taking control of leadership. This is unfortunate. At the same time, both sides verbally justify their behavior as expressing greater "loyalty" to me. It is not at all unlikely that these are dishonest approaches.[5] This is something that must be clarified.

I would be glad about and be fully supportive of a situation in which I am no longer necessary and have been surpassed. I am also ready to support the faction that succeeds in a positive way. A coup is not necessary, because the circumstances of my incarceration make it superfluous. If people fan hostile flames against me within the organization, this will only serve the purpose of liquidation; our strong and vital support for any individual or group that wants to be successful is explicit. It is also clear that no attempt to wear me out can be anything but an attempt at liquidation. Although I am known to be the fiercest opponent of family coteries and dynasticism, the emphasis on Osman is not quite correct. The attempt to build an organization within the organization under this cloak is doomed to failure. It would seem that this approach has been tried. Therefore, the factions should be very sensitive about this and demonstrate practical self-critical behavior with an awareness of its objective meaning. The core of the cadre policy is the correct coming together with an understanding of the actuality of leadership. In any case, the necessary steps must be successfully carried out immediately.

6

It might make sense to criticize me in relation to the topics of war and peace. My call for the immediate end of the armed actions under the influence of the plot was not entirely appropriate.[6] The decisive factor in issuing my call was the fact that the plot was directed against all of our structures, and that the traitors were already lying in wait. It is well known that this call, which was not made for my own personal benefit, was used *against* me. Even though, from that point on, our forces were inactive for a long time, in part as a result of my call, for the most part, the decisive factor was the concrete situation of our forces and commanders. In all of this, there was a fundamental error, namely, the impression some people created that everything happened as a result of my orders. Many completely incorrect actions and much fallacious praxis were carried out in my name. Of course, I never wanted to be misused in this way. This is an issue that I will pay serious attention to from now on. I was not very sensitive in that regard. I continuously emphasized that our forces should seek the conditions for war and peace based on their own reality—not for me, but for the people. Had this been the basis for the formation of factions, it might have made sense.

With my most recent court submission, my views on war and peace have been clearly laid on the table. I am not in a position to give orders for war or peace. Even if I wanted to, the necessary conditions are quite obviously absent. I considered it a manifestation of respect that my request was complied with for a long time. It turned out, however, that the representatives of the state didn't attach very much importance to this. Their attitude amounts to saying: "If they have the power let them fight." Even under the most modest circumstances, there is neither a bilateral ceasefire nor the expression of any will for peace on the part of the state. The state seems determined to liquidate us. It is also trying to involve the United States. You thus have two alternatives: complete capitulation or resistance. Since you have not capitulated, you will have to resist. Therefore, you must immediately end your factionalism. Otherwise, those who want to persist cannot avoid playing a provocative role. It is entirely your responsibility to develop a multifaceted war strategy and tactics. You are in a position to assess and analyze not only the Turkish armed forces but all armed and political forces that may attack you. You should keep each other focused on the fact that the war must be intense and must encompass the urban, rural, and mountain dimensions. You should warn the people of the coming war beforehand, and you should offer peace and a ceasefire one last time. You should determine and address the problems of the various regions of the war and the necessary logistics, and you should consolidate your forces both quantitatively and qualitatively. In short, all these issues depend entirely on you and your own efforts.

Do not expect me to remain silent about the way you have used me until now. I want to emphasize that my situation doesn't allow me to evaluate your course of action. You must try to attain results solely on the basis of your own strategic and tactical strength. Anything else would amount to expecting a miracle from the saints, and that would be a little anachronistic. It is important that you are the force for both war and peace. As long as the state or the states don't see your actual fighting capacity, they won't undertake the steps necessary for peace. It seems that there is a formula for this: "The more war there is, the more peace there will be." This is the reality, however grim. I once said that not a single additional soldier or guerrilla should die. That was a very humane attitude, but the state doesn't take it seriously. The state seems to see military success as essential. Thus, a fierce guerrilla war on your part may contribute to peace.

In this context, one can think about tactical considerations such as defensive warfare and taking prisoners instead of killing as many people as possible, about inflicting material damage rather than taking lives, and of adopting a line of action that compels peace. In addition, it is also more humane to proclaim the conditions for a bilateral ceasefire and the rules to be adhered to in the war *beforehand*. I hope that the door to dialogue will open at the last moment.

Of course, we all know that war and peace are the most difficult topics. Nobody can deny that I have made great efforts in both areas. However, now I am obviously in no position to contribute to either war or peace. Among your tasks today is to develop a correct evaluation of your own reality in times of war, as well as an accurate assessment of the Turkish army. The difficulty for me comes from the fact that both sides put the whole burden of war and peace on me. This is cruel. Now you have no choice but to try to settle accounts with one another, between yourselves and the state forces, using all of your skills. You cannot rid yourself of this burden simply by liquidating yourself. The duration, extent, and style of war depends solely on your skills. This burden cannot be reduced either by emotional loyalty to or hostile reactions against me. Let me emphasize this once again: this war will be waged on the basis of your will and your intellectual clarity. Approach it properly and competently. Don't suicidally throw yourselves or others into the deep end. You must comprehend the difficulties that I would be facing if it fell to me alone to answer all your questions about war and peace.

I think you still don't understand the extent to which you sustain yourselves by leaning on me. Be realistic and capable. By forming such poor factions, you will only dig your own graves. You will only have a chance to lead if your achievements are recognized by the people, as well as by your friends and your foes. Anything else is just mischief. Do not address leadership issues until you have achieved success in historic offensives. Let me again emphasize that the two factions need each other in the way the fingernail needs the finger. If people fail to understand that, it would be a huge personal catastrophe if members of these factions rose deliberately or spontaneously to leadership positions. It appears that you have no choice but to embrace the tasks you are able to successfully complete.

7

In today's Middle East, the theoretical and practical development of the democracy movement is a historical necessity. Such a foray against the tradition of the despotic state is the most appropriate political option for the most fundamental demands of all groups of people. The transition of the peoples of the Middle East to the era of democratic civilization would signify a qualitative leap to a new stage of global geopolitics and history. Overcoming the chaos in the Middle East with democracy would be the decisive factor for the turn from the era of the warrior ruling power to the era of peace and democratization. Therefore, the democratization in Kurdistan will play a key role. The road to democracy in the Middle East depends on the success of the people of Kurdistan and their democratic option against the despotic state. That is why it is so important that the people in every part of Kurdistan set up democratic parties. Success in this regard would lead to a chain reaction that accelerates the democratization of the peoples of the Middle East.

Even more important in this connection is the question of how a democratic party can be founded. Undoubtedly, any top-down approach goes against both the form and the essence of democracy. Persons and groups can earn the attribute "democratic" only if they continuously educate and organize the popular base and lead it into action. This has to involve a passion for democracy bordering on love. The democratic system has a different paradigm of life and is characterized by a wholeness of philosophy and practice. For democracies, elections and positions of authority have only a limited significance. Basically, democracy denotes the conscious and organized state of the population in its struggle for freedom and dignity. Democracy expresses people's attainment of self-governance, authority, and sovereignty. A truly democratic party can prove its merits by carrying out the most comprehensive grassroots organizing and action in accordance with this framework. A state of affairs in which the people are driven like a herd of sheep is the result of the despotic state culture and must be overcome by a constant struggle on the part of the democratic party.

No cadre and no leader can be worthy of the attribute "democrat" without proving themselves in the democratic organization of the people and its activity. Seen from this point of view, it is obvious that the factionalizing tendencies that have emerged are not aware of the line on democratization but, rather, insist on forming coteries and cliques, the approach familiar to them. This understanding and behavior is rooted in the fact that the phenomenon of the democratic social leadership analyzed a long time ago was not grasped, and that people have, therefore, not adapted themselves to it. One underlying aspect is reactionary social mentality in its various forms. These people have not been able to overcome this through education and practice, because their will for freedom is not strong enough. This shows up not only in their party work in the narrow sense but also in the line developed by the congress and the legal parties regarding organization and action. These basic institutions show the extent to which one is integrated with the people and with society. In general, all hierarchical and statist power holders share a top-down approach to the appointment of people, staying out of sight while covertly holding the reigns of control, all under the cloak of secrecy. Only circles, powers, and representatives of classes that are not democratic but want to exercise hierarchy, authority, and power over society can behave in this way. Contemporary state-focused organizational mechanisms, including real socialism, also subscribe to this line in their approach.

I am convinced that we as a movement and I personally have made great efforts to overcome this traditional understanding of rule based on hierarchy, authority, and small cliques, however, there is not a sufficient understanding of how we elaborated this democratic stance into a process that attained a more conscious, theoretical, and structural quality, having in the beginning only subscribed to it spontaneously, in response to the plotting of the powerful states. The audacious acts shown by the formation of these recent factions confirms this observation. A system, including the selection of candidates, that should have been organized by the people's democratic decision-making was instead carried out by appointments in a way that came close to exceeding a sultan's authority. Such top-down approaches are very harmful to the highly valuable democratic stance of our popular base. Those who lack the passion for organizing the people and for democracy are strikingly exposed as a result.

Given such attitudes, working democratically is difficult and cannot lead to success. The situation of the left in Turkey proves this well. Imposing top-down approaches on the Kurdish people, who are developing into a truly democratic people, must definitely be overcome. This is the real reason why, from HEP to DEHAP, a democratic organization has not developed, democratic cadres have not been trained, that the potential far-reaching progress in democratization has failed to materialize. This is a situation experienced by the entire left. The main factor underlying this is the hierarchical statist culture and its utopia.

Based on my most recent court submission, our movement has turned toward a deeply democratic line, both theoretically and practically. This democratic line has been internalized, and, thus, with this knowledge and a self-critical stance, everyone should join anew and make a fresh start. Prolonging the present state of affairs with superficial self-critique and an authoritarian and sectarian practice, while wasting time by pretending to be marching together, will only result in a loss. Our line on democratization is the antithesis to the five-thousand-year-old line of hierarchical and statist society and represents the democratic ascendancy of a people formed by a comprehensive theory and a noble practice. Regardless of how many groups people set up within the organization or how many cliques and gangs they form, they must know that they will lose against the people's commitment to democratic leadership. Ultimately, it will not be possible to keep the people under the old relationships of slavery and demagogic authorities or deceived by false revolutionary socialist dogmas as long as their sons and daughters love democracy.

In the end, if there is insistent factionalization, and the factions are not integrated into structures with clear form and content, then these factions, which in a way should have been considered natural since the beginning of the PKK movement, can only result in liquidationism. Not every faction is necessarily bad. But the criteria for positive factions are unification on a higher level, the capacity to be constructive, to solve problems, and to transcend reactionary views and organizational forms.

I believe that I have clarified the ideological, political, organizational, and moral line that I hoped to develop. By ideology, I mean a revolutionary mentality, a new paradigm for viewing the world and the universe. The great belief and thought struggles resulted in an enhanced understanding of the core of the functioning laws of the universe. In my most recent court submission, I have tried to convey some of this understanding. Although the European Renaissance lies at its core, I also attempted to surpass it. I think I have delivered a useful analysis of the hierarchical and statist paradigm that emerged and developed in the Middle East. I have tried to show how individualism, which deteriorated into extreme forms after the European Renaissance, can actually be unified with the almost complete negation of individualism in Eastern societies once a correct social definition is provided. In doing so, I paid due attention to establishing a healthy equilibrium between the individual and society. Society should not be shortchanged in the name of the individual nor should the individual be abandoned in the name of society.

There are two ways to engage with the theoretical and ideological level that has been achieved; either one rallies around it with full trust, sincerity, and modesty or intentionally participates in the theoretical essence and ideological substance on a deeply conscious level. Thousands of comrades who represent the greatest values of the PKK—Haki Karer, Kemal Pir, Mazlum Doğan, Hayri Durmuş, and Mahsum Korkmaz among them—have exhibited a well-balanced harmony of these two approaches. This genuine participation made them an example of the most heroic behavior until the end. On the other hand, those who neither managed to rally sincerely and modestly nor to make a sufficient theoretical and ideological effort always failed badly. Sometimes they turned into coteries, sometimes they became liquidators, and sometimes they succumbed to the tendency to form gangs. It is difficult for me to arrive at a common mentality with those who are unable to comprehend my basic mentality, who do not respect it, and who are unable to participate modestly and display a high theoretical participation. Here we are talking about embracing a high level of mentality. Esteeming a backward mentality leads to aberrations.

The second basic point is that my political line has made great progress in an evolution from our natural democratic stance to a conscious and active democratization, and a unification with the people has been attained. It should be noted that the institutionalization of the PKK's leadership that I represent has liberated itself from the national liberation and real socialist stumbling without pandering to the tendencies of bourgeois life. In this way, both in terms of understanding and in practice, a democratic, free, and equal political line has been achieved in Kurdistan under its present conditions that neither leads to capitulation nor, on the basis of nationalism, fixates on achieving a state. The cadres of the PKK are expected to internalize this political line and to take it to the people. A political approach that does not actually integrate this understanding and fails to make practical efforts in this direction will sooner or later come back to haunt its practitioners in the form of liquidationism. Politics is an art that requires a high level of sensitivity and decency. The biggest weaknesses of our structures in this regard are arbitrariness and an insistence on behavior that lacks sensitivity and a dynamic attitude. This will only result in early defeat, becoming the instruments of liquidators, and cronyism. To be successful, we must always remember that politics does not tolerate a vacuum, and that we must, therefore, live a life full of action.

Since the age of seven, I've been trying to live actively and in an organized fashion. Indeed, being organized requires action, and action requires being organized. In all of this, being constructive outweighs being destructive. Construction and production are the decisive factors. We have not particularly tried to be destructive, and when we did it was to destroy the structures that were an obstacle to important developments. We are talking about an active personality that condemns destruction, extortion, and confiscation of all sorts. My conception of friendship has always been based on achieving noble goals. I never entered into relations with people to distract myself, to amuse myself, or to attain personal benefit. This aspect of the actuality of leadership that I represent must be carefully understood and followed. Otherwise, it is impossible to talk about political unity and an organizational and activist life under my leadership. It is close to impossible for people whose lives are not thoroughly organized and primarily determined by positive activism to successfully play a role within the leadership institution.

Organization and activism should be understood less as an obligation than as a way of life. One should try to understand the reality of our leadership by keeping in mind that just as it is impossible to live without water and air, it is impossible to live without organization and action. Otherwise, the rise of an organization within the organization, arbitrary destructive actions, and meaningless and aimless activism will always create problems. The only correct form of commitment is to organize competently and to do so concretely, in keeping with the essence of the ideological and political line, and to integrate this organizing with targeted and productive activism. Doing so serves our goals, avoids the squandering of historical efforts, and erects the building stone by stone. There is no other way to succeed besides increasing the understanding of organization and action of our forces, including in terms of armed struggle to this position of ours.

In the reality of the leadership of the PKK, moral behavior doesn't simply mean conforming to the laws and rules; it means being passionately committed to the new sociality that has emerged on the basis of the ideological, political, and organizational line. The reality of PKK leadership perceives this new sociality as the form of being that life takes. Life is our new sociality. Pursuing life outside of this or walking away from this means emptiness and loss. The correct moral attitude is not meant to lead to a life like that of a disciple or member of a sect, but to a life that is based on a scientific understanding and a mastery of and wisdom about life that perceives political freedom as an effort to create the new—i.e., being a contemporary "believer." Those who fail to display the necessary moral strength will lose their way in everything they do. A moral life is essentially continuously displaying the ability to use our mentality and free will to take part in society's way of being. The truly great values of the PKK were produced by those who exercised this kind of moral attitude. Anyone who wants to live according to the PKK's line must have this moral strength.

In brief, this definition of leadership, which I found that I had to represent, shows that everyone must again take a critical look at their own participation and must once more reintegrate themselves into the whole. A leadership that follows this line carries within itself the whole universe, the whole of human existence, our social reality, and the democratic freedom of our people. It is not just national but is universal. If the leadership has flaws and shortcomings, they are to be found in these fundamental categories. To live in the shadow of this leadership and to think that by building simple selfish worlds or worlds characterized by slavery one could actually live is thoughtless, even perverse. This court defense reflects all of the fundamental features of a leadership that have been realized. Those who are interested must first fully grasp this. If there are points that are flawed or inadequate, it is a requirement of comradeship to point this out and to address these flaws and inadequacies. Acting so as to appear to be participating, while doing something else in practice, is either, to use two old-fashioned words, *sanctimony* or *hypocrisy*. The reality of my leadership may not be accepted. In that case, those who do not accept it have the right to leave after having provided an appropriate explanation. But to say yes I understand and then to refuse to participate or to say, "I will participate," and then to refuse to live up to the requirements only denotes a decadent and irresponsible way of life, which cannot endure or be meaningful.

My style of leadership never consists of forcing people to do things. It is nurtured with great belief and wisdom. Those who lack these traits should stay away. The individuals who have been made sick by our age cannot participate in a leadership of this style, and when they do cannot attain results. One aspect of the latest formation of factions was the fact that right from the start the people involved could not participate in this leadership reality as I redefined it. If people are interested in and respect us, if people actually have the desire and the determination to connect with us and share a common ideological, political, and organizational line, then it is not me who has to join them, but they who must join me. For this, it is immaterial whether I am physically alive or dead. The decisive factors are the meaning, will, and morality that have been attained. This doesn't concern just me, but the whole universe, humanity, and our social reality, which find their expression in me. This is the basis for a renewed democratic, free, and egalitarian formation of our people.

Our martyrs, before whom I am always shaken, our poor and long-suffering people, our understanding of friendship and humanity—these and all other noble values are calling on the comrades to rally around our line, which paves the way to productivity and allows no place for other walks of life that cannot attain success. My regards and my love to all those who assemble under the flag of these noble values.

ANNEX A

Modern History of Turkey

1914—World War I begins. The Ottoman Empire allies with Germany.

1919—World War I ends, the Ottoman Empire is defeated.

1923—Foundation of the Republic of Turkey.

1923–1950—The CHP holds power.

1950–1960—The DP holds power.

May 27, 1960—Military coup.

1961—Execution of deposed prime minister Adnan Menderes at the prison on İmralı Island.

1965–1971, 1975–1977, 1979–1980—The AP holds power during these three periods.

March 12, 1971—Military coup.

May 6, 1972—Execution of the Turkish revolutionaries Deniz Gezmiş, Hüseyin İnan, and Yusuf Aslan. Öcalan himself was imprisoned on April 7, 1972, for a short time, and, thus, followed these developments closely.

September 12, 1980—Military coup.

1982—The constitution resulting from the coup, which remains in force, and which declares all people in Turkey to be Turks and prohibits the use of any language except Turkish, comes in to effect.

1983—Turgut Özal becomes prime minister when his ANAP wins the first elections following the coup.

1989—Turgut Özal becomes state president.

1993—The first unilateral ceasefire is declared by the PKK, and at a press conference in Lebanon Öcalan declares the movement's intention to resolve the Kurdish question within the borders of Turkey. Turgut Özal responds favorably but then dies under unclear circumstances later that year.

November 3, 1996—In the aftermath of a traffic accident near the village of Susurluk, the entanglement of politics, security agencies, the fascist mafia, and Kurdish village guards becomes broader public knowledge for the first time, in what is known as the Susurluk scandal.

April 1999—Bülent Ecevit is reelected, having previously been elected in 1974, 1977, and 1978, and leads a coalition government made up of the of the DSP, the ANAP, and the MHP.

2001—Abolition of the death penalty in peace time.

November 2, 2002—The AKP wins the parliamentary elections, and Recep Tayyip Erdoğan becomes prime minister, with the CHP as the only parliamentary opposition.

ANNEX B

Chronology of the Recent History of Kurdistan

1639—Partition of Kurdistan by the demarcation of the border between the Ottoman and Iranian Empires in the Treaty of Kasr-I Shirin.

1806—Baban uprising.

1846–1947—Bedirhan uprising.

1879—Nehri uprising in Şemzînan under the leadership of Sheikh Ubeydullah.

1915—Genocide of Armenians and Assyrians begins.

August 10, 1920—Treaty of Sèvres, which envisages independence for both Kurdistan and Armenia. It is never ratified.

1923—Mahmud Barzanji revolts.

July 24, 1923—Peace Treaty of Lausanne and foundation of the Republic of Turkey.

1925—Sheikh Said uprising.

June 29, 1925—Execution of Sheikh Said.

1926–1932—Ararat uprising.

1936–1938—Dersim uprising under the leadership of Seyid Riza. Bombardment of Dersim.

January 22, 1946—Proclamation of the Republic of Kurdistan in Mahabad, with Ghazi Mohammed as president. The Republic only exists until December 16, 1946.

March 30, 1947—Ghazi Mohammed is hanged.

1975—Algiers Agreement between Iran and Iraq. The KDP is forced to capitulate.

May 16, 1988—Poison gas attack by Saddam Hussein's army kills five thousand people in the Kurdish town of Halabja.

1991—Creation of the Iraqi Kurdistan parliament in South Kurdistan.

Since 1991—Popular uprisings (*Serhildan*).

February 15, 1999—Abdullah Öcalan is kidnapped from Nairobi, Kenya, in a NATO operation.

April 18, 1999—Kurdish HDP is successful in the municipal elections.

2003—Iraqi Kurdistan becomes a federal state in Iraq.

March 2009—The Kurdish DTP scores a major success in municipal elections.

Beginning April 2009—Arrest of more than 1,400 DTP members and voters.

November 2009—The DTP is banned.

August 2014—ISIS attacks Sinjar. The YPJ/YPG and the HPG rush to liberate Sinjar from ISIS.

September 13, 2014—ISIS begins the siege of Kobani. On January 27, 2015, Kobani is taken back.

October 10, 2015—Ankara bombings kill ninety-seven people and injure more than four hundred at a peace rally for the resolution of the Kurdish question.

December 2015 through the first half of 2016—In response to a campaign for "democratic autonomy," the Turkish state unleashes a monstrous wave of state terror. Curfews are declared in Sur, Diyarbakır, Cizre, Silopi, as well as in Mardin and Hakkari. Cities are bombed by the Turkish army; the old town of Amed (Diyarbakır) is completely destroyed. More than two hundred people are killed in Amed alone.

October 2016—Mayors and many members of parliament, including the cochairs of HDP, are arrested.

January 2018—Turkey occupies Efrin in North-Syria.

October 2019—Turkey occupies Serê Kanîyê (Ras al-Ayn).

ANNEX C

Chronology of the PKK

with particular focus on events mentioned in this book

Late 1973—Abdullah Öcalan decides to found his own political group.

May 18, 1977—Murder of Haki Karer in Antep.

November 27, 1978—Foundation of the PKK in the village of Fis near Diyarbakır.

Mid-1979—Öcalan leaves Turkey and begins to establish contact with Palestinian groups in Lebanon.

September 12, 1980—Military coup in Turkey. Hundreds of thousands are arrested and tortured, including most of the PKK cadres.

March 21, 1982—Mazlum Doğan, a member of the central committee of the PKK, sets his cell on fire and hangs himself in protest of the torture in the military prison no. 5, in Diyarbakır, where most of the Kurdish political prisoners are incarcerated.

May 18, 1982—Self-immolation of the PKK prisoners Ferhat Kurtay, Eşref Anyık, Necmi Önen, and Mahmut Zengin in the military prison Diyarbakır.

July 14, 1982—PKK prisoners in Diyarbakır begin a hunger strike. Central committee members Kemal Pir, Mehmet Hayri Durmuş, Akıf Yılmaz, and Ali Çiçek die before the strike ends.

August 15, 1984—Beginning of the PKK's armed struggle with simultaneous attacks on two military posts, one in Eruh (province of Siirt) and the other in Şemdinli (province of Hakkâri).

March 21, 1985—Proclamation of the ERNK.

March 28, 1986—Mahsum Korkmaz is killed in battle under circumstances that remain unclear.

March 20, 1993—First unilateral PKK ceasefire.

May 24, 1993—Massacre of thirty-three unarmed soldiers by Şemdin Sakık, leading to the end of the ceasefire.

January 1995—At its fifth congress, the PKK removes the demand for an independent state from its program.

December 14, 1995—Second unilateral PKK ceasefire ended in May 1996 due to state violence.

September 2, 1998—Third unilateral PKK ceasefire. It was presumed that it would end when Abdullah Öcalan was abducted in Kenya and taken to Turkey, but Öcalan requested that the ceasefire continue.

October 9, 1998—Öcalan leaves Syria, arriving in Rome in November.

February 15, 1999—Öcalan is kidnapped from Nairobi, Kenya. Since then, he has been held in solitary confinement in the one-person prison on İmralı Island, which was completely evacuated for this purpose.

May 6, 1999—Beginning of the show trial against Öcalan. Öcalan expresses his sympathy for the relatives of the victims of the war. In his defense speech, he says that the mission of armed struggle has been accomplished and calls for a political solution, with the goal of a "democratic republic" for all people living in Turkey.

June 29, 1999—Öcalan is sentenced to death on the anniversary of the 1925 execution of Sheikh Said.

August 1999—On Öcalan's recommendation all PKK armed forces withdraw from Turkey, marking the beginning of a unilateral ceasefire that will last for several years. During the withdrawal and ceasefire, more than five hundred members of the guerrilla are killed in Turkish military attacks. Up to this point, approximately forty thousand people have been killed in the war.

January 2000—At its seventh congress, the PKK decides to strategically reorient in line with Öcalan's proposals concerning the primacy of the political struggle over the military option. The ARGK is dissolved and the HPG is founded as a defensive army to take its place.

2001—Öcalan's essential two-volume work on the history of civilization *The Roots of Civilization*, and *The PKK and the Kurdish Question* is published. In it, he presents his ideas about the peaceful building of a democratic civilization. The PKK agrees with his ideas and confirms its commitment to "unity in freedom" with Turkey.

2002—Dissolution of the PKK and founding of the KADEK.

September 2003—Dissolution of the KADEK and founding of the Kongra Gel, which would later split as a result of internal tensions, with several hundred members gathering around Nizamettin Taş and Osman Öcalan, who advocated cooperation with the US and the Iraqi Kurdish parties.

May 2004—Publication of the Turkish original of the present book.

June 1, 2004—The 1998 unilateral ceasefire is officially ended, but no major military engagement follows.

2005—The PKK is refounded and the KKK is founded.

2006—Renewed flare-up of fighting after numerous attacks by the Turkish military.

August 2006—Prime Minister Erdoğan speaks for the first time about the Kurdish question, conceding that mistakes have been made by the state.

October 2006—The PKK declares its fifth unilateral ceasefire. Turkey responds with it most massive attack in ten years.

2007—Dissolution of the KKK and founding of the KCK.

October 2007—Massive air strikes by the Turkish army on PKK positions in South Kurdistan/North Iraq. Guerilla attacks on Turkish military positions intensify.

February 2008—Turkish ground troops invade South Kurdistan/North Iraq. After surprisingly strong resistance, there is quick withdrawal.

August 15, 2009—Öcalan finishes penning *The Road Map to Negotiations*, which was presented to the Turkish state for talks and only transmitted to the court at the end of 2010. It was first published in Turkish, in 2011, and then in English, in 2012.

April 13, 2009—The KCK declares a unilateral ceasefire.

June 1, 2010—End of the ceasefire. Numerous guerrilla attacks and Turkish military operations ensue.

August 2010—The KCK and the Turkish government confirm that the authorities are in "dialogue" with Öcalan. The result is the renewed cessation of the armed activities beginning on August 13, 2010.

January 2013–April 2015—Abdullah Öcalan and the PKK begin one of the most serious series of talks aimed at realizing a political solution to the Kurdish question and a negotiated resolution of the conflict with the Turkish state. The talks collapse in April 2015, ushering in a new wave of violence and brutality on the part of the Turkish state and a total and aggravated isolation of Abdullah Öcalan.

January 9, 2013—Sakine Cansız, one of the founders of the PKK, and two other Kurdish women revolutionaries, Fidan Doğan and Leyla Şaylemez, are murdered in Paris, France, by the MIT (National Intelligence Organization of Turkey) just as the talks involving the Turkish state, Abdullah Öcalan, and the PKK are about to begin.

Notes

Editor's note: the Turkish original does not contain any notes; all notes were added by the editors of the German and/or English translations of the book.

Foreword

1 Perhaps this was what T.S. Eliot meant when he said that there are men who have an incapacity for what we ordinarily call thinking. We have poisoned humanity almost to death with rational "understanding."

2 William McNeill, *Mythhistory and Other Essays* (Chicago: University of Chicago Press, 1986), 5–6.

3 One can recognize this elective affinity in the architectural collaboration between the Soviet and US American empires, something that had been written out of the history of both countries by the end of the 1950s. One of my favorite examples is that of Soviet poet Gastev, whose work faithfully mimicked Taylor's system of scientific management, in which workers' movements were measured and remunerated with piece rates. Concrete grain silos that dominated industrial cities like Buffalo were celebrated in the Soviet Union almost as much as the unsightly cupola of the Singer Building.

4 Another important influence on Abdullah Öcalan is French historian Fernand Braudel. As Braudel is not explicitly mentioned in this book, I will leave his analysis of the plurality of social times to another reviewer. But Braudel's impatience with occurrences (especially the "vexing" ones) and his sensitivity to time as depth (multiple temporalities of event/long term/structural time) are very much present in Öcalan's thinking in *The Sociology of Freedom* (PM Press, 2020), where he looks at the continuity that exists on the deeper level, below and beyond the "surface disturbances" of *l'histoire eventuelle*.

Preface

1   These defenses were published as *Prison Writings: The Roots of Civilization* (London: Pluto Press, 2007) and *Prison Writings: The PKK and the Kurdish Question in the 21st Century* (London: Pluto Press, 2011).

2   *Özgür İnsan Savunması* (Neuss: Mezopotamien Verlag, 2003).

3   This book was first published in Turkish in 2004.

4   At the Helsinki summit of the European Council on December 12, 1999, Turkey was officially recognized as a candidate for full membership. Before the summit, both Abdullah Öcalan and the PKK made statements of support for such a process.

Social Reality and the Individual

1   In 2005, the European Court of Human Rights (ECtHR) ruled that the 1999 trial during which Öcalan was sentenced to death violated the fundamental right to a fair trial, and that there should be a retrial. Therefore, pending a new trial, Öcalan's sentence was deemed to be inconclusive.

2   These are submissions to the court that have been published in the two-volume *Sümer Rahip Devletinden Demokratik Uygarlığa: AİHM Savunmaları I. ve II. Cilt* (Neuss: Mezopotamien Verlag, 2002) and in English in two volumes under the title *Prison Writings: The Roots of Civilization* (London: Pluto Press, 2007) and *Prison Writings: The PKK and the Kurdish Question in the 21st Century* (London: Pluto Press, 2011).

3   Jürgen Habermas, *Inclusion of the Other: Studies in Political Theory* (Cambridge: Polity Press, 1999).

4   A term coined by Michel Foucault to describe political action based on "scientific," biologically constructed criteria. People are divided into "we" and "the others" according to certain criteria (race, sexuality), and then subjected to particular forms of discipline; Michel Foucault, *Discipline and Punish: The Birth of the Prison* (New York: Pantheon Books, 1977).

5   This line of argument follows Murray Bookchin, *Ecology of Freedom: The Emergence and Dissolution of Hierarchy* (Buckley, UK: Cheshire Books, 1982).

6   For Öcalan's interpretation of Abraham as the leader of a religiously based rebellion against the ruling powers and their polytheism, see Abdullah Öcalan, *Sümer Rahip Devletinden Demokratik Uygarlığa* (Neuss: Mezopotamien Verlag, 2001); Abdullah Öcalan, *Kutsallık ve Lanetin Simgesi Urfa* (Neuss: Mezopotamien Verlag, 2001).

7   This term quite obviously alludes to Murray Bookchin's "organic society"; Bookchin, *Ecology of Freedom*.

8   The historian Anthony Giddens formulated this as follows: "If we can think of the entire span of human existence thus far as a 24-hour day, agriculture would have come into existence at 11:56 p.m.—four minutes to midnight—and civilizations at 11:57 p.m."; Anthony Giddens, *Sociology*, 6th edition (Cambridge: Polity Press, 2009), 109.

9   The author often criticizes real socialist and vulgar materialist interpretations of dialectics. This criticism also shows up in his dispute with the Stalinist

concepts that were dominant within the socialist movement in Turkey at the time the PKK was founded.

Hierarchical Statist Society: The Birth of Slave Society

1   "For as becoming is between being and not being, so that which is becoming is always between that which is and that which is not"; Aristotle, *Metaphysics*, trans by W.D. Ross, (Whitefish, MT: Kessinger Publishing, 2008), Book 2, part 2).

2   Here, Öcalan quotes the definition of human nature rendered self-conscious in Murray Bookchin, The *Philosophy of Social Ecology—Essays on Dialectical Naturalism* (Montréal: Black Rose Books, 1995).

3   Similar value judgments are also found in sagas such as the Nibelungenlied (Song of the Nibelungs), where the ones who hoard treasures are evil dragons.

4   This example, familiar to readers in the Middle East, is based on the idea that snakes eat mice, and mice in their turn eat snake eggs, which in the end leads to an equilibrium.

5   The Inanna epic, the role of the Sumerian priests, and the function of the ziggurat are extensively treated and addressed in Abdullah Öcalan, *Sümer Rahip Devletinden Demokratik Uygarlığa: AİHM Savunmaları I. Cilt.* (Neuss: Mezopotamien Verlag, 2002); in English, see *Prison Writings: The Roots of Civilization* (London: Pluto Press, 2007).

6   *Enuma Elish: The Seven Tablets of the History of Creation*, trans. L.W. King (London: Luzac, 1902), accessed July 7, 2021, https://archive.org/details/seventabletsofcro2kinguoft/page/n12.

7   In classical Greek philosophy, men were seen as the actors who formed, while women were regarded as matter to be formed; see Genevieve Lloyd, *The Man of Reason: "Male" and "Female" in Western Philosophy* (Minneapolis: University of Minnesota Press, 1993).

8   "Your wives are a tilth for you; so approach your wives when and how you like." (Koran 2: 223).

9   In Jewish mythology, Lilith is regarded as the first wife of Adam, whom he repudiated, because, according to one of the transmissions, she wanted to lie on top of him during sexual intercourse. Predecessors of this figure can also be found in the Sumerian transmissions.

10 El is the main god in the Canaanite pantheon.

11 One of the great Indian epics, along with the Mahabharata, was written between the fourth century BCE and the second century CE.

12 The title of one of the works of by the Sumerologist Samuel Noah Kramer, *History Begins at Sumer* (Philadelphia: University of Pennsylvania Press, 1988) Kramer.

13 Thomas Hobbes, *Leviathan* (Harmondsworth, UK: Penguin Classics, 2017 [1651]).

14 This is the dating that Öcalan uses, but sources generally put the end of the most recent Ice Age at between ten and fifteen thousand years ago.

The Statist Society: The Formation of Slave Society

1 Unlike Upper Mesopotamia, the country of the Sumerians in today's southern Iraq required artificial irrigation to develop and a great deal of well-organized labor, rendering it extremely fertile. The mill wheel in the text should, therefore, be understood in a literal sense.

2 For a comprehensive presentation, see Abdullah Öcalan, *Sümer Rahip Devletinden Demokratik Uygarlığa: AİHM Savunmaları I. Cilt I.* (Neuss: Mezopotamien Verlag, 2002); in English, see *Prison Writings: The Roots of Civilization* (London: Pluto Press, 2007).

3 This is a reference to Sultan Mehmed III (1566–1603), but fratricide was a fairly frequent phenomenon among Ottoman sultanates.

4 Murray Bookchin, *The Ecology of Freedom: The Emergence and Dissolution of Hierarchy* (Cheshire Books, 1982).

5 In the patriarchal pantheon of the Sumerians, En was the god of the heavens and Enlil the god of the wind. Ra was the Egyptian god of the sun.

6 The term "surplus product" describes all products that exceed the immediate needs for survival.

7 The latter term, "private prostitution," refers to the institution of marriage; see Öcalan, *Sümer Rahip Devletinden Demokratik Uygarlığa*; in English, see *Prison Writings: The Roots of Civilization* (London: Pluto Press, 2007).

8 Giordano Bruno advocated a pantheism according to which God was present in everything. At the time, the Church treated pantheism as equivalent of atheism.

9 "Perhaps, too, we should abandon a whole tradition that allows us to imagine that knowledge can exist only where the power relations are suspended and that knowledge can develop only outside its injunctions, its demands and its interests.... We should admit rather that power produces knowledge...; that power and knowledge directly imply one another; that there is no power relation without the correlative constitution of a field of knowledge, nor any knowledge that does not presuppose and constitute at the same time power relations. These 'power-knowledge relations' are to be analyzed, therefore, not on the basis of a subject of knowledge who is or is not free in relation to the power system, but, on the contrary, the subject who knows, the objects to be known and the modalities of knowledge must be regarded as so many effects of these fundamental implications of power-knowledge and their historical transformations"; Michel Foucault, *Discipline and Punish: The Birth of the Prison* (New York: Pantheon Books, 1977), 8.

Feudal Statist Society

1 The use of the term "ethnic" might be considered as problematic, as it has come to be used almost synonymously with "race" in expressions such as "ethnic cleansing." The author uses "ethnic" in the sense of "autochthonous." Here, it is not the relation to a certain location that is important but the organizational form that lies somewhere between the tribal society and societies organized in the form of the state.

2 *El* is an old Semitic word for *spirit* which underwent an evolution from the *Elohim* of Abraham to *Ilah*, and then to *Allah*, see Abdullah Öcalan, *Sümer*

Rahip Devletinden Demokratik Uygarlığa: AİHM Savunmaları I. Cilt I. (Neuss: Mezopotamien Verlag, 2002); in English, see *Prison Writings: The Roots of Civilization* (London: Pluto Press, 2007).

3   *"Shadow of God,"* or *zillullah,* was one of the designations of the caliph.

4   G.W.F. Hegel, *Outlines of the Philosophy of Right* (New York: Oxford University Press, 2008), 233-34.

5   The *ilmiye* was one of four institutions that existed within the state organization of the Ottoman Empire, the other three were: the imperial (*mülkiye*) institution; the military (*seyfiye*) institution; and the administrative (*kalemiye*) institution. The function of the ilmiye was to propagate the Muslim religion, to ensure that Islamic law was enforced properly within the courts, as well as to ensure that it was interpreted and taught properly within the Ottoman school system. The development of the ilmiye took place over the course of the sixteenth century, absorbing the *ulema,* the educated class of Muslim legal scholars in the process.

6   This refers to the religious community of the Yazidi. The charge that they were devil worshippers was mostly made by Muslims who hoped to defame and discredit them. Actually, the Yazidi believed that God later forgave the fallen angel and brought him back to the place by his side.

7   In Sumerian mythology, the goddess Inanna chose her lovers and consummated the sacred nuptials with them. It was through the act of love that the earth became fertile again each year.

8   Miriam was herself a prophet (Exodus 15:20). She criticized Moses (Numbers 12:1) on the grounds that God also spoke to her and to Aaron. God, however, clearly places Moses above Miriam and punishes her with leprosy (Numbers 12:10-14). Miriam's fate is seen as a warning not to transgress against the priestly orders (Deuteronomy 24:9).

9   There was a great controversy around Aisha, because she became enmeshed in a situation that gave the appearance of infidelity. Ali, therefore, demanded her execution.

10 "The state, therefore, has not existed from all eternity. There have been societies which have managed without it, which had no notion of the state or state power. At a definite stage of economic development, which necessarily involved the cleavage of society into classes, the state became a necessity because of this cleavage. We are now rapidly approaching a stage in the development of production at which the existence of these classes has not only ceased to be a necessity, but becomes a positive hindrance to production. They will fall as inevitably as they once arose. The state inevitably falls with them. The society which organizes production anew on the basis of free and equal association of the producers will put the whole state machinery where it will then belong—into the museum of antiquities, next to the spinning wheel and the bronze ax"; Frederick Engels, "The Origin of the Family, Private Property and the State," in Karl Marx and Frederick Engels, *Selected Works,* vol. 3 (Moscow: Progress Publishers, 1977), accessed November 1, 2021, https://www.marxists. org/archive/marx/works/download/pdf/originfamily.pdf.

11 See Immanuel Wallerstein, *Utopistics or Historical Choices of the Twenty-First Century* (New York: New Press, 1998).

12 In Islam, *ijtihad* is the name of an independent religious-philosophical discussion to find the solution to questions of law. From the eleventh century onward, it was massively limited by conservative imams, particularly Imam al-Ghazali; see Öcalan, *Sümer Rahip Devletinden Demokratik Uygarlığa*, 277.

13 The return to the Greek philosophy, known as "classical philosophy" since then, was a result of the engagement of Albertus Magnus, Thomas Aquinas, and others with its Islamic interpretation. Thus, in the thirteenth century, the texts of Aristotle, for example, were translated into Latin, not from Greek but from Arabic.

14 The Levh-i Mahfûz, Arabic for the *protected tablet*, is the divine Islamic book where all that has happened and will happen is written.

15 The Mu'tazilites are an unorthodox current of Islam that believes, among other things, that humans are in the possession of free will.

16 The Ishraqiyun are an Islamic current, which is also called "illuminationist (*ishraqi*)" philosophy, that can be traced back to the philosopher Suhrawardi (1153–1191).

17 For example, there is also an open form of slavery in Thomas More, *Utopia* (Mineola, NY: Dover Publications, 1997 [1516]).

18 The preceding sentence is: "The bourgeoisie, historically, has played a most revolutionary role"; Karl Marx and Frederick Engels, "Manifesto of the Communist Party," in Karl Marx and Frederick Engels, *Selected Works*, vol. 1 (Moscow: Progress Publishers, 1969), accessed July 8, 2021, https://www.marxists.org/archive/marx/works/download/pdf/Manifesto.pdf.

19 Thomas Hobbes, *Leviathan* (London, Oxford University Press, 1909 [1651]), accessed July 8, 2021, http://files.libertyfund.org/files/869/0161_Bk.pdf.

20 In the Revelations (13:11) of St. John, this false messiah is an animal with two horns like a lamb that speaks like a dragon. Later on, it is called a false prophet (Revelations 16:13). The Islamic tradition refers to the Dajjal, the false messiah who will deceive the world. The Dajjal is not, however, mentioned in the Koran.

21 This was written in 2004, while George W. Bush was in power.

22 This is a Turkish play on words. In Turkish *genelev* euphemistically means *a brothel* and literally means *a public house*, whereas *özelev* means *a private home* and refers to the institution of the family.

The Democratic and Ecological Society

1 Here, the author refers to the legend of Abraham in the Koran, 21:51–70; cf. Abdullah Öcalan, *Sümer Rahip Devletinden Demokratik Uygarlığa: AİHM Savunmaları I. Cilt I.* (Neuss: Mezopotamien Verlag, 2002); Abdullah Öcalan, *Kutsallık ve Lanetin Simgesi Urfa* (Neuss: Mezopotamien Verlag, 2001).

2 Tiamat, Marduk's mother, is depicted as a dragon, and gets killed and cut to pieces by him, after which Marduk becomes the most powerful of all gods.

3 This references state formations in the Middle East, such as the Samaritans and the Hurrians, among others, in their struggle with the Sumerian city-states, that faced the alternative of submission or of founding their own states.

4   An *aşiret* is a federation of tribal communities.

5   Big landowners and princes.

6   Thus, even the god-king Gilgamesh was unable to carry out his personal crusade against the monster Humbaba, who lived in the forest, without previously getting the assent of the council of the elders. Quite obviously, here, Humbaba represents a tribe defending the forest against the attackers from Uruk.

7   The Hyksos were a Semitic people who conquered Egypt in 1648 BCE. The country was governed by a Hyksos dynasty until circa 1540 BCE.

8   The legend of the Newroz celebration (March 21) recounts the victory over the tyrant Dehak, a symbol for the end of the Assyrian Empire in 612 BCE.

9   In the legend, Medea, who was kidnapped from the eastern coast of the Black Sea by Jason, appears as the daughter of a king and a powerful sorceress. Looking at the drama of Euripides, Evelyn Reed interprets her struggle with Theseus over their common children as the struggle of a matricentric culture against the patriarchal tradition of Athens. Medea is also regarded as the ancestress of the Medes; Euripides, "Medea," in *Medea and Other Plays*, trans. Philip Vellacott (Baltimore: Penguin Books, 1963), accessed July 9, 2021, https://vemos.typepad. com/files/medea.pdf; Evelyn Reed, *Woman's Evolution: From Matriarchal Clan to Patriarchal Family* (New York: Pathfinder Press, 1975).

10 Here, the author refers to the Sumerian myth of the flood, which was also the apparent model for versions in the Bible and the Koran.

11 Koran, 11:44.

12 See Abdullah Öcalan, *Kutsallık ve Lanetin Simgesi Urfa* (Cologne: Mezopotamien Verlag, 2001).

13 At the time, the name of Urfa was Edessa.

14 In Islam, Idris is the biblical Enoch.

15 This is the Koranic version of history.

16 According to Koran 21:69, God saved him by preventing the flames from burning him.

17 In Islam, Abraham is regarded as the first prophet.

18 Corresponding to the interpretation of a column of clouds, a column of fire, and the splendor on Moses's face as the signs of a volcano.

19 This is an allusion to the giant "Office for Religious Affairs" in "laicist" Turkey.

20 The author is referring to the "Anatolia hypothesis" of Professor Colin Renfrew, who postulates a connection between the spreading of both a proto-Indo-European language and agricultural techniques from a core area in Anatolia. He regards terms that are closely connected to these cultural techniques and are found in the entire Indo-European language area as a significant support for his thesis. Opposed to this is the older hypothesis, according to which the speakers of the Indo-European languages only later immigrated into Mesopotamia and the region of today's Iran.

21 At one time *Sephardim* designated Jews on the Iberian Peninsula. After the Jews were driven out of Spain from the seventh to the tenth century, collections of poetry emerged that gave comprehensive descriptions of Sephardic life and the lives of their ancestors.

22 Mawlana (1207–1273), also known as Rumi, was the founder of a mystic Sufi order and a poet.

23 The *dergah* is an Islamic monastery, particularly of Sufi orders.

24 Batiniyya refers to groups that distinguish between an outer, or exoteric, and an inner, or esoteric (*bāṭin*), meaning in Islamic scriptures.

25 Kharijites (the outsiders) were adherents of one of the three original schools of Islam. They did not acknowledge any of the caliphs and were held responsible for the death of Ali. Later on, the word became a common designation for infidels in general.

26 The Qarmatians (also: Karmathians) were a militant İsmaili communal movement that organized protracted uprisings in the ninth century. Hassan Sabah was the leader of the famous İsmaili congregation, the Assassins, who fought the Abbasid caliphs in the twelfth-century Shia counter-dynasty in Egypt. The religious community of the Alawites is often forcibly "co-opted" by Muslims and subjected to great pressure to assimilate. At this point, there are strong efforts in both Turkey and Germany to have them recognized as an autonomous religious community. In Turkey and in Kurdistan, the Alawites were often persecuted by Sunnis and fascists. Hundreds of Alawites were murdered during the 1978 Maraş massacre.

27 On the metaphor of the flow of civilization, see Abdullah Öcalan, *Sümer Rahip Devletinden Demokratik Uygarlığa: AİHM Savunmaları I. Cilt I.* (Neuss: Mezopotamien Verlag, 2002).

28 The 1982 Turkish constitution was adopted two years into the military coup, includes the phrase "inseparable identity of the state and the nation." Because of this doctrine, the mere act of mentioning the existence of another nation within Turkey is immediately regarded as separatism.

29 The term *"iç oğlan"* (lads of the interior [palace]) refers to the boy servants or pages who had been received from Christian parents in the Balkans and converted, according to the *devşirme* system in the Ottoman Empire—the staff serving in the private apartments of the Sultan and his family.

30 Tommaso Campanello (1568–1639), *The City of the Sun* (1623); Thomas More (1478–1535), *Utopia* (London: Cassell and Company, 1901 [1516]), accessed July 10, 2021, https://www.gutenberg.org/files/2130/2130-h/2130-h.htm; Francis Bacon (1561–1626), *New Atlantis*, (London: John Crooke, 1660 [1626]), accessed July 10, 2021, https://archive.org/details/fnewatlantisoobaco/page/n4; Charles Fourier (1772–1837), *The Utopian Vision of Charles Fourier: Selected Texts on Work, Love, and Passionate Attraction* (Boston: Beacon Press, 1971), accessed July 10, 2021, https://archive.org/details/TheUtopianVisionOfCharlesFourierSelectedTe xtsOnWorkLoveAndPassionateAttraction; Robert Owen (1771–1858), *A New Conception of Society* (London: Cadell and Davies, Strand, 1813), accessed July 10, 2021, https://archive.org/details/anewviewsocietyooowengoog/page/n4; Pierre-Joseph Proudhon (1809–1865), *What Is Property?* (Princeton, MA: Benj. R. Tucker, 1876), accessed July 10, 2021, https://libcom.org/files/Proudhon%20 -%20What%20is%20Property.pdf.

31 Karl Marx and Frederick Engels, "Manifesto of the Communist Party," in *Selected Works*, vol. 1 (Moscow: Progress Publishers, 1969 [1848]), 98–137, accessed July

10, 2021, https://www.marxists.org/archive/marx/works/download/pdf/Manifesto.pdf.

32 Karl Marx, *Capital*, vol. 1, (Moscow: Progress Publishers, 1965 [1867]), accessed July 10, 2021, https://www.marxists.org/archive/marx/works/download/pdf/Capital-Volume-I.pdf.

33 Frederick Engels, *The Origin of the Family, Private Property and the State* (Chicago: Charles Kerr & Co., 1908 [1884]), accessed July 10, 2021, https://archive.org/stream/theoriginofthefa33111gut/33111-8.txt.

34 In the Middle East green is normally identified as the color of Islam.

A Blueprint for a Democratic and Ecological Society

1 See Murray Bookchin, *Urbanization without Cities: The Rise and Decline of Citizenship* (Montréal: Black Rose Books, 1992), accessed July 10, 2021, https://libcom.org/files/Urbanization_Without_Cities_-_Ebook.pdf.

2 Immanuel Wallerstein, *Utopistics, or, Historical Choices of the Twenty-First Century* (New York: New Press, 1988).

3 Here the author uses *devletli*, which literally means *with the state* but among the people has the meaning of *great and wealthy*.

4 The original quote reads: "The psyche of the great masses is not receptive to anything that is half-hearted and weak. Like the woman, whose psychic state is determined less by grounds of abstract reason than by an indefinable emotional longing for a force which will complement her nature, and who, consequently, would rather bow to a strong man than dominate a weakling, likewise the masses love a commander more than a petitioner and feel inwardly more satisfied by a doctrine, tolerating no other beside itself, than by the granting of liberalistic freedom with which, as a rule, they can do little, and are prone to feel that they have been abandoned"; Adolf Hitler, *Mein Kampf*, translated by Ralph Manheim (Boston: Houghton Mifflin Company, 1943), 42.

5 The Greek *oikos* and the Roman *familia* are systems in which the man of the house has total control over the house, the farm, and the farmhands, a control that includes sexual control.

6 In Turkish, "women's sickness" is a common expression for menstruation.

7 Samuel N. Kramer, *History Begins at Sumer: Thirty-Nine Firsts in Recorded History* (Philadelphia: University of Pennsylvania Press, 1988).

8 Since March 8, 1996, the ideology of independent women's organization within the Kurdish freedom movement has been called the ideology of women's freedom.

9 This alludes to the group around Osman Öcalan, who married a woman thirty years younger than himself and openly admitted to having sabotaged the women's movement.

10 Laila and Majnun are the main characters in a medieval epic about two lovers who never unite. Majnun despairs for his love and slides into madness. Sufism is a mystical Islamic current in which the love to Allah plays a huge role.

11 See Murray Bookchin, *The Ecology of Freedom: The Emergence and Dissolution of Hierarchy* (Montréal: Black Rose Books, 1990), 316.

12 See Bookchin, ibid., 319.

Chaos in the Middle East Civilization and Ways Out

1   This refers to Samuel Huntington, *The Clash of Civilizations and the Remaking of World Order* (New York: Simon & Schuster, 1996).

2   This remark refers to the coalition troops that occupied Iraq and toppled the regime of Saddam Hussein in 2003.

3   In the legend of Noah in the Koran, the ark lands at the mountain of Cûdî in Northern Kurdistan.

4   Independent or original interpretations of problems not covered by the Koran, Hadith, or scholarly consensus.

5   A secondary educational institution, founded in lieu of a vocational school to train government employed imams.

6   In the valley of Hinnom (Ge-Hinnom), South of Jerusalem, where sacrifices were offered to the Moloch. *Hinnom* is the source of the word from which the Arab word for *hell* developed (2 Kings 23:10).

7   See Abdullah Öcalan, *Sümer Rahip Devletinden Demokratik Uygarlığa: AİHM Savunmaları Cilt I* (Neuss: Mezopotamien Verlag, 2002), 52.

8   One of four institutions that existed in the Ottoman empire. Its role was to propagate the Muslim religion, to ensure that Islamic law was enforced properly by the courts, and that it was interpreted and taught properly in the Ottoman school system.

9   We must name Albertus Magnus, in particular, who translated many works from Arabic.

10 Here we need to mention, for example, Dante's *Divine Comedy*, which draws heavily on mythological and religious motifs, accessed July 13, 2021, http://www.gutenberg.org/files/8800/8800-h/8800-h.htm.

11 "Shadow of God" was the title of Ottoman sultans.

12 As in the Book of Revelation, chapter 20.

13 "Compradors" are the local profiteers within an imperialist economic relationship.

14 Memê Alan is an older version of the legend of the two lovers Mem and Zîn, the main work of the poet Ehmedê Xanî, which is written in verse. It was written in 1692 and is renowned as a Kurdish national epic. In it, Xanî openly complains about the inability of the Kurdish princes to develop any form of unity. This historic Yazidi leader lived at the end of the seventeenth century. Even today, Kurdish bards sing the story of his struggles and his unfulfilled love to Adulê.

15 In the original myth, Inanna had two companions. In later narratives, Dumuzi, the biblical Tammuz (Ezekiel 8:15), rises to the position of coregent, while Enkimdu is reduced to being her son. The comparison with the story of the farmer Cain and the shepherd Abel (Genesis 4), who compete for God's affection, is interesting.

16 The three goddesses are Lat, Manāt, and Uzza, the goddesses of the three most important cities: of Mecca, Medina, and Taif.

17 This formulation is meant as a criticism of the Kurdish men who defend the "honor" and virginity of female family members, while Kurdistan as a whole is being materially and culturally plundered, or, one might say, "raped."

18   *Tariqa* (plural *tariqat*) is Arabic for *road(s)* and is the name for religious brother-hoods or orders in the Sufi tradition. Within them, the clear hierarchy is primarily between the enlightened *murshid* and his followers, the *murid*. A *silsila*, or ancestral lineage, is often traced back to Mohammad. The leader or *murshid* himself appoints his successor, who is frequently a son or other rela-tive. These orders often enjoy considerable political and economic influence. In Turkey and Kurdistan, different branches of the *tariqa* of the Naqshbandi are particularly widespread.

19   In Islam, the *umma* is the community of all faithful Muslims, independently of the affiliation to a tribe or a nation.

20   For the Shiites, Mohammad's family plays a particularly important role. Thus, the Shiite imams are regarded as descendants of Ali, Mohammad's son-in-law.

21   Arius, a priest from Alexandria, taught that Jesus was not consubstantial with God, merely his most noble creation. Under the influence of Constantine the Great, Arius was excommunicated and condemned at the Council of Nicaea in 325, but Arianism lived on until the sixth century among the Goths, Vandals, and Lombards.

22   Murray Bookchin defines usufruct in organic societies as "the freedom of indi-viduals in a community to appropriate resources merely by virtue of the fact that they are using them. Such resources belong to the user as long as they are being used.… [T]he collective claim is implicit in the primacy of usufruct over proprietorship"; Murray Bookchin, *The Ecology of Freedom: The Emergence and Dissolution of Hierarchy* (Montréal: Black Rose Books, 1990), 50.

23   The word *Ayyubids* is derived from Ayyub, the father of Saladin the Great and the founder of a Kurdish dynasty. The Barmakids were a Persian family of highly placed state functionaries under the Abbasids (750–803).

24   The word *mezhep* is used to describe the various main denominations of Islam, for example, the Sunni and the Shite denominations.

25   Genesis 1:28.

The Current Situation in the Middle East and Probable Developments

1   One of the humanity's oldest traditional narratives is the "Curse of Agade." It was written in the twenty-second century BCE after Akkadian troops had laid the Sumerian city of Nippur to waste.

2   Books like *The Art of War* by Sun Tzu.

3   The original title of this book is *In Defense of the People*.

4   Samuel Huntington, *The Clash of Civilizations and the Remaking of World Order* (New York: Simon & Schuster, 1996).

5   The main work of the Dutch humanist Desiderius Erasmus of Rotterdam; see Desiderius Erasmus, *In Praise of Folly* (Grand Rapids: University of Michigan Press, 1958 [1509]), accessed July 17, 2021, http://www.documentacatholicaomnia. eu/03d/1466-1536,_Erasmus_Roterodamus,_In_Praise_Of_Folly,_EN.pdf.

6   Mawlana is the honorary title given the Islamic mystic Jalāl ad-Dīn Rumi (1207–1273). Mani (216–276) was the founder of Manichaeism, which unified elements of Christianity, Buddhism, and Zoroastrianism. Suhrawardi (1153–1191) was an

Islamic mystic; see Shihāb al-Din al-Suhrawardi, *The Philosophy of Illumination* (Chicago: University of Chicago Press, 2000).

7   This thesis about the emergence of the state is extensively developed in Abdullah Öcalan, *Sümer Rahip Devletinden Demokratik Uygarlığa: AİHM Savunmaları I. Cilt I.* (Neuss: Mezopotamien Verlag, 2002).

8   Called *kahvehane* or *kıraathane*, it is an exclusively male place, where tobacco products, but not food or alcohol, are served, card games among other games are played, and discussions and many different activities take place. These cafés have served different purposes over time but have become a sites of decay rather than enlightenment over the last fifty years or so.

9   Superficially, the dispute known as the Arianus controversy was about theological questions. For a long time, the followers of Arius were primarily found in the Eastern Church.

10 Emperor Constantine claimed to owe his victory in the Battle at the Milvian Bridge in 312 CE to a vision of Christ. This victory made him the sole ruler of the Western Roman Empire. His tolerance edict of the following year is regarded as the end of the persecution of the Christians.

11 The *höyük* are hills where the remnants of Neolithic settlements have been found.

12 Mazlum Doğan and Kemal Pir were both founding members of the PKK. At the age of twenty-four, Mazlum Doğan began the resistance in the Diyarbakır prison to end the severe repression both in prisons and outside, he is famously quoted as saying: "We love life to the point of dying for it when necessary." He lost his life on Newroz, March 21, 1982, while protesting the repression. Ferhat Kurtay, one of the leading PKK cadres, immolated himself along with three others on May 18, 1982, in the infamous Diyarbakır prison, following Mazlum Doğan's lead in protesting both the brutality in prison and against the society at large and the freedom movement. Kemal Pir, from the Black Sea region and Laz, lost his life on hunger strike on July 14, 1982, in the same prison.

13 "War is simply a continuation of political intercourse, with the addition of other means"; Carl von Clausewitz, *On War*, ed. and trans. Michael Howard and Peter Paret, (Princeton, NJ: Princeton University Press, 1976), accessed July 21, 2021, https://antilogicalism.com/wp-content/uploads/2019/04/on-war.pdf, generally quoted in its shorter form as "war is the continuation of politics with other means"; ibid.

14 Mazdak was a religious leader whose followers (the Mazdakites) formed a social revolutionary movement during the fifth century that lasted for several centuries. They promoted equality and communal property. Babak Khorramdin (798–838) led a twenty-year uprising against the Abbasids.

15 In the Turkish original, *baş bağlama* is an expression that refers to getting engaged or married, literally meaning *tying* or *covering the head*, in this sentence Öcalan uses a word play and paraphrases this expression to include the mind as well as the head not being tied down or covered, which is, of course, also the literal meaning for a headscarf.

16 The term "yellow union" refers to a union that works hand in hand with the state and the employers and not in the interests of the workers it allegedly represents.

17 In the aftermath of the defeat and collapse of the Ottoman Empire following World War I, a war of independence was waged under the leadership of Mustafa Kemal Atatürk from May 1919 to June 1923. In those years and the early years of the Republic of Turkey, many radical reforms were implemented. The 1920s were therefore a transitional period in which the ultimate direction of the republic was not yet clear.

The Kurdish Phenomenon and the Kurdish Question in the Chaos of the Middle East

1 The PKK dissolved itself at its eighth congress, and, on April 4, 2002, the Kongreya Azadi u Demokrasiya Kurdistan (KADEK: Congress for Freedom and Democracy Kurdistan) was founded. It was in turn dissolved in October 2003. The Kongra Gel (KGK: People's Congress of Kurdistan), founded in October 2003, was conceived of as a broad direct democratic structure. "Civilians," i.e., people who had not been active in the guerrilla, were elected to leading positions.

2 The detailed discussion of the name *Kurdistan* is necessary in response to a decades-old assimilation policy in Turkey. It is still widely believed that "there is no Kurdistan" and that "there has never been a Kurdistan."

3 Urartu is the name of an empire that existed from around 900 BCE to approximately 600 BCE, with Tušpa, today's Van, as its capital. The ethnic and linguistic structure of Urartu is unclear; the Urartian language is related both to Hurrian and the Eastern Caucasian languages. Incorrectly pronounced, *Urartu* became *Ararat*.

4 The word appears in Sumerian written sources and refers to tribes living in the Zagros Mountains.

5 1876–1878 and 1908–1918.

6 In Kurdish, the grammatical gender of most nouns is feminine. Among the Sumerians, we encounter Star as Inanna and among the Akkadians, as Ishtar (later, Astarte). Even today, in Kurdish, she is called "Ya Star!"

7 Many Zoroastrian concepts were adopted by Jewish thought and Greek philosophy.

8 The Medes, who have often been regarded as the predecessors of the Kurds, destroyed the Great Assyrian Empire of the seventh century BCE. In 585 BCE, they expanded their empire to the Halys (today, Kızılırmak) in Western Anatolia. Later on, under Cyrus II, the Achaemenid dynasty rose to power.

9 Herodotus, *The Histories*, trans. George Rawlinson (Moscow, ID: Roman Roads Media, 2013), accessed July 24, 2021, https://files.romanroadsstatic.com/materials/herodotus.pdf.

10 Manichaeism contains elements from Zoroastrianism, Christianity, and Buddhism.

11 See Abdullah Öcalan, *Sümer Rahip Devletinden Demokratik Uygarlığa: AİHM Savunmaları I. Cilt I.* (Neuss: Mezopotamien Verlag, 2002) Öcalan.

12 The most important representative of the Ayyubid dynasty was Sultan Saladin.

13 The Şerefhanoğulları are descendants of Şerefhan (1543–1599 CE), the author of the *Şerefnama*.

14 The Shammar are one of the largest tribes in the Arab world. A major part of the Arab population of Iraq traces its roots back to the Shammar. Some of their extended families have long been among the elite of the country, both under the Ottomans and under British rule, and later under Saddam's regime. In 2004, Ghazi al-Yawear, a Shammarn emir became the president of Iraq.

15 İdris of Bitlis (1452 to 1520 CE) was a high ranking official and a military leader under the Ottoman sultan Selim I. After the battle of Chaldiran, he convinced the Kurdish princes to cooperate with the sultan. Şerefhan, the prince of Bitlis, was one of his descendants.

16 The Naqshbandi Brotherhood has existed since the fourteenth century and is one of today's most influential brotherhoods in the Middle East. Its leaders always try to move in circles close to political power. The former Turkish prime minister, now president, Erdogan, is close to the Naqshbandi, and the Barzani family is a clan of Naqshbandi sheiks.

17 In the Sumerian cities, including Uruk, wood was rare. Therefore, in the Sumerian original version of the epic, Gilgamesh's aim is the forests of the Zagros Mountains. Lebanon only becomes the goal of the expedition in the later Babylonian versions.

18 Elbistan is a district in the province of Maraş.

19 The peace treaty following the Battle of Kadesh, concluded between the Egyptian and the Hittite Empires in 1270 BCE, is the oldest known peace treaty.

20 See Herodotus, *The Histories.*

21 Ctesiphon, which was forty kilometers [approximately twenty-five miles] south of Baghdad, was the capital of the Parthian Empire. The battle itself took place at Carrhae, today's Harran.

22 Pir Sultan Abdal was a popular Alevi cleric. He authored many poems and songs that are recited and sung to this day and is regarded as a symbol of resistance.

23 In 1416, the Sunni Sheikh Bedreddin led a major popular uprising against the Ottoman sultan. He was hanged in 1420. The Turkish writer Nazim Hikmet devoted one of his best-known works to him.

24 The Celali rebellions were uprisings in Anatolia over a two-hundred-year period. The first of these took place in Bozok, in 1510, and was led by Sheikh Celal. The following sequence of uprisings were all named after him.

25 Ismail Agha Simko, the Kurdish tribal leader of the Shikak (1887–1930), organized uprisings against the Persian Shah Reza Pahlavi. Between 1918 and 1922, he controlled a large territory in East Kurdistan. He was murdered in 1930 at a sham "meeting" with an Iranian general. In January 1946, a Kurdish republic was proclaimed and was crushed by the Iranian military the same year.

26 Erdoğan'dan bir işçiye: Kürt sorunu yok, December 24, 2002, accessed July 26, 2021, https://www.hurriyet.com.tr/gundem/erdogan-dan-bir-isciye-kurt-sorunu-yok-117716.

27 Big land owners, princes, Muslim pilgrims, and Muslim scholars.

28 When this book was first published (2004), the ceasefire proclaimed by the Hêzên Parastina Gel (HPG; the People's Defense Forces) had been in force for five and a half years.

29 Abdullah Öcalan, *Kürdistan'da Zorun Rolü* (Cologne: Weşanên Serxwebûn, 1982). This book played a key role in the development of the Kurdish guerrilla.

30 This likely refers to the Hittite cuneiform texts that present the oldest written examples of an Indo-European language. The oldest findings date back to around 1600 BCE.

31 The Turkish terminology used by the author does not exactly correspond to the English one. In English, the ethnological concepts are rendered as follows: clan (*klan*), lineage (*soy*), tribe (*kabile*), federation of tribal communities (*aşiret*), tribe (*boy*), a community that shares a common territory irrespective of ethnic make-up (*kavim*), people (*halk*).

32 See Murray Bookchin, *Urbanization without Cities: The Rise and Decline of Citizenship* (Montréal: Black Rose Books, 1992).

33 As is visible from the definition the author gives here, he is not talking about the Kurmanji-speaking Kurds.

34 Abdullah Öcalan himself belongs to the Kurmanj group, in whose development aşiret relationships play no role. The PKK, which he cofounded, from the beginning radically opposed the Kurdish aşiret aristocracy and aşiret structures in general. The subtler perspective on the aşiret sketched out in this text represents a significant shift in Öcalan's thinking.

35 Kurdish for *worker*, as in Partiya Karkerên Kurdistan (PKK: Kurdistan Workers' Party).

36 See Öcalan, *Sümer Rahip Devletinden Demokratik Uygarlığa*.

37 In Kurdistan, it is customary that the followers of a sheikh work on his manors for free.

38 Thus, the Kurd Ziya Gökalp (1876–1924) is regarded as one of the intellectual fathers of Turkish nationalism.

39 In Turkish these are: "alavere dalavere, Kürt Mehmet nöbete" and "Kürt ne bilir bayramı, hor hor içer ayranı"; ayran is a drink made of water and yogurt.

40 Even though Turkey calls itself a "laic" state, there is no genuine separation of state and religion, and the state tries to exert total control over religion. Only the Sunni Islam is promoted, while all other religions and denominations face massive obstruction.

41 They were founded as schools to train government-employed imams.

42 Mustafa Kemal Atatürk was the founder of the Republic of Turkey and its president from 1923 until his death in 1938.

43 Until 1946, Turkey was ruled by a one-party system. When the Demokrat Parti (DP: Democrat Party) arose as the first opposition party, it immediately won the parliamentary elections of 1950 and became the only party in government. After the military coup of 1960, it was banned, and three of its leading members, among them the former prime minister Adnan Menderes, were executed on the prison island of İmralı. The Adalet Partisi (AP: Justice Party) was the successor party to the DP and was also removed from power in a coup, in 1980.

44 The Adalet ve Kalkınma Partisi (AKP: Justice and Development Party) emerged as the successor party of the banned Refah and Fazilet Partisi (FP: Virtue Party) when Recep Tayyip Erdoğan parted ways with his political mentor Necmettin Erbakan. In the first elections in which it ran, in 2002, the AKP won an absolute majority of the seats and has governed without a coalition partner since then.

45 This strategy aimed at hemming in the Soviet Union on its southern flank in the Caucasus and in Central Asia with a "green belt" of Islamic movements. With that goal in mind, the US also supported movements like the mujaheddin in Afghanistan.

46 Fethullah Gülen has been living in the USA since 1999, before there were any criminal proceedings opened against him. Since 2000, he is faced with a trial in Turkey. Gülen exercises control over an enormous international media and educational empire that once included Turkey's most widely circulated newspaper, *Zaman*. Gülen has acted as the representative of "moderate Islam." His adherents had considerable political influence in Turkey before the AKP and Fethullah Gülen fell out. Fethullah Gülen was particularly ferocious in Kurdish areas, where he was trying to attain significant political influence.

47 The conservative Anavatan Partisi (ANAP: Motherland Party) was founded in 1983 by Turgut Özal, the first prime minister following the military coup and later the president. After Turgut Özal, Mesut Yılmaz became chairman of the party. The ANAP, was the governing party from 1999 to 2002 but splintered thereafter and dissolved in 2009.

48 Abdülmelik Fırat is one of the grandsons of Sheikh Said. He was an MP of the DP and later the chairman of the Kurdish HAK-PAR. He died on September 29, 2009. Cüneyd Zapsu was one of the most influential members of the AKP. He is regarded as the architect of relations between the AKP and the US. After claims that his company was involved in financing al-Qaeda, he left politics. Hüseyin Çelik was minister of education in Recep Tayyip Erdoğan's first cabinet. Even though he is a Kurd, as minister of education, he did all he could to prevent Kurdish from being taught at state schools or universities. Zeki Ergezen is also a Kurd, but he has never done anything to defend the interests of the Kurds. He has been in parliament representing various political parties since 1991 and was the minister for public works and housing from 2002 to 2005.

49 Thus, both Barzani and Talabani openly called on the Kurds in Turkey to vote for the AKP in the parliamentary and municipal elections.

50 The Cumhuriyet Halk Partisi (CHP: Republican People's Party) was founded by Mustafa Kemal Atatürk and was the ruling party during the one-party system that existed until 1946. In the 1960s and 1970s, the CHP pursued a nationalist social democratic policy. But, in recent years, under the chairmanship of Deniz Baykall, it has entirely banked on Turkish nationalism.

51 Saudi Wahhabism is the extremely conservative variety of Sunnism that, among other things, provided the roots for al-Qaeda.

52 "Tanzimat reforms" (salutary reforms) is the name for a period of radical reforms in the Ottoman Empire from 1838 to 1876. It is closely connected with the viziers Mustafa Reşid Pasha, Ali Pasha, and Fuad Pasha.

53 During the last years of the Ottoman Empire, the Ottoman army was reorganized by German officers. The genocide of the Armenians and Assyrians in 1915 took place under the eyes of the German army.

54 The Milliyetçi Hareket Partisi (MHP: Nationalist Movement Party) of Alpaslan Türkeş, one of the 1960 coup plotters, is a militantly fascist party whose members are also called the Bozkurtlar (Grey Wolves). It entered the government in 1999, after having promised during its electoral campaign to have Abdullah Öcalan executed.

55 A nationalist rhetoric taken up by all officials in Turkey, including Prime Minister Tansu Çiller, who is also quoted as saying, "We give our lives, but not a pebble," meaning any territory, not even as small as a pebble. She made this statement in 1996 when Turkey took war on Kurds to another level.

56 In many electoral districts, parties did not run their own candidates, instead supporting the candidate of a pro-state party in order to prevent a victory of the pro-Kurdish Demokratik Toplum Partisi (DTP: Democratic Society Party).

57 During the Iraqi military's chemical weapons attack of the Kurdish town of Halabja, on March 16, 1988, at least five thousand people died.

58 Since 1991 in particular, thousands of Kurdish civilians, including journalists and intellectuals, have been murdered in broad daylight. These state-sponsored crimes have been classified as "murders by unknown perpetrators." They were executed by paramilitary units, including the constabulary secret service, the JITEM, as well as by PKK deserters, village guards, and the Turkish Hezbollah. It is generally assumed that this represented a targeted and deliberate state policy. In an article in the liberal daily *Radikal*, on December 6, 1996, the journalist İsmet Berkan provided concrete proofs: "I am writing these lines based on a document that I was allowed to read only briefly, without being permitted to copy it or to make notes.... Actually, everything began in 1992. At that time, the Turkish general staff radically changed its strategy for fighting the PKK. The technique now used had actually been invented by the Brits. This new technique had two important features. One was to capture terrorists before they could carry out any actions and to kill them, if necessary. The second important pillar was to equate all those who support terrorists materially or ideologically with the terrorists themselves. This change of strategy became part of the agenda of the Milli Güvenlik Kurulu (MGK: National Security Council) at the end of 1992. In an MGK document that the author of these lines personally inspected, both the outlook of the organization to be founded and the persons meant to take over tasks in it were listed. One of the names was Abdullah Çatlı [a killer wanted on an international warrant and one of the key figures in the Susurluk scandal]. Police officers from special units, a few soldiers, and some of Çatlı's friends are also believed to be part of the organization"; Radikal, accessed November 30, 2021, http://www.radikal.com.tr/yazarlar/ismet-berkan/6-yil-sonra-gladio-itirafi-626716. Even though Turkey now claims to have caught the perpetrators of some of the murders, there has actually never been a real reappraisal of or accounting for this state policy. The victims still wait for a resolution of these cases and an apology.

59 The term "execution without a verdict" refers to murdering people during their arrests. What its meant here is that there is no real justice if a case goes to trial.

60 This was a period of reform in the Ottoman Empire that ended with the First Constitutional Era in 1876.

61 The Ottoman Empire's First Constitutional Era, the 1876 promulgation of the Ottoman constitution by members of the Young Ottomans, began on December 23, 1876, and lasted until January 14, 1878. The Young Ottomans were dissatisfied with the Tanzimat and opted instead for a constitutional government similar to those in Europe. The Second Constitutional Era forced Sultan Abdul Hamid II to restore the constitutional monarchy by reviving the Ottoman parliament and the General Assembly of the Ottoman Empire and reinstating the 1876 constitution.

62 Deniz Gezmiş was one of the revolutionary student leaders and the founder of the Türkiye Halk Kurtuluş Ordusu (THKO: People's Liberation Army of Turkey). He was hanged in Ankara on May 6, 1972. Abdullah Öcalan was also detained and in prison at the time.

63 Mahir Çayan was a revolutionary Turkish student leader and the founder of the Türkiye Halk Kurtuluş Partisi-Cephesi (THKP-C: People's Liberation Party-Front of Turkey). He was killed in a massacre in the village Kızıldere on March 30, 1972. İbrahim Kaypakkaya was a revolutionary Maoist. In the 1970s, he founded the Türkiye Komünist Partisi-Marksist-Leninist (TKP/ML: Communist Party of Turkey/Marxist-Leninist) and the Türkiye İşçi ve Köylü Kurtuluş Ordusu (TİKKO: Liberation Army of the Workers and Peasants of Turkey). In 1973, he was brutally tortured to death.

64 In this way, Selim secured the loyalty of the Kurds, which he needed for his campaign against the Iranian Safavids, followed by Egypt, and later, via the Balkans, against the West.

The PKK Movement: Critique, Self-Critique, and Its Reconstruction

1 Together with Abdullah Öcalan, the students Haki Karer and Kemal Pir, who were not ethnically Kurdish but Laz and Turkish, formed the core group from which the PKK later emerged.

2 See Immanuel Wallerstein, *Utopistics or Historical Choices of the Twenty-First Century* (New York: New Press, 1998).

3 Unlike other Kurdish organizations, the PKK did not just fight for an independent state but for a socialist "Federation of the Middle East."

4 "Free areas" was the name given to regions that were under the de facto control of the guerrilla.

5 The first armed actions against the Bucak tribe took place in Hilvan/Siverek in 1979.

6 Mahsum Korkmaz (Agit) became the first commander of the Artêşa Rizgariya Gelê Kurdistan (ARGK: Kurdistan People's Liberation Army). He was killed under suspicious circumstances in a battle in 1986.

7   This remark probably refers to the relative lack of success of the Palestinian groups and the necessity for the PKK to develop its own distinct guerrilla strategy.

8   Mazlum Doğan was cofounder of the PKK and a member of the central committee. In the night of March 20 to March 21, 1982, he set fire to his cell and took his own life to protest against the torture practiced in the Diyarbakır military prison. This was the beginning of the 1982 resistance actions. For more on the conditions in the Diyarbakır military prison, see Muzaffer Ayata, *Diyarbakır Zindanı—Tarihe ateşten bir sayfa* (Cologne: Weşanên Serxwebûn, 1999); Mehdi Zana, *Prison No 5: Eleven Years in Turkish Jails* (Watertown, MA: Blue Crane Books, 1997); Fuat Kav, *Mavi Ring* (Yenişehir/Diyarbakır, Turkey: Aram Yayınları, 2013).

9   Ferhat Kurtay, Eşref Anyık, Mahmut Zengin, and Necmi Önen were cellmates who immolated themselves on the night of May 17 to May 18, 1982, to protest against the prison conditions. Also see Muzaffer Ayata, *Diyarbakır Zindanı*; Fuat Kav, *Mavi Ring*; Mehdi Zana, *Prison No 5*.

10 Guerrilla commander Cemil Işık (Hogir) was noted for his extreme cruelty. He later defected and worked for the notorious military secret service the JITEM. Among other things, he participated in the murder of the Kurdish intellectual Musa Anter.

11 This unauthorized massacre led to the end of the 1993 ceasefire.

12 This intervention by the Turkish army, in which "Islamic reaction" was pronounced the biggest security threat in the country, led to the resignation of Prime Minister Necmettin Erbakan.

13 See Abdullah Öcalan, *Özgür İnsan Savunması* (Cologne: Mezopotamien Verlag, 2003).

14 Allusion to Enkidu of the Gilgamesh epic, who was part human, part animal.

15 The title was also an allusion to Mahir Çayan, *The Path of Revolution in Turkey*.

16 Early on, Öcalan pointed to the parallel between the excesses of the warfare on the part of the state in the form of the "deep state," the Jandarma İstihbarat ve Terörle Mücadele (JITEM: Gendarmerie Intelligence and Counter-Terrorism), the Turkish Hezbollah, and the Ergenekon terror network, on one hand, and the excesses of the gang culture within the PKK, on the other hand. In the course of the investigation against Ergenekon, a number of interconnections between the two structures emerged.

17 *İtirafçı*, a "defector" or a "repenter," is a former PKK member who has shown "active remorse," that is, has provided extensive legal testimony to the judiciary. A particularity of Turkey is that the itirafçı are sometimes released from prison to participate in military operations against the guerrilla. They were also often used to do the extralegal work of the security forces, particularly in the case of JITEM.

18 Öcalan resided outside of Kurdistan after mid-1979, at first in Lebanon and then in Syria.

19 In 1992, the KDP switched sides and joined the Turkish army to fight against the PKK. This two-front war, which the PKK called the "southern war," led to enormous losses for the ARGK guerrilla.

20 These would-be talks held together with the cadres that have come from different areas of praxis, from the mountains to the cities, and this education would include visiting civilians. These analyses would concentrate on expanding upon the ideological issues and political developments and, ultimately, would include an analysis of the reasons the circumstances were not overcome.

21 Abdullah Öcalan, *Declaration on the Democratic Solution of the Kurdish Question* (London: Mesopotamian Publishers, 1999); Abdullah Öcalan, *Sümer Rahip Devletinden Demokratik Uygarlığa: AİHM Savunmaları I. Cilt* (Neuss: Mezopotamien Verlag, 2002); Abdullah Öcalan, *Özgür İnsan Savunması* (Cologne: Mezopotamien Verlag, 2003); Abdullah Öcalan, *Kutsallık ve Lanetin Simgesi Urfa* (Neuss: Mezopotamien Verlag, 2001).

22 Frederick Engels, *Anti-Dühring* (Moscow: Progress Publishers, 1947), part 3, chapter 2, accessed August 7, 2021, https://www.marxists.org/archive/marx/works/1877/anti-duhring.

23 In Turkish, the word *iktidar* refers both to power in general and the persons who are in power. In this translation, it is rendered by the words *power* and *ruler*. But the reader should also keep in mind that both meanings are often simultaneously intended.

24 See Herodotus, *The Histories*, trans. George Rawlinson (Moscow, ID: Roman Roads Media, 2013), accessed July 24, 2021, https://files.romanroadsstatic.com/materials/herodotus.pdf.

25 In the Middle East, Turkey in particular, holding a job as a civil servant is seen as a guarantee of lifetime employment that offers significant protection. However, it demands bureaucratism and a colorless life that leaves no room for any radical change and obliges one to always mind one's own business and never challenge the ruling power.

26 The ceasefire had taken effect on September 1, 1998. After Abdullah Öcalan was abducted, he affirmed that the ceasefire was still in force. In August of that same year, he had called for the guerrilla units to withdraw from the national territory of Turkey. What followed was a phase of relative détente that lasted for several years. When this book was first published in 2004, the ceasefire was still in effect.

27 From 1999 to 2002, Öcalan made various efforts to bring about a solution of the Kurdish question in talks with representatives of Turkey's military and political leadership, including writing letters to the prime ministers Bülent Ecevit, Abdullah Gül, and Recep Tayyip Erdoğan and engaging in talks with representatives of the military and the secret services on İmralı Island.

28 The KNK, however, did not join the Kongra Gel but carried on as an autonomous organization.

29 Within the KADEK, a group formed around the former central committee members Nizamettin Taş, Osman Öcalan, Hıdır Yalçın, Kani Yılmaz, and Hıdır Sarıkaya. It advocated a rapprochement with the US and the South Kurdish parties. The present book was written at a time when this conflict was still limited to the formation of an internal tendency. During 2004, the group around Nizamettin Taş split from the tendency and founded the Partîya Welatparêzên Demokratên (PWD: Patriotic Democratic Party), which, however, soon slipped

into obscurity. In the course of the split, around 1,500 members left the PKK, but only a small number of them joined the PWD.

30 In the autumn and winter of 2003-2004, Öcalan was unable to receive visits for six months and was thus completely isolated from the outside world.

31 Amr ibn Hishām, a pagan Quraysh leader whose epithet, Abu al-Hakam, meant Father of Wisdom, rejected Mohammad's message. He showed relentless animosity to Islam and, therefore, Mohammad referred to him as Abu Jahl, meaning Father of Ignorance.

32 Metehan, or Modun Chanyu, (234-174 BCE) was the ruler of the Xiongnu Empire, which put incredible pressure on the Chinese army. His ascension to the throne is eternalized in the emblem of the Turkish army.

33 Afrasiab was the name of a mythical king of Iranian popular mythology. Afrasiab, the king of Turan, was a descendant of Ahriman and the bitterest and most powerful enemy of Iran and Ahura Mazda. He conducted several campaigns against Iran and was, among other things, responsible for the death of the hero Siyâvash. Finally, the Iranian king Khosrow personally confronted Afrasiab, who was defeated and killed following a long battle with Rostam. The name *Afrasiab* is mentioned several times in Avestan. The word *Turan* originally comes from Persian and is the name of the southern area of South Asia. It is probably derived from the Old-Iranian word stem *târ/tur* (*dark/black*). The battle between Iran and Turan, the land of light and the land of darkness, is an important part of Iranian-Avestan mythology. Turan is also regarded as the mythological aboriginal home of the Turks.

34 Biopower is a term coined by French philosopher and social theorist Michel Foucault and relates to the practice of modern nation-states and their regulation of their subjects through "an explosion of numerous and diverse techniques for achieving the subjugation of bodies and the control of populations."

35 The İttihat ve Terakki Cemiyeti, also known as the Young Turks, existed from 1860 to 1918 and as a government party had a decisive impact on the final phase of the Ottoman Empire. None of the five founders of this Turkish-nationalist movement was Turkish. Their protagonists, Enver Pasha among them, played decisive roles in the genocide of the Armenians and the Arameans in 1915.

36 Members of Christian peoples who were recruited into the regiments of the Janissaries through the so-called "blood tax" or "boys' recruitment" and Islamized in the process.

37 This was a particularly explosive claim, because during the time of the Janissaries, the leading cadres of the military and the secret services were, for the most part, recruited from these non-Turkish ethnic groups. Paradoxically, these services have often advocated a particularly radical Turkish nationalism.

38 The Cumhuriyet Halk Fırkası was found by Mustafa Kemal Atatürk and was later renamed Cumhuriyet Halk Partisi (CHP).

39 The Misak-ı Millî pact defines the settlement areas of Turks and Kurds as the "national border" and, therefore, reaches beyond today's Turkey and into Mosul and Kirkuk in Iraq.

40 During the war of liberation, there was only talk about "nation" (*millet*) and "fatherland" (*vatan*). Both are Islamically tinged concepts with which both Turks and Kurds could identify.

41 Ahmet Aznavur (1834–1921) led two uprisings in the west of Turkey in 1919 and 1920, both of which were suppressed with much bloodshed by the republican national liberation troops.

42 After World War I, Syria became a French mandate area. This mandate ended after twenty years. The area around Antakya (Antioch) and İskenderun was claimed by both Syria and Turkey, and on July 23, 1939, was turned over to Turkey following a dubious referendum.

43 Here we must mention in particular Radio Erivan, which regularly broadcast Kurdish music.

44 The village guards (*köy korucusu*) are paramilitary Kurdish tribal militias armed and paid by the state whose task consists of fighting the PKK. Many of the approximately 4,500 villages were depopulated, because the inhabitants did not want to become village guards. According to human rights activists, this system, which at times involved more than one hundred thousand village guards is a big problem, because at this point a large number of people are financially dependent on this system.

45 Süleyman Demirel, Tansu Çiller, and Mehmet Ağar's Doğru Yol Partisi (DYP: True Path Party) was regarded as a counterguerrilla party with close ties to the mafia. At the end of the 1990s, it declined in importance.

46 This is a reference to a book of poetry titled *Kızıl Elma* (Red Apple), by the nationalist theorist Ziya Gökalp.

47 Bülent Ecevit's left nationalist Demokratik Sol Parti (DSP: Democratic Left Party) split from the CHP and was the ruling party from 1997 to 2002 but has since shrunk to a small splinter party.

48 In the elections in November 2002, none of the three governing parties, the DSP, ANAP, and MHP, were reelected. Bülent Ecevit's DSP, which was the strongest party in 1999, with 22 percent of the vote, only got around 2 percent of the vote in 2002.

49 Öcalan suggested to change the name of the Kongra Gel, founded in 2003, to "Koma Gel" or "Koma Gelan" (Commune of the Peoples), a change in which the word *"Kurdistan"* would not have been included, but this proposal did not receive majority support at the Kongra Gel.

50 In Islam, the practice of concealing one's belief and foregoing ordinary religious duties when under threat of death or injury.

51 This concept, which draws upon the work of Murray Bookchin, goes beyond environmental protection and aims at a society that is free from hierarchies between sexes, classes, and peoples, and in which there are no power relations between humans and nature; see Murray Bookchin, *Ecology of Freedom: The Emergence and Dissolution of Hierarchy* (Buckley, UK: Cheshire Books, 1982).

52 In Turkey, to be represented in parliament a party must garner at least 10 percent of the vote, the main purpose of which is to prevent Kurdish parties from entering parliament.

53 In the communal elections of March 28, 2004, the Unity of the Democratic Forces alliance ran on the SHP list. The pro-Kurdish DEHAP is the successor party to the Halkın Demokrasi Partisi (HADEP: People's Democracy Party) and the predecessor to the Demokratik Toplum Partisi (DTP: Democratic Society Party). Parties in Turkey that address the Kurdish question are regularly banned and have to found themselves anew under new names.

Contribution to the Debate About the Refoundation of the PKK

1 This section was meant as a contribution to the then pending summer of 2004 general assembly of the Kongra Gel.
2 In Turkey, provincial governors appointed by the state have much more authority than the regionally elected representatives of the people. This is a particularly serious problem in the Kurdish provinces, because municipal politicians have very little influence and are, among other things, prevented from promoting the Kurdish language at a local level.
3 A feudal unit governed by an aga or a lord.
4 The Partiya Azadiya Jin a Kurdistan, the political-ideological organization of the women's movement, was founded in 2004.
5 In this phrase, the author uses the neologism karılaşma, which in English would be something like "housewifization."
6 Öcalan proposed a preparatory committee for the reconstruction of the PKK but did not name any potential participants.
7 The Demokratik Güçler Birliği (DGB: Union of Democratic Forces) was an electoral alliance of Kurdish and left-wing parties during the 2002 parliamentary election.
8 After the congress, a group led by Nizamettin Taş, Kani Yılmaz, Hıdır Yalçın, and Osman Öcalan split from the Kongra Gel.
9 Like the AKP, Necmettin Erbakan and Recai Kutan's Islamist Millî Selâmet Partisi (MSP: National Salvation Party) came out of their predecessor parties, the Refah Partisi (RP: Welfare Party) and the Fazilet Partisi (FP: Virtue Party).
10 The term "special warfare" refers to all forms of irregular, psychological, and economic warfare.
11 Green is the color of Islam.
12 See Abdullah Öcalan, Özgür İnsan Savunması (Neuss: Mezopotamien Verlag, 2003).
13 The Kongra Gel published a document to this effect in August 2006.
14 The HPG said that it would abide by the Geneva Convention, and after the mediation of the NGO Geneva Call, it signed the Ottawa Convention against anti-personnel mines, on July 18, 2006.

The Role of the ECtHR and the EU in the Lawsuit against Abdullah Öcalan

1 Savvas Kalenteridis was a colonel in the Greek secret service. He accompanied Öcalan during the second sojourn in Greece and Kenya.
2 See Abdullah Öcalan, Özgür İnsan Savunması (Cologne: Mezopotamien Verlag, 2003).

3   In 1991, Leyla Zana became the first Kurdish woman to win a seat and speak Kurdish in the Turkish Parliament. When the Democracy Party (DEP) was banned by the Turkish government in 1994, her parliamentary immunity was lifted, along with that of five other DEP deputies. Leyla Zana, Orhan Doğan, Hatip Dicle, and Selim Sadak were arrested and convicted in 1994. They were initially charged with "treason against the integrity of the state," which was later changed to "membership in an armed gang." In July 2001, the European Court of Human Rights ruled that they had not received a fair, independent, and impartial trial.

4   Abdullah Öcalan was at the Greek embassy in Kenya when the operation to abduct him took place.

5   Şemsi Kılıç, one of the European spokespersons of the ERNK, accompanied Öcalan on his odyssey.

6   The Kurds, who had been mentioned in the 1920 Treaty of Sèvres, were not acknowledged in the 1923 Treaty of Lausanne between Turkey and the victorious powers of World War I.

7   This refers to the instrumentalization of the trade agreements between the European states and the Ottoman Empire.

An Identity That Must Be Accurately Defined

1   It is quite possible that material from proto-Kurdish narrations found its way into the epic. For example, in Kurdish, the name *Gilgamesh* means *big buffalo* (author's note).

2   See Samuel N. Kramer and John Maier, *Myths of Enki, the Crafty God* (New York: Oxford University Press, 1989).

3   The driver did this to delay the flight and notify Öcalan of the plot.

4   Hasan Bindal was a childhood friend of Öcalan, from a household that was an adversary of Öcalan's family. Despite objections, especially from his mother and grandmother, Öcalan pursued this friendship, and they became best friends. Bindal was killed during a military exercise in Beqaa Valley, Lebanon, in 1990.

5   Duran Kalkan is of Turkmen origin.

6   Cihangır Hazır is better known as "Sarı Baran."

7   See note 4 above.

8   Nikolai Bukharin and Grigory Zinoviev, both leading cadres of the Russian October Revolution, were sentenced to death at the 1936–1938 Moscow trials and subsequently executed.

9   During the November 3, 2002, elections, none of the three government parties passed the 10 percent hurdle necessary to be represented in parliament.

10 Öcalan had exerted pressure for a democratic selection of candidates by the local base, but many candidates were determined by various cliques. This created a lot of discontent at the base and led to the loss of many DEHAP strongholds at the polls.

11 The term "social life" is sometimes used as a synonym for "sex life."

12 Osman Öcalan signed a ceasefire agreement without party consent.

13 He was sentenced to death by a party court but was later pardoned.

14 At the time, Osman Öcalan, along with others around him, entered into talks with the US that seemed to be preparing for the collapse of the PKK. The group engaged in these talks, without the participation of others in the organization.

15 Immediately after he commented positively on the PKK's ceasefire, Özal died mysteriously. His family insists to this day that he was murdered.

16 Osman Öcalan had demanded an immediate unconditional dissolution of the guerrilla.

17 When, at fifty, Osman Öcalan married a nineteen-year-old, the response was widespread disgust.

18 In 1992, Osman Öcalan picked up a weapon and threatened to shoot himself and planned to flee and take shelter with Iranian state.

19 The group around Osman Öcalan talked about a coup.

20 This was written shortly before the Second Plenary Session of the Kongra Gel, in spring 2004.

21 After Abdullah Öcalan left Syria, many members and supporters of the Kurdish movement in Syria were arrested, tortured, and extradited to Turkey.

22 During his fast to the death, Kemal Pir said: "We love life so much that we are ready to die for it."

23 At the time, one pillar of the policy toward South Kurdistan was to downplay national identity and call for a union under the banner of Islam. The long-term aim of this was to add the Kurdish territory of Iraq to Turkey. Ever since, Turkey has expanded its military presence in South Kurdistan.

24 *Yavuz* refers to "Selim the Grim," the nickname of Sultan Selim I; see pages 380 and 433, this volume.

25 "Idealists" is what the Turkish fascists call themselves.

26 During the 2004 local elections, Jalal Talabani and Masoud Barzani called on the Kurds in Turkey to vote for the AKP.

27 The DGB was an electoral alliance of the DEHAP, the SHP, the ÖDP, and the EMEP. The alliance candidates ran on the SHP list, which led to a criticism that was particularly pronounced among the DEHAP's base, because the SHP had been a part of Tansu Çiller's "war government."

28 The SHP, whose electoral potential was far smaller than that of the DEHAP, chose the candidates for all of the electoral districts.

Afterword

1 In 1992, the PKK was enmeshed in a two-front war with both the Turkish army and the South Kurdish KDP, suffering many losses. Following this, the part of the front under the command of Osman Öcalan capitulated without any previous discussion with Abdullah Öcalan or the central committee. Osman was heavily criticized for this, but he did save the lives of the units commanded by Murat Karayılan and Cemil Bayık in the process.

2 At that time, a Turkish-language—and, later on, Kurdish-language—Central Party School was opened near Damascus.

Appendix

1   In 2004, this letter was submitted as an appendix in the original edition of this book but was inserted into the main text in later editions. It was not included in the first German edition published by the Mezopotamien-Verlag.

2   In the summer of 2004, Yalçın and Taş split from the movement for good and joined Osman Öcalan to form the Patriotic Democratic Party (PWD), which rapidly faded into insignificance.

3   Zeki Okçuoğlu was one of Öcalan's attorneys but soon distanced himself and accused Öcalan of betraying the "Kurdish cause." Later on, he peddled absurd conspiracy theories, including the claim that Öcalan was actually not incarcerated on İmralı but was only flown there every now and then to meet his lawyers.

4   At the municipal elections of 2003, the candidates of DEHAP ran on the list of the SHP. For the selection process of the candidates, see notes 27 and 28, page 637.

5   After the group around Osman Öcalan, Taş, Yalçın, and Yılmaz split, it shifted its rhetoric into furious attacks on Abdullah Öcalan.

6   Immediately after his abduction on February 15, 1999, Öcalan called on the guerrilla to continue the ceasefire that had been declared on September 1, 1998. By doing so, he opposed almost the whole movement, which followed his call only very reluctantly. On August 2, 1999, five weeks after the death sentence pronounced against him, he called for a retreat from Turkey. This step also gave rise to a lot of dissatisfaction within the guerrilla.

Index

"Passim" (literally "scattered") indicates intermittent discussion of a topic over a cluster of pages.

Abbasids, 321, 333, 334, 619n26, 622n23, 623n14

Abraham (biblical figure), 95, 96, 99, 119, 120, 126, 217–18, 328

accumulation, 17, 76–77, 101, 139–40, 274; war and, 110

action, civil. *See* civil action (direct action)

Adalet Partisi (AP), 364, 436, 437, 452, 626n43

Adam (biblical figure), 118, 120, 238

adolescents. *See* youth

Afghanistan, 172, 231, 270, 275, 280, 281–82, 301

agriculture: Aryan, 124; birth of, 113, 234, 324–25; irrigation, 34

Aisha, 99–100

Akkadian Empire, 82, 116, 161, 261

AKP (Adalet ve Kalkınma Partisi), 437, 452–55 passim, 459, 503, 553, 565, 571, 573; elections, 422; Öcalan letter to, 422; silence of, 422, 496; theocracy, 497

Alawites, 322, 619n26

Alexander the Great, 56, 114, 117, 215, 330, 405

Alevism, 321, 333, 335, 352

Allah, 58, 60, 61, 70, 96, 97, 127, 255

Alp Arslan, Sultan of the Seljuks, 431–32

Altun, Rıza, 563, 585

analytical intelligence, 40–41, 148, 149, 196–97, 237, 263, 405

Anatolia, 329, 331, 334, 344, 430–34 passim. *See also* West Anatolia

Anavatan Partisi (ANAP), 365, 436, 437, 452, 453, 503, 553, 571, 627n47

animism, 39, 41, 43, 47, 95, 126

Anter, Musa, 630n10

AP. *See* Adalet Partisi (AP)

Arab Empire, 333–34

Arabic, 343–45

Arabs, 113–14, 190, 450, 533–34; colonial Turkey and, 337; defeat of the Sasanian Empire, 333; Islamic conquests, 359; Israeli conflict, 282, 299; Kurdish relations, 114, 380, 533–34; nationalism, 231, 244, 299; Reconquista, 523; states, 298–99, 494

Aramaic, 343

Arameans, 121, 435, 442, 632n35

Ararat uprising, 442
Arianism, 247, 287, 622n21
Aristotle, 135, 330, 614n1
Armenia and Armenians, 322, 323, 331, 334; "liquidation"/genocide, 323, 335, 367, 523–24, 628n53, 632n35; nationalism, 355; Xoybûn, 442
arts, 51, 52, 72, 74, 86, 187, 209; as defense mechanism, 169; war and, 111, 112; women in, 147. *See also* music
Aryan language group, 96, 124
Aryans, 113, 114, 124, 129, 325
Aşkın, Saime, 551
Assassins, 132, 619n26
Assyrians, 124, 320, 322, 323, 329–35 passim, 520–24 passim; language, 343–44; "liquidation"/genocide, 367, 442, 523, 628n53, 632n35; nationalism, 355
Atatürk, Mustafa Kemal, 381, 435, 440–43 passim, 450–53 passim, 458–59, 534, 535; CHP, 627n50; nationalism, 367, 375, 381, 438, 451–53 passim; recognition of Kurds and Kurdistan, 315; religious policy, 364. *See also* Kemalism
Athens, ancient, 56, 107, 117, 180–81, 185
Atsız, Nihal, 438
authority and hierarchy. *See* hierarchy and authority
Ayyubid dynasty, 321, 353–54, 622n23
Azadi Cemiyeti, 441
Aznavur, Ahmet, 441, 633n41

Babylon, 119, 134, 261, 327–30 passim; Abraham, 217; cities, 353; conquest of, 114; culture of violence, 237; imperial power, 116
Babylonian mythology, 22, 29, 99, 236
Bakunin, Mikhail, 36
Baliç, Şahin, 392, 550
"barbarians" and "savages," 53, 54, 55, 112–13

Barzani, Masoud, 365, 367, 393, 455, 570, 571–72
Barzanji, Mahmud, 434
Bayık, Cemil, 391, 397, 425, 550–58 passim, 563, 580, 585
Baykal, Deniz, 574, 627n50
Berkan, İsmet, 628n58
Bible, 78, 152–53, 257, 270. *See also* Abraham (biblical figure); Adam (biblical figure); Eve (biblical figure); Job (biblical figure); Miriam (biblical figure); Moses (biblical figure); Noah (biblical figure); Sarah (biblical figure)
Bindal, Hasan, 393, 547, 550, 635n4 ("An Identity")
Bolshevik Revolution. *See* Russian Revolution
Bookchin, Murray, xvi, 622n22
bourgeoisie. *See* middle class (bourgeoisie)
Braudel, Fernand, 612n4
Britain. *See* Great Britain
Bruno, Giordano, 43, 136
Bush, George W., 287, 371
Byzantium and Byzantine Empire, 57, 129, 332–34 passim, 348, 431, 520, 522

Calanus (Kalanos), 405
Capital (Marx), 152
capitalism, 65–68 passim, 75–81 passim, 85–86, 140–45 passim, 149–50, 154–60 passim, 164–71 passim, 178; Christianity and, 520; Marx and Engels's view, 158; morality and, 157, 168; nature and, 78, 149; Ottoman Empire and Turkey, 434–40 passim; Renaissance, 140–41
Catholic Church, 73, 239–40. *See also* Inquisition
Çatlı, Abdullah, 628n58
Çayan, Mahir, 376, 386, 629n63
Çelik, Hüseyin, 365, 571, 627n48
Cemal, Kör, 392

"chaos interval," 19, 154, 164, 165, 204, 290; in quantum physics, 68; Renaissance as, 160

children, 79, 168; girls, 194; mother relationship, 18; subjugation of, 24–25, 52, 63; violence against, 258. *See also* youth

CHF. *See* Cumhuriyet Halk Fırkası (CHF)

China, ancient, 429

CHP. *See* Cumhuriyet Halk Partisi (CHP)

Christianity, 53–59 passim, 66–71 passim, 118, 127, 153, 226, 288, 290; Alexander the Great and, 117; capitalism and, 520; class division, 246, 247; Constantine, 229; dogmatism, 67, 69; earliest years, 331; episcopacy, 123; fourth and fifth centuries, 332; Hellenistic era, 319–20; manifestos, 152–53; Middle Ages, 69, 128–32 passim, 135–36, 384; Middle East, 287; party/ religion of the poor, 53, 57, 122, 153; theocracy, 270; Trinity, 56; Urfa, 119; women and, 99. *See also* Bible; Catholic Church; Protestantism

Çiçek, Ali, 391

Çiller, Tansu, 525, 565, 628n55

citizenship, 144–45, 245

city-states, 21, 30, 34–35, 113, 161, 541. *See also* Athens, ancient

civil action (direct action), 189–90

clans, Paleolithic and Neolithic, 6–11, 123

"clash of civilizations," 211, 212, 263, 280, 386, 440

class, 20, 26, 38–39, 41, 58, 63, 79, 103, 245–46; birth of, 125, 347–51 passim; Kurds, 436; Middle Ages, 132, 133; Middle East, 246–48; religion and, 219. *See also* middle class (bourgeoisie)

class struggle, 89, 108, 129, 158, 246, 305, 520

Clausewitz, Carl von, 295, 623n13

Clinton, Bill, 402

collective property, 248–49

Commagene kingdom, 315, 319, 331, 332, 352

commodification, 85, 167, 479; of women, 84, 147, 239–40

common good and safety, 35–36, 93, 107, 168, 184, 246, 270, 271, 414; contravention of, 231

communality and communal society, 93–94, 101, 115, 150–51, 156, 182, 184

Communist Manifesto (Marx and Engels), 78, 140, 152, 398

Communist Party of Turkey. *See* TKP (Communist Party of Turkey)

confederation. *See* federation and federalism

conquest, right of. *See* right of conquest

Constantine the Great, 54, 57, 127, 229, 623n10

cosmology, 7–8

coups: Turkey, 364, 372, 436, 626n43

crisis and crises, 19, 81, 89, 164–92 passim, 201, 207; ecological/ environmental, 201, 204

Cumhuriyet Halk Fırkası (CHF), 438, 632n38

Cumhuriyet Halk Partisi (CHP), 366, 396, 444, 452, 503, 571, 574, 627n50, 632n38

Çürükkaya, Selim, 399, 589

Cyprus, 299, 458, 494–95, 497, 535, 570

DDKO. *See* Devrimci Doğu Kültür Ocakları (DDKO)

DEHAP. *See* Demokratik Halk Partisi (DEHAP)

Demirel, Süleyman, 393, 633n45

democracy and democratization, 36, 111–17 passim, 176–92, 307, 413–15, 509–11 passim, 515–18 passim, 599; economy and, 185; Middle East, 276, 279, 285, 294–302, 309–11 passim; politics and, 80, 294–302; roots, 43;

Turkey, 450, 455–60, 472, 480, 517.
See also people's congresses
Demokrat Parti (DP), 364, 436, 437,
439, 443–44, 452, 459, 626n43
Demokratik Güçler Birliği (DGB), 460,
496, 573, 574, 634n7, 636n27
Demokratik Halk Partisi (DEHAP),
460, 473, 503, 563, 573–74, 592,
634n53, 636n27, 637n4
Demokratik Sol Parti (DSP), 553, 571,
633nn47–48
Demokratik Toplum Partisi (DTP),
628n56, 634n53
Dersim uprising, 443
Derweşê Evdî, 236, 321, 492
"devilry," 61–62. *See also* witch hunts
and witch trials
Devrimci Doğu Kültür Ocakları
(DDKO), 386, 444
DGB. *See* Demokratik Güçler Birliği
(DGB)
Dicle, Hatip, 635n3 ("Role of the
ECtHR")
dictatorship, 158, 180, 184, 254
dictatorship of the proletariat, 157,
158, 389, 408, 411
direct action. *See* civil action (direct
action)
Doğan, Mazlum, 390, 391, 514, 609,
623n12, 630n8
Doğan, Orhan, 635n3 ("Role of the
ECtHR")
Doğru Yol Partisi (DYP), 452, 503, 571,
633n45
Dönmez, Şahin, 400
Dostoevsky, Fyodor, 521
DP. *See* Demokrat Parti (DP)
DSP. *See* Demokratik Sol Parti (DSP)
DTP. *See* Demokratik Toplum Partisi
(DTP)
Dumuzi (Tammuz), 236, 621n15
Durmuş, Mehmet Hayri, 390, 391, 395,
397, 514
DYP. *See* Doğru Yol Partisi (DYP)

Ecevit, Bülent, 365, 395, 454, 553,
633nn47–48
ECHR. *See* European Convention on
Human Rights (ECHR)
ECtHR. *See* European Court of
Human Rights (ECtHR)
ecological destruction, 81, 83, 149, 167;
capitalism and, 138–39
ecology, 204–6, 305–7, 478–79. *See
also* reforestation; social ecology
economy and economics, 478–79;
Middle East, 215, 249–50, 274–75,
304–5; as weapon, 80. *See also*
capitalism
Egypt, 38, 39, 71, 120, 223–24, 239, 328,
433
elderly, 148, 168. *See also* gerontocracy
elections, 422–25 passim, 455–58
passim, 472–74 passim, 509,
553, 571, 599, 634n53; Bingöl,
322; DEHAP and, 592; local,
322, 571, 636n26; manipulation,
504; municipal, 365, 371, 425,
455–57 passim, 473, 504, 553,
592; Naqshbandi and, 365, 496;
parliamentary, 365, 422, 513,
626n43
Elohim, 29, 97, 615n2 ("Feudal Statist
Society")
Emek Partisi (EMEP), 460, 636n27
emotional intelligence, 40–41, 148,
196–97, 263, 405
empire and empires, 161; Arab,
333–34; Islamic, 333; Middle East,
276–78 passim. *See also* Akkadian
Empire; Byzantium and Byzantine
Empire; German Empire; Great
Britain: empire; Holy Roman
Empire; Parthian Empire; Persian
Empire; Rome (empire); Ottoman
Empire; United States (US): empire
Engels, Friedrich, 65, 151–52, 156,
158; *Communist Manifesto*, 78, 140,
152, 398; *Origin of Family, Private
Property and the State*, 152, 616n10
England, 375, 437, 439, 441, 443

Enki (god), 21–22, 99, 103, 118, 235, 542
Enkidu, 44, 112, 326, 541–42, 546, 547
Enkimdu, 236
Enlightenment, 68, 151, 221, 231, 265, 526–27
Enuma Elish (Babylonian creation myth), 22, 236
Enver Pasha, 632n35
environment. *See* ecology
environmental destruction. *See* ecological destruction
Epic of Gilgamesh. *See* Gilgamesh
epistemology, 8–9, 65
Erbakan, Necmettin, 365, 627n44
Erdoğan, Recep Tayyip, 322, 337, 365, 454, 571, 625n16, 627n44
Ergenekon, 630n16
Ergezen, Zeki, 365, 571, 627n48
Essenes, 57, 467, 519
"ethnic" (word), 615n1 ("Feudal Statist Society")
Etruscans, 125, 135
European Convention on Human Rights (ECHR), 528, 530, 531, 540
European Court of Human Rights (ECtHR), xxiv, xxv, 1, 518, 526–31 passim, 539–40, 613n1 ("Social Reality"), 635n3 ("Role of the ECtHR")
European Union (EU), xxi–xxv passim, 174, 183, 207, 258, 453–55 passim, 529–30, 535; norms, 3. *See also* European Court of Human Rights (ECtHR)
Eve (biblical figure), 25–26, 118, 238
evolution, 7, 8, 27, 201

family, 475; disintegration, 168; dynasties, 251; Middle East, 214, 233–42; patriarchal, 79, 85, 198, 233–42 passim, 251
fate and fatalism, 20, 68, 69, 73, 150, 578. *See also* Lehv-i Mahfûz
Fazilet Partisi (FP), 627n44, 634n9
federation and federalism, 245, 282, 347, 430; empires and, 161; Iraq, 300,

312–13; Medes, 416; Middle East, 276–82 passim, 300, 301, 480, 537, 573; Nairi, 315, 328–29; US, 494
feminine culture. *See* mother-goddess culture
feminism, 195–97 passim, 206, 477
feudalism and serfdom, 121, 128, 133, 228–29; demise, 166
Fırat, Abdülmelik, 365, 571, 627n48
Foucault, Michel, 615n9
France, 336, 337, 437, 439, 443, 530
Frankish Empire, 129
freedom, 11, 19, 68, 69, 289; free will, 67; in science, 72; of speech, 362; state and, 51; unthinkable nature of, 63; young people's urge for, 24–25. *See also* women's freedom and liberation
Freedom and Solidarity Party. *See* Özgürlük ve Dayanışma Partisi (ÖDP)
French Revolution, 141, 212, 231, 296, 367; influence on Atatürk, 435, 593
friendship, 545–47 passim, 579, 602, 635n4; gender and, 23, 560

gender, 10–11, 233–42, 487–93; friendship and, 23, 560; intelligence and, 196–97, 237, 477; man as appendage of woman, 196, 488. *See also* matriarchy; patriarchy; women, subjugation of; women's freedom and liberation
German Empire, 437–38, 628n53
gerontocracy, 23–26
Gezmiş, Deniz, 376, 386, 629n62
Gilgamesh, 30–31, 42, 43, 104, 112, 326, 541–42, 547
God, 61, 225–28 passim; alienation from nature and, 202, 203; Christianity, 56, 57, 58, 217; politicization of, 218; Renaissance, 138; Trinity, 239. *See also* Allah
goddess culture. *See* mother-goddess culture
goddess Inanna. *See* Inanna (goddess)

goddess Tiamat. *See* Tiamat (goddess)
god-kings, 44, 56, 58, 66, 106, 120, 126–29 passim, 166, 224–28 passim; contemporary version, 232; property and, 249; warrior ruling power, 115
gods, 13, 29, 39–44 passim, 58, 67, 95–97, 103; excrement of, 42, 43, 225; pantheon, 61, 103, 105. *See also* Enki (god); God; Marduk (god)
god-state. *See* theocracy (god-state)
Gökalp, Ziya, 535
Great Britain, 336, 337, 434, 441–42, 443; counterterrorism, 628n58; empire, 181, 523; Öcalan and, 525, 530; Treaty of Lausanne, 531. *See also* England
Greater Middle East Initiative, 173, 275–79 passim, 283, 295, 299; Arab states and, 309; Kurds and, 313, 449, 532; Turkey and, 428, 535, 538
Greece, 397, 521–22, 526, 530, 531
Greece, ancient, 125, 135, 317, 330, 520. *See also* Athens, ancient; Hellenistic era
Greek, 127, 319, 320, 343, 344
Gülen, Fethullah, 365, 571, 627n46

Halkın Demokrasi Partisi (HADEP), 634n53
Hazır, Cihangır, 550, 551, 635n6 ("An Identity")
heaven and hell, 41, 52, 59, 67, 218–19
Hebrew, 96, 343
Hebrews, 97, 127, 238–40 passim, 255, 269–70, 334, 519; Moses, 120–21, 152, 246
Hegel, G.W.F., 59, 546
Heisenberg uncertainty principle, 65
Hellenism, 215, 229, 343, 352
Hellenistic era, 319, 331, 344, 353, 420
Herodotus: *Histories*, 117, 317, 318, 352
Hezbollah, 366, 503, 571
Hêzên Parastina Gel (HPG), 507–15 passim

hierarchy and authority, 15–20, 26, 100–103 passim, 140
Hitler, Adolf, 193, 620n4
Hittites, 135, 327–28, 329, 351, 625n19
Hobbes, Thomas, 30, 78
Hogir. *See* Işık, Cemil (Hogir)
Holy Roman Empire, 129, 229
homeland, 244–45
"honor killing," 21, 241, 398, 475
human intelligence. *See* intelligence
human rights, 480–82, 527. *See also* European Convention on Human Rights; European Court of Human Rights (ECtHR)
Huns, 53, 129, 429
hunting, 26, 581, 582; as basis for patriarchy and militarism, 16, 21, 25, 27, 347; subsistence, 6–7, 10–11
Hurrians, 117, 124, 317, 327, 328, 351
Hussein, Saddam, 261, 380, 569

İmralı Island prison, 499, 528, 586, 626n43, 637n3
Inanna (goddess), 21–22, 45, 62, 99, 103, 235, 542, 616n7
individual rights, 474, 480–82, 539
individuality and individualism, 1–2, 76, 156, 178, 184, 280, 481
Industrial Revolution, 142, 149, 151, 160, 279
İnönü, İsmet, 436, 443, 534
Inquisition, 67, 72–73, 130, 134
Iran, 231, 300–301, 344, 390, 433, 572, 625n25; Hezbollah, 366; Pahlavi dynasty, 337; theocracy, 270, 363
intelligence, 13, 40–41, 76, 148, 149, 405; gender and, 196–97, 237, 477; scientism and, 263
internationalism, 479–80; of Jesus Christ, 520
Iraq, 172, 299, 535; Arab nationalism, 231; bicultural state creation, 114; Britain and France in, 337; democracy, 300; federation (proposed), 281–82; Kurds and Kurdistan, 283, 312–16 passim,

336, 357, 367, 380, 532, 569; military power reliance, 536; Turkish relations, 533; US in, xxiv, 177, 264, 275, 280, 295, 357, 402, 553
Işık, Cemil (Hogir), 392, 630n10
Islam, 57–59 passim, 66–70 passim, 127, 163, 230, 264, 321, 386; Aisha, 99–100; class and, 53, 247; empire, 333; influence on Kurds, 353, 377–78; jihad, 333; Middle Ages, 66, 69–70, 128, 131, 132, 264, 320–21, 334–36 passim; party-like movements in, 467; radical/extremist (Islamism), 173, 175, 221, 292, 364, 375, 436; as state ideology, 363–64; theocracy, 270; Turkey, 430, 431, 439; women, 240. *See also* Alevism; Allah; Koran; Naqshbandi; Pan-Islamism; Shiite Islam; Sunni Islam
Islamic Conference. *See* Organization of Islamic Cooperation (Islamic Conference)
İsmailis, 619n26
Israel, 231, 503, 532, 533; nationalism, 244, 245, 356; Syrian relations, 300; Turkish relations, 525
İttihat ve Terakki Cemiyeti (İTC) (Young Turks), 366, 375, 435, 632n35
İttihat ve Terakkiperver Fırkası (İTF), 438

Japan, 207
Jerusalem, 126, 127, 519
Jesus Christ, 56–57, 74, 118, 121, 127, 226, 290; apostles, 331; arrest and crucifixion, 255, 519–22 passim; class and, 246; party-like movement of, 467
JITEM (Jandarma İstihbarat ve Terörle Mücadele), 628n58, 630n10, 630nn16–17
Job (biblical figure), 119, 226, 227
John the Baptist, Saint, 57, 519
Judaea, 519, 520, 522

Judaism, 57, 70, 152

KADEK (Kongreya Azadi u Demokrasiya Kurdistan), 422–23, 552, 553, 624n1, 631n29
Kalenteridis, Savvas, 522, 528, 634n1 ("Role of the ECtHR")
Kalkan, Duran, 391, 425, 549–50, 551, 563, 579, 585
Kapan, Alaattin, 395
Karasungur, Mehmet, 390–91, 579
Karayılan, Murat, 558, 580
Karer, Haki, 383, 395, 549
Kaypakkaya, Ibrahim, 376, 629n63
Kaytan, Ali Haydar, 391, 551, 579
KDP (Kurdistan Democratic Party), 392, 393, 395, 417, 559, 579, 630n19
Kemal, Namık, 366
Kemalism, 451–52, 453, 459, 593–94
Khorramdin, Babak, 577, 623n14
Kılıç, Şemsi, 528, 635n5
Kılınç, Tuncer, 566
knowledge monopolization by state, 71–72
Koçgiri rebellion, 440
Koma Gel (Kongra Gel) (People's Congress), 422, 455, 458, 493–507, 553, 554, 572, 573, 624n1
Koran, 58, 153, 227, 255, 614n8
Korkmaz, Mahsum, 391, 392, 550, 629n6
"Kurdistan" (term), 315–16
Kurdistan Democratic Party. *See* KDP (Kurdistan Democratic Party)
Kurmanj, 354
Kürt Teali Cemiyetleri, 441
Kurtay, Ferhat, 391, 514, 623n12

Labor Party (Turkey). *See* Emek Partisi (EMEP)
language and languages, 342–45; establishment of, 123–24. *See also* Aryan language group; Greek; Hebrew
Layla, 240, 266

Lenin, Vladimir, xvii, 51, 64, 89, 158, 179, 180, 195, 260–61; *State and Revolution*, 411
Leninism, xvi, 196, 261
Levh-i Mahfûz, 67, 73
Leviathan, 30, 37, 53, 66
Lilith, 25–26, 614n9
literature, 220–21
love, 199, 240, 266, 273–74, 488–93 passim, 545, 560–62 passim; nature and humans, 205

Majnun, 240, 266
male dominance. *See* patriarchy
Mamluks, 323, 432, 433
Mani and Manicheism, 53, 54, 319, 320, 332, 622n6
Marduk (god), 99, 100, 103, 236, 617n2
marriage, 45, 168, 198, 304, 475, 490, 492, 560–62; monogamy, 239; Öcalan's, 396–97, 545
Marshall Plan, 173, 279, 284
Marwanid dynasty, 321, 353–54, 432
Marx, Karl, 151–52, 158; *Capital*, 152; *Communist Manifesto*, 78, 140, 152, 398
Marxism, xvi, 12, 14, 26, 49, 54–55, 68–69, 73, 78, 151–59 passim; analysis of war lacking, 508; dialectics, 18; early Christianity compared, 57; view of bourgeoisie, 77; view of class, 20; view of nations, 142; view of natural society, 89; view of religion, 105; view of slavery, 48; view of state, 36; views of history, 139
Mary, Saint, 238–39
matriarchy, 10–11; primordial, 10, 15–18, 21, 25–28 passim, 34, 45, 100, 103
Mawlana (Rumi), 131, 266, 267, 344
Mazdak and Mazdakites, 623n14
McNeill, William, xv
meat-eating, 26–27
Medea (mythological character), 117, 618n9

Medes and Medians, 117, 124, 125, 180–81, 317–18, 329–30, 352, 431, 624n8; Deioces, 416; timeline, 135
Mem û Zîn, 345, 354, 433, 621n14
men's rule. *See* patriarchy
menstruation, 196, 205
MGK. *See* Milli Güvenlik Kurulu (MGK)
MHP. *See* Milliyetçi Hareket Partisi (MHP)
Middle Ages, 63–64, 71, 121, 166, 217, 354–55; Christianity, 28–32 passim, 69, 135–36, 384; class, 132, 133; Islam, 66, 69–70, 128, 131, 132, 264, 320–21, 334–36 passim; Kurds, 315, 316, 322, 434; religion, 128–32 passim; war, 336
middle class (bourgeoisie), 64, 74–78 passim, 183, 453–55, 503
militaries, primordial roots of, 25, 27–28
military occupation. *See* occupation, military
Milli Güvenlik Kurulu (MGK), 628n58
Millî Selâmet Partisi (MSP), 503, 634n9
Milliyetçi Hareket Partisi (MHP), 367, 438, 452, 503, 565, 628n54; in coalition government, 454, 553, 571, 633n48
Miriam (biblical figure), 62, 99, 238, 240, 616n8
Mitanni, 316, 327, 328, 343, 344
Mohammad, 54, 58, 75, 121, 127, 227–28, 255, 332, 578; Aisha and, 99–100, 240; *jihad sughra*, 405; Koran, 153
monasteries, 131–34, 141, 143, 157, 179, 287
morality, 100–101, 156–57, 206, 291, 308, 466, 476, 603; bourgeoisie and, 77; capitalism and, 157, 168, 205; Enlightenment, 151; love and, 199; of natural society, 89; origin of, 9; people's congresses and, 209; unraveling of, 79; war and, 158

Moses (biblical figure), 99, 120–21, 152, 238, 328, 578; class and 246; Miriam and, 99, 238, 240, 616n8

mother-goddess culture, 15–25 passim, 70, 100, 234–36, 487; archaeological finds, 30, 235; assimilation/dissipation of, 42, 45, 98, 103, 236–39 passim

music, 70, 318–19, 326

mutual dependence, 19, 201, 537

mythology, Babylonian. *See* Babylonian mythology

mythology, Sumerian. *See* Sumerian mythology

Nairi, 117, 124, 315, 318, 328–29

Naqshbandi, 322, 364–67 passim, 433, 441, 449, 503, 571–72, 625n16; Kurdish collaborators, 454; Sheikh Said uprising, 365, 443

national liberation, 419–22, 508

national state and nation-states, 80, 82, 142, 144, 338, 349; Europe, 494; Middle East, 279, 283, 284, 285, 301, 345; rise of, 64, 73, 142; twenty-first century, 174, 207, 278. *See also* priest state (Sumer)

nationalism, 75, 79–82 passim, 142–43, 169, 345–49 passim, 355–57 passim, 480; Anatolian, 438; Arab, 231, 244, 299; Israeli and Palestinian, 356; Kurdish, 355, 357, 436, 503, 534, 565, 572, 595; Middle East, 231, 243–44, 365; right of conquest and, 508; Turkish, 345, 366–67, 371, 375, 431, 435–38 passim, 448–53 passim, 534, 535

nationhood, 130, 348; Kurdish, 355, 356; of women, 193

NATO, 174, 175, 275–76, 281, 284, 439, 440

natural society, 6–11 passim, 17–63 passim, 71, 88–92 passim, 109, 134–37 passim, 149, 204–5; fundamental moral principle, 76–77; memories of, 66–70 passim;

re-creation of, 306. *See also* mother-goddess culture

nature, 71, 582; alienation from, 5, 26–27, 149, 167, 201–3 passim, 478; bourgeoisie and, 78; capitalism and, 149, 203–4; Christian view of, 67; nomadic communities and, 96. *See also* ecological destruction

Neo-Assyrian language, 343

Neolithic clans. *See* clans, Paleolithic and Neolithic

Neolithic mother-goddess culture. *See* mother-goddess culture

Nietzsche, Friedrich, 85

Nimrod, 95, 119, 120, 217–18, 224, 226

Nineveh, 328, 329

Ninhursag, 235, 542

Noah (biblical figure), 118

nomadism and sedentarism. *See* sedentarism and nomadism

North Atlantic Treaty Organization. *See* NATO

nuclear weapons, 94, 263; atomic bomb, 86, 144, 409

Nursî, Said, 365

Öcalan, Abdullah, 575–83; assassination plot and attempt, 524, 525, 550; capture/abduction, 386, 521, 522, 525, 528, 581; İmralı Island imprisonment, 499, 528; MHP and, 628n54; mother, xix–xx, 425, 546, 559, 575; legal case, 526–31 passim

Öcalan, Osman, 425, 553–58 passim, 563, 580, 585–92 passim, 631n29, 636nn14–19, 636n1; marriage, 562, 636n17

occupation, military, 190–91, 360

ODP. *See* Özgürlük ve Dayanışma Partisi (ÖDP)

Okçuoğlu, Ahmet Zeki, 590, 637n3

old people. *See* elderly; gerontocracy

Organization of Islamic Cooperation (Islamic Conference), 301

Origin of Family, Private Property and the State (Engels), 152, 616n10

Ottoman Empire, 229, 323, 324, 334–37 passim, 355, 432–37 passim, 441; agas, 354; birth, 431; decline and fall, 372, 443, 523; despotism, 254; Kurds, 315; Napoleon I and, 522; Tanzimat reforms, 366, 375, 431, 627n52, 629n61

ownership. See collective property; private property; state property

Özal, Turgut, 365, 391, 393, 453, 454, 558, 572, 627n47

Özgürlük ve Dayanışma Partisi (ÖDP), 460, 573, 636n27

PAJK (Partiya Azadiya Jin a Kurdistan), 477, 487–93 passim, 634n4

Pakistan: theocracy, 270, 301

Paleolithic clans. See clans, Paleolithic and Neolithic

Palestine, 231, 282, 356, 503, 532

Palmyra, 319, 331, 332

Pan-Islamism, 378, 435, 437, 535

Pan-Turkism, 437, 535

Parthian Empire, 331, 352, 625n21

"The Path of Revolution in Kurdistan" (Öcalan), 397–98

patriarchy, 83–85, 145–48, 206, 560; family, 79, 85, 147, 251, 475, 487; Middle East, 223, 233–42, 272–74, 303–4; roots of, 10, 21–23, 29–31 passim, 42–46 passim, 98–100 passim, 155, 346–47, 541–42; Turkey, 438

Patriotic Democratic Party. See PWD (Partîya Welatparêzên Demokratên)

PDK (Partiya Demokrat a Kurdistanê). See KDP (Kurdistan Democratic Party)

"peace and stability," 109, 110, 114

people's congresses, 187, 188–89, 208–9. See also Koma Gel (Kongra Gel) (People's Congress)

People's Defense Forces. See Hêzên Parastina Gel (HPG)

Persian Empire, 317, 318, 329, 352; fall, 330

Persian language, 343, 344, 345

Persians, 318, 329, 330, 353, 359; Kurdish relations, 380

Phrygians, 125, 328

physics, 153–54. See also quantum physics

Pir, Kemal, 391, 392, 397, 514, 547, 549, 564, 567, 629n1; death, 391, 514, 623n12, 636n22; in hindsight, 579

PKK (Partiya Karkerên Kurdistanê), 91, 314, 401–9 passim, 415–28 passim, 444, 448–55 passim, 533–38 passim, 548–55 passim, 572, 601–3; cadres, 482–93, 602; critique and self-critique, 405–22; defectors, 557; dissolution, 624n1; emergence, 383–90 passim, 576; front against, 367; low-intensity warfare, 420; party program, 467–82 passim; political objectives, 469–74; refoundation of, 461–518 passim, 585; second phase, 391–95, 577; social objectives, 474–76; "terrorist" label, 373, 455, 525, 535, 565; withdrawal to South Kurdistan, xxiv. See also Hêzên Parastina Gel (HPG)

Plato, 85, 297

population explosion, 167–68, 204

priest state (Sumer), 51, 54, 215

"primitive" (word), 93

primitive communal society. See natural society

private property, 28, 47, 101–2, 248–49

proletariat, dictatorship of. See dictatorship of the proletariat

property. See collective property; private property; state property

prophets and prophecy, 118–22 passim, 126–27, 218, 226–28 passim, 262

prostitution, 42, 542; creation of, 197; temple prostitution, 22; Uruk, 541

Protestantism, 73, 130, 137
public good and safety. *See* common good and safety
PUK (Patriotic Union of Kurdistan), 417, 559, 579, 580
PWD (Partîya Welatparêzên Demokratên), 631–32n29, 637n2

Qarmatians, 132, 467, 577, 619n26
quantum physics, 7, 13, 19, 65, 68
Quran. *See* Koran

rebellions. *See* uprisings
Refah Partisi (RP), 437, 627n44, 634n9
reforestation, 206, 306, 479
Reformation, 231, 292
religion, 41–42, 56–70 passim, 95–103 passim, 217–31 passim, 340, 363–64; assimilation and, 377–38; beholden to power, 170; ethnic groups and, 297–98; George W. Bush, 287; gnostic currents, 53; Middle Ages, 128–32 passim; politicization, 301; primordial and nature-based, 205, 206, 228; prophets and prophecy, 118–22 passim, 126–27; Renaissance, 137–39 passim; roots of, 10; slavery and, 54; twenty-first century, 169, 170, 476. *See also* Christianity; gods; heaven and hell; Islam; Judaism; monasteries; Zoroastrianism
Renaissance, 67–74 passim, 81, 133–41 passim, 203, 220, 231
revolt and revolutions, 73–76 passim, 90, 141, 181, 190, 212, 296, 307; secular state and, 230, 231. *See also* French Revolution; Russian Revolution
right of conquest, 360, 508–9
rights of people. *See* human rights; individual rights
Rıza, Seyid, 434
Roman Catholic Church. *See* Catholic Church

Rome (empire), 54, 55, 56, 57, 117–18, 122–23, 135, 229; conquests, 331; decline and fall, 128, 129–30, 179, 229, 287, 332; Christianity and, 153; Jesus Christ and, 519–22 passim; Julian II, 286–87; US compared, 207
Rumi. *See* Mawlana (Rumi)
Russia (czarist era), 261, 415, 437, 523
Russian Revolution, 76, 89, 179, 212, 439, 551

Sadak, Selim, 635n3 ("Role of the ECtHR")
Safavids, 323, 334, 432–33
Sakık, Şemdin, 392, 393, 415, 550–51
Sarah (biblical figure), 99, 238
Sargon, 115–16, 161, 369
Sarıkaya, Hıdır, 631n29
Sasanian Empire, 318, 319, 320, 331, 333, 352, 520
Saudi Arabia, 299, 366
science, 5–6, 13, 14, 49, 51, 86, 174, 204, 209; beholden to power, 169, 170; freedom in, 72; mentality, 202; religion and, 363; Renaissance, 136–37; scientism, 69; sexism of, 83. *See also* evolution; scientism
scientism, 69, 221, 263, 287
Scythes and Scythians, 327, 329, 431
sedentarism and nomadism, 103, 114, 235
self-defense, 110, 111, 169, 190–92 passim, 361, 554. *See also* war and wars: of self-defense
Selim I, Sultan of the Turks, 315, 322, 323, 334, 335, 371, 380, 432–33, 534
Seljuks, 315, 321, 334, 344, 430, 431, 445
Şener, Mehmet, 399, 550, 551, 589
servitude, 61–62, 63
sexism, 62, 83, 194, 456, 490
sexuality, 199, 235–36, 372, 489, 492, 561; women's 238, 239–40
shamans and shamanism, 16, 25, 28, 98, 102
Sheikh Said uprising, 1925, 365, 434, 441, 443

sheikhdom, 97, 354–55
Shiite Islam, 247, 270, 364, 433,
    622n20; İsmailis, 619n26
SHP. *See* Sosyaldemokrat Halk Partisi
    (SHP)
Simko, Ismail Agha, 337, 625n25
slavery, 38–41 passim, 45–57 passim,
    108, 138, 181–82, 223–25; family,
    85; Middle Ages and, 121, 128;
    patriarchal roots, 22, 45–46, 62–63;
    state roots, 223–24; Sumer and
    Egypt, 122; Ten Commandments
    and, 152; women's, 22, 147, 193–98
    passim, 233–34, 242, 273
social class. *See* class
Social Democratic People's Party. *See*
    Sosyaldemokrat Halk Partisi (SHP)
social ecology, 149, 201–10
Sosyaldemokrat Halk Partisi (SHP),
    460, 573, 634n53, 636nn27–28
Soviet Union, xvi, 76, 174, 261, 288,
    481; Bukharin and Zinoviev, 551,
    635n8 collapse/dissolution, 51, 76,
    89, 276, 385, 402, 403, 440; military
    power reliance, 536; Turkish
    relations, 371
sports and cultural events, 79, 169,
    170, 187, 371, 372, 453
state, 26, 32–55 passim, 64–66
    passim, 408–10 passim, 502; birth
    of, 107–8; David and Solomon, 227;
    democracy and, 182–83; elections,
    509; Engels view, 157, 616n10; Hegel
    view, 59, 546; Hobbes view, 78;
    knowledge monopolization, 71–72;
    as Leviathan, 30, 37, 53; Middle
    East, 222–33; political parties and,
    79, 447–48; in real socialism, 157;
    Sumer, 51, 106; Turkey, 445–51
    passim, 456, 457, 470; ziggurats and,
    105. *See also* city-states; national
    state and nation-states; theocracy
    (god-state)
State and Revolution (Lenin), 411
state citizenship. *See* citizenship
state property, 147, 248–49

subjugation of children. *See* children:
    subjugation of
subjugation of women. *See* women:
    subjugation of
subjugation of youth. *See* youth:
    subjugation of
Sufi Naqshbandi order. *See*
    Naqshbandi
Sufi philosophers and poets, 131, 220,
    266, 267, 344
Suhrawardi, 220, 266–67, 617n16,
    622–23n6
Sumer (ancient civilization), 21, 25–35
    passim, 39–59 passim, 82, 99, 103–6
    passim, 124–27 passim, 134–35;
    accumulation, 139; Adam, 118; birth
    of, 326; cities, 30, 104, 119; god-kings,
    44, 106, 120, 127; as model state,
    51, 106; mother-goddess cult, 235;
    music, 318; priests, 94, 106; religion,
    39, 41; Sargon, 115–16; wars, 113. *See
    also* Sumerian mythology
Sumerian language, 343
Sumerian mythology, 42, 45, 58, 59,
    99–104 passim, 218, 239; god-kings,
    127; human creation in, 42, 225. *See
    also* Enki (god); Inanna (goddess)
Sunni Islam, 321, 333, 334, 335, 364. *See
    also* Naqshbandi; Wahhabism
Sykes-Picot Agreement, xxii
Syria, 300, 525–26, 533, 534, 572;
    French mandate, 634; Hellenistic
    era, 319; Öcalan in, 394, 402, 512,
    526; twenty-first century, 373

Talabani, Jalal, 365, 367, 393, 455, 558,
    570, 571–72
Tanzimat reforms, 366, 375, 431,
    627n52, 629n61
tariqat, 252–53
Taş, Nizamettin, 585, 631n29, 637n2
temple (Sumerian institution). *See*
    ziggurats
Ten Commandments, 152
"terrorist" (label), 373, 449, 455, 505–6,
    525, 530, 535, 565

theocracy (god-state), 255, 370; Middle East, 269–72; Turkey, 397

THKO. *See* Türkiye Halk Kurtuluş Ordusu (THKO)

THKP-C. *See* Türkiye Devrimci Kurtuluş Partisi-Cephesi (THKP-C)

Tiamat (goddess), 22, 99, 100, 103, 236

TİİKP. *See* Türkiye İhtilâlci İşçi Köylü Partisi (TİİKP)

TKP (Communist Party of Turkey), 460

totems and totemism, 9–10, 28–29, 38, 95, 97

Treaty of Lausanne, 531, 635n6 ("Role of the ECtHR")

Türk Sanayicileri ve İş İnsanları Derneği (TÜSIAD), 454

Türkiye Devrimci Kurtuluş Partisi-Cephesi (THKP-C), 386, 629n63

Türkiye Halk Kurtuluş Ordusu (THKO), 368, 629n62

Türkiye İhtilâlci İşçi Köylü Partisi (TİİKP), 368

Türkiye Kürdistan Demokrat Partisi. *See* KDP

Turkmens, 322, 335, 338, 430, 433

Umayyads, 75, 228, 333–34

unemployment, 145, 167, 168, 185, 305, 371, 479

United Kingdom. *See* Great Britain

United States (US), 65, 86, 172–75 passim, 183, 208; anticommunism, 436; Bush II, 287, 371; empire, 81, 160–62 passim, 207, 215, 277, 287–90 passim; as hegemon, 82, 207; in Iraq, xxiv, 177, 215, 264, 275, 280, 295, 357, 402, 553; Middle East relations and policy, xxii–xxiii, 87, 275–95 passim, 356, 402–3, 450, 462, 503–4, 536; after 9/11, 552; Öcalan arrest and, 522; Turkish relations, 338, 364, 365, 371, 439, 452–55 passim, 525, 565. *See also* Greater Middle East Initiative

uprisings, 189–90, 229. *See also* revolt and revolutions

Urartu and Urartians, 117, 124, 125, 318, 329, 624n3; influence on Greeks, 318; language, 343, 624n3

urbanization, 353, 430, 541–45 passim, 575–76

Urfa, 96, 119, 126, 217, 319, 321, 331, 334, 591; resistance against English and French occupation, 440

Uruk, 30, 104, 235, 541–42

USSR. *See* Soviet Union

utopian systems and utopic visions, 150–51, 310, 582

violence, 28, 36, 86, 111, 237; Middle East, 253–59; in slavery, 46–47, 52, 63; twentieth-century, 65–66; against women, 241, 258, 475. *See also* war and wars

vulgar materialism, 13, 55, 139

Wahhabism, 366, 627n51

war and wars, 60, 109–14 passim, 237, 256–57, 419–22 passim, 445, 464, 502–3, 507–9 passim, 569–70; anti-Kurd, 565–66; asymmetrical, 529–30; basis of state and power, 412–13; Clausewitz on, 295, 623n14; as existential threat, 5; "holy wars," 60–61, 73, 110, 332–33; immorality of, 158; Iraq, 295; land and, 64; Middle Ages, 336; nationalism and, 80–81; PKK and, 507–8, 512–13, 516–17; plunder, 60, 237, 326; of self-defense, 190–91, 512–13, 516–17; roots, 16, 27; Sumer, 326–27; twentieth-century, 65–66, 76, 81, 143, 176; US, 173; viewed as necessary, 3, 257

West Anatolia, 137, 328

witch hunts and witch trials, 72, 130

women, commodification of. *See* commodification: of women

women, subjugation of, 22, 52, 62–63, 83–84, 100, 145–48, 155, 168, 193; in

Abrahamic tradition, 99; Middle
East, 233–42, 272–74. *See also*
patriarchy
women, violence against. *See*
violence: against women
women as a people (or nation). *See*
nationhood: of women
women's freedom and liberation,
192–201, 206–7, 302–4, 351, 456,
476–78, 488, 559–62 passim
women's rule. *See* matriarchy
World War I, 143, 171, 276–80 passim,
284, 439, 523
World War II, 76, 81, 89, 143, 171, 276,
279, 280, 284
"World War III," 207, 211, 275, 276

Xanî, Ehmedê: Mem û Zîn, 345, 354,
433, 621n14
Xoybûn, 442

Yalçın, Hıdır, 585, 631n29, 637n2,
637n5
Yavuz Selim. *See* Selim I, Sultan of the
Turks
Yazidis, 321, 352, 616n6
Yıldırım, Kesire, 392, 396–97, 399, 400,
545, 559
Yılmaz, Akıf, 391
Yılmaz, Kani, 631n29, 634n8, 637n5
Yılmaz, Mesut, 627n47
Young Ottomans, 375, 629n61
Young Turks. *See* İttihad ve Terakki
Cemiyeti (İTC) (Young Turks)
youth, 186; subjugation of, 23–28
passim, 63

Zana, Leyla, 527, 529, 635n3 ("Role of
the ECtHR")
Zapsu, Cüneyd, 365, 571, 627n48
ziggurats, 33, 105, 106
Zoroaster, 59, 431
Zoroastrianism, 318, 319–20, 321, 333,
335, 352, 547

About the Contributors

Abdullah Öcalan actively led the Kurdish liberation struggle as the head of the PKK from its foundation in 1978 until his abduction on February 15, 1999. He is still regarded as a leading strategist and the most important political representative of the Kurdish freedom movement. In isolation conditions at Imralı Island Prison, Öcalan authored more than ten books that revolutionized Kurdish politics. Several times he initiated unilateral cease-fires of the guerrilla and presented constructive proposals for a political solution to the Kurdish question. For several years, Turkish state authorities led a "dialogue" with Öcalan. Ever since the government broke off the talks in April 2015, he has been held in total isolation at Imralı Island Prison, with no contact whatsoever with the outside world.

Andrej Grubačić is the Founding Chair of the Anthropology and Social Change department at CIIS-San Francisco, an academic program with an exclusive focus on anarchist anthropology. He is the editor of the *Journal of World-Systems Research* and is an affiliated faculty member at the Berkeley Center for Social Medicine, UC Berkeley. He is the author of several books, including *Living at the Edges of Capitalism: Adventures in Exile and Mutual Aid* (coauthored with Denis O'Hearn), *Don't Mourn, Balkanize!*, and *Wobblies and Zapatistas* (with Staughton Lynd). He is the editor of the PM Press Kairos imprint.

International Initiative "Freedom for Abdullah Öcalan—Peace in Kurdistan" is a multinational peace initiative for the release of Abdullah

Öcalan and a peaceful solution to the Kurdish question. It was established immediately after he was abducted in Nairobi and handed over to the Republic of Turkey on February 15, 1999, following a clandestine operation by an alliance of secret services. Part of its activity is the publication of Öcalan's works.

Publications by Abdullah Öcalan in English

Books
Declaration on the Democratic Solution of the Kurdish Question (Neuss: Mesopotamia Publishers, 1999).
Prison Writings I: The Roots of Civilization (London: Pluto Press, 2007).
Prison Writings II: The PKK and the Kurdish Question in the 21st Century (London: Pluto Press, 2011).
Prison Writings III: The Road Map to Negotiations (Neuss: Mesopotamia Publishers, 2012).

Building Free Life: Dialogues with Öcalan (Oakland: PM Press, 2020).
Manifesto of the Democratic Civilization newly edited and published by PM Press
Volume I: Civilization: The Age of Masked Gods and Disguised Kings (2023).
Volume II: Capitalism: The Age of Unmasked Gods and Naked Kings (2023).
Volume III: The Sociology of Freedom (2021).
Volume IV: The Civilizational Crisis in the Middle East and the Democratic Civilization Solution (forthcoming).
Volume V: The Manifesto of the Kurdistan Revolution (forthcoming).

Pamphlets Compiled from the Prison Writings
War and Peace in Kurdistan (Cologne: International Initiative Edition, revised edition, 2017).
Democratic Confederalism (Cologne: International Initiative Edition, revised edition, 2017).

Liberating Life: Woman's Revolution (Cologne: International Initiative Edition, 2013).

Democratic Nation (Cologne: International Initiative Edition, 2016).

ABOUT PM PRESS

PM Press is an independent, radical publisher of books and
media to educate, entertain, and inspire. Founded in 2007
by a small group of people with decades of publishing,
media, and organizing experience, PM Press amplifies the
voices of radical authors, artists, and activists. Our aim is to
deliver bold political ideas and vital stories to all walks of life and arm the dreamers
to demand the impossible. We have sold millions of copies of our books, most
often one at a time, face to face. We're old enough to know what we're doing and
young enough to know what's at stake. Join us to create a better world.

PM Press
PO Box 23912
Oakland, CA 94623
www.pmpress.org

PM Press in Europe
europe@pmpress.org
www.pmpress.org.uk

FRIENDS OF PM PRESS

These are indisputably momentous times—the financial system is melting down globally and the Empire is stumbling. Now more than ever there is a vital need for radical ideas.

In the many years since its founding—and on a mere shoestring—PM Press has risen to the formidable challenge of publishing and distributing knowledge and entertainment for the struggles ahead. With hundreds of releases to date, we have published an impressive and stimulating array of literature, art, music, politics, and culture. Using every available medium, we've succeeded in connecting those hungry for ideas and information to those putting them into practice.

Friends of PM allows you to directly help impact, amplify, and revitalize the discourse and actions of radical writers, filmmakers, and artists. It provides us with a stable foundation from which we can build upon our early successes and provides a much-needed subsidy for the materials that can't necessarily pay their own way. You can help make that happen—and receive every new title automatically delivered to your door once a month—by joining as a Friend of PM Press. And, we'll throw in a free T-shirt when you sign up.

Here are your options:

- **$30 a month** Get all books and pamphlets plus 50% discount on all webstore purchases

- **$40 a month** Get all PM Press releases (including CDs and DVDs) plus 50% discount on all webstore purchases

- **$100 a month** Superstar—Everything plus PM merchandise, free downloads, and 50% discount on all webstore purchases

For those who can't afford $30 or more a month, we have **Sustainer Rates** at $15, $10, and $5. Sustainers get a free PM Press T-shirt and a 50% discount on all purchases from our website.

Your Visa or Mastercard will be billed once a month, until you tell us to stop. Or until our efforts succeed in bringing the revolution around. Or the financial meltdown of Capital makes plastic redundant. Whichever comes first.

DEPARTMENT OF ANTHROPOLOGY & SOCIAL CHANGE

Anthropology and Social Change, housed within the California Institute of Integral Studies, is a small innovative graduate department with a particular focus on activist scholarship, militant research, and social change. We offer both masters and doctoral degree programs.

Our unique approach to collaborative research methodology dissolves traditional barriers between research and political activism, between insiders and outsiders, and between researchers and protagonists. Activist research is a tool for "creating the conditions we describe." We engage in the process of co-research to explore existing alternatives and possibilities for social change.

Anthropology and Social Change
anth@ciis.edu
1453 Mission Street
94103
San Francisco, California
www.ciis.edu/academics/graduate-programs/anthropology-and-social-change

The Sociology of Freedom: Manifesto of the Democratic Civilization, Volume III

Abdullah Öcalan
with a Foreword by John Holloway
Edited by International Initiative

ISBN: 978-1-62963-710-5 (paperback)
      978-1-62963-765-5 (hardcover)
$28.95/$59.95   480 pages

When scientific socialism, which for many years was implemented by Abdullah Öcalan and the Kurdistan Workers' Party (PKK), became too narrow for his purposes, Öcalan deftly answered the call for a radical redefinition of the social sciences. Writing from his solitary cell in İmralı Prison, Öcalan offered a new and astute analysis of what is happening to the Kurdish people, the Kurdish freedom movement, and future prospects for humanity.

The Sociology of Freedom is the fascinating third volume of a five-volume work titled *The Manifesto of the Democratic Civilization*. The general aim of the two earlier volumes was to clarify what power and capitalist modernity entailed. Here, Öcalan presents his stunningly original thesis of the Democratic Civilization, based on his criticism of Capitalist Modernity. Ambitious in scope and encyclopedic in execution, *The Sociology of Freedom* is a one-of-a-kind exploration that reveals the remarkable range of one of the Left's most original thinkers with topics such as existence and freedom, nature and philosophy, anarchism and ecology. Öcalan goes back to the origins of human culture to present a penetrating reinterpretation of the basic problems facing the twenty-first century and an examination of their solutions. Öcalan convincingly argues that industrialism, capitalism, and the nation-state cannot be conquered within the narrow confines of a socialist context.

Recognizing the need for more than just a critique, Öcalan has advanced what is the most radical, far-reaching definition of democracy today and argues that a democratic civilization, as an alternative system, already exists but systemic power and knowledge structures, along with a perverse sectarianism, do not allow it to be seen.

The Sociology of Freedom is a truly monumental work that gives profuse evidence of Öcalan's position as one of the most influential thinkers of our day. It deserves the careful attention of anyone seriously interested in constructive thought or the future of the Left.

"Öcalan's works make many intellectuals uncomfortable because they represent a form of thought which is not only inextricable from action, but which directly grapples with the knowledge that it is."
—David Graeber author of *Debt: The First 500 Years*

Building Free Life:
Dialogues with Öcalan

Edited by International Initiative

ISBN: 978-1-62963-704-4 (paperback)
 978-1-62963-764-8 (hardcover)
$20.00/$49.95   256 pages

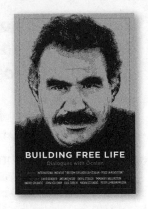

From Socrates to Antonio Gramsci, imprisoned
philosophers have marked the history of thought
and changed how we view power and politics. From
his solitary jail cell, Abdullah Öcalan has penned
daringly innovative works that give profuse evidence of his position as one of the
most significant thinkers of our day. His prison writings have mobilized tens of
thousands of people and inspired a revolution in the making in Rojava, northern
Syria, while also penetrating the insular walls of academia and triggering debate
and reflection among countless scholars.

So how do you engage in a meaningful dialogue with Abdullah Öcalan when he has
been held in total isolation since April 2015? You compile a book of essays written
by a globally diverse cast of the most imaginative luminaries of our time, send it to
Öcalan's jailers, and hope that they deliver it to him.

Featured in this extraordinary volume are over a dozen writers, activists, dreamers,
and scholars whose ideas have been investigated in Öcalan's own writings. Now
these same people have the unique opportunity to enter into a dialogue with his
ideas. Building Free Life is a rich and wholly original exploration of the most critical
issues facing humanity today. In the broad sweep of this one-of-a-kind dialogue,
the contributors explore topics ranging from democratic confederalism to women's
revolution, from the philosophy of history to the crisis of the capitalist system,
from religion to Marxism and anarchism, all in an effort to better understand the
liberatory social forms that are boldly confronting capitalism and the state.

Contributors include: Shannon Brincat, Radha D'Souza, Mechthild Exo, Damian
Gerber, Barry K. Gills, Muriel González Athenas, David Graeber, Andrej Grubačić,
John Holloway, Patrick Huff, Donald H. Matthews, Thomas Jeffrey Miley, Antonio
Negri, Norman Paech, Ekkehard Sauermann, Fabian Scheidler, Nazan Üstündağ,
Immanuel Wallerstein, Peter Lamborn Wilson, and Raúl Zibechi.

There can be no boundaries or restrictions for the development of thought. Thus,
in the midst of different realities—from closed prisons to open-air prisons—
the human mind will find a way to seek the truth. Building Free Life stands as
a monument of radical thought, a testament of resilience, and a searchlight
illuminating the impulse for freedom.

The Art of Freedom: A Brief History of the Kurdish Liberation Struggle

Havin Guneser with an Introduction by Andrej Grubačić and Interview by Sasha Lilley

ISBN: 978-1-62963-781-5 (paperback)
       978-1-62963-907-9
$15.95/$39.95   192 pages

The Revolution in Rojava captured the imagination of the Left sparking a worldwide interest in the Kurdish Freedom Movement. *The Art of Freedom* demonstrates that this explosive movement is firmly rooted in several decades of organized struggle.

In 2018, one of the most important spokespersons for the struggle of Kurdish Freedom, Havin Guneser, held three groundbreaking seminars on the historical background and guiding ideology of the movement. Much to the chagrin of career academics, the theoretical foundation of the Kurdish Freedom Movement is far too fluid and dynamic to be neatly stuffed into an ivory-tower filing cabinet. A vital introduction to the Kurdish struggle, *The Art of Freedom* is the first English-language book to deliver a distillation of the ideas and sensibilities that gave rise to the most important political event of the twenty-first century.

The book is broken into three sections: "Critique and Self-Critique: The rise of the Kurdish freedom movement from the rubbles of two world wars" provides an accessible explanation of the origins and theoretical foundation of the movement. "The Rebellion of the Oldest Colony: Jineology—the Science of Women" describes the undercurrents and nuance of the Kurdish women's movement and how they have managed to create the most vibrant and successful feminist movement in the Middle East. "Democratic Confederalism and Democratic Nation: Defense of Society Against Societycide" deals with the attacks on the fabric of society and new concepts beyond national liberation to counter it. Centering on notions of "a shared homeland" and "a nation made up of nations," these rousing ideas find deep international resonation.

Havin Guneser has provided an expansive definition of freedom and democracy and a road map to help usher in a new era of struggle against capitalism, imperialism, and the State.

"Havin Guneser is not just the world's leading authority on the thought of Abdullah Öcalan; she is a profound, sensitive, and challenging revolutionary thinker with a message the world desperately needs to hear."
—David Graeber author of *Debt: The First 500 Years* and *Bullshit Jobs: A Theory*

The Battle for the Mountain of the Kurds: Self-Determination and Ethnic Cleansing in the Afrin Region of Rojava

Thomas Schmidinger
with a Preface by Andrej Grubačić

ISBN: 978-1-62963-651-1
$19.95   192 pages

In early 2018, Turkey invaded the autonomous Kurdish region of Afrin in Syria and is currently threatening to ethnically cleanse the region. Between 2012 and 2018, the "Mountain of the Kurds" (Kurd Dagh) as the area has been called for centuries, had been one of the quietest regions in a country otherwise torn by civil war.

After the outbreak of the Syrian civil war in 2011, the Syrian army withdrew from the region in 2012, enabling the Party of Democratic Union (PYD), the Syrian sister party of Abdullah Öcalan's outlawed Turkish Kurdistan Workers' Party (PKK) to first introduce a Kurdish self-administration and then, in 2014, to establish the Canton Afrin as one of the three parts of the heavily Kurdish Democratic Federation of Northern Syria, which is better known under the name Rojava.

This self-administration—which had seen multiparty municipal and regionwide elections in the summer and autumn of 2017, which included a far-reaching autonomy for a number of ethnic and religious groups, and which had provided a safe haven for up to 300,000 refugees from other parts of Syria—is now at risk of being annihilated by the Turkish invasion and occupation.

Thomas Schmidinger is one of the very few Europeans to have visited the Canton of Afrin. In this book, he gives an account of the history and the present situation of the region. In a number of interviews, he also gives inhabitants of the region from a variety of ethnicities, religions, political orientations, and walks of life the opportunity to speak for themselves. As things stand now, the book might seem to be in danger of becoming an epitaph for the "Mountain of the Kurds," but as the author writes, "the battle for the Mountain of the Kurds is far from over yet."

"Preferable to most journalistic accounts that reduce the Rojava revolution to a single narrative. It will remain an informative resource even when the realities have further changed."
—Martin van Bruinessen, Kurdish Studies on *Rojava: Revolution, War and the Future of Syria's Kurds*